Cisco Networking Academy Program: Computer Networking Essentials

Debra Littlejohn Shinder

CISCO SYSTEMS

CISCO PRESS

Cisco Press
201 West 103rd Street
Indianapolis, IN 46290

Cisco Networking Academy Program: Computer Networking Essentials

Debra Littlejohn Shinder

Copyright © 2000 Cisco Systems, Inc.

Cisco Press logo is a trademark of Cisco Systems, Inc.

Published by:
Cisco Press
201 West 103rd Street
Indianapolis, IN 46290 USA

Printed in the United States of America 1 2 3 4 5 6 7 8 9 0

Library of Congress Cataloging-in-Publication Number: 00-100257

ISBN: 1-58713-000-9

Trademark Acknowledgments

All terms mentioned in this book that are known to be trademarks or service marks have been appropriately capitalized. Cisco Press or Cisco Systems, Inc., cannot attest to the accuracy of this information. Use of a term in this book should not be regarded as affecting the validity of any trademark or service mark.

Warning and Disclaimer

This book is designed to provide information about basic networking and operating system technologies. Every effort has been made to make this book as complete and as accurate as possible, but no warranty or fitness is implied.

The information is provided on an "as is" basis. The author, Cisco Press, and Cisco Systems, Inc., shall have neither liability nor responsibility to any person or entity with respect to any loss or damages arising from the information contained in this book or from the use of the discs or programs that may accompany it.

The opinions expressed in this book belong to the author and are not necessarily those of Cisco Systems, Inc.

Feedback Information

At Cisco Press, our goal is to create in-depth technical books of the highest quality and value. Each book is crafted with care and precision, undergoing rigorous development that involves the unique expertise of members from the professional technical community.

Readers' feedback is a natural continuation of this process. If you have any comments regarding how we could improve the quality of this book or otherwise alter it to better suit your needs, you can contact us through e-mail at ciscopress@mcp.com. Please make sure to include the book title and ISBN in your message.

We greatly appreciate your assistance.

Publisher	*John Wait*
Editor-in-Chief	*John Kane*
Executive Editor	*Dave Dusthimer*
Cisco Systems Program Manager	*Jim LeValley*
Managing Editor	*Patrick Kanouse*
Development Editor	*Kitty Wilson Jarrett*
Senior Editor	*Jennifer Chisholm*
Copy Editor	*Jill Batistick*
Technical Editor	*Dr. Thomas W. Shinder*
Reviewers	*Lynn Bloomer* *Wayne Jarvimaki* *Michael R. Hanson*
Associate Editor	*Shannon Gross*
Cover Designer	*Louisa Klucznik*
Composition	*Steve Gifford*
Indexer	*Tim Wright*

About the Author

Debra Littlejohn Shinder is a Microsoft Certified Systems Engineer and trainer who teaches, writes, and consults in the Dallas-Ft. Worth, Texas, area. She has been an instructor in the Dallas County Community College District since 1992 and is the webmaster for the cities of Seagoville and Sunnyvale, Texas. She also designed the family website at www.shinder.net. Prior to entering the IT field, Deb was a police sergeant and police academy instructor.

Deb and her husband, Dr. Thomas Shinder, met online in 1994 and have worked together on numerous training and writing projects. Deb is the proud mom of two great kids. Her daughter, Kristen, is serving the U.S. Navy and is stationed in Sardinia, Italy, and her son, Kristoffer, is a high-school chess champion. Deb has been a writer for most of her life and has published articles in both technical and nontechnical fields. She can be contacted through e-mail at deb@shinder.net.

About the Technical Reviewer

Dr. Thomas W. Shinder has co-authored several books on Windows 2000 networking with his wife, Deb, and is an IT columnist for Swynk.com and a series editor for Syngress Media. He teaches at Eastfield College in Mesquite, Texas, and he has provided training and consulting services for major Dallas area firms, including Exxon, Computer Learning Center, Xerox, CompUSA, and others. Dr. Shinder attended the University of California at Berkeley and the University of Illinois Medical School and practiced neurology for several years before making a career change that allowed him to work with computers, his long-time hobby. Tom can be contacted through e-mail at tshinder@dallas.net.

Dedications

To Mom, Kris, and Kniki, and especially to Dad, who still lives in my memory and in my heart.

To Neal, who saw me through the transition, and to Johnnie and Irene, who opened the door.

To all the little piglets, especially Bob Brenson and the other three of the original fearsome foursome: Chief Al, "Lil Brother" Tom C., and the Buerger King.

Finally and foremost, to my tech editor, my best friend, and my husband, who happen to be conveniently all rolled up in the same person. Tom, I couldn't do it without you, and even if I could, I wouldn't want to.

Acknowledgments

It is impossible to name all the people who made this book possible. Special thanks go out to the authors and IT professionals from whom I have learned so much, especially Mark Minasi and Thomas Lee. I also want to thank those who were so patient with me, and who got used to hearing that I would get around to their projects "just as soon as I finish the Cisco Press book." That goes double for Julie.

There is no way I can adequately thank Tom, who not only kept me technically on target, but who also took on more than his share of the load in other areas so I could focus on writing this book.

A big thank you goes to Kent Jones and Jearl Goodnight, who went out of their ways in their attempts to dig up some obscure information I needed for the book.

Many thanks to my students in the Eastfield College networking classes, who taught me to be a better teacher, whose support inspired me, and whose questions provided a wealth of material for this book. I'm lucky to have many good friends "in the biz," from Cash, who installed that first modem and planted the seed, to Darkcat, who introduced me to a new way to "think." I also appreciate the support of Jim T., Jolie, and the "ladies in the office," especially Beth.

Special thanks to all the reviewers who waded through the first draft and offered valuable feedback on how to make the book better. In this regard, I especially want to thank Michael R. Hanson, who went above and beyond the call of duty and whose suggestions contributed a great deal to the finished product.

Finally, I want to thank the wonderful editors at Cisco Press, especially Dave Dusthimer, who gave me the opportunity to write it, and Kitty Wilson Jarrett, who made what I had written better.

Overview

Contents

Introduction

Cisco Networking Academy Program: Computer Networking Essentials is designed to provide entry-level students with a solid foundation of knowledge on which to build a career in computer networking.

This book helps you understand the fundamentals of computer networking concepts and implementation and introduces you to the client and server operating systems that run on networked PCs.

Concepts covered in this book include the history of networking, networking terminology, networking theory and established standards, and implementation of local-area and wide-area networks. Special emphasis is placed on understanding network protocols and how they operate at all layers of the networking model. Emphasis also is placed on the interoperability of networks that run on multiple protocols, platforms, and operating systems.

Specialty areas such as security, remote access, virtual private networking, thin client networking, monitoring, management, and troubleshooting are covered thoroughly. Emerging technologies that are expected to impact the future of networking are also introduced.

Who Should Read This Book

This book's primary audience is students who are beginning training in the networking industry and those who need a review of basic concepts. This includes those enrolled or planning to enroll in networking technology programs in high schools, community colleges, universities, or private technical schools. It also includes those pursuing generic or vendor-specific networking certifications such as CompTIA's Network+, Cisco's CCNA, Microsoft's MCP/MCSE, Novell's CNA/CNE, and similar programs.

The secondary audience includes corporate training faculties and staff and members of the business world who work with information technology personnel and require a broad overview of the concepts involved in networking from the small business to the enterprise-level corporation.

A third target audience is the general user who wants to know more about how computers communicate over networks. The book's approach is designed to be user-friendly and accessible to the non-technical reader who is overwhelmed by the jargon found in vendor documentation and technical manuals.

This Book's Organization

This book is organized into four parts and includes 19 chapters, an appendix, and a glossary. The following sections describe the contents of each part of the book.

Part I: Introduction to Networking Concepts

Chapter 1, "Introduction to PC Networking," introduces you to the basic concepts of PC networking by providing a brief history of electronic communications and networking and a summary of where PC networking is today.

Chapter 2, "Categorizing Networks," discusses the categorization of networks according to physical scope, administrative model, network operating system, protocols in use, topology, and architecture.

Chapter 3, "Networking Concepts, Models, and Standards," provides an overview of binary communications and introduces two popular networking models: the Department of Defense (DoD) model on which the TCP/IP protocols are based and the Open Systems Interconnection (OSI) model, which was developed by the International Organization for Standardization (ISO). Specifications set forth by the Institute of Electrical and Electronics Engineers (IEEE) and vendor-specific models are also covered.

Chapter 4, "Networking Communications Methods," discusses signaling methods and provides an understanding of analog, digital, broadband, baseband, asynchronous, synchronous, simplex, duplex, and multiplexed signaling. Media access methods are described, including CSMA/CD, CSMA/CA, token passing, and demand priority.

Chapter 5, "LAN Links," discusses popular LAN types, including Ethernet, Token Ring, FDDI, AppleTalk, and ARCnet.

Chapter 6, "WAN Links," provides an overview of WAN connections such as PSTN, ISDN, t-carriers, Frame Relay, X.25, and CATV network, as well as high-speed connectivity solutions such as ATM, SONET, and SMDS. This chapter also covers LAN-to-WAN connection solutions, including Internet Connection Sharing (ICS), Network Address Translation (NAT), proxy servers, and routed connections.

Part II: Networking Hardware and Software

Chapter 7, "Physical Components of the Network," introduces students to the many types of networking media, including coax, twisted-pair cable, and fiber-optic cable, as well as to wireless technologies such as laser, infrared, radio, and satellite/microwave communications. Connectivity devices such as repeaters, hubs, bridges, routers, and switches are also discussed.

Chapter 8, "Networking Protocols and Services," describes common LAN protocols—TCP/IP, NetBEUI, IPX/SPX—and discusses the OSI protocol suite. PPP and SLIP, which are WAN link protocols, and PPTP and L2TP, which are common tunneling protocols, are also presented.

Chapter 9, "The Widest Area Network: The Global Internet," discusses the evolution of the Internet, the protocols used for Internet communications—HTTP, FTP, NNTP, SMTP, and POP—and the TCP/IP protocol suite.

Chapter 10, "Network Operating Systems," discusses general network administration practices and then looks at the specifics of common server operating systems, including Windows NT, Windows 2000, NetWare, UNIX, and Linux.

Chapter 11, "Directory Services," describes the Directory Services Protocol (DAP) and the Lightweight Directory Access Protocol (LDAP), as well as the X.500 standards developed by the ISO to promote directory services compatibility and interoperability. Novell's NDS, Microsoft's Active Directory, and Banyan VINES' StreetTalk directory services are covered in some depth.

Chapter 12, "Desktop Operating Systems," looks at the client side of the client/server network and discusses the advantages and disadvantages of common desktop clients, such as DOS, Windows, Linux, Macintosh, and OS/2, and how each can be integrated into popular NOS environments.

Chapter 13, "Hybrid Networks," provides information about interoperability solutions and protocol gateways that allow PCs running different operating systems, protocols, and platforms to communicate with one another. This chapter also looks at PC-to-mainframe communications using Systems Network Architecture (SNA) solutions.

Part III: Network Specialty Areas

Chapter 14, "Protecting the Network," addresses security issues and provides an overview of basic cryptography concepts, public and private key encryption, certificate services, firewalls and proxies, and internal security measures such as "smart cards" and advanced authentication technologies. It also provides guidance for developing security policies for your network. The second half of the chapter discusses disaster recovery plans, including implementation of disk fault tolerance (or RAID), regular scheduled backups, and server clustering.

Chapter 15, "Remote Access," discusses methods of connecting to a server from a remote location using remote connectivity devices such as modems, ISDN terminal adapters, and customer premises equipment (CPE) for dedicated lines. Dial-in server configuration and special security considerations are also covered.

Chapter 16, "Virtual Private Networking," provides an overview of VPN concepts and discusses the tunneling protocols used to provide VPN security.

Chapter 17, "Thin Client Networking," discusses Network Computers, Net PCs, and Windows-based terminals. Windows terminal services, Citrix Metaframe, web-based computing, the X Window system and Java virtual machines—and the role each plays in thin client networking—are also discussed.

Chapter 18, "Monitoring, Management, and Troubleshooting Tools," presents an introduction to the TCP/IP utilities and other tools built into the various operating systems. This chapter also examines commercial products such as Sniffer Pro, LANanalzyer, Microsoft's Systems Management Server, Novell's ManageWise, and IBM's Tivoli.

Part IV: The Future of Networking

Chapter 19, "Tomorrow's Technologies," takes a look into the future of PC networking. It discusses ways of overcoming the current limits of IP, including the new version of IP—IPv6. The goal of universal connectivity is addressed, and more exotic possibilities such as artificial intelligence, quantum computing, and cybernetic life forms are presented as possible components of tomorrow's networks.

This Book's Features

This book contains several elements that help you learn about operating systems and networking:

- **Figures, listings, and tables**—This book contains figures, listings, and tables that help to explain concepts, commands, and procedural sequences. Diagrams illustrate network layouts and processes, and screenshots assist students in visualization configuration procedures. In addition, listings and tables provide summaries and comparisons of features and characteristics.

- **Author's notes, tips, sidebars, and cautions**—These elements are included to provide you with extra information on a subject. You will probably find these asides to be very beneficial in real-world implementations.

- **Chapter summaries**—At the end of each chapter is a summary of the concepts covered in the chapter, which provides a synopsis of the chapter and can serve as a study aid.

- **Further Reading**—Each chapter includes a list of resources for additional information about the topics covered in the chapter, including website URLs and books and articles that cover the topic in more detail.

- **Review questions**—After the Further Reading section in each chapter are 10 review questions that serve as an end-of-chapter assessment. The questions are designed to reinforce the concepts introduced in the chapter and to help students evaluate their understanding before moving on to the next chapter.

The conventions used to present command syntax in this book are the same conventions used in the *Cisco IOS Command Reference*, as follows:

- **Boldface** indicates commands and keywords that are entered literally as shown. In examples (not syntax), boldface indicates user input (for example, a **show** command).
- *Italics* indicates arguments for which you supply values.
- Square brackets [ ] indicate optional elements.
- Vertical bars (|) separate alternative, mutually exclusive elements.
- Braces and vertical bars within square brackets—for example, [x {y | z}]— indicate a required choice within an optional element. You do not need to enter what is in the brackets, but if you do, you have some required choices in the braces.

Part I

Introduction to Networking Concepts

Chapter 1

Introduction to PC Networking

Welcome to the world of personal computer (PC) networking. In this world, it is no longer enough to simply have and use PCs; today it is imperative that you also "get connected." The real power and usability of PCs becomes apparent only when they are linked so that they can communicate with one another. From the simple two-computer home or small office local-area network (LAN) to the ever-growing global Internet, networking is *the future* of computing, and that future is here today.

In many areas of the United States, the demand for trained networking professionals far exceeds the supply. According to projections of the U.S. Department of Labor, computer networking as an occupation has a bright future. Businesses and individuals are buying PCs, and those computers are linking within LANs and wide-area networks (WANs) at an astonishing pace. We literally are "networking the world."

Because network communications is quickly becoming a part of our lives, even those not directly involved in the information technology (IT) industry should know something about the basics of networking. Just as it would be difficult to function in today's world if you knew nothing about a telephone and its features, in the not-too-distant future, knowing how to "get on the network" will be a requirement for many individuals, both at work and at home.

A Brief History of PC Networking

The desire to communicate with others is a driving force among human beings, and the sophisticated means we have developed to communicate sets us apart from other species. From the moment it became possible to link two computers and get them to talk to one another, the concept of the Internet was inevitable.

In the early days of computing, computers were enormous machines that filled entire rooms—sometimes entire city blocks—and cost hundreds of thousands of dollars. Although these expensive behemoths had less processing power and memory than today's tiny handheld computers, they were state-of-the-art technology in the 1950s and 1960s. In a world in which human beings who were slow and prone to error had done calculations manually, the capabilities of the computer were amazing.

At the midpoint of the twentieth century, computers were still rare, exotic, mysterious machines owned only by large companies, governmental bodies, and educational institutions. For the most part, computers were standalone systems, isolated from one another.

In the 1940s, Thomas Watson, the chairman of IBM, said that a market existed in the world for approximately five computers. Even as recently as 1977, Ken Olson, president of Digital Equipment Corporation, said, "There is no reason anyone would want a computer in their home" (ISBC [International Small Business Consortium], www.isbc.com/isbc/business/wisdom.cfm). Of course, both have been proven not just wrong, but *very* wrong. However, no one would have predicted, even a decade ago, that PCs would proliferate as they have or that computer networking would become a mainstream topic.

The First Communications Networks

By the mid-1900s, electronic communications had been around for over a century and was being implemented in both Europe and the United States. These early networks took many forms and sent only coded signals. They later became capable of sending voice across the wire.

This section provides a rough time line of how the first networks were developed.

Telegraph Cables

In the early 1800s, the French developed the first optical telegraph network, which sent information at the blazing speed of 20 characters per second, and Samuel Morse demonstrated the electrical telegraph, which spurred the development of networked communications in the United States.

The Telephone Network: Circuit-Switching Technology

In the late 1800s, a vast telephone network began to be built. Technology leaders of the day, however, were no more farsighted than those of the early computer age. In 1876 an internal memo at Western Union stated that "This 'telephone' has too many shortcomings to be seriously considered as a means of communication. The device is inherently of no value to us" (www.isbc.com/isbc/business/wisdom.cfm).

Despite that attitude, there were more than 50,000 telephone lines in the U.S. by 1880, and by 1960, telephone lines covered urban areas, and the telephone network became a global communications network.

A telephone system uses circuit-switching technology, in which a circuit, or virtual pathway, is established when one telephone connects to another on a network. This works well for voice transmission because the sounds being transferred over the wire flow at a relatively constant rate.

In a circuit-switched network, a connection is established, as shown in Figure 1-1. All signals are passed over this circuit for the duration of the session. If you disconnect and reconnect, a different circuit can be used, as represented by the dotted line.

FIGURE 1-1
In a circuit-switched network, a connection is established, as represented by the solid line.

The technology works less well for transfer of computer data, which has a tendency to be sent in bursts; that is, periods of high activity are interspersed with intervals of low activity or inactivity.

Packet-Switching Technology

During the 1960s, the U.S. government became interested in developing a computer network that would enable systems at military installations and major educational institutions to communicate with one another. Because this was during the middle of the Cold War, they wanted the network to have robustness, reliability, and redundancy so that the network would survive a nuclear war.

Researchers working at the Massachusetts Institute of Technology (MIT), the RAND Institute, and the National Physical Laboratory (NPL) in England invented a new technology called *packet switching*, which worked better for bursty transmissions than did the traditional circuit-switching technologies. Their work created a foundation for the communications technology used on the Internet today.

In a packet-switched network, as shown in Figure 1-2, a connection is not established for the entire transmission. Instead, each individual packet of data can take a different path. Communications from different sources can share the same line, rather than the line being dedicated to one end-to-end communication for the duration of a session, as is the case with circuit switching.

FIGURE 1-2
In a packet-switched network, each individual packet of data can take a different path, as represented by the dotted lines.

Circuit Switching Versus Packet Switching

The terms *circuit switching* and *packet switching* sound alike but have different meanings.

The public telephone system, sometimes referred to as POTS (plain old telephone service), is a switched-circuit communications network. When you place a telephone call in this type of network, only one physical path from your telephone to the one you're dialing is used for the duration of that call. This pathway, or *circuit,* is maintained for your exclusive use, until you end the connection by hanging up your telephone.

Note, however, that if you call the same friend at the same number tomorrow, and do so at the same location from which you placed today's call, the path is not necessarily the same. That's why the circuit is referred to as *switched*. It also explains why you can get a clear connection one day and noise and static on another.

With a packet-switching network, no dedicated pathway or circuit is established. Packet switching is sometimes referred to as a *connectionless* technology because of the lack of a dedicated pathway. If you transfer data, such as a word processing file, from your computer to another using a packet-switched network, each individual *packet* (that is, each small chunk of data) can take a different route. Although it all arrives at the same destination, it doesn't all travel the same path to get there. Internet traffic generally uses packet-switching technology.

The difference between circuit and packet switching can be compared to the different ways in which a large group of people traveling from Dallas to San Francisco can reach their destination. For example, circuit switching is similar to loading the entire group on a bus, a train, or an airplane. The route is plotted out, and the whole group travels over that same route.

Packet switching is like having each person travel in an automobile. The group is broken down into individual components as the data communication is broken into packets. Some travelers can take interstate highways, and others can use back roads. Some can drive straight through, and others can take a more roundabout path. Eventually, they all end up at the same destination. The group is put back together, just as packets are reassembled at the endpoint of the communication.

The ARPAnet

The first packet-switched computer network was conceived in the late 1960s, under the auspices of the U.S. Department of Defense (DoD). It was christened the ARPAnet (for Advanced Research Projects Agency network). The ARPAnet's first *node*, or connection point, was installed at the University of California at Los Angeles in 1969. In just three years, the network spread across the United States, and two years after that, it spread to Europe.

As the network grew, it split into two parts. The military called its part of the internetwork *Milnet,* and ARPAnet continued to be used to describe the part of the network that connected research and university sites. In the 1980s the Defense Data Network (a separate military network) and NSFNet (a network of scientific and academic sites funded by the National Science Foundation) replaced ARPAnet. Eventually this WAN grew into what we today call the Internet.

Yesterday's Networks

Computer networking didn't begin on such a large scale as the ARPAnet project; that is, the LAN came before the WAN. As computers became less expensive and more powerful, businesses of all sizes more commonly used them. Although the first machines were useful for only very limited types of data processing, as software development flourished, new programs enabled users to do much more than just collect and sort data.

With early mainframe systems, for instance, multiple users could access the same stored data from *terminals,* which were stations with input and output devices (for example, keyboards and monitors). These stations had no computing power of their own; they were points from which the mainframe computer could be accessed.

Using mainframes worked well in many respects, but they had several disadvantages when compared to smaller computers (then called microcomputers). Expense was one disadvantage; large mainframe systems cost far more than the so-called "personal" computers designed to sit on a desktop and function independently.

Another disadvantage of mainframes was the *single point of failure* concept. With mainframe computing, if the computer was down, it was down for everyone. Nobody could access data, and nobody who depended on the computer could get any work done. The use of individual PCs, on the other hand, circumvented this problem.

PCs were full-fledged computers that ran programs and performed tasks entirely on their own. They also provided some measure of *fault tolerance*, which is the capability of a system to continue to function and ensure data integrity when failures occur. If one employee's computer crashed, it didn't affect the capability of the rest of the employees, who had their own PCs, to continue working. In fact, if an employee had saved data to a floppy disk, he or she could move to a functioning machine and continue working.

These factors contributed to the increased popularity of PCs as a computing solution for small and large businesses (and everything in between). However, once everyone had a PC on the desktop, companies were faced with a dilemma: How could workers share information as they had with the old mainframe computing model? The solution was networking.

Disadvantages of Standalone Systems

In the early days of desktop PCs, networking hardware and software were not readily available, and many businesses used the machines as standalone systems. If all users needed to print documents on occasion, there were three possible ways to provide that ability:

- A printer could be attached to each machine. This was a costly solution because it necessitated buying multiple printers, even though it was unlikely that they all would be in use at the same time.
- The file to be printed could be saved to floppy disk and transferred to a machine that had an attached printer. This was a less-expensive option, but it was an inconvenience both to the person who had to go begging for a printer and to the person with the printer, whose work was interrupted while someone else used his or her machine to print.
- A printer could be moved from one workstation to another, depending on who needed to print. This was a somewhat cumbersome solution; nonetheless, it was widely implemented, using rolling printer carts that were wheeled around the office. Each move required that cables be disconnected

and reconnected, and sometimes, a move involved software reconfiguration as well.

High cost, inconvenience, and extra work are the primary disadvantages of standalone, or non-networked, solutions.

What Is a Network, Anyway?

The *American Heritage Dictionary* defines a *network* as "a system of lines or channels that cross or interconnect." Earlier we mentioned the telegraph and telephone networks, and of course, we've all heard references to the television networks. Using the dictionary definition, we can call even the state highway system, or the railways that crisscross the country, a network.

That being said, what is a computer network? Simply, it is two or more devices linked for the purpose of sharing information, resources, or both. The link can be through cable (coaxial, twisted-pair, or fiber optics, as you'll learn later in this chapter), or it can be a wireless connection that uses radio signals, laser or infrared technology, or satellite transmission. The information and resources shared can be data files, application programs, printers, modems, or other hardware devices. See Figure 1-3 for an illustration.

FIGURE 1-3
Networked computers share data, software, and hardware resources.

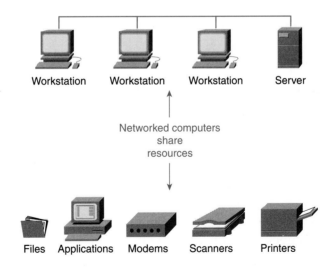

Workstation   Workstation   Workstation   Server

Networked computers
share
resources

Files   Applications   Modems   Scanners   Printers

Why Network Computers?

If the advantage of PCs were each user having an independent computer, why would we want to turn around and link them again? We link them because networked PCs give us, in many ways, the best of both worlds. Each user has independent processing power, but still can enjoy all the benefits of sharing. On the other hand, a company sees a significant cost savings when expensive, occasionally used peripherals are shared over the network. For example, an expensive color laser printer might be used only for special projects, yet many different members of the organization will need to print to it from time to time. With network access, it's easy for them to do so.

Benefits of Getting Connected

Many business owners and managers state that the primary reason for networking their PCs was the need to share printers, as described in the earlier example. Of course, once the systems were linked, people discovered the usefulness of being able to share much more than printers.

The cost involved in linking computers in a LAN—the network interface cards (NICs) for the computers, the cabling or wireless media, the hubs and other connectivity devices—often pays for itself many times over by reducing expenditures and lost production time.

Sharing Output Devices

As discussed, printers and other output devices can be shared on a network, saving time, money, and a great deal of aggravation. Items that can be shared include plotters, which are devices used to draw diagrams, and charts. They also include line-based graphics that use pens or electrostatic charges and toner. Fax machines, which can be either input or output devices, also are easy to share.

Sharing Input Devices

You can share scanners, digital cameras, and other input devices across the network. Because these devices, even more so than printers, are generally used on an occasional basis and are often relatively expensive, it makes sense to configure them for multiple users on the network.

Sharing Storage Devices

Networked computers can share the use of hard disks and floppy and CD-ROM drives. With this type of sharing, you can save files to the disk of another computer across the network if you run out of hard disk space on your computer. In addition, if your computer doesn't have a CD-ROM drive installed, you can access the shared CD drive of another computer. This ability to share also occurs with Zip and Jaz drives, magneto-optical drives, tape drives, and just about any other type of storage device that can be connected to a PC.

Sharing Modems and Internet Connections

Another important feature of networking is the ability of networked PCs to share modems, ISDN lines, cable modems, and DSL adapters. With the proper software—such as proxy or Network Address Translation (NAT) software, which we discuss in detail in Chapter 9, "The Widest Area Network: The Global Internet"—an entire LAN can connect to the Internet through one phone line and a single ISP account.

Sharing Data and Applications

Hardware devices are not the only, or even the most important, resources that can be shared on a network. Data files and application programs also can be made available to multiple users. This sharing results in the efficient use of disk space and easier collaboration on multiuser projects. For example, if several managers need to access and revise a spreadsheet containing a department's budget, the file can be stored in a central location. After each manager makes the desired changes, the file can be saved to the network location so that the updated version is available for the next manager.

Application programs, such as word processing programs, can be installed to a network server. Users can connect to the share and run the application on their own machines, without using space on their local hard disks for the program files.

Be aware that software vendors' licensing agreements can require that you purchase additional licenses for each workstation that uses a network application, even though only one copy is actually installed and all users are accessing that same copy.

The Birth of the Internet

As mentioned previously, back in the 1960s, usable networking technologies became available, and in the early 1970s, the ARPAnet was created by a collaborative effort between the U.S. government (primarily the DoD) and several large universities.

The Role of the DoD

As the Cold War between the United States and the Soviet Union intensified in the 1960s, the DoD recognized the need to establish communications links between major U.S. military installations. The primary motivation was to maintain communications if a nuclear war resulted in mass destruction and breakdown of traditional communications channels. Major universities, such as the University of California and MIT, were already involved in networking projects too.

The DoD funded research sites throughout the United States, and in 1968, ARPA contracted with BNN, a private company, to build a network based on the packet-switching technology that had been developed for better transmission of computer data.

NOTE

Although some applications can be accessed and run across the network without running the setup program on the local machines, this does not work for all applications. Many Windows applications, for example, must write initialization information to the Registry (a hierarchical database in which initialization information is saved). In this case, you must run the setup program on each local machine, but you can choose to install the program files to the network drive. This action also saves disk space on the workstations.

The 1970s: The Growth Spurt Begins

When the ARPAnet project began, no one anticipated that the network would grow to the extent it did. Throughout the 1970s, more nodes were added, both domestically and abroad.

The 1980s: More Is Better

In 1983, the ARPAnet network was split, and 68 of the 113 existing nodes were taken by Milnet, which was integrated with the Defense Data Network. The Defense Data Network had been created the previous year.

The Domain Name System (DNS) was introduced in 1984, providing a way to map "friendly" host names to IP addresses that was much more efficient and convenient than previous methods. We discuss these previous methods in Chapter 8, "Networking Protocols and Services." In 1984, there were more than 1000 host computers on the network.

During the last half of the 1980s, the networking picked up considerably. For instance, the NSF created supercomputer centers at Princeton, in Pittsburgh, at the University of California at San Diego, at the University of Illinois at Urbana-Champaign, and at Cornell. The Internet Engineering Task Force (IETF) also came into being during this time. By 1987, there were 10,000 hosts on the network, and by 1989, that number increased to over 100,000.

The 1990s: The Net Becomes Big Business

The phenomenal growth rate of the 1980s was nothing compared to what came in the 1990s. ARPAnet ceased to exist, and the Internet was "invented," with the U.S. government getting involved in pushing the development of the so-called information superhighway. The NSFnet backbone was upgraded to T3 speed (that is, 44.736 Mbps), and in 1991 it sent more than 1 trillion bytes per month. The Internet Society (ISOC) was formed, and in 1992 more than 1 million hosts existed on the Internet.

The 1990s was the decade that the Internet went commercial. As more and more college students and faculty, individual home users, and companies of all sizes got connected, the business world recognized the opportunity to reach a large and expanding affluent market. By 1995, online advertising had caught on, online banking had arrived, and you could even order a pizza over the Internet.

The last half of the last decade of the century ushered in new major developments almost on a daily basis. Streaming audio and video, "push" technologies, and Java and ActiveX scripting took advantage of higher-performance connectivity available at lower and lower prices. Domain names became big business, with particularly desirable names selling for upwards of $1 million.

In December 1999, almost 1 billion sites existed on the Word Wide Web, with well over 50 million host computers participating in this great linking.

Figure 1-4 shows a time line of significant events in PC networking history.

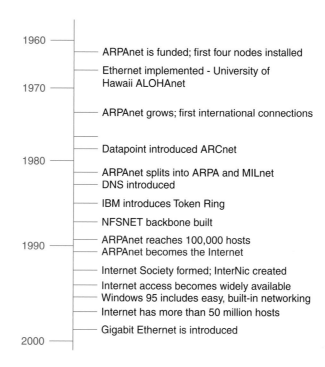

FIGURE 1-4
This time line shows significant events in PC networking history.

1960	ARPAnet is funded; first four nodes installed
	Ethernet implemented - University of Hawaii ALOHAnet
1970	
	ARPAnet grows; first international connections
	Datapoint introduced ARCnet
1980	ARPAnet splits into ARPA and MILnet
	DNS introduced
	IBM introduces Token Ring
	NFSNET backbone built
	ARPAnet reaches 100,000 hosts
1990	ARPAnet becomes the Internet
	Internet Society formed; InterNic created
	Internet access becomes widely available
	Windows 95 includes easy, built-in networking
	Internet has more than 50 million hosts
	Gigabit Ethernet is introduced
2000	

The Cost of Technology: More and More for Less and Less

As computer and networking technology have advanced over the past few decades, the cost of that increasingly sophisticated technology has fallen dramatically. Those falling prices are at least partially responsible for the rising popularity of connectivity solutions in the business world and in personal lives.

In the 1970s and 1980s, a PC that was considered state of the art for the time cost several thousand dollars. Online services existed, but with fees of $25 or more *per hour* of access, only big businesses and the wealthy could afford them. PC veterans still can remember the announcement of Prodigy's "bargain rates" of only $9.95 an hour for online access. This was at blazing speeds of 1200 or 2400 baud.

Today, of course, for under $1000, you can buy a computer system capable of doing much more, and doing it better and faster, than the $500,000 mainframe of 20 years ago. Internet access at speeds equivalent to T1 is available through DSL or cable modem for $30 to $40 per month, and the price is falling all the time. Basic Internet access at 56 kbps can be had for much less—even for free, if you can tolerate a bit of advertising taking up space on your screen.

PC Networking Today

As we enter the 2000s, we are on our way to networking the world (and beyond). The Net is beginning to permeate almost every area of our lives. We have computers at work, computers at home, and portable computers that we carry with us on airplanes and to the beach.

As always, where there are multiple computers, networking usually follows. Indeed, a primary function of many of these computers is to connect to the Internet. In this section, we look at some of the ways in which networked computers are changing our lives.

Home Computing

Home PCs are commonplace, and many of these PCs are being marketed specifically as e-machines, ready to connect to the Internet. Many households have multiple computers, and where two or more computers exist under the same roof, the desire to link them is sure to rear its head sooner or later. There is a new, booming market in home LAN technology, which uses wireless solutions or the house's telephone or electrical wiring in place of traditional Ethernet cabling.

Web Presence and E-commerce

Businesses of all sizes and types are finding that having a Web site is beneficial—or even essential—to their advertising strategies. Even small companies are turning to e-commerce (that is, selling their products or services directly over the Internet) as a cost-effective solution. Large corporations are running *enterprise networks* (that is, large multisite networks) that connect offices around the world to their own internal intranets as well as to the Internet.

High-Performance Business Solutions

As high-speed connectivity over fiber-optic and other fast media becomes commonplace, live videoconferencing is becoming a viable replacement for face-to-face meetings. Executives are staying in close touch with their offices even while traveling, thanks to the availability of remote dial-in access and virtual private networking. Employees at all levels of the organization are telecommuting, enjoying more flexibility in their work schedules while the company benefits from savings in facilities and onsite equipment. In addition, transfer of large data files can now be accomplished quickly and efficiently. Even traditional low-bandwidth activities such as scheduling and e-mail access are improved by emerging and affordable high-performance technologies.

Online Learning

Public schools are getting wired, and online learning is becoming a reality as major colleges and universities offer credit courses that can be completed either partially or wholly over the Internet. In addition, hardware and software vendors, led by big players such as Microsoft Corporation and Cisco Systems, are partnering with commercial and nonprofit organizations to bring networked computers and Internet access within the reach of almost everyone who wants it.

Tomorrow's Networks

At the end of this book, we look at emerging technologies in the networking field. Some of these are still on the drawing board, and others have been tested and found feasible in the lab or in limited scope in the field.

As political entities and large corporations get behind the push to develop new, better, and faster means of bringing networked communications into the daily lives of people at all socioeconomic levels, exciting new developments in both software and hardware are being announced on a regular basis. The way we work and play is being transformed, and optimists predict that international and cultural barriers will melt as global connectivity makes the world a smaller—or at least more accessible—place. Many people seek to establish shared technology centers that provide access and training to groups that traditionally have not had the opportunity to benefit from computer technology and connectivity.

Speculation about where networking is headed is an attempt to predict the unpredictable. Twenty years ago, many of the technologies we now take for granted were unthinkable to anyone but science fiction writers. It's likely that twenty years in the future, computing and networking will have gone in drastically new directions that we can't begin to imagine today. There are, however, some interesting possibilities on the horizon, as discussed in the following sections.

"Smart" Appliances and Homes

Although not yet widely available, the concept of smart appliances and homes is already a reality. You can buy kitchen appliances today that have embedded microprocessors, or miniature computers, that control temperature, cooking time, and so forth. The next step—and it's not a very big one—is connecting those tiny computers to a network so that you can issue commands remotely. It's likely that in the not-too-distant future, you will get online at the office, access your oven, and tell it what time to start preheating in preparation for your arrival home.

This concept logically leads to the next: the integrated smart house, which is computer-controlled and wired to a central network. The prime example of this is the multimillion-dollar estate of Microsoft chairman Bill Gates. This estate features computerized climate control and customized music "zones" that follow a person from room to room.

Numerous companies can make your present home smart by wiring it for Ethernet connectivity and by integrating your home computers with your phone, security, home theater, heating and air conditioning, and lighting systems. You can control these systems with the click of a mouse or even through voice command. Figure 1-5 illustrates some features currently available in smart house technology.

FIGURE 1-5
Smart house technology brings the network of the future home today.

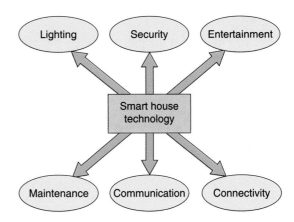

We discuss the house of the future a bit more in Chapter 19, "Tomorrow's Technologies."

Phoning Home

Telephone technology has been quietly advancing over the past few decades. The developments in this area, however, have been marketed and integrated into our lives so smoothly and gradually that their impact has not received the sort of attention it might have otherwise.

Providers of mobile phones have built cellular- and satellite-based networks that now offer sophisticated services, such as wireless Internet access, at affordable prices. The technology is improving all the time.

Regular telephone companies (referred to within the industry as *telcos*), spurred by competition from cable TV companies, are implementing high-speed services for data transfer, such as Asynchronous Digital Subscriber Line (ADSL), at a cost low enough to market to home users.

Telephony applications are integrating the PC and the telephone in a variety of ways that allow for automatic answering, message storage, and message retrieval through the computer.

Internet phone programs using voice over IP enable you to bypass the telephone lines entirely (if you have an Internet connection through cable, wireless, or some other medium) to make long distance calls from your computer without paying long distance charges.

New operating systems, such as the latest version of Microsoft Windows, include support for IP telephony, which blends voice, video, and data transmission over TCP/IP connections with improved quality of service.

We take a closer look at personal communications systems of the future in Chapter 19.

The Wired Workplace

It seems that in any business facility you enter, there is a computer (or several) on every desktop, all of them linked to an internal LAN, the external Internet, and a few remote private networks for good measure. We can only wonder how the work environment of the future will be *more* network-centric than it is today.

The office of tomorrow will be even more reliant on network technology. As business environments are wired with fiber-optic and other high-performance media, increasing bandwidth and real-time video will make teleconferencing an attractive alternative to face-to-face meetings. It's likely that more and more employees will work from home. They will not, however, be isolated with their own little individual projects. Instead, they will share documents over the network to foster a more team-oriented environment.

As full-featured computers shrink in size while growing in capability, it will become easier to "take the office on the road." Handheld systems that today integrate e-mail, Web access, calendaring, and task management will no doubt in the future provide for on-the-go video on demand, voice communications, and notification services—combining the functions now performed by separate devices. No longer will you need to carry a palm computer, mobile phone, and

> **NOTE**
>
> *Telephony* applications are those that combine telecommunications technologies with computing technologies. This includes implementations in accordance with the Telephony Applications Programmers Interface (TAPI) specifications and the standards of the Internet and Telecoms Convergence Consortium (ITC).

pager; one machine, small enough to wear on your belt or slip into a purse, will do it all.

This universal connectivity and accessibility have the potential to increase the productivity of businesses of all types.

Schools of the Future

The future of education will be impacted by developments in networking technology. In fact, it is already commonplace for libraries from elementary to university level to include one or more Internet-connected computers for students.

The most dramatic effect of technology on schools is the availability of information on a scale that was never before possible. As more public and private schools get wired, the way in which students do research for papers will change. In fact, the very nature of those assignments can change as well, to require the inclusion of multimedia material.

New learning methodologies that involve more of the senses are likely to become more popular. At the lower age levels, this can mean educational interactive games that engage the attention of students and contribute to the development of hand-eye coordination.

At the college and university levels, offsite learning seems to be the trend. Students can attend class through computer, downloading assigned reading material, submitting completed assignments through e-mail, and participating in class discussions through live chat. There are already a small percentage of courses offered in this way, and we expect that in the next decade, this will become a standard way to gain college credit or even complete degrees.

Networking Health Care

The advancement of computer and networking technology will make an enormous impact in medicine and health care. The most obvious benefit of networking to the healthcare industry is the capability of physicians to share patient records and diagnostic and treatment information.

Other ambitious and exciting developments are already taking place or are expected to become reality in the near future. For instance, long-distance surgery—in which the physician performing the operation from a remote location controls the robotic device that is actually operating on the patient—has been successful in experimental situations.

A related concept is the tele-examination, in which the physician conducts a preliminary physical exam over two-way video, perhaps aided by a proxy or stand-in such as a physician's assistant or nurse practitioner who is actually with the patient. The idea of telemedicine is especially attractive in rural areas where physicians are in short supply.

Technology and the Law

Legal research and courtroom procedures have become more efficient because of networking and the subsequent improvement in record keeping and information sharing abilities.

Law enforcement, in particular, has put the new technologies to work. Many police agencies now have mobile data terminals (MDTs) installed in squad cars, allowing officers to quickly and directly access criminal history files, license records, and departmental references and resources. MDTs also make it possible for officers to communicate with one another over the network in a fashion that is more secure than broadcasting over open radio channels. Departments are also making use of global positioning system (GPS) technology, combined with computer-aided dispatch, to provide accurate information to dispatchers and supervisors at the station about where each unit is located at any given time. This gives command staff more control for better deployment of officers.

Intergalactic Networking?

Now that Internet connectivity has permeated almost every corner of the globe, the next logical step is to network the final frontier: outer space. The idea is not as futuristic as it sounds; in fact, computer communications are already sending signals to satellites orbiting high over the earth, and there are projects underway that broadcast signals into deep space in hopes of catching the attention of life, if it exists, on other planets.

Computers on Earth already control the activities of unmanned space missions and play a huge role in the journeys of manned shuttles. Networked communications make interplanetary exploration feasible.

A Brief Overview of Networking Terminology

When you visit another country, the first task to tackle is learning the language. The same is true of entering a new area of study or a new career field.

Computer networking, like most professions, has its own jargon, such as technical terms, abbreviations, and acronyms, that can, at first glance, look as foreign to the uninitiated as does the alphabet of a country halfway around the world.

Without a good grasp of the terminology, you will have difficulty understanding the concepts and processes in this book. This section gives you a head start on deciphering some of the tech talk in this and other introductory guides to networking and network operating systems.

This is not intended to be a comprehensive glossary of networking terms, but a quick reference that defines and briefly discusses some of the most important and most basic words, phrases, and acronyms that enable you to navigate through the next few chapters. Each definition is expanded on in the chapters that follow. Please refer to the book's glossary for a more comprehensive list of definitions.

Concept-Related Terminology

networking model—A networking model is a graphical representation of the processes involved in network communications. The popular models represent these processes as layers or levels; thus, they are called *layered models*. The most commonly referenced are the Open System Interconnection (OSI) seven-layer model, the four-layer DoD model (sometimes called the TCP/IP networking model), and the Microsoft Windows networking model. We discuss each in detail in Chapter 2, "Categorizing Networks."

client/server networking—In computer networking terms, a *client* computer is one that sends a request to another computer for access to its data or resources. The computer that responds to that request and shares its data or resources over the network is called the *server*. In a *peer-to-peer network* (also called a *workgroup*), all computers on the network act as both clients and servers. In a *server-based network* (sometimes called a client/server network, and in Microsoft Windows networking, called a *domain*), there is a dedicated server computer running special server software, which performs user authentication/security functions. We discuss both peer-to-peer and server-based networking in Chapter 2.

Network Hardware-Related Terminology

NIC—It is pronounced "nick" and refers to the network interface card, also called the network adapter card (but for some reason never called a NAC), or just the network interface. This card typically goes into an ISA, PCI, or PCM-CIA (PC card) slot in a computer and connects to the network *medium*, which in turn is connected to other computers on the network.

media—Media are the means by which signals are sent from one computer to another by cable or *wireless* means.

wireless media—Wireless media, such as the radio, laser, infrared, and satellite/microwave technologies, carry signals from one computer to another without a permanent tangible physical connection (cable).

coax—Coaxial cable, or coax, is similar to cable TV cable, which is copper-cored cable surrounded by a heavy shielding that is used to connect computers in a network. Either thin or thick coax can be used.

twisted-pair—Twisted-pair is a type of cabling, also used for telephone communications, that consists of pairs of copper wires twisted inside an outer jacket. There are two basic types: UTP (unshielded twisted pair) and STP (shielded twisted pair). UTP is the most commonly used cabling in modern Ethernet networks. It comes in different category ratings depending on whether it is considered voice or data grade and the transmission speed it supports. "Cat 5" refers to a category 5 rating, which can be used for voice (telephone) or data and which supports speeds up to 100 Mbps.

plenum—The plenum in a building is the space between a false ceiling and the floor above, through which cabling can be run. *Plenum-grade* cable, often called plenum cable, refers to cable with an outer jacket made of Teflon or other material that complies with fire and building codes for installation in the plenum area.

PVC—In the context of network hardware and cabling, PVC stands for polyvinyl chloride, the material out of which the jacket on non-plenum-grade cable is made. It is less expensive than plenum-grade materials but does not meet most safety codes for installation in the ceiling because it gives off a poisonous gas when burned.

fiber optics—Often shorted to just *fiber*, fiber optics refers to cabling that has a core made of strands of glass or plastic (instead of copper), through which light pulses carry signals. Fiber has many advantages over copper in terms of transmission speed and signal integrity over distance; however, it is more expensive and more difficult to work with.

connectivity devices—This term refers to several different device types, all of which are used to connect cable segments, connect two or more smaller networks (or subnets) into a larger network, or divide a large network into smaller ones. The term encompasses repeaters, hubs, switches, bridges, routers, and brouters. Each is discussed in detail in Chapter 7, "Physical Components of the Network."

Software-Related Terminology

protocol—A network protocol is a set of rules by which computers communicate. Protocols are sometimes compared to languages, but a better analogy is that the protocol is like the syntax of a language, which is the order in which processes occur. There are many different types of computer protocols. A *protocol stack* refers to two or more protocols working together. The term *protocol suite* describes a set of several protocols that perform different functions related to different aspects of the communication process.

NOS—*NOS*, which stands for network operating system, usually refers to server software, such as Windows NT, Windows 2000 Server, Novell NetWare, and UNIX. The term sometimes refers to the networking components of a client operating system such as Windows 95 or the Macintosh OS.

client operating system—Also referred to as the desktop operating system, *client operating system* refers to the operating system software that runs on the network's workstations, which access the server and/or log onto the network as clients.

hybrid network—A hybrid network (also called a multivendor network) is one in which the software products of different vendors interoperate, especially in regard to the server operating systems. For example, a network that has Windows NT domain controllers, NetWare file servers, and a UNIX Web server is a hybrid network.

Design and Topology Terminology

LAN—A local-area network (LAN) is a network that is confined to a limited geographic area. This can be a room, a floor, a building, or even an entire campus.

WAN—A wide-area network (WAN) is made up of interconnected LANs. It spans wide geographic areas by using WAN links such as telephone lines or satellite technology to connect computers in different cities, countries, or even different continents.

MAN—A MAN (metropolitan-area network) is a network that is between the LAN and the WAN in size. This is a network that covers roughly the area of a large city or metropolitan area.

physical topology—This refers to the layout or physical shape of the network, whether the computers are arranged so that cabling goes from one to another in a linear fashion (linear bus topology), the last connects back to the first to form a ring (ring topology), the systems "meet in the middle" by connecting to a central hub (star topology), or multiple redundant connections make pathways (mesh topology). The characteristics of each are discussed in Chapter 3, "Networking Concepts, Models, and Standards."

logical topology—The logical topology is the path that signals take from one computer to another. This can correspond to the physical topology. For instance, a network can be a physical *star*, in which each computer connects to a central hub, but inside the hub, the data can travel in a circle, making it a *logical ring.* The difference between physical and logical topologies is discussed in Chapter 3.

Measurement-Related Terminology

bit—The smallest unit of data in a computer. A bit equals 1 or 0, and it is the binary format in which data is processed by computers.

byte—A byte is a unit of measure used to describe the size of a data file, the amount of space on a disk or other storage medium, or the amount of data being sent over a network. 1 byte generally equals 8 bits of data.

KB (kilobyte)—A kilobyte is approximately 1000 bytes (actually, it's 1024 bytes). It can be abbreviated as "K."

KBps (kilobytes per second)—This is a standard measurement of the amount of data transferred over a network connection.

kbps (kilobits per second)—This is a standard measurement of the amount of data transferred over a network connection.

MB (megabyte)—A megabyte is approximately 1 million bytes (actually 1,048,576). A megabyte is sometimes referred to as a "meg."

MBps (megabytes per second)—This is a standard measurement of the amount of data transferred over a network connection.

Mbps (megabits per second)—This is a standard measurement of the amount of data transferred over a network connection.

Hz (Hertz)—A unit of frequency. It is the rate of change in the state or cycle in a sound wave, alternating current, or other cyclical waveform. It has one cycle per second and is used to describe the speed of a computer's microprocessor.

MHz (megahertz)—One million cycles per second. This is a common measurement of the speed of a processing chip such as a computer's microprocessor.

GHz (gigahertz)—One thousand million, or 1 billion (1,000,000,000), cycles per second. This is a common measurement of the speed of a processing chip such as a computer's microprocessor.

> **NOTE**
>
> A common error is confusing KB with kb and MB with Mb. Remember to do the proper calculations when comparing transmission speeds that are measured in KB with those measured in kb. For example, modem software usually shows your connection speed in *kilobits* per second (for example, 45 kbps). However, popular browsers display file-download speeds in *kilobytes* per second, meaning with a 45 kbps connection, your download speed would be a maximum of 5.76 KBps. In practice, you cannot reach this download speed because of other factors consuming bandwidth at the same time. We discuss data transfer rates in more detail in Chapter 7.

What This Book Covers and What It Doesn't

This book provides an overview of networking fundamentals and popular server and client operating systems in use on networks today. Because the scope is broad, we are not able to go into the depth or detail on individual topics in a manner possible in more specialized books.

NOTE

PC processors are getting faster all the time. The micropro-cessors used on PCs in the 1980s typically ran under 10 MHz (the origi-nal IBM PC was 4.77 MHz). As the year 2000 began, PC processors approached the speed of 1 GHz.

Throughout the book, we provide a resource list at the end of each chapter to point you toward sources of more detailed information on each of the topics introduced.

Networking Certifications

Because of the shortage of qualified professionals and the high demand for personnel in the networking industry, certification has become a popular means of measuring basic knowledge and qualifications, especially for entry-level positions. Many organizations offer certification examinations to test your grasp of networking technologies.

Vendor-Specific Certifications

Some certification programs are *vendor-specific;* exam candidates are tested on their abilities with particular hardware or software products and are expected to know the "party line" and answer exam questions in keeping with the par-ticular vendor's philosophy and focus. Many of these certifications, such as the Cisco CCIE and the Microsoft MCSE, are well respected in the industry.

Some of the most popular vendor-specific certification programs include the following:

NOTE

Vendor-specific certifications are useful for demon-strating specific capabilities with a particular com-pany's products and in many instances are desired or even required by employers.

- Cisco Certified Network Associate (CCNA), Cisco Certified Network Pro-fessional (CCNP), and Cisco Certified Internetwork Expert (CCIE)
- Microsoft Certified Professional (MCP) and Microsoft Certified Systems Engineer (MCSE)
- Novell Certified NetWare Administrator (CNA) and Novell Certified Net-Ware Engineer (CNE)

Other companies, such as Sun, Lotus, IBM, and RedHat and other Linux ven-dors, also offer certification exams for their networking software. There are also vendor-specific hardware certifications offered by IBM, Compaq Comput-ers, Digital Equipment Corporation, and others.

Non-Vendor-Specific Certifications

Non-vendor-specific certification programs attempt to measure general knowl-edge and skills applicable to the networking products of a wide range of vendors.

The most popular non-vendor-specific networking skills certification is Net-work+, which is offered by the Computing Technology Industry Association (CompTIA). This association also developed the vendor-neutral A+ PC hard-ware technician's exam.

Non-vendor-specific certifications are useful for demonstrating a broad base of knowledge and skills pertaining to generic networking concepts, practices, and terminology.

This Book and Certification

This book was designed to give you a broad overview of the essential elements of PC networking. It can serve as an introductory guide for those new to the IT industry and those who plan to seek vendor-specific certification such as the CCNA, MCSE, or CNA.

It can also be used as a study guide, in conjunction with other preparatory material, for the Network+ exam. We have covered all topics included in the exam objectives. We also have covered the objectives specified by Microsoft for the Networking Essentials exam, which is generally prescribed as the first of the six exams required to obtain the MCSE under the Windows NT 4.0 track.

Although the new Windows 2000 MCSE certification track does not include an exam devoted exclusively to networking essentials, much of the material in this book is useful in studying for the Windows 2000 core examination 70-216, *Implementing and Administering a Microsoft Windows 2000 Network Infrastructure.*

> **NOTE**
>
> The Network+ certification was supported and sponsored by such companies as Microsoft, Novell, IBM, Lotus, and many more.

Summary

This chapter introduced you to the world of computer networking and how standalone systems began to be linked into networks. You learned about early LANs and the development of the ARPAnet, which was the joint DoD/university project that became today's global Internet.

This chapter touched on some of the ways in which technologies are affecting our lives, and it provided an overview of some of the concepts that are explored in depth in later chapters of this book. You learned some common networking terms and about the role of technical certifications in the networking industry.

In upcoming chapters, you will build on this information as you learn about the models and standards on which today's networks are built. We will go under the hoods of small LANs and complex WANs, and you will become familiar with the signaling methods, architectures, hardware, protocol operating systems, and services that provide the foundation of modern networking.

You will learn about hot topics such as security and troubleshooting, and we will discuss specialty areas such as remote access, virtual private networking, and thin client networking. We will look at emerging technologies that promise that the networks of the future will be even more fascinating, and more practically useful, than the networks of today.

Further Reading

An excellent Web-based resource for definitions of networking terms and acronyms is www.whatis.com.

A good reference for additional information about the history of networking is www.silkroad.com/net-history.html.

For more information about CompTIA and the Network+ certification program, see CompTIA's Web site at www.comptia.com.

For more information about vendor-specific certification training and exams, see the following Web sites:

- Cisco: www.cisco.com/warp/public/10/wwtraining/certprog
- Microsoft: www.microsoft.com/train_cert
- Novell: education.novell.com/certinfo

Review Questions

The following questions test your knowledge on the material covered in this chapter. Be sure to read each question carefully and select the *best* correct answer or answers.

1. What was the early implementation of networking technology developed by the French in the early 1800s?

   A. The telephone network

   B. The optical telegraph network

   C. The Ethernet network

   D. The ARPAnet

2. What is the name of the technology that the telephone network uses?

   A. Packet switching

   B. Layer 2 switching

   C. Layer 3 switching

   D. Circuit switching

3. What is the technology that works best for bursty data transmissions?

   A. Packet switching

   B. Analog transmission

   C. Circuit switching

   D. Switchboard technology

4. Which of the following is a disadvantage of mainframe-based networks? (Select all that apply.)

   A. The mainframe hardware is more expensive than PC hardware.

   B. Mainframes are incapable of processing the large amounts of data that are processed by PC servers.

   C. Mainframes represent a single point of failure.

   D. Mainframe terminals are less secure than networked PCs.

5. Which of the following can be shared across a computer network? (Select all that apply.)

    A. Data

    B. Applications

    C. Printers

    D. Modems

6. Which of the following is classified as an input device? (Select all that apply.)

    A. Plotter

    B. Fax machine

    C. Digital camera

    D. Printer

7. What is the name of the method introduced in the 1980s to provide a means for mapping friendly host names to IP addresses?

    A. DoD

    B. DHCP

    C. DSL

    D. DNS

8. What are the applications that combine telecommunications and computer technologies called?

    A. Computel technologies

    B. Telephony technologies

    C. TPI technologies

    D. ITC technologies

9. What type of computer sends a request to another computer for access to its data or resources?

    A. Server

    B. Workstation

    C. Client

    D. Terminal

10. What is the set of rules by which computers communicate?

    A. Protocol

    B. Media type

    C. Byte

    D. Topology

Chapter 2

Categorizing Networks

Technology professionals break networks into categories based on characteristics required to administer or troubleshoot a particular network. You can break down types of networks according to physical properties or characteristics of the software running on them. For example, categorization can be based on the following:

- Physical scope
- Administrative method
- Network operating system
- Networking protocols
- Topology
- Architecture

We look at each classification method in the following sections.

Categorizing Networks by Physical Scope

One network categorization method is based on the physical scope of the network, which includes the geographic area it spans and, to a lesser extent, the size of the network. Using this method, you can generally place a network into one of three categories:

- Local-area network (LAN)
- Metropolitan-area network (MAN)
- Wide-area network (WAN)

These categorizations correlate somewhat with the network size, which is the number of computers and users (a LAN tends to be smaller than a MAN, which is in turn smaller than a WAN). They also correlate to some degree with financial resources (a WAN is generally much more expensive to set up and maintain than a LAN), but the most important determining factor is the geographic area covered by the network.

Characteristics of a LAN

The *American Heritage Dictionary* defines the word *local* as "of, related to, or characteristic of a particular place, rather than a larger area." Similarly, the term *LAN* describes a network that spans a limited area; the computers that belong to the network are physically close to one another. However, LANs can vary drastically in their numbers of computers and users. For instance, a LAN could consist of two PCs sitting a few feet apart in a home or office, or it could include hundreds of computers spanning several floors of a skyscraper, or even in some cases, multiple office buildings in close proximity. Figure 2-1 shows a graphical representation of the layout of a simple LAN.

FIGURE 2-1
A LAN is limited to a specific geographic area.

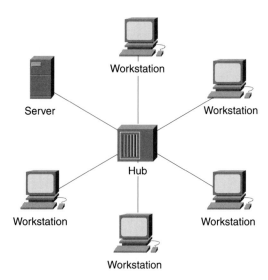

Large LANs can be divided into *workgroups* for easier management. In this context, a workgroup consists of users who share the same resources, such as files, printers, and applications. For example, within a company LAN, you can create workgroups for different departments, such as Sales, Finance, and Human Resources. Figure 2-2 shows how a LAN can be divided into workgroups.

LANs are the basis of larger networks (MANs and WANs), which are created by networking two or more LANs together.

Characteristics of a MAN

A MAN consists of two or more LANs networked together within the confines of a space roughly corresponding to a metropolitan area, hence the name. The typical MAN is a high-performance, public network. See Figure 2-3 for an illustration of a MAN.

The term *MAN* is used less frequently to define networks than are the terms *LAN* and *WAN* because it is less frequently implemented. Most networks are contained within a building or campus and thus fall into the category of LAN, or they span a greater distance, with nodes in different cities, states, or even countries, and thus qualify as a WAN. The maximum distance defining a MAN is approximately 50 miles, or 80 kilometers.

NOTE

Network architecture and cable type can limit the number of computers a LAN can contain. You'll learn about these limitations later in this chapter, in the section "Categorizing Networks by Architecture."

NOTE

When networks are networked to one another, the result is referred to as an *internetwork*, or *internet*. When you see the word internet beginning with a lowercase letter, it refers to any network of networks. When the first letter is capitalized, the word pertains to the global public network of networks we call the Internet.

Related terms that evolved from the term internet are intranet and extranet. An *intranet* is a private network within an enterprise that uses the same protocols (such as TCP, HTTP, and FTP) and technologies used on the Internet. An *extranet* also uses Internet technologies, but is made accessible across remote links to a business's customers, employees, vendors, and partners.

FIGURE 2-2
LANs can be divided into workgroups.

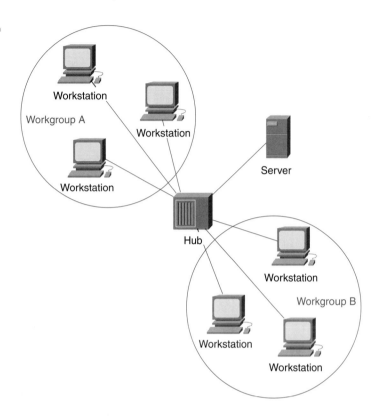

Characteristics of a WAN

A WAN is a network that spans a large geographic area. The best and most familiar example of a WAN is the Internet. However, a WAN can also be a private network. For example, a company with offices in many countries can have a corporate WAN connecting locations through telephone lines, satellites, or other technologies. The WAN generally consists of many interconnected LANs.

Although WANs can use private links to connect networks, they often use public transports such as the public telephone system. Consequently, transmission speed is often slower than on a LAN; typical speed over analog phone lines using a top-of-the-line modem is at or under 50 kbps. Even the high-speed WAN links, such as T1, cable modem, and digital subscriber lines (DSL) top out between 1 and 6 Mbps. On the other hand, the slowest Ethernet LAN links sends at 10 Mbps.

FIGURE 2-3
A MAN covers a wider area than a LAN, but it is more geographically limited than a WAN.

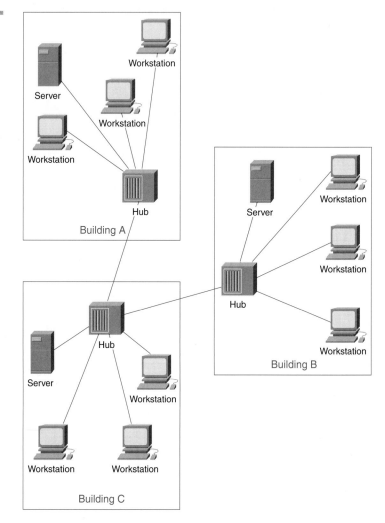

Another characteristic of the WAN is that a connection to it may not be permanently wired, as with a cabled LAN. Instead, WAN links are often, but not always, dialed "on demand." Many WAN links are in fact dedicated, always-on connections, but temporary connections are more common on the WAN than on the LAN.

In summary, WANs can use either private or public transports and can consist of permanently dedicated or dial-up connections. WAN links are usually slow when compared to LAN links. WANs are categorized as either distributed or centralized. A *distributed* WAN, such as the Internet, has no central point of control. A *centralized* WAN, on the other hand, is based on a central server or a centralized site (such as company headquarters) to which all other computers are connected. Figure 2-4 shows a centralized WAN.

FIGURE 2-4
A centralized WAN is built around a "master" computer or site to which others connect.

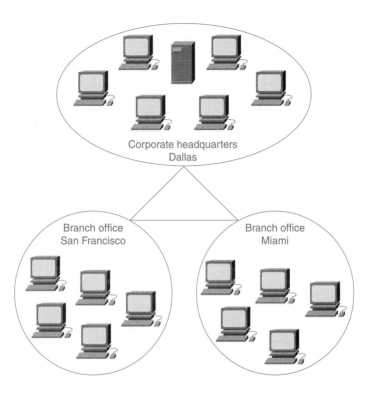

Corporate headquarters
Dallas

Branch office
San Francisco

Branch office
Miami

WANs are *routed* networks, which means that in order for messages to get from one LAN to another, the packets must go through a *gateway*. The gateway is a router, or computer that is configured to perform routing functions. We discuss how routing works in much more detail in Chapter 9, "The Widest Area Network: The Global Internet."

Categorizing Networks by Administrative Method

You can categorize networks based on administrative method, that is, how and by whom shared resources are managed. A network can be organized as follows:

■ As a peer-to-peer workgroup in which each computer functions as both client and server and each user administers the resources on his or her computer

■ As a client/server, or server-based, network in which administration is centralized on a computer running special network operating system (NOS) server software that authenticates username and password information to enable authorized users to log on and access resources

Which of these is better? It depends on the situation. Each has advantages and disadvantages, which are summarized in Table 2-1.

TABLE 2-1   Advantages and Disadvantages of Peer-to-Peer and Client/Server Networks

Advantages of a Peer-to-Peer Network	Advantages of a Client/Server Network
Less expensive to implement.	Provides for better security.
Does not require NOS server software.	Easier to administer when the network is large because administration is centralized.
Does not require a dedicated network administrator.	All data can be backed up on one central location.
Disadvantages of a Peer-to-Peer Network	**Disadvantages of a Client/Server Network**
Does not scale well to large networks; administration becomes unmanageable.	Requires expensive NOS software such as NT or Windows 2000 Server or Novell NetWare.
Each user must be trained to perform administrative tasks.	Requires expensive, more powerful hardware for the server machine.
Less secure.	Requires a professional administrator.
All machines sharing the resources negatively impact performance.	Has a single point of failure if there is only one server; users' data can be unavailable if the server is down.

As you can see, choosing the method of administrative organization depends on factors such as the number of computers and users, the security requirements, the hardware, the personnel, and the available budget.

Servers and Clients

Before we look more closely at the characteristics of each type of network and how each is implemented, let's review the terms used to describe the roles of computers on a network.

A *server* is a computer that makes its resources (data, software, or attached peripherals such as printers) available for access by other computers on the network. On the other hand, a *client* is a computer that accesses the resources of a server.

It's easy to become confused by these terms; although we sometimes use the word server to describe a dedicated server computer that is usually a powerful computer running NOS software that enables centralized management of the network, in reality, *any* computer that shares its resources is acting as a server.

Servers Sharing "Shares"

The operating systems that we think of as client or desktop operating systems—Windows 95/98, NT Workstation, and Windows 2000 Professional, for example—can and do function as servers when you create *shares* on them to enable other computers to use their resources.

To enable resources to be accessed by others, you must specifically designate the resource as shared and give it a *share name* that identifies it on the network. This name does not necessarily have to be the same as the name of the resource itself. For example, if you had a folder called Administration that you wanted to share over the network, you could name the share "Admin." Admin is the name others would see when they browse the network. They would also use this name when they connect to your share.

Figure 2-5 shows the dialog box used in Windows 2000 to create a share for the folder named My Documents.

FIGURE 2-5
Creating a share in Windows 2000.

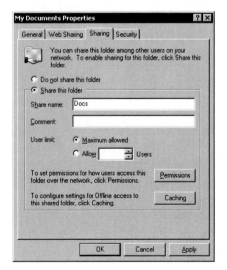

TIP

Remember the two this way: Servers give (that is, share their resources) and clients take (that is, access the resources of servers).

NOTE

Some operating system vendors use the term *share* to describe the resources that have been made available to other computers, while others vendors stay with the more traditional terminology *shared resource.*

Notice that the folder name appears in the title bar, but the share is named Docs. When another computer on the network consults the *browse list*, which is the list of available shared resources, the share appears as shown in Figure 2-6.

FIGURE 2-6
The share named Docs appears in the browse list for the server named Constellation.

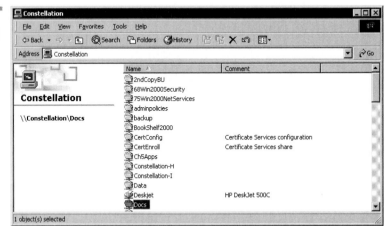

NOTE

Some NOSs allow for shared resources to be "published" to the directory (for example, shared folders and printers can be published to the Active Directory in Windows 2000 and to the NDS tree in Novell NetWare). This enables users to locate the shared resources without requiring that they know on which server the resource is physically located.

Dedicated Servers

Any computer that shares its resources is a server. The term is often used, however, to refer to machines that are *dedicated* to sharing their files, applications, or peripherals. A *dedicated server* is usually a powerful machine with a fast processor and a large amount of memory that is not used to do day-to-day productivity tasks; it is dedicated to being a server. Access is usually restricted to administrators who use the server to perform management, monitoring, and maintenance of the network.

In a large network, a dedicated server may serve only one function, as in the following situations:

- File servers are servers on which data files are stored. Users save their application data to a hard disk on the server instead of saving to the local hard disks on their workstation machines. Files on the server are easier to locate because they are all in a central location; they also are easier to back up.

- Print servers are machines that control one or several printers to which users can send documents across the network to be printed.

- Application servers are computers on which network applications are installed. Users can run the application (such as a word processing or database program) across the network, even though it is not installed on their local machines.

■ Logon servers (called *domain controllers* on Windows networks) hold a *security database*, which contains information comprising user accounts. The server checks user credentials against the database and controls access to the network and its resources.

■ Web servers run Web server software on top of the operating system in combinations such as Microsoft Internet Information Server on NT and Windows 2000, Apache on Linux and UNIX servers, and Netscape's Enterprise Server on various platforms. Many operating systems come with built-in Web server software. Web server software often includes both File Transfer Protocol (FTP) and Network News Transfer Protocol (NNTP) server software.

> **NOTE**
>
> A *daemon*, in UNIX terminology, is a program that runs continuously and handles periodic requests for service.

■ Mail servers provide mailboxes to collect e-mail sent to users of the network. This e-mail then can be downloaded to the mail client software on the users' individual machines. Examples of mail server software include Microsoft Exchange for Windows networks and sendmail, a popular UNIX mail daemon.

■ Remote access servers enable dial-in connections so that other computers can access the server or the entire network from a distant location over the telephone lines.

■ Terminal servers run software that enables client applications to be run on the server so that "thin client" computers (low-powered, inexpensive systems) can function as terminals rather than as independent systems. The server provides a multisession environment and runs the application programs being used on the clients.

■ Telephony servers provide answering machine and voice mail services and also route calls.

■ Cluster servers run software that enables multiple servers to be joined in *clusters*, which are groups of independent computer systems, also known as *nodes*, working together as a single system to ensure that mission-critical applications and resources remain available to clients.

■ Proxy servers act as intermediaries between workstation users and the Internet to ensure security and provide administrative control and caching services.

■ Fax servers provide a central point on the network to send and receive facsimile messages and to distribute incoming faxes to the appropriate users.

- BOOTP servers use the bootstrap protocol to enable client computers to boot an operating system and receive IP configuration information over the network.

- DHCP servers assign IP addresses and TCP/IP configuration information to computers configured to be DHCP clients so that administrators do not have to manually assign a unique IP address to each client machine on the network.

- Name resolution servers provide mapping of friendly network names, which enable users to identify computers without having to remember numerical identifiers. These names map to IP addresses, which are used by the TCP/IP protocol suite to locate computers on the network. Name resolution servers include *Domain Name System (DNS) servers*, which map hierarchically structured host names to IP addresses, and *NetBIOS Name servers* (such as Microsoft's WINS server) that map flat NetBIOS names to IP addresses.

> **NOTE**
>
> We discuss BOOTP, DHCP, and name resolution services in more detail in Chapter 8, "Networking Protocols and Services," in the section "The TCP/IP Suite."

Clients, Workstations, Hosts, and Nodes

As you have learned, a network client is a computer or other network device that requests access to network resources. A client is usually, but not always, a computer. Note that a printer or other network device that can request resources is also technically a client.

The term *client* can also refer to software programs that access the resources of server programs. For example, the e-mail program that runs on your desktop computer and that sends a request to download your new messages from a server computer running e-mail server software is called a *mail client*.

A *client operating system* is commonly installed on desktop computers, or *workstations*, which are either networked as peers in a workgroup or logged on to a logon authentication server to access the network. Examples of client operating systems are Windows 95/98 and Windows NT Workstation.

> **NOTE**
>
> When used as a verb, *host* generally refers to providing a service to another device or computer. For instance, a Web server hosts users' Web pages.

The term *workstation* is used in many ways. It refers to the NT client operating system, and it is sometimes used to mean any desktop computer running any client operating system. Workstation also has a secondary meaning: a powerful computer used to run resource-intensive application software. Such a computer is a graphics workstation or a computer-aided design (CAD) workstation.

Another term you hear used to refer to computers on a network is *hosts*. This term is often used in reference to TCP/IP-based networks and can include any network device that is assigned an IP address.

A *node* is a connection point on a network. In some contexts, the word refers to any computer or other network device. In other cases, it indicates a redistribution point, or device, that is programmed or engineered to recognize and process transmissions to other nodes.

Characteristics of Peer-to-Peer Networks

The peer-to-peer structure is appropriate for small networks, where strict security is not required. Most networking books recommend a maximum of ten computers for this type of administrative model.

Implementing a small peer-to-peer network is inexpensive and relatively easy with modern operating systems such as Windows 95/98, NT Workstation, Windows 2000, and various versions of Linux, all of which have networking components built in.

If you want to participate on a peer-to-peer network, you configure the computer to join a *workgroup* in the networking configuration properties in Windows 9*x*, Windows NT, and Windows 2000. All computers that share their resources with one another must have the same workgroup name entered in this field.

Administration in Peer-to-Peer Networks

Administration over users and resources is *decentralized* in a peer-to-peer network. Every computer on the network can act as both client and server; that is, every computer can share its own resources with the rest of the network and access the resources of others.

The user of each computer is responsible for administration of that computer's resources (creating user accounts, creating shares, and assigning permissions to access those shares). Each user is responsible also for backing up the data on that computer. Unfortunately, locating a resource can be difficult in a peer-to-peer network that has more than a few computers.

Security in Peer-to-Peer Networks

A peer-to-peer network has no central database where user account information is kept. All security is local. User accounts and passwords must be created and maintained on each individual machine. This is both inconvenient and inherently less secure than the centralized security model used in client/server networks.

For example, consider a workgroup consisting of four NT Workstation machines belonging to Mary, Joe, John, and Jane. For Mary to access files stored on Joe's machine, Joe must create a user account for her on his computer. If she also wants to access a shared printer on Jane's computer, Jane must create a user account for Mary, and so on.

If Joe, Jane, and John assign different usernames and passwords to these accounts, Mary can be in the position of having to remember to use the name *maryjohnson* and the password *tree* when she accesses resources on Joe's machine, username *maryj* and password *Shelton* when she accesses resources on Jane's machine, and username *mjohnson* and password *flute* when she accesses resources located on John's computer. You can see how unmanageable all those accounts can get as the network grows.

Share-Level versus User-Level Security. In a Windows for Workgroups or Windows 95/98 workgroup, security is implemented at the *share level* rather than at the *user level*. Table 2-2 outlines the differences between share- and user-level security.

TABLE 2-2   Characteristics of Share- and User-Level Security

Share-Level Security	User-Level Security
Used by Windows for Workgroups 3.11, Windows 95, and Windows 98.	Used by Windows NT and Windows 2000.
A password is assigned to each shared resource.	A password is assigned to each individual user.
To access a resource across the network, the user must enter the password for that resource.	To access a resource across the network, the user's account must have permissions assigned to access that resource.
Users must remember multiple passwords.	Users must remember only one password.

In our small workgroup example from before, if Mary, Joe, Jane, and John are running Windows 95 on their computers, they need not create user accounts for each person who will access their resources. Instead they assign a password to every shared resource. This means if Mary wants Jane to be able to access the Documents folder, but doesn't want Joe or John to have access to it, she must give the folder a password (for example, "health") and tell only Jane the password. Jane is prompted to enter the password when she tries to access the folder.

If Mary has another folder, named Pix, that she wants John and Jane to access, but not Joe, she must assign that folder a different password (let's say "crate") and give that password only to John and Jane.

Suppose Mary has 20 shared folders on her hard disk. She has to remember 20 different passwords that grant access to those folders, and the other users have to remember multiple passwords *and* keep track of which password goes with which folder. (And you thought the multiple user account scenario with the NT workgroup was bad!) Figure 2-7 illustrates this situation.

FIGURE 2-7
With share-level security, the number of passwords that must be remembered can quickly get out of hand.

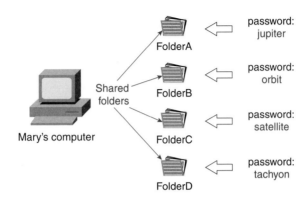

Because this situation becomes intolerable as the network grows, most users in Windows 9*x* workgroups soon resort to the easiest solution—not securing resources at all. Obviously, leaving resources unsecured does not work in a network environment that contains highly sensitive data to which access must be restricted. It is better to use a server-based network, as described in the following section.

Characteristics of Server-Based Networks

The defining characteristic of a server-based (also called a client/server network) network is *centralized control*. In such a network, at least one machine runs an NOS such as Windows NT, Windows 2000 Server, or NetWare. User accounts are created on the server, and the network administrator can control the entire network from this central location.

Server-based networking solves the problem of performance degradation that occurs on workgroup computers when other users are accessing a system's resource while a user is working at the station. Generally, performance and throughput are better on a server-based network.

Server operating systems generally provide for additional sophisticated services. For example, a Windows NT/2000 server can function as a remote access (dial-in) server to which multiple users simultaneously can connect over phone lines. Note that Windows 9*x* and NT Workstation allow one incoming connection at a time. The server also has other services built in, such as the capability to

NOTE

A better way to manage permissions, instead of assigning them to individual user accounts, is to organize the user accounts into *security groups* and assign permissions to the groups. We discuss use of groups in more detail in Chapter 10, "Network Operating Systems," in the section "General Network Administration."

provide name resolution services, to allocate IP addresses as a DHCP server, and to host websites with add-on or built-in Web server software.

Administration in Server-Based Networks

The server-based networking model simplifies administration, especially for networks with many computers and a large number of shared resources. Shared files are stored on the server so that they can be easily located and backed up.

One important characteristic of server-based computing, which can be seen as either a drawback or a blessing, is the requirement for a dedicated professional network administrator. Although this can increase the cost of maintaining the network, having all network operations under the control of a trained administrator, rather than having end-users manage their own resources, can actually reduce overall costs in the long run.

Security in Server-Based Networks

Server-based security is inherently more secure than that of peer-to-peer networks. To log on to the network, each user must have a valid user account and password created on the server. This enables access to resources throughout the network, and there is no need for multiple user accounts on different machines, as is the case with an NT Workstation workgroup. There is also no need to remember passwords for different shared resources, as is the case with Windows 9*x* workgroups, because server-based networks rely on *user authentication* and *permissions* to control access.

NOTE

This is a simplified explanation to illustrate the difference between server-based and workgroup-based *share permissions*. Windows 2000 can implement several different layers of security, depending on the file system and protocols used. The permissions assigned to the share make up only one of the locks on the door to a shared resource.

The network administrator can assign permissions for each shared resource to individual users or groups. Those permissions can enable different levels of access for different users. For example, let's say there is a shared folder on the server called Sales. We want Mary, who is a secretary in the Sales department, to be able to read the documents in the folder, but she should not be able to make changes to them. We want Jane, who is vice president in charge of Sales, to be able to read, change, delete, and otherwise fully control the documents in the Sales folder. To accomplish this in a Windows 2000 network, we can edit the share's properties and assign read permissions to Mary's user account and full control permissions to Jane's.

When we assign permissions for the Sales folder to Mary and Jane (or groups to which they belong), we must remove the default share permission, as shown in Figure 2-8.

As you can see in Figure 2-8, when you create a new share, the Everyone group is automatically given Full Control. This group includes all users who have a valid account to log on to the network. Luckily, you can easily delete this permission to restrict access to only those who should have it.

FIGURE 2-8
In Windows networks, the default share permission gives Full Control to Everyone.

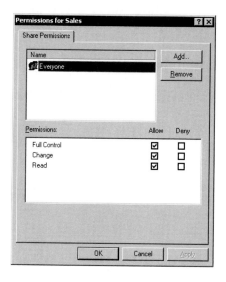

Categorizing Networks by NOS

Networks are sometimes categorized based on the NOS that is installed on the servers and that is used to control the network. Examples of network types based on the server operating system include the following:

- Windows (Windows NT and Windows 2000)
- NetWare
- UNIX

Many networks combine two or more server types on the network; these are often referred to as *hybrid networks*.

Windows Networks

Windows server-based networks are called *domains*. In Windows NT 4.0 domains, a master computer called a *primary domain controller* holds the only read/write copy of the security accounts manager (SAM) database. Since the release of Windows 2000, Microsoft has referred to NT 4.0 domains as *down-level domains*.

Windows 2000 domains are based on the Active Directory, a copy of which is held on each domain controller and which contains security account information and objects representing network resources. A network can have multiple domain controllers; all can read and write to the directory database.

NOTE

Each popular network operating system is discussed in detail in Chapter 10.

Windows 2000 Professional, Windows NT Workstation, Windows 95 and 98, Windows for Workgroups, and MS-DOS all can be clients to both Windows NT and Windows 2000 servers. Non-Microsoft operating systems, such as Macintosh and Linux, also can access resources on Windows servers with the proper additional software installed.

NetWare Networks

Novell NetWare is a popular NOS that provides logon security and functions as a file and print server. Windows desktop operating systems can access NetWare servers if they have the proper client software installed. Windows 9*x*, NT, and 2000 all include client services for NetWare. Novell also makes an add-on client program, Client32, that can be installed on Windows 32-bit operating systems to provide greater functionality.

NetWare versions 4.*x* and 5.*x* provide directory services through NetWare Directory Services (NDS), a hierarchical database similar to (and which preceded and perhaps inspired) Microsoft's Active Directory. Older versions of NetWare (3.x and later) are still in use on some networks and use a database called the *Bindery* to organize network objects.

UNIX Networks

UNIX was the NOS originally used by most hosts on the ARPAnet, the predecessor to the Internet. UNIX was developed by Bell Labs in 1969 and comes in many flavors because of its open code distribution. It is a powerful NOS, but most UNIX implementations are text-based and are relatively difficult to learn.

Linux is a variation on UNIX that recently has become popular both as a server and as a desktop operating system. Like its older brother UNIX, Linux is an open standard, and many different companies market their own versions. Popular versions include RedHat, Caldera, and Corel.

Hybrid Networks

Most medium to large networks today can be considered hybrid networks. They run software made by different vendors, use multiple protocols, and can even combine the domain and workgroup concepts.

A Microsoft network in which clients log on to a Windows NT domain controller may also have a NetWare file server that those same clients access and a UNIX machine that is used to provide Web hosting services. The PCs can even connect to an IBM AS/400 mainframe to access certain applications and records.

Most vendors provide software interoperability tools, either included with the operating system or available as add-ons, to facilitate their integration into this type of multivendor environment. For instance, Microsoft's Windows NT and

2000 Server products include Gateway Services for NetWare and Services for Macintosh.

Some popular interoperability programs include the following:

- **Client Services for NetWare (CSNW) and Gateway Services for NetWare (GSNW)**—CSNW enables individual Microsoft client computers to directly access NetWare servers. GSNW enables a Microsoft server's clients to access the NetWare server's resources by going through the gateway software installed on the NT or Windows 2000 server.

- **File and print services for NetWare**—This enables clients to a NetWare server to access resources on a Windows server.

- **Services for Macintosh**—This enables Macintosh computers to access files and printers on a Microsoft network.

- **Systems Network Architecture (SNA)**—SNA enables PC networks to connect to IBM mainframes.

- **SAMBA**—SAMBA is a set of utilities that enables Microsoft computers to access files and print services on UNIX servers.

These interoperability solutions are discussed in greater detail in Chapter 13, "Hybrid Networks."

Categorizing Networks by Protocol

Sometimes networks are categorized according to the protocols they use for communications. The network protocols are the rules of order followed by the linked computers in establishing and maintaining communication over the network. The three most popular LAN protocols are NetBEUI, IPX/SPX, and TCP/IP, as described in the following sections. Other LAN protocols include AppleTalk and the OSI protocol suite.

NetBEUI Networks

A small, simple LAN using Microsoft operating systems can communicate using the NetBEUI protocol. NetBEUI (which stands for NetBIOS Extended User Interface) is based on the NetBIOS (Network Basic Input/Output System) protocols developed by IBM for workgroups. Note that a NetBEUI network cannot be routed because the protocol is nonroutable. This means if your network is divided into subnets, you have to use a different LAN protocol for computers to be able to communicate with computers in a different subnet.

You will learn more about why and how networks are subnetted in Chapter 8 in the section "IP Subnetting and Supernetting."

Advantages of NetBEUI include its simplicity and low resource overhead. It is fast and requires no complicated configuration information to set up.

IPX/SPX Networks

Novell uses the Internet Package Exchange/Sequenced Packet Exchange (IPX/SPX) protocol stack as its LAN protocol, and it is required for NetWare networks before version 5.0.

IPX/SPX is usually associated with NetWare networks, but is not limited to that purpose. A workgroup or domain of Microsoft computers can use the IPX/SPX protocol as well. Microsoft includes its own implementation of IPX/SPX-compatible protocols, called NWLink, in the Windows 9*x*, NT, and 2000 operating systems. A Microsoft client must have NWLink or IPX/SPX installed to connect to a NetWare server running NetWare 4.x or below.

IPX/SPX requires minimal configuration (more than NetBEUI, but less than TCP/IP) and offers faster performance than TCP/IP. IPX/SPX is sometimes run on internal Microsoft networks that are connected to the Internet for security purposes. We discuss this option in more detail in Chapter 13 in the section "Security Aspects of Using Multiple Protocols."

TCP/IP Networks

Despite the fact that it is the slowest and most difficult to configure of the popular LAN protocols, TCP/IP is the most widely used. There are several good reasons for this:

- TCP/IP uses a flexible addressing scheme that is extremely routable, even over the largest networks.
- Almost all operating systems and platforms can use TCP/IP.
- A huge number of utilities and tools are available, some of which are included with the protocol suite and some of which are add-on programs for monitoring and managing TCP/IP.
- TCP/IP is *the* protocol of the global Internet. A system must run TCP/IP to connect to the Internet.

Most enterprise level networks run on TCP/IP, and it is imperative that network administrators be familiar with its protocols. We cover the individual components of the TCP/IP suite in Chapter 8.

Other LAN Protocols Used in Networks

Most LANs use one of the three protocols, but you might encounter a few other protocols and protocol suites in your study of PC networking.

AppleTalk

AppleTalk is the set of protocols developed by Apple for networking its Macintosh machines. The AppleTalk suite includes the following protocols:

- **LocalTalk**—Used for connecting Macintosh computers in small workgroups. It is relatively slow (230.4 kbps) and supports only 32 devices.
- **EtherTalk**—Used to connect Macintosh workgroups to Ethernet networks.
- **TokenTalk**—Used to connect Macintosh workgroups to Token Ring networks.

AppleTalk networks use AppleTalk Address Resolution Protocol (AARP) to map AppleTalk addresses to Ethernet and Token Ring physical Media Access Control (MAC) addresses.

The OSI Protocol Suite

The Open System Interconnection (OSI) protocol suite was intended to be a replacement for TCP/IP, which was expected to be phased out. The OSI suite was developed by the International Organization for Standardization (ISO) to provide an improved set of protocols for less confusion and easier standardization of networking products among multiple vendors.

Phasing out TCP/IP and using OSI instead sounded good in theory, but TCP/IP proved to be a little harder to kill off than anticipated. The U.S. government got behind the OSI suite, and in the late 1980s the Department of Defense decreed that by August 1990, all its computer communications would use OSI protocols. But it didn't happen. Networks didn't make the change, and TCP/IP still reigns as king of the Internet. Its position seems strong, especially with its capability to evolve (demonstrated by the planned transition to IPv6) to meet the challenges of future growth.

> **NOTE**
>
> The International Organization for Standardization is also called the ISO. No, that's not a typo—"ISO" is not an acronym, but a word derived from the Greek *isos*, meaning "equal."

Categorizing Networks by Topology

Networks are sometimes categorized based on the physical or logical *topology* of the network. The *physical topology* refers to the shape of the network—the way in which the cable is laid out. The *logical topology* refers to the path the signals travel as they make their way from one point on the network to another.

The physical and logical topologies can be the same; in a network physically shaped as a linear bus (that is, in a straight line), the data travels in a straight line from one computer to the next. A network also can have physical and logical topologies that are not the same. The cable segments can connect all computers to a central hub in a star shape, but inside the hub, the connections can be wired so that the signal travels around in a circle from one port to the next, creating a logical ring.

The following are the most popular LAN topologies for networks:

- Linear bus
- Ring
- Star bus
- Mesh
- Hybrid

They are described in more detail in the following sections.

Linear Bus Networks

A linear bus (sometimes called just a *bus*), as the name implies, is a network that is laid out in a straight line. The line doesn't actually have to be physically straight; rather, the cable proceeds from one computer to the next, and then to the next, and so on. Figure 2-9 illustrates a linear bus.

FIGURE 2-9
Computers in a linear bus network are connected in a line from one to the next.

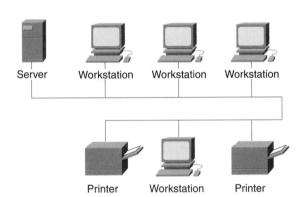

Server   Workstation   Workstation   Workstation

Printer   Workstation   Printer

NOTE

To end a bus, a device called a terminator is attached to the "empty" side of the NIC T-connector on the first and last computers on the linear cable.

Because it has a beginning and an end, a linear bus network requires *termination* at each end. Failure to terminate both ends of the cable results in *signal bounce*, which can disrupt or prevent communications on the network. One end of a linear bus—but *not both*—should be grounded.

Bus networks usually use thick or thin coax cable and the Ethernet 10Base2 or 10Base5 architecture. You learn more about the characteristics of different cable types in Chapter 7, "Physical Components of the Network."

Communications on a Bus Network

On a bus network, when a computer sends a message, that message goes to every computer on the bus. Each network interface card (NIC) examines the headers of the message to determine whether the message is addressed to that computer. If it is not, the message is discarded.

Advantages of Bus Networks

The bus topology is very simple and easy to set up. It is relatively inexpensive because it uses less cable than other topologies. The bus is especially suitable for small, temporary networks, such as in a classroom that might be used for only a few days or weeks.

Disadvantages of Bus Networks

A bus is known as a *passive* topology because the computers do not regenerate the signal and pass it on as they do in a ring. This makes the network vulnerable to *attenuation*, which is the loss of signal strength over distance. *Repeaters* can be used to address this problem. We discuss repeaters in more detail in Chapter 7.

Another disadvantage of the bus is that if there is a break in the cable (or one user decides to unplug his or her computer from the network), the line is broken. This means not only that computers on opposite sides of the break cannot communicate, but also that two new ends are not terminated and the resulting signal bounce can bring the entire network down.

Ring Networks

If you connect the last computer in a bus back to the first, you have a *ring* topology. In a ring, every computer is connected to two other computers, and the signal can travel around and around the circle (see Figure 2-10). Because a ring has no endpoint, termination is not necessary (or possible).

A physical ring network generally uses coax cable, as with the bus. A Token Ring network, which is a logical ring, uses STP cable (IBM type) and complies with IEEE 802.5 specifications.

Communications on a Ring Network

On a ring network, the signal travels in one direction. Each computer receives the signal from its *upstream neighbor* and sends it to its *downstream neighbor*. The ring is considered an *active topology* because each computer regenerates the signal before passing it on to the next.

The ring topology is most commonly associated with the Token Ring architecture. In this implementation, the ring is generally a *logical* ring, the circle being wired inside the Token Ring hub, which is called a multistation access unit (MSAU).

FIGURE 2-10
In a ring net-
work, computers
are connected in
a circle, with the
last connected
back to the first.

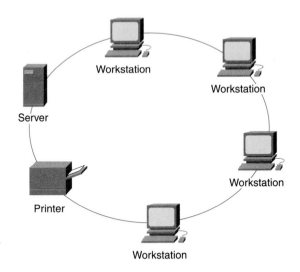

Advantages of Ring Networks

The ring is relatively easy to troubleshoot, and like the bus, is simple to set up. A physical ring requires more cable than a bus and less than a star topology.

Disadvantages of Ring Networks

The ring suffers from some of the same drawbacks as the bus. If the circle stays unbroken, it is a reliable topology. If a break or disconnection of the cable occurs anywhere on the network, however, it brings all network communications to a screeching halt.

Another disadvantage of the ring is the difficulty in adding more computers to the network. Because the cabling runs in a closed circle, it is necessary to break the ring at some point to insert the new computers. This means the network is out of commission while you make the additions.

Star Bus Networks

The *star* (also called a *star bus*) is one of the most popular LAN topologies. It is implemented by connecting each computer to a central hub, as shown in Figure 2-11.

The hub can be *active*, *passive*, or *intelligent*. A passive hub is just a connection point. It does not require electrical power. An active hub (the most common) is actually a *repeater* with multiple ports; it boosts the signal before passing it to the other computers. An intelligent hub is an active hub with diagnostic capabilities. It has a processing chip built in. We discuss hubs in more detail in Chapter 7.

FIGURE 2-11
The star topology connects all computers to a central hub.

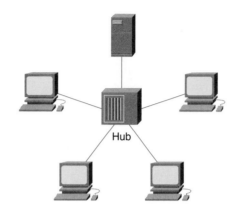

Hub

The star topology is generally used with unshielded twisted-pair (UTP) cabling and the Ethernet 10BaseT or 100BaseT architecture.

Communications on a Star Network

On a typical star network, the signal is passed from the sending computer's NIC to the hub, boosted (that is, amplified), and sent back out all ports. On a star, in a manner similar to a bus, all computers receive the message, but only the computer whose address matches the destination address in the message's header pays attention.

Advantages of Star Networks

The star topology has two big advantages over the bus and ring. First, it is far more *fault tolerant*; that is, if one computer becomes disconnected or there is a break in its cable, only *that* computer is affected, and the rest of the network can communicate normally. Second, it offers ease of reconfiguration. Adding more computers to the network, or removing computers, is as simple as plugging in or unplugging a cable. Troubleshooting physical layer problems in a star network is also easy, especially with an intelligent hub that provides diagnostic information. You learn more about the physical and other layers defined by the standard networking models in Chapter 3, "Networking Concepts, Models, and Standards."

Disadvantages of Star Networks

Despite the star's benefits, it does have a few disadvantages, primarily related to cost. First, it uses more cable than the linear bus or ring because there must be a separate length of cable going all the way from the hub to each computer. Another source of additional expense is the hub itself, which must be purchased in addition to the cable. The good news is that UTP cable is relatively inexpensive, and there is no need for terminators on a star network.

Mesh Networks

The *mesh* is a topology you won't see as often as the three discussed so far. In a mesh network, every computer has a direct connection to every other computer on the network, as shown in Figure 2-12.

FIGURE 2-12
In a mesh network, every computer is connected to every other computer.

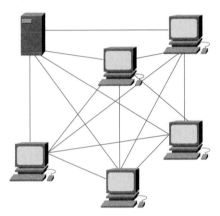

These redundant connections make the mesh the most fault-tolerant of all topologies. If one pathway from the sending to the destination computer is down, the signal can take another path.

Unfortunately, this advantage is offset by both the high cost of the huge amount of cable required to implement a mesh and the complexity of the network if more than a few computers are involved. The number of connections increases exponentially as each new computer is added. It is no coincidence that "mesh" sounds a lot like "mess"—that's exactly what you have as a mesh network grows.

Hybrid Topologies

The word *hybrid* is used in a couple of different ways in reference to network topology. In Chapter 13, we examine the use of the term *hybrid* to describe networks that run multiple protocols, operating systems, or computing platforms. In this chapter, the word is used in reference to a topology that combines elements of two or more of the standard topologies (for example, hybrid mesh, star bus, or ring bus).

Hybrid Mesh Networks

Because the mesh topology quickly grows complex and unmanageable, many networks are based on a semi-mesh topology, in which there are redundant connections between some of the computers, but not all; this type of network is often referred to as a *hybrid mesh*. The redundant connections should be made between the computers that have the greatest need for a fault tolerant connection. Figure 2-13 shows an example.

FIGURE 2-13
A hybrid mesh provides for redundant connections between some computers, but not all.

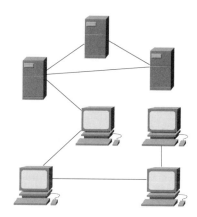

The hybrid mesh provides much of the benefit of the mesh at less expense, and it is easier to set up and manage.

Combined Topologies

Hybrid is also used to refer to networks that use multiple topologies. Many networks combine one or more topologies. For instance, you can have several hubs with computers connected to each in a star configuration, and then network the hubs in a linear bus. Many hubs include a BNC connector for thin coax cable, along with several RJ-45 ports for the UTP connections, for this purpose.

In this type of connection (see Figure 2-14), the coax cable connecting the hubs is called the *backbone*. The backbone is the part of the network that connects all smaller parts, or *segments*. Several segments can be connected to one backbone to create a larger network.

FIGURE 2-14
The coax cable
connecting the
hubs is called the
backbone of the
network.

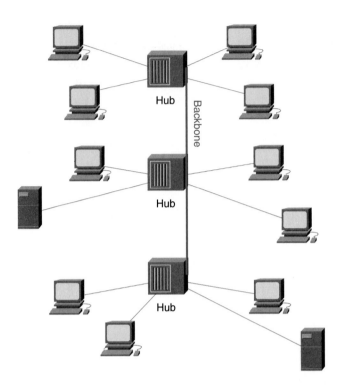

Categorizing Networks by Architecture

Yet another way to describe a network is by its architecture. Generally speaking, the *network architecture* includes a set of specifications that take into account its physical and logical topologies, the type of cable used, distance limitations, media access methods, packet size and headers, and other factors. You might see these specifications referred to as the *data link layer protocols*.

The most popular current LAN architectures are Ethernet and Token Ring. Other common LAN architectures are AppleTalk and ARCnet. All are described in the following sections.

Ethernet Networks

Ethernet, developed in the 1960s and refined by Xerox, Digital, and Intel to form the basis of the IEEE 802.3 specifications, is today's most popular networking architecture. We examine the role of IEEE specifications in Chapter 3.

Ethernet networks are configured as a physical bus or star, and use the carrier sense multiple access collision detect (CSMA/CD) method of media access.

Standard Ethernet was limited to 10 Mbps, but *Fast Ethernet*, which runs at 100 Mbps, is now commonplace, and *Gigabit Ethernet*—capable of speeds exceeding 1 Gbps—is emerging as a new and exciting technology.

There are different subcategories of Ethernet networks, depending on the cable type used. They include the following:

- 10Base5
- 10Base2
- 10BaseT
- 100BaseT
- 1000BaseT
- 100BaseVG-AnyLAN
- 10BaseFL
- 100BaseFL

In the next sections, we discuss characteristics of each type of Ethernet network.

10Base5 Ethernet Networks

Referred to as standard Ethernet, although it is no longer as popular as some of the other types, 10Base5 networks use thick coaxial cable (approximately one-half inch in diameter) and are also called *thicknet networks*. Thick coaxial cable is also called *RG-8* or *RG-11*.

The 10 in 10Base5 refers to its maximum speed: 10 Mbps. The 5 refers to maximum segment length, which is 500 meters. Thicknet networks use the bus topology.

Thicknet is more difficult to work with than other Ethernet cabling for a couple of reasons. First, it is less flexible because of the larger diameter. Second, connections are made using a device called a *vampire tap*, which requires that you drill a small hole into the cable to attach the connector. 10Base5 networks use *external transceivers*. A transceiver is a device that generates and receives the data signals; in other Ethernet architectures, the transceiver is built into the network card. 10Base5 technology uses DIX connectors with AUI cable to connect the transceiver to the NIC.

Thicknet often is used in conjunction with other Ethernet cable types to provide a *backbone* linking thinnet segments or 10BaseT hubs.

10Base2 Ethernet Networks

A popular coax-based network type is 10Base2 Ethernet, which uses thinner (approximately one-quarter inch in diameter), less expensive, and more flexible

NOTE

Specifications about maximum and minimum segment lengths are given in meters in most books because it is standard practice in the scientific community to use metric measurements rather than the U.S. measurement system. We follow that convention in this book. However, popular certification exams have been known to mix measurement types. For example, one question can give a cable length in meters, while another gives the measurement in feet, so it is important to know how to make the conversion: One meter equals 3.28 feet.

NOTE

We discuss NICs and the various connector types in detail in Chapter 7.

cable than 10Base5. The 2 in this case is a bit misleading; it is actually a rounded up approximation of the maximum segment length, which is 185 meters. Like 10Base5, these thinnet networks are physically structured as a linear bus, which requires termination at each end.

10Base2 networks are easier to set up and work with at the physical level than thicknet networks. Twist-and-push connectors (called *BNC connectors*) are used to connect the cable to a *T-connector* on the network card, as shown in Figure 2-15, and the transceiver is built into the network card.

FIGURE 2-15
Thinnet connects to the NIC's T-connector with a BNC twistlock device on the end of the cable.

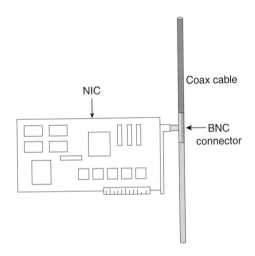

NIC

Coax cable

BNC connector

WARNING

Although RG-58 cable is similar in appearance to RG-59, which is used for cable television installations, don't confuse the two. RG-59 is 75-ohm cable and should *not* be used for computer networking. RG-58U is a similar cable type that does not meet IEEE specifications and should be avoided.

Thin coaxial cable for a 10Base2 network is 50-ohm RG-58A/U or RG-58C/U. (The first is most often used; the latter is a military specification.)

Thinnet cable is sometimes called *cheapernet* because it costs less to implement than thick coax cable. Thinnet is generally more expensive per foot than UTP, but less cable is required for a coax network because of the bus configuration.

UTP Ethernet Networks

The most popular media for new LAN installations is UTP cable, which is used in 10BaseT (T for *twisted*) networks. Most of us are already familiar with twisted-pair cabling, which is used for telephone cabling.

UTP comes in different grades, identified as numbered *categories* that follow the pattern of Cat 1, Cat 2, and so on. Table 2-3 shows the UTP categories and the use and characteristics of each.

TABLE 2-3   Available Categories of UTP Cable

UTP Category	Maximum Transmission Speed	Characteristics and Uses
Cat 1	Voice only	Used in old telephone installations
Cat 2	4 Mbps	Not recommended for data transmission
Cat 3	16 Mbps	Lowest recognized data grade; used for most telephone wiring
Cat 4	20 Mbps	Suitable for networking 10 Mbps Ethernet networks
Cat 5	100 Mbps–1 Gbps	Most popular grade for LAN networking; used for Fast Ethernet (100 Mbps)
*Cat 5 Enhanced (Cat 5e)	155 Mbps	Used for Fast Ethernet and 155 Mbps Asynchronous Transfer Mode (ATM)
*Cat 6 & 7	1 Gbps and up	Used for new Gigabit Ethernet technologies

   *   You often do not see Cat 6, Cat 7, and enhanced Cat 5 mentioned in networking texts because these new cable types have specifications that have been only recently established.

As you can see, UTP supports higher transmission speeds than coax. UTP is also highly flexible and easy to install. It uses RJ connectors, which are the modular plug types used for telephones. Although telephone cables usually use the smaller RJ-11 connector, most Ethernet cables connect with the slightly larger RJ-45 connector.

In a UTP-based network, each computer has a length of cable connecting it to a central *hub* in a star topology. We discuss various types of hubs in Chapter 7.

10BaseT Networks. The 10BaseT specification is popular for LANs of all sizes. It can run on Cat 3 cable, which is already installed in many buildings for telephone communications. New 10BaseT networks are usually set up using Cat 5 or 5e cable so that it is easy to upgrade to 100 Mbps later.

100BaseT Networks. The 100BaseT classification refers to Ethernet networks running at 100 Mbps over Cat 5 or 5e cable. These networks use the same topology and access methods as 10BaseT. Indeed, the only differences are the requirement for the higher-grade cable and the fact that the network cards and hubs must support the 100-Mbps transmission speed.

Many NICs and hubs are made to support both 10- and 100-Mbps transmission speeds, which makes it easy to upgrade incrementally. In addition, with the proper hardware, you can run part of the network at 100 Mbps while other parts still run at 10 Mbps.

NOTE

The IEEE 802.3ab standard sets specifications for the operation, testing, and usage requirements for Gigabit Ethernet for distances of up to 100 m, using four pairs of Cat 5 copper cabling. This includes most of the cabling already installed in buildings for 10BaseT and 100BaseT networks.

1000BaseT (Gigabit Ethernet) Networks. The initial standards for very high speed Ethernet, most commonly called Gigabit Ethernet, were established by the IEEE in 1996 and published as the 802.3z specifications. These standards provide for 1000-Mbps (1-Gbps) transmission, using the 802.3 Ethernet frame format and the CSMA/CD access method.

A big advantage of Gigabit Ethernet is its interoperability and backward compatibility with its predecessors. Gigabit Ethernet makes an excellent backbone technology in conjunction with 10BaseT and 100BaseT LANs.

NICs and hubs that support the 1000 BaseT standards are available, although at a cost that is several times that of 100-Mbps Ethernet components.

100BaseVG-AnyLAN Networks. Hewlett Packard developed 100BaseVG-AnyLAN technology as a fast, reliable networking architecture that uses a special type of hub that functions as an intelligent central controller. This hub manages network access by continually performing a rapid round-robin scan of network port requests to check for service requests from the nodes that are attached to them. The hub receives the incoming data packet and directs it only to the port with a matching destination address. This matching provides inherent network data security.

Hubs can be linked together, and each hub can be configured to support either 802.3 Ethernet or 802.5 Token Ring frame formats. However, all hubs on the same network segment must be configured to use the same frame format.

100BaseVG-AnyLAN networks often are placed into the Ethernet category, but they use a different media access method, called *demand priority*, that is defined in IEEE specification 802.12.

10BaseFL and 100BaseFL Networks. The FL in 10BaseFL stands for *fiber link*, and these networks use baseband signaling over fiber optic cable. You learn more about signaling methods in Chapter 4, "Networking Communications Methods."

Fiber-optic cabling uses pulses of light instead of electrical signals to represent the 0s and 1s of binary communication used by computers. A big advantage of fiber optics over copper cabling is its resistance to interference and *attenuation* (that is, loss of signal strength over distance). A cable segment under the FL specifications can be 2000 meters in length, which is 4 times that of 10Base5, over 10 times that of 10Base2, and 20 times the limit for 10BaseT!

Token Ring Networks

Token Ring is a networking architecture that was developed by IBM in the 1980s. It was designed to overcome some of the problems inherent in a *contention*-type network such as Ethernet, where the computers on the network compete or contend for the chance to broadcast. We discuss this more in Chapter 4 in the section "Media Access Methods."

In a Token Ring network, which uses a logical ring topology, a signal called a *token* is passed around the circle and a computer cannot broadcast until the token gets around to it. This means that, unlike Ethernet networks, Token Ring networks do not experience *data collisions*. A data collision occurs when two computers send at the same time.

Although logically a ring, Token Ring networks are physically laid out as star topologies. Computers connect to a central hub or concentrator called an MSAU. The ring is actually inside the hub, where the wiring connects the ports in a continuous circle and the data travels in a circular path.

The standards for Token Ring networks are defined in IEEE 802.5. IBM cable types, primarily shielded twisted-pair (STP), are used. Token Ring network cards and other components are generally more expensive than those made for Ethernet networks. However, Token Ring is a highly reliable architecture that is still in use in many LANs.

Older Token Ring components supported only 4-Mbps transmissions, but newer implementations can transfer data at 16 Mbps.

Advantages of Token Ring include the following:

- As a Token Ring network gets overloaded, its performance degrades gracefully. That is, the network gradually gets slower but does not fail suddenly, as can happen with Ethernet.

NOTE

Efforts are under way to develop an effective high-speed Token Ring technology that runs Token Ring over FDDI or ATM. For more information, see the white papers provided by the High-Speed Token Ring Alliance at www.hstra.com/ whitepapers.html.

■ Token Ring uses an *active topology*, in which each computer in the circle regenerates the signal as the signal travels around the ring. Ethernet networks require *repeaters* to boost the signal as distance increases.

AppleTalk Networks

Apple Computers developed the AppleTalk protocol suite to network its Macintosh machines for file and print sharing in a workgroup environment. AppleShare is a suite of application layer protocols that provide this functionality. AppleShare components, which are built into the Macintosh operating system, include the following:

■ **AppleShare File Server**—Enables users to access the computer's resources

■ **AppleShare Print Server**—Provides for sharing of printers

AppleShare PC is a service that runs on DOS computers to enable them to access files on an AppleShare file server or print to a shared AppleShare print server.

AppleTalk networks are often referred to as *LocalTalk* networks. The Local-Talk Link Access Protocol (LLAP) is the basic protocol used, and it supports dynamic addressing.

AppleTalk networks can be divided into groups, called *zones*, and serve a purpose similar to dividing a large network into workgroups. Users only see those shared resources that are in the zone to which he or she belongs. Routers use the Zone Information Protocol (ZIP) to communicate between zones.

ARCnet Networks

Attached Resource Computer Network (ARCnet) is an older LAN architecture that has, for the most part, been replaced by Ethernet and Token Ring. ARCnet uses a token-passing access method, but implements the network topology as a bus or star instead of as a ring.

> **NOTE**
>
> ARCnet networks are slow compared to most LAN technologies: 2.5 Mbps for standard ARCnet, although a newer standard called *ARCnet Plus* improves on this considerably, with a top speed of 20 Mbps.

In an ARCnet network, the token is passed in numerical order according to the *node address*, which is an eight-digit binary number set on the ARCnet NIC using DIP switches or jumpers. If the cards are not numbered carefully so that the signal travels in a logical order—or if computers are later moved to different locations without the addresses being changed—you can end up with the signal traveling greater distances than necessary. Figure 2-16 illustrates this problem.

ARCnet can use coax, UTP, or even fiber-optic cable, but it is most commonly associated with RG-62/U 90-ohm coax cable. One of the drawbacks of ARCnet, and a reason it is no longer a popular choice for local-area networking, is its very proprietary nature. It is, however, a stable and reliable architecture.

FIGURE 2-16
If the addresses on ARCnet NICs are not set properly, the path taken by the token can be very inefficient.

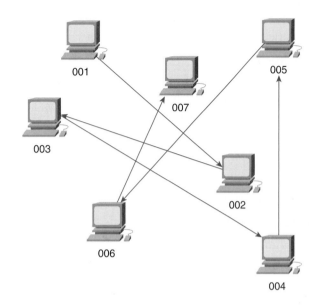

Summary

In this chapter, we have looked at many different ways in which networks can be categorized, including the following:

- The physical scope of the network
- The administrative model used to manage the network
- The NOS run on the servers that control the network
- The protocols used by the network to communicate
- The topology or layout of the network
- The architecture, which encompasses the standards and specifications by which the network operates

There are, of course, other ways in which networks can be categorized. This book focuses on networking PCs, but in the bigger picture, networks could also be categorized as PC networks and mainframe networks.

Many of the categories we have discussed can be broken down further; for instance, UNIX networks can be broken down into HP-UX networks, SUN Solaris networks, AIX networks, SCO networks, and so on. Microsoft networks can be divided into Windows 2000 networks, Windows NT 4.0 networks, and Windows NT 3.51 networks—not to mention Windows 9x workgroups.

As we examined each method of categorization, you might have noticed that certain architectures are associated with certain topologies, or that particular NOSs use specific administrative models, or that some protocols are used more often in networks of a particular physical scope. In later chapters, we build on these observations.

You will learn about the different signaling methods used by different technologies and the different cable types associated with different media access methods. Chapter 3 provides a look at the popular models used to describe the complex process in which all these components engage. We also discuss the specifications and standards on which networks are based.

Further Reading

A good resource for information on Gigabit Ethernet is the Gigabit Ethernet Consortium homepage: www.iol.unh.edu/consortiums/ge/main.html.

GEC2000 is an annual conference addressing Gigabit Ethernet, most recently held March 27–29, 2000, in San Jose, California. See the GEC2000 website, at www.etherconference.com/English/Main_Splash.html.

An excellent resource for information about Hewlett Packard's 100BaseVG-AnyLAN is available at www.100vg.com.

For general information on how LANs operate, see www.net-engineer.com/lanbasics1.html.

Review Questions

The following questions test your knowledge on the material covered in this chapter. Be sure to read each question carefully and select the *best* correct answer or answers.

1. Which of the following is a category used when classifying networks according to the physical scope of the network?

   A. 10Base2

   B. WAN

   C. IPX/SPX

   D. Ring

2. Which of the following is true of the typical LAN? (Select all that apply.)

   A. A LAN is a large network comprised of many small networks.

   B. A LAN typically spans a dispersed geographic area, with nodes in different cities, states, or countries.

   C. A LAN is typically confined to a limited area, with the computers in close physical proximity.

   D. LANs can be divided into workgroups for easier management.

3. What is a group of networks that are networked to each other called?

   A. An internet

   B. An intranet

   C. An extranet

   D. A workgroup

4. Which of the following is true of a client/server (or server-based) network but not true of a peer-to-peer network? (Select all that apply.)

   A. Client/server networks are generally less expensive to implement.

   B. Client/server networks provide for centralized data storage, making backups easier.

   C. Client/server networks generally require a dedicated network administrator.

   D. Client/server networks offer better security.

5. Which of the following terms is used to identify a logon authentication server in a Microsoft client/server network?

 A. Daemon

 B. Security Accounts Manager

 C. Domain controller

 D. Cluster server

6. Which of the following is true of security in a peer-to-peer (workgroup) environment? (Select all that apply.)

 A. Security is centralized and administered by a network administrator.

 B. Security is stronger and more difficult to defeat than in a client/server environment.

 C. Each machine in the workgroup maintains its own local security database.

 D. Security is implemented at the share level rather than at the user level.

7. Which of the following is a characteristic of Windows 2000 domains that is a change from the Windows NT domain model? (Select all that apply.)

 A. Windows 2000 domains are based on a directory service called the Active Directory.

 B. Windows 2000 domains are based on a directory service called the Bindery.

 C. Windows 2000 domains are referred to as downlevel domains.

 D. Windows 2000 domains can contain multiple domain controllers, all of which can read and write to the directory database.

8. Which of the following is true of TCP/IP networks?

 A. TCP/IP networks are typically medium- to large-sized networks that contain multiple subnets.

 B. The global Internet is a TCP/IP network.

 C. Few tools and utilities are available for TCP/IP networks.

 D. TCP/IP networks are easier to administer than NetBEUI networks.

9. What is the name for the network topology that has a beginning and an end and that requires termination to prevent signal bounce?

   A. Star

   B. Hybrid mesh

   C. Linear bus

   D. Token Ring

10. Which of the following network architectures uses unshielded twisted-pair cabling?

   A. 10Base2

   B. 10BaseT

   C. 100BaseFL

   D. Token Ring

Chapter 3

Networking Concepts, Models, and Standards

Learning, especially learning about a new and complex subject such as computer networking, is easier when we start with theory and concepts and then move on to the more concrete aspects of implementation. Just as an aspiring doctor learns the theories of biology, biochemistry, and human physiology before seeing a patient, aspiring network professionals learn the theory of how network communications take place before attempting to set up, manage, or troubleshoot networked computers.

This chapter presents basic concepts involved in computer networking and discusses ways of representing, understanding, and remembering them. Specifically, we discuss networking models, standards, specifications (and the entities that establish them), and the well-known rules of networking engagement that you should keep in mind as you read about network design, hardware, and software in later chapters.

Computer Communication Concepts

Regardless of the size and scope of the network, the topology, the architecture, the media type, or the administrative model used, we link computers for one basic reason: to enable them to communicate with one another. That sounds simple, but in reality it is a complex process. Before you can understand how communication takes place across the network, you must first understand how computers process information.

In the following sections, we discuss the concepts behind network communication, including the following:

- The binary language used to communicate with machines (also called *machine language*)
- Networking models that have been devised to graphically represent the communications process
- The standards and specifications established to make it easier for the networking products of different vendors to communicate with one another

Our first step is to look at the language or *code* that computers speak and how it enables us to program them to perform the tasks we desire.

The Language of the Machine

Modern computers are sophisticated machines capable of performing a myriad of complicated tasks. When you enter a letter or report into a word processing program, not only can the computer save your work and enable you to make changes to it later, but also it can check the spelling and grammar, format the appearance according to your preset preferences, and even enable you to send the document to someone working at another computer across the room or across the globe.

With the proper software, a PC can display amazing graphic designs, keep track of your schedule, and remind you when you have an appointment. It can run maintenance utilities to keep its operating system and file tables in good order, log on to the Internet (with or without your intervention), and retrieve updates for its software. It can even out-think a world-champion chess player.

A computer accomplishes all these functions, and more, by performing high-speed mathematical calculations using only 1s and 0s. "Under the hood," computers process commands and return results using *binary*, a *base 2* number system, which, as you'll see in a moment, is uniquely suited for electronic communication. Binary code is sometimes referred to as machine language.

Common Numbering Systems

There are quite a few numbering and counting systems. We most commonly use *decimal* for everyday transactions, but other systems that are used extensively in the scientific field include *hexadecimal* and *binary*. We look at each in the following sections.

The Decimal System

NOTE

Don't be confused by the name. A decimal number does not necessarily contain a decimal point.

The *decimal* numbering system is also called *base 10* because it is based on 10 numeric digits (0 through 9) that can be organized to represent numbers that are even too large to name.

In a decimal number such as 342, the "3" represents three *hundreds*, the "4" represents four *tens*, and the "2" represents two *ones*, based on the place occupied by each digit in relation to the others.

The Hexadecimal System

Another numbering system, which is also used in the computer industry, is hexadecimal. *Hex*, as it is called, is not an evil spell invoked by a broomstick-riding witch, although working with it can seem a little like black magic to the uninitiated. The hexadecimal system is *base 16*, using the same 10 digits as the decimal system, plus the alphabetic characters A through F.

In hex, the numbers 0 through 9 have the same meaning as they have in decimal notation. However, the number we ordinarily represent as 10 (9 plus 1 more) is noted in hexadecimal as A. The decimal 11 is B in hexadecimal; 12 is C; 13 is D; 14 is E; and 15 is F. Okay, that's relatively simple, but when we run out of allotted letters, it gets a little more confusing. For instance, the number we call 16 in decimal is 10 in hex, and 17 is 11.

How do we make the conversion? Well, the easiest way is to use the Windows calculator in scientific mode or any other scientific calculator. Counting actually works the same way in hexadecimal as in decimal, except that we have those extra six digits to contend with. Table 3-1 shows how decimal and hexadecimal numbers correspond. The decimal equivalent is shown in parentheses.

Hexadecimal notation is used in the computer industry because it is easier to convert between hex and binary than between decimal and binary. Because hexadecimal is base 16, you can use two hex digits to represent each *byte* (which is made up of 8 binary *bits*). We come back to bits and bytes in the next section of this chapter.

Note that in Table 3-1, some hexadecimal numbers look like decimal numbers, even when they don't represent the same value. If we see the number 12 sitting there all by itself, how do we know whether it represents the decimal number 12, or if it is a hexadecimal representation of the decimal number 18? We need a way to identify the base system being used. Fortunately, hexadecimal notation is indicated in one of two ways:

- By appending an H to the end of the number, for example, 12H
- By prefixing the number with 0x, for example, 0x12

Note that the second method is the standard way of indicating hex notation in C++ and some other programming languages.

NOTE

If you attempt to research the origins of hexadecimal, you'll find it's a hybrid of the Greek *hexa*, which means six, and the Latin *decem*, which means ten.

TABLE 3-1   How Hexadecimal Corresponds to Decimal (Decimal numbers are in parentheses)

0 (0)	1 (1)	2 (2)	3 (3)	4 (4)	5 (5)	6 (6)	7 (7)	8 (8)
10 (16)	11 (17)	12 (18)	13 (19)	14 (20)	15 (21)	16 (22)	17 (23)	18 (24)
20 (32)	21 (33)	22 (34)	23 (35)	24 (36)	25 (37)	26 (38)	27 (39)	28 (40)
9 (9)	A (10)	B (11)	C (12)	D (13)	E (14)	F (15)		
19 (25)	1A (26)	1B (27)	1C (28)	1D (29)	1E (30)	1F (31)		
29 (41)	2A (42)	2B (43)	2C (44)	2D (45)	2E (46)	2F (47)		

The Binary System

In one way, the binary numbering system is the height of simplicity; it uses only two digits: 0 and 1. Because all numbers must be represented with just these two digits, however, the numbers get very large, very quickly. For example, the decimal number 519 in binary becomes 10000000111.

The word *binary* comes from the Latin *bi*, meaning two, and binary is called a *base 2* numbering system. An example of a binary number is 01001100.

0s and 1s. If you've never been exposed to binary numbering, you may wonder how it is possible to represent all possible numbers using only two digits. Of course, the same question could be asked about the practice of using only 10 digits, but we have been doing that all our lives. To us, it seems normal to use places to indicate the value of each digit by designating, for instance, the third place from the right as representing hundreds. Binary works similarly.

Bits and Bytes. A binary digit (a single 1 or 0) is called a bit. In most computer systems, a byte equals 8 bits. The *byte* is a string of bits grouped for convenience and is the unit that computers generally use to represent a *character* (that is, an alphabetic letter, a numeric digit, or a symbol).

Converting Binary to Decimal. Look again at our sample binary number: 01001100. To determine what this number represents in decimal notation, you must know how to interpret the value of each digit, according to its place.

In binary notation, each bit is turned "on" or "off." A 0 indicates that a bit is off, and a bit that is turned off has no value (0). A bit that is turned on has a value according to its place. Just as with the decimal system with which we are so familiar, we determine the place by counting from the right.

In binary, as in decimal, a 1 in the first (far right) place has a value of 1. That's where the similarity between decimal and binary ends, however. In binary, which is a base 2 system, the value of a turned-on bit increases by a power of 2 each time we move one place to the left. Thus, the decimal equivalent of each

NOTE

Remember that in binary language, 0 and 1 are the only digits that exist.

NOTE

The term "byte" comes from the phrase "binary term" and refers to the amount of computer memory required to store one character of a specified size. This character size has become standardized as 8 bits for microcomputers, but a byte represents 16 bits on some larger computers (minicomputers and mainframes).

binary value (when the bit is turned on or designated as 1) is shown in Table 3-2.

TABLE 3-2   Determining the Value of Binary Bits

Binary	1	1	1	1	1	1	1	1
Decimal	128	64	32	16	8	4	2	1

If the digit is a 0, the bit for that place is off and its value is 0 as well. So, to convert the original binary number 01001100 to decimal, we simply add up the values for each bit that is turned on. Table 3-3 illustrates this.

TABLE 3-3   Converting a Binary Number to Its Decimal Equivalent

Binary	0	1	0	0	1	1	0	0
Decimal	0	64	0	0	8	4	0	0

To get the decimal equivalent of 01001100, we add 64 + 8 + 4, which gives us a value of 76. You can check the answer by entering the binary number in a scientific calculator and selecting the Dec option to perform the conversion.

Why Use Binary? All this makes for interesting small talk (if you're attending a party full of network engineers), but you may still be wondering why computer communications are based on the binary system in the first place. Why not hexadecimal? Or even better, why not use decimal, so you don't have to spend time learning to work in other numbering systems?

There is a reason. Think about this fact: Computers are electronic machines, and they represent data by using electrical impulses. Computers use *digital* signals. In Chapter 4, "Networking Communications Methods," we talk more about digital signals and how they differ from the *analog* signals broadcast by radios.

For purposes of this discussion, note that digital signaling is a *discrete state* form of signal. Discrete state works like a simple light bulb: It can be either on or off. It cannot be both at the same time, and there are no degrees of "on-ness" or "off-ness" between the states.

You can see how binary notation is very easy to represent using digital electronic signals. As with the light bulb, an electrical current is either present or not present. If it is present (on), the computer sees a 1. If it is not present (off), the computer sees a 0.

Binary calculation and how it relates to digital signaling is the first and most basic concept that you need to master to understand how computer networking works. See the "Further Reading" section at the end of the chapter for in-depth information on binary communications.

Using Packets

Before data can be sent across a network as electrical impulses, it first must be broken into manageable chunks. An entire word processing document or e-mail message cannot be sent in one long, continuous stream. This would tie up the network, and other computers would be unable to send. For many computers to use the network simultaneously, large files must be divided into smaller sections before being sent over cable or other media.

Consider an analogy: Suppose you need to mail a 100-page report to a colleague, but you have only letter-sized envelopes, each of which is already metered with enough postage to deliver a 1-ounce document. One solution is to break the large document into parts that weigh 1 ounce each, put each part in a separate envelope, address them all to your colleague, and put them all in the mailbox. Your recipient can reassemble the report when all the envelopes arrive.

In a perfect world, all the envelopes would arrive in the correct order. However, the postal service doesn't work this way. Your colleague might not even receive all the envelopes on the same day because of the complex routing process that mail goes through at the post office. The envelope containing the first pages of the document won't necessarily arrive first, either. How will your colleague put the report back together in the proper order? You can make your colleague's job much easier if you number the pages so that he or she doesn't have to figure out the sequence.

In the section "Putting the Data Back Together Again," we discuss how the networking protocols provide sequencing information so that packets are reassembled correctly at the receiving end.

The small, easily transmitted units into which computer data is broken for transmission across a network are called *packets.* Depending on the networking architecture and the point in the communications process the unit has reached, the term *frames* can be used to talk about packets. In addition, the word *segment* refers to a unit of data transmitted by the Transmission Control Protocol (TCP). We use the term *packet* to refer to these manageable chunks in general.

NOTE

You might have noticed that we use the word data to describe the signals being sent across the network. *Information* and *data* are two terms that are sometimes used interchangeably, but they are not the same. *Information* is data in usable form, such as a message produced by your e-mail program. The *data* is not the information itself; it is the encoded form of the information, which is the series of electrical impulses into which the information is translated for sending.

Advantages of Dividing Data into Packets

Transmitting data in small packets has several advantages:

- Computers on the network can take turns sending packets, and one computer with a large amount of data to transmit won't monopolize the network's bandwidth.

- If network communication is disrupted and a packet is lost, only that small amount of data, rather than the entire file, has to be retransmitted.

- Depending on the network's topology and link type, each packet may be able to take a different path to reach the destination. Thus, if one pathway becomes congested or slows down, subsequent packets can take a more efficient route.

Putting the Data Back Together Again

If we separate data into chunks and then send each chunk individually, what happens when they arrive at their destination? Refer back to our post office analogy; the networking components do something similar. Each data packet has information added to the raw data itself, in the form of *packet headers*. The headers contain addressing information so that the packets reach the correct destination. They also contain sequencing information so that the data can be reassembled accurately when all packets reach the receiving computer.

Header information is placed at the *head* of the packet, in front of the original data. Packets can also include *trailer information*, which is appended to the back of the packet, following the original data. This often includes error-checking information. Figure 3-1 shows the structure of a typical data packet.

NOTE

The error-checking component in the trailer is called a *cyclical redundancy check (CRC)*. The CRC performs calculations—in binary, of course—on the packet before it leaves the source computer and again when it reaches the destination. If the results of these calculations are different, the data has changed. This can occur because of a disruption of the electrical signals that represent the 0s and 1s making up the data. If a discrepancy is found, that packet can be resent.

FIGURE 3-1
A typical data packet includes header and trailer information.

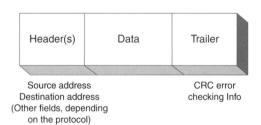

The exact fields in the header and trailer portions of the packet depend on the networking architecture and protocols, as does the size of each field. For example, on an Ethernet network, the data unit is called a frame. An Ethernet frame can be between 64 and 1518 bytes in size, but 18 bytes is used for the Ethernet frame itself. This means that there is a maximum of 1500 bytes of data per frame (packet). A Token Ring frame or packet is quite a bit larger, typically holding 4202 bytes of data.

A Layered Communication Process

As if the way a standalone computer functions internally—converting data into 0s and 1s for processing—wasn't complicated enough, we then expect the computer to send the data to another computer, even if the other computer is not using the same operating system or application program. For example, if you want to use a Windows NT PC to send an e-mail message composed in the Microsoft Outlook Express mail program to a recipient who uses the Eudora Pro mail program on an Apple Macintosh, you expect the message to be transferred quickly and accurately!

The network communication process is complex. All those words you enter, along with information necessary to get it to its correct destination with the attached graphics or other files, must somehow be reduced to a series of electronic impulses representing 0s and 1s.

The data, in the form of electronic signals, must travel across a cable to the correct destination computer and then be converted to its original form to be read by the recipient. As you can imagine, there are several steps involved in this process. For this reason, developers of hardware, software, and protocols recognized that the most efficient way to implement network communications would be as a *layered* process.

Network Teamwork

Building a car, like transferring data across a network, is a *process* that involves many individual functions. One person *could* take all the parts and, with the proper tools, assemble them into a functioning automobile, but cars are not built that way. Why?

Experience has shown that it is more efficient to use an assembly line to put together automobiles. On an assembly line, the car is built in layers. Each worker, at each station along the way, has a specific responsibility. The steps required to assemble the car are broken down into very basic functions: One person can put a hubcap in place, the next person on the line can insert a screw, and the third can tighten the screw. This methodology gives the following advantages:

- Each worker can focus exclusively on his or her own area of responsibility.
- Because each worker repeats the same task over and over, all become very proficient at their respective tasks.

> **NOTE**
>
> Pulses of electricity constitute the typical means of LAN communications, although we could substitute pulses of light or radio transmissions, depending on the networking media used. We examine different media types in Chapter 7, "Physical Components of the Network."

- By working as a team, the workers can produce their final product more quickly and efficiently than would be possible by one person or a group of people with no assigned responsibilities.

- It is easy to track accountability. If there is a problem at one layer (for example, if a particular screw was not tightened), it is simple to determine who is responsible.

A layered communication process works in a similar manner. Each layer (that is, each component of the networking system) performs a specific task. As with the automobile assembly line example, this results in the process being completed more quickly and more efficiently. In addition, just as the supervisor knows whom to blame when a mistake is made, the network administrator is able to narrow down the troubleshooting scope when something goes wrong.

Processes and Protocols

Using the layered model, the network communication process is broken into steps somewhat like the automobile assembly process. In our automotive factory, someone must first interact with the designer, interpret the specifications, and get the assembly process started. Likewise, in networking, one "worker" takes care of interacting with the user application and starting the process of sending data out over the network. Another handles tasks such as compressing the data, encrypting it, or otherwise packaging it for transport. Yet another deals with ensuring accuracy, the next with making sure the data is addressed correctly so it will reach its intended destination, and so on.

The assembly line workers in this process are the *protocols* that operate at each layer of our model. As we look at the models in detail in the following sections, it is important for you to understand which networking protocols operate at which layers; this not only indicates the protocols' functions, but also provides you with valuable information for troubleshooting when the communications process does not proceed smoothly.

Networking Models

Most human beings are dependent on visual stimuli. We understand better when we can see something for ourselves. Abstract concepts that have no concrete form can still be represented in a *model*, however, to make it easier for us to visualize a structure, a process, or a relationship.

Models are all around us. Geneticists use the double helix to represent the structure of a DNA molecule. Physicists represent the relationships of protons and electrons at the atomic level. Atoms are too small to be seen, but scientists use models to assist in understanding ideas that cannot be seen directly.

The Purpose of Models

If we look up the word model in a dictionary, we find that it has many meanings, for instance, "a schematic description of a system, theory, or phenomenon that accounts for its known or inferred properties and can be used for further study of its characteristics" (*American Heritage Dictionary*). This definition captures one of the purposes of networking models: to help us describe, understand and study the network communications process.

A model is also "one serving as an example to be imitated or compared" (*American Heritage Dictionary*). Networking models are the basis for *standardization*; if the same model is used by vendors of networking products, those products are compatible with one another. The models describe how data communications should take place. If a vendor who makes networking products adheres to the standards at each layer, the networking components should work with those made by other vendors. We discuss other aspects of standardization, and who sets the standards, later in this chapter.

The OSI Model

The "model of models" in the networking world is the Open System Interconnection (OSI) model. Practically every computer networking book discusses this model, which was developed by the International Organization for Standardization (ISO).

The Structure of the OSI Model

The OSI model is made up of seven layers, each representing a step in the network communications process. The seven layers of the OSI model are shown in Figure 3-2.

The protocols that make up a *protocol suite* operate at different layers. You will learn more about networking protocols in Chapter 8, "Networking Protocols and Services."

Each layer in the OSI model performs a specific task in the network communication process, and then passes the data up or down to the next layer (depending on whether the layer is operating in the sending or receiving computer). As the data passes through the layers, each layer adds its own information in the form of *headers*, which are added in front of the original data. Refer to Figure 3-1 for an illustration of how headers are affixed.

Communication Between Peer Layers

The network communication process works like this: On the sending side, an application creates data to be transferred across the network. It then hands it off to the application layer of the operating system's networking component.

NOTE

In some books, the OSI model is referred to as Open System *Interconnect*, rather than *Interconnection*. The latter, however, is the usage on the Web site of the ISO, and we figure they should know best.

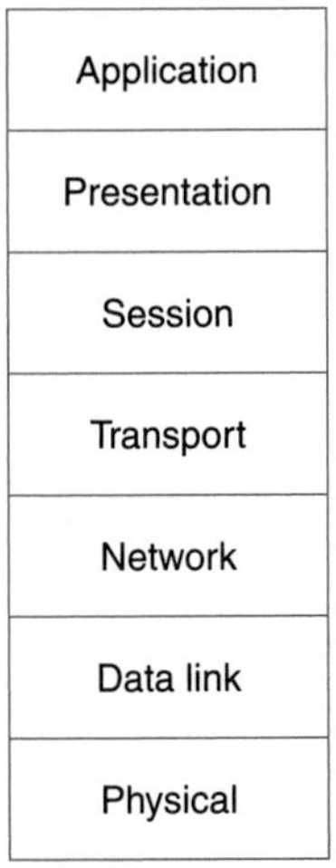

FIGURE 3-2
The OSI model
has seven layers.

Application
Presentation
Session
Transport
Network
Data link
Physical

As the data travels down through the layers, it is *encapsulated,* or enclosed within a larger unit, as each layer adds header information. When the data reaches the receiving computer, the process occurs in reverse; the information is passed upward through each layer, and as it does so, the encapsulation information is stripped off, one layer at a time, in the reverse order in which it was added.

The data link layer on the receiving end reads and strips off the header added by the data link layer on the sending side. Then, the network layer on the receiving side processes the header information added by its corresponding layer at the sending computer, and so on. In essence, each layer communicates only with the layer bearing the same name on the other side.

Figure 3-3 illustrates how this communication process works.

When the data has worked its way through the layers at the receiving computer, all header information has been removed and the data is in its original form, as created by the sender's application program. In that form, it is presented to the recipient's application in the form of information.

Figure 3-4 shows how the header information is added as the data progresses through the layers.

Note that the physical layer does not add header information. Its function does not require the addition of this information because it deals primarily with the networking hardware and signaling.

FIGURE 3-3
Each layer communicates directly with its peer layer on the other side.

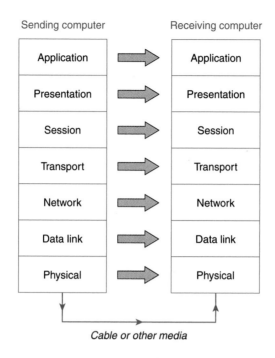

FIGURE 3-4
Each layer adds header information to the data as it travels down through the layers.

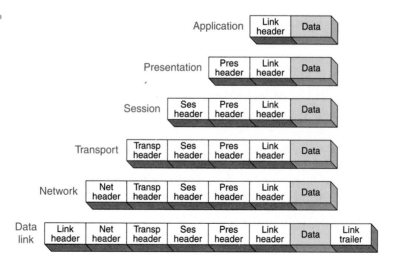

Let's take a look at the specific tasks performed by each of the OSI layers. We start at the top, where the process begins on the sending computer.

NOTE

Although the communication process begins on the sending computer at the top of the model, many networking courses teach the OSI layers "from the bottom up." You might see references to Layer 1, Layer 2, and so on. In standard networking terminology, the numbering begins at the bottom, with the physical layer as Layer 1.

The Application Layer. The first and most important thing to understand about the application layer is that it is not the user application that creates the message. Rather, this layer provides for interaction between that application program and the network. Protocols that function at the application layer perform functions such as file transfers, printing access, and messaging services.

Protocols that function at the application layer include the following:

- **File Transfer Protocol (FTP)**—FTP is used to transfer files between computers that do not necessarily run on the same operating system or platform. FTP server software runs on the computer hosting the files, and an FTP *client program* is used to connect to, upload to, or download from the server. A command-line FTP client is included in most vendors' implementations of the TCP/IP protocol suite. There are many popular graphical FTP clients, such as WSFTP, CuteFTP, and FTP Voyager. Modern versions of Web browsers such as the Microsoft Internet Explorer and Netscape's Navigator/Communicator also include built-in file transfer capabilities.

- **Telnet**—Telnet is used for terminal emulation and to enable access to applications and files on another computer. Unlike FTP, it cannot be used to copy the files from one computer to another, only to read or run them on the remote host. Telnet software includes the Telnet *server* software that runs on the remote computer being accessed, and the Telnet *client*, which runs on the accessing computer.

- **Simple Mail Transfer Protocol (SMTP)**—SMTP is a non-vendor-specific, simple ASCII protocol used for sending e-mail on the Internet. Many popular e-mail programs use SMTP for sending mail and the Post Office Protocol (POP3 is the current version) or the Internet Message Access Protocol (IMAP) for downloading mail from the user's mailbox on the mail server.

- **Simple Network Management Protocol (SNMP)**—SNMP gathers information about the network. SNMP can be used with different platforms and operating systems. It is often thought of as a TCP/IP protocol, but it can also be run over Internet Packet Exchange (IPX) and OSI. SNMP uses a Management Information Base (MIB), which is a database that contains information about a networked computer. SNMP has two parts: the *agent* software that runs on the computer being monitored and the *management* software that runs on the computer doing the monitoring.

These are only a few application-layer protocols. We discuss others, such as the Hypertext Transfer Protocol (HTTP) and the Network News Transfer

Protocol (NNTP), in Chapter 9, "The Widest Area Network: The Global Internet."

Don't confuse the application programs themselves with the protocols by the same name, on which they are based. For example, there are a variety of application programs called FTP (such as FTP Voyager, FTP Explorer, Fetch for Macintosh, and GREED for Linux) provided by different vendors. These programs use the FTP protocol to transfer files, but the applications also include features such as graphical interfaces (which differ from one implementation to the next) or additional functions such as file search engines.

The Presentation Layer. The application layer protocol receives the data from the user application and passes it down the stack to the presentation layer. As its name suggests, this layer handles issues that have to do with the packaging or *presentation* of the data. These issues include the following:

- **Data compression**—This is the reduction of the size of the data to facilitate faster transmission over the network. Different types of data can be compressed at different ratios.

- **Data encryption**—This is the conversion of data into an encoded form that cannot be read by unauthorized persons.

- **Protocol translation**—This is the conversion of data from one protocol to another so that it can be transferred between dissimilar platforms or operating systems.

The presentation layer on the receiving computer is responsible for uncompressing, decrypting, and otherwise translating data into a format understandable by the application and presenting it to the application layer.

Many gateways operate at the presentation layer. A *gateway* is a device or software program that serves as a connection point between two different networks. Popular gateways include the following:

- **Gateway Services for Netware (GSNW)**—This software is included with the Windows NT and Windows 2000 Server operating systems to enable the server's clients to access files on a Novell Netware server. It translates between the Server Message Block (SMB) used on the Microsoft software to Netware Core Protocol (NCP), which is the file sharing protocol used by Netware.

- **E-mail gateway**—This is a type of software that translates messages from diverse, incompatible e-mail systems into a common Internet format such as SMTP. This enables you to send an e-mail message from a Macintosh computer using the Eudora mail client to a recipient using, for example,

Lotus Notes on a NetWare network. Despite the difference in mail systems, the message goes through and is readable.

- **Systems Network Architecture (SNA) gateway**—SNA is a proprietary IBM architecture that is used in mainframe computer systems such as the AS/400. SNA gateway software enables PCs on a LAN to access files and applications on a mainframe computer from their PC desktops.

Redirectors, software that determines whether a request should be handled by the local computer or by a network device, redirect input/output requests appropriately and generally operate at the presentation layer.

The Session Layer. The next layer on the way down the stack in the OSI model is the session layer. The protocols at this layer have the duty of establishing a one-to-one session between the sending and receiving computers. The session layer sets up and tears down application-to-application dialogs. It also provides for *checkpointing* to synchronize the data flow for the applications. This involves placing markers in the stream of data. If there is a communication failure, only the data from the most recent marker, or *checkpoint*, need be resent.

Another function of the session layer is to control whether a transmission is sent as *half duplex* or *full duplex*. Full duplex is bidirectional communication, in which both sides can send and receive simultaneously. Half duplex is bidirectional too, but the signals can flow only in one direction at a time.

A full-duplex session works something like a conversation on a regular analog telephone. Both parties can talk at once, and you can still hear the other person's voice while you're talking. Half duplex is more like a conversation over a two-way radio. When you key the microphone so that you can transmit, you won't be able to hear anything said by the other person while you're talking. Transmission can go in either direction, but not both directions at the same time.

The session layer has many responsibilities, such as establishing the rules that are used to exchange data between the applications during the session. This is somewhat like the job of a referee, or a mediation expert, who ensures that both parties know the rules of the game and agree to follow them—at least for the duration of that session.

What else does this busy layer do? The session layer provides data expedition, class of service, and the reporting of problems in itself and the layers above it in the networking model.

Session layer protocols include the following:

- **Network Basic Input/Output System (NetBIOS) interface**—In session mode, NetBIOS lets two computers establish a connection, enables large

NOTE

Unidirectional communication, in which the signal can go only one way and can never go back in the other direction, is referred to as *simplex*. AM/FM radio broadcasts and television transmissions are simplex transmissions. Emerging "interactive TV" technologies require bidirectional communications, however, and many CATV companies are modifying their infrastructures to enable two-way signaling.

messages to be handled, and provides error detection and recovery. It also frees the application from having to understand the details of the network.

- **Windows Sockets (Winsock) interface**—This interface handles input/output requests for Internet applications in a Windows environment. Winsock is derived from the Berkeley UNIX sockets interface, which is used for establishing connections with and exchanging data between two program processes within the same computer or across a network. We discuss sockets more thoroughly in the next section.

The session layer can also perform security functions and name recognition.

The Transport Layer. The transport layer performs several important functions and is an essential element in network communications. The primary responsibility of this layer is to provide for reliable end-to-end error control and flow control. Transport layer protocols handle structuring of messages.

The transport layer keeps track of such things as validity of data packets, sequencing, and the handling of duplicate packets. The transport layer on the receiving end can send an acknowledgment back to the sending computer to let the sender know that the packet arrived. This only happens if the transport layer is using a *connection-oriented* protocol to send the message.

There are two protocol types used by the transport layer—*connection-oriented* and *connectionless*—as described in the following sections. Other important transport layer concepts are *name resolution* and *ports and sockets*.

Connection-Oriented Transport Protocols

TCP is a connection-oriented protocol that works at the transport layer as part of the TCP/IP protocol stack. Connection-oriented services establish a connection before sending the data, and use *acknowledgments* to verify that the data arrived safely at its destination.

Here's an analogy: If you wanted to mail a package to a friend, you could do so in one of two ways. In the first way, if the contents are important, you might first call your friend to let him know the package is on the way. This is similar to what connection-oriented protocols do; they establish a connection before sending.

In the second way, you might send it through certified mail with a return receipt requested. This means that you would be notified that the friend did indeed receive the package. The return receipt that comes back to you is like the acknowledgment that a connection-oriented protocol returns to the sending computer.

Connectionless Transport Protocols

User Datagram Protocol (UDP), also a member of the TCP/IP suite, is a connectionless transport protocol. Connectionless protocols work more like the regular mail service. When you put first class postage on a letter and mail it, you trust that it will reach the destination to which it is addressed, but there is no mechanism provided to let you know that it did.

Connectionless transport services are used to send messages that are not critical or that are short and simple and easily resent if lost. For example, broadcast messages, which are sent to all computers on a subnet, use UDP.

What is the advantage of the connectionless protocols if they are less reliable? The advantage is speed; simplicity and low overhead result in faster performance.

Name Resolution

Another duty of the transport layer is the resolution of computer (host) names to logical network addresses. Both TCP/IP and Internet Package Exchange/ Sequenced Packet Exchange (IPX/SPX) assign logical names to network computers and use assigned logical addresses to identify the computers on the network.

The Domain Name System (DNS) operates at the transport layer. We discuss DNS and other name resolution services in Chapter 9.

Ports and Sockets

Multitasking in networked applications is an advantage that modern operating systems have over older ones (such as MS-DOS); multitasking enables a user to run more than one network program at a time. For example, you can use your Web browser to access a website at the same time your e-mail software is downloading your e-mail messages.

The transport layer includes a mechanism to separate the response to your browser's request from your incoming mail when both arrive at the same network address. Transport layer protocols such as TCP and UDP use ports to make this distinction.

Port numbers break down a network address. In Chapter 9, we discuss IP addressing, used by TCP/IP to route data to a destination computer, in detail. For now, think of IP addressing this way: the IP address, or logical network address, has parts that represent the network identification (what network the computer is on) and the host (individual computer) identification.

IP addresses work somewhat like the way a street name and an individual street number identifies an apartment building or office location. Continuing this analogy, a port number would be like the number that identifies the specific apartment or suite within the building. Thus, TCP and UDP, the transport layer protocols, assign port numbers to each application. This ensures that the data intended for the Web browser in Apartment B doesn't get sent to the e-mail program that lives in Apartment D.

The Network Layer. The network layer is responsible for getting the data packets to their destinations. This layer handles *routing*. You can compare the duty of the network layer protocols to that of a navigator who plots a course from one location to another using the most efficient pathway possible. Most routing protocols (discussed in Chapter 9) operate at the network layer.

This layer also handles prioritization of data types (the basis of Quality of Service [QoS]), which assures some level of guarantee for sufficient network resources for high-bandwidth applications such as live video.

Network Layer Devices

Devices that work at the network layer include routers and *Layer 3 switches*. (Remember that the layer numbers start at the bottom, which makes the network layer the third layer.) These network connectivity devices are discussed in more detail in Chapter 7.

The Data Link Layer. Layer 2 is defined as the data link layer by the original OSI specifications; however, this layer has been further divided into two sublayers:

- Media Access Control (MAC)
- Logical Link Control (LLC)

MAC Addressing

The MAC sublayer handles *physical addressing* issues. In fact, the physical address, which on an Ethernet or a Token Ring network is a hexadecimal number that is permanently burned into the chip on the network interface card (NIC), is called the *MAC address.*

The MAC address on an Ethernet network (sometimes called by yet another name: the Ethernet address) is generally expressed as 12 hexadecimal digits arranged in pairs, with a colon separating each pair (for example, 17:A4:2C:43:2F:09).

These 12 digits in hexadecimal represent 48-bit (that is, 6-byte) binary numbers. The first 3 bytes contain a manufacturer code, which is assigned by the

NOTE

The MAC address, or physical address, is also referred to as the *hardware address*. It differs from the logical address (that is, the IP address on a TCP/IP network) in that it generally cannot be changed. The logical address is assigned through software and is simple to modify. Both identify the computer's location on the network. Think of the logical address as a street address that can be changed by edict of the city council. The MAC address is more like a latitude and longitude coordinate, which always remains the same.

Institute of Electrical and Electronics Engineers (IEEE). The last 3 bytes are assigned by the manufacturer and represent that particular card.

In theory, there should never be two cards with the same MAC address. In practice, however, there have been manufacturing errors that created cards with duplicate addresses. Additionally, some vendors have begun recycling their numbers. Duplicate MAC addresses cause problems if both cards with the same address are on the same network, much like having two homes on the same street with the same house number. The post office does not know where to deliver mail addressed to 150 Main Street if there are two such addresses.

If two NICs on your network have the same address, you need to replace one of the cards or change the address of one of them. Some vendors provide software that makes it possible to do this by "flashing" the chip on the network card.

The *media access control method* allocates access to the network by computers. Media access control occurs, appropriately enough, at the MAC sublayer. We examine various methods and how they work in Chapter 4.

The LLC Layer and Logical Topology

At the LLC sublayer, the *logical topology* of the network is defined. As discussed, this might not be the same as the physical topology. This sublayer is responsible also for providing a link, or interface, between the MAC sublayer following it and the network layer above it.

Data Link Layer Devices

Both *bridges* and *Layer 2 switches* (also called *switching hubs*) operate at the data link layer. Both are discussed in detail in Chapter 7.

The Physical Layer. Finally, we arrive at Layer 1, the physical layer. This is where the data and headers that have come down from the layers above are translated into transmittable signals and put on the wire to travel across the network (or, in the case of wireless media, sent over the airwaves or by other means). The physical layer protocols turn all those 0s and 1s into electrical impulses or pulses of light.

The physical layer deals with *signaling issues*, including the following:

- Analog versus digital signaling
- Baseband versus broadband technology
- Asynchronous versus synchronous transmission
- Multiplexing

In Chapter 4, we will look at signaling methods and characteristics in detail.

Another physical layer issue is network topology. At the physical layer, this refers to the physical layout of the network, as opposed to the logical topology addressed at the data link layer. You might recall from Chapter 2 that the most common LAN topologies are the linear bus, the star bus, the ring, and the mesh.

Physical layer devices are those that deal with basic signaling. The NIC operates at the physical layer, as do repeaters and *hubs*. These hubs include the Token Ring network hub, which is referred to as a multistation access unit (MSAU), and the passive, active, and intelligent hubs. It does not include the *switching hub*, which operates at the data link layer. (Note that "MSAU" is sometimes written as "MAU.")

NICs

The NIC is a basic component that is generally required for establishing communication between computers. We say *generally* because there are situations in which a computer can participate on a network without a NIC. These situations include remote access in which a modem and phone lines are used to connect to the network and a simple connection between two computers using a special serial cable called a *null* modem cable. The NIC is responsible for preparing data to be sent out over network media.

NICs come in many different types, and choosing the correct card can be a challenge. You must consider each of the following when you select a NIC:

- **Network architecture**—The card must be designed to work with the architecture used by your network. A Token Ring card does work on an Ethernet network, for example.

- **Media type**—Ethernet networks can use thin coax cable, thick coaxial cable, twisted-pair cable, and even fiber-optic cable. Your card must have the correct connector type to attach to your network's media. (If you have a wireless connection, the card must be of the correct media type, such as infrared, laser, or radio.)

- **Bus architecture**— The card must be designed to work with the architecture used by your computer. You must have a matching bus type and PCI, ISA, or PC card for the NIC to work in the computer.

> **NOTE**
>
> It is also possible, and often desirable, to buy a combo card that has connectors for two or even three Ethernet cable types. This is especially handy if you expect to upgrade your thinnet network, for example, to UTP.

NOTE

Ethernet cards with connectors for UTP come in 10-Mbps, 100-Mbps, and 10/100-Mbps varieties. Although more costly, the 10/100-Mbps variety has obvious advantages. Note that if your hub is a 100-Mbps hub, you can use either a 100-Mbps or a 10/100-Mbps card with it, but a 10-Mbps card will not work.

- **Speed**—An Ethernet network running on Cat 5 unshielded twisted-pair cable could be running at 10 Mbps or at 100 Mbps. A Token Ring network using IBM cable can run at either 4 Mbps or 16 Mbps. You should match the speed of the card to that of the other network components.

Networking Transceivers

A transceiver is so named because it is a device that *transmits* and *receives*. A 10Base5 network (thicknet) uses an *external transceiver*, which is a device that is attached to the NIC through an AUI connector (also called a DIX connector). The AUI connector, which is a 15-pin DIN type, also enables the conversion to a different media type by attaching an external transceiver for the desired cable type.

All network cards use a transceiver, and a transceiver is built into cards intended for use on 10Base2, 10BaseT, or 100BaseT networks.

Repeaters

A repeater connects two lengths of network cable and boosts the signal before passing it from the first to the second cable segment. A repeater enables you to make a network's cable length longer than would otherwise be possible, by addressing the problem of *attenuation* (signal loss) that occurs with distance.

Repeaters do not filter the signals. They pass on noise as well as the data. This is why only a limited number of repeaters can be used without communication problems. Use of repeaters on a coax-cable network is governed by the 5-4-3 rule, which we will discuss in Chapter 5, "LAN Links," in the section "Rules of Ethernet Engagement."

Hubs

Hubs are also called *concentrators* because they serve as a central connection point. Most hubs are actually *multistation repeaters*. Where a repeater typically has only two ports, a hub generally has from four to twenty or more ports. Hubs are used most commonly in Ethernet 10BaseT or 100BaseT networks, although there are other network architectures that use them as well.

Hubs come in three basic types:

- **Passive**—A passive hub serves as a physical connection point only. A passive hub does not need electrical power because it does not boost or clean the signal; it merely passes it through. Passive hubs are not very common today.
- **Active**—An active hub needs to be plugged into electricity because it must use power to amplify the incoming signal before passing it back out the other ports. The active hub is a multiport repeater and is the most common

type of hub you will encounter. Note that all Ethernet hubs require electrical power and are thus classified as active hubs.

- **Intelligent or "smart"**—These devices function as active hubs but also include a microprocessor chip and diagnostic capabilities. They are more costly than active hubs (without extra features), but can be useful in troubleshooting situations.

Another special device, which is often referred to as a Token Ring hub, is actually an MSAU. A unique feature of the MSAU is the *logical ring* topology that it creates by virtue of the wiring inside the device. Several MSAUs can be linked to provide a continuous circular pathway for the signal to travel, as shown in Figure 3-5.

FIGURE 3-5
MSAUs connected in a Token Ring network provide a continuous circular data pathway.

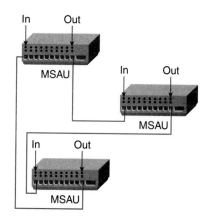

The DoD Model

Although the OSI model is the most popular, it is neither the only nor the first networking model. In fact, the U.S. Department of Defense (DoD) model—sometimes referred to as the TCP/IP model—was developed approximately a decade earlier than the OSI model, in the 1970s.

The DoD model was developed in conjunction with TCP/IP itself, as part of the ARPAnet project. It is a simpler model that consists of only four layers, which can be mapped roughly to the seven layers of the OSI reference model. As you can see in Figure 3-6, the DoD's top and bottom layers combine the functions of more than one OSI layer.

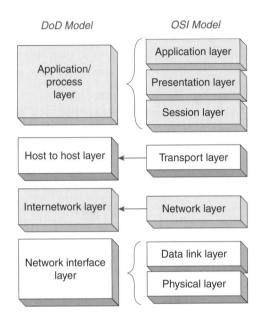

FIGURE 3-6
The four layers of
the DoD model
are shown as
they correspond
to OSI reference
model layers.

The function of each layer is as follows:

- **The application/process layer**—The top layer of the DoD model encompasses the functions of all three OSI upper layers: application, presentation, and session. In texts referring to TCP/IP, you might read that encryption of data, or checkpointing, and dialog control take place at the application layer. If you remember that this does *not* mean the OSI application layer, you'll avoid confusion.

- **The host to host (transport) layer**—The host to host layer is labeled the transport Layer in some resources, even on four-layer DoD diagrams, and it maps to the transport layer of the OSI model. TCP, UDP, and DNS operate here.

- **The internetworking layer**—This layer corresponds very closely to the OSI network layer. It deals with routing based on logical addresses. Address Resolution Protocol (ARP) translates logical addresses to MAC addresses. This translation is necessary because the lower layers can process only the MAC addresses.

- **The network interface layer**—The network interface layer maps to both the data link and physical layers of the OSI reference model. The standard Ethernet and Token Ring data link layer protocols and physical layer protocols operate in this layer.

One goal of the ISO in developing the OSI model was to more specifically define the networking functions designated by the DoD model in creating TCP/IP. The TCP/IP protocols, however, were designed to fit the DoD model, not the OSI model.

Vendor-Specific Models

Vendors that provide network operating system software can have their own networking models to describe the way in which the operating system's networking components work. For example, the Microsoft Windows networking model for NT and Windows 2000 is shown in Figure 3-7.

FIGURE 3-7
Microsoft developed its own network communications model for Windows networking.

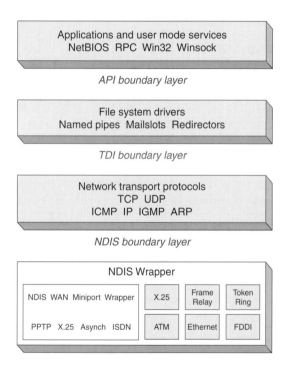

As you can see, the Microsoft model is difficult to map directly to the other models. It includes a new type of layer called a *boundary layer*, which is an interface between the actual networking component layers. The boundary layers are open specifications, while the component layers between them are operating-system specific.

Other NOS vendors have their own models, but the OSI model is a standard with which all are compatible.

Networking Standards and Specifications

The models are not the only standards and specifications to which networking components are developed. Numerous standards-setting bodies publish specifications for network-related hardware and software. Of course, these specifications are not *law*. The standards-setting bodies are not government entities and have no way to force compliance. A vendor is free to deviate from the standards as much as is desired, but it is not in the vendor's self-interest to do so. Proprietary products, which work only with other products made by the same vendor, are generally unpopular. In the early days of networking, manufacturers could get away with creating them, but the industry today demands compatibility.

Why Standardize?

The ISO (www.iso.ch) defines standards as "documented agreements containing technical specifications or other precise criteria to be used consistently as rules, guidelines, or definitions of characteristics, to ensure that materials, products, processes and services are fit for their purpose."

Marketing, as you have seen, is one reason for vendors to standardize, but other advantages exist as well. For instance, standards provide guidelines that make designing and manufacturing products easier, and from the consumer's point of view, standardization ensures reliability of products and services.

Standards-Setting Bodies

The ISO is a long-standing and well-recognized standard-setting body, but it is by no means the only organization that provides standardized specifications for computer and networking components. Some of the major international standards-setting organizations include the following and are described in subsequent sections in this chapter:

- The ISO
- The IEC
- The ITU
- The IETF
- The IEEE

The ISO

The ISO is a worldwide federation of national standards-setting bodies, with one representative from each of over 100 different countries. It was formed in 1947 to develop international standards in a variety of fields. One ISO standard with which many people have been familiar for years is the "ISO number" on a box of photographic film that designates the film speed. The international country codes are another example of the ISO's work.

The ISO operates in partnership with other organizations, such as the International Electrotechnical Commission (IEC), the World Trade Commission (WTO), and the International Telecommunications Union (ITU).

More information about the ISO is available on the ISO's official website, at www.iso.ch.

The IEC

The IEC has been around longer than the ISO, since 1906, but is more specialized. Whereas the ISO addresses standards of all kinds, the IEC's purpose is the promotion and establishment of standards in the fields of electrical and electronic engineering.

The IEC is made up of 47 national committees, and in 1967, it entered into an agreement to work in conjunction with the ISO in the development of standards and specifications.

The IEC's Web site can be accessed at www.hike.te.chiba-u.ac.jp/ikeda/IEC/home.html.

The ITU

The ITU is another international organization that has focused on sponsoring events, publishing documents, and setting standards for telecom-related products and services.

The ITU's website, at www.itu.int, has information about the organization's structure and activities.

The IETF

The Internet Engineering Task Force (IETF) is part of the Internet Architecture Board (IAB), which in turn is a technical advisory group that belongs to the Internet Society (ISOC).

The IETF is divided into *working groups*, each of which addresses a different issue related to the establishment of Internet standards. The membership is open; any interested party can join.

The primary task of the IETF groups involves developing and submitting Internet Drafts, which evolve into official Request For Comments (RFC) documents, which in turn go through an established approval process to become Internet standards.

RFCs and Internet Standards. As a networking professional, you might see references to "RFC [*number*]" for more information on the characteristics of certain networking services and protocols. These services and protocols include items such as the following:

- Implementation of the Domain Name System (DNS)
- TCP/IP extensions
- Specifications for Network Address Translation (NAT) software

Although many RFCs originate with the IETF, any interested party can submit RFC proposals. Not all RFCs describe standards, but if a document is to become a standard, it goes through three stages:

- Proposed Standard
- Draft Standard
- Internet Standard

There is even an RFC, number 2226, "Instructions to Authors," that contains information on how to write and format a draft. Once submitted, the Internet Engineering Steering Group (IESG), which is a part of the IETF, reviews the document. For more information about this process, see the IETF Website, at www.ietf.org/home.html.

After review, if the draft is approved, it is edited and published. The RFC editor, who is employed by the Internet Society, maintains and publishes a master list of RFCs. The editor is also responsible for final editing of the documents. The RFC editor's homepage is located at www.rfc-editor.org.

Following review by technical experts or a task force, each RFC is classified into one of the following categories:

- **Required Status**—Must be implemented
- **Recommended Status**—Encouraged
- **Elective Status**—Can be implemented, but implementation is not required
- **Limited Use Status**—Not intended for general implementation
- **Not Recommended Status**—Implementation discouraged

If you would like more information about the RFC submission and approval process, you can download RFC 2026, at ftp://ftp.isi.edu/in-notes/rfc2026.txt.

The IEEE

The IEEE (often called the "Eye-triple E" by members of the industry) promotes the exchange of information and develops standards and specifications for lower level networking technologies (those at the physical and data link layers).

Of particular interest to networking professionals are the specifications that make up the IEEE 802 project. The name is based on the date of the committee meeting. The 80 designates the year (1980) and the 2 designates the month (February). The physical and data link protocols for which the 802 committee set standards are as follows:

- 802.1—Standards introduction: LAN and MAN management, bridges that operate at the MAC sublayer, and the Spanning-Tree Algorithm that prevents a communications problem called *bridge looping*.

- 802.2—Logical Link Control (LLC): These specifications were designed to prevent senders from overwhelming receivers. This standard provided for division of the OSI data link layer into two sublayers, with the LLC sublayer providing an interface between the MAC sublayer and the network layer.

- 802.3—CSMA/CD: This specification governs Ethernet networks using the carrier sense multiple access collision detect media (CSMA/CD) access method, and sets standards for Ethernet packet (frame) format. It originally defined a linear bus network running on coax cable, but has been updated to include 10BaseT (star topology) networks.

- 802.4—Token Bus: Sets standards for networks implementing a physical and logical bus topology using 75-ohm CATV coax or fiber-optic cable and using token-passing as the access method.

- 802.5—Token Ring: This specification sets the physical standard and media access method for a physical star, logical ring topology that can use shielded or unshielded twisted-pair cabling and use token-passing as its access method. This standard was developed based on IBM's Token Ring technology.

- 802.6—MAN: Sets standards for networks that are larger than LANs and smaller than WANs.

- 802.7—Broadband: Addresses networking with broadband transmission technologies, such as CATV, using Frequency Division Multiplexing (FDM) to send different signals on separate frequencies using the same cable.

- 802.8—Fiber Optics: Provides specifications for networks using fiber-optic cabling, including Fiber Distributed Data Interface (FDDI).

- 802.9—Integrated Voice and Data: Sometimes called just "integrated services," this standard addresses transmission of voice and data over ISDN.

- 802.10—LAN Security: These specifications pertain to virtual private networking (VPN), a way of establishing a secure connection to a private network over the public Internet.

- 802.11—Wireless: Provides guidelines for implementing wireless (non-cabled) LAN technologies
- 802.12—100 VG AnyLAN: This standard pertains to the demand priority media access method developed by Hewlett Packard to combine advantages of Ethernet, Token Ring, and ATM technologies into a high-speed LAN solution.

The IEEE can be accessed online (including a catalog of its standards, available by subscription) at standards.ieee.org.

Summary

This chapter briefly covers most of the concepts involved in computer networking. We started with the basic tenets of computer communication, comparing the binary, hexadecimal, and decimal numbering systems to gain an understanding of why binary machine language is best suited for the computer's way of processing data. You have learned that data is broken down into small, manageable chunks to be sent across a network, and we discussed how a layered approach to network communications simplifies the process and maintains the integrity of the information being sent.

We have explored the purposes and uses of networking models and mapped the four layers of the DoD model to the seven layers of the OSI version. Next, we examined the benefits of standardization in the networking world, and looked at some specific standards, such as RFCs and the project 802 specifications, that you are likely to encounter in your study of PC networking technology.

In the next chapter, we go back to the source; that is, we examine the signal that represents our transferred data. We'll learn about signaling types and characteristics, and then we will discuss media access methods and how all those signals, from multiple computers on the network, avoid ending up in a massive electronic traffic jam.

Further Reading

For a more in-depth discussion of binary and hexadecimal calculations, see *A Practical Guide to Binary, Decimal and Hexadecimal Numbers*, at www.myhome.org/pg/numbers.html.

The World Standards Services Network (WSSN) is a network of publicly accessible World Wide Web servers belong to standards organizations around the world. For more information, visit www.wssn.net/WSSN.

A good, brief tutorial on the OSI model, along with a quiz, is available at www.lex-con.com/osimodel.htm.

For a chart that maps protocols to the OSI model, see www.lex-con.com/osimodel.htm.

Review Questions

The following questions test your knowledge on the material covered in this chapter. Be sure to read each question carefully and select the *best* correct answer or answers.

1. What is the name of the numbering system that uses 16 digits to represent numerical values?

   A. Decimal

   B. Hexadecimal

   C. Binary

   D. Machine code

2. What is a binary digit (a single 0 or 1) called?

   A. Bit

   B. Byte

   C. Qubit

   D. Gig

3. Which of the following is the decimal equivalent of the binary number 10010001?

   A. 256

   B. 128

   C. 145

   D. 64

4. What is the name for the small, easily transmitted units into which computer data is broken for transmission over a network?

   A. Hexadecimals

   B. Packets

   C. Headers

   D. Bits

5. What is the name for an error-checking component sometimes included in the trailer of a data packet?

   A. Verification bit

   B. Frame

   C. UDP

   D. CRC

6. "A schematic description of a system, theory, or phenomenon that accounts for its known or inferred properties and can be used for further study of its characteristics" is the definition of which of the following?

   A. Protocol

   B. Model

   C. Process

   D. Layer

7. Which layer of the OSI model is divided into two sublayers?

   A. Physical Layer

   B. Data Link Layer

   C. Network Layer

   D. Transport Layer

8. Which layer of the OSI model does not add header information to the data packet as the packet travels down the stack?

   A. Physical layer

   B. Data link layer

   C. Session layer

   D. Application layer

9. Which of the following is a session-layer protocol?

   A. TCP

   B. IPX

   C. NetBIOS

   D. Telnet

10. What is another name for a multistation repeater?

A. Bridge

B. Router

C. Switch

D. Hub

Chapter 4

Networking Communications Methods

So far in this book, we have taken a broad view of how computers can be connected to communicate with one another. You now know how computers process information in binary format and that the binary digits are transformed into electronic signals to travel over the network media. In this chapter, we get down to the core of network communication—the signal itself. Then we examine the methods used in different network architectures for controlling access to the transmission media.

Signaling Methods and Characteristics

As mentioned previously, there are many ways in which a signal can be physically created: as electrical impulses that travel over copper wire, as pulses of light that travel through strands of glass or plastic, as radio transmissions that travel over the airwaves, as laser or satellite transmissions, and as infrared pulses. When the 1s and 0s that represent computer data are turned into pulses of energy, they are *encoded,* or *modulated.*

Just as we categorized networks in different ways, we can categorize encoded signals according to different characteristics, such as the following:

- Analog or digital
- Baseband or broadband
- Synchronous or asynchronous
- Simplex, half duplex, full duplex, or multiplexed

We take a look at each signal type in the following sections.

Analog and Digital

Signaling methods are classified as either analog or digital, which are two very different forms of encoding. You are probably familiar with the terms in relation to electronic equipment such as tape recorders, stereo receivers, and television tuners.

You might think of analog equipment as the old style and digital as the new style. Remember that one type of signaling is not necessarily better than the other; each has advantages and disadvantages, and each is best suited for certain types of transmission. It is unlikely that digital signaling will ever completely replace analog, although digital technologies are certainly gaining popularity.

Characteristics of Analog Signaling

Analog signals can be graphically illustrated as waveforms because they change gradually and continuously. Figure 4-1 is a pictorial representation of an analog signal.

FIGURE 4-1
An analog signal is an electromagnetic wave that constantly changes.

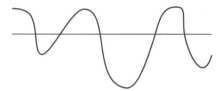

Many processes are essentially analog in nature. Voice patterns, for example, are analog because tone and pitch vary in increments along a wave path. To further envision analog information, think of a traditional car speedometer. As you increase the car's speed, the needle moves gradually from one number to the next. Another example is an old-style radio tuner. When you move the dial through the frequency range from one station to the next, the radio picks up static or weak signals between stations.

Analog signals are measured in *cycles,* with one cycle representing the change from high to low and back again (or vice versa). The following three characteristics are measured:

- **Amplitude**—The strength of the signal, represented by the height of the wave.
- **Frequency**—The time required for a wave to complete a cycle. Frequency is represented as *hertz* (cycles per second).
- **Phase**—The relative state of one wave to another, measured in *degrees.*

As you can see, analog signaling is fairly complex.

Characteristics of Digital Signaling

Digital signaling is also called *discrete state* signaling. Digital signals change from one state to another almost instantaneously, without stopping at an in-between state. Figure 4-2 illustrates digital signaling.

As an example of digital information, consider new radio tuners in which you enter an exact frequency number to access a station. In addition, the speed display on some new cars in which an LED or LCD readout shows miles or kilometers per hour in whole numbers also is an example of digital information.

FIGURE 4-2
Digital signaling represents fixed, discrete states.

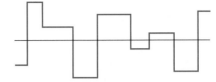

Comparing Analog and Digital

Computers are digital machines. The information they process is based on 1s and 0s. A binary digit is either a 1 or a 0, and there is nothing between them. Thus, digital signaling often is the most appropriate format for transmitting computer data, and most networks use digital signaling methods for that reason.

Digital signaling is obviously simpler than analog. To illustrate this statement, imagine that you are taking an exam. True-or-false and multiple-choice questions are discrete-state questions; the answer is either true or it's false, or the answer is A, B, C, or D. An essay question is more like an analog question. Your answer could be completely incorrect, completely correct, or somewhere in between.

Because it is a simpler technology, digital signaling has some advantages over analog:

- It is generally less expensive to make digital equipment, and that's why digital clocks and watches cost less than their analog counterparts.
- Digital signals are generally less vulnerable to errors caused by interference. The discrete state of on or off is not as easily affected by a small distortion as is a continuous waveform.

Analog signals also have advantages:

- Analog signals can be easily *multiplexed*; that is, signals can be combined to increase bandwidth.
- Analog signals are less vulnerable to the problem of *attenuation* (that is, signal loss) because of distance, so they can travel farther without becoming too weak for reliable transmission.

Both analog and digital signaling are useful. Digital connectivity solutions generally offer better security, faster performance, and higher reliability. In addition, digital lines are far less error-prone than are analog lines.

LANs generally rely on cabling over which digital signals are transmitted. Some WAN technologies use analog signaling methods. A third transmission

> **NOTE**
>
> Interestingly, information that is inherently analog can be represented digitally, and vice versa. For an illustration, let's return to the speedometer example. Note that your car's speed doesn't go directly from 51 mph to 52 mph; it increases gradually. The new-style speedometer, however, skips the fractional increases and shows the information in digital format.
>
> In contrast, an electroencephalograph (EEG) provides a brain-wave readout in analog format. It is actually representing, however, the discrete states of neurons in the brain, which are either on or off at a given time.

technology used for wide-area networking, which we discuss in Chapter 6, "WAN Links," is *packet switching*.

Baseband and Broadband

Another signaling issue pertains to how bandwidth is allocated over the networking media. *Bandwidth* generally refers to the speed or capacity of a network link. For example, the entire capacity of an Ethernet cable is used for transmitting the data in one channel. This makes Ethernet a *baseband* technology.

You can divide bandwidth into multiple channels and send different data streams over each channel. Consider cable television (CATV), in which dozens of separate channels, each sending a different program, come into your television set over one coaxial cable. CATV is a *broadband* technology.

Characteristics of Baseband Technology

Baseband transmission is simple—one signal at a time goes over the cable. That signal enjoys the benefits of having the entire bandwidth to itself. Baseband is usually associated with digital signaling (although it can be used with analog).

Most computer communications are baseband; for example, the signal from a computer to monitors, printers, and other peripherals is baseband because they are analog communications. ISDN, on the other hand, is broadband because multiple signals can be carried over separate channels on a single wire. Baseband signaling is bidirectional; the signal can flow both ways so that you can transmit and receive over the same cable.

Characteristics of Broadband Technology

Broadband technologies allow for dividing the capacity of a link into two or more channels, each of which can carry a different signal. All channels can send simultaneously.

Broadband signaling is unidirectional. The signal flows only one way, but the bandwidth can be divided into two channels, one for transmitting and one for receiving. This is called a *midsplit broadband configuration*. Another option is to attach two separate cables to the device and use one for transmitting signals and the other for receiving signals.

In addition to CATV, broadband technologies include Digital Subscriber Line (DSL) telephone service, in which data and voice can simultaneously travel over the same line, satellite, and other wireless technologies.

To divide bandwidth, multiplexing is used, as described in the following section.

Multiplexing

Multiplexing is a method of sending different streams of information on a link at the same time, in the form of a single, complex signal. The separate streams are then recovered at the receiving end. Returning to our example of CATV transmission, a CATV tuner built into the TV or cable box that decodes the signals enables you to select the channel you want to watch.

Although some networking texts associate multiplexing with analog signaling only, both analog and digital signals can be multiplexed. Multiplexing can be accomplished with the following methods:

- Frequency-division multiplexing (FDM)
- Time-division multiplexing (TDM)
- Dense wavelength division multiplexing (DWDM)

We discuss each in the following sections.

FDM

Analog signals are typically multiplexed using FDM. Multiple channels are combined on a single line for transmission, and each channel is assigned a different frequency. A two-way communications circuit requires a multiplexer/demultiplexer at each end, as shown in Figure 4-3.

FIGURE 4-3
FDM assigns each channel a separate frequency and combines all frequencies for transmission on a single line.

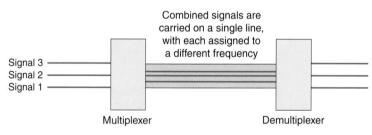

TDM

Digital signals usually use TDM. This method combines signals for transmission on a single communications line and breaks each signal into segments with short durations. The signals are then carried over the line in alternating time slots, one after another. At the other end, they are separated by a demultiplexer, as shown in Figure 4-4.

DWDM

Networks that run over fiber-optic cable can use yet another type of multiplexing, DWDM. With DWDM, each signal is carried on a separate wavelength of light. Different data formats (for instance, SONET and ATM) can simultaneously travel over the same fiber-optic cable, as shown in Figure 4-5.

FIGURE 4-4
TDM breaks each signal into segments of short duration and transmits all segments over a single line.

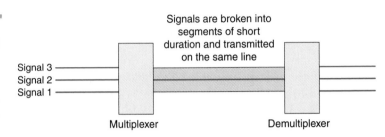

Signals are broken into segments of short duration and transmitted on the same line

Signal 3
Signal 2
Signal 1

Multiplexer

Demultiplexer

FIGURE 4-5
DWDM carries each signal on a separate wavelength of light.

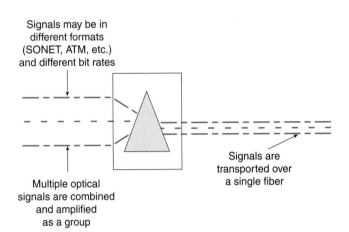

Signals may be in different formats (SONET, ATM, etc.) and different bit rates

Multiple optical signals are combined and amplified as a group

Signals are transported over a single fiber

Asynchronous and Synchronous Transmission

Remember that data that is encoded as analog or digital depends on changes in state, or modulations, to represent the binary data. To correctly interpret the signals, the receiving network device must know exactly when the signal should be measured. Timing, in networking as in many other aspects of life, is vitally important.

In computer networking, this timing factor is called *bit synchronization*. Devices can synchronize the bits by using an *asynchronous* method or a *synchronous* method, as described in the following sections.

Characteristics of Asynchronous Transmission

Asynchronous transmissions use a *start bit* at the beginning of each message. When the receiving device receives the start bit, it can synchronize its internal clock with the sender's clock.

Characteristics of Synchronous Transmission

In synchronous transmissions, a built-in timing mechanism coordinates the clocks of the sender and receiver. For instance, the clocking information can be embedded in the data signal. This is called *guaranteed state change* synchronization and is the most common type of synchronous methods.

Two other synchronous methods are *separate clock signal,* in which there is a separate channel between the sender and receiver over which clocking information is sent, and *oversampling,* in which the receiving device samples the signal at a much faster speed than the data is being sent. It does so by using the extra measurements to determine if the clocks are synchronized.

Simplex, Half-Duplex, and Full-Duplex Transmission

The data channels over which a signal is sent can operate in one of three ways: *simplex*, *half-duplex*, or *full-duplex* (often just called *duplex*). The distinction between these three is in the way the signal can travel.

Simplex Transmission

Simplex transmission, as its name implies, is simple. It is also called *unidirectional* because the signal travels in only one direction, just like traffic flows on a one-way street. Figure 4-6 illustrates this transmission type.

FIGURE 4-6
In simplex transmission, the signal can travel in one direction only.

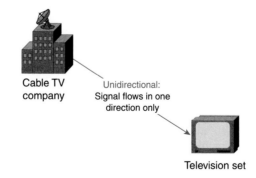

Cable TV company

Unidirectional: Signal flows in one direction only

Television set

Television transmission is an example of simplex communication. The data (that is, the television programs) are sent to your TV. No signals are transmitted back from the television to the broadcaster or cable company. This is why a TV has a *receiver*, but no transmitter.

Because traditional television transmission (before the development of interactive TV technologies) had no need for two-way communication, the equipment of many cable companies supports only simplex transmissions. When cable Internet access was developed, this presented a problem. The capability already existed to send the signals *down* the cable to the user, but there was no way for the user to *upload* data.

This deficiency affected the user's ability to access a website, for example, because the user's browser application had to send a small amount of data to request a particular web page. Cable companies had two choices for solving this problem:

- Implement technologies that used the cable bandwidth for downstream transmissions and the user's phone lines for upstream
- Install a new two-way infrastructure

Most companies used the first option until they could accomplish the second. With simplex cable access, the user benefits from the high speed of cable technology only when downloading data to his or her machine; the sending of data is done through a 56-kbps modem over the phone line.

Many cable companies have upgraded their infrastructures to support two-way communications, but many other companies still offer only downstream Internet communication over cable. Customers in those areas must use a cable modem that also includes an analog modem, to which a phone line must be connected.

Half-Duplex Transmission

Half-duplex transmission is an improvement over simplex; the traffic can travel in both directions. Unfortunately, the road isn't wide enough to accommodate bidirectional signals simultaneously. This means that only one side can transmit at a time, as shown in Figure 4-7.

Two-way radios, such as citizens band (CB) and police/emergency communications mobile radios, work with half-duplex transmissions. When you press the button on the microphone to transmit, you can't hear anything being said on the other end. If people at both ends try to talk at the same time, neither transmission gets through.

Full-Duplex Transmission

Full-duplex transmission operates like a two-way, two-lane street. Traffic can travel in both directions at the same time, as shown in Figure 4-8.

NOTE

Modems are half-duplex devices. They can send and receive, but not at the same time. However, it is possible to create a full-duplex modem connection with two telephone lines and two modems.

FIGURE 4-7
Half-duplex trans-
mission enables
signals to travel
in either direc-
tion, but not in
both directions
simultaneously.

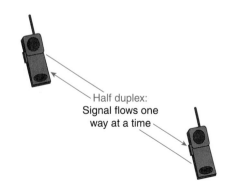

Half duplex:
Signal flows one
way at a time

FIGURE 4-8
With full-duplex
transmission, sig-
nals can travel in
both directions
simultaneously.

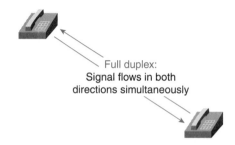

Full duplex:
Signal flows in both
directions simultaneously

A regular telephone conversation is an example of full-duplex communication.
Both parties can talk at the same time, and you can still hear the person on the
other end while you're talking (although you might not be able to understand
what's being said).

Full-duplex networking technology increases performance because data can be
sent and received at the same time. DSL, two-way cable modem, and other
broadband technologies operate in full-duplex mode. With DSL, for example,
you can download data to your computer at the same time you are sending a
voice message over the line.

Signaling and Communications Problems

The signals that make computer communications possible are subject to various problems and limitations. Some cable types and signaling methods are

more susceptible to certain problems than others. When troubleshooting network connectivity, you should keep the following issues in mind.

Electromagnetic Interference

Electromagnetic interference (EMI) is the intrusion of outside electromagnetic signals that affect the signal being sent over the network media. When outside interference encroaches on the network signals, the receiving computer has difficulty interpreting the signals.

EMI is similar to the problem you might have if you are listening to a car radio while driving through an industrial area with a great deal of electronic equipment. The previously clear channel is suddenly covered up with noise and static caused by other signals interfering with receipt of the radio transmission. This is why EMI is sometimes referred to as *noise.*

Interfering signals do not necessarily come from the sources you would expect. Cell phones, radios, and walkie-talkies work by transmitting signals, but other types of electrical equipment also emit a silent, invisible electromagnetic field that can extend for up to two miles.

EMI is not a problem that is confined to computer communications. EMI has been blamed for poor TV reception, malfunctioning cordless telephones, airplane crashes, deaths caused by failure of pacemakers and medical equipment, and even long-term effects such as cancer or leukemia attributed to the electromagnetic field created by an electric company's power wires.

Copper wire is especially susceptible to EMI. Coaxial cable's thick outer jacket offers some protection from EMI, as does the shielding material on shielded twisted-pair (STP). Unshielded twisted-pair (UTP) is fairly vulnerable to EMI, but the twisting of the wire pairs inside the cable helps reduce it. Fiber-optic cable, because it uses pulses of light instead of pulses of electricity to send its signal, is the best choice for a high-EMI environment.

Radio Frequency Interference

Radio frequency interference (RFI) refers to signal interference caused by radio transmitters and other types of equipment that generate signals on radio frequencies. This includes computer processors and monitors. Electromagnetic radiation with frequencies between about 10 kHz and 100 GHz are referred to as radio frequencies (RFs). Frequencies between around 2 GHz and 10 GHz are called microwaves (because their wavelengths are so short).

Interference filters to address the problem are available for various network types.

Crosstalk

Crosstalk is a particular type of interference in which signals from wires in close proximity "bleed" over one another. You might have experienced something similar if you've ever had the experience of talking on the telephone and hearing a low, barely audible conversation taking place in the background.

Reducing this crossover of signals from adjacent wires is another reason for the twists in twisted-pair cabling. The more twists per foot, the better the protection. Once again, fiber-optic cable is the cable type to choose if you want to eliminate this problem. Multiple fibers can run inside the same jacket without crossing the signals because each glass or plastic thread contains a light wave, rather than electronic pulses, as copper cable does.

Attenuation

Electrical signals grow weaker as they travel down the cable; the greater the distance from the source, the weaker the signal. This is easy to understand if you imagine you are shouting at another person. If that person is 3 feet away, your voice (that is, the signal) is loud and clear, but if the person is 100 yards away, he may hardly be able to hear you. The term for loss of signal strength is *attenuation.*

Attenuation is the reason that specifications for different network architectures place limitations on cable length. The limits generally ensure that the effects of attenuation are not great enough to cause significant degradation of the signal.

Attenuation increases at higher temperatures and higher frequencies. According to the laws of physics, atoms move faster as temperature increases, and they use more energy. The same is true of high frequencies; more energy is expended to achieve the higher frequency. Compare this to running versus walking; running requires you to expend more energy to travel the same distance, so you tire more quickly, whereas you may be able to walk a much greater distance without wearing out. Similarly, the signal will "wear out" at a shorter distance if more energy is being expended.

Fiber-optic cable is not completely immune to attenuation; signal loss in glass fiber can be caused by impurities in the glass, and *scattering* can result from small variations in density that are created when the glass is manufactured. Fiber-optic cable, however, can run much longer distances than copper cable and can do so without unacceptable signal loss because of attenuation.

Bandwidth Capacity Issues

Capacity of network bandwidth is usually measured in megabits per second (Mbps). The signaling type and the distance over which the signal is transmitted affect the throughput of a particular media type.

> **NOTE**
>
> A signal can be strengthened, or *boosted,* to increase the maximum allowed distance. *Repeaters* are used to boost digital signals, and *amplifiers* serve the same purpose for analog signals. We discuss these devices in Chapter 7, "Physical Components of the Network."

Classification of high and low bandwidth is a relative concept. 10-Mbps Ethernet is a blazing fast medium compared to the 40–50 Kbps average transfer rate over analog phone lines, but it seems woefully slow when held up against 1-Gbps or better speeds attainable with high-speed WAN links such as SONET and ATM.

One important criterion in selecting cable type and architecture for a network is the amount of bandwidth needed, both currently and in the future.

PLANNING A NETWORK WITH FUTURE GROWTH IN MIND

A good rule of thumb to keep in mind during the planning stage is that network bandwidth is like funding, in that you almost always end up needing more than you anticipated.

Computer and communications technologies advance at a rapid pace. In the 1980s, when wide-area connections typically enjoyed a bandwidth of less than 10 Kbps, and many LANs ran at 2.5 Mbps or less, few people thought there would ever be a need for transfer rates of 100 Mbps and up. This was before the bandwidth-hungry technologies such as videoconferencing, streaming audio, and large file transfers that are common today.

It is much easier to make upgrades at the time you install cable than to do it all over in the future. For example, you might save a few dollars by using Cat 3 cable instead of Cat 5 for a 10BaseT network (which requires only 10-Mbps transfer rates, of which Cat 3 is capable). However, if you find five years later that you need to upgrade your LAN to 100 Mbps, you will spend much more than you originally saved to tear out the Cat 3 cabling and install the higher grade.

Media Access Methods

Now that you know about the various signaling methods and their characteristics, let's examine how a network handles the transmission of signals from multiple computers so that the data packets reach their destinations.

Imagine a busy roadway. If there were no traffic control devices or rules of the road to guide us, drivers would just barrel ahead to their destinations. Collisions would probably occur, and the roads would become so congested that movement would slow to a crawl.

Traffic lights, stop and yield signs, police officers directing traffic, and the right-of-way rules that we all must learn to get a driver's license are *access methods* that control which car can proceed at a given time. Access methods are designed to ensure that traffic moves in an orderly fashion and that everyone reaches his or her destination as quickly as possible.

In networking, we likewise need a way to control access to the media. Several different access methods are associated with different network architectures and topologies. In the following sections, we examine the most popular of these:

- Carrier sense multiple access collision detect (CSMA/CD)
- Carrier sense multiple access collision avoidance (CSMA/CA)
- Token passing
- Demand priority

CSMA/CD

The most popular access control method used on LANs today is carrier sense multiple access collision detect (CSMA/CD). That's quite a mouthful, so it is usually shortened to its acronym. It is popular because it is the access method used by Ethernet, which is the most common LAN architecture.

CSMA/CD is a relatively fast and efficient method of allocating access to the Ethernet cable. To understand how it works, let's first break the name into its component parts:

- **Carrier sense**—When a computer wants to transmit on a network using CSMA/CD, it first listens to the cable to determine whether another computer is currently sending data. Thus, it senses the state of the carrier—that is, whether the carrier is presently in use.
- **Multiple access**—This indicates that more than one computer can begin transmitting on the network at the same time.
- **Collision detection**—Here we get the real story about how CSMA/CD works. When a computer is ready to transmit, it senses the state of the carrier, and if the cable is occupied, it does not send its signal. If the computer does not sense a signal already on the wire, it transmits. This works fine, unless two computers listen, both sense that there is no signal on the line, and then send at the exact same time. When this happens, a *collision* occurs.

When signals collide on a network wired with coaxial cable, the data packets are destroyed. But all is not lost; with CSMA/CD, each computer waits a *random amount of time* and then resends the same signal. Why a random amount? Obviously, if they were both set to wait X number of milliseconds, the same thing would happen again. The computer that resends first (the one that chose the shortest random amount of time) "wins" access to the cable.

With CSMA/CD, the data *does* eventually get through, and because the signal travels quickly (either at 10 Mbps or 100 Mbps on a typical Ethernet network), performance remains high.

The specifications for implementation of CSMA/CD are contained in IEEE 802.3.

CSMA/CA

Carrier sense multiple access collision avoidance (CSMA/CA) is, as you might guess, related in some ways to CSMA/CD. Once again, the first step is for the computer with data to send to monitor the cable and determine whether it is free.

CSMA/CA, however, is a less-trusting access method. If the computer senses that there is no signal on the wire, it does not assume that it's safe and then send its precious data out there, risking its annihilation if another computer has decided to do the same thing at the same time. Instead, the computer sends a signal called a *request to send (RTS)* first. This signal announces the computer's intention to send. If another computer has the same idea, these signals will collide, but there is no loss of data because the data packets themselves can never collide. This is known as *collision avoidance*.

CSMA/CA can, at first glance, seem superior to collision detection. However, it has a negative impact on performance because of all the RTS messages (many of them unnecessary) that must be sent in addition to the data itself. In essence, you double the amount of signal that goes out on the cable.

AppleTalk networks use the CSMA/CA access method.

Token Passing

What if there were an access method that enabled you to do away with collisions altogether? Well, there is: token passing.

Token passing is a *noncontention* method in that two computers cannot transmit a signal at the same time. It works somewhat like a formal committee meeting, where a member is not allowed to speak unless he or she has the floor. Likewise, a computer on a token-passing network must wait until it has the token before it can speak.

Token passing is a very polite and civilized method of access control. A signal called a *token* circulates on the network (most commonly a ring topology, but token passing can also be used on a bus network) until it reaches a computer that has data to send.

Figure 4-9 illustrates the token-passing process.

NOTE

Both CSMA/CD and CSMA/CA are known as *contention* methods because the signals must contend, or compete, for use of the cable.

FIGURE 4-9
A computer in a token-passing network cannot transmit until it gets the token.

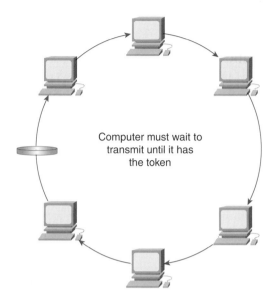

Computer must wait to
transmit until it has
the token

The most common token-passing network is Token Ring. Here's how it works: When the token gets around the network to the computer that is waiting to send, that computer takes control of the token. Specifically, it appends its data to the token signal and puts it back out on the network. The data packet has addressing information, and as the signal proceeds once again around the network, those stations whose addresses don't match the one in the header send it on.

When the token finally reaches the destination in the header address, that computer's network card copies the data. It then appends information to the token, acknowledging that the data was received, and sends the token back around. The original sending computer gets the token and either sends more data or releases the token by marking it to indicate that it is once again free to circulate, and then the computer puts the token back out on the network.

In some token-passing architectures, such as Fiber Distributed Data Interface (FDDI), multiple tokens can circulate on the network at the same time. We discuss both Token Ring and FDDI in more detail in Chapter 5, "LAN Links." Token Ring standards are outlined in the IEEE 802.3 specification.

Demand Priority

The demand-priority access method was developed by Hewlett-Packard to be used with a LAN architecture called 100VG-AnyLAN. This architecture is also referred to as VG-AnyLAN, or simply AnyLAN. VG-AnyLAN was designed to be a high-speed, flexible, and efficient replacement for Ethernet.

The demand-priority method of controlling access to the media uses multiport repeaters (hubs) that conduct round-robin searches of the connected nodes (computers, routers, or other network devices), monitoring for requests to transmit. The topology of a VG-AnyLAN network is a star-wired tree. The hubs can be cascaded off a root hub (also called a parent hub) for centralized control.

Figure 4-10 illustrates a 100VG-AnyLAN network.

FIGURE 4-10
A 100VG-Any-LAN network uses a series of hubs to implement the demand-priority access method.

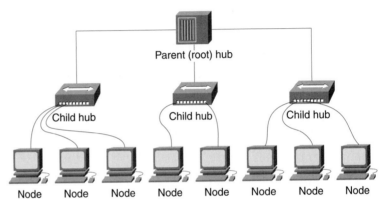

Parent (root) hub

Child hub   Child hub   Child hub

Node   Node   Node   Node   Node   Node   Node   Node

The *priority* part of demand priority refers to the fact that you can set a priority on a certain type of data so that it is processed first if the hub simultaneously receives two requests to send. This ensures a guaranteed bandwidth for high-usage applications such as live video.

Demand priority is more efficient than CSMA/CD because the cabling that it uses (four pairs of wires, with each pair capable of carrying signals) enables a computer to transmit and receive at the same time. Additionally, this method avoids CSMA/CD's practice of broadcasting to the entire network. Instead, only the computers attached to a particular hub receive a broadcast. The hubs communicate with one another; each hub deals only with the nodes attached to it, and it is not aware of nodes attached to other hubs.

Because not all data goes through all stations, as is normally the case with both Ethernet and Token Ring, a VG-AnyLAN network is inherently somewhat more secure.

VG-AnyLAN networks can use two- or four-pair UTP, two-pair STP, or fiber-optic cabling. IEEE 802.12 contains specifications for demand priority.

Unfortunately, 100VG-AnyLAN products are available from only a small number of vendors, and the architecture has not been widely implemented. Thus, most network administrators do not encounter a VG-AnyLAN network in the field.

Summary

This chapter examined computer data transmission at the signaling level and introduced the common ways in which signals are classified.

You learned the differences between analog and digital transmissions and how baseband technologies are distinguished from broadband. We also discussed the characteristics of both synchronous and asynchronous communications, and we learned to recognize the three descriptors relating to direction of signal flow: simplex transmission, half-duplex transmission, and full-duplex transmission. We discussed some common signal-related problems, such as EMI, RFI, crosstalk, and attenuation.

Next we took a look at the most common methods PC networks use for controlling access to the media, including CSMA/CD, CSMA/CA, token passing, and demand priority.

In the next chapters, we build on this knowledge as we explore the theory and practice of implementing different network link types. We will look at LAN links (Ethernet, Token Ring, and AppleTalk) in Chapter 5 and common WAN links (ATM, FDDI, and SONET) in Chapter 6.

Further Reading

An overview of communication systems and the transmission of information is available at www.cs.ucl.ac.uk/staff/S.Bhatti/D51-notes/node1.html.

The Georgia Tech Broadband Institute's home page, containing useful information and links related to broadband technologies, is located at www.broadband.gatech.edu/top.html.

An excellent tutorial on 100VG-AnyLAN can be accessed at www.iol.unh.edu/training/vganylan.

Review Questions

The following questions test your knowledge of the material covered in this chapter. Be sure to read each question carefully and select the *best* correct answer or answers.

1. When the 1s and 0s that represent computer data are turned into pulses of electricity or light, what do they become?

   A. Encrypted

   B. Modulated

   C. Secured

   D. Pulsated

2. Which of the following is true of digital signaling?

   A. A digital signal is an electromagnetic wave that is constantly changing.

   B. Digital signals are measured in amplitude, frequency, and phase.

   C. Digital signals are measured in cycles.

   D. Digital signaling is called discrete-state signaling.

3. Which of the following is an advantage of analog signaling over digital? (Select all that apply.)

   A. Analog signals are generally less vulnerable to errors caused by interference.

   B. Analog devices are less expensive to make than digital devices.

   C. Analog signals are easier to multiplex.

   D. Analog signals are less vulnerable to attenuation.

4. When the entire capacity of the medium is used to transmit data in one channel, what is the technology called?

   A. Baseband

   B. Broadband

   C. Multiplexed

   D. Multilinked

5. Which of the following is true of baseband signaling? (Select all that apply.)

   A. Baseband signaling is bidirectional.

   B. CATV is a baseband technology.

   C. Baseband signaling is unidirectional.

   D. Baseband is usually associated with digital signaling.

6. Which of the following types of multiplexing is used on fiber-optic networks, in which each signal is carried on a separate wavelength of light?

   A. FDM

   B. TDM

   C. DWDM

   D. MPPE

7. Which of the following is true of asynchronous transmission?

   A. Asynchronous transmissions include a built-in timing mechanism.

   B. Asynchronous transmissions use guaranteed state change synchronization.

   C. Asynchronous transmissions use the oversampling synchronization method.

   D. Asynchronous transmissions use a start bit to synchronize the clocks of the sending and receiving devices.

8. Which of the following is an example of half-duplex transmission?

   A. Traditional television broadcasts

   B. Citizens band radio

   C. Telephone communications

   D. Digital Subscriber Line (DSL)

9. Which of the following media is most vulnerable to electromagnetic interference (EMI)?

   A. UTP

   B. Coaxial cable

   C. Fiber-optic cable

   D. STP

10. Which media access method is used on Ethernet networks?

A. CSMA/CA

B. CSMA/CD

C. Token passing

D. Demand priority

Chapter 5

LAN Links

In the first four chapters of this book, you learned about the purpose and structure of networks, networking models and standards, how signals are sent across network media, and the methods used for controlling access to those media.

In this chapter, we put together some of these concepts as we discuss how they all fit into the specifications that make up a particular type of network link (also referred to as the networking *architecture).*

Generally, we can divide link types into two categories:

- Those used to connect local-area networks (LANs) or metropolitan-area networks (MANs); that is, networks of limited geographic scope
- Those used to connect wide-area networks (WANs), which span cities, countries, or even continents

In this chapter, we look at the characteristics of the first link type, and how to best make choices about which is easiest, most cost effective, and otherwise the optimum solution for a given situation. The second type is covered in Chapter 6, "WAN Links."

There are several link types used for connecting computers over a LAN or MAN. Because these networks span relatively short distances, cable types can be used that would not work with WANS because of their susceptibility to attenuation.

You are already familiar with most of the LAN architectures from earlier chapters, but this chapter outlines the specifications and standards for each, including:

- Ethernet
- Token Ring
- Fiber Distributed Data Interface (FDDI)
- AppleTalk
- ARCnet

Ethernet

The Ethernet architecture is the most popular type of LAN link today. It is based on the 802.3 standard, which specifies a network that implements the CSMA/CD access control method using baseband transmission over coaxial or twisted-pair cable laid out in a bus topology (that is, a linear or star bus). Standard transfer

NOTE

There is some disagreement in the networking industry about the origins of the abbreviation BNC. You might see it defined in some texts as *British Naval Connector.* Others define it as *Bayonet Nut Connector.* Many sources attribute the abbreviation to the names of those who designed it: Neil and Concelman. Among those who advocate the last definition, there is further contention over whether the name is spelled *Neil* or *Neill.* Research indicates that Paul Neill, an employee of Bell Labs, created a connector he called an "N" connector, which was used by the British Navy. Carl Concelman later adapted the design to create a bayonet-mount connector, which he called the "C" connector. Finally, Neill and Concelman got together and created a smaller version, the BNC connector.

rates are 10 Mbps or 100 Mbps, but new standards provide for *Gigabit Ethernet,* capable of attaining speeds up to 1 Gbps over fiber-optic cable or other high-speed media.

Ethernet originated with the ALOHA WAN at the University of Hawaii, which used the CSMA/CD access control method. In the 1970s the Palo Alto Research Center (PARC), owned by Xerox, developed a 2.95-Mbps Ethernet design. Soon afterward, Xerox, Intel, and Digital collaborated on a standard for Ethernet that transmitted at 10 Mbps.

Today there are numerous Ethernet topologies in use, including the following widely implemented forms:

- 10Base2 (thinnet)
- 10Base5 (thicknet)
- 10BaseT (UTP)
- 100BaseT (Fast Ethernet)
- 100BaseFX (Ethernet over fiber-optic cable)
- 1000BaseT (Gigabit Ethernet)

10Base2

The 10Base2 Ethernet topology implements the CSMA/CD access method in a linear bus layout as specified in IEEE standard 802.3, using thin coax cable. This topology is also referred to as *thinnet.*

The 10 in the name refers to the transfer speed of thinnet, which is 10 Mbps. Ethernet is a baseband transmission network. The 2 is a little trickier to figure out; it indicates a rough approximation of the maximum cable segment length for this topology, which is 185 meters (rounding that up to 200 gives you the 2).

A 10Base2 network is limited to 30 *nodes* (that is, computers or other network devices) per 185-meter segment. Thinnet uses barrel connectors and T-connectors (both of which are called *BNC* connectors) and BNC-type terminators on each end of the bus. Figure 5-1 illustrates how a barrel connector is used to extend the length of the cable.

FIGURE 5-1
A BNC barrel connector can be used to extend the length of a piece of thin coax cable.

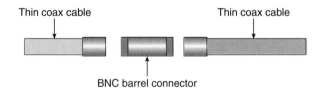

Advantages of 10Base2

The 10Base2 topology is easy to install and configure. For this reason, it is appropriate for small temporary networks (such as classrooms that must be set up and torn down regularly). 10Base2 uses less cable than 10BaseT, and the cable it uses costs less per foot than that which is used with 10Base5. It does not require extra components such as hubs or external transceivers. Thus, 10Base2 is a relatively inexpensive network to implement.

Disadvantages of 10Base2

Unfortunately, 10Base2 is not appropriate for large networks because of the limitations on cable segment length and the number of nodes per segment. In addition, its transfer speed, 10 Mbps, is relatively slow in today's bandwidth-intensive world.

10Base5

10Base5 is sometimes referred to as *standard* Ethernet. It is also called *thicknet*. Thicknet cable is approximately one-half inch in diameter, which is about twice the thickness of thinnet. Thicknet uses the linear bus topology, but because of the thicker coax cable used, it is capable of transmitting for a greater distance (500 meters) without signal loss. Thicknet specifications mandate a minimum segment length of 2.5 meters.

Setting up a network with thicknet is more complex than doing so with thinnet. 10Base5 uses external transceivers, which provide for transmission and reception. They are attached to the network card through a *transceiver cable*, using AUI (DIX) 15-pin connectors, and to the coax cable through a *vampire tap*. See Figure 5-2 for an illustration of this connection.

> **NOTE**
>
> Network specifications mandate a maximum cable segment length because a signal loses strength over distance (attenuation). Minimum length specifications are also important because if the cable segment between two computers is too short, the signals of the two devices will overlap, resulting in an abnormal voltage on the cable that is called a *collision*.

FIGURE 5-2
A NIC attaches to thicknet through an external transceiver and a vampire tap.

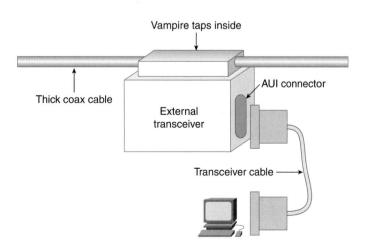

10Base5 is often used as a *backbone,* with the thicknet used to span long distances, such as connecting repeaters on different floors, to which thinnet is then attached and the computers on each floor are connected to the thin coax. Figure 5-3 shows how this works.

FIGURE 5-3
Thick coax can be used as a backbone in combination with thinnet segments.

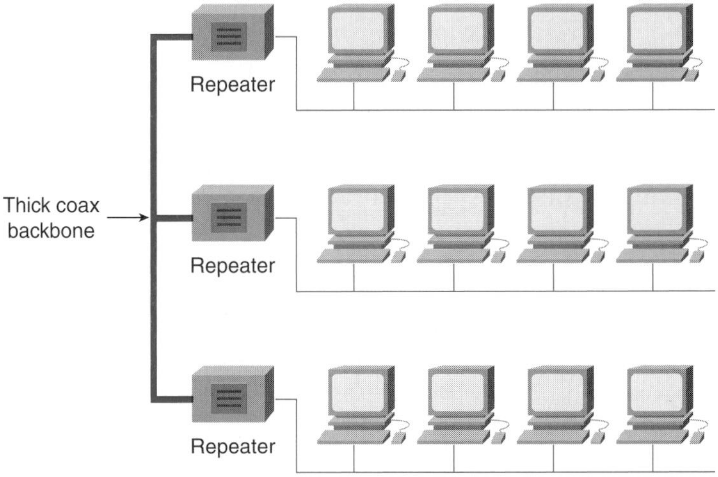

Like other Ethernet networks, 10Base5 uses the CSMA/CD media access method and baseband transmission. A length of cable can be extended using an N-series barrel connector, and the bus is terminated with N-series terminators.

Advantages of 10Base5

Thicknet offers two big advantages over thinnet:

- Capability to span a greater distance between repeaters
- Capacity for more nodes (computers) on each segment

An advantage of thick (and thin) coax over UTP is the partial protection against EMI that the thick outer jacket affords.

Disadvantages of 10Base5

Thick coax does have some disadvantages. Its inflexibility makes it difficult to work with, and adding stations requires drilling into the cable to make the tap.

Thicknet is also relatively expensive. Not only does the thick cable cost more than thin coax or UTP, but also you must purchase the additional equipment (for example, transceiver and transceiver cable) for each computer on the network.

10BaseT

Currently 10BaseT is one of the most popular Ethernet implementations. You could say it is the star of the PC networking world—especially since it uses a star bus topology.

In fact, you will probably hear the term *Ethernet cable* used to describe the unshielded twisted-pair (UTP) cabling generally used in this architecture (shielded twisted-pair [STP] also can be used). 10BaseT and its cousin, 100BaseX, make for networks that are easy to set up and expand.

Advantages of 10BaseT

Networks based on the 10BaseT specifications are relatively inexpensive. Although a hub is required if you are connecting more than two computers, small hubs are available at a low cost, and 10BaseT network cards are inexpensive and widely available.

Twisted-pair cabling, especially the UTP mostly commonly used, is thin, flexible, and easier to work with than coax. It uses modular RJ-45 plugs and jacks, so it is literally a "snap" to connect the cable to the NIC or hub.

Another big advantage of 10BaseT is upgradability. Although by definition a 10BaseT network runs at 10 Mbps, by using Category 5 or above cable and 10/100-Mbps dual-speed NICs, you can easily upgrade to 100 Mbps by simply replacing the hubs.

Disadvantages of 10BaseT

The maximum length for a 10BaseT segment (without repeaters) is only 100 meters (about 328 feet). The UTP used in such a network is more vulnerable to EMI and attenuation than other cable types. Finally, the extra cost of a hub may make this solution slightly more expensive than a thin coax network.

100BaseX

The high-bandwidth demands of many modern applications, such as live video conferencing and streaming audio, have created a need for speed, and many networks require more throughput than is possible with 10-Mbps Ethernet. This is where 100BaseX, also called *Fast Ethernet*, comes into play.

100BaseX comes in several different flavors. It can be implemented over 4-pair Cat 3, 4, or 5 UTP (100BaseT), over 2-pair Cat 5 UTP or STP (100BaseTX), or as Ethernet over 2-strand fiber-optic cable (100BaseFX).

Advantages of 100BaseX

Regardless of the implementation, the big advantage of 100BaseX is high-speed performance. At 100 Mbps, transfer rates are 10 times that of 10Base2, 10Base5, and 10BaseT.

NOTE

Inside the Ethernet hub, the signaling system is a bus, as with coax Ethernet networks.

NOTE

10BaseT specifications require a hub. However, if you wish to connect only two computers (for example, for a home network), and you want to use UTP rather than thinnet, you can do so using a *crossover cable*. This is a type of cable in which the wire pairs are cross-connected, and it is used also to connect two hubs to each other if the hubs do not have uplink ports.

Because it uses twisted-pair cabling, 100BaseX also shares the same advantages enjoyed by 10BaseT: low cost, flexibility, and ease of implementation and expansion.

Disadvantages of 100BaseX

100BaseX shares the disadvantages of 10BaseT, which are inherent to twisted-pair cabling, such as susceptibility to EMI and attenuation. 100-Mbps NICs and hubs are generally somewhat more expensive than those designed for 10-Mbps networks, but prices have dropped as 100BaseX has gained in popularity.

Fiber-optic cable remains an expensive cabling option, not so much because of the cost of the cable itself, but because of the training and expertise required to install it. We discuss cabling more in Chapter 6.

1000BaseT

If 100BaseX is known as *Fast Ethernet*, this new addition to the Ethernet family, 1000BaseT, must be considered a speed demon. Its common nickname is *Gigabit Ethernet*. Although not yet in widespread implementation in production networks, this architecture supports data transfer rates of 1 Gbps, which is almost seven times faster than a T-1 line. Gigabit Ethernet is, for the most part, a LAN architecture, although its implementation over fiber-optic cable makes it suitable for MANs as well.

Advantages of 1000BaseT

The greatest advantage of 1000BaseT is, of course, performance. At 1 Gbps, it is 10 times as fast as Fast Ethernet and 100 times as fast as standard Ethernet. This makes it possible to implement bandwidth-intensive applications, such as live video, throughout an intranet.

Disadvantages of 1000BaseT

The only disadvantages associated with 1000BaseT are those common to all UTP networks, as detailed in the sections on 10BaseT and 100BaseT.

The Structure of an Ethernet Frame

The package into which data is broken for transmission is called a *frame* in Ethernet terminology. The frame contains header information, the data being transmitted, and trailer information.

ETHERNET FRAME TYPES

There are four different frame types (Ethernet_802.2, Ethernet_802.3, Ethernet II, and Ethernet_SNAP) associated with Ethernet communications. The two frame types generally used on a TCP/IP network are Ethernet_II and Ethernet_SNAP (Subnetwork Access Protocol). The frame type is defined by the structure of the frame (that is, the number of bytes allocated to each field in the header, data field, and trailer field). For example, the Ethernet_II header is simpler, containing only four fields. The Ethernet_SNAP header contains nine fields.

Figure 5-4 illustrates the structure of an Ethernet frame (Ethernet II type).

FIGURE 5-4
An Ethernet II frame contains four header fields and a trailer.

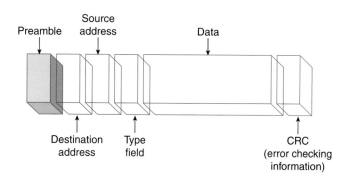

The first header field, which is simply an indicator of the beginning of the frame, is the *preamble*. The next two fields contain the destination and source addresses (that is, the receiving and sending computers), and the fourth field is used to identify the protocol operating at the network layer (typically IP or IPX). The data follows, and can be from 46 to 1500 bytes in length. Ethernet uses an additional 18 bytes for construction of the frame itself. Finally, the trailer contains a cyclic redundancy check (CRC), which is a calculation used to verify that the frame that is received matches what was sent.

CHECKING FOR ERRORS USING CRC

The CRC is a standard way of checking for errors in the data after it has been transmitted over a network. Here's how it works: The computer that is transmitting the data treats the data as one long polynomial. A polynomial is an algebraic expression consisting of one or more summed terms, each term consisting of a constant multiplier and one or more variables raised to integral powers. The transmitting computer divides that polynomial by a predefined 16- or 32-bit polynomial. The quotient from that division is the CRC, and it is appended to the block of data before transmission. Then the computer on the receiving side uses the same predefined 16- or 32-bit polynomial, which it applies to the incoming data. The receiving system compares its result with the result that was appended to the data by the sending system. If the two are the same, the receiving computer concludes that the data has been received successfully. If they are different, the sending computer is notified so that it can resend that block of data.

Rules of Ethernet Engagement

To ensure that the network operates properly, it is important to comply with the rules of engagement laid forth in the specifications for each implementation. These are restrictions and limitations imposed by the characteristics of the media. Note that it may be possible to break or bend these rules and still have functional network communication; however, the network would not be in compliance with standards, and you could experience connectivity problems from pushing beyond the limits.

We discuss two important rules in this section:

- The 5-4-3 rule
- 10BaseT node capacity limitations

The 5-4-3 Rule

One well-known limitation on coax-based Ethernet networks is referred to as the 5-4-3 rule. The numbers represent the following limitations:

- **5**—The maximum number of cable segments allowed in a thinnet or thicknet network is five (each segment can be up to 185 meters for thinnet or 500 meters for thicknet).
- **4**—The maximum number of repeaters that can be used to connect the segments is four.
- **3**—The maximum number of segments that can be *populated* (that is, contain nodes) is three. The other two segments are for purposes of extending the distance only.

> **NOTE**
>
> When applying the 5-4-3 rule to a 10Base5 (thicknet) network, the length of the thick coax cable is used to measure the distance. The transceiver cable does not count in this measurement.

5-4-3 and 10BaseT. Does the 5-4-3 rule apply to twisted-pair Ethernet networks? Many books lead you to believe it doesn't. However, the limitation on the number of hubs that can be uplinked is really an application of this same rule.

Applying the 5-4-3 rule to a UTP star-bus network means that a populated hub, for purposes of this rule, counts as a segment, and the maximum number of cascaded populated hubs allowed in a twisted-pair network is three.

If you think about the fact that the wiring inside each hub is a bus with computers connected to it, just as in a cable segment between repeaters on a linear bus network, this makes sense, as shown in Figure 5-5. This is the reason the topology is called a *star bus*.

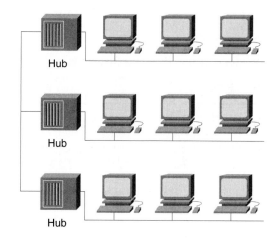

FIGURE 5-5
Each hub to which computers are connected represents a populated segment.

5-4-3 and Expansion of the Network. At this point, you might be wondering how large Ethernet networks can ever be created within the parameters of this rule. Although it is possible to have hundreds of computers connected through twisted-pair or coax cabling, how do those networks circumvent the 5-4-3 limitations?

To understand how Ethernet networks can be expanded, we must first really understand the rule itself. The 5-4-3 rule is often stated as "no more than five segments, four repeaters, and three populated segments per *network*." In this case, a "network" is defined as a *collision domain*, that is, a network within which there will be a collision if two computers transmit at the same time.

The reality of the collision domain is the key to connecting more devices than the 5-4-3 rule would seem to allow. We can create many separate collision domains on a network by dividing the network by using connectivity devices such as switches and routers. In Chapter 7, we look in detail at how these devices work.

10BaseT Node Capacity

The number of nodes per segment on a twisted-pair star-wired bus is always exactly two: the computer or device at one end of the cable and the hub at the other. The maximum number of nodes in a hub-based network should not exceed 100 because of the exponential increase of collisions after 100 nodes. This limit can be extended with connectivity devices such as bridges and switches. The theoretical total number of network devices on a 10BaseT network is 1024.

Summary of Ethernet Characteristics

Table 5-1 is a brief summary of specifications for the most widely used Ethernet implementations.

TABLE 5-1   Ethernet Specifications Summary

	10Base2	10Base5	10BaseT	100BaseX
Cable Type	Thin coax RG-58 A/U	Thick coax RG-8 or RG-11	UTP Cat 3, 4, 5, and 5e	UTP Cat 3, 4, 5, and 5e
Connector Type	BNC connector	AUI/DIX (to transceiver)	RJ-45 modular	RJ-45 modular
Maximum Segment Length	185 meters (607 ft)	500 meters (1640 ft)	100 meters (328 ft)	100 meters (328 ft)
Maximum Network Length	925 meters (3035 ft)	2500 meters (8200 ft)	Star-bus topology	Star-bus topology
Nodes per Segment	30	100	2 (1024 per network)*	2 (1024 per network)*
Transfer Rate	10 Mbps	10 Mbps	10 Mbps	100 Mbps

*   Because a hub is used as a central connection point with UTP-based networks, each segment of cable has only the computer or network device at one end and the hub at the other as nodes on that segment.

Ethernet is a popular LAN architecture that works with almost all popular network server and client operating systems, including Windows for Workgroups, Windows 9x, Windows NT, Windows 2000, Novell NetWare, AppleTalk/AppleShare, and UNIX/Linux.

Token Ring

Token Ring was originally developed by IBM and was designed to be a reliable network architecture based on the token-passing access control method. It is often integrated with IBM mainframe systems such as the AS/400, and it was intended to be used with PCs, minicomputers, and mainframes. It works well with Systems Network Architecture (SNA), the IBM architecture used for connecting to mainframe networks.

The Token Ring standards are provided in IEEE 802.5.

Token Ring Topology

Token Ring's topology can be confusing at first. It is a prime example of an architecture whose physical topology is different from its logical topology. The Token Ring topology is referred to as a *star-wired ring* because the outer appearance of the network design is a star, with computers connecting to a central hub, called a multistation access unit (MSAU). Inside the device, however, the wiring forms a circular data path, creating a logical ring.

Token Ring is so named because of its logical topology and its media access control method: token passing. The transfer rate for Token Ring can be either 4 Mbps or 16 Mbps.

Token Ring is a baseband architecture using digital signaling. In that way it resembles Ethernet, but the communication process is quite different in many respects. Token Ring is an *active* topology: As the signal travels around the circle to each network card, it is regenerated before being sent on its way.

The Token Ring Communication Process

In an Ethernet network, all computers are created physically equal. At the software level, some may act as servers and control network accounts and access, but the servers communicate physically on the network in exactly the same way as the clients.

The Monitor of the Ring

In a Token Ring network, the first computer that comes online becomes the "hall monitor" and must keep track of how many times each frame circles the ring, and it has the responsibility of ensuring that only one token is out on the network at a time.

The monitor computer periodically sends a signal called a *beacon*, which circulates around the ring as does any other signal. Each computer on the network looks for the beacon. If a computer does not receive the beacon from its nearest active upstream neighbor (NAUN) when expected, it puts a message on the network that notifies the monitoring computer of the beacon that was not received, along with its own address and that of the NAUN that failed to send when expected. In many cases, this caused an automatic reconfiguration that restores the communications.

Data Transfer

A Token Ring network uses a *token* (that is, a special signal) to control access to the cable. A token is initially generated when the first computer on the network comes online. As you learned in Chapter 4, when a computer wants to transmit, it waits for and then takes control of the token.

The token can travel in either direction around the ring, but only in one direction at a time. The hardware configuration determines the direction of travel.

Token Ring Hardware Components

Token Ring networks use special hardware. One reason Token Ring is less widely implemented than Ethernet is the higher cost of the Token Ring components.

The MSAU

The Token Ring hub is called a MSAU or smart MSAU (SMSAU). The distinguishing characteristic of an MSAU is the ring configuration of the wiring inside. Multiple MSAUs can be joined together, as long as the "out" port of one is connected to the "in" port of the next, maintaining the integrity of the ring topology. The data must travel in a continuous circle.

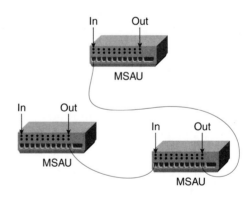

FIGURE 5-6
Multiple MSAUs can be connected, as long as the ring is maintained by ensuring that the ring cable goes in and out properly.

The Cabling and Network Card

Token Ring uses IBM type 1, 2, or 3 cabling. IBM labels its twisted-pair cabling as "types" rather than as "categories." See Table 5-2 for complete descriptions.

TABLE 5-2   IBM Cable Types

IBM Cable Type	Description
Type 1	STP; two pairs of wires with outer shield
Type 2	STP; two pairs of wires for data and four pairs of wires for voice
Type 3	UTP; uses RJ-45 or RJ-11 connectors; four wire pairs
Type 5	Fiber-optic cable
Type 6	STP; used as data patch cable
Type 9	Plenum-grade STP cable

NOTE

IBM cable uses a special IBM connector, called a type A connector, that is not compatible with standard BNC connectors.

Token Ring network cards, such as Ethernet UTP cards, come in different speeds, designed to run at either 4 Mbps or 16 Mbps. If the network runs at 4 Mbps, you can use a 16-Mbps card (although it will run only at the slower speed).

Other Components

A variety of other hardware components are used with Token Ring. Media interface connectors (MICs), for instance, are used to connect type 1 and type 2 IBM cable. Media filters are used to connect a Token Ring NIC to a modular jack and to reduce noise on the line.

Repeaters can be used to regenerate the digital signal, as in Ethernet networks, and extend the length of the network.

CAUTION

You *cannot* use a card designed to run at 4 Mbps on a 16-Mbps Token Ring network. The computer will not be able to communicate at all.

Advantages of Token Ring

Token Ring is a highly reliable architecture, and its token-passing scheme eliminates data collisions. Additionally, the MSAUs can detect the failure of a network card and automatically disconnect it from the ring, thus enabling the token to continue around the ring. Hence, the network is not brought down by the failure of one computer.

Another advantage is the capability to easily interoperate with PC and mainframe networks.

Disadvantages of Token Ring

The major disadvantages of the Token Ring architecture are its higher cost when compared to 10BaseT or 100BaseT and its slower relative speeds.

The Structure of the Token Ring Frame

Token Ring networks use three different types of frames:

- **Data Frame**—Carries information being sent from one computer to another

- **Token Frame**—Circulates on the network until it is captured by a computer that is ready to send information

- **Management Frame**—Transmits error or other management information

The Token Ring data frame structure is a bit more complex than that of the Ethernet II data frame. Figure 5-7 illustrates a Token Ring data frame, which is sometimes also called an LLC (logical link control) frame.

FIGURE 5-7
The Token Ring data frame is more complex than the standard Ethernet frame.

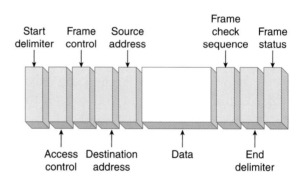

The *start delimiter* in a Token Ring frame serves the same purpose as the preamble on an Ethernet frame. The other fields function as follows:

- **Access control field**—Signifies whether the frame is a token or a data frame, and its priority

- **Frame control field**—Contains access control information

- **Destination address**—The address(es) of the computer(s) to which the data is being sent

- **Source address**—The address of the sending computer

- **Data**—The actual information being sent (for example, the contents of an e-mail message)
- **Frame check sequence (FCS)**—CRC error-checking bits
- **End delimiter**—Signifies the end of the frame
- **Frame status field**—Indicates whether the address was recognized and the frame copied (marked by the receiving computer before being sent back around the ring)

Rules of the Ring

Specifications for Token Ring place some limitations on its implementation:

- Distance between MSAUs is limited to 365 meters for type 3 cable and to 730 meters for type 1 or 2 cable.
- Maximum length for a cable segment depends on the cable type and varies from 45 to 200 meters.
- Maximum length for type 6 patch cable is 46 meters.
- Minimum segment length is 2.5 meters.
- Maximum number of computers per segment, per IBM specifications, is 72 with unshielded cable and 260 with shielded.
- Maximum number of segments (that is, MSAUs) that can be connected is 33 (again, according to IBM specifications).

Summary of Token Ring Characteristics

Token Ring is a reliable technology, but less popular than Ethernet because of the relatively higher cost and slower transfer rates. However, specifications are being developed for 100-Mbps Token Ring and Gigabit Token Ring, so this architecture should not be counted out just yet.

> **NOTE**
>
> The token frame (sometimes just called the "token") circulates on the network until it is captured by a computer that is ready to transmit. A token frame has only three fields: the start delimiter, the access control field, and the end delimiter.

FDDI

FDDI is a type of Token Ring network. Its implementation and topology differ from IBM's Token Ring LAN architecture, which is governed by IEEE 802.5. FDDI is often used for MANs or larger LANs, such as those connecting several buildings in an office complex or campus.

How FDDI Works

As its name implies, FDDI runs on fiber-optic cable, and thus combines high-speed performance with the advantages of the token-passing ring topology. FDDI runs at 100 Mbps, and its topology is a *dual ring*. The outer ring is called the *primary ring* and the inner is the *secondary ring*.

Normally, traffic flows only on the primary ring, but if it fails, the data automatically flows onto the secondary ring, in the opposite direction. The network is said to be in a *wrapped state* when this occurs. This provides fault tolerance for the link. Figure 5-8 illustrates how FDDI works.

FIGURE 5-8
FDDI uses a dual-ring fault-tolerant topology.

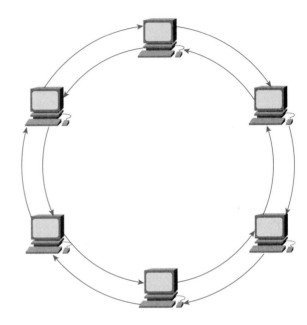

Computers on a FDDI network are divided into two classes:

- **Class A**—Computers connected to the cables of both rings
- **Class B**—Computers connected to only one ring

Another difference between FDDI and 802.5 Token Ring is the allowed number of frames on the network. A FDDI network enables multiple frames to circulate on the ring simultaneously. More than one computer can transmit at the same time. This is called *shared network technology.*

Like 802.5 Token Ring, FDDI uses beaconing to detect and isolate problems within the ring.

FDDI Specifications

A FDDI dual ring supports a maximum of 500 nodes per ring. The total distance of each length of the cable ring is 100 kilometers, or 62 miles. A repeater is needed every 2 kilometers, which is why FDDI is not considered to be a WAN link.

NOTE

These specifications refer to FDDI implemented over fiber-optic cable. It is also possible to use the FDDI technology with copper cabling. This is called *Copper Distributed Data Interface (CDDI)*. The maximum distances for CDDI are considerably lower than those for FDDI.

FDDI's ring topology can be implemented as a physical ring or as a star-wired logical ring by using a hub.

Advantages of FDDI

FDDI combines the advantages of token passing on the ring topology with the high speed of fiber-optic transmission. Its dual ring topology provides redundancy and fault tolerance. The fiber-optic cable is not susceptible to EMI and noise, and it is more secure than copper wiring. It can send data for greater distances between repeaters than can Ethernet and traditional Token Ring.

Disadvantages of FDDI

As always, high speed and reliability come with a price. FDDI is relatively expensive to implement, and its distance limitations, though less restrictive than those of other LAN links, make it unsuitable for true WAN communications.

The FDDI Frame Structure

The FDDI frame structure is similar to that of Token Ring; however, FDDI uses a timed token protocol, while Token Ring uses a priority/reservation token access method. The maximum size for a FDDI frame is 4500 bytes.

The FDDI token is a special frame consisting of three octets. A computer that has data to transmit waits for the token frame, takes possession of it, transmits one or more data frames, and then releases the token.

Summary of FDDI Characteristics

FDDI is a good choice for medium-sized networks—MANs and large LANs. It is good for networks that require high bandwidth, such as engineering, graphics, and video applications.

AppleTalk

AppleTalk networking is designed, not surprisingly, to connect Apple computers, and its software components are built into the Macintosh operating systems. AppleTalk is the name of the architecture. It comes in two varieties: Phase 1 (included in early versions of the Mac OS) and Phase 2 (the current release).

LocalTalk is the term used to refer to the cables, the hardware, and the data link layer protocol used in AppleTalk networks.

AppleTalk Specifications

AppleTalk/LocalTalk networks use the CSMA/CA media access control method. STP cabling is most commonly used, but it is also possible to use UTP

NOTE

Vendors besides Apple also offer cabling and connection components that enable more computers on an AppleTalk network.

or fiber-optic cable. The network topology is a bus or tree, and a LocalTalk network (using Apple components) is limited to 32 nodes.

AppleShare is the protocol that provides file and print sharing on an Apple-Talk network.

How AppleTalk Works

AppleTalk networks use an addressing scheme in which each computer that comes on the network first looks for a stored address (one that it used in a previous session). If it finds one, it uses that; if not, it assigns itself an address, chosen at random from the range of allocated addresses. Then it broadcasts the address to determine if another computer is using it. If so, it repeats the process. If not, it stores the address to be used again the next time it comes on the network.

AppleTalk was designed for small networks. However, separate networks can be connected to one another. Each subnetwork is called a *zone* and has a zone name to identify it. Zones function somewhat like workgroups. You can access resources in a different zone by clicking the zone name.

AppleTalk networks can also be connected to networks using other architectures, such as Ethernet or Token Ring. Apple provides EtherTalk and Token-Talk, which are cards that enable Macintosh computers to connect to networks operating under the 802.3 and 802.5 specifications, respectively.

Advantages of AppleTalk

Because Apple included AppleTalk in the Macintosh operating system, it is easy to implement and configure. Setting up a small workgroup of Macintosh computers is simple and inexpensive.

Disadvantages of AppleTalk

AppleTalk is not suitable for very large networks. It is very slow compared to other LAN links (230.4 Kbps), and thus not suitable for bandwidth-intensive applications.

LocalTalk Data Transmission

LocalTalk is the data link layer protocol originally used by AppleTalk. Macintosh computers using LocalTalk are linked to one another through their printer ports.

Summary of AppleTalk Characteristics

Despite performance limitations, the AppleTalk protocol suite provides a quick, easy way to connect Macintosh computers in small workgroups for sharing of files, printers, and other resources.

NOTE

Although Apple-Talk networks originally used LocalTalk cabling, AppleTalk runs also over Ethernet. The latter has become the popular choice because LocalTalk is slow (230.4 kbps) and was designed for small, low-traffic workgroups.

ARCnet

Attached Resource Computer Network (ARCnet) is an older LAN technology that uses a special token-passing access control method over a star-bus topology.

Some books associate ARCnet with the 802.4 token bus specifications, but actually ARCnet was developed before the 802 standards and does not map completely to this specification. It was designed for small workgroups and is a very simple and inexpensive architecture.

How ARCnet Works

The token-passing method used by ARCnet differs from that of Token Ring. On an ARCnet network, the token does not move along a path based on physical location. It instead goes from one computer to another based on that computer's position in the assigned numbering order. This makes ARCnet an inefficient transmission medium in that the data may travel a much longer path than necessary to reach its destination. Figure 5-9 illustrates how ARCnet works.

FIGURE 5-9
ARCnet's token-passing method can result in data taking an inefficient route to its destination.

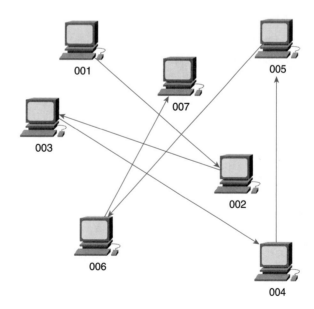

ARCnet Specifications

ARCnet uses a hub to connect computers in a star bus configuration, and it generally uses 93-ohm coax cable specified as RG-62 A/U. However, ARCnet can run also on twisted-pair or fiber-optic cabling.

Using the more common coax cable, the maximum segment length (computer to hub) is 610 meters. Using UTP, the maximum segment length drops to 244 meters.

Standard ARCnet suffers from slow performance; the transfer rate is only 2.5 Mbps. A later implementation, ARCnet Plus, can transmit at 20 Mbps.

Advantages of ARCnet

ARCnet is inexpensive and works adequately for small networks. ARCnet Plus offers a higher data transmission rate than standard Ethernet.

Disadvantages of ARCnet

ARCnet is an older technology that is not as popular as Ethernet and Token Ring. Its networking components are not as widely available, and it is more difficult to find technicians who are experienced in working with ARCnet technology. Even in its faster variety, it is not nearly as fast or efficient as 100BaseT, and it is not suitable for high-bandwidth applications.

The ARCnet Packet Structure

A unit of data transmitted across the network is called a *packet* on an ARCnet network. This equates to the Ethernet or Token Ring *frame*. The standard ARCnet packet is very simple in structure, as shown in Figure 5-10.

FIGURE 5-10
The ARCnet packet contains addressing information and data.

As you can see, the header and trailer fields contain the addresses of the source and destination computers, with the data between the addresses. A standard ARCnet packet is limited to 506 bytes of data, and ARCnet Plus packets can contain up to 4096 bytes.

Summary of ARCnet Characteristics

ARCnet is a simple technology that is being replaced, in many environments, by Ethernet or Token Ring. Although ARCnet is relatively inexpensive and provides adequate performance for small, low-bandwidth networks, its limited transmission speed and inefficient token-passing method have led to a decline in popularity.

Comparing Networking Architectures

Table 5-3 summarizes the characteristics of the networking architectures.

TABLE 5-3   Networking Architectures Compared

Networking Architecture	Cabling Type(s)	Transfer Speed	Access Method	Topology
Ethernet 10Base2	Thin coaxial	10 Mbps	CSMA/CD	Linear bus
Ethernet 10Base5	Thick coaxial	10 Mbps	CSMA/CD	Linear bus
Ethernet 10baseT	UTP Cat 3–5	10 Mbps	CSMA/CD	Star
Ethernet 100BaseT	UTP Cat 5	100 Mbps	CSMA/CD	Star
Ethernet 100BaseFX	Fiber-optic	100 Mbps	CSMA/CD	Star
Ethernet 1000BaseT	UTP Cat7	1 Gbps	CSMA/CD	Star
Token Ring	STP or UTP	4 Mbps or 16 Mbps	Token passing	Physical star, logical ring
FDDI	Fiber optic	100 Mbps	Token passing	Dual ring
AppleTalk	STP or UTP	LocalTalk: 230.4 Mbps Ethernet: 10 Mbps	CDMA/CA	LocalTalk: Linear bus Ethernet: Star

Summary

In this chapter, we have examined the characteristics, specifications, and implementations of several popular LAN architectures.

You learned that Ethernet is one of the most popular LAN links and that it is based on the CSMA/CD access method and governed by IEEE 802.3 standards. We discussed the many varieties of Ethernet, including:

- 10Base2 (thinnet)
- 10Base5 (thicknet)
- 10BaseT, 100BaseT, and 1000BaseT

We also discussed the Token Ring architecture governed by IEEE 802.5 and how communication occurs on a Token Ring network. Next, we looked at FDDI, a token-passing architecture that runs over fiber-optic cable and that is appropriate for large LANs and MANs. Then we took a look at AppleTalk and the components that make up the architecture: LocalTalk, AppleShare, EtherTalk, and TokenTalk. Finally, we discussed ARCnet, an older technology that uses a unique token-passing scheme in which data follows a logical, rather than physical, path.

In the next chapter, we will expand our horizons a bit and look beyond the LAN to the concepts and practices of wide area networking. We will discuss popular WAN links and how they are implemented, and we will examine how you can connect your LAN to a WAN (including the widest area network of all, the Internet).

Further Reading

For more information on LAN links, see the following:

- Charles Spurgeon's Ethernet (802.3) website at wwwhost.ots.utexas.edu/ethernet/ethernet-home.html.
- The Token Ring Consortium at www.iol.unh.edu/consortiums/tokenring/main.html.
- The Interoperability Lab's FDDI tutorial at www.iol.unh.edu/training/fddi/htmls/index.html.
- Core Competence AppleTalk whitepaper at www.corecom.com/html/appletalk.html.
- The ARCNET trade association website at www.arcnet.com/home.html.

Review Questions

The following questions test your knowledge of the material covered in this chapter. Be sure to read each question carefully and select the *best* correct answer or answers.

1. IEEE 802.3 defines specifications for which of the following network architectures?

   A. Token Ring

   B. Ethernet

   C. ARCnet

   D. FDDI

2. Which media access method is used by Ethernet networks?

   A. CSMA/CD

   B. CSMA/CA

   C. Token Passing

   D. Demand priority

3. 10Base2 Ethernet specifications limit the number of nodes on a segment of cable to what number?

   A. 30

   B. 100

   C. 185

   D. 1024

4. Which of the following cable types uses a BNC connector?

   A. UTP

   B. thick coax

   C. thin coax

   D. Fiber optic

5. The term "standard Ethernet" is used to refer to which of the following?

   A. 10BaseT networks

   B. 100BaseT networks

    C. 10Base2 networks

    ▸**D.** 10Base5 networks

6. What is the specified maximum cable distance for a 10Base5 network?

    A. 100 meters

    ▸**B.** 500 meters

    C. 100 feet

    D. 500 feet

7. Which of the following is true of the Token Ring architecture? (Select all that apply.)

    A. Token Ring is a passive topology.

    B. Token Ring networks run at 4 or 16 Mbps.

    C. Token Ring hubs are called multistation access units.

    ▸**D.** Token Ring is a broadband architecture.

8. What is the name of the circulating signal sent by the monitor computer in a Token Ring network, whose purpose is to detect when a station fails so that the network can reconfigure itself to restore communications?

    A. token

    B. data frame

    ▸**C.** beacon

    D. NAUN

9. Which of the following is the data link layer protocol originally designed for AppleTalk networks?

    A. Ethernet

    ▸**B.** LocalTalk

    C. EtherTalk

    D. TokenTalk

10. What is the transfer speed for standard ARCnet?

    ▸**A.** 2.5 Mbps

    B. 25 Mbps

    C. 16 Mbps

    D. 10 Mbps

Chapter 6

WAN Links

The technologies, media, and equipment that work well for the short distances spanned by a LAN or MAN are generally not suitable for long-distance wide-area networks (WANs). In today's very mobile world, high-performance, cost-effective WAN technologies are a necessity for many reasons:

- Executives and other employees need access to their corporate networks while on the road or at home.
- Companies with branch offices in widely dispersed geographic locations need network connectivity between locations.
- Organizations want to share information with other organizations physically separated by long distances.
- Commercial, governmental, and educational bodies and individuals need access to the resources available on the global Internet.

It is obviously impossible to string Ethernet cable from the home office in Denver to the branch office in Houston. Even if cabling distance limitations did not apply, this would not be a viable solution for connecting international sites.

WANs require a whole new set of technologies and rules of implementation. In this chapter, we discuss the concept of networking over long distances and the technologies commonly used to connect computers that are located in different states, countries, or even different continents. These range from the Public Switched Telephone Network (PSTN) already in place in most of the world to modern high-tech solutions such as satellite communications technologies that enable us to "talk" to computers in space.

Wide-area networking presents many challenges not encountered in implementing a network that is confined to one geographic area. A WAN is *not* just a really big LAN. Rather, it is a collection of many separate LANs, connected by links that are different in many ways from LAN links. WANs that span international boundaries require consideration of even more factors, including time zones and language differences.

Designing a WAN is a complex task. Choosing the appropriate technology involves analyzing the purpose(s) the WAN will serve, the number of users, the bandwidth requirements, and the patterns of use. We can categorize these considerations as follows:

- WAN hardware
- WAN topologies

- Network switching types
- New and emerging WAN technologies
- LAN/WAN connectivity

We look at each issue in the sections that follow.

WAN Hardware

The hardware necessary to implement a WAN link can be as simple and inexpensive as a telephone line and a modem at each end. On the other hand, it can be complex and costly. In general, equipment cost and complexity increases with increased speed and reliability.

In the following sections, we discuss common WAN devices, including modems, ISDN and digital subscriber line (DSL) terminal adapters, and customer premises equipment (CPE) used with dedicated links such as T-carrier connections and X.25.

Modems

To establish a network connection (to an Internet service provider or to a dial-up server on a private network) over public telephone lines, you use a device called a *modem*.

Modems come in two physical types: *internal* and *external*. Each has advantages and disadvantages, and configuration is slightly different depending on the type. Either way, modems are *serial* devices, which means bits are sent one at a time. This can be contrasted with *parallel* devices, such as printers, to which multiple bits can be sent simultaneously. A serial transmission is analogous to a group of people marching in a straight line, and a parallel transmission is like having the same group marching in rows of three across.

Internal Modems

One advantage of the internal modem is compactness. It is a circuit board card that fits in an ISA (Industry Standard Architecture) or PCI (Peripheral Component Interconnect) slot inside the computer, as shown in Figure 6-1. This means that you don't have to find room for an extra device on your desk. In addition, you are not required to buy a serial cable, which you might be forced to do if you use an external model that doesn't include one in the box.

> **TIP**
>
> The word "modem" is derived from the actions it performs; a modem *modulates* and *demodulates* a signal. In other words, it converts the sending computer's digital signal to analog for transmission over the analog line and then converts it back to digital for processing by the receiving computer.

FIGURE 6-1
An internal modem is a circuit board that fits inside the computer.

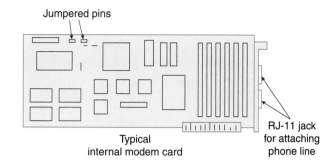

Jumpered pins

Typical internal modem card

RJ-11 jack for attaching phone line

Internal Modem Configuration Parameters. Internal modems are traditionally more difficult to configure than external modems. You must set the IRQ, the input/output addresses, and the virtual com ports to ensure that they don't conflict with the settings of some other device in your computer. Let's look more closely at each setting and how it is used:

- **Interrupt Request (IRQ)**—This is an assigned location that designates where the system expects the device to interrupt it when the device sends a signal. Signals from different devices that go to the processor on the same interrupt line would interfere with each other, so a separate IRQ must be assigned to each device.

- **Input/Output (I/O) address**—This is the location where data sent from the device is stored before it is processed by the CPU. As with the IRQ, if multiple devices attempt to use the same I/O address, one or both devices might not work properly.

- **Virtual com port**—This is a logical port number, by which the operating system identifies a serial port. You must set each serial device to use a different com port.

All popular operating systems provide a means by which you can view how resources are being used, and which ones are not in use, so that you can choose free resources to assign to your new device.

Changing the Internal Modem Settings. Internal modems generally provide a way to change the configuration settings. Depending on the manufacturer and model, you can change IRQ, I/O, and com port settings with the following:

- **Dip switches**—These are small switches on the circuit board that can be moved to a different position. The position of the switch designates which setting is to be used.

- **Jumpers**—Pairs of metal pins built into the circuit board, these represent an electrical contact point. Jumpers are configured by placing a small plug on the pins to complete the circuit. The instructions that come with your internal modem tell you how the jumpers should be set to use a specific IRQ, I/O address, or com port.

- **Software**—Some modems do not have physical switches or jumpers, but do come with a software program that is run to change the configuration.

Plug and Play. Many modern modems support *Plug and Play (PnP)* technology, which enables the operating system to detect the device, install the necessary software drivers, detect what resources are free on the computer, and assign those resources to the device automatically. Little or no intervention is required from the user.

PnP is great—when it works and when you are aware of a few caveats. If you buy a modem or other device that is advertised as Plug and Play, it is automatically configured *only* if the following is true:

- Your computer's BIOS (Basic Input/Output System) supports PnP.
- You are running a PnP operating system.

Both criteria must be met. Computer motherboards produced after 1995 usually support PnP. Operating systems that support PnP include Windows 95, 98, ME, and 2000.

External Modems

External modems have a couple advantages over the internal variety:

- Most external modems provide status lights, which indicate when the modem is powered on, connected, or transferring data. See Figure 6-2.
- External modems are generally easier to install and configure. There are no switches or jumpers to set, and you don't have to open the computer case.

External modems require power cords to plug into an electrical outlet, but internal modems run off the computer's power. A serial cable connects the modem to one of the serial ports on the back of the computer.

NOTE

Windows NT is *not* a PnP operating system. However, it does have limited PnP functionality and detects some modem types.

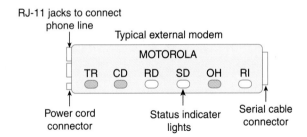

FIGURE 6-2
External modems
provide status
indicator lights.

Serial Port Considerations. To use an external modem, you need a free *serial port*. Most computers have two built-in serial ports, labeled COM 1 and COM 2, with connectors on the back of the computer.

Many devices, such as scanners, digital cameras, and serial pointing devices, also use serial ports. If your computer does not have a free serial port, you have a few options:

- Use an internal modem.
- Install an expansion card in your computer, which enables you to add serial port connections.
- If your computer's motherboard supports universal serial bus (USB), you can chain multiple serial devices, such as modems, off a single serial port. You might have to add a card to provide a USB connector, and you need a USB modem.

UART Chips. Serial ports use a chip called a UART (Universal Asynchronous Receiver/Transmitter) to handle serial communications. This chip comes in different types, and the type used determines how fast data can be transferred over that serial port.

The first PCs had 8250 UART chips. The top speed for this chip is 9600 bps, which means that even if you attach a high speed (56 kbps) modem to one of these ports, your speed would be limited by the UART.

Modern computers have UART chips in the 16450 or 16550 series. These serial ports can support transfer speeds of up to 115,200 bps.

16650 and 16750 UART chips are also available as add-on "enhanced serial port" cards. Internal modems have their own UART chips built into the card, so the speed of the computer's com port is irrelevant.

NOTE

If you have a high-speed modem and a modern computer, but are able to connect only at low speeds, check the com port configuration settings. Some operating systems set the com ports to 9600 bps by default; you need to change this setting to realize the port's full capacity.

Modem Drivers

Drivers are software programs that act as a liaison between the hardware device and the operating system. Driver software is usually supplied by the modem manufacturer with the device, or it can be downloaded from the manufacturer's website.

You must install the correct driver software for your device because if operating system code included support for all hardware devices that could possibly be used with it, the operating system would require significantly more disk space—much of it wasted on driver software that would never be used.

Modem Configuration

In addition to installing the driver software that enables the operating system to recognize the modem, and setting the IRQ, I/O address, and com port that the modem will use, you have to configure the modem to dial and maintain a connection. Modern operating systems have built-in support for dialup networking. You might have to install the remote access services if the modem was not present when the operating system was installed.

Modem Banks

A computer can be configured as a *dialup server* (also called a *remote access server*) to enable other computers to dial into it and connect to it over the phone lines. Computers running powerful server software can support many incoming remote access connections simultaneously; for instance, Windows NT Server supports up to 256 connections.

How can you connect 256 modems to a remote server? When you have many simultaneous dial-in connections (for example, when the server belongs to a company with many telecommuters who need to connect to the corporate network from home), you can use a *modem bank*. Modem banks are also called *modem nests* or *modem pools*.

A modem bank enables you to use a group of modems (usually mounted together in a rack) with a single server, and host multiple remote connections. The rack of modem cards is controlled by an interface that connects to the server, to a router, or directly to the local network. Of course, you need a phone line for each separate connection.

ISDN and DSL Adapters

The device used to connect a computer to an Integrated Services Digital Network (ISDN) or DSL telephone line is often referred to as a modem. It is more accurately called a *terminal adapter* because it does not modulate and demodulate signals because ISDN lines are digital, unlike the analog PSTN lines.

ISDN Adapters

ISDN adapters, such as modems, come in both internal and external varieties. They are configured similarly to modems, but the typical 128-kbps ISDN service consists of two data channels that each run at 64 kbps. The two channels are commonly used in a *multilink* configuration to provide the 128-kbps bandwidth. We discuss ISDN technology later in this chapter in the "ISDN" section.

The two data channels have separate telephone numbers in most cases. ISDN adapters are configured with information about the *service profile identifier (SPID)* for each channel, which consists of the telephone number, a two-digit sharing terminal identifier, and a two-digit terminal identifier (TID). Some modern ISDN adapters support automated SPID selection and do not require you to enter this information.

DSL Adapters

Both ends of a DSL connection require a device called an *endpoint* (and often referred to as a *DSL modem*), which connects to an Ethernet NIC installed in the computer. In some cases, the endpoint/modem is external. In others, the endpoint and the NIC are placed together on the same card.

Customer Premises Equipment

Customer premises equipment (CPE) is a general term that encompasses several different devices. The customer's site requires this hardware to process incoming transmissions from WAN links such as T-carrier lines, X.25 connections, and Frame Relay links.

Common types of CPE include the following:

- A channel service unit/digital service unit (CSU/DSU), used with circuit-switched connections such as a T-1 line. The CSU receives and transmits signals to and from the WAN line. The DSU manages line control, timing errors, and signal regeneration.
- A packet assembler/disassembler (PAD), used with packet-switched connections such as X.25. The PAD is an asynchronous device that enables multiple terminals to share a network line. Users dial into PADs through modems.

WAN Topologies

We discussed LAN topologies in Chapter 2, "Categorizing Networks," and some of those same concepts apply to WANs. In the context of WANs, however, the *topology* describes the arrangement of the transmission facilities.

The simplest WAN topology is a simple point-to-point connection. The WAN, like the LAN, also can use traditional networking topologies such as a ring or star.

The Point-to-Point WAN

A point-to-point WAN is similar to the LAN topology referred to as a linear bus. A remote access link, which can be anything from a 56-kbps dial-up modem connection to a dedicated T-1 line, connects each point on the WAN to the next. See Figure 6-3 for an illustration of this.

FIGURE 6-3
A point-to-point WAN directly connects two endpoints.

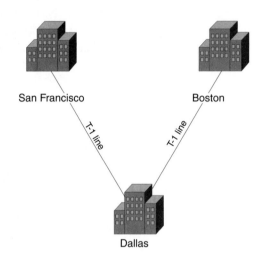

San Francisco

Boston

T-1 line

T-1 line

Dallas

This is a relatively inexpensive way to connect a small number of WAN sites. However, it is not fault tolerant. For example, in Figure 6-3, if the equipment at the Dallas office fails, San Francisco and Boston cannot communicate with one another. Limited scalability (the capability to "grow gracefully," that is, to continue to function efficiently as the network grows larger) is another disadvantage. If you add another point to the WAN at Nashville, between Dallas and Boston, you increase the number of hops required for Boston to communicate with Dallas or San Francisco.

The point-to-point link works best for small WANs with only two or three locations.

The WAN Ring

A ring is constructed by establishing a point-to-point connection from Point A to Point B, from Point B to Point C, and from Point C back to Point A, as shown in Figure 6-4.

NOTE

In wide-area networking, a *hop* is defined as the trip from one router to the next. The *hop count* is the number of routers the packet passes through from source to destination.

FIGURE 6-4
A WAN can use a
ring topology.

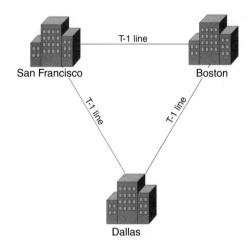

FIGURE 6-4
A WAN can use a
ring topology.

The ring topology provides redundancy. In the example shown in Figure 6-4, if the line between Dallas and San Francisco goes down, data can still be transferred between the two cities by going through Boston.

The ring topology is more expensive to implement than the single point-to-point topology, and it suffers from the same scalability problem as the point-to-point topology.

The ring topology works well for WANs that connect only a few locations and that need the reliability offered by the redundant pathways.

The WAN Star

When a WAN is laid out in a star configuration, a device called a *concentrator router* is used; it serves as a central point to which all network routers are connected. In Figure 6-5, for example, the concentrator router is located at the Dallas headquarters.

The star topology is more scalable than the ring, and in a star, it is easier to add locations to the WAN.

The disadvantage of the star is its single point of failure. In the case shown in Figure 6-5, this point of failure is the Dallas concentrator router. If this device fails, communications cease among all points on the network.

Full- and Partial-Mesh WANs

A mesh topology, where there are multiple connections between points, provides the most fault-tolerant and reliable WAN. Unfortunately, it is also the most expensive to implement, and it becomes cumbersome if there are a large number of sites.

FIGURE 6-5
A WAN arranged in a star topology is scalable.

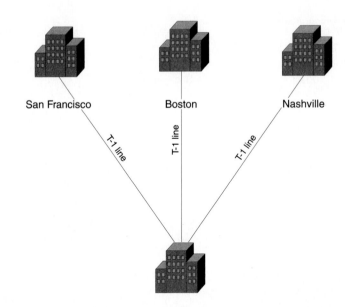

A full mesh topology requires that every site in the network be connected to every other site. With a partial mesh, a smaller number of redundant connections exist. This provides reliability approaching that of the full mesh, at significantly lower cost.

Refer to Figures 2-10 and 2-11 in Chapter 2 for an illustration of mesh and partial (hybrid) mesh topologies.

Multitiered WANs

A multitiered WAN is similar to the star in that it uses concentrator routers, but is more reliable because it links two or more of these concentrators with other locations "cascaded" off the main routers. See Figure 6-6 for an illustration.

The multitiered WAN is scalable because additional locations (and even additional tiers) can be added to the network relatively easily. This topology is used for large, fast-growing networks.

Traffic flow can become a problem on large, multitiered WANs. Flow patterns should be carefully analyzed to ensure the most efficient placement of equipment for best performance.

FIGURE 6-6
A multitiered
WAN offers more
reliability than a
simple star.

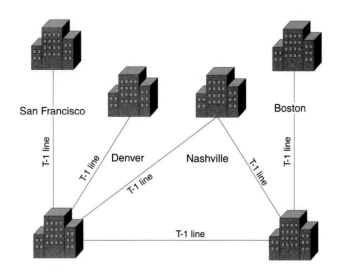

Network Switching Types

Data can travel to a distant destination over several different types of lines, using one of two popular switching technologies:

- Circuit switching
- Packet switching

In the next sections, we examine how each technology works.

CIRCUIT SWITCHING VERSUS PACKET SWITCHING

Many people confuse circuit switching and packet switching. An example of a circuit-switched network is the telephone network. When you place a call to a branch office in Boston, a circuit is established for the duration of the call. The signal uses that circuit, or pathway, until you break the connection by hanging up. If you call again tomorrow, a different pathway might be taken.

An example of a packet-switched network is the Internet. When you send an e-mail message to the Boston office, it is broken down into chunks called *packets*. Each packet might take a different pathway to reach the destination computer; they are reassembled at the other end.

Circuit-Switching Networks

The first switching type we examine is the *circuit-switched* network.

DIALUP VERSUS DEDICATED CONNECTIONS

Circuit-switched networks include both dialup and dedicated leased lines.

A dialup connection is a *temporary* connection, established for the duration of the session. Dialup connections can, however, be implemented as "always-on" connections with which you dial up the remote server and then do not end the connection. With a dialup connection, it is possible to hang up and dial a different location if you choose to do so. For example, you can end the connection to one ISP and then dial in and connect to another.

A dedicated connection is one that goes only from one specific point to another (for example, from your business office to your ISP).

Circuit-switching technology has a long history and is older than packet switching. Circuit switching is most appropriate when data must be transmitted in real time (as with a telephone conversation). Circuit-switched networks are connection-oriented networks because a connection is established before transmission begins.

We briefly examine the following circuit-switched technologies in the following subsections of this chapter:

- PSTN
- ISDN
- DSL
- Leased lines
- Digital data service (DDS)
- T-carriers
- Switched 56

PSTN

The most common type of dialup WAN link is made by using the PSTN—the analog phone lines that are installed in most residences and businesses.

PSTN has two big advantages:

- It is available almost all over the world.
- It is inexpensive.

A dialup connection using ordinary phone lines is easy to implement. Besides a modem, no special equipment is required, and analog modems are readily available, simple to configure, and inexpensive.

The telephone system was not originally created with data transfer in mind; it was designed to transmit voice. High speed was not an issue, so there is an inherent limit to the attainable transfer rate.

Line quality is also a factor. Even with top-of-the-line 56-kbps modems, many telephone lines are capable of providing no more than 40 kbps–45 kbps.

ISDN

ISDN was designed to eventually replace POTS and provide a reliable digital connection suitable for both voice and data. Although that hasn't happened, and the recent advent of faster technologies at lower cost means it probably won't, ISDN still offers some advantages.

The characteristics of ISDN include the following:

- As its name implies, ISDN is a digital link. Because it does not have to convert data from digital to analog format and back, performance and reliability are high.
- It is more readily available than some of its newer competitors, such as DSL.
- Although it is a dialup technology, ISDN can be used as an always-on link (that is, dedicated ISDN).
- ISDN service is more expensive than analog service (PSTN) and requires specialized equipment, both at the telephone company central office (that is, at the digital switch) and at the customer's premise (that is, at the ISDN terminal adapter).

An ISDN circuit is made up of one or more channels that carry data (called bearer channels, or B channels) and a control channel (called the Delta channel, or D channel).

Each B channel provides 64 kbps of bandwidth, and B channels can be aggregated by using *inverse multiplexing*. This enables you to combine the bandwidth of multiple channels to create one high-speed connection. The D channel provides either 16 or 64 kbps, depending on the interface implementation.

ISDN is offered by most telephone companies in two standard access interfaces:

- **Basic Rate ISDN (BRI)**—This interface consists of two 64-kbps B channels (for an aggregate usable bandwidth of 128 kbps) and one 16-kbps D channel.
- **Primary Rate ISDN (PRI)**—This consists of 23 64-kbps B channels (for an aggregate bandwidth of 1.472 Mbps) and one 64-kbps D channel.

BRI is often implemented for residential or small business high-speed data transfer, and PRI is commonly used for digital voice transmission in conjunction with private branch exchange (PBX) telephone systems.

DSL

DSL is a relatively new technology, offered by telephone companies as an add-on service over existing copper wires. DSL offers several advantages over other WAN link types.

The following list contains characteristics of DSL:

- DSL offers speeds up to and exceeding those of T-1, at a fraction of the cost. In many areas, DSL service costs less than ISDN.
- DSL is an always-on technology. There is no need to dial up each time you wish to connect.
- Both voice and data can be transmitted over the same line simultaneously.
- At present, availability is limited. The telephone company central office (CO) that is servicing the location must have DSL equipment installed, and for most "flavors" of DSL, you must be within a specified number of feet from the CO to get DSL service.

DSL comes in several varieties:

- **ADSL (Asymmetric DSL)**—This is the most common implementation. Speeds vary from 384 kbps to 6 Mbps (or more) downstream, typically combined with a lower upstream speed.
- **SDSL (Symmetric DSL)**—This provides the same speed for downloads and uploads.
- **HDSL (High Data Rate DSL)**—This variety typically provides bandwidth of 768 kbps in both directions.
- **VDSL (Very High Data Rate DSL)**—This is capable of bandwidths between 13 Mbps and 52 Mbps.
- **IDSL**—This is DSL over ISDN lines. It has a top speed of 144 kbps, but is available in areas that don't qualify for other DSL implementations.

The generic term for DSL, encompassing all implementations, is *xDSL*.

NOTE

A *PBX* is a private telephone network operated within an organization. Internal users share outside lines, and calling within the organization requires dialing only a four-digit extension. A traditional PBX required a switchboard operator, who answered all incoming calls and then routed each to the appropriate extension. Modern equipment automates this process.

ADSL, currently the most popular DSL implementation, generally provides a fast downstream transfer rate (typically 1.5 Mbps) and a slower upstream rate. This is based on the theory that most users of the Internet primarily access e-mail and surf the Web, which are download-intensive tasks. The lower upload rates do not work as well, however, if you wish to host a Web or FTP server, or engage in other upload-intensive tasks.

ADSL typically uses frequency-division multiplexing (FDM) to split the bandwidth and create multiple channels. Some ADSL implementations use a different method, called *echo cancellation*. It is more efficient, but also more complex and more costly.

Table 6-1 summarizes currently available DSL implementations.

TABLE 6-1   Comparison of DSL Implementations

DSL Type	Average Speeds	Advantages	Disadvantages
ADSL	384 kbps to 6 Mbps (downstream)	Relatively inexpensive; more widely implemented than other types.	Can be installed only within 17,500 ft of a telephone company CO; upstream speed is usually much slower.
SDSL	Up to 3 Mbps	Offers the same data rate upstream and downstream.	Generally more expensive and less widely available than ADSL.
IDSL	144 kbps	Can be installed in many locations where other DSL types are not available because of distance.	More expensive than ADSL; considerably slower speed.
HDSL	768 kbps up and downstream	Faster than IDSL and some implementations of ADSL.	Not widely available.
VDSL	13 Mbps to 52 Mbps	Extremely high speed for live audio and video.	Not widely available; most expensive DSL type.

Leased Lines

For WAN links that require guaranteed high performance and reliability, an option is to lease lines from the telephone company for private use. A leased line provides a permanent connection from one point to another (for example, from one branch office to another, or from your company LAN to your ISP).

DDS

DDS was one of the first digital services made available to the public. DDS provided a 56-kbps transfer rate. It lost the popularity contest to T-carrier technology because a T-1 line typically provides more bandwidth per dollar.

T-carriers

T-carriers are dedicated digital circuits that are typically leased by large companies to provide high-speed data, voice, audio, and video over a highly reliable point-to-point connection.

T-carrier circuits are typically established over copper wires, but they can also run over fiber-optic cable, coaxial cable, and even wireless technologies.

A CSU/DSU is used at each end of the connection to encode the data to be sent over the T-carrier.

Although prices for T-1 lines have fallen dramatically over the last decade, it is still an expensive option. A T-1 line typically costs 10 to 20 times that of DSL service for comparable speed (1.5 Mbps).

Why would anyone pay for T-1 when low-cost high-speed options are available? Availability itself is one reason; DSL has only recently become widespread, and even in areas where it is offered, many businesses and residences are not within the distance limitations required to order the service.

Another reason to pay extra for T-1 is guaranteed bandwidth. This is called the *committed information rate* (*CIR*). With 1.5-Mbps DSL service, the telephone company sells you a service that has a maximum transfer rate of 1.5 Mbps. Your line might or might not actually perform at that speed at a given time. When you lease a T-1 connection, the telephone company guarantees the data rate of 1.544 Mbps. This can be an important consideration for corporate enterprises that depend on network performance.

The T in T-carrier refers to transmission channel; the signal itself is more accurately referred to as the data signal (DS) rate. You hear both DS-1 and T-1 used to refer to the same line type. Table 6-2 lists common T-carrier implementations.

TABLE 6-2   Common T-Carrier Implementations

Carrier Designation	Data Signal Rate	Data Transfer Speed
T-1	DS-1	1.544 Mbps
T-2	DS-2	6.312 Mbps
T-3	DS-3	44.736 Mbps
T-4	DS-4	274.760 Mbps

T-carrier lines consist of multiple 64 kbps channels. It is possible to lease just part of a T-1 line (in 64 kbps increments) if you don't need the entire 1.544 Mbps bandwidth; this is called *fractional T-1*.

Switched 56

Switched 56 is an enhanced version of PSTN. It is a digital switched-circuit connection that transfers data over one 56 kbps channel. Switched 56 is less expensive—but also much slower—than a T-1 line. It is a dialup technology, thus it can be appropriate in cases in which a dedicated connection is unnecessary.

Unlike PSTN, which is theoretically capable of data rates of 56 kbps but in practice generally attains speeds no higher than 50 kbps (and often falls far short of that), Switched 56 can provide a reliable full 56 kbps connection. Because it is a digital connection, error rates are lower than on a regular PSTN (analog) line.

The connection is called "switched" because individual 56 kbps channels are switched out of a T-1 circuit and sent to a specific user location.

The popularity of Switched 56 has suffered as other low-cost, high-bandwidth options (such as ISDN and DSL) have become more widely available.

Packet-Switching Networks

Packet-switching networks are networks in which data packets can take different routes to reach the same destination. At the receiving end, the packets are put back together in the correct order. Packet-switched networks are often depicted as a cloud because the exact route of travel of the data is unknown.

Packet-switching technologies include the following:

- X.25
- Frame Relay
- Asynchronous Transfer Mode (ATM)

We discuss each in more detail in the following sections.

NOTE

Although you often hear the term *X.25 network*, the technically correct term is *Public Switched Data Network (PSDN)*. X.25 is the protocol that is used for communication between the data terminal equipment and the network.

X.25

NOTE

The CCITT changed its name to the International Telecommunications Union (ITU) in 1993.

X.25 was one of the first packet-switching networks and was designed to work with IBM mainframes, such as the IBM 360, and use analog transmission.

X.25 was originally called the ARPAnet 1822 protocol; the name X.25 came from the specifications for the protocols used by this technology, established by the International Telegraph and Telephone Consultative Committee (CCITT) in 1976.

PSDN technology operates at the first three layers of the OSI model. The technology called X.25 is actually made up of several protocols:

- PSDN uses a protocol called X.21 at the physical layer (a variation of the X.21 physical layer protocol, X.21bis, is used in the United States).
- A protocol named Link Access Procedure Balanced (LAPB) is used at the data link layer.
- At the network layer, the Packet Layer Protocol (PLP) is used to assemble frames from the data link layer into packets.

The primary objective in designing the X.25 protocol was reliability. At the time it was designed in the 1970s, both the computers in use and the telephone lines were prone to error. Thus, the PSDN running on X.25 included redundant error-checking to compensate for these problems. The result was a highly reliable means of data transfer, but performance was slowed by the extra error-checking activity. The PSDN usually transfers at 64 kbps or below.

There are still public switched data networks in use today. To make a WAN connection over a PSDN, you can do one of the following:

- Dial into a packet assembler/disassembler (PAD) with an asynchronous modem
- Make a synchronous connection using the X.32 protocol
- Use an X.25 smart card to connect directly to the PSDN

Frame Relay

Frame Relay is a newer packet switching technology, which was designed to be used over digital lines and which grew out of X.25. Frame relay is a variation on and improvement to the X.25 technology, developed by the CCITT. Frame Relay uses only the first two OSI layers rather than the first three (as X.25 does). It was developed to take advantage of modern computers and telephone lines, which are far more reliable than those in use when X.25 originated. It has become a popular option for WAN links, and it generally offers a higher-performance, more cost-effective solution than does X.25.

Frame Relay operates only at the two lowest levels of the OSI model, the physical and data link layers. Frame Relay uses less overhead than X.25, and thus, it is faster. Frame Relay can run at T-1 and T-3 speeds (from 1.5 Mbps to almost 45 Mbps).

Frame relay is called a *fast packet* technology.

A typical Frame Relay implementation uses a *permanent virtual circuit (PVC)* to provide an always-on connection. Because service providers generally charge fees based on usage (referred to as *bandwidth on demand*), you can avoid the cost of a dedicated leased line.

Frame relay has high performance because it does not include the extensive error checking and correction of X.25. Frames with errors are discarded, and it is up to the endpoints (communication computers) to detect the missing packet and request retransmission. Because transmission is digital, there are relatively few errors to contend with, and Frame Relay works well in a WAN environment over T-1 lines.

ATM

ATM is a popular packet-switching technology that was designed to support high-speed applications such as streaming audio and video. An important concept for ATM networks is quality of service (QoS), which is a way to control the allocation of network bandwidth to specific applications to provide guaranteed bandwidth where it is most important.

ATM is hardware based, which means that all equipment on the network must be designed to work with ATM. The advantage is that this results in high speeds for processing and switching. Standard ATM transfer rates are 25 Mbps, 155.520 Mbps, and 622.080 Mbps, and ATM is capable of speeds of 10 Gbps. Unfortunately, that performance comes at a high price. ATM is expensive to implement because all network hardware must support ATM, and network interface cards (NICs), hubs, and other ATM-compatible equipment is costly.

ATM is a modern digital technology that breaks data into 53-byte fixed-length units called *cells*. Five bytes are used for the ATM header, which contains addressing information.

ATM can be used for both LANs and WANs, and it uses multiplexing to transfer voice, data, and video simultaneously over the network. Cell switching is a function of the ATM hardware (unlike Frame Relay, in which it is a software function).

You can connect to an ATM network through a direct connection or an on-demand connection. The connection between the two endpoints is a *virtual circuit*; it can be either a PVC or a switched virtual circuit (SVC). With either a PVC or an SVC, ATM uses predefined circuits instead of establishing the virtual circuits at the time of connection, as X.25 and Frame Relay do. This saves a great deal of time and is another factor in ATM's high speed.

Many networking experts predict that in the future, ATM will become the technology of choice for both LANs and WANs.

Emerging WAN Technologies

New, faster, and more efficient WAN technologies are being developed all the time. Many of these interoperate with one another to provide support for the high-bandwidth applications in use today and those expected to be in demand in the future.

In the following sections, we look at new high-speed technologies, including OC-SONET, Broadband ISDN, CATV, and SMDS.

OC-SONET

OC stands for *optical carrier*, and SONET stands for *Synchronous Optical Network*. SONET is a physical layer protocol that provides for high-speed transmission using fiber-optic media. SONET is capable of rates of almost 20 Gbps, and ATM can run over SONET to achieve very high data transfer speeds.

The SONET signal rate is measured by OC standards. Table 6-3 illustrates the available transmission rates (called optical carrier levels).

TABLE 6-3   OC Signal Transmission Rates

OC Level	Signal Transmission Rate
OC-1 (base rate)	51.84 Mbps
OC-3	155.52 Mbps
OC-12	622.08 Mbps
OC-48	2.488 Gbps

SONET is used as the physical basis for another technology, broadband ISDN, which is discussed in the next section.

Broadband ISDN

Broadband ISDN (BISDN) is an emerging technology designed to use fiber-optic cable and radio waves to transmit data at high speeds over SONET, FDDI (the Fiber Distributed Data Interface), and Frame Relay.

Broadband technologies, which can send multiple channels of data, video, and voice over the same medium, are growing in popularity as Internet connectivity and other high-bandwidth network usage increases. Other broadband technologies include DSL and cable modem.

CATV

Cable TV (CATV) companies saw a great opportunity: They already had a vast infrastructure of coaxial cable in most major cities and many rural areas, and this cable could be used not only to transmit television signals, but also to transmit computer data. Numerous cable providers now offer Internet access accounts.

Cable is not a general WAN technology. It was originally designed to enable you to communicate only with the cable company/service provider's server (in the form of receiving incoming television channels). Although customers were all connected to the same network through the coax cable running through their neighborhood, the network was not designed to enable them to communicate with one another. In fact, the network was not designed to enable its users to send data at all—only to receive it. Cable modem changes all that.

Cable Internet access requires a cable modem that connects both to the incoming coax cable and to a NIC in the user's PC (typically this is a 10BaseT Ethernet NIC).

In this scenario, the cable company is also the user's ISP. There is no option to separate the provision of the physical line from the access service as there is with access over telephone lines. In other words, you cannot lease the line from the cable company and use it to connect to some other ISP's server.

On the other hand, when you pay a telco for the use of a phone line (whether an analog PSTN line or a dedicated T-1 line), you can purchase an Internet account from any ISP you choose (including the phone company that provides the line). Although this same method is technically possible with cable, the cable companies have packaged the two services together and the terms of their service contracts require that you use the cable company as your ISP.

Cable infrastructure can support either one-way or two-way transmissions. *One-way cable* provides only downstream transmission over the coax. Uploading must be done over a regular analog phone line that also plugs into the cable modem. With one-way cable, upload speeds are limited to standard rates attainable over PSTN, which is less than 56 kbps. Download speeds vary from 364 kbps to 1.5 Mbps.

Two-way cable provides both uploads and downloads over the coax. Nonetheless, many cable companies limit the upstream speed to 128 kbps to discourage customers from running servers (which is often prohibited by the CATV terms of service contract).

Cable is an always-on technology, but one-way cable still requires you to dial up to establish a connection. A big advantage of CATV is its low cost; however, in many areas, users experience reliability problems. Because cable is a "shared-bandwidth" technology (that is, the entire bandwidth of the cable is divided between all users on that cable segment at a given time), performance might degrade as more users in the neighborhood are added to the network. There are also security issues that, at this time, make CATV more viable for residential use than for business.

SMDS

Switched Multimegabit Data Service (SMDS) is a new packet-switching technology that is designed especially for WAN links that experience a lot of "bursty" traffic. (*Bursty* refers to transmission that comes in "bursts" rather than in a constant, even stream.)

SMDS is connectionless; that is, there is no requirement that a connection or circuit be established before transmitting the data. It uses relatively large packets, up to 7168 bytes in length. SMDS addresses, which are ten-digit numbers (such as a telephone number), are used to identify the SMDS subnetwork. SMDS links are connected to an SMDS switch on the telephone company's backbone network, typically by multiple OC-3 SONET links.

SMDS was designed as a public network to provide services similar to those of a LAN, except that it spans a metropolitan area. Data transfer speeds typically range from 1.544 Mbps to 45 Mbps. It is scalable and can be used in conjunction with ATM. However, SMDS is not as widely available as Frame Relay and other services, and SMDS equipment may be more difficult to find.

Wireless WAN

In many cases, it is impossible—or at least inconvenient or expensive—to run a wired link to connect WAN sites. Wireless solutions are especially appropriate when it is important that data be communicated in real time, or when users are on the move. Wireless works best for communicating small amounts of data.

The wireless technologies used for WANs include the following:

- **Radio frequency (RF) technologies**—Specialized Mobile Radio (SMR) provides data rates of 1200 bps to 19,200 bps. Enhanced SMR (ESMR) is the digital implementation.
- **Satellite technologies**—This provides both circuit-switched and packet-switched services at speeds of 4800 to 9600 bps.

- **Microwave technologies**—This technology uses cellular techniques over microwave frequencies to provide higher speed and capacity (wireless broadband).

- **Cellular technologies**—This provides a circuit-switched connection over analog or digital cellular links.

- **Packet data network technologies**—This technology provides a packet-switched WAN with no call setup involved.

Compared to wired links, wireless communications are often more costly and relatively slow. For example, analog cellular systems typically provide no more than 14,400 bps transfer rates, while digital cellular offers up to 64 kbps.

LAN/WAN Connectivity

In today's wired world, local connectivity often is not enough. No LAN is an island, or at least, fewer and fewer of them are islands as it becomes vital to business interests that a LAN be able to communicate with the outside. This can mean connecting the LAN to a corporate WAN, the global Internet, or both.

There are several ways to connect your LAN to the outside world, depending upon your budget and needs. Of course, the most obvious way to provide network users with access to other networks is to equip each PC with a modem and phone line. In this manner, each user can establish a dialup connection to an ISP or other remote server. However, this solution has many drawbacks:

- It becomes prohibitively expensive as the number of users increases. Not only must you purchase hardware (the modem) for every computer, you must also pay for a separate telephone line *and* if users are to connect to the Internet, a separate ISP account for each.

- Allowing users to dial out using a modem can create serious security risks if the nature of the data on your network is confidential. The company has little control over which networks the user connects to and the audience to which the company's data might be exposed.

- A high degree of user sophistication is required, which means a significant expense for training users to configure and manage their own dialup connections.

There is a better way. In fact, several alternatives offer advantages over the old-fashioned way of connecting LAN users to a WAN. Each has advantages and disadvantages, and which is best depends on your particular situation.

In the following sections, we briefly discuss the following LAN/WAN connectivity options:

- Translated connections
- Proxy servers
- Routed connections

Translated Connections

One of the most cost-effective ways to connect all computers on a small LAN to the Internet or to another WAN link is through address translation. *Address translation* enables all computers to access the WAN through a single host computer, using only one telephone line and ISP account (or other WAN link) and only one registered public IP address.

How Address Translation Works

A computer running address translation software sits between the public WAN and the private LAN. It has interfaces to both networks. This computer has a private IP address used for communications with other computers on the LAN and a public IP address (which can be assigned through Dynamic Host Configuration Protocol [DHCP] from an ISP's server at the time the WAN connection is established). We refer to this computer as the *address translation host*.

Address translation works by mapping the private IP address of each computer on the LAN that sends data "outside" to a port number on the host computer. This information is added to the IP header of the packet, which is then sent out over the WAN with the IP address of the host computer (the one that has the physical connection to the WAN) as the source address.

When a computer on the local network opens a web browser and sends a request to view a URL, for example, the host computer assigns a port number to that request, which identifies the original sending computer. Then the host sends the request out to the ISP's web server. When the page is returned to the host computer (whose IP address is listed in the header as the source of the request), the host consults its address translation table, matches up the packets with the computer that originally sent the request, and then forwards the web page to that computer.

The information in the address translation table includes the following:

- The original source and destination IP addresses (identifying the sending computer within the network and the computer outside the network to which the data is sent)

- The original source and destination port numbers (identifying the application making or receiving the request; for example, HTTP requests for web pages are normally sent to TCP port 80)
- Sequence numbers (identifying the order in which the packets are sent)
- A timestamp

Network address translation (NAT) is the common term for which standards have been developed and published as RFC 1631. Not all address translation technologies comply with these standards. Figure 6-7 illustrates the steps in the address translation process.

FIGURE 6-7
The NAT process involves translating private addresses to a public address.

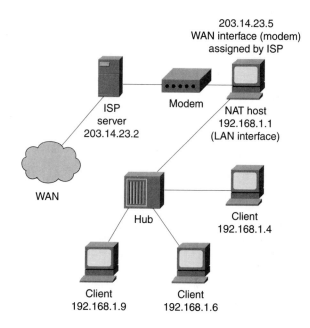

1. The user at the client computer (IP address 192.168.1.9) opens a web browser application and enters the URL www.tacteam.net into the address box. The browser software sends an HTTP request to the IP address associated with the www.tacteam.net "friendly name."

2. The NAT host on the client's LAN maps the request from 192.168.1.9 for www.tacteam.net to a port number in the mapping table. The table contains the original source and destination IP addresses and original source and destination TCP/UDP port numbers.

3. The NAT host changes the header so that to the outside network, the packet appears to originate not from 192.168.1.9, but from the public IP address assigned to the NAT host's external network adapter by the ISP.

4. The NAT host sends the request for www.tacteam.net to the ISP server. Domain Name System (DNS) maps the name to the IP address of the server on which the www.tacteam.net homepage is stored.

5. The request is received by the www.tacteam.net server and the page is returned to the public IP address used by the NAT host.

6. The NAT host consults its address translation table to determine whether the page should be sent to the client at 192.168.1.9 (and the TCP/UDP port number to which it should be sent).

NAT Software

Some operating systems, such as Windows 98/2000 and current versions of Linux, have built-in support for address translation. In Linux it is referred to as *IP masquerading*. Windows 98 and 2000 Professional call the feature *Internet Connection Sharing (ICS)*, although it can be used to share a connection to a private remote network or to a VPN as well. Windows 2000 Server supports the more flexible and robust version of address translation, NAT. If an operating system does not include address translation, you can use an add-on NAT program to provide the same functionality. Examples of these programs include:

- **Sygate, from Sybergen Software**—www.sygate.com
- **NAT32, from A.C.T. Software**—www.nat32.com

Another, more sophisticated (and slightly more difficult to configure) type of software that you can use to share a connection is a *proxy*. We discuss this option in the next section.

Proxy Servers

A proxy server does more than provide a shared connection to the WAN, although it does serve this purpose. A proxy server acts as an intermediary, separating the LAN from the outside network, and it can provide protection by filtering incoming and outgoing packets. It also enhances web performance by *caching* often-requested web pages.

Proxies use an address translation method, but do not necessarily comply with the NAT specifications in RFC 1631.

How Proxies Work

The proxy server receives requests for Internet resources from proxy clients, similar to the way in which NAT works. The proxy server checks its filter settings (which are configured by the administrator). If the request meets filter requirements, the server looks first in its cache of stored pages. If the requested page is there, the proxy server returns the page to the requesting client. There is no need to send the request on to the ISP server. If the page is not there, the proxy server requests the page from the ISP server, receives it, and returns it to the client.

As with NAT, the internal clients that access the Internet through a proxy server are invisible to the Internet; all outside communication is done by the proxy server.

Proxy Software

Proxy software typically provides more protection and performance enhancement than NAT. However, it might also be more expensive, and it is typically more difficult to set up because the Internet applications on all the client machines (such as the web browser) must be individually configured to use a proxy server.

To use NAT, you need only set the client's TCP/IP configuration to obtain an IP address through DHCP, and other necessary information can be automatically distributed to the clients by the DHCP server.

Numerous proxy server applications are available for popular operating systems, and they include the following:

- **Rideway, from DGL**—dgl.com/rideway
- **Winproxy, from Ositis**—www.winproxy.com/toc
- **Microsoft Proxy Server, from Microsoft**—www.microsoft.com
- **Squid for UNIX, from SCO**—www.sco.com

Some proxy programs, such as Microsoft Proxy Server, run only on a network operating system (NOS) such as Windows NT or Windows 2000 Server. Others, such as Rideway and Winproxy, can be used on desktop operating systems such as Windows 95/98, Windows NT Workstation, and Windows 2000 Professional.

Software that combines proxy and NAT technologies are sometimes referred to as *transparent proxies*.

Routed Connections

A *routed connection* is another way to provide the computers on the LAN with access to a WAN. A routed connection enables each computer to participate directly on the Internet, unlike NAT and proxy connections, where the individual computers must go through an intermediary.

Configuring a routed connection requires extensive knowledge of TCP/IP addressing, and you must purchase and configure a *router*. Additionally, every

NOTE

See Chapter 8 for more information on TCP/IP and IP addressing and Chapter 9, "The Widest Area Network: The Global Internet," for more information on routing.

computer on the LAN that connects to the outside network must have a "legal" registered public IP address.

Why Use a Routed Connection?

A big advantage of the NAT and proxy solutions is the capability to connect the small LAN to a public WAN by using only a single IP address. However, this might not be the best solution in some situations.

Because of the way address translation works, protocols that do not store the addressing information in the IP header do not work with NAT. In some cases, *NAT editors* can be added to make modifications to the IP packet so that NAT will work. In other cases (for example, when packets are authenticated and encrypted using IP Security [IPSec]), address translation is not possible.

Configuring a Routed Connection

A routed connection requires either a dedicated routing device such as a router or the use of a computer running an operating system that enables IP forwarding (in the latter case, the computer acts as the router).

Computers that use TCP/IP to communicate must have the following properties configured:

- An IP address that is valid for the network on which they will communicate
- A subnet mask that designates what part of the IP address identifies the computer and what part identifies the network

Computers participating on a *routed* network must also have a *default gateway* configured. This is the address of the router, which has two network connections: one to the LAN and one to the outside network.

NOTE

The address for a DNS server must be entered if you want to use "friendly" host names (for example, URLs such as www.tac-team.net) instead of IP addresses. You learn more about DNS in Chapter 8.

To set up a routed connection to the Internet, the TCP/IP protocol on the router is configured with an IP address, a subnet mask, and a DNS server address obtained from the ISP, and a static default route is configured to use the Internet interface.

The computers on the LAN that connect to the Internet are likewise configured with IP addresses, a subnet mask, and a DNS server address obtained from the ISP. They are also configured to use the IP address of the router on its LAN interface as their default gateway address.

Summary

In this chapter, you have learned about wide-area networking and the established and emerging technologies that can be used to connect computers in distant locations.

We discussed WAN hardware, and then we moved on to WAN topologies and discussed the advantages and disadvantages of WAN configurations such as the point-to-point connection, the ring, the star, the full or partial mesh, and the multitiered WAN.

We then delved into the differences between circuit-switched and packet-switched networks, and we discussed the characteristics and technologies associated with PSTN, ISDN, xDSL, DDS, T-carriers, X.25, Frame Relay, ATM, OC-SONET, BISDN, CATV, SMDS, and wireless WAN technologies.

We next discussed how to connect a LAN to a WAN. Specifically, we learned several ways to provide all computers on a local network with access to the Internet or another outside network. We learned about translated connections that use NAT, which is sometimes called connection sharing or IP masquerading. Then we discussed how to set up a routed connection for those circumstances in which address translation is undesirable or impossible.

This chapter wraps up Part I of this book. You should now have a grasp of basic networking concepts. In Part II, we look at the hardware and software that makes the network run. Chapter 7 introduces you to the components of the physical network.

Further Reading

An excellent resource for information on various WAN technologies is WAN-sites, at www.networkcomputing.com/wansites/default.html.

Thorough, clear explanations of the different WAN technologies can be found at the High Performance Networking Unleashed website, at www.officewizard.com/books/network.

An excellent, detailed discussion of NAT is available online at www.suse.de/~mha/linux-ip-nat/diplom.

Review Questions

The following questions test your knowledge of the material covered in this chapter. Be sure to read each question carefully and select the *best* correct answer or answers.

1. Which of the following hardware settings commonly must be configured on an internal modem?(Select all that apply.)

    A. I/O address

    B. IP address

    C. IRQ

    D. Virtual com port

2. The CSU/DSU and the PAD are examples of which of the following?

    A. ISDN terminal adapters

    B. Customer premises equipment

    C. Terminal identifiers

    D. Concentrator routers

3. PSTN, ISDN, DSL, DDS, and T-carrier links are all examples of what type of network?

    A. Circuit-switched networks

    B. Packet-switched networks

    C. Switched 56 networks

    D. LANs

4. Which of the following are true of ISDN? (Select all that apply.)

    A. It is an analog link.

    B. It is generally more expensive than PSTN.

    C. It requires special equipment at the CO and the customer's premise.

    D. It uses a circuit consisting of only one channel.

    E. It can transfer both voice and data.

5. Which WAN topology is the most scalable?

   A. Point-to-point.

   B. Ring.

   C. Star.

   D. All of the above are equally scalable.

6. What was the first packet switching technology that was based on the ARPAnet 1822 protocol?

   A. Frame Relay

   B. X.25

   C. ATM

   D. DSL

7. Which of the following are characteristics of Frame Relay that distinguish it from X.25? (Select all that apply.)

   A. Frame Relay offers high performance.

   B. Frame Relay uses packet switching.

   C. Frame Relay uses digital signaling.

   D. Frame Relay does not include extensive error checking.

8. Which of the following describes ATM? (Select all that apply.)

   A. It uses variable length packets.

   B. It uses 53 byte units of data called cells.

   C. It can transfer video, voice, and data simultaneously.

   D. It uses predefined circuits.

   E. It is less expensive than other WAN technologies.

9. Which of the following technologies is capable of transmission rates of up to 2.488 Gbps?

   A. ADSL

   B. T-1

   C. ISDN BRI

   D. OC-SONET

10. Which of the following is true of NAT? (Select all that apply.)

A. NAT requires that each computer on the internal network have a registered public IP address.

B. NAT is compatible with all applications.

'C. NAT is incompatible with technologies that encrypt IP data.

' D. NAT uses a table to map private internal IP addresses to one or more external public addresses.

Part II

Networking Hardware and Software

Chapter 7

Physical Components of the Network

Now that you have an understanding of the basic concepts involved in computer networking, we turn our attention to something more concrete: the physical components used to link PCs so that they can share resources.

The components required to link the computers in a network can be as simple and inexpensive as a few low-cost network interface cards (NICs) and a length of Ethernet cable. On the other hand, your network design can be complex enough to require the services of a *network architect* to designate the necessary devices, with a budget running to six figures or beyond.

In this chapter, we discuss some of the most common network hardware devices and networking media, including NICs, cable and wireless media, and connectivity devices.

NICs

The most basic piece of hardware required to network computers is the NIC, also called a network adapter or network card. NICs come in several varieties, which will be discussed in the section "Selecting a NIC."

The NIC is generally referred to as a physical layer device, and the NIC drivers (the software that interfaces between the NIC and the computer operating system) work at the data link layer of the OSI model.

In the following sections, we examine the role of the NIC in network communications, and you will learn how to select the appropriate network adapter and how NICs are configured and used to send and receive data on the network.

The Role of the NIC in Network Communications

Some sort of network interface is always required to communicate over a network. When you connect to a network remotely over analog phone lines, the modem is your network interface and serves the function that a NIC serves on a local network.

The NIC is the basic hardware component of network communications. It translates the *parallel* signal produced by the computer into the *serial* format that is sent over the network cable. The 1s and 0s of binary communication are turned into electrical impulses, pulses of light, radio waves, or whatever signaling scheme is used by the network media.

An important part of the network interface is the *transceiver*. Some NICs, such as those made for 10Base2 and 10BaseT networks, have the transceiver built onto the card itself. Others, such as those made for 10Base5 networks, have an attachment unit interface (AUI) connector by which a cable is attached to an external transceiver. The transceiver, as its name indicates, sends and receives signals.

Along with preparing the data to go onto the network media, the NIC is responsible for controlling the flow of data between computers and media and for receiving incoming data.

Selecting a NIC

When selecting a NIC for a computer, you should consider the following:

- **Network architecture**—The NIC should be made to work with the existing transmission technology. However, it is possible to use a *media filter* that enables you, for example, to use a Token Ring card on an Ethernet network. Refer to Chapter 6, "WAN Links," for more information on the popular LAN architectures.

- **Media type**—Ethernet can be run over thick coax (10Base5), thin coax (10Base2), or twisted-pair cable (10BaseT). The connector on the card must match the connector on the cable. Fiber-optic and wireless NICs are also available. We cover cable and wireless media later in this chapter, in the section "Network Media."

- **Data transfer speed**—If you have 100-Mbps hubs, a 10-Mbps network card does not work. However, you can get dual-speed components (that is, hubs or NICs) that work at either 10 Mbps or 100 Mbps. Likewise, a 4-Mbps Token Ring card does not work on a 16-Mbps network. However, a 16-Mbps card *does* work on the slower network, but its speed drops to 4-Mbps.

- **Available bus type**—Do you have a free ISA or PCI slot? Is the computer a laptop that must use a PCMCIA (that is, a PC card) interface? Do you need a special card that can connect through a serial or SCSI port? Note that if you have both ISA and PCI slots free, the PCI bus is faster.

PC BUS TYPES

The *data bus* is a transmission path on the computer's motherboard. Signals are picked up or delivered at each device that is attached to this path or line. There are several different bus architectures for which NICs are made:

- **ISA (Industry Standard Architecture)**—A 16-bit expansion slot on the motherboard. The plastic surrounding the slot is usually black, and the slot (actually two slots, one behind the other) is longer than the PCI slot.

- **EISA (Extended ISA)**—A 32-bit architecture compatible with ISA. Most modern "ISA" slots are actually EISA.

- **PCI (Peripheral Component Interconnect)**—A 32-bit bus used in modern computers (that is, Pentium-class PCs and above and the Macintosh). PCI architecture supports Plug and Play (PnP) devices. The slots on the motherboard are usually surrounded by beige or light-colored plastic and are shorter than ISA/EISA slots.

- **MCA (Micro Channel Architecture)**—A proprietary bus used on IBM computers, which can function as 16- or 32-bit. It is rarely seen today.

- **PCMCIA (Personal Computer Memory Card International Association; also called the PC card)**—An input/output (I/O) bus that uses devices the size and shape of credit cards. Usually used in laptop or notebook computers, PC card adapters for desktop computers are also available.

There are also NICs that connect through the SCSI bus. A few USB (universal serial bus) network cards are available, but these are not common. Also note that some computer motherboards come with an *onboard NIC,* that is, the network interface card is integrated into the motherboard.

- **Operating system**—You must ensure that the manufacturer of the NIC makes drivers for the operating system you are using. If you are using one of the Windows operating systems, check the Microsoft Hardware Compatibility List (HCL) at www.microsoft.com for a list of NICs that have been tested and found to work with the operating system. We discuss the popular desktop operating systems in Chapter 12, "Desktop Operating Systems."

Configuring and Using a NIC

Configuring a NIC is similar to the process of configuring a modem, as discussed in Chapter 6. Remember that the NIC and modem perform essentially the same basic function.

As with the modem, you might need to set the following:

- IRQ
- I/O address
- Memory address

You can set these through dip switches, jumpers, or software configuration programs that come with the card. PnP NICs can be detected and automatically configured by a PnP operating system, as long as the computer's BIOS also supports PnP.

Additional configuration parameters may be required if the NIC is a *combo card,* which can be used with different media types. A combo card typically has a BNC connector for thin coax cable, an RJ-45 connector ("RJ" stands for registered jack) for twisted-pair cable, and sometimes, an AUI connector for thick coax cable as well. This means that the same card works on 10Base2, 10Base5, and 10BaseT networks. However, only one media type can be used at a time. You might have to manually select the media type, or the card might autodetect the type of media that is attached.

Figure 7-1 shows a three-way combo card.

FIGURE 7-1
A combo NIC can be used with 10Base2, 10Base5, and 10BaseT networks.

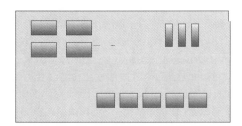

Configuring the IRQ

Typically, a NIC uses IRQ 3 or IRQ 5. Many cards are set to use one of these by default. If you have another device using the predefined IRQ, you need to change the settings for one of the devices so that they do not conflict.

It is a good idea to memorize the following table, which shows the standard default IRQ settings for a typical PC. Note that in early PCs, only the first eight IRQs were available. IRQ 2 is used as an IRQ controller, to "redirect" an interrupt request to IRQ 9, through which the high-numbered IRQs can be accessed.

TABLE 7-1   Standard Default IRQ Settings for PCs

Device	Default IRQ Used
VGA graphics adapter	2 (9)
COM 2 and COM 4 (secondary serial port)	3*
COM 1 and COM 3 (primary serial port)	4
Secondary parallel port (LPT2) or sound card	5*
Floppy disk controller	6
Primary parallel port (LPT1)	7
Real-time clock	8
Primary SCSI controller	10*
Secondary SCSI controller	11*
PS/2 mouse	12
Math coprocessor	13
Primary IDE controller	14
Secondary IDE controller	15*

* These devices are optional and might not be present on many computers. If these devices are not present, the corresponding IRQs are free. For example, if the computer has no SCSI controllers, IRQs 10 and 11 are probably free and can be assigned to the NIC.

Configuring the I/O Port and Memory Address

In addition to a unique IRQ, each device must have a different I/O port setting. The *I/O port* is a channel through which data is transferred between the hardware device and the processor. Port numbers are designated by hexadecimal numbers. The following ports are usually available for use by the NIC:

- 300 to 30F
- 310 to 31F

Others may also be available. Generally, the default I/O port settings (to which the NIC was set at the factory) work.

A *memory address* is a location in RAM that is used for storage of incoming and outgoing data. Some NICs do not use the computer's memory for this purpose and thus do not have a memory address setting. Otherwise, the default factory settings generally work.

Network Media

The network *media* is the means by which the signals travel from one networked device to another. The most common media type is cable, but newer wireless media are now available as well (for example, radio waves, laser and infrared beams, satellite, and microwaves).

In this section, we first discuss different cable types commonly used to join networked computers, and then we look at wireless options.

Cable Types

Most networks today are cabled, and the most common types of cable in use are coaxial, twisted-pair, and fiber-optic.

Coaxial Cable

Coaxial cable is familiar to most persons who have cable TV. It has a copper core (which can be either stranded wire or solid copper). The signal travels on the copper, which is wrapped in insulation. Surrounding the insulation is another conductor of metal foil or braid. This outer conductor runs the length of the cable, hence the name coaxial, because two physical channels, one carrying the signal and the other serving as a ground, run together ("co") along the same *axis* ("axial"). The outer conductor acts as a shield against outside electromagnetic interference (EMI). These components are then wrapped in an outer shielding of plastic, rubber, or—in the case of *plenum grade* cable—Teflon or other fire-resistant material.

Because of its thick insulation and shielding, coax is less vulnerable to outside EMI than is twisted pair.

There are thousands of different types and grades of coax cable, as a glance at any cable manufacturer's catalog shows. Many are used for special-purpose networks, such as connecting scientific instruments or other dedicated devices. The types discussed in the following sections and summarized in Table 7-2 are the only ones with which you must be familiar for most PC LAN networking tasks.

NOTE

Plenum-grade cable is required by most local building and fire codes when cable is installed in the *plenum*, the space between a false ceiling and the floor above it, because standard grade coaxial cable is covered with polyvinyl chloride (PVC), which emits toxic gases when burned.

TABLE 7-2   Coax Cable Types and Characteristics

Designation	Common Name	Description	Network Use
RG-8, RG-11	Thicknet	One-half inch diameter thick coaxial cable	10Base5
RG-58 A/U	Thinnet	One-quarter inch diameter thin coaxial cable	10Base2
RG-58 C/U	Thinnet (military spec)	One-quarter inch diameter thin coaxial cable	10Base2 (military use)
RG-62	ARCnet	Thin coaxial cable	ARCnet networks

> **NOTE**
>
> Cable TV (CATV) coax looks very much like thinnet, but they are not interchangeable. CATV cable is RG-59, 75-ohm cable.

In early implementations of Ethernet, coaxial cable was the most popular type. However, twisted-pair coaxial cable has surpassed it in popularity. Coaxial cable for Ethernet networking comes in two basic types: thin coax and thick coax, also called *thinnet* and *thicknet.*

Thin Coax. Thin coax cable is approximately one-quarter inch in diameter and more flexible than thicknet. It is used in Ethernet 10Base2 networks, and it can transmit signals for approximately 185 meters without suffering from attenuation (that is, signal weakening).

Thin coax cable is sometimes called RG-58 cabling. Its *impedance* (that is, its resistance to current flowing through the wire) is 50 ohms.

BASIC ELECTRONICS TERMINOLOGY

Electrical current is a flow of electrons, or electron-deficient atoms, that carry an electrical charge. An *ampere* (amp) is the basic unit used in the measurement of electrical current.

Resistance (also called impedance) is a way of measuring the amount of opposition to the flow of electrical current. Different substances offer different levels of resistance. Resistance is measured in *ohms,* named after German scientist Georg Simon Ohm, who postulated the mathematical relationship among electrical current, resistance, and voltage (Ohm's Law). The symbol for ohm is the Greek letter omega (Ω).

Voltage or *electromotive force* (EMF) is also called the electric potential. It is a measurement of the force that causes movement of electrons in a conductor (a medium that conducts, or transmits, an electric charge).

Frequency is the measure of how often a periodic event takes place (for example, a signal completing a cycle). *Hertz* is a unit used to measure frequency.

Coax cable is standardized throughout the industry according to RG (Registered Grade) specifications. Only a few of the hundreds of coax grades are used in PC networking.

10Base2 networks use type RG-58 A/U thin coax. This type has a stranded wire core. The military specification for the same cable type is RG-58 C/U. The military grade cable has a slightly thicker outer covering, making it more resistant to heat, cold, liquid, and other elements.

RG-58 /U is similar in appearance to RG-58 A/U, but the copper core is solid. It does not meet 10Base2 specifications, and you should *not* use RG-58 /U on a computer network. It is used only for antenna wiring and other purposes. See Figure 7-2 for an illustration of the difference between the two.

FIGURE 7-2
The difference between stranded and solid core copper cable

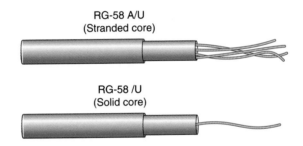

RG-58 A/U
(Stranded core)

RG-58 /U
(Solid core)

Thinnet cable connects to the network card through a BNC T-connector that attaches to the NIC's BNC connector, as shown in Figure 7-3.

A terminator is required at each end of a thinnet network. The terminator connects to the unused side of the T-connector.

Thick Coax. Thick coaxial cable, also called thicknet, is approximately twice the diameter of thinnet—about one-half inch. Thicknet was the original cable typed used in early Ethernet networks, and thus is referred to as *standard Ethernet*.

FIGURE 7-3
Thin coax connects to the NIC with a BNC T-connector.

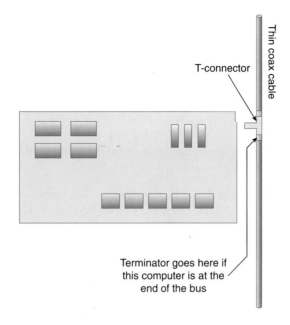

T-connector

Thin coax cable

Terminator goes here if this computer is at the end of the bus

Thick coax is type RG-8 or RG-11 cable. Because of the thicker core, it can transmit signals for a longer distance—500 meters— without attenuation. It is, however, more expensive and more difficult to work with than thin coax because it is less flexible and it uses an external transceiver that must be connected to the cable with a device called a *vampire tap*. The tap drills into the core of the cable. Making the connection is more complex than using twist-on BNC connectors on thinnet, as shown in Figure 7-4.

NOTE

Another type of coax cable, commonly used in the past in ARCnet networks, is RG-62 90-ohm cabling. The ARCnet architecture has become less popular in recent years, as discussed in Chapter 5, "LAN Links."

FIGURE 7-4
A 10Base5 network uses an external transceiver, connected to thick coax by vampire taps.

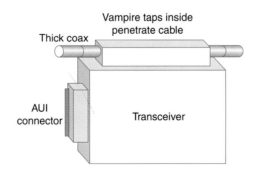

Vampire taps inside penetrate cable

Thick coax

AUI connector

Transceiver

Twisted-Pair Cable

Many people today, when they use the term *Ethernet cable,* are referring to the twisted-pair cabling used in a huge number of Ethernet networks. It is called *twisted pair* because, inside the cable's outer sheath, pairs of insulated copper wires are twisted around one another to prevent *crosstalk* (that is, the "leaking" of signal from one wire to another). As the number of twists per foot increases, so does the degree of protection against crosstalk.

Telephone companies use twisted-pair cable for internal wiring; this contributes to its popularity because most buildings are already wired with twisted-pair cable for telephone systems.

Twisted-pair cable comes in two basic types: unshielded twisted-pair (UTP) cable and shielded twisted-pair (STP) cable, as shown in Figure 7-5. Telephone communications and most Ethernet networks use UTP. STP is used in Token Ring and AppleTalk networks.

FIGURE 7-5
The difference between STP and UTP.

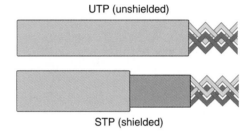

UTP (unshielded)

STP (shielded)

When shielding is added to twisted-pair cable, it reduces the effect of outside electromagnetic interference. However, it increases attenuation and can affect the resistance of the wire and cause loss of data.

UTP Cable. UTP is a very popular cable type for LANs, for several reasons:

- It is relatively inexpensive.
- It is flexible and easy to work with.
- It uses familiar RJ-45 connectors that look and work like the smaller RJ-11 modular telephone connectors.
- It is used in a star topology, which offers advantages that are discussed in Chapter 2, "Categorizing Networks."

UTP cabling is rated by category, according to its use and data transmission speed. Refer to Table 2-3 in Chapter 2 for a listing of UTP categories and the uses and transmission speeds of each.

Like coax, UTP comes in both standard and plenum-grade versions.

STP Cable. *Shielding* is made of woven copper or foil, and it wraps the insulated copper pairs inside the outer covering. This reduces the effect of EMI, but causes STP to be more expensive than UTP and introduces other problems, as discussed in previous sections of this chapter.

STP is often used for AppleTalk and IBM Token Ring networks.

Fiber-Optic Cable

Fiber-optic cable (also called *optical fiber*, *optical cable*, or *fiber*) is a newer, faster, but relatively expensive transmission medium that is growing in popularity as high-bandwidth applications become more common. Although often implemented at 100 Mbps, optical fiber is capable of speeds of 1 Gbps or more.

In lieu of copper, fiber-optic cable uses tiny strands of glass or plastic through which the signal is transmitted in the form of light pulses.

Fiber-optic cable has several advantages, in addition to speed:

- It is more secure than coax and twisted-pair cable because there is no electrical signal that can be tapped.
- It is less susceptible than other cable types to attenuation and thus can span long distances—2000 meters or more.
- It is not vulnerable to outside electrical interference such as EMI and radio frequency interference (RFI).

Fiber-optic cable is costly compared to more traditional cable types. Although the cable itself is somewhat more expensive, the largest expense is labor; fiber-optic cable is much more difficult to work with and requires specially trained technicians to splice the tiny strands of glass or plastic.

Fiber-Optic Mode Types. Fiber-optic cable operates in one of two modes:

- **Single mode**—Single mode is also called *axial* because the light travels down the axis of the cable.
- **Multimode**—In multimode fiber, light waves enter the glass pipe at different angles and travel *nonaxially*, which means that they bounce back and forth off the walls of the glass tube.

NOTE

UTP is the telephone wiring that is inside walls and that connects to an outlet called an RJ-11 receptacle (jack). The common telephone wire that runs from the wall to the phone is *untwisted* flat copper pair, often called "silver satin" because of its shiny gray color.

NOTE

Lucent Technologies has documented data transmission speeds of over 3 *terabits* per second in the laboratory, using multiple lasers with fiber-optic cable. A terabit is one trillion bits.

Single-mode fiber is faster than multimode (up to 10 Gbps) because of the *dispersion* (scattering or separation of light waves) in multimode caused by the light pulses arriving at the end of the cable at different times. Single mode is typically used for WANs (for example, telephone company switch-to-switch connections). Multimode is often used in LANs.

Fiber-Optic Cable Light Sources. Fiber-optic cable can be categorized by the type of light source used:

- **LED (light emitting diode)**—LED is commonly used with single-mode fiber. It is relatively weak.
- **ILD (injection laser diode)**—ILD emits a strong, intense, narrowly focused light beam. It is commonly used with multimode fiber, which helps counteract multimode's lower performance.

LEDs are widely used in displays for digital clocks, remote controls, and electronic instruments. The LED is a semiconductor device. When a current of electricity passes through it, the LED gives off light. This light is typically red but can range through the spectrum to a blue-violet color depending on the wavelength. LEDs that emit infrared energy are called *infrared emitting diodes (IREDs)*.

ILDs are sometimes used in hand-held laser scanners.

Wireless Media

Wireless technologies are becoming a popular networking alternative. Although wireless transmission methods are often much slower than cabled connections, there are significant advantages to wireless networking under certain circumstances, as discussed in Chapter 6. The same basic concepts that affect wireless WANs also affect wireless LANs.

NOTE

Cisco Systems, in partnership with other companies such as Motorola, EDS, Samsung, and Texas Instruments, is leading the way in developing high-speed, reliable, and widely available wireless technologies.

Typically, a "wireless" network is not completely without cables, but incorporates wireless devices that communicate with a traditional cabled network. Transceivers, which are called *access points*, are used to transmit and receive data between the wireless device or devices and the wired network, as shown in Figure 7-6.

Wireless LAN communication is a category that includes a variety of transmission methods, including the following:

- Laser
- Infrared
- Radio

We look at some of the characteristics of each in the following sections.

FIGURE 7-6
Wireless net-
working uses
transceivers to
transmit and
receive data with-
out cables.

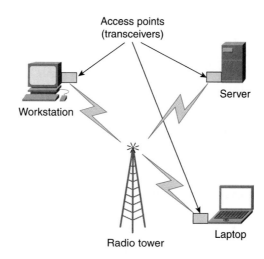

Access points
(transceivers)

Server

Workstation

Radio tower

Laptop

Laser

Laser is an acronym for "light amplification by stimulated emission of radiation." A laser outputs a coherent electromagnetic energy field, in which all
waves are at the same frequency and are aligned in phase. A *phase* is a fraction
of a complete cycle that has elapsed and that is measured from a specific point
of reference. Different types of lasers produce beams of different wavelengths.

Lasers are used for many purposes, ranging from cheap pointing devices to
highly accurate pistol sights, printers, electronic games, remote control
devices, surgical procedures, and network communications.

Laser networking works by using pulses of laser light to represent the data signals. Laser is a *line-of-sight* technology, which means that there must be an
unobstructed pathway between the transmitting and receiving devices. The
need for this unobstructed pathway is a drawback of laser-based wireless communications.

Infrared

Infrared (IR) technology is familiar to many people because of its use in TV
remote control units. It can also be used to network wireless LANs by using
cones or beams of light in the IR frequency spectrum to carry the data signal.
IR uses very high frequencies that are just below the visible light spectrum.

The Infrared Data Association (IrDA) is an organization that sets standards
for IR hardware and software. IrDA-compliant devices are designed so that

NOTE

Most people think of
laser light as a "red
dot," but argon
lasers (so called
because they use
argon gas as the
laser medium) pro-
duce a blue or green
light. Krypton lasers
(using gas by the
same name) pro-
duce red light, and
"mixed gas" lasers
combine the two
gases, which pro-
duces red, green,
and blue output
simultaneously. This
simultaneous output
results in a white
beam.

when a user breaks the infrared connection, the connection is reinstated when the devices move back into IR range.

IR networking requires a transceiver in both communicating devices and might require synchronization software as well. Some operating systems, such as Windows 98 and 2000, have built-in IR support. Transfer speeds range from 4 Mbps to 16 Mbps.

IR, like laser, is normally a line-of-sight technology. However, in some implementations of IR, such as scatter and reflective, the signal can be bounced or redirected. Even in these implementations, however, IR cannot go through opaque objects such as walls.

Disadvantages of IR for networking include the following:

- **Distance limitations**—Although it is possible to implement IR at distances greater than one mile, the more common distance is less than 100 feet.
- **Vulnerability**—Ambient light can cause interference.

Broadband optical telepoint is an IR technology designed to support high-bandwidth multimedia applications.

Radio

We know that telephone lines, originally used to transmit voice, can transmit data as well. Likewise, radio waves—a medium we associate with audio transmission—can be used to carry data signals.

Data transmission over radio can be implemented with a range of technologies. We look at two broad categories in the following sections:

- Narrowband radio
- Spread spectrum radio

Narrowband Radio. Narrowband radio is familiar to most of us. A transmitter sends a signal on a specified frequency, and a receiver tuned to that frequency picks up the signal. This is how broadcast radios, two-way radios, and traditional emergency channel communications work.

When data is transferred over narrowband radio, it is easy for an unauthorized listener to intercept the signals. A more secure and more reliable radio technology, originally developed by the military, is called *spread spectrum.*

Spread-Spectrum Radio. Spread-spectrum radio is a *wideband* technology. Although it is less efficient than narrowband (that is, it uses more bandwidth), it is more secure because it uses multiple frequencies. Narrowband receivers are not able to pick up spread-spectrum transmissions. There are two main types of spread spectrum radio:

- **Frequency hopping spread spectrum (FHSS)**—With FHSS, the transmitter hops from one frequency to another. The receiver must know the frequencies, the pattern, and the timing of the hops. This makes it difficult for an unauthorized person to intercept the signal.

- **Direct sequence spread spectrum (DSSS)**—This technique uses special encoding (calling *chipping*) that creates a redundant bit pattern for each bit of transmitted data. This provides fault tolerance because if some bits are damaged during transmission, the original data can still be recovered without retransmission.

Network Connectivity Devices

Connectivity device is a general term that includes the simple and complex devices used to connect one part of a network to another. In most cases, this means two or more lengths of cable are connected to a device.

In the next sections of this chapter, we examine three types of connectivity devices:

- Simple connectors
- Complex connectors
- Segmenting and subnetting devices

Simple Connectors

Simple connectivity devices are those that provide only a connection point and that do not amplify or otherwise modify the signal. These include the following:

- BNC connectors
- RJ connectors
- Fiber-optic connectors
- Patch panels
- Passive hubs

The following sections describe these connectors in more detail.

BNC Connectors

10Base2 (that is, thin coax) networks use BNC connectors to connect the NIC to the cable. A BNC connector is a small cylindrical device with a pin that connects to the conduction wire in the cable. The connector locks into place by the twisting of an outer ring.

BNC devices include the following:

- **BNC T-connector**—With this connector, the stem of the T attaches to the NIC, and a piece of cable attaches to each side of the top bar. If only one cable is to be connected, a terminator must be connected to the other side of the T-connector.

- **BNC barrel connector**—This connector is a straight cylindrical unit to which a cable attaches at each end, thus enabling you to join two pieces of cable to increase the total cable length.

The BNC *terminator* is a 50-ohm termination device, which is installed at each end of a coax bus. The terminator prevents a signal from bouncing back when it reaches the end of the cable, which causes interference. Both ends of the cable should be terminated, and one end should be *grounded* by attaching a conductor such as a wire to a position of zero electrical potential. The term "ground" is used because, in many cases, the conductor is physically con-nected to the actual ground (the earth).

RJ Connectors

RJ (registered jack) connectors are so called because they are registered with the Federal Communications Commission (FCC). RJ connectors consist of a *plug* and a *receptacle*. The receptacle is sometimes referred to as the *jack*.

Ordinary analog telephone wires in the United States generally use RJ-11 con-nectors. These are modular plugs connected to "silver satin," the familiar flat gray phone cord that runs from the wall outlet to the telephone. Inside the wall, the jack connects to UTP (usually Cat 3 or 5 in modern buildings). Modems have RJ-11 jacks.

RJ-45 connectors are used on UTP cable designed for Ethernet networks. The RJ-45 plug and receptacle look like the RJ-11, but are slightly larger. A special crimping tool is used to attach the wire pairs to the RJ plug.

There are numerous RJ designations, but RJ-11 and RJ-45 are the ones com-monly encountered in computer networking.

Fiber-Optic Connectors

Connectors for optical cable are the most difficult to install because each indi-vidual strand of glass or plastic must be precisely aligned. Once they are aligned, the cable is attached to the connector with hot melt glue, epoxy, or anaerobic adhesive.

Common fiber-optic connectors include the following:

- **SC**—A push-pull type
- **ST**—A keyed, bayonet type
- **FC**—A keyed, threaded-lock type
- **SMA**—A threaded type
- **FSD**—A fixed shroud device, used with FDDI

Patch Panels and Passive Hubs

A *patch panel* is a connection and distribution point used to organize cables that come together at a central location. This works somewhat like early telephone switchboards, in which a connection was completed by plugging a wire into a specific jack.

For a star topology network, cables from computers at various locations in the building come into a wiring closet, which is where the patch panel is located. The cables are connected to a punch down block on the back of the panel. On the front are RJ-45 jacks, from which patch cables run from the panel to the hub.

A patch panel serves the same function as a passive hub. A passive hub is a central connection device where the cables from computers and other network devices meet. It contains no electronic parts and does not require electrical power. It does not regenerate the signal, but merely sends it out through all ports of the hub.

Complex Connectors

Simple connectivity devices merely connect cables; complex devices do more. For example, they might strengthen the signal before passing it on and even convert the signal from one media type to another.

In the following sections, we discuss the following types of complex connectors:

- Media converters
- Repeaters
- Active/intelligent hubs

Media Converters

Media converters are also called *media adapters* or *media translators*. They are used to convert one segment type to another; for example, they can convert 10Base2 to 10BaseT, 100BaseT Ethernet to fiber optics, or Token Ring to fiber optics.

Repeaters

A repeater connects two network segments or lengths of cable. Unlike a barrel connector, however, it doesn't just pass the signal on from one cable to the next—it *regenerates* the signal. Thus a signal that has weakened because of attenuation is strengthened, and the effective distance of the cable is increased.

Repeaters do not filter the data that passes through them. They regenerate *all* signals, including broadcast messages, noise, and interference, and pass them on. Repeaters operate at the physical layer of the OSI reference model.

Active and Intelligent Hubs

Active hubs are also called *multiport repeaters* because they have multiple ports (like a passive hub), and they regenerate the signal coming into one port before sending it back out the other port (like a repeater). Active hubs require electrical power.

The intelligent hub is a special type of active hub. It not only regenerates the signal but also has an onboard processor that enables you to perform diagnostics and detect if there is a problem with a particular port. Hubs operate at the physical layer of the OSI reference model.

Segmenting and Subnetting Devices

Segmenting and subnetting devices are the most complex of the network connectivity devices. Although the terms are sometimes used interchangeably, *segmenting* the network refers to dividing it into segments that are still part of the same network. *Subnetting* goes a step further and divides the network into separate networks called *subnetworks* (based on network address information). We discuss subnetting in more detail in Chapter 8, "Networking Protocols and Services," and Chapter 9, "The Widest Area Network: The Global Internet."

Bridges

A traditional bridge (also called a *simple transparent bridge*) joins two network segments and performs *filtering* of traffic, based on the media access control (MAC) address on the packet. When used properly, this enables you to reduce congestion. The network is divided into two segments, with the bridge in between, as shown in Figure 7-7. MAC addresses are indicated as hexadecimal numbers.

The bridge builds an address table by executing the following steps:

1. When a packet is sent on the network, the bridge checks the source and destination address (that is, the MAC address). The table tells the bridge on which segment (that is, which side of the bridge) each address is located.

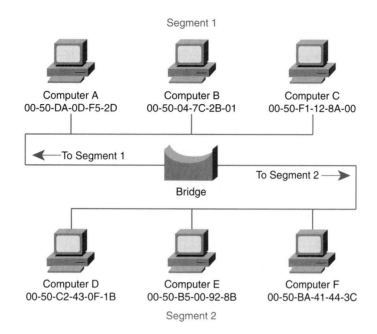

FIGURE 7-7
A bridge divides the network into two segments.

Segment 1

Computer A
00-50-DA-0D-F5-2D

Computer B
00-50-04-7C-2B-01

Computer C
00-50-F1-12-8A-00

To Segment 1

Bridge

To Segment 2

Computer D
00-50-C2-43-0F-1B

Computer E
00-50-B5-00-92-8B

Computer F
00-50-BA-41-44-3C

Segment 2

2. If the destination address of a packet is not in the bridge's table, the bridge forwards it to both segments. If the source address is not in the table, the bridge adds it to the table.

3. If the destination address is in the table, the bridge forwards the packet to the appropriate segment *unless* the source and destination computer are on the same segment.

4. If the table shows that the source and destination are on the same segment, the bridge does not forward the packet.

In the example shown in Figure 7-7, if Computer B sends a message to Computer F, the bridge forwards the packet to Segment 2. It does this regardless of whether Computer F's address is in the table because the packet is forwarded to all segments if there is no address entry.

However, if Computer B sends a message to Computer A, the bridge checks its table. If Computer A's address is not there, the packet goes across the bridge to the other segment. If Computer A's address has been entered (because Computer A previously sent a message), the message does *not* go across the bridge. You can see how this reduces unnecessary traffic on Segment 2.

The bridge is called *transparent* because the computers on an Ethernet network are not aware of its presence.

NOTE

The address table built by the bridge is called a *routing table* because it is used to determine to which side the packets should be routed. Don't confuse this with the routing table used by a router. The bridge's routing table uses hardware addresses, but the router's table is based on higher-level IP addresses.

Bridges forward broadcast messages, which are those that are addressed to the hardware *broadcast address* (FF-FF-FF-FF-FF-FF).

TRANSLATION AND ENCAPSULATION BRIDGES

Unlike repeaters, some bridges can connect network segments using different media access methods (for example, Ethernet and FDDI), as long as they use the same network protocol (for example, TCP/IP). These are called *translation bridges* or *encapsulation bridges.*

The translation bridge translates the Ethernet addresses into FDDI addresses. You can also bridge unlike networks by using encapsulation bridging, in which the Ethernet frame is *encapsulated,* or wrapped, inside a FDDI frame.

A *source routing bridge* is a special type of bridge used on Token Ring networks. It is unlike standard transparent bridges because it depends on the host computer to make the routing decision.

Bridges operate at the data link layer of the OSI reference model. Thus, *nonroutable* protocols, such as NetBEUI, can cross bridges. (You learn more about routable and nonroutable protocols in Chapter 8.) Like repeaters, bridges regenerate data, but they do so at the *packet* level.

A network can have more than one bridge. This provides fault tolerance, but can lead to a *bridging loop* problem, which occurs when there are multiple paths between two points, and packets end up going around in circles. This creates unnecessary traffic (see Figure 7-8).

The *Spanning-Tree Algorithm (STA)* was developed to solve the bridging loop problem. STA creates a subset of bridged links that eliminates looping. The technical details of bridge looping and STA are beyond the scope of this book, but excellent resources are listed at the end of this chapter.

Routers

As we work our way up the OSI reference model, we encounter the connectivity device that works at the network layer: the *router*. Routers connect separate networks to one another. This can occur within a LAN (in which case the individual networks are called *subnets*) or between unrelated networks in a WAN such as the global Internet.

Like a bridge, a router filters traffic. Unlike a bridge, it does so using the logical network address (IP or IPX address) instead of the physical hardware address. Routers are more intelligent than bridges; they make complex decisions by selecting the best route to a given destination from among multiple paths.

NOTE

Dedicated routing devices are actually special-purpose computers; they contain microprocessors and run their own operating system. PCs can also be configured to act as routers if the operating system supports IP or IPX forwarding.

FIGURE 7-8
Multiple paths between bridges can result in a bridging loop.

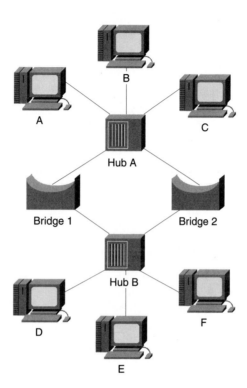

Routers maintain routing tables that contain the network addresses of other routers. A router must have at least two network interfaces because it serves as a *gateway* from one network to another. The address of the router's interface that serves a particular subnet is called that subnet's *default gateway*. (Note that the term "gateway" is also used to describe software and devices that function at the higher OSI layers to translate between protocols.)

Router Functionality. Routers can be used to join multiple networks into one larger one or to separate a large network into several smaller ones. In Chapter 9, we discuss why networks should be subnetted.

When a data packet travels from one router to another, the data link layer headers (that is, the pieces of addressing information) are stripped off and recreated. This enables routers to exchange packets between unlike networks, such as Ethernet and Token Ring. This process does require overhead, however, which makes the network performance slower than it would be with lower-level devices.

When multiple paths exist on a network, a bridge chooses one and always uses that path to reach a specific destination. Routers consider all available paths for each packet sent and make the decision on a packet-by-packet basis. Thus, if one route is very busy at that time, the router chooses another, more efficient one.

Another advantage of the router is its capability to filter both Layer 2 and Layer 3 broadcast packets. By default, routers do *not* forward messages that were sent to the broadcast IP address (255.255.255.255) across the router. This reduces network traffic significantly and prevents the propagation of *broadcast storms*. A broadcast storm occurs when there are so many broadcasts that the network cannot function properly.

Routable Protocols Versus Routing Protocols. Routers work only with *routable* protocols, including IP, IPX, OSI, XNS, DECnet, and DDP. A nonroutable protocol, such as NetBEUI, does not use an addressing scheme that enables the router to identify the network; thus, the protocol cannot be routed.

It is important to distinguish between routable protocols (discussed previously) and *routing* protocols. The latter are used by the router and are required for *dynamic routing*.

In the following sections of this chapter, we compare routing types and routing protocols, including the following pairings:

- Static versus dynamic routing
- Interior versus exterior routing protocols

Static and Dynamic Routing

There are two basic ways of routing:

- **Static routing**—This requires that an administrator manually enter addresses into the routing table and keep that table updated.
- **Dynamic routing**—This uses protocols such as Routing Information Protocol (RIP), Open Shortest Path First (OSPF), or NetWare Link Services Protocol (NLSP) to enable routers to automatically and dynamically exchange routing table information with one another.

You will learn more about dynamic routing, and these protocols, in Chapter 9.

Interior and Exterior Routing Protocols

Routing protocols are classified as either *interior gateway protocols (IGP)* or *exterior gateway protocols (EGP)*. These are discussed in more detail in Chapter 9.

Routing protocols that operate within an *autonomous system*—that is, a network under the control of a particular company or organization—are IGPs.

Brouters

A brouter can function as either a bridge or a router, depending on the network transport protocol in use. A brouter acts like a bridge for messages sent with NetBEUI or other nonroutable protocols, but it provides the functionality of a router for routable protocols such as TCP/IP. Modern routers are capable of bridging and routing.

Switches

The basic functionality of a switch is deceptively simple: choosing a path across which to send data to its destination.

Ethernet switches are becoming a popular connectivity solution, and for good reason. They increase performance (speed) and are relatively inexpensive.

Switches use one of two switching schemes:

- **Cut-through switching**—The switch starts forwarding the packet to its destination before it has received the entire packet. This method is faster, but it can result in bad packets getting through.
- **Store-and-forward switching**—The switch does not send the packet until it has been completely received and its integrity has been checked. This is slower, but more reliable.

There are different types of switches. Switches are sometimes categorized based on the layer of the OSI reference model at which they function. In the next sections, we discuss the differences between Layer 2, Layer 3, and Layer 4 switching.

Layer 2 Switching. Standard Layer 2 switches act like hubs—with an important difference. Where a hub sends messages out all its ports, a switch (referred to as a *switching hub)* is "smart" enough to determine which port is connected to the computer to which the message is addressed and to send it only to that port. This has several positive effects:

- The overall amount of unnecessary network traffic is reduced, which decreases congestion.

- Separate collision domains are created, which prevents data collisions that slow performance and that require resending of messages.

- Security is increased because messages are not going out all ports. Messages that are going out on all ports are easier to intercept.

These switching hubs are also called *port switches* because a computer or network device connects to each port. Each device has its own dedicated pathway to the switch.

Another type of switch is the *segment switch,* which enables you to connect an entire network segment to each port.

Switches can be used to create *virtual LANs (VLANs),* which divide the physical network connected to a switch into multiple logical networks. This can increase both performance and security.

Layer 3 Switching. Layer 3 switches, as the name implies, operate at the network layer of the OSI reference model. This device was first developed by 3Com in 1992, when it started to integrate its switching and routing devices to reduce the number of devices that needed to be managed.

The most important thing to understand about Layer 3 switches is that they are routers, but of a special type. A Layer 3 switch (or *switched router,* as it is sometimes called) performs the same functions as a dedicated router and uses routing protocols, such as RIP and OSPF.

The difference is that Layer 3 switches perform the functions that a Layer 2 switch performs. The switch uses a hardware-based architecture to apply policies based on network layer information in the packet header.

Layer 3 switches are generally easier to set up and configure than are routers and can be used in most situations (within a local network) where a router can be used. Surprisingly, despite the added functionality and ease of use, Layer 3 switches are generally less expensive than comparable routers.

Layer 4 Switching. Recent enhancements to Layer 3 switches enable them to use information, such as port numbers, from the TCP and UDP headers. These enhancements are referred to by some as *Layer 4 switching* because TCP and UDP operate at the transport layer (Layer 4) of the OSI reference model. Despite the name, these switches are often capable of using information at higher layers as well.

An important use of Layer 4 switching is providing access control list (ACL) filtering for security purposes. Although traditional routers can "see" Layer 4 information—and some routers (such as the Cisco 7500) can perform Layer 4 functions—enabling ACLs results in a significant performance hit. Because the packet processing is done in the hardware with Layer 4 switches, there is not a corresponding reduction in performance.

Layer 4 switches have the capability to manage allocation of bandwidth for quality of service (QoS) implementations and to perform load balancing.

Layer 4 switching functions are available on many modern routers.

Summary

In this chapter, we discussed a broad range of network hardware devices. You learned how to select, install, configure, and troubleshoot various types of NICs.

We also discussed the many choices available in selecting networking media, both cabled and wireless. Specifically, we addressed the characteristics of the three common cable types: coax cable (thin and thick), twisted-pair cable (shielded and unshielded), and fiber-optic cable. You learned about some of the advantages and disadvantages of each, and how they can be used in different LAN configurations.

Then we examined the popular devices that can be used to connect segments or subnetworks. We first looked at simple, nonelectronic devices, such as cable connectors, patch panels, and passive hubs. Then we took a closer look at more complex devices such as repeaters, active hubs, and intelligent hubs. Finally, we learned about segmenting and subnetting solutions such as bridges, routers, and switches.

Now that you have a good understanding of the hardware components that can be involved in the typical networking scenario, in the next chapter we take an in-depth look at networking protocols and services on which the network runs.

Further Reading

An excellent tutorial on wireless networking is available on the Web at www.proxim.com/wireless/whiteppr/whatwlan.shtml.

For more detailed information on bridges, bridge loops, and the Spanning-Tree Algorithm, see www.officewizard.com/books/network/ch07.htm.

An excellent explanation of Layer 3 switching can be found at www.3com.com/technology/tech_net/white_papers/500660.html.

Review Questions

The following questions test your knowledge of the material covered in this chapter. Be sure to read each question carefully and select the *best* correct answer or answers.

1. What is the most basic piece of hardware required to network computers?

    A. Router

    B. Cable

    C. NIC

    D. Hub

2. Which type of network uses an external transceiver?

    A. 10Base2

    B. 10Base5

    C. 10BaseT

    D. All of the above

3. If you want to install a NIC in a computer that has a PS/2 mouse, keyboard, a printer, and two IDE controllers, all using default IRQs, and a sound card set to IRQ 10, which of the following IRQs should be available for the NIC?

    A. 5

    B. 7

    C. 12

    D. 14

4. What type of cable is required by most fire codes when you install cable in the space between the false ceiling and the floor above?

    A. Cat 5

    B. Thick coax

    C. Military grade

    D. Plenum grade

5. Which cable type is specified for use on the typical 10Base2 network?

   A. RG-58 /U

   B. RG-58 A/U

   C. RG-58 C/U

   D. RG-59

6. What cable type is associated with the use of a vampire tap?

   A. UTP

   B. STP

   C. Thick coax

   D. Thin coax

7. What is the leaking of signal from one wire to another, which can be diminished by twisting wires around one another?

   A. RFI

   B. Attenuation

   C. Distortion

   D. Crosstalk

8. What connector type is generally used with UTP Cat 5 cabling on Ethernet networks?

   A. RJ-45

   B. RJ-11

   C. BNC connector

   D. F connector

9. Which of the following is true of fiber-optic cable? (Select all that apply.)

   A. Fiber-optic cable is the easiest of all cable types to work with and to install.

   B. Fiber-optic cable provides better security than does copper cable.

   C. Fiber-optic cable is more susceptible to attenuation than is copper cable.

   D. Single-mode fiber-optic cable is faster than multimode fiber-optic cable.

10. Which of the following is used to connect two segments of network cable and to regenerate the signal as it passes through, thus countering the effects of attenuation?

A. Barrel connector

B. Patch panel

C. Repeater

D. Passive hub

Chapter 8

Networking Protocols and Services

If the network's hardware is analogous to its bones and organs, and the signals that run through it can be compared to its lifeblood, we can think of the protocols and services on which the network runs as the mind of the network. The protocols tell the network how to perform its functions. They control it just as the mind controls the body.

The network protocols are sets of rules—the logic by which the network operates. Network *services,* such as name resolution or address allocation services, perform specific functions and control particular tasks. This is somewhat similar to the way different areas of the brain govern hearing, seeing, breathing, speech, and so on.

There are many different types of computer protocols. Each operates at a different layer of the OSI reference model. In the context of PC networking, the term "protocol" is often used to identify the *network/transport* protocols, which are those that work at Layers 3 and 4 of the OSI reference model. Networked computers must use a common protocol to communicate.

We discuss three network/transport protocols in this chapter:

- The NetBIOS Extended User Interface (NetBEUI)
- The Internet Packet Exchange/Sequenced Packet Exchange (IPX/SPX)
- The Transmission Control Protocol/Internet Protocol (TCP/IP)

These are the three standard stacks supported by many popular PC operating systems. Each has advantages and disadvantages, depending on the LAN environment.

In this chapter, we also examine networking services such as Domain Name System (DNS), Windows Internet Name Service (WINS), and Dynamic Host Configuration Protocol (DHCP) that work with TCP/IP to enhance its functionality.

NetBIOS/NetBEUI

You might hear references to NetBIOS and NetBEUI that imply they are the same thing. In fact, at one time this was true. NetBIOS (Network Basic Input/Output System) was developed by IBM and adopted by Microsoft for early LAN

NOTE

A *protocol stack* is a group of two or more protocols that work together, with each operating at a different layer of the OSI reference model.

communications. At that time, the term referred to both the application programming interface (API) and the network/transport protocol stack.

Subsequently, these components were split into NetBIOS (referring to the API) and NetBEUI (which encompasses the network/transport layer protocols). NetBIOS does not provide a frame or data format for network transmission; NetBEUI does.

NETBIOS: THE API

NetBIOS can run over NetBEUI, IPX/SPX or TCP/IP. NetBIOS enables applications to deal with a common programming interface so that information can be shared over different lower-level protocols.

Operating at the upper layers (that is, the application layer of the Department of Defense (DoD) model and the session layer of the OSI reference model), NetBIOS provides for two communication modes: session mode and datagram mode.

When running in session mode, NetBIOS enables the communicating computers to establish a connection, or *session,* with error detection and recovery. When NetBIOS is used in datagram mode, the individual messages are sent separately in a connectionless manner, meaning that error detection and correction must be handled by the application itself.

NetBIOS also provides a name service (that is, NetBIOS names) by which computers and applications can be identified on the network.

NetBEUI is the simplest of the three protocol stacks. Its simplicity makes it the highest performer in terms of sheer speed, but the simplicity also limits its functionality. Because NetBEUI does not include a means of logical addressing for addresses at the network layer, it cannot be routed from one network or subnet to another. It works well, however, for communication within a single LAN, and it is easy to set up. It can be used in conjunction with another routable protocol such as TCP/IP. This gives you the advantages of NetBEUI's high performance within the local network and the capability to communicate beyond the LAN over TCP/IP.

NOTE

IPX/SPX or NWLink is required for connecting Microsoft clients to NetWare 4.*x* and older servers. Some NetWare 5.*x* servers can communicate through TCP/IP only.

IPX/SPX

IPX works in conjunction with SPX to provide routable network communications. Novell developed IPX/SPX for its NetWare servers and clients, but it can also be used with other operating systems (such as Microsoft Windows LANs). Novell based IPX/SPX on the Xerox Network System (XNS) protocols.

Performance is higher and configuration is easier for IPX/SPX than it is for TCP/IP. IPX/SPX is sometimes used for internal LAN communications as part of a security plan. "Outside" computers accessing the LAN from the Internet, which are running only TCP/IP, are not able to access LAN systems that run only IPX/SPX.

Microsoft provides an IPX/SPX-compatible protocol stack called NWLink, which is included with all modern Windows operating systems, although it is not installed by default.

IPX works at the network layer of the OSI reference model and is connection-less. SPX operates at the transport layer of the OSI reference model and provides for acknowledgments, reassembly of packets, and other connection-oriented services.

The Network Layer Protocol: IPX

In Chapter 3, "Networking Concepts, Models, and Standards," you learned that the network layer of the OSI reference model is responsible for logical addressing and routing functions, that is, for getting messages to the correct destinations. This is the primary function of IPX.

For a protocol to be routable, there must be a means of identifying the network on which the computer resides. IPX uses hexadecimal *network numbers* to identify the network (subnet). A typical IPX network number would look like this: 805609a0. The administrator assigns the network number.

An IPX address consists of two parts: the network number and the *node number*, as shown in Figure 8-1. The node number identifies the specific device, and it is based on the Media Access Control (MAC) address of the interface.

FIGURE 8-1
An IPX address is made up of two parts: a network number and a node number.

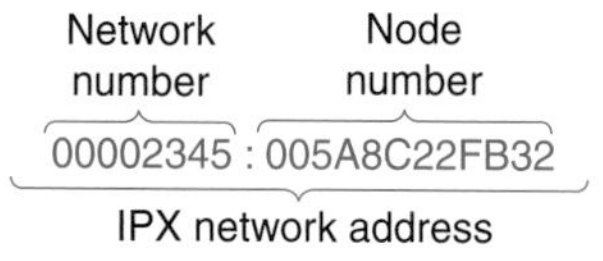

Network number   Node number

00002345 : 005A8C22FB32

IPX network address

In networks running both TCP/IP and IPX/SPX, the network numbers are often derived from the IP addresses by simply converting the IP address from decimal to hexadecimal (for example, 214.12.1.42 in hex is D6C12A).

> **NOTE**
>
> *Connection-oriented* communication is similar to a person-to-person telephone call. If you wish to speak to Mr. Jones, you dial his number and then ask for him by name. You do not begin to communicate your message until you know you have Mr. Jones on the line (in other words, not until you have established your session).
>
> *Connectionless* communication works more like using a public address system to communicate your message to a member of a large crowd. You speak into the microphone and your message is transmitted. You hope Mr. Jones was in the crowd and heard the message, but you have no way of knowing if the message did indeed reach its intended destination because no session was established.

The Role of the Service Advertising Protocol

IPX uses the Service Advertising Protocol (SAP) to advertise the addresses of network services such as file servers. A number called a SAP ID or SAP identifier is assigned to each service, and SAP broadcasts are transmitted every 60 seconds. Routers and servers keep tables that match SAP IDs to the services and update the tables dynamically with each broadcast. This keeps the tables up to date, but it also uses a great deal of network bandwidth. SAP broadcasts are not forwarded across routers, although routers can forward their SAP tables to other routers.

The Transport Layer Protocol: SPX

SPX operates above IPX, at the transport layer. Where IPX is a connectionless protocol, SPX is a connection-oriented protocol. This makes SPX more reliable, which makes sense when you think about the fact that the transport layer is responsible for acknowledgments, error checking, and other reliability issues.

IPX gets the packet to its destination. SPX concerns itself with ensuring that the packet arrives complete and in good condition. SPX handles sequencing and keeps count of the packets transmitted. It guarantees delivery by verifying the receipt of the data.

TCP/IP

The TCP/IP stack is the foundation of Internet communications. It is quickly becoming the most common network/transport solution for networks of all sizes and configurations. Thus, we focus on it in this discussion of network/transport protocols.

The following sections of this chapter talk about the concepts and theory behind the various members of the TCP/IP suite, what each one does, and how each one works. In Chapter 12, "Desktop Operating Systems," you will learn how to configure TCP/IP for various desktop operating systems.

The TCP/IP Suite

TCP/IP is not only a protocol stack that consists of a network layer protocol and a transport layer protocol, but also a complete suite of protocols that operates at many layers of the networking model. A protocol suite, by definition, includes "extras" that are not required for network communication. These extras include, for example, the application layer utilities that are part of the TCP/IP suite.

Many of the protocols included in the suite function as information-gathering or troubleshooting utilities. In the following sections of this chapter, we examine each in turn, beginning with the main players: the network layer and transport layer protocols.

The Network Layer Protocol: IP

You know that the network layer handles routing tasks. The TCP/IP protocols enable this routing by using IP addresses to identify network devices. Every computer, network-attached printer, router, and other network device has a unique IP address.

Understanding IP Addressing

Each IP address has two parts. Together, they identify the network on which the device resides and the particular device on that network. One section of the IP address represents the *network* and the second section represents the *host* (individual computer). This is much like the way in which a two-part postal address identifies a particular house to which mail is delivered:

- The street name tells the post office the general area where the house is located. Many different houses share the street name "Elm" as part of their addresses.

- The street number is unique for each individual house on that street. There can be many houses in a town with the street number "101," but only one house on Elm Street has that number.

Similarly, many computers share the same network address, but the combined network and host address is unique to one computer (or more accurately, to one network interface). In the IP address 201.32.0.4, for example, the first three sections (called *octets,* which are discussed in the "IP Address Classes" section of this chapter) identify the network. The last section identifies the individual computer's network interface. All computers on the same subnet have the same network ID (201.32.0), but each has a different host ID (that is, there can be only one .4 on the subnet).

If you mail a letter from Dallas to San Francisco, the post office in Dallas is not concerned with the street number in San Francisco. The first task is to get the letter to the correct city. Likewise, when you send a message across the Internet to a different LAN, the routers are not concerned with the host portion of the IP address; only the network portion is of interest. After the packet reaches the correct network (subnet), the host address is used to forward it to a specific computer—much as the local post office in San Francisco uses the street address to ensure that your letter reaches its destination.

> **NOTE**
>
> One device can actually have multiple IP addresses, one for each of its *network interfaces.* Routers have a minimum of two interfaces, which are attached to different subnets. Each has a unique IP address. *Multi-homed* computers have more than one network interface card (NIC), and each card is assigned an IP address.

Likewise, if a computer sends a message to IP address 201.32.0.4, in which 204.32.0 represents the network and 4 represents the host, the first step is to get the packet to the proper network. After it arrives there, it is routed internally within the network to the computer represented by the host ID (which is 4).

In our example, the first three octets identify the network. This is not always the case. In the traditional IP addressing scheme, the portion of the address that represents the network and the portion that represents the host is determined by the address *class*, as discussed in the next section.

IP Address Classes. IP addresses, like other information processed by computers, are made up of binary numbers, or *bits*. Because long strings of ones and zeros are difficult for most humans to work with, we usually denote IP addresses in *dotted-decimal* format. (See Chapter 3 if you need a review of numbering systems and how binary is converted to decimal.) The dotted-decimal format is sometimes called *dotted quad* because there are four sets of numbers separated by dots, with each set representing an octet.

An *octet* is eight bits long; there are eight digits, each of which is a one or a zero. The four octets are sometimes designated as w.x.y.z. With this designation, the far right octet is called the "z" octet, the next one is called the "y" octet, and so on.

Because there are eight bits in each of the four octets, each IP address is a 32-bit number. This means that there are over four billion possible IP addresses (4,294,967,296, to be exact, or 2^{32}). An IP address usually looks something like this: 192.168.1.12.

We know that part of the IP address identifies the network and part identifies the individual device (host), but which part represents which? Unfortunately, the answer is that it depends. Traditionally, it depended upon the class to which the network belonged (a newer method of addressing, called *classless addressing*, will be discussed in the section titled "Understanding Classless Addressing").

The Internet Assigned Numbers Authority (IANA) hands out IP addresses. In the early days of Internet communications, it seemed logical to assign IP addresses to companies and organizations in blocks because each computer on the LAN needed a unique address with which to communicate on the Internet.

Blocks of addresses were assigned based on the size of the local network. Large enterprise-level networks needed larger blocks of addresses, and small networks with only a few devices required smaller blocks. *Address classes* were

> **NOTE**
>
> This discussion is based on version 4 of the Internet Protocol (IPv4), which is in common use today. A new proposed standard, IPv6, or IPng (which stands for IP, Next Generation), would use a 128-bit address and provide 2^{128} useable addresses.

> **NOTE**
>
> With the advent of technologies such as Network Address Translation (NAT), which was discussed in Chapter 6, "WAN Links," it is no longer strictly true that every computer on the local network needs a public IP address.

designated based on network size (number of host addresses). Table 8-1 shows the traditional IP address classes.

TABLE 8-1   IP Address Classes

Address Class	Number of Networks	Number of Hosts per Network
A	126*	16,777,216
B	16,384	65,535
C	2,097,152	254
D (Multicast)	N/A	N/A

*   The 127.x.x.x address range is reserved as a *loopback address,* used for testing and diagnostic purposes.

As you can see in Table 8-1, there are only 126 Class A addresses available. These addresses were used up some time ago; they were assigned to very large corporations and educational institutes, including IBM, Hewlett Packard, Xerox, Massachusetts Institute of Technology (MIT), Columbia University, Digital Equipment Corporation, General Electric, and Apple. Each network has more than 16 million host addresses that can be assigned to computers within it.

The IP address class scheme creates more than 2 million Class C networks, but each of those networks can have no more than 254 host addresses. Class C network addresses are often assigned to Internet service providers, which subdivide their allocation into smaller blocks of addresses for companies that have only 10 to 20 host machines on their networks.

Class B addresses fall between Class A and Class C addresses. They are assigned primarily to large companies that were too small (or nonexistent) to have received Class A addresses back in the early days of the Internet. Microsoft Corporation is an example of a company that has a Class B network.

Class D addresses are not used for networks, but for *multicast messaging,* which is a means of sending a single message to multiple recipients simultaneously. A Class D address is assigned to a specified group of computers, and multicast protocols handle the distribution of the packets.

The method of dividing IP addresses into classes based on network size is called *classful addressing.* (The *classless addressing* method of addressing is discussed in the "Understanding Classless Addressing" section of this chapter.)

MULTICASTING AND THE MBONE

Multicast messages serve a function on the Internet that is similar to that of broadcast messages on a LAN. However, rather than being sent to *all* computers on the network, multicast messages are sent only to the computers that belong to predefined multicast groups.

There are several advantages to multicast messaging:

- It conserves bandwidth because you send the same packet to multiple addresses instead of sending the packet once for each address.

- You don't have to know the address of every computer to which you send the packet; you only have to know the multicast address.

Traditional, single-destination transmissions are called *unicast messages.* Traditional Internet routers are configured for unicast transmissions, and many cannot handle multicast packets. To solve this problem, the Internet Engineering Task Force (IETF) developed a virtual network called the MBONE (multicast backbone) that runs on top of the Internet. Using the same hardware as the Internet, the MBONE software transmits multicast packets inside unicast packets. This *encapsulation* (also referred to as *tunneling)* hides the multicast packet from routers that cannot process it and enables it to travel through the traditional nonmulticast routers.

Understanding Classful Addressing. Remember that although we commonly use decimal notation, IP addresses are actually made up of binary numbers. Table 8-2 shows how address classes can be identified based on the first octet address range. To understand Table 8-2, it is necessary to go back to the binary for a moment.

Remember that the address class is identified by the *high-order bits,* or the first few bits in the leftmost octet (sometimes referred to as the "w" octet).

TABLE 8-2   Identifying Address Classes

IP Address Class	High-Order Bits	First Octet Address Range	Number of Bits in the Network Address
Class A	0	0–127*	7
Class B	10	128–191	14
Class C	110	192–223	21
Class D	1110	224–239	28

* The 127.x.x.x address range is reserved as a *loopback address,* used for testing and diagnostic purposes.

As you can see in Table 8-2, Class A addresses are identified by the first bit of 0, Class B addresses are designated by the first two bits of 10, Class C addresses have the first three bits of 110, and multicast (Class D) addresses use 1110 as the first four bits.

Consider the following IP address: 11001111.00101100.01010001.11100111. Because the first three far-left (high-order) bits are 110, we know that this is a Class C address. If we convert the binary address to dotted-decimal notation (using a scientific calculator or the method described in Chapter 3), we get the following: 207.44.81.231.

Notice that the first octet, 207, falls into the 192–223 range shown in Table 8-2. Because all Class C addresses have 110 as the first three bits, they all have a "w" octet that falls into this range. This means that we can identify which class an IP address belongs to merely by its first octet.

In the previous example, 207.44.81 identifies the network (subnet) on which the computer resides. All computers on that subnet have these numbers as the first three octets of their IP addresses. The number 231 designates the specific host computer. No other device on that subnet can have this number as the far-right octet of its IP address. Figure 8-2 shows an example of how an IP address is divided into network and host IDs.

FIGURE 8-2
In a Class C address, the first three octets represent the network ID.

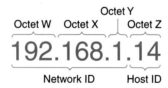

Now, how do we determine the number of networks and hosts that are available for each class? Traditionally, a Class A address uses the first octet as the network address and the remaining three as the host address. Because the very first bit (the high-order bit) in a Class A address is used to identify the address class, that leaves seven bits in the first octet that can be used for the network identification.

A Class B address uses the first two octets for the network and the last two for the host. There are 16 bits in the first two octets, but the first 2 bits are used to identify the class. Thus, we have 14 bits left for the network ID.

Following the same logic, Class C uses the first three octets (8 bits times three octets, or 24 bits) to identify the network, and only the last octet is available to identify hosts. The 3 high-order bits identify the class, so we subtract 3 from 24 and end up with 21 bits for the network ID portion of the address.

Let's go back to our Class A network. We know that 7 bits are available for the network ID. If all 7 bits are turned "on," (designated by 1s), the highest number we can have for the network ID is 1111111. When we convert this number to decimal, we have 127, which is the number of possible Class A networks (the 127 range is reserved for loopback testing). The 0.0.0.0 address is reserved for representing all IP addresses.

An easier way to arrive at this number is to raise 2 to the power of x, where x is the number of bits available for the network ID. If we use this method, we get 2^7, or 128. When we exclude the 0.0.0.0 network address and the loopback network address, we arrive at 126, the number of possible Class A addresses.

The same process can be used for Class B and Class C networks:

- **Class B**—14 bits = 2^{14} = 16,384
- **Class C**—21 bits = 2^{21} = 2,097,252

You might have determined by now that classful addressing is not the most efficient use of the finite number of IP addresses available within the 32-bit addressing scheme. To illustrate this determination, let's use the example of a company that has 2000 computers it wants to connect to the Internet. A Class C address won't do because that would limit the network to 254 hosts. The next step up is a Class B address—but if the company obtains one, it would take over 65,000 addresses out of commission. Because it needs only 2000 of those addresses, more than 63,000 IP addresses would be wasted. *Classless addressing*, discussed in the next section, addresses this problem.

Understanding Classless Addressing. The waste of addresses associated with classful addressing has contributed to the shortage of public IP addresses. One proposed solution is the implementation of IPv6, which uses a larger address space (128 bits). However, the transition to a new version of IP is not simple and will take some time to accomplish. Meanwhile, another solution exists: classless addressing based on classless interdomain routing (CIDR).

Rather than using address classes, CIDR uses a designation appended to each IP address that specifies the number of bits used for the network portion of the address. CIDR networks are sometimes called "slash x" networks because the IP address is separated from the suffix by a slash. Thus, a CIDR address looks like this: 192.168.1.0/24. The "slash 24" means that the far-left 24 bits are used to identify the network, and the remaining eight bits are used to identify the host. In other words, the first three octets indicate the network, and the last octet specifies the host computer. In classful addressing, this would be a Class C network.

Table 8-3 shows how CIDR addresses correspond to traditional classful addresses.

TABLE 8-3   CIDR (Classless) Addresses and Traditional Classful Addresses

CIDR Address	Classful Address
/8	Class A
/16	Class B
/24	Class C

CIDR enables much more efficient allocation of IP addresses. In addition to the slash-x designations in Table 8-3, CIDR networks can be designated as /12, /20, /21, /28, and so on; that is, whatever number of bits you wish to use for the network ID can follow the slash. This enables network sizes that fall between the traditional network classes.

CIDR also supports the practice of combining small contiguous blocks of network addresses into one larger one. This is called *supernetting* and is discussed later in this chapter in the section "IP Subnetting and Supernetting."

Automatic Address Allocation

To communicate using TCP/IP, a computer or other network device must have a unique IP address. This is a *logical* address and is processed at the network layer.

The network portion of the address must be the same as that of other computers on its subnet. For example, if you were using the default subnet mask for Class C networks, 192.168.1.12 and 192.168.1.34 would be two computers on the same subnet because the network ID, represented by the first three octets, is the same.

In contrast, the host portion must *not* be the same as that of any other computer on the same subnet. For example, there could not be two computers with host address .6 on the same subnet.

There are two ways to obtain an IP address:

- The address can be manually entered into the operating system's TCP/IP properties configuration. This requires that the network administrator assigning the address understand TCP/IP addressing and know how to choose a valid address for the particular network.

- The address can be automatically assigned. Generally, this means a computer on the network is configured as a DHCP server to hand out IP addresses from a pool of valid addresses. In other cases, an operating system feature called Automatic Private IP Addressing (APIPA) enables a computer to assign itself an address if it is unable to contact a DHCP server.

DHCP. DHCP is a protocol that runs on a machine designated as a DHCP server, which allocates IP addresses to machines that are configured to be DHCP clients. Figure 8-3 illustrates the process.

FIGURE 8-3
The DHCP server leases an address to the DHCP client.

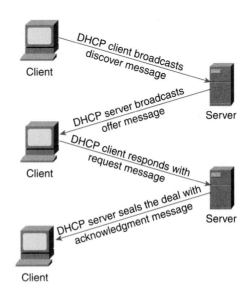

The steps involved when a DHCP client obtains an IP address lease from a DHCP server is as follows:

1. A computer whose TCP/IP properties are set to obtain an IP address through DHCP comes onto the network. This computer broadcasts a message called a DHCP discover message to the entire network or subnet. (Broadcast messages are sent to all computers by using a special broadcast address.)

2. If a DHCP server is present on the network, it receives the broadcast message and responds with a message called a DHCP offer. The message offers the client an IP address from the server's range of addresses that are available for allocation. The offered address is temporarily reserved until the server receives a response from the client. The offer message is also

sent as a broadcast because the client does not yet have an IP address of its own to which a one-to-one message can be sent.

3. The client can receive multiple offers if there are multiple DHCP servers on the network. When the first offer arrives, the client responds with a message called a *DHCP request*. This is an acceptance of the first offer received. Again, it is a broadcast message; thus, all DHCP servers receive it and those who made late offers will subsequently know that their offers were not accepted. They can then place the offered addresses they had reserved for the client back into their available address pools.

4. The last step in this negotiation is the *DHCP acknowledgment* (also called the *ACK*). The DHCP server whose offer was accepted receives the client's request message. The server acknowledges the acceptance and assigns the IP address to that client for the duration of a preset "lease" period. It can send the client additional TCP/IP configuration information, such as the IP addresses of DNS and WINS servers. (We discuss the role of those servers later in this chapter.)

NOTE

The DHCP server might send a NACK if, for example, the client machine has moved to a different subnet and the address it is trying to renew is no longer valid for its location.

When these steps are completed, the client can use the assigned IP address to communicate with other computers running the TCP/IP protocols and do so until the lease period expires. Note that the length of the lease can be set by an administrator on the DHCP server.

Before the expiration of the lease, the client begins negotiations to renew it so that it can continue to use the address. Normally the DHCP server grants this request. If the DHCP server has gone offline, however, or if the server sends a Negative Acknowledgment response (NACK), the client must start the DHCP process all over again.

DHCP has many advantages over manual IP addressing:

- It saves time because the administrator does not have to enter the addresses into each computer's property settings.
- It ensures greater accuracy because the administrator does not have to keep up with which addresses have already been assigned and which are still free.

If computers on a network must have the same IP address (this is often true of servers), they can still use DHCP. In this case, you must configure those computers to use a *reserved address*. The DHCP server always assigns the same address to a client that has such a reservation. The reservation is made based on the DHCP client's MAC (that is, physical) address.

THE ORIGINS OF DHCP

DHCP grew out of an earlier protocol, the Bootstrap Protocol (BOOTP). BOOTP was originally developed to enable diskless workstations to boot up, be assigned an IP address, and then load an operating system over the network.

DHCP is much more advanced than BOOTP, and it enables the administrator to configure many options and set lease durations. DHCP adds dynamic allocation of addresses. Some DHCP servers are configured to support BOOTP clients.

DHCP is not operating system specific. It can be used with Microsoft, UNIX, NetWare, and other popular network types. However, vendor implementation of the DHCP services may differ. For example, Windows 2000 DHCP servers are integrated with Active Directory. This enables administrators to prevent unauthorized DHCP servers (sometimes referred to as "rogue" DHCP servers) from handing out IP addresses on the network.

APIPA. Another means of automatically obtaining an IP address is APIPA. The TCP/IP implementation of recent Microsoft operating systems, such as Windows 98 and Windows 2000, include this feature.

Traditionally, if a computer was configured to be a DHCP client, and it was unable to contact a DHCP server when it came onto the network, that computer would have no IP address and would not be able to communicate over TCP/IP. APIPA was introduced to solve this problem.

When an APIPA-enabled computer cannot locate a DHCP server to obtain an address, it assigns itself one from a range of addresses reserved for that purpose (the Class B 169.254.0.0 network range). The self-assigned address can be used until the DHCP server is functional again.

IP Subnetting and Supernetting

To *subnet* a network means to divide it into parts. Subnetting turns the two-level address hierarchy described earlier into a three-level addressing system. To subnet a network, you "borrow" some of the bits that are normally used for the host portion of the address and use them for the second level of the network address (that is, the subnet address).

The Subnet Mask. Subnetting involves borrowing from one part of the address to give to the other. When we subnet, IP must have a means of determining which bits identify the network and which are still being used to indicate the host. IP determines this by using the *subnet mask,* a 32-bit number entered by the administrator in the TCP/IP properties configuration. The subnet mask sets the bits representing the network ID to 1s and those representing the host ID to 0s. The network ID portion of the address is said to be "masked" by the bits that are turned on.

By default, Class A networks use the bits in the first octet for the network ID, Class B networks use the bits in the first two octets to identify the network, and Class C addresses use the first three octets for this purpose. The *default subnet masks* resulting from this pattern are shown in Table 8-4.

TABLE 8-4   Default Subnet Masks

Address Class	Binary Subnet Mask	Decimal Subnet Mask
Class A	11111111.00000000.00000000.00000000	255.0.0.0
Class B	11111111.11111111.00000000.00000000	255.255.0.0
Class C	11111111.11111111.11111111.00000000	255.255.255.0

The subnet masks in Table 8-4 apply to *unsubnetted* networks, and as long as we stick with the defaults, this is simple enough.

What happens, however, if we want to divide a network? Let's say we have been assigned a Class B network address, such as 181.25.0.0. We know that a Class B network can contain 65,535 host computers. However, if we had that many computers on one network, broadcast traffic would be unmanageable.

As a solution, let's suppose we have decided to divide the network into six subnets. To do so, we must borrow bits from the host address portion of the address, which is used to indicate the subnets, and we must calculate the correct subnet mask that indicates to IP that our network has six subnets (or eight possible subnets).

Calculating the Subnet Mask. A subnet mask other than the default masks is referred to as a *variable-length* or *custom* subnet mask. To calculate the correct subnet mask for our scenario in which six separate subnets are desired, we must first determine how many bits we need to borrow from the host portion of the address.

Because binary is a base 2 numbering system, subnets must be created in blocks of powers of 2. To calculate the subnet mask, we must find out what power of 2 gives us 6 (or more) subnets.

If we raise 2 to the second power (2×2), we get 4. We need more subnets than that, so let's try 2 to the third power ($2 \times 2 \times 2 = 8$). If we subtract 2, to comply with the old rule that says we can't use network IDs that consist of all 0s or all 1s, we have 6 remaining usable subnets. Therefore, we need to borrow three bits from the host portion of the address. This means we must turn the first three 0s, which indicate the host ID, into 1s, which indicate the network ID. Our original default subnet mask, with the borrowed bits, now looks like this: 11111111.11111111.11100000.00000000. If we convert it to decimal, we have this: 255.255.224.0.

How many host computers can we have on each subnet? Look at the remaining 0s that indicate the host portion of the address. You'll find there are 13 of them, which gives us $2^{13} = 8192$. This means that we can have 8190 hosts on each subnet, after subtracting 2 so that no host address is all 0s or all 1s. (Remember that the prohibition against all 0s and 1s has been removed only in regard to network IDs. The host IDs still follow this rule.)

Table 8-5 provides a quick reference for the number of subnets and hosts enabled with each subnet mask.

TABLE 8-5   Quick Reference Subnetting Chart

Decimal Notation for First Octet	Number of Subnets	Number of Class A Hosts	Number of Class B Hosts	Number of Class C Hosts
.192	2	4,194,302	16,382	62
.224	6	2,097,150	8190	30
.240	14	1,048,574	4094	14
.248	30	524,286	2046	6
.252	62	262,142	1022	2
.254	126	131,070	510	—
.255	254	65,534	254	—

ANDing. When a network transmission is sent using TCP/IP, IP must determine whether the destination computer is on the same subnet as the sending computer. If both computers are on the same subnet, the message is broadcast. If the destination computer is on a different subnet, the message is sent to the *default gateway* address, which is the address of the router's interface (the router serves as the gateway out of the subnet).

IP uses a process called ANDing to ascertain whether the sending and destination computers are on the same subnet. ANDing is done by combining the binary versions of the IP address for each computer with the subnet mask. In combining these binary numbers, the calculations are made as follows:

- 1 AND 1 = 1
- 1 AND 0 = 0
- 0 AND 0 = 0

Here is an example of ANDing: The IP address for the sending computer is 192.168.1.1, with a subnet mask of 255.255.255.0. The IP address for the destination computer is 192.168.3.1 with a subnet mask of 255.255.255.0.

First, we AND the sending computer's IP address with the subnet mask:

```
192.168.1.1 = 11000000.10101000.00000001.00000001
255.255.255.0 =11111111.11111111.11111111.00000000
ANDed result =11000000.10101000.00000001.00000000
```

Then, we do the same calculation for the destination computer and subnet mask:

```
192.168.3.1 =11000000.10101000.00000011.00000001
255.255.255.0 =11111111.11111111.11111111.00000000
ANDed result =11000000.10101000.00000011.00000000
```

The results are different, so we know (and more importantly, IP knows) that these two computers reside on different subnets. The message is then sent to the router (default gateway) to be forwarded to the correct subnet.

If the result had been the same, IP would know the destination computer was on the local subnet and the message would be sent using an Address Resolution Protocol (ARP) broadcast. We discuss more about ARP later in this chapter.

Benefits of Subnetting. The benefits of separating a large network into two or more subnetworks (subnets) include the following:

- It reduces broadcast traffic. Subnets are connected to one another by routers, and most routers are configured by default not to pass on broadcast messages. This can substantially conserve network bandwidth.
- It organizes computers at different locations into separate subnets for easier management.

- It isolates a part of the network for security or filtering purposes.
- It provides more efficient use of available addresses and fewer "wasted" addresses.

IP subnetting is the subject of entire books. It is a complex topic and all the details involved are beyond the scope of this introductory text (the list at the end of this chapter has several good subnetting tutorials). This section provided, however, a very basic overview of subnetting concepts.

The Transport Layer Protocols: TCP and UDP

Recall from Chapter 3 that the transport layer (called the *host-to-host* layer in the DoD model) is responsible for providing reliable end-to-end communication. This is accomplished by mechanisms such as acknowledgments, which verify that data has arrived at the destination without damage or loss.

Transport layer protocols also differentiate between messages that arrive at the same destination computer. Because different applications can be sending or receiving messages at the same time, the transport layer protocols use *ports* to keep these messages separate. We discuss ports and a related concept, *sockets*, later in this section.

The TCP/IP suite includes not one, but two transport layer protocols:

- **Transmission Control Protocol (TCP)**—A connection-oriented protocol
- **User Datagram Protocol (UDP)**—A connectionless protocol

Which of the two transport protocols is used to send a particular message? It depends on the needs for that transmission. TCP is appropriate when reliability is of utmost importance, and UDP is used if performance (speed) is the highest priority. We examine the characteristics and functions of each in the following sections.

The Transport Layer Protocol: TCP

TCP, because it is a connection-oriented protocol, establishes a session between the two communicating computers before sending data. Acknowledgment and response messages are used to establish the session. Error checking and correction are then performed, and the data is broken down into packets.

Sequencing information is added to each packet so that the parts of the message can be put back together in the correct order. This information also enables the receiving computer to detect if packets are missing. This makes TCP more reliable than UDP, but at a price: all these extra duties slow down performance.

The Transport Layer Protocol: UDP

UDP is connectionless. It does not sequence the packets in which data arrives; this means it is more appropriate for small messages that can be transmitted in one packet. UDP also doesn't keep track of what it has sent or guaranteed. It does provide for a checksum, however, to ensure that data is intact upon arrival. Like TCP, it provides port numbers to differentiate between the requests sent by or being delivered to different applications.

Because it does not have to bother with sequencing and error checking, UDP is fast. Its header is less complex than the header added by TCP. The Routing Information Protocol (RIP), the Trivial File Transfer Protocol (TFTP), and name lookup messages use UDP.

Ports and Sockets

TCP/IP uses a two-part logical address—the IP address—to identify the source and destination computers in network communication. What happens, however, if two network applications running on the same computer are sending requests and receiving responses simultaneously? For example, what happens if one incoming message is intended for your email program, while another is a web page being returned to your web browser? The protocols need a way to differentiate between them. That's where TCP and UDP ports come in.

The Role of Port Numbers. Remember that the IP address of a destination computer contains two parts: a network address that functions somewhat like a street name, and a host address that functions somewhat like a street number. You can think of port numbers as specific routing information within an address. It is an addendum to the IP address, just as the name of an addressee on an envelope is an addendum to the street address. Likewise, you can think of separate applications as separate residents.

A port is a *logical connection point*. Ports are used by the transport protocols, TCP and UDP, to identify the specific application that is sending or receiving the message.

Commonly used Internet applications have predefined port numbers. This standardization makes communication easier. The preassigned port numbers are called *well-known ports*. Table 8-6 lists examples of these commonly used port numbers.

> **NOTE**
>
> What is a *datagram*? The term is defined in RFC 1594 as "a self contained, independent entity of data carrying sufficient information to be routed from the source to the destination computer without reliance on earlier exchanges between this source and destination computer and the transporting network."
>
> The terms datagram and *packet* are sometimes used interchangeably. "Packet" describes a unit of data that is part of a sequenced group of units or "chunks" into which a message is broken. Packets can take different routes over the network to reach the destination. They are then reassembled at the destination. Datagram is used to describe the simpler, nonsequenced data units transmitted by UDP.

TABLE 8-6   **TCP/UDP Well-Known Ports**

Preassigned Port	Protocol	Application
80	TCP	HTTP
21	TCP/UDP	FTP
23	TCP/UDP	Telnet
25	TCP/UDP	SMTP
110	TCP/UDP	POP3
119	TCP/UDP	NNTP
137	TCP/UDP	NetBIOS name service
161	TCP/UDP	SNMP
194	TCP/UDP	IRC
389	TCP/UDP	LDAP
396	TCP/UDP	NetWare over IP
458	TCP/UDP	Apple QuickTime
500	TCP/UDP	ISAKMP

There are 65,536 useable ports. Ports 0 through 1024 (the "well-known ports") are reserved for predefined services, such as the ones shown in Table 8-6.

What Is a Socket? Now that you understand the function of ports, we will discuss the concept of sockets. The common definition of socket is "the endpoint of a connection"; a socket must be created for communication to take place.

Different socket types use different addressing methods. The most common method uses an IP address combined with a port number to identify the socket. In UNIX terminology, this is called AF_INET addressing. A second addressing method, AF_UNIX, uses pathnames to identify the sockets.

Berkeley (BSD) Sockets became the standard API for TCP/IP communications. A popular adaptation of the sockets interface is *Windows Sockets*, or *Winsock*. This implementation provides an API for Internet applications running on Windows operating systems. Winsock is loaded as a dynamic link library (DLL).

Addressing the Envelope: Packet Headers

You now know that the TCP/IP protocols use addressing information to get a message to the correct destination. You might be wondering, however, where the protocols find all this addressing information. Just as a letter you send through the postal service must be placed in an envelope and the sender's and recipient's addresses noted on the outside, a message sent through TCP/IP must be placed "inside an envelope."

When the message is placed in the "envelope," the data is encapsulated in protocol *headers*, which contain the addresses. The headers can also include other information and special instructions, just as you can write "Handle with Care" or "Special Delivery" on your postal envelope to aid in proper delivery.

By default, the IP header is 20 bytes long, and it includes fields that indicate the following (see Figure 8-4 for more details):

- Type of service
- Total length of the datagram
- Unique identification of the datagram
- Flags and fragmentation offset to aid in reassembly
- Time To Live (TTL) to limit the number of routers through which the datagram can pass
- Upper-layer protocol that is to receive the data (ICMP, TCP, UDP, IGRP, or OSPF)
- Checksum for detection of corruption
- Source IP address (sending computer)
- Destination IP address (receiving computer)

The header can include options such as security restrictions, timestamps, and routing restrictions. The header *without* options is 20 bytes long.

Name Resolution

We have discussed how TCP/IP uses IP addresses and port numbers to identify networks, computers, and specific network applications to which messages are sent. Most human beings, however, prefer to use names instead of numbers for identification purposes. That preference is why we never want to imagine having to memorize our friends' social security numbers to designate to whom we are talking!

FIGURE 8-4
The IP header is made up of 12 fields, plus options.

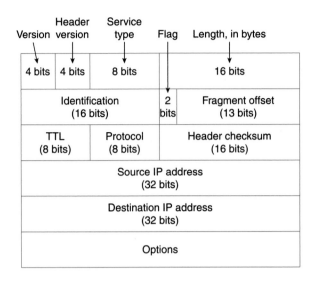

Although we like to use names when we access a computer on the network or type a web server location into a web browser, computers can work only with numbers. Because of this incompatibility, we need services that translate "friendly" names into IP addresses. Using these services, we can type www.xerox.com into our browser's address box instead of 208.134.240.50 when we want to view the Xerox website. It's certainly easier to remember. Regardless of our actions, however, our browser is converting the host name to an IP address to find the web server on the Internet and to retrieve the requested page.

What's in a Name?

Different name types are used in computer network communications. The Internet arranges host (computer) names in a hierarchical structure within *domains*. The most common top-level domains in the United States are as follows:

- **com**—Originally intended for commercial organizations
- **net**—Originally intended for networks such as ISPs
- **org**—Originally intended for nonprofit organizations
- **edu**—Restricted for use by educational institutions
- **gov**—Restricted for use by U.S. governmental entities
- **mil**—Restricted for use by U.S. military units
- **int**—Restricted for use by international organizations

Outside the United States, the following country codes are used to identify domains:

- **uk**—United Kingdom
- **au**—Australia
- **ca**—Canada

Businesses, organizations, and individuals register *second-level domain names*, for example, ibm.com, whitehouse.gov, or dallas.net, within these top-level domains. At one time, second-level domain names were assigned by InterNIC, but that task has now been distributed to several authorized name registrars.

Within your second-level domain, individual computers are identified by the hostname, the second-level domain name, and the top-level domain name— with dots separating each section. Thus, a web server named "www" in the dallas.net domain is identified as www.dallas.net. This "dotted" hierarchical name is called the *fully qualified domain name (FQDN)*.

On Microsoft networks, each computer is also assigned a NetBIOS name. This is a 16-character name, assigned by the administrator, used to identify resources on the local network.

Both types of names must be translated into IP addresses before TCP/IP communication can take place.

Translating Names to Numbers

You can use the following to translate names into IP addresses:

- HOSTS and LMHOSTS files, which are text files stored on computer hard disks
- DNS or Dynamic DNS (DDNS)
- WINS

The following sections describe these means of translation.

HOSTS and LMHOSTS Files. In the early days of the Internet, the method for matching host (computer) names to IP addresses for TCP/IP communication was the HOSTS file. This is a text file, stored on the local hard drive, which lists host names and their corresponding IP addresses. Example 8-1 shows an example of a HOSTS file.

EXAMPLE 8-1 A Local HOSTS File Maps IP Addresses to Host Names

```
102.54.94.97    rhino.acme.com    # source server
38.25.63.10     x.acme.com        # x client host
127.0.0.1       localhost
```

NOTE

The pound sign (#) in the HOSTS file indicates a comment. Any information that follows the # will be ignored by the computer.

The HOSTS file worked when there were only a few computers on the Internet. It is simple to construct and it can be modified with any text editor (for example, Windows Notepad, and vi or Emacs in UNIX or Linux). When a user attempted to access another computer using its "friendly" host name, the operating system consulted the HOSTS file for the "real" identification, the IP address.

However, each time another host was added to the network, the HOSTS file had to be manually updated, and the new file saved to all the computers on the network. As the Internet grew, this became an impossible task.

LMHOSTS serves a similar function in Microsoft networks by mapping IP addresses to NetBIOS names instead of to computer names. It suffers from the same disadvantages as HOSTS, however; it is a static file, and it must be manually updated. See Example 8-2 for an illustration of a typical LMHOSTS file.

EXAMPLE 8-2 The LMHOSTS File Matches IP Addresses to NetBIOS Names

```
102.54.94.97   rhino    #PRE #DOM:networking  #net group's DC
102.54.94.102  "appname  \0x14"    #special app server
102.54.94.123  popular #PRE     #source server
102.54.94.117  localsrv #PRE    #needed for the include
```

A better means of matching up names to IP addresses was obviously needed.

DNS and DDNS. The DNS was devised to solve the problems inherent in using HOSTS files. DNS servers store databases of IP-to-hostname mappings, and clients' TCP/IP properties are configured with the address of the DNS server. When a friendly hostname needs to be translated to its IP address, the client contacts the DNS server.

A hierarchy of DNS servers exists on the Internet, with different servers maintaining DNS information for their own "zones," or areas of authority. If the DNS server consulted by your computer does not have an IP mapping for the hostname you entered, it can pass the query to another DNS server until the information is obtained.

DNS is not absolutely required to communicate on the Internet, but without it, all communications must use IP addresses instead of hostnames. For example, if you do not have a DNS server address configured in your computer's TCP/IP properties, you can still access a website by typing its IP address into the URL field. However, if you type in the hostname instead, the browser is unable to return the page. The DNS server address can be entered manually, or it can be obtained from a DHCP server if your computer is set up as a DHCP client.

DNS is a big improvement over local HOSTS files because the database is stored on a central server and you need only update it there instead of on all client machines. However, the server's database still must be updated manually. *Dynamic DNS* addresses this problem by enabling automatic updates of the DNS database. Using this enhanced form of DNS, client computers can register and update their resource records on the DNS server when changes occur.

Windows 2000 DNS servers support the DDNS protocol extension, as does BIND version 8. RFC 2136 contains specifications for DDNS standards.

THE DNS DATABASE TABLE

DNS uses different types of records in the database table. The following are some of the common record types:

- **Address (A) Record**—Maps a host name to an IP address

- **Mail Exchange (MX) Record**—Points to a mail exchange server for a specific host

- **Canonical Name (CNAME) Record**—Maps *aliases,* or additional names, to a host

All these record types (and others for specialized purposes) are combined in the DNS table.

WINS. WINS is another method for resolving names to IP addresses. In this case, NetBIOS names (used to identify computers and services on Microsoft networks) are mapped in a database on a WINS server. Windows NT and Windows 2000 servers can function as WINS servers.

NetBIOS names are flat rather than hierarchical as are FQDNs (DNS host names). Where the FQDN for a particular server might be exeter.tacteam.net, a NetBIOS name would be simply Exeter. TCP/IP doesn't understand NetBIOS names; again, it needs an IP address to communicate with the server. WINS, like the static LMHOST file, can translate the name to the required IP number.

WINS, unlike the original DNS, uses a dynamically updated database. When WINS clients come onto the network, they announce themselves to the WINS server, giving their names and IP addresses. The WINS server builds its database from this information.

DHCP, DNS, and WINS can all work together on the same network. In new operating systems such as Microsoft Windows 2000, the three services are integrated to interoperate efficiently.

Summarizing Name Resolution Methods. It is easy to confuse the various name resolution methods. Table 8-7 summarizes the features and uses of each.

TABLE 8-7   Name Resolution Methods

Name Resolution Method	Name Type Resolved	Characteristics
HOSTS file	Host names to IP addresses	Text file; must be updated manually on each computer
LMHOSTS file	NetBIOS names to IP addresses	Text file; must be updated manually on each computer
DNS	Host names to IP addresses	Centralized database managed by DNS server; must be updated manually
DDNS	Host names to IP addresses	Centralized database managed by DNS server; can be updated dynamically
WINS	NetBIOS names to IP addresses	Centralized database managed by WINS server; can be updated dynamically

TCP/IP Utilities

TCP/IP is a complex collection of protocols. Most vendors' implementations of the suite include a variety of utilities for viewing configuration information and troubleshooting problems. In the following section, we look at the following common TCP/IP utilities:

- Packet Internet groper (ping)
- Address Resolution Protocol (ARP) and Reverse ARP (RARP)
- Netstat and tpcon
- Nbtstat
- IP configuration utilities: ipconfig, winipcfg, config, and ifconfig
- Route-tracing utilities: traceroute, tracert, and iptrace

Note that utilities that perform the same function(s) may be given different names by different vendors.

Ping

A simple but highly useful command-line utility included in most implementations of TCP/IP is ping. Ping can be used with either the hostname or the IP address to test IP connectivity.

Ping works by sending an ICMP echo request to the destination computer. That receiving computer then sends back an ICMP echo reply message.

It is also possible to use ping to find out the IP address of a host when you know the name. If you type the **ping apple.com** command as shown in Example 8-3, you will see the IP address from which the reply is returned.

EXAMPLE 8-3 Information Returned in Response to a ping of apple.com

```
c:\>ping apple.com
Pinging apple.com [17.254.3.183] with 32 bytes of data:
Reply from 17.254.3.183: bytes=32 time=430ms TTL=90
Reply from 17.254.3.183: bytes=32 time=371ms TTL=90
Reply from 17.254.3.183: bytes=32 time=370ms TTL=90
Reply from 17.254.3.183: bytes=32 time=371ms TTL=90

Ping statistics for 17.254.3.183:
    Packets: Sent = 4, Received = 4, Lost = 0 <0% loss.,
Approximate round trip times in milli-seconds:
    Minimum = 370ms, Maximum = 430ms, Average = 385ms
```

Another utility, nslookup, returns the IP address for a given host name and a host name for a given IP address.

Novell implements ping as a NetWare Loadable Module (NLM). Windows and UNIX/Linux operating systems use the **ping** command at the command line. Third-party ping utilities are available, some of which provide a graphical interface.

ARP and RARP

ARP refers to the protocol itself and to the command-line utility used to view and manipulate the ARP cache. You must understand the function of the protocol to properly use the utility.

ARP: The Protocol. ARP is the means by which networked computers map logical IP addresses to physical hardware (MAC) addresses. ARP builds and maintains a table called the *ARP cache,* which contains these mappings. RARP is used by a machine that doesn't know its IP address to obtain the information based on its MAC address.

ARP: The Utility. ARP is also a command-line utility provided with Windows and UNIX/Linux TCP/IP stacks that can be used to view and change ARP's IP-to-MAC address mappings. (Novell implements this as an NLM called tpcon.) With the ARP utility, you can display the contents of the cache and add or delete specific mappings, as shown in Example 8-4.

EXAMPLE 8-4 The arp Command Is Used to View the ARP Cache

```
c:>arp -a
Interface: 192.168.1.201 on Interface 0x2
    Internet Address      Physical Address      Type
    192.168.1.16          00-40-f6-54-d7-43     dynamic
    192.168.1.185         00-50-da-0d-f5-2d     dynamic
```

The following switches can be used with the **arp** command:

- **arp –a**—Displays the cache
- **arp –s**—Adds a permanent IP-to-MAC mapping
- **arp –d**—Deletes an entry

There are other switches included with specific vendors' implementations of ARP.

Netstat/Tpcon

It is often useful to view network statistics. The **netstat** command is used in Windows and UNIX/Linux to display TCP/IP connection and protocol information. Novell uses the tpcon NLM to accomplish this.

The **netstat** command provides a list of connections that are currently active, as shown in Example 8-5.

EXAMPLE 8-5 The netstat Command Is Used to View Connection Information.

```
c:>netstat
Active Connections
    Proto   Local Address   Foreign Address                 State
    TCP     DS2000:3301     msgr-ns18.hotmail.com:1863      ESTABLISHED
    TCP     DS2000:3450     constellation.tacteam.net:3389  ESTABLISHED
    TCP     DS2000:3860     ultra1.dallas.net:pop3          TIME_WAIT
    TCP     DS2000:3861     aux153.plano.net:pop3           TIME WAIT
```

In Example 8-5, you can see the protocol used for each connection, the local computer name and port number used for the connection, the "foreign" address (the remote computer name), and the state of the connection.

Several switches can be used with **netstat**, as shown in Table 8-8.

TABLE 8-8   netstat Switches and Their Functions

Switch	Function
-a	Shows all connections and listening ports
-e	Shows Ethernet statistics
-n	Shows addresses and ports
-p*	Enables you to display information only for selected protocol
-t, -u, -w, -x**	Enables you to display information for TCP, UDP, RAW, or sockets
-r	Shows the routing table
-s	Provides a summary of statistics for each protocol

* Used with Microsoft TCP/IP implementation

** Used with Linux TCP/IP implementation

Netstat statistics can be useful in troubleshooting TCP/IP connectivity problems. Example 8-6 shows the wealth of information available in summary (-s switch) mode. These error reports are especially helpful in diagnosing hardware and routing problems.

EXAMPLE 8-6 The netstat -s Command Displays TCP/IP Statistics

```
C:>netstat -s
IP Statistics
  Packets Received                  = 1091043
  Received Header Errors            = 0
  Received Address Errors           = 7
  Datagrams Forwarded               = 0
  Unknown Protocols Received        = 0
  Received Packets Discarded        = 0
  Received Packets Delivered        = 1091034
  Output Requests                   = 420049
  Routing Discards                  = 0
```

continues

EXAMPLE 8-6 The netstat -s Command Displays TCP/IP Statistics (Continued)

```
Discarded Output Packets                      = 0
Output Packets No Route                       = 0
Reassembly Required                           = 6
Reassembly Successful                         = 3
Reassembly Failures                           = 0
Datagrams Successfully Fragmented             = 12
Datagrams Failing Fragmentation               = 0
Fragments Created                             = 24
ICMP Statistics
```

	Received	Sent
Messages	994	1129
Errors	0	0
Destination Unreachable	12	82
Time Exceeded	0	0
Parameter Problems	0	0
Source Quenches	0	0
Redirects	0	0
Echoes	37	1010
Echo Replies	945	37
Timestamps	0	0
Timestamp Replies	0	0
Address Masks	0	0
Address Mask Replies	0	0

```
TCP Statistics
Active Opens                       = 3940
Passive Opens                      = 42
Failed Connection Attempts         = 77
Reset Connections                  = 930
Current Connections                = 2
Segments Received                  = 577343
Segments Sent                      = 388999
Segments Retransmitted             = 361


UDP Statistics
```

EXAMPLE 8-6 The netstat -s Command Displays TCP/IP Statistics (Continued)

```
Datagrams Received                   =  38481
No Ports                             =  475173
Receive Errors                       =  0
Datagrams Sent                       =  29404
```

Nbtstat

The Microsoft TCP/IP stacks included in Windows operating systems provide the nbtstat utility, which is used to display NetBIOS information. Example 8-7 shows the syntax and switches available with the **nbtstat** command.

EXAMPLE 8-7 Type nbtstat at the Command Line for a Display of the Syntax and a List of Available Switches

```
c:\>nbtstat


Displays protocol statistics and current TCP/IP connections using NBT
(NetBIOS over TCP/IP).


NBTSTAT [ [-a RemoteName] [-A IP address] [-c] [-n]
        [-r] [-R] [-RR] [-s] [-S] [interval] ]


  -a   (adapter status) Lists the remote machine's name table given its name
  -A   (Adapter status) Lists the remote machine's name table given its
                        IP address.
  -c   (cache)          Lists NBT's cache of remote [machine] names and their IP
                        addresses
  -n   (names)          Lists local NetBIOS names.
  -r   (resolved)       Lists names resolved by broadcast and via WINS
  -R   (Reload)         Purges and reloads the remote cache name table
  -S   (Sessions)       Lists sessions table with the destination IP addresses
  -s   (sessions)       Lists sessions table converting destination IP
                        addresses to computer NETBIOS names.
  -RR  (ReleaseRefresh) Sends Name Release packets to WINs and then, starts
                        Refresh


  RemoteName   Remote host machine name.
  IP address   Dotted decimal representation of the IP address.
```

continues

EXAMPLE 8-7 Type nbtstat at the Command Line for a Display of the Syntax and a List of Available Switches (Continued)

```
interval     Redisplays selected statistics, pausing interval seconds
             between each display. Press Ctrl+C to stop redisplaying
             statistics.
```

Ipconfig, Winipcfg, Config, and Ifconfig

TCP/IP configuration information can be displayed using the following utilities, depending on the operating system:

- **Ipconfig**—Windows NT and Windows 2000 (command-line)
- **Winipcfg**—Windows 95 and 98 (graphical interface)
- **Ifconfig**—UNIX and Linux (command-line)
- **Config**—NetWare (server console)

The configuration utilities can provide a wealth of information, including currently used IP address, MAC address, subnet mask, and default gateway; addresses of DNS and WINS servers; DHCP information; and services enabled. There is a variety of switches available, depending on the vendor and specific utility. See Example 8-8 for the results of using the **ipconfig** command with the **/all** switch in Windows 2000.

EXAMPLE 8-8 Configuration Information Is Displayed by the Windows 2000 ipconfig /all Command

```
c:\>ipconfig/all
Windows 2000 IP Configuration

        Host Name . . . . . . . . . . . : DS2000
        Primary DNS Suffix  . . . . . . : tacteam.net
        Node Type . . . . . . . . . . . : Hybrid
        IP Routing Enabled. . . . . . . : Yes
        WINS Proxy Enabled. . . . . . . : No
        DNS Suffix Search List. . . . . : tacteam.net


Ethernet adapter Local Area Connection:

        Connection-specific DNS Suffix  . :
        Description . . . . . . . . . . : 3Com EtherLink XL 10/100 PCI TX NIC
(3C905B-TX)
        Physical Address. . . . . . . . : 00-50-04-7C-C0-D2
```

EXAMPLE 8-8 Configuration Information Is Displayed by the Windows 2000 ipconfig /all Command (Continued)

```
DHCP Enabled. . . . . . . . . . . : No
IP Address. . . . . . . . . . . : 192.168.1.201
Subnet Mask . . . . . . . . . . : 255.255.255.0
Default Gateway . . . . . . . . : 192.168.1.16
DNS Servers . . . . . . . . . . : 192.150.87.2
                                   216.87.128.131
Primary WINS Server . . . . . . : 192.168.1.185
```

Tracert, Iptrace, and Traceroute

It is often useful to trace the route a packet takes on its journey from source computer to destination host. TCP/IP stacks include a route tracing utility that enables you to identify the routers through which the message passes. Depending on your operating system, you can use one of the following:

- **Tracert**—Windows
- **Iptrace**—NetWare NLM
- **Traceroute**—UNIX/Linux

Example 8-9 show the results of a trace using the **tracert** command, which has the following syntax:

tracert *destination hostname*

EXAMPLE 8-9 You Use tracert to Trace the Route of a Packet from Source to Destination

```
c:\>tracert dallas.net


Tracing route to dallas.net [204.215.60.1]
over a maximum of 30 hops:


 1   <10 ms   <10 ms   <10 ms   STARBLAZER [192.168.1.16]
 2    60 ms    90 ms    60 ms   dal-isdn0.august.net [216.87.128.117]
 3    80 ms    60 ms   100 ms   dal-gw-eth0.august.net [216.87.128.126]
 4    60 ms    70 ms    61 ms   dal-gw2-fe2-0.august.net [216.87.128.86]
 5    60 ms    70 ms   100 ms   500.Serial2-7.GW6.DFW9.ALTER.NET [157.130.216.157]
 6    80 ms    70 ms    60 ms   158.at-5-0-0.XR1.DFW9.ALTER.NET [152.63.100.186]
 7    60 ms   110 ms    70 ms   185.ATM6-0.XR1.DFW4.ALTER.NET [152.63.96.137]
 8    80 ms    70 ms    80 ms   195.ATM11-0-0.GW1.DFW1.ALTER.NET [146.188.240.41]
```

continues

EXAMPLE 8-9 You Use tracert to Trace the Route of a Packet from Source to Destination (Continued)

```
 9   90 ms   320 ms   171 ms   savvis-dfw-gw.customer.ALTER.NET [157.130.128.54]

10   90 ms    90 ms   100 ms   ETHOS-1.usdlls.savvis.net [209.44.32.10]

11  150 ms   130 ms   131 ms   cisco-plano-e0.dallas.net [204.215.60.1]


Trace complete.
```

As you can see, the trace shows the IP address and the name of the forwarding computer or router. The packet required five hops to reach its destination, which was a host named www.dallas.net. Roundtrip times (in milliseconds) are shown for each hop.

Summarizing TCP/IP Utilities

TCP/IP is a large and complex suite of protocols. Most implementations include a variety of utilities that can be used for information gathering and troubleshooting. Table 8-9 offers a summarization of the common utilities.

TABLE 8-9   TCP/IP Utilities

Utility	Use
ARP/RARP	To view IP address to MAC address entries that have been resolved by ARP protocol, to delete entries from the ARP cache, and to add permanent IP-to-MAC mappings
Netstat (Windows/UNIX), tpcon (NetWare)	To view network connections and protocol statistics
Netbtstat (Windows)	To view connections and statistics for NetBIOS over TCP/IP (NetBT)
Ipconfig (Windows NT/2000), Winipcfg (Windows 95/98), Config (NetWare), Ifconfig (UNIX)	To view TCP/IP configuration information such as IP address, subnet mask, default gateway, MAC address, services enabled, and more
Tracert (Windows), Iptrace (NetWare), Traceroute (UNIX)	To discover the route taken by a packet on its journey from the source to the destination computer and to identify the routers through which it passes
Ping	To determine IP connectivity between two systems

Application Layer Protocols

The TCP/IP suite includes a variety of application layer protocols that provide services such as terminal emulation, the uploading and downloading of files, and access to pages published on the World Wide Web. Most implementations include applications that use the following protocols:

- HTTP (Hypertext Transfer Protocol)
- SMTP (Simple Mail Transfer Protocol)
- NNTP (Network News Transfer Protocol)
- FTP (File Transfer Protocol)
- Telnet

The Internet application layer protocols and the programs that run on them are discussed in more detail in Chapter 9, "The Widest Area Network: The Global Internet."

Summary

Many protocols work in conjunction with the network/transport and higher-layer protocols to provide LAN and WAN communications. It takes many protocols, working together, to establish and maintain network communications between computers on a LAN or WAN. In this chapter, we discussed the three most popular network/transport protocol stacks: NetBEUI, IPX/SPX, and TCP/IP.

You learned that computer communication is based on binary numbers, yet humans prefer to use names to identify systems and resources. We discussed the available methods for resolving these "friendly" names to IP addresses that can be used by the computers.

This chapter focuses primarily on TCP/IP because it is the protocol of the global Internet and of most medium-sized to large LANs today. You learned about the suite of protocols that make up TCP/IP.

This chapter covers the basic concepts of IP addressing, and you learned about traditional address classes and CIDR, which is a new routing method that uses classless addressing. You learned about the two parts of an IP address, the role of TCP and UDP ports in getting a message to its destination, and how and why to subnet an IP network. You also learned about DHCP, which automatically assigns IP addresses to computers configured as DHCP clients.

The protocols used for network communications are complex. This chapter can provide only a limited overview. Many excellent books, websites, and classroom and online training courses cover these topics in depth.

Now that you have a basic understanding of how network protocols work, in the next chapter we discuss the largest and most complex network of all: the global Internet.

Further Reading

For an overview of IPv6, the next generation of the Internet Protocol, see playground.sun.com/pub/ipng/html/ipng-main.html.

An excellent resource on multicasting and the MBONE is available at www.savetz.com/mbone/ch3.html.

3Com provides a good basic overview of IP addressing, including subnetting, at www.3com.com/nsc/501302.html.

Review Questions

The following questions test your knowledge of the material covered in this chapter. Be sure to read each question carefully and select the *best* correct answer or answers.

1. Which of the following is the fastest and easiest to configure, but is a non-routable, network/transport protocol?

    A. NWLink

    B. NetBIOS

    C. NetBEUI

    D. IPX/SPX

2. Which of the following parts of an IPX address is based on the MAC address of the device?

    A. Node number

    B. Network number

    C. Subnet number

    D. Host number

3. Which of the following are connection-oriented? (Select all that apply.)

    A. TCP

    B. UDP

    C. IP

    D. SPX

    E. IPX

4. Which of the following is true of IP addresses? (Select all that apply.)

    A. IP addresses are made up of two octets.

    B. An octet in an IP address that consists of eight bits.

    C. IP addresses are 32-bit binary numbers.

    D. IP addresses are usually notated in hexadecimal format.

5. How many host computers can a Class B network theoretically have?

   A. 16,384

   B. 254

   C. 65,535

   D. 2,097,152

   E. Over 16 million

6. What is the default subnet mask for a Class C network?

   A. 255.255.255.255

   B. 255.255.255.0

   C. 255.255.0.0

   D. 255.0.0.0

7. Assuming classful addressing, to what address class does the IP address 190.23.201.6 belong?

   A. Class A

   B. Class B

   C. Class C

   D. Class D

8. What is the routing method that uses classless addressing, with the network ID following the IP address indicated by a "slash x"?

   A. CIR

   B. CD-R

   C. CIDR

   D. RIP

9. What is the function of DHCP?

   A. It resolves NetBIOS names to IP addresses.

   B. It translates private IP addresses to public addresses.

   C. It resolves IP addresses to MAC addresses.

   D. It automatically assigns IP addresses to client computers.

10. Which of the following TCP/IP utilities can be used to view the cache of IP addresses that have been resolved to MAC addresses?

A. Ipconfig

B. Iptrace

C. ARP

D. Nbtstat

Chapter 9

The Widest Area Network: The Global Internet

In Chapter 8, "Networking Protocols and Services," you learned about networking protocols. You learned that some protocols are more appropriate for small networks and others scale to very large multisite networks. The Transmission Control Protocol/Internet Protocol (TCP/IP) stack serves as the foundation for communications over the largest and most complex network of all: the global Internet.

In this chapter, we explore the evolution of the Internet as you learn more about popular Internet applications, such as the World Wide Web, e-mail, newsgroups, and file transfer. In addition, we discuss sophisticated modern technologies such as streaming media and live audio and video conferencing.

Next, we look at how packets are routed on the Internet. We discuss basic routing concepts, static and dynamic routing, and popular route discovery protocols. Toward the end of the chapter, you learn about the many organizations that oversee the operations of the Internet and keep it running smoothly.

The Evolution of the Internet

By definition, an *internet* is a network of networks, and the *Internet* is made up of thousands of large and small networks that are themselves all over the world. As you learned in Chapter 1, "Introduction to PC Networking," the Internet originated in the 1960s with ARPAnet, a joint project of the U.S. Department of Defense and major educational institutions.

In the early days of ARPAnet, which was during the peak of the cold war era, only a handful of elite government and university personnel had access to ARPAnet's "super network." A major goal of the military side of the so-called "internetting project" was to design a network that could survive nuclear devastation and provide continued communications. The universities, on the other hand, were interested in a way for researchers to quickly and easily share data.

The Development of the Backbone

The National Science Foundation (NSF) began to develop the backbone of the Internet in the mid-1980s, and it still provides some Internet services in the United States today. Other backbone facilities have developed as the Internet has

NOTE

An Internet *back-bone* is a group of pathways used by local networks to connect over long distances. The Internet backbones are made up of connection points called *nodes*.

grown to be a truly global network, and in 1995, the backbone project was privatized and the funding was distributed to regional networks. During the period from 1986 to 1995, the NSF spent approximately $200 million on development of the backbone.

As you can see in Figure 9-1, the Internet infrastructure uses a hybrid mesh topology. This topology provides redundancy so that if one link goes down, packets can take an alternate route to reach their destinations.

FIGURE 9-1
The Internet backbone is arranged in a hybrid mesh topology.

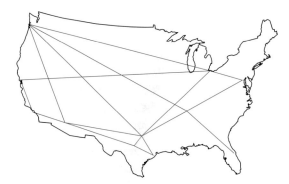

The U.S. infrastructure of today's Internet consists of a commercial backbone and a high-speed service called vBNS, Very High-speed Backbone Network Service.

The Commercial Backbone

The commercial backbone is an internetwork of commercially operated networks that are provided by companies such as AT&T, Sprint, UUNET (a division of WorldCom), BBN Planet, and Cable & Wireless USA. Internet service providers (ISPs) connect to these commercial networks.

The backbone providers and ISPs establish *peering agreements* to carry one another's network traffic. These agreements govern the interconnection and exchange of data.

The Regional Bell Operating Companies (RBOCs) own much of the physical cabling in this country, and they lease it to the providers. The provider networks connect with T-1, T-3, or OC-3 lines.

The vBNS and the Supercomputer Centers

The vBNS is used for scientific purposes. It connects five "supercomputer" centers, which are at the following locations:

- National Center for Supercomputing Applications (NCSA), Urbana, Illinois

- National Partnership for an Advanced Computational Infrastructure (NPACI), San Diego, California
- Cornell Theory Center, Ithaca, New York
- National Center for Atmospheric Research, Boulder, Colorado
- Pittsburgh Supercomputing Center, Pittsburgh, Pennsylvania

The vBNS is funded by the NSF through a contract with MCI. It is made up of OC-3 connections running at 155 Mbps and up. The vBNS network is connected to national network access points, or NAPs, which are discussed later in this chapter. The commercial backbone also uses the NAPs.

The Internet2 Project

The vBNS is part of the Internet2 Project, a joint effort of U.S. universities and the U.S. government. It is aimed at developing a high-speed backbone that can be used as a test bed for deployment of new technologies. For example, Internet2 has deployed IPv6, and sponsored the Qbone, a quality of service (QoS) testing initiative.

Internet2 is not a separate physical network, and it is not intended to replace the "old" Internet. Rather, it is a consortium of entities that have banded together to develop and test new technologies before they are deployed on the commercial Internet.

The Components of the Internet

To modern users, the Internet seems simple. You plug your computer's modem into a phone line, configure the software to dial up an ISP or online service, type in an account name and password, and you're there. If your computer is connected to a LAN with dedicated Internet access, it's even less complicated.

Most people don't appreciate or understand the sophistication of the technology that makes this possible any more than they understand what *really* happens when they turn on the television and tune to a favorite program. They just accept it as one of those miracles of modern science.

Because you're a student of technology, however, we're guessing that you want to learn about the components that are involved in accessing a website or sending an e-mail message to someone across the street or even across the world. Thus, in the following sections, we discuss the interaction of the following elements that make up the Internet:

- Local computer or LAN connected to the Internet
- ISP

- Regional network
- NAPs
- Metropolitan area exchanges (MAEs)

The Local Computer or LAN

The first element required for initiating an Internet connection and communication is a local computer running the appropriate protocols and software or connecting to a LAN that has a proxy/NAT connection.

TCP/IP is the protocol stack of the Internet, so it must be installed and configured on the local computer or proxy/NAT machine. For a dialup connection, dialer software is needed. Modern operating systems have dialers, such as Microsoft's Dialup Networking component, built in.

The ISP

When the connection is made with an ISP, a computer becomes a remote client on the ISP's local network.

In the beginning of the Internet era, your local computer or LAN had to have a direct connection to the Internet backbone. This was expensive and not feasible for individuals and small companies.

ISPs own or rent the costly and complex equipment used to establish a *point of presence*, or access point, on the Internet. ISPs lease dedicated high-speed lines from the telephone company or, in the case of large ISPs, own their own. Small local ISPs might not be connected directly to the backbone, but instead might go through a larger regional ISP that is directly connected.

The Regional Network

ISPs that aren't directly connected to the national backbone pay a *regional provider* to connect to a regional network that in turn is plugged into the national backbone. Major regional networks in the U.S. include the following:

- **BARRNet**—Located in north-central California
- **Westnet**—Covers the western part of United States
- **NEARNET and NYSERNet**—Covers the northeastern part of the United States
- **MIDnet**—Covers the central part of the United States
- **SURAnet**—Covers the southeastern part of the United States
- **CICnet**—Covers the midwestern part of the United States

NAPs

NAPs are the locations at which the access providers are interconnected. The NSF developed and funded the four original NAPs in the United States. They are located in or near the following cities and are operated by the listed companies:

- **New York**—Sprint
- **Washington, D.C.**—WorldCom
- **Chicago**—Ameritech
- **San Francisco**—Pacific Bell

The NAPs provide switching facilities, but not all Internet traffic must go through NAPs. ISPs within geographic areas can make their own interconnections and peering arrangements with one another.

MAEs

A MAE is a point where ISPs connect to each other and traffic is switched between them. The Washington, D.C., NAP is also known as MAE EAST. WorldCom operates an access point, MAE WEST, in Silicon Valley, California. MAE EAST and MAE WEST are the first-tier MAEs.

There are five second-tier MAEs: MAE CHICAGO, MAE DALLAS, MAE HOUSTON, MAE LOS ANGELES, and MAE NEW YORK. The MAE itself does not route data; ISPs connected to the MAE perform the routing. However, the MAEs do provide *collocation*, or housing, for the routers belonging to the ISPs.

The MAE-connected routers require very large routing tables, using top-of-the-line routers such as those from the Cisco 7000 series. WorldCom owns the switching platforms, which are linked in a Fiber Distributed Data Interface (FDDI) network. MAE devices are administered through Sun workstations, using the Simple Network Management Protocol (SNMP) and customized monitoring applications.

Major national ISPs, such as Sprint and Netcom, connect to the two first-tier MAEs. Regional and smaller ISPs connect to the second-tier MAEs, where smaller routers (for example, the Cisco 4500-M) are used.

How Internet Components Work Together

How do the components of the Internet relate to the typical Internet user? When you click to send an e-mail message, the e-mail client application formats the data, and it goes through the process you learned about in Chapter 3, "Networking Concepts, Models, and Standards." Figure 9-2 shows a simplified version of this sequence of events.

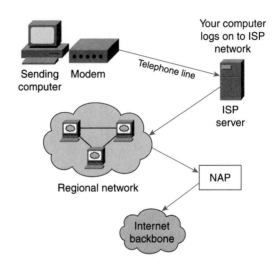

FIGURE 9-2
A message is
sent across the
Internet.

1. The data is broken into manageable chunks, which are called packets.

2. The networking protocols add header and trailer information.

3. The binary 1s and 0s are converted to electrical signals or light pulses to travel over the physical medium.

4. If your computer is on a LAN, the data travels over the local network to a server or router that is connected to a phone line or dedicated leased line.

5. If a modem connection is used, the packets are encapsulated inside a link protocol, such as Point-to-Point Protocol (PPP) or Serial Line Internet Protocol (SLIP), and the digital signals are *modulated* to travel over the analog phone line.

6. The signals reach the ISP's *remote access server (RAS)*, which is configured to accept dial-in connections, or you might have a direct dedicated link to the ISP. With a dial-in account, you log on to the server by entering a user name and password.

7. The computer becomes a remote node on the ISP's local network.

8. The data travels from the ISP's server to the regional network to which the ISP is connected (if you use one of the largest national ISPs, this step may be skipped).

9. Your data travels through one of the major NAPs, if necessary, and onto the commercial Internet backbone.

10. At the other end, the data goes through another NAP, another regional network, and then the ISP at the receiving side, which delivers the data to the destination computer (for example, the ISP's mail server).

11. The data is finally delivered to the intended user when the user's e-mail client connects to the ISP's or company's mail server and downloads the contents of the mailbox set up for that user account.

As you can see, the process is complex and your data packet must travel through numerous servers and routers, across a variety of physical media, to reach its location. Yet the typical e-mail message can go across the country in a matter of minutes. No wonder it seems a bit miraculous.

Now that you understand *how* packets travel across this very wide-area network (WAN) from one city or country to another, in the next section we look at some of the uses to which this technology has been applied. What does the Internet *do* and what can you do with the Internet? Perhaps more importantly, after you've decided *what* you want to accomplish, how do you do it?

What the Internet Does

If you had to sum up the purpose of the Internet in one word, it would probably be *communication*. Communication can be one-way or two-way, for business or for pleasure, conducted in real-time or not. In addition, the communication can take many different forms.

Just a few of the things that users can accomplish via the Internet are

- Surf the World Wide Web for information or entertainment and create web pages for others to access.
- Send and receive e-mail messages in a fraction of the time it takes a letter to make its way through the postal system.
- Join a mailing list and exchange messages with people who share a common interest, occupation, or characteristic.
- Participate in or start a newsgroup, which serves as a type of virtual bulletin board where interested parties can read and post messages.
- Transfer files such as documents, graphics, and sounds from another computer to your own, or from your computer to another, using the File Transfer Protocol (FTP).
- Use a terminal emulation program such as Telnet to connect to a remote computer to run applications or to read the data on its hard disk.
- Listen to radio broadcasts or watch streaming video productions.

- Chat in real time with one or more persons in distant locations.
- Have a virtual meeting sharing documents, whiteboard drawings, and communicating via text, audio, and video.
- Make long distance telephone calls without incurring telephone company long distances charges by using *telephony* technologies that combine telecommunications and computer technology.
- Establish a secure virtual private network by tunneling through the Internet to a private server or local-area network (LAN).

In the following sections, we examine each of these possibilities and discuss the applications and protocols that make them possible.

The World Wide Web

To many people, the Internet is synonymous with the World Wide Web. The term *Internet address* is sometimes used to describe web page URLs, such as www.yahoo.com. Despite the many other applications that run over the Internet, the Web *is* the Internet for a large number of network users.

In the following sections of this chapter, we discuss the components of the Web:

- Hypertext Transfer Protocol (HTTP)
- Hypertext Markup Language (HTML)
- Web servers
- Domain Name System (DNS)
- Web browsers

We also look at what's on the Web, who's using the Web, and how you can navigate your way around the millions of pages that make up the Web without getting hopelessly lost.

HTTP

The protocol of the Web is HTTP. As you know, a protocol is a set of rules, and HTTP governs how files (for example, text, graphics, sounds, and video) are exchanged on the Web. HTTP is an application layer protocol. The standards for HTTP were developed by the Internet Engineering Task Force (IETF), and the current version is HTTP 1.1.

As its name implies, HTTP is used to exchange *hypertext* files. These files can include links to other files. A web server runs an HTTP service or *daemon*, which is a program that services HTTP requests. These requests are transmitted by HTTP client software—another name for a web browser.

When a user types a web address or URL into a browser's address box or clicks a hyperlink, the browser sends the request to the web server at that address. The web server processes the request and returns the requested resource. The resource might be an HTML page, a graphic, a sound file, or some other type of file.

If the requested resource is not on the web server, or if the user did not have proper permissions to access the resource, the web server returns an error message. Common HTTP error messages include the following:

- **401/Unauthorized**—Access denied because of an improper authorization header.
- **403/Forbidden**—Access denied for unknown reasons.
- **404/File not found**—The resource is not on this server.
- **500/Internal error**—The server had a problem that prevented it from processing the request.

HTML

Web pages are created by *web designers*, who use HTML to indicate to web browser software how the page should look. HTML includes tags to indicate boldface type, italics, line breaks, paragraph breaks, hyperlinks, insertion of tables, and so forth. Example 9-1 shows source code for a web page, and Figure 9-3 shows that page as displayed by the Microsoft Internet Explorer web browser.

EXAMPLE 9-1 The HTML Source Code Defines How a Web Page Is Displayed

```
<html>

<head>
<meta name="GENERATOR" content="Microsoft FrontPage 4.0">
<bgsound src="picflute.mid" loop="-1">
<title>Welcome to www.shinder.net</title>
</head>

<body bgcolor="#000000" link="#C0C0C0">
<div align="center"><center>

<table border="0" width="644" height="605">
  <tr>
    <td width="13" height="601" rowspan="2"></td>
    <td width="682" valign="top" style="margin-left: 4px; margin-right: 4px;
```

continues

EXAMPLE 9-1 The HTML Source Code Defines How a Web Page Is Displayed (Continued)

```
margin-top: 4px; padding-left: 2px; padding-right: 2px" colspan="3"
height="330"><p align="center"> </p>
  <p align="center"> </p>
  <p align="center"><img src="welcomegold.jpg" alt="welcomegold.jpg
(12428 bytes)" WIDTH="307" HEIGHT="108"><br>
  <big><font color="#808000"><strong>to<br>
  <a href="http://www.shinder.net">www.shinder.net</a></strong>
</font></big></p>
  <p align="center"><img src="goldtube1.jpg" alt="goldtube1.jpg (2642 bytes)"
WIDTH="450" HEIGHT="10"></p>
  <p align="center"><font color="#808000"> This is the starting point<br>
  to our many<br>
  diverse and sundry websites.<br>
  <br>
  <big><strong><em>Thank you for visiting our place in cyberspace</em>
</strong>. </big></font></p>
  <p align="center"><strong><font face="Arial" color="#FFFFFF"><small>NOTE:
These pages are designed for 800x600 resolution or better</small><br>
  <small>and are best viewed using Microsoft Internet Explorer 4.0 or above.
</small><br>
  <small>Click the icon to download the latest version.</small></font></strong>
</p>
  <p align="center"><a href="http://www.microsoft.com/windows/ie/
default.htm">
  <img src="Eastfield/ieget_animated1.gif" alt="ieget_animated[1].gif
(7090 bytes)" WIDTH="88" HEIGHT="31"></a></p>
  <p align="center"> </td>
</tr>
<tr>
  <td width="200" valign="middle" style="margin-left: 4px; margin-right: 4px;
margin-top: 4px; padding-left: 15px; padding-right: 15px" height="267">
<p align="center"><img border="0" src="tom0400.jpg" width="206" height="212">
</td>
  <td width="207" valign="middle" style="margin-left: 4px; margin-right: 4px;
margin-top: 4px; padding-left: 2px; padding-right: 2px" height="267"><em>
<font color="#408080"><strong><p align="center"><img src="swirl_mask.gif"
```

EXAMPLE 9-1 The HTML Source Code Defines How a Web Page Is Displayed (Continued)

```
alt="swirl_mask.gif (34856 bytes)" WIDTH="201" HEIGHT="187"></strong></font>
</em></p>
  <p align="center"><a href="http://www.dallas.net/~shinder">
<img src="goldframebutton.jpg" alt="goldframebutton.jpg (4461 bytes)"
WIDTH="184" HEIGHT="65"></a></td>
  <td width="247" valign="middle" style="margin-left: 4px; margin-right:
4px; margin-top: 4px; padding-left: 15px; padding-right: 15px" height="267">
<p align="center"><img src="family/me0399.jpg" width="209" height="221"
alt="me0399.jpg (5916 bytes)"></td>
```

FIGURE 9-3
The page shown
in Example 9-1.

The HTML source code can be created with *web authoring software* (also referred to as an *HTML editor*), such as Adobe Pagemill, Macromedia Dreamweaver, Microsoft FrontPage, SoftQuad HoTMetaL Pro, and Sausage Software HotDog. Many web designers prefer to write the code manually in a simple text editor (for example, Notepad in Windows or vi in UNIX or Linux).

Web Servers

Once created, the HTML source pages are uploaded to a *web server,* a computer that is connected to the Internet or an intranet and that runs web server software such as Apache (for Linux/UNIX), Internet Information Server (IIS) (for Microsoft), Domino (for Lotus), or Suitespot (for Netscape). The web server *hosts* the web documents. All graphics, sound files, and other embedded files that appear in the document are also uploaded to the web server.

The web server must have a connection to the Internet and a public IP address by which it can be identified. Remember that each server on the Internet has a host name, such as *www,* a second-level domain name, such as *tacteam,* and a top-level domain, such as *net.* Together they make up the fully qualified domain name (in this example, www.tacteam.net) that serves as the web site's URL.

The Domain Name System (DNS)

When a web surfer types the URL "www.tacteam.net" into a web browser and prefaces it with "http://" (which indicates HTTP, the protocol used for web documents), the request goes to a DNS server that translates the name into an IP address. The browser uses the IP address to locate the web server on the Internet and then sends a message requesting the page. The web server returns the files that make up the requested page. The page is displayed in the user's browser.

Web Browsers

The two most popular web browsers (HTTP client software) are Microsoft Internet Explorer and Netscape Communicator. Numerous other browsers are available, such as the following:

- **Lynx**—A text-only browser that can be used on various platforms, including DOS, Macintosh, Windows, OS/2, AIX, SCO, Linux, and others
- **Amaya**—A browser distributed by the World Wide Web Consortium (also called W3C)
- **Emacs/W3**—A web browser for UNIX, Windows, AmigaDOS, OS/2, and VMS
- **QNX Voyager**—A web browser for the QNX operating system
- **Opera**—A small, fast web browser that works in Windows, Linux, and BeOS (see Figure 9-4)

Some web browsers are *freeware* (that is, they cost nothing) or *shareware* (that is, you can try before you buy) and are available for download from the Web. Online services may have their own proprietary browsers, and ISPs often customize the versions of Internet Explorer or Netscape that they distribute to their customers.

FIGURE 9-4
Opera is a small, fast web browser that is available for multiple platforms.

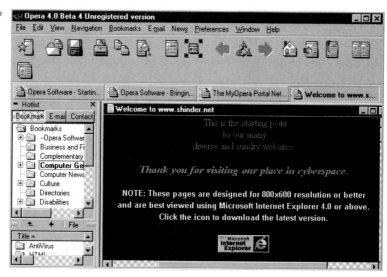

What's on the Web?

From simple text documents to animated Java- or ActiveX-powered multimedia shows, the Web seems to have it all. To say the Web has increased our ability to gather information quickly and easily would be an understatement. Having Web access is a bit like having the entire Library of Congress at your fingertips—and more.

The Web has come a long way since its humble beginnings. The term hypertext was first coined by Ted Nelson, who included it as part of his software project called Xanadu. Tim Berners-Lee (often called the father of the Internet) is recognized as the visionary who used this interactive technology to create the World Wide Web. Berners-Lee remains active in the World Wide Web Consortium, which is an international organization that promotes the development of standards for web technologies.

Who's Using the Web?

Increasingly, it seems as if almost everyone is on the Web. Having a web presence is becoming almost mandatory for many types of businesses. Personal and family home pages are commonplace. Even those who don't have their own pages are busy surfing and examining others' offerings.

The National Science Foundation Network (NSFNET) kept statistical information on the types of traffic that passed through the backbone and did so until 1995, which is when the NSF stopped operating the backbone and commercial interests took over. According to their data, in June 1993 the Web accounted for only 0.5 percent of Internet traffic. By March 1995 that figure had grown to 23.9 percent. According to a survey of NUA, an internationally respected Internet consulting company, as of April 2000, roughly 52 percent of U.S. homes had access to the Web. According to many sources, the number of pages posted on the Web roughly doubles every year. In addition, as of January 2000, the Web was believed to contain approximately 2 billion pages and over 450 million images. These estimates are, of course, dynamic—hundreds of thousands of web pages are added daily, and others are removed or changed.

The price of personal computers has fallen and Internet service has become affordable. Some companies even offer the service for free; it is supported by advertising. This means that more people are getting connected all the time. Schools are incorporating Internet-connected computers into the classrooms and computer literacy into the curriculum. Cybercafes, where users can rent surf time, are also appearing.

Those who have Internet access use the Web for a variety of purposes, and many use it daily. Consumers use the Web to learn about products and make purchases. Students use it to research papers. Educators use it to disseminate reading lists and course materials. Travelers use it to make flight and hotel reservations and to assist in choosing vacation destinations. Patients use it to learn more about their medical conditions and treatments. Business people use it to learn about their industry and their competitors and to market their own goods and services.

The Web is evolving into a technology that is changing our society and our lives in the same profound manner as did electricity, television, and the telephone. Already the question isn't so much "Who's using the Web?" as it is "Who's *not* using it?"

Finding Your Way Around the Web

The incredible amount of information available to the public on the Web is both its greatest strength and its biggest weakness. Locating all the relevant data on a given topic—and *only* the data that's relevant—can be a daunting task.

In the following sections, we look at how search engines, metasearch engines, and portals can help you navigate through the vast amount of data available on the Web.

Search Engines. Hundreds of *search engines* have been developed in an attempt to make web navigation easier. Search engines are sites that contain interactive indexed databases that categorize web sites, usually by *metatags*. A metatag is a keyword designated by the page designers in the HTML code. According to www.wwwmetrics.com, a site devoted to web statistics, 85 percent of users make use of search engines, but less than 20 percent of the public web is indexed by search engines.

Yahoo (www.yahoo.com) was the first major search engine and is still used by many today. Other popular search engines include the following:

- **Lycos**—www.lycos.com
- **DirectHit**—www.directhit.com
- **Excite**—www.excite.com
- **AltaVista**—www.altavista.com
- **Northern Light**—www.northernlight.com
- **Google**—www.google.com

Most search engines work by referencing the keywords or metatags placed in the HTML source code by the designer of the web page. These keywords represent terms that a person would be likely to use when searching for documents related to the topic of the web pages. For example, if you designed a web page that featured your Siamese cat breeding business, you might place the following keywords into the HTML code as metatags: cat, Siamese, and breeding.

Search engines have three basic components:

- The *spider*—A program that travels from one link to another on the Web, gathering indexing information
- The *index*—A database that stores a copy of each web page that the spider collects
- The *search/retrieval* mechanism—An interface that provides a way for users to enter their queries and receive the results

Some search engines can actually search the entire text of each document rather than only the keywords. This results in many more *hits* (a page that matches the search criteria), but also might result in many irrelevant matches. For example, if you need information on dessert recipes and type in the word "dessert," you would get back a list of pages that contain the word "dessert" anywhere on the page. Thus, a page containing a comment about someone getting his "just desserts" shows up as a match.

It is important to read the instructions for using a particular search engine. Some allow Boolean searches, which are arguments that use AND, OR, or NOT. In the previous example, you could have narrowed your search by entering "dessert AND recipe" into the query field.

NOTE

Most search engines cannot index the contents of websites that are password-protected. Also, be aware that it takes some time for documents to be indexed after they are uploaded to a web server, so search engines often do not contain documents that were posted recently.

Metasearch Engines. *Metasearch* engines, such as the following, compile the results from several engines:

- MetaCrawler—www.metacrawler.com
- SavvySearch—www.savvysearch.com
- Ask Jeeves—www.askjeeves.com

A metasearch engine (sometimes referred to as a *meta engine)* does not maintain its own index. It utilizes the indexes of other engines by searching multiple databases simultaneously and then collating the results into one comprehensive list. Sophisticated meta engines can detect and remove duplicate results.

Web Portals. Many search engine sites also serve as web *portals.* A portal is a web site that aspires to become the "start page" for users, a point to which they frequently return for links, news, web mail, maps, phone directories, and community forums. Users can customize their personal start pages to reflect their own interests. For example, you can choose to have the portal page display local news and weather for your area. In addition, you can select specialty topics such as sports, business, technology, and entertainment for which current news and features are displayed when you access the page.

Online services (such as AOL and MSN) and ISPs often provide portals for their users.

Other Web Services

In addition to text-and-graphics pages with links to other pages, the Web offers sophisticated services such as the following:

- Animations
- Real-time chat boards
- Live and replayed video (using web cams and RealVideo)
- Live and replayed audio broadcasts (using RealAudio)
- Virtual reality (VRML) games
- 3-D "walkarounds" and panoramas
- E-commerce sites (that is, interactive shopping)
- Web-based e-mail services

Many services (such as those that allow you to send e-mail, read newsgroup postings, chat, and transfer files) that at one time required separate applications are now available as functions built into web browsers.

E-mail and Mailing Lists

E-mail is one of the most-used services on the Internet. According to some sources, more than 6 billion e-mail messages per year travel over the Internet and through online services.

In the following sections, we examine the advantages and disadvantages of e-mail compared to other forms of communication, examine how e-mail client and server software works, and discuss the uses of Internet mailing lists, which are mass e-mail distribution lists.

The Advantages of E-mail

E-mail has many advantages over other forms of communication. It combines many of the benefits of traditional "snail mail" (that is, postal delivery) with the benefits of telecommunications, and it manages to avoid some of the downsides of both.

Like telephone calls, e-mail communications can be quick and informal. Like postal letters, e-mail messages can be read at the recipient's leisure, and they can be printed so that a permanent record is preserved. In many ways, it's the best of both worlds.

E-mail need not be plain text. Modern e-mail client programs allow you to attach files (such as word processing documents, pictures, and audio and video files) and format text with special fonts, colors, and backgrounds.

E-mail is also significantly less expensive than postal mail, especially for very large documents. It is also less expensive than long distance telephone calls. E-mail provides a way for friends and relatives to keep in touch, for companies to engage in business correspondence in a convenient and cost-effective way, and for advertisers to distribute bulk mailings at a fraction of the expense of postal mailings. (This last benefit causes one of the inevitable *disadvantages* of electronic mail, which we discuss next.)

Disadvantages of E-mail

Spam, or unsolicited commercial e-mail, is a growing problem for users and ISPs. Many organizations now attempt to curb the flow of mass-mailed messages. Many modern e-mail programs have built in "junk mail" filters that flag suspicious messages, move them to a separate folder, or even delete them automatically on arrival.

E-mail shares a disadvantage with all written communication: the potential for misinterpretation. Studies show that human beings are very dependent on visual and tonal clues to interpret the meanings of one another's spoken words. Body language, facial expression, and changes in vocal pitch tell us whether the speaker is sincere, sarcastic, playful, angry, and so on. E-mail and other written communications often leave us unsure as to the intent of the writer. To address this problem, the use of *emoticons* (also called *smileys,* although they encompass a broad range of emotions), text-based icons representing smiles, frowns, and other body language indicators, has become common among e-mail users.

Because it is informal, e-mail is sometimes sent impulsively because there is less of an inclination to "think about it before you send it." This has resulted in e-mail's reputation for rudeness in some circles. E-mail *flame wars* (that is, back-and-forth personal attacks, often escalating to vulgarity) are common on the Internet.

Finally, privacy issues are a concern with e-mail, and the laws in most jurisdictions about e-mail are still in flux. Generally, e-mail messages can be intercepted at any point along the journey from sender to receiver. (There are encryption methods available, which will be discussed in Chapter 14, "Protecting the Network.") Nonetheless, it is advisable for e-mail users to consider anything sent across the Internet to be more like a postcard (which can be read by anyone whose path it crosses) than like a sealed, private letter.

E-mail Software

The phrase "e-mail software" can mean one of two things: e-mail server software or e-mail client software. Both are discussed in the following sections.

E-mail Servers and Internet Mail Protocols. E-mail servers use standards-based protocols such as Simple Mail Transfer Protocol (SMTP), Post Office Protocol (POP, of which version 3 [POP3] is the current implementation), and Internet Message Access Protocol (IMAP, of which the latest version is 4 [IMAP4]).

An SMTP server is usually used for sending e-mail. When you compose and send a message in your e-mail client software, the message goes to the ISP's SMTP server, which then sends it out onto the Internet using the TCP/IP standard—SMTP.

Sendmail is a popular UNIX SMTP server program. If you are connected to a company LAN, the company might maintain its own internal e-mail servers (for example, Exchange Server). In that case, messages go through the local mail server, which routes internal mail to the correct recipient and forwards mail to the ISP if the address is outside the company.

POP servers receive e-mail addressed to a specific account name (such as deb@shinder.net) and hold it in a folder called a *mailbox*. When the POP3 mail client on the local computer connects to the server, the mail is downloaded to the local hard disk. Normally, it is deleted from the server at the

NOTE

SMTP is used for transferring mail from one point to another across the Internet. POP and IMAP are used to read and manipulate incoming e-mail messages after they have been delivered to your mail server.

same time (although you might be able to configure your mail client to leave a copy of each message on the server).

IMAP servers also receive mail, but they are more sophisticated than POP servers. With IMAP, a mail client can view the headers of messages and choose which ones to download. You can delete messages on the server without ever downloading them to your local machine.

Examples of popular mail servers include Microsoft Exchange, Netscape Messaging Server, Post Office, Sendmail, SLmail, IMail, and MDaemon.

E-mail Clients. E-mail client software is an application that allows you to compose and read e-mail. The application must be configured to connect to mail servers. Some of the many e-mail client applications available include the following:

- Eudora
- Pegasus
- Microsoft Outlook Express
- Netscape Mail

There are also personal organizer and collaboration programs, such as Microsoft's Outlook 2000 and Lotus Notes, that combine e-mail with other functions such as calendaring/scheduling, task lists, and contacts databases. Figure 9-5 shows an example of a popular e-mail client, Eudora.

Most modern e-mail clients allow you to organize received mail into folders. Some allow you to set up rules or filters to automatically sort the mail as it comes in. Many allow you to send and receive e-mail that is formatted in HTML so that an e-mail message can use some or all the elements of a web page (embedded graphics, sound, backgrounds, and even scripts).

Mailing Lists

Electronic discussion lists are a popular use of e-mail on the Internet. Don't confuse them with unsolicited mass mailings; mailing lists are distributed to large numbers of addresses, but to get the mail from a list, you must join the list. In some cases, the list owner or moderator must approve your membership request because many lists have defined membership criteria.

There are mailing lists devoted to almost every topic imaginable. Numerous professional lists exist. Through these lists, groups of doctors, attorneys, police officers, artists, writers, computer engineers, and so on can discuss issues pertaining to their fields. There are also lists for hobbyists, such as coin collectors, chess players, video gamers, amateur photographers, and pet owners. There are even lists devoted to books, sports, entertainers, television shows, and software programs—the list of lists goes on almost endlessly.

NOTE

You don't always have to have e-mail client software installed to send and read e-mail. Many web-based e-mail sites are available. These sites allow you to compose, send, and receive e-mail using your web browser. In many cases, web-based e-mail accounts are free—although you do have to have a way to connect to the web to use them.

NOTE

A directory of mailing lists is maintained at www.liszt.com. It provides instructions on how to join a list or start one of your own.

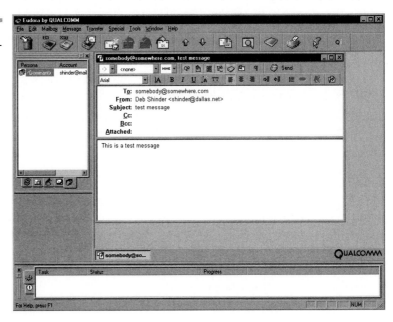

FIGURE 9-5
Eudora is a popular e-mail client program available for download at www.qualcomm.com.

Mailing lists can be small and informal, with mail distributed manually to a group of e-mail addresses using the cc (that is, carbon copy) function of e-mail client software. Larger lists are distributed through automated mailing list programs called list servers such as the following:

- **Majordomo**—Often run on UNIX servers.
- **ListServ**—Made by L-Soft, which runs on Windows NT.
- **Web-based list servers**—These include Egroups (www.egroups.com) and Topica (www.topica.com).

Newsgroups

Newsgroups are similar to mailing lists in that they are usually organized around specific interests or topics. The biggest difference is that once you join a mailing list (usually by sending an e-mail to a special "subscribe" address), all list messages are sent to the e-mail address under which you subscribed. To stop the messages, you must unsubscribe from the list.

In most cases, you aren't required to join a newsgroup (although there are some restricted newsgroups that require a username and password to gain access); you need only configure your newsreader software (such as Outlook Express, Netscape News, or Free Agent) to connect to a particular news server. You can then browse through all the messages posted there, read them, and post messages of your own.

If you decide you don't want to read the newsgroup anymore, you simply don't connect to it. Your e-mail box is not flooded with additional messages, which can happen with high-volume mailing lists.

Network News Protocol

The protocol used by most news servers and newsreaders to communicate with one another and manage newsgroups is Network News Protocol (NNTP). NNTP was originally called *Usenet*, and it used the UNIX-to-UNIX Copy Protocol (UUCP). NNTP has replaced UUCP as the standard for distribution of news. NNTP is an application layer protocol.

Newsgroup Software

As with e-mail, newsgroups require two types of software: *news server* software running on the machine that hosts the newsgroup and *news client* software, also called a *newsreader*. (Figure 9-6 shows a newsreader.)

News server software is often included with web server programs such as Microsoft IIS. Some e-mail programs and web browsers, such as Netscape Communicator, Microsoft Internet Explorer/Outlook Express, and Opera, come with built-in newsreaders.

FIGURE 9-6
Microsoft Outlook Express allows you to read news posted to a newsgroup on a news server.

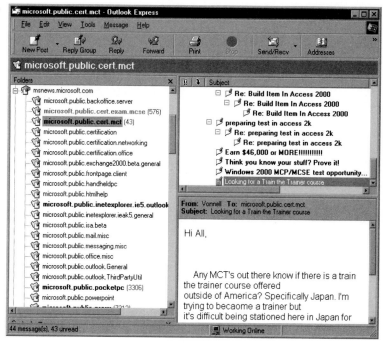

The news server shown in Figure 9-6 is named msnews.microsoft.com. (You can see the name in the left pane.) The list of newsgroups on that server to which the user is subscribed is shown under the server name. In the top-right pane is a list of messages posted to the selected newsgroup, microsoft.public.cert.mct. The selected message is displayed in the bottom right pane.

File Transfer

FTP allows you to upload files from your computer to a remote machine and download files from the remote system to your own hard disk.

FTP is used for many purposes, such as uploading web pages from a local computer to a remote web server and downloading drivers from a manufacturer's FTP server to your system.

Command-line FTP client software is included with the TCP/IP stacks of most operating systems. Numerous third-party FTP client programs offer easy-to-use graphical user interfaces. The latest versions of popular web browsers, such as Internet Explorer, Netscape, and Opera, include FTP functionality.

Example 9-2 shows a command-line FTP interface in which a connection was established with the Xerox FTP server by using FTP. The command has the following syntax:

```
ftp
open ftp_server_name
```

EXAMPLE 9-2 You Use the Command-Line FTP Client to Connect to an FTP Server

```
G:\>ftp

ftp> open ftp.xerox.com

Connected to ftp.xerox.com.

220 FTP.XEROX.COM

User (ftp.xerox.com:(none)): anonymous

331 Anonymous login ok, send your complete e-mail address as password.

Password:

230-


WELCOME TO THE DOCUMENT COMPANY - XEROX FTP SERVER.


Information about your login and any transfers you do are logged on this

server.  If you do not wish to be logged, please disconnect now.


Any comments, questions, etc. regarding this archive should be directed to
```

EXAMPLE 9-2 You Use the Command-Line FTP Client to Connect to an FTP Server (Continued)

```
webmaster@xerox.com.
230 Anonymous access granted, restrictions apply.
ftp> dir
200 PORT command successful.
150 Opening ASCII mode data connection for file list.
drwxr-xr-x 138 xerox      grpXerox     3072 Aug  3 04:55 pub
-rw-r--r--   1 root       other         293 Dec  3 1999 welcome.msg
226 Transfer complete.
ftp: 128 bytes received in 1.48Seconds 0.09Kbytes/sec.
ftp>
```

The first line in Example 9-2 starts the FTP client software. The second line opens the connection with the named FTP server (in this case, ftp.xerox.com).

Many FTP servers allow anonymous logins, but request that you use your e-mail address as your login password. When login is completed, the **dir** command provides a list of available directories that you can access. The **get** command downloads a file, and the **put** command uploads a file to the server.

Popular, graphical, stand-alone FTP clients include WSFTP, CuteFTP, and FTP Voyager. You can download these and other FTP applications from the Web. Some are freeware (such as the "lite" version of WSFTP), but most are shareware.

Telnet

Terminal emulation software allows a PC to appear and function as a "dumb terminal" to another computer (typically a mainframe). Users can then access programs on the host computer. Telnet is a terminal emulation client that uses the Telnet protocol, and it is included with most implementations of TCP/IP.

The Telnet protocol allows a computer running Telnet client software to connect to a Telnet server and interact with the remote server through a terminal window. Telnet does not allow the transfer of files from one machine to another; it does allow the user to run programs or view files on the server.

Figure 9-7 shows a Telnet session using the Telnet client included in Windows 2000. In this example, a remote session has been established with Fedworld, the National Technical Information Service of the U.S. government.

FIGURE 9-7
Telnet is a TCP/IP application layer protocol used to connect to remote servers.

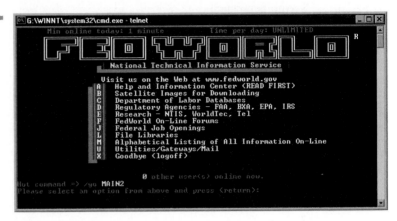

Streaming Media

With high-speed Internet connections becoming more available and using modern technologies such as ISDN, T-1, cable modem, and DSL, it has become possible to transmit audio or video signals in a continuous stream. This means that instead of downloading an entire file before you can hear or see it, you can use a continuous connection and get the data bit by bit.

To play streaming media without annoying pauses in audio or distracting movements in video, you need not only a fast connection, but also a computer with enough memory and processor power to handle the ongoing data flow. The falling prices of high-end PCs and Macintosh systems have contributed to the growing popularity of streaming media.

Applications such as Apple's QuickTime, Real Audio/Real Video, and the Windows Media Player are used to access and play streamed music and video clips.

Live Chat

Communication in real time is possible over the Internet using the Internet Relay Chat (IRC) system, web chat, or one of various "instant messaging" programs, as described in the following sections.

IRC and Web-Based Chat Rooms

IRC provides an environment where IRC clients connect to an IRC server and participate in real-time text "conversations" with one or more other users. IRC servers host "channels," or separate forums, usually devoted to specific topics or common interests. Popular IRC client applications include mIRC (one of the most popular shareware IRC programs), Visual IRC, and PIRCH (includes real-time video).

Web-based chat rooms are websites that use Java or other scripting languages to provide a forum in which web surfers can enter "chat communities" and send real-time text messages to one another.

Instant Messaging

Instant messaging programs allow you to send one-to-one messages to other people who are online and who have the correct software installed. In most cases, a dialog box pops up on the recipient's monitor screen and your text message appears as you type it. Some messaging services include "voice chat" or two-way video capabilities. (These capabilities are similar to audio conferencing tools, which we discuss in the next section of this chapter.)

Popular instant messaging applications include Mirabilis ICQ ("I seek you"), AOL/Netscape Instant Messenger, Microsoft MSN Messenger, Yahoo Messenger, Tribal Voice PowWow, and Elf Communications WinTalk.

Audio/Videoconferencing

Audio/video conferencing technologies enable you to conduct a meeting with people in remote locations. The technologies are growing in popularity in business, and they are used in educational circles to create a "virtual classroom" for online training.

Depending on the software used, you might be able to display documents during the conference and have those documents seen by all participants on their screens. You might also be able to mark on a virtual whiteboard that can be displayed on each participant's monitor.

Each participant in a conference must run the conferencing software and have a soundcard, microphone, and digital camera attached to the PC. Popular videoconferencing programs include CUseeMe (formerly White Pine Software) and Microsoft NetMeeting.

Standards have been developed for videoconferencing applications, and H.323 is an International Telecommunications Union (ITU) standard that governs various multimedia communications over IP and IPX that do not provide QoS. Conferencing applications that are H.323 compliant should be able to interoperate with one another.

Videoconferencing software can be divided into two categories:

- **Point-to-point**—A one-to-one connect that works somewhat like a video telephone
- **Multipoint**—Software in which more than two participants can communicate simultaneously

The International Multimedia Teleconferencing Consortium (IMTC) develops standards, sponsors events, and provides information. It is a nonprofit organization and membership is open to interested parties. The IMTC website is at www.imtc.org.

Internet Telephony

Internet telephony applications enable you to place long distance telephone calls using *voice over IP* technology without incurring telephone company charges for the calls. Early telephony applications were poor quality, and both the caller and the person being called had to have the same telephony software.

Newer technologies allow you to use Internet gateway servers to place calls to a regular telephone number. The person on the receiving end is not even required to have a computer or an Internet connection.

The following steps are involved in placing a call:

1. The caller dials the IP address of an Internet gateway server.

2. The call is routed over the Internet to the gateway server.

3. The gateway server routes the call to a PBX in the city being called.

4. The call is transferred to an outbound line to call the recipient's telephone number.

5. The call is recognized by the telephone company as a local call because it originates within the PBX in the same city.

NOTE

You can also use Internet telephony to send faxes over the Internet.

Some popular telephony applications include Internet Phone (for Windows), Webphone (for Windows), NetPhone (for Macintosh), Cyberphone (for UNIX and Windows), PGPhone (for Windows and Macintosh), and Speak Freely (for UNIX and Windows).

Most telephony applications use proprietary technology, and users can communicate only with others who have the same vendor software installed. Applications that are available for multiple platforms generally work across platforms as well. For example, a PGPhone user with a Macintosh computer can communicate with a PGPhone user with a Windows computer.

Virtual Private Networking

An exciting way to use the Internet is through *virtual private networking*, which is growing steadily in popularity because it saves companies money. VPN technology uses the Internet as a conduit, through which a secure connection can be established between a remote client and a private LAN, without incurring long distance charges that might result from dialing in to the LAN's server directly.

We discuss VPNs in detail in Chapter 16, "Virtual Private Networking."

TCP/IP Routing and the Internet

The Internet applications we have discussed in this chapter are dependent on the TCP/IP protocols that link the different operating systems and platforms that are on the Internet. In Chapter 8, you learned about the components of the TCP/IP protocol suite and how they work in a LAN environment. In this section, we focus on how TCP/IP operates on the global WAN.

Routability is an aspect of TCP/IP that is especially important to internetworking and Internet communications. *Routing* means forwarding packets from one network (or subnet) to another. However simple it might be in concept, IP routing is anything but simple in implementation. Some routing protocols or specialty areas, such as router configuration, require entire books of explanation. This chapter covers only the very basic routing concepts; see the resource list at the end of the chapter for more detailed sources of information.

How IP Routing Works

You learned in Chapter 8 that there are several reasons to divide a large TCP/IP network into subnets. One reason is that subnets cut down on broadcast traffic by allowing broadcast messages only to those computers that are on the same subnet as the sender. This increases network efficiency.

How do messages addressed to a computer on a different subnet get to their destinations? They get there by a process called *IP forwarding*.

IP handles logical addressing and routing of packets. When a packet is sent, IP looks at the source and destination IP address and subnet mask and performs the ANDing calculation (discussed in Chapter 8). This determines if the destination computer is on the same subnet or on a different one. If it is on the same subnet, the packet is delivered to the destination computer. If it is on a different subnet, IP sends the packet to the *default gateway*.

The default gateway is the IP address of a router connected to the local network and to at least one other network. The router consults its routing table to determine the best path to take to reach the destination network. The packet might travel through many routers to reach the network on which the destination computer resides. When the packet does reach the network, IP uses the host portion of the IP address to deliver it to the correct computer on that network.

> **NOTE**
>
> As you know, IPX/SPX is a routable protocol stack, just like TCP/IP. Most routers support both IP and IPX forwarding.

An Example of a Simple Routed Network

Let's look at a simple routed network. Network A's ID is 198.1.1.0. Network B's ID is 203.13.4.0. Both are unsubnetted Class C networks, and a Windows NT *multihomed* computer (that is, a computer with two network interfaces) connects them. The NT computer has IP forwarding enabled in its TCP/IP properties, which allows it to function as a router, as shown in Figure 9-8.

FIGURE 9-8
A packet is routed from a computer on Network A to a computer on Network B.

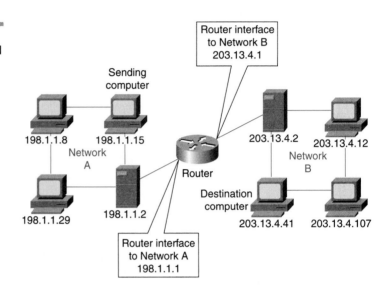

NOTE

It is customary to assign the first IP address of the network to the router. This is not required; it is merely a way to easily identify the router's address on the network.

A router (whether a dedicated device or a computer acting as a router) must belong to at least two networks. That means that the IP addresses assigned to its two network interface cards (NICs) are on different networks or subnets. In our example, one NIC is configured as 198.1.1.1 and the second is configured as 203.13.4.1.

If a computer on the first network, with an IP address of 198.1.1.15, sends a packet addressed to 203.13.4.41, IP examines the header to determine the IP addresses and subnet masks. The subnet mask for each is 255.255.255.0 because they are on unsubnetted Class C networks.

ANDing takes place:

```
   198.1.1.15  = 1000110 00000001 00000001 00001111
255.255.255.0  =11111111 11111111 11111111 00000000
      ANDed1    1000110 00000001 00000001 00000000
   203.13.4.41 =11001011 00001101 00000100 00101001
255.255.255.0  =11111111 11111111 11111111 00000000
      ANDed1    1001011 00001101 00000100 00000000
```

As you can see, the ANDed results are different; thus, IP concludes that the source and destination hosts are on different networks. The packet is sent to 198.1.1.1, the default gateway for the first network.

The packet is then passed across the gateway to the second network. Now the source address becomes the IP address on that side of the router, 203.13.4.1.

Let's try ANDing again:

```
   203.13.4.1  =11001011 00001101 00000100 00000001
255.255.255.0 =11111111 11111111 11111111 00000000
        ANDed  11001011 00001101 00000100 00000000
  203.13.4.41 =11001011 00001101 00000100 00101001
255.255.255.0 = 1111111 11111111 11111111 00000000
        ANDed  11001011 00001101 00000100 00000000
```

The ANDed results match; the source and destination are on the same network, so the packet is delivered directly to the destination host. See Figure 9-8 for a graphical illustration of this process.

Types of Routing Interfaces

A router must have an interface on more than one network; the networks can be LANs or WANs. A WAN interface can be a modem or an ISDN adapter, or it can be another WAN device instead of a NIC.

For example, when a LAN is connected to the Internet over a dialup connection, the router (or the computer functioning as a router) has a NIC that is connected to the LAN and a modem (the WAN interface) that connects to the "outside" network. Each interface is separately configured and each has its own IP address.

Static versus Dynamic Routing

Routers use *routing tables*, which are databases containing the routes to various networks. Figure 9-9 shows a routing table in a Windows 2000 Server computer. Note the Destination entry labeled "0.0.0.0." This is the *default route*, which is the IP address of the default gateway. Packets addressed to hosts outside the 192.168.1.0 network are sent to the default gateway address (192.168.1.16) for forwarding.

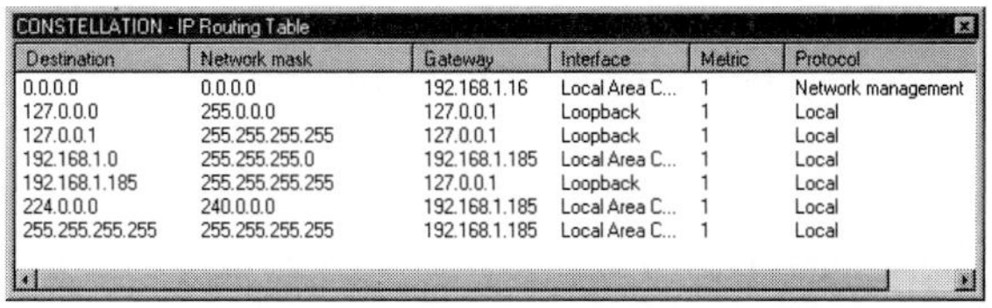

FIGURE 9-9
The routing table for a Windows 2000 Server contains routes to other networks.

Destination	Network mask	Gateway	Interface	Metric	Protocol
0.0.0.0	0.0.0.0	192.168.1.16	Local Area C...	1	Network management
127.0.0.0	255.0.0.0	127.0.0.1	Loopback	1	Local
127.0.0.1	255.255.255.255	127.0.0.1	Loopback	1	Local
192.168.1.0	255.255.255.0	192.168.1.185	Local Area C...	1	Local
192.168.1.185	255.255.255.255	127.0.0.1	Loopback	1	Local
224.0.0.0	240.0.0.0	192.168.1.185	Local Area C...	1	Local
255.255.255.255	255.255.255.255	192.168.1.185	Local Area C...	1	Local

Where does the router get the routes in its routing table? It depends on whether it is using static or dynamic routing, both of which are described in the following sections.

Static Routing

Static routing requires that the administrator manually enter into the routing table the IP addresses that define network routes. This can be done with the **route** command that comes with TCP/IP. This command-line utility allows you to add or delete routing table entries.

You can also use this utility and the **route print** command to view the routing table, as shown in Example 9-3.

EXAMPLE 9-3 You Use the route print Command to View the Static Routing Table

```
c:\>route print

===========================================================================
Interface List
0x1 ........................ MS TCP Loopback interface
0x2 ...00 50 04 7c c0 d2 ...... 3Com EtherLink PCI
===========================================================================
===========================================================================
Active Routes:
Network Destination        Netmask          Gateway       Interface  Metric
          0.0.0.0          0.0.0.0     192.168.1.16   192.168.1.201       1
        127.0.0.0        255.0.0.0        127.0.0.1       127.0.0.1       1
      192.168.1.0    255.255.255.0    192.168.1.201   192.168.1.201       1
    192.168.1.201  255.255.255.255        127.0.0.1       127.0.0.1       1
    192.168.1.255  255.255.255.255    192.168.1.201   192.168.1.201       1
        224.0.0.0        224.0.0.0    192.168.1.201   192.168.1.201       1
  255.255.255.255  255.255.255.255    192.168.1.201   192.168.1.201       1
Default Gateway:      192.168.1.16
===========================================================================
Persistent Routes:
  None
```

Static routing gives the administrator more control over the routes that are used. However, it requires a great deal of ongoing, painstaking effort to maintain the table because you must update it every time routes are added or changed. For large networks, this can become unmanageable.

Dynamic Routing

Dynamic routing uses protocols (which we discuss in the next section) to build and change routing tables automatically. These protocols allow routers on the network to communicate with each other and to exchange their routing table information. This offers several advantages:

- Less administrative overhead
- More fault tolerance (if a router goes down, others are informed and can take different pathways to the destination)
- Less chance for errors in routing table entries

Dynamic routing is the appropriate choice for all but the smallest routed networks.

Distance-Vector versus Link-State Protocols

Routing protocols fall into two categories: *distance-vector* protocols and *link-state* protocols. Distance-vector protocols are an established standard for dynamic routing. They are based on algorithms developed in the 1960s for ARPAnet routing. The basis of these protocols is "Bellman's equation," and the algorithms are often called the Bellman-Ford algorithms.

Distance-vector protocols assume that each router or host on the network has access to information about all destinations on the network. The routing tables include gateway addresses and a *metric* for each. The metric represents the total distance (in number of "hops") to the destination network. The algorithms calculate the best route to a specific destination based on these distances.

The "dynamic" aspect comes into play when the protocol sends an updated routing table to its adjacent neighbors. When an update is received, the routing information is compared to that which is already in the router's table. If the neighboring router's updated route has a lower metric than the route to that network in the router's current table, it adopts the lower-cost route.

Disadvantages of distance-vector protocols include the following:

- They are vulnerable to routing loops.
- The maximum distance for a route is 15 hops.
- They do not scale well for large networks.

The link-state protocol is a newer type of dynamic routing protocol. The algorithms used by these protocols create a "map" of the network's topology and maintain a *link-state database* that is based on this map. When changes occur, the database is updated.

With link-state protocols, routers broadcast route data and distribute the information to the rest of the network. This is more efficient than the distance-vector method and eliminates some of its problems. However, it creates problems of its own. The link-state database, for instance, can grow very large, resulting in high processor and memory overhead.

Convergence, or the dissemination of the update information to other routers, occurs more quickly with link-state protocols than with distance-vector protocols.

Common Routing Protocols

Dedicated routing devices, such as Cisco routers, support dynamic routing protocols. Some operating systems, such as Windows 2000, allow the use of dynamic protocols when the computer is functioning as a router. Dynamic routing protocols for IP include Routing Information Protocol (RIP) versions 1 and 2 and Open Shortest Path First (OSPF). The following sections describe these protocols in detail.

RIP

RIP, a distance-vector protocol, was one of the earliest dynamic routing protocols. (RFC 1058 provides detailed specifications.) The origins of RIP can be traced to a program called Routed, which was part of BSD UNIX 4.3. One advantage of RIP is its status as a recognized standard.

RIP routers "announce" their routing table information to other routers at periodic intervals. RIPv1 uses broadcast packets to send the announcement messages, and RIPv2 adds the use of multicast.

To address some of the problems inherent in RIP's distance-vector algorithms, the protocol supports the following features:

- Split horizon
- Poison reverse
- Triggered updates

Each feature is discussed in the following sections.

Split Horizon. *Split horizon* is a means of avoiding problems encountered when a router, after receiving an update from a neighboring router that has bad information, propagates that information *back* to the same neighboring router. This can cause the bad route to be propagated indefinitely. Figure 9-10 illustrates this problem, in which the following process occurs:

1. Router B receives information that Router C is down and sends that information to Router A.

> **NOTE**
>
> The NetWare Link Services Protocol (NLSP) is a dynamic routing protocol for IPX. It works in a manner similar to OSPF. The acronym "NLSP" is also used to refer to the Network Layer Security Protocol.

FIGURE 9-10
Split horizon addresses the problem of bad information being propagated back and forth between routers.

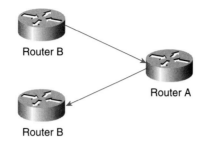

Router B

Router A

Router B

2. Router A updates its routing table to show that Router C is unavailable.

3. Router B receives information that Router C is back up, but before Router B can send its update to Router A, Router A sends Router B its own update, which shows that Router C is down.

4. Router B updates its routing table with Router A's information, which is now invalid.

With split horizon enabled, when Router A sends its updates to Router B, it does *not* include those routes that it received *from* Router B.

Poison Reverse. *Poison reverse* works similarly to split horizon. However, instead of omitting the routes received from Router B, Router A gives those routes a metric of 16. RIP has a distance limit of 15 hops, so the routes are considered unreachable.

Triggered Updates. With *triggered updates*, convergence of changes to the routing table takes place more quickly. For instance, you can specify a rule that if Router A changes the metric for a particular route, it must send the update immediately instead of waiting for the update interval to pass. This means that other routers get the new, correct information sooner and that problems caused by some routers having outdated route information are prevented.

OSPF

RIP works well for medium-sized networks, but a more sophisticated protocol is needed for large networks. Cisco and other routers, as well as some operating systems that support IP forwarding, use OSPF for this purpose.

OSPF is a link-state protocol that handles large, complex internetworks more efficiently than does RIP. The standards for OSPF can be found in RFCs 1247 and 1583. The link-state algorithm used by OSPF is not prone to routing loops and is generally more efficient than RIP.

A reason for this increased efficiency (despite the problems caused by large databases) is OSPF's method of dividing the network into *areas*. This provides a hierarchical structure for OSPF's routing tables, in contrast to the flat databases used by RIP.

Each OSPF router belongs to an area and maintains a database only for the gateways in its area. A special router, called an *area border router (ABR)*, connects every area to a special *backbone area*. When a packet needs to travel from one area to another, it goes through this backbone area. This method reduces the size of the routing tables and decreases the time spent recalculating routes when changes are made.

Who Owns the Internet?

Although the global Internet was built by the Department of Defense (DoD) and later managed by the NSF, each entity gave up its role years ago. The Internet today is a commercial enterprise, but an atypical one. Although the answer to "Who owns the Internet?" is "No one," hundreds of thousands of governments, companies, organizations, and individuals do own pieces of the network. For instance, the infrastructure runs on wiring and equipment owned by telephone companies, private businesses, and public agencies.

Although no one "owns" the Internet, many bodies, including the following, oversee aspects of its operations or set standards:

- Internet Society (ISOC)
- Internet Architecture Board (IAB)
- Internet Engineering Task Force (IETF)
- Internet Engineering Steering Group (IESG)
- Internet Assigned Numbers Authority (IANA) and Internet Corporation for Assigned Names and Numbers (ICANN)
- World Wide Web Consortium (W3C)

The following sections describe these organizations in detail.

ISOC

ISOC is made up of organizations and individuals devoted to the mission of providing leadership and developing standards to ensure that the Internet continues to evolve and benefit societies throughout the world.

ISOC coordinates Internet-related activities, funds the RFC Editor position, and provides a home base for organizations such as the IAB and IETF.

IAB

The IAB (originally the Internet Activities Board) is made up of 13 voting members, one of whom is the chairperson of the IETF. Other members are nominated by the IETF. The IAB publishes Internet Drafts and RFCs, forms research groups, and discusses issues affecting the Internet's infrastructure, community, and operation.

IETF

The IETF is made up of "working groups" devoted to specific internetworking issues. For instance, an active group is concerned with standards and implementation of the IPv6 transition. The IETF is open to anyone who wishes to participate; most of the discussion takes place, appropriately enough, over the Internet. Each working group has one or more mailing lists through which members communicate.

IESG

The IESG is part of ISOC and operates in conjunction with the IAB. It administers the process by which proposals become Internet standards, as defined in RFC 2026.

IANA/ICANN

IANA is responsible for the assignment of IP addresses and other unique identifiers on the Internet.

ICANN is a nonprofit organization made up of governmental, commercial, and technical members. ICANN coordinates the management of the Internet's domain name system and the allocation of IP addresses.

W3C

W3C develops common protocols and standards applicable to the Web. It is an international organization devoted to providing leadership and to creating technical specifications for the operation and infrastructure of the Web.

Summary

In this chapter, we discussed the evolution of the Internet, from ARPAnet to the present. You learned about the Internet backbone, which provides the pathways used by local and regional networks to connect over long distances. We discussed both the commercial backbone and the vBNS, which is reserved for scientific purposes. You learned about the Internet2 project, a consortium of universities and government entities devoted to developing and testing new technologies.

We discussed the ways in which an Internet connection can be established and the roles of ISPs, regional networks, NAPs, and MAEs. After discussing how packets travel across the physical infrastructure, we turned our attention to the many applications used on the Internet and the protocols on which they run. We took a look at the World Wide Web, search engines, e-mail, newsgroups, file transfer, and Telnet. We also discussed modern technologies such as streaming media, live chat, audio/videoconferencing, and Internet telephony.

We addressed the role of TCP/IP routing on the Internet, and you learned some very basic routing concepts, such as the difference between static and dynamic routing. We briefly discussed distance-vector and link-state protocols in general, and RIP and OSPF in particular.

Finally, we talked about the bodies that oversee various aspects of the Internet, including the ISOC, IAB, IETF, IESG, IANA, ICANN, and W3C.

Now that you understand more about networking hardware and protocols and the largest network of them all, in the next chapter you will be introduced to the Network Operating Systems (NOSs) that run on servers to make their resources available on LANs and on the Internet.

Further Reading

For more information on WorldCom's MAE system, see http://208.234.102.97/MAE/doc/maedesc/maedesc1.html.

For a collection of maps showing the Internet backbones in the United States and Europe, as well as other useful Internet-related maps and graphical representations, see "An Atlas of Cyberspace" at www.cybergeography.org/atlas/atlas.html.

For more information about the World Wide Web and Web standards, see the W3C web site at www.w3.org.

For more information about Internet mail standards, see the Internet Mail Consortium website at www.imc.org.

For links to tutorials and resources related to videoconferencing, see http://netconference.about.com/internet/netconference/msub1.htm.

Review Questions

The following questions test your knowledge of the material covered in this chapter. Be sure to read each question carefully and select the *best* correct answer or answers.

1. The Internet backbones are groups of pathways used by local networks to make long distance connections. What are the related connection points called?

   A. Hosts

   B. Nodes

   C. Subnets

   D. Servers

2. What are the locations at which major Internet providers are connected to one another?

   A. ISPs

   B. vBNS

   C. Supercomputers

   D. NAPs

3. Which of the following is the defining characteristic of hypertext files?

   A. They are located on a web server.

   B. They are accessed through a URL address.

   C. They contain links to other files.

   D. They cannot contain embedded graphics.

4. Which of the following is the correct syntax for typing the URL of a remote website into a web browser?

   A. http:\www.acme\

   B. html://www.acme.com

   C. http://bigserver.acme.com/

   D. html:\acme.com

5. Which of the following is a web site that serves as a "starting point" for users and that is often provided by ISPs or online services for their customers and by major search engine sites?

    A. Metasearch engine

    B. Portal

    C. Default gateway

    D. Hyperlink

6. Which Internet mail protocol is run on servers receiving mail and allows you to view headers on the server and choose which ones to download?

    A. SMTP

    B. SNMP

    C. POP

    D. IMAP

7. NNTP is used for which of the following?

    A. Managing Internet mailing lists

    B. Running Novell NetWare over TCP/IP

    C. Accessing newsgroup posts

    D. Connecting to a remote computer to view files and run applications

8. Which of the following is used for engaging in text-based "live chat" over the Internet?

    A. IRC

    B. Telnet

    C. IGMP

    D. FTP

9. To what does the H.323 ITU standard apply?

    A. Web-page formatting

    B. Videoconferencing

    C. Transfer of files over the Internet

    D. Search engines

10. Which of the following is true of RIP? (Select all that apply.)

   A. RIP is a dynamic routing protocol.

   B. RIP divides the network into areas, including a backbone area to which all other areas are connected.

   C. RIP is more efficient and scalable than OSPF.

   D. RIP is a distance-vector protocol.

Network Operating Systems

A computer operating system is the software that provides the foundation on which the computer's applications and services run. Similarly, a *network operating system (NOS)* enables devices to communicate with other devices and to share resources across the network.

NOS is sometimes used to describe any operating system that has built-in networking components. This is in contrast to a *standalone* operating system, which is designed to be used in isolation. Generally, however, an NOS is an operating system, such as NetWare or NT Server, that runs on a network server. We use this latter definition in this chapter as we look at the following popular server operating systems:

- Microsoft Windows NT 4.0
- Microsoft Windows 2000
- Novell NetWare
- UNIX
- Linux
- Banyan Vines
- OS/2 Warp Server
- Apple NOS
- LANtastic

Before we address the characteristics of each NOS and the networks on which they run, we discuss some general principles of network administration in a client/server environment.

General Network Administration

A server-based network has one or more dedicated servers. The server is usually (but not necessarily) a machine with a faster processor, a larger amount of RAM, and a larger hard disk or disks than the client workstations that connect to it.

Although a server operating system can provide centralized administration and a centralized location for storing data, server-based computing is different from *centralized* computing, which is a term usually applied to mainframe networking. In a mainframe network, terminals connect to one large, powerful computer that does all the processing. In contrast, client workstations in a server-based network are powerful computers in their own right. Depending on the application, all processing may be done on the client machine, or the processing may be shared between client and server.

The client/server environment differs also from the *peer-to-peer* (or *workgroup*) environment, which we discussed in Chapter 2 (see Figure 10-1).

FIGURE 10-1
The workgroup, client/server, and mainframe environments

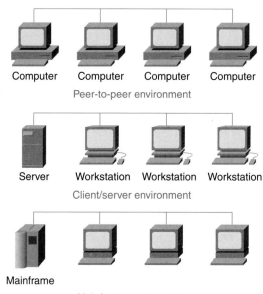

In the following sections, we discuss the characteristics of the client/server environment and how network resources are shared and managed.

The Client/Server Environment

The server-based network offers an environment that is easy to administer, back up, and secure. In this environment, the client machines request data and resources from the server. This server might share only files, or it might share printers, applications, modems, Internet connections, and other resources.

In the following sections, we discuss client/server applications and how a client/server network is configured.

Client/Server Applications

Client/server applications utilize the processing power of a server, such as a Microsoft Structured Query Language (SQL) database server, to optimize tasks such as database queries. Most large database applications use SQL; here's how it works:

1. A client, running a database client (called the "front end") such as Microsoft Access, requests data from the SQL server (called the "back end"). The request is then translated into SQL.

2. The SQL request is transmitted to the server, which conducts a search for the requested information on the computer where the database itself resides.

3. The server returns the results of the search to the client, which is then presented to the user by the client application.

Contrast the client/server application method to the one in which users create databases in Access (which is running on their local machines) and then store the databases on a file server. When a request is made, the entire database is downloaded to the client machine and the search process is conducted there. You can see that network bandwidth is conserved by the client/server application method.

The disadvantage of client/server applications is the initial cost. Client/server database programs, such as SQL Server or Oracle, are relatively expensive and might not be cost-effective in small networks where database queries are simple and infrequent.

Client/Server Network Configuration

The client/server network can be configured in one of two ways:

- The data can be located on one database server.
- The data can be *distributed*, or spread across, multiple database servers.

Figure 10-2 illustrates the difference between these two configurations.

A *data warehouse* is a central location where large amounts of data are stored. Traditionally, data warehouses were mainframe-based, but some PC NOSs, such as Microsoft's Windows 2000 Datacenter Server, are designed especially for this purpose. In data warehousing, the data can be stored on an array of disks on a single server or spread across the disks of multiple servers in a *server farm*.

Sharing Network Resources

The process for sharing resources over the network depends on the NOS. Some NOSs, such as those in the Windows family, share nothing by default. If you want resources to be available across the network, they must be explicitly shared in a process called *creating a share*. Other NOSs, such as NetWare, behave in the opposite fashion—resources are shared by default.

For a Windows 9*x* computer to share its resources, it must have *File and Print Sharing* enabled. A Windows NT or Windows 2000 computer must have the *server service* installed and started.

> **NOTE**
>
> Some network servers can run *terminal services* software, which allows a network client computer running the terminal client software to connect to the server and to run programs in which the server handles the processing. This is similar in some ways to the centralized computing environment.

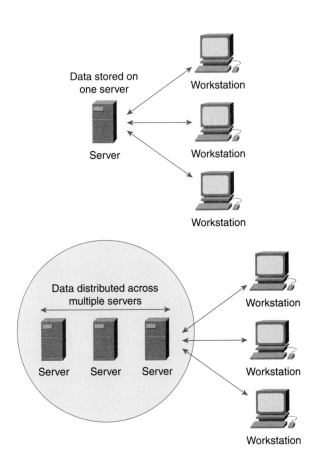

FIGURE 10-2
Data can be located on one server or distributed across multiple servers.

Data stored on one server

Server

Workstation

Workstation

Workstation

Data distributed across multiple servers

Server   Server   Server

Workstation

Workstation

Workstation

Computers are networked for the purpose of sharing resources, but this doesn't mean that every resource should be shared with every user. Thus, an NOS must provide a means for controlling access to files, folders, printers, and other resources. There are two ways to do this: share-level security and user-level security.

Share-level security is generally used on peer-to-peer networks using operating systems such as Windows 95 and 98. With share-level security, when you elect to share over the network a resource such as a folder, you set a password on that resource. For someone to access the shared folder, he or she must know and enter the correct password when prompted.

Despite its simplicity, share-level security becomes a nightmare when there are many users and many shares on the network. Each shared resource has a different password, and those passwords must be given to all people who are authorized to access those shares (see Figure 10-3).

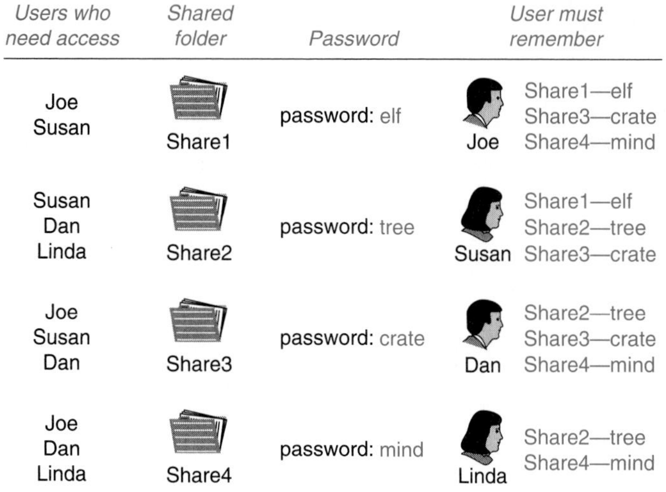

FIGURE 10-3
In share-level security, a password is assigned to each shared resource.

Users who need access	Shared folder	Password	User must remember
Joe Susan	Share1	password: elf	Joe — Share1—elf Share3—crate Share4—mind
Susan Dan Linda	Share2	password: tree	Susan — Share1—elf Share2—tree Share3—crate
Joe Susan Dan	Share3	password: crate	Dan — Share2—tree Share3—crate Share4—mind
Joe Dan Linda	Share4	password: mind	Linda — Share2—tree Share4—mind

User-level security is much easier to manage in a medium or large network than is share-level security. In user-level security, every user has a *user account* that is password-protected. The user logs on to the computer with that account. Each shared resource is configured to allow access for users who are authorized. When a user attempts to access a resource, the *access control list* associated with the resource, which contains the authorized accounts that have permissions for that resource, is checked against the account with which the user is logged on.

With user-level security, each user must remember only one password, instead of many, to access different network resources (see Figure 10-4).

User-level security provides more security than share-level security because the user must be logged in with an authorized account to access a resource. With share-level security, anyone who knows (or guesses) the password for a resource can access it. User-level security also allows you to *audit*, or track, who accesses network resources.

Managing Network Accounts

User-level security requires the creation of user accounts. Most NOSs enable you to arrange these user accounts in *groups* for easier management. Some NOSs also require that each computer that logs in to the network has a *computer account* (also called a *machine account*). This provides an added layer of protection and enhances the security of the network. In the following sections, we look at these three types of accounts: user accounts, group accounts, and computer accounts.

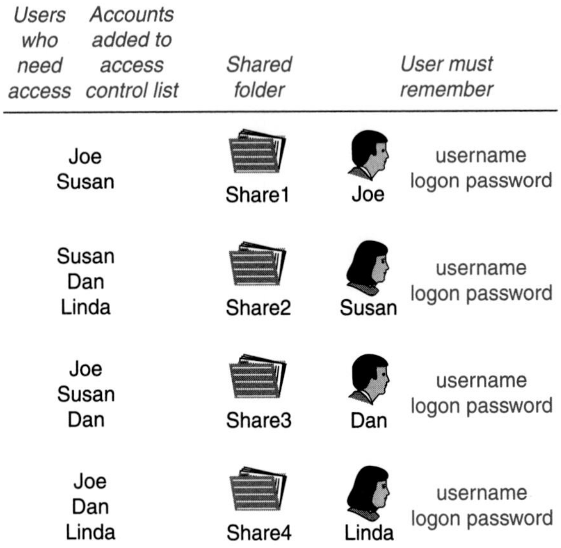

FIGURE 10-4
User-level security works by creating access control lists for each shared resource.

Users who need access	Accounts added to access control list	Shared folder		User must remember
Joe Susan	Share1	Joe	username logon password
Susan Dan Linda	Share2	Susan	username logon password
Joe Susan Dan	Share3	Dan	username logon password
Joe Dan Linda	Share4	Linda	username logon password

User Accounts. User-level security relies on the creation of separate user accounts for each person who accesses resources. User-level security is supported by some operating systems, such as Windows NT and 2000, at the *local level*. However, user-level security is more often associated with *network-level security*, which in Microsoft Windows networks is referred to as *domain-level security*.

Although implementation varies depending on the NOS, in general, network-level security utilizes user accounts and access control lists, which work together as follows:

1. During installation of the NOS, a special user account called the *administrator account* (referred to as the *supervisor account* in older versions of NetWare and *root* in UNIX and Linux) is created.

2. By using the administrator account, the network administrator can create user accounts for others who will use the network's resources.

3. When a user logs in to the network, he enters a user account name and password, and it is checked against the *security accounts database*. This database is located on a *logon authentication server*. (In Microsoft Windows networks, this server is called a *domain controller*.)

4. If the credentials are found to be valid, the user is issued an *access token*, which identifies the user and groups to which he belongs.

5. Each shared resource has an access control list, which contains the individual users and groups that are authorized to access it and the level of access that each is permitted. When a user attempts to access a resource (for example, print to a shared printer), the access token is compared to the access control list, as shown in Figure 10-5.

FIGURE 10-5
The user's access token is compared to the resource's access control list.

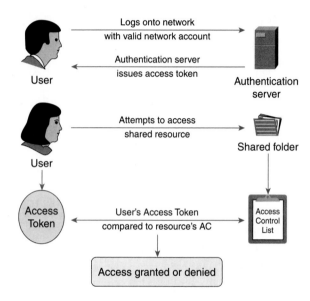

6. If the user account, or a group account to which the user belongs, is found to be authorized in the access control list, the user can use the resource. If the user does not have the appropriate permissions, access is denied.

This is a simplified version of how network-level security works. In Chapter 14, "Protecting the Network," we discuss security in more depth, and you will learn about some of the methods used to authenticate users on the network.

Creating User Accounts

A user account consists of the following:

- A user name
- A password (in some cases the password can be blank)

- User conditions and limitations (the computers from which the user can log in, hour/date restrictions, whether remote logon is allowed, and so on)

- User security information (groups to which the user belongs and user rights)

- Optional information (the user's full name, a title or job description, directory information such as telephone numbers and e-mail address, and so on)

The exact method for creating user accounts depends on the NOS, but all have utilities, or *administrative tools*, that can be used to add a new user to the security database. Regardless of the NOS, the principles involved are the same:

- User names should be unique.

- In general, uppercase and lowercase alphabetical and numeric characters can be used.

- In most cases, you should avoid using the following symbols in user names: " \ / : | = , + * ? < >.

- The operating system can restrict the number of characters used in a name.

- You should avoid including spaces in a username.

Group Accounts. You can manage access permissions and user rights by assigning them to individual user accounts, but most NOSs allow you to use groups to simplify account management.

Most company networks contain hundreds or even thousands of users. Let's suppose we have ten shared folders in which all sales department documents are stored, and 200 users who work in sales and who need access to those documents.

In our scenario, we *could* configure each of the ten folders so that each of the 200 user accounts has access, but imagine what a time-consuming and tedious task that would be. Furthermore, every time we created a new folder to which sales personnel needed access, we would have to add 200 user accounts to that folder's access list. There has to be a better way.

Fortunately, there *is* a better way. If we place all user accounts for employees in the sales department into a group named Sales, we can then assign access permissions for each of those ten folders to *1* group account instead of to *200* user accounts. If we create a new folder, it takes only a minute to add the Sales group to its access list—instead of hours to add all 200 user accounts.

Groups can also be used to easily send multiple copies of a message to a large number of users.

Groups to which access permissions are assigned are called *security groups*.
Groups created for use only by applications such as e-mail programs, to which
no permissions are attached, are called *distribution groups*.

Some operating systems divide groups into categories based on scope, such as
local and global, depending on whether they are applicable on the individual
server or throughout the entire domain. Windows 2000 also includes a group
scope called *universal* that can be used across all domains in a tree or forest of
domains, as shown in Figure 10-6. NetWare and UNIX don't distinguish
between local and global groups.

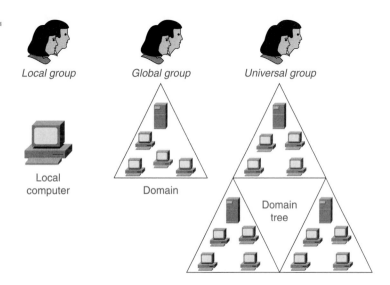

FIGURE 10-6
Windows 2000
networks include
three group
scopes.

Most NOSs create one or more *default groups* during installation. One of
these groups is usually an all-encompassing group into which all user accounts
are automatically placed. In Windows NT, Windows 2000, and NetWare 3*x*,
this is called the *Everyone* group (there is no such group in later versions of
NetWare). In UNIX, it is called the *World*. Other default groups include *Users*,
Administrators, *Backup Operators*, and so on.

All users who belong to a group have the rights and permissions assigned to that
group. Because in most NOSs users can belong to more than one group at a time
(and some operating systems enable the *nesting* of groups inside other groups), it
can get interesting if the rights and permissions of one group conflict with those
of another to which the user belongs. Learning how these conflicts are resolved
is an important part of learning to work with a particular NOS.

Computer Accounts. NOSs that are designed for high-security environments might require not only that users have accounts to log in to the network, but also that computers connected to the network have machine accounts. For example, in a Windows domain, each system running Windows NT or Windows 2000 must have a computer account created by an administrator before it can join the domain. Windows 9*x* computers, however, were designed for homes and smaller businesses with lower security environments; these machines cannot join a domain, although a user with a valid user account *can* log in to a Windows domain from a Windows 9*x* system.

The operating system uses the computer account to validate the identity of the computer and to audit actions performed while using the computer account.

Managing Shared Resources

In some NOSs, such as Windows, when you create a shared resource, it is automatically shared by default with the Everyone group, which contains *all* users. If this is not what you want, be sure to modify the permissions when you create the share.

Shared resources are generally given *share names*, which can be—but don't have to be—the same as the actual name of the resource. For example, if you share a folder named salesdocs, you can name the share Sales Documents if you want; this does *not* change the name of the folder itself.

After resources have been shared, they must be managed. Management of resources involves the following:

- Making shared resources easily accessible to those who are authorized to access them
- Making shared resources secure against unauthorized access

These objectives are in some ways contradictory, but you can accomplish both by using *directory services*, such as Novell's NDS (Novell Directory Services) or Microsoft's Active Directory. You will learn more about directory services in Chapter 11, "Directory Services."

All sorts of devices, including scanners, fax functions, and external storage devices, can be shared. If something is attached to a computer and that computer is attached to a network, someone probably has figured out a way to share it—or soon will. Regardless of the resource, however, the goals of sharing are the same: accessibility and access control.

In the following sections, we review the types of shared resources that must be managed by the network administrator, including:

- Files and folders
- Printers
- Applications
- Connections

Shared Files and Folders. There are several reasons for making files and folders accessible across the network. Documents that need to be viewed or edited by multiple users must be shared so that everyone accesses the same copy of the document. This prevents confusion that results from different people having unique copies on their own hard disks.

You *could* have the person who created the document store it on his or her computer's disk and then create a share. However, a better way is to store the document in a centralized location, on a *file server*. This is more efficient than having shared documents stored on different computers all over the network for several reasons:

- The administrator can ensure that all documents are backed up regularly.
- If one person's workstation is down, it won't affect access to the documents.
- It is easier for everyone to locate the shared documents if they are all on one server.

Another reason for using shared network folders is to give each user a secure but centralized location to store documents. This is sometimes referred to as a *home directory*. All data created by the user goes into his or her home directory, which is located on the network server. No one else has access to the directory, but all users' home directories are backed up each time the server's scheduled backup occurs.

A shared folder can be mapped as a network drive to make it easier to access. This means that to the user, the remote folder appears as a drive letter in the local file management tool (such as Windows Explorer). For example, if Joe often needs to access files in a folder called Marketing stored on the file server, he can map a drive to that folder so that it appears as drive K in Windows Explorer. If he double-clicks K, the contents of the remote folder are displayed. This is much easier than navigating through the network to locate and access the folder each time he needs it.

> **NOTE**
>
> Later in this chapter, you will learn how to map network drives in each operating system.

Shared Printers. A driving force for networking business computers is the ability to share printers and other expensive peripherals. With printer sharing, anyone on the network can print to a printer attached to any other computer on the network (or directly connected to the network, as with some laser printers).

Depending on the operating system, there are several ways to connect to a remote shared printer. One way, *capturing the printer port*, redirects print jobs away from the local printer port to the network printer. Later in this chapter, you will learn how to do this in different operating systems.

Shared Applications. An *application server* can allow network users to use its application programs. This means that the applications are installed only on the server machine and do not take up hard disk space on the local workstations. Performance with an application server is usually slower than running the application with the local computer, but several advantages offset this:

- Smaller hard disks are required for the workstations.
- Administrators have control over the configuration of the application programs.
- Administrators can ensure that everyone in the organization is using the same version of the application.
- The application can be upgraded once, on the server, instead of at every workstation.

Application sharing also can be accomplished by using *terminal services*, which will be discussed in Chapter 17, "Thin Client Networking."

Shared Connections. Another reason for networking computers in a business or home is to share an Internet connection. Instead of having a modem, a telephone line, and an Internet service provider (ISP) account for every computer in the organization, all networked computers can connect to the Internet through a single line and account. There are several ways to do this:

- Using a router that connects all computers to the Internet connection, each using a separate public IP address
- Using Network Address Translation (NAT) software that allows computers on the local network to connect to the Internet through a NAT host, using only one public IP address
- Using a proxy server, which uses a form of address translation and provides security for incoming and outgoing packets

LAN/WAN connections using routing or NAT were discussed in detail in Chapter 6, "WAN Links."

Overview of NOSs

Choosing an NOS can be a complex decision. Each popular NOS has strengths and weaknesses, and because network operating systems are generally much more costly than desktop varieties (often costing several thousand dollars, depending on the number of clients that connect to the server), it is a decision not to be taken lightly.

Network administrators need to know at least some basics about the three most popular NOS families: Windows, NetWare, and UNIX/Linux. Many of today's networks include more than one server type, and knowing how to get these diverse systems to interoperate is an important skill for network personnel. For that reason, we have devoted Chapter 13, "Hybrid Networks," to hybrid networks and interoperability issues.

It is important for a network administrator to learn to "speak the language" of the operating systems on the network. Different NOS vendors use the same terms in different ways. For example, "root" refers to the master administrative account in a UNIX environment, but it is used to identify an NDS object in NetWare networks. In the Windows world, "root" can pertain to the domain at the top of a Windows 2000 domain tree or to the basic component of a Distributed File System (Dfs).

In the following sections, we discuss the popular NOS-based networks, including:

- Windows NT and Windows 2000 networks
- NetWare networks
- UNIX/Linux networks

Windows NT and Windows 2000 Networks

Windows server-based networks, running Windows NT Server or Windows 2000 Server, are based on the concept of the domain. A *domain* is a grouping of computers and users that serves as a boundary of administrative authority. Windows NT domains and Windows 2000 domains, although similar in function, interact with one another differently.

Windows Terminology

Microsoft uses the term "domain" to describe groups of computers, users, and resources that form an administrative boundary, and it uses "domain controller" to describe the logon authentication servers that hold a copy of the security accounts database. Also peculiar to Microsoft networks is the distinction between the *printer*, used to describe a logical software construct, and the *print device*, which refers to the actual piece of hardware that prints the document.

Windows 2000 networking terminology is familiar to those who have worked with Windows NT 4.0, but some new terms and concepts, such as the *domain tree* and *forest*, might be unfamiliar to seasoned NT administrators. In addition, administrators who come to Windows networking from a NetWare environment might find that some familiar terms, such as "*tree,*" have a different meaning.

In the following sections, we look at specific characteristics of Windows NT 4.0 and Windows 2000 and discuss how to perform common administrative tasks, including mapping network drives and sharing printers, on Windows networks.

Windows NT 4.0

The Windows NT 4.0 graphical interface is similar to that of Windows 95 and thus familiar to those who have used this popular desktop operating system. Each NT domain requires one (and only one) *primary domain controller (PDC)*. This is a "master" server that contains the security accounts management database (often called the SAM). A domain also can have one or more *backup domain controllers (BDCs)*, each of which contains a read-only copy of the SAM.

Users can log in to and then be authenticated by either the PDC or a BDC, but changes to the SAM can be made only on the PDC. These changes are then replicated to the BDCs on a regular basis. BDCs balance the load of authentication traffic and serve as a backup in case the PDC goes down. If the PDC goes down permanently, a BDC can be "promoted" to become the PDC.

Creating and Managing User Accounts in Windows NT 4.0. Microsoft provides an administrative tool called the User Manager for Domains that you access from the domain controller and use to create, manage, and remove domain user accounts. To access it, choose Start, Programs, Administrative Tools, User Manager for Domains.

The User Manager for Domains allows the administrator to create new user and group accounts; rename, modify and delete accounts; assign passwords; set account policies; and set restrictions on users. Restrictions on users include specifying when and from which workstations they can log in. See Figure 10-7.

Notice the groups shown in Figure 10-7. All are built-in default groups for Windows NT 4.0 domains. The two built-in default user accounts are Administrator and Guest.

FIGURE 10-7
User Manager for Domains enables you to create and manage accounts.

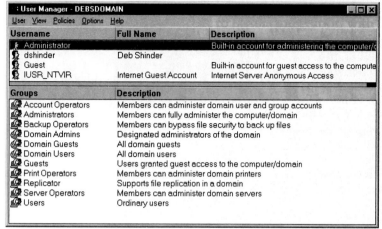

Windows 2000

Windows 2000 networks use *Active Directory*, a directory service similar to Novell's NDS, to store security information. (You learn more about the many functions of Active Directory in Chapter 11.) Whereas the NT security database is flat, the Active Directory is hierarchical in nature.

Windows 2000 domains can be joined in domain trees, which are groups of domains that share a contiguous namespace. Multiple trees can be joined into forests, which makes the network structure scalable to almost any size.

Windows 2000 domains do not have a PDC or any BDCs. All domain controllers have a copy of the Active Directory partition, and changes can be made on any domain controller. The changes are then replicated to the other domain controllers.

Account Administration in Windows 2000. Administrative tasks in Windows 2000 use a common framework, the *Microsoft Management Console (MMC)*. This tool uses *snap-ins*, which are modules that contain the tools for specific administrative functions. Users and groups are created and managed with the Active Directory Users and Computers MMC snap-in. You can access it by choosing Start, Programs, Administrative Tools, Active Directory Users and Computers. See Figure 10-8.

Windows 2000, unlike Windows NT 4.0, enables you to place objects such as users and resources into container objects called *organizational units (OUs)*. You can delegate administrative authority over each OU to a user or group.

This makes for much more granularity (that is, specificity) of control than was possible with Windows NT 4.0.

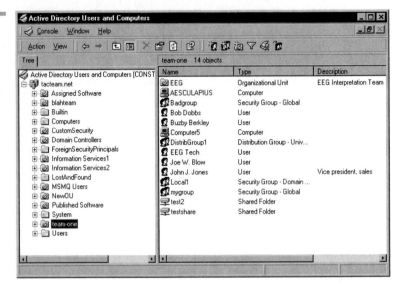

FIGURE 10-8
Windows 2000 user and group accounts are administered through the Active Directory Users and Computers MMC snap-in.

Mapping Drives in Windows Networks

Mapping a network drive in the Windows NOSs is easy. You can do it in one of two ways:

- By using Windows Explorer
- By using the **net use** command

Mapping a Drive with Windows Explorer. To map a drive with Windows Explorer, you need only navigate to the folder on the remote system in Windows Explorer (choose Network Neighborhood, *Server name*, *Shared folder name*), choose the Tools menu, and then choose Map Network Drive, as shown in Figure 10-9. Note that if you have installed Internet Explorer 4.0 or later, another option is to right-click the shared folder name in Windows Explorer and then choose Map Network Drive from the right context menu.

The mapped drive shows up as the assigned drive letter in the left pane of Explorer, along with your floppy and CD drives and hard disk partitions. You can access it from Windows Explorer, My Computer, and, if you create a shortcut for it, from your desktop.

FIGURE 10-9
You can map a network drive in Windows NT 4.0 by using Windows Explorer.

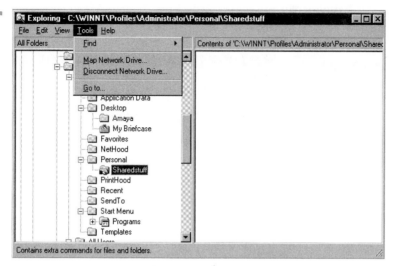

Mapping a Drive with the net use Command. Another way to map a drive in Windows operating systems utilizes the *Universal Naming Convention (UNC) path.* You can identify the share by using the following syntax:

`\\computername\sharename`

To map a network drive to the shared resource, enter the following at the command prompt:

`net use <driveletter: \\computername\sharename`

If you are comfortable with command-line administration, you might prefer using the **net use** command instead of mapping drives through Windows Explorer.

Sharing Printers in Windows Networks

Sharing printers and attaching to shared printers on a Windows network is simple. In the next sections, we look at how to share a local printer (one that is attached to the machine at which you are working) and how to connect to a shared printer on the network.

Sharing a Local Printer. To share a printer that is attached to the local computer, go to the Printers folder, which is accessible through the Control Panel, and then right-click the printer name. Choose Sharing, click the Shared as option button, and then either enter a share name or accept the default. Figure 10-10 shows this process in Windows 2000.

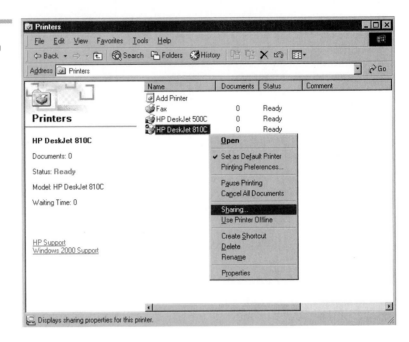

FIGURE 10-10
You can share a local printer in Windows 2000.

Connecting to a Shared Printer. As with mapping network drives, there are two ways to connect to a shared network printer: using the Add Printer Wizard and using the **net use** command at the command line. In the following sections, we examine each method in detail.

Using the Add Printer Wizard

The easiest way to use a remote printer in Windows is to add it with the Add Printer Wizard. To do so, double-click the Add Printer icon in the Printers folder and follow the instructions of the wizard.

When the wizard is finished, the network printer appears in your Printers folder, and you can print to it from your applications as if it were a local printer.

Print jobs are *spooled* (stored in memory or on the hard disk) to "wait in line" to be printed. The list of pending print jobs is referred to as the *print spool*.

NOTE

Microsoft uses *wizards*, which are made up of a systematic series of dialog boxes, to guide you through many administrative tasks.

Using net use to Capture a Printer Port

The **net use** command can be used to capture a printer port and redirect print jobs from the local port (LPT1) to the network printer. The syntax for the command, which is entered at the command prompt, is as follows:

```
net use LPT1: \\computername\printername
```

computername is the print server to which the printing device (*printername*) is physically attached.

NetWare Networks

As with Windows NT and Windows 2000, there are significant differences in the administration of different versions of NetWare. Although numerous networks still use NetWare 3.*x* servers, the most current version is NetWare 5.1.

NetWare Terminology

Novell uses many terms that might not be familiar to those who have not worked with NetWare products. For instance, the *bindery* might sound mysterious, but it's really only a database, similar to the SAM on Windows NT domain controllers.

NetWare 3.*x* and the Bindery

NetWare 3.x uses a database, called the bindery, on each server. Each bindery stores the security account information for only that machine. If two (or more) NetWare servers are on the network, a user must have an account created on each server in order to access resources on all of them. There is no replication of account information. This makes administration increasingly difficult as more servers are added to the network.

NetWare version 3.11 introduced support for add-on software components called NetWare loadable modules (NLMs). These utilities and drivers are installed on the server to enhance its functionality.

NetWare 4.x and NDS

NetWare 4 introduced a sophisticated directory service called NDS (which stands for Novell Directory Services) that solved the administrative problem caused by having individual binderies on each server. NDS is a distributed database that allows users to log in to any server with one user account and access all network resources. The bindery is a flat database; NDS is hierarchical and arranged like a tree. In fact, Novell calls network resources such as users, groups, printers, and volumes *leaf objects*.

NDS was released prior to Microsoft's Active Directory. The two have a lot in common, including the concept of OUs and the ability to locate objects in the tree directory structure without having to know where the resources are

NOTE

The meanings of the terms "tree" and "root" are different in NetWare than in Windows 2000 or UNIX.

physically located on the network. Both NDS and Active Directory are Lightweight Directory Access Protocol (LDAP)-compatible directory services. (You will learn about LDAP in Chapter 11.)

Account Administration in NetWare 4.x. When you install NetWare 3.*x*, two default accounts are created: Guest and Supervisor. The Guest account has limited access, and the Supervisor account is an administrative account. NetWare 4 and 5 have only one default account called Admin.

NetWare 4.*x* accounts are created and managed with one of two tools:

- **NetWare Administrator**—Run from a Windows client that is running the Novell NDS client software
- **NETADMIN**—A character-based utility that can be run from DOS

NetWare 5.x

NetWare 5.x provides a graphical Java-based administration console called ConsoleOne that allows for remote administration. It resembles the UNIX X Window interface, and it is designed to eventually provide the framework for NetWare's administrative tools in the same way that the MMC provides a framework in Windows 2000. NetWare 5 also can be administered through the standard command-line console or a menu-based utility called the Monitor.

NetWare 5.1 introduces the NetWare Management Portal, a web-based tool that allows you to manage NetWare 5.1 servers from a client machine through a Web browser.

NetWare Clients

NetWare is a server operating system. Client workstations must run a desktop operating system for which NetWare client software is available. Novell makes client software for DOS and all versions of Windows, and Microsoft builds a NetWare client into its Windows operating systems. Third-party NetWare clients are available for Macintosh and Linux.

For operating systems such as BeOS that do not have NetWare client software, you might still be able to access NetWare servers by using Server Message Block (SMB) client support. SMB client support enables you to go through a Linux computer that runs both Samba software and the Linux NetWare client. We discuss Samba in Chapter 13.

NOTE

You can use either the Microsoft Client for Netware (called Client Services for NetWare [CSNW] in Windows NT and Windows 2000) or the Novell client software, but you *cannot* run both clients on one machine. The Novell client provides greater functionality than the built-in Microsoft client.

When you install and configure NetWare client software, you must provide the following information:

- **For NetWare 3.x**—The preferred server, which is selected from a drop-down list of available servers
- **For NetWare 4/5.x**—The preferred tree and context

Mapping Drives in NetWare Networks. Mapping a drive on a NetWare server can be done with Windows Explorer. You need to follow the same process described for mapping drives on a Microsoft network, if your NetWare client machines are running Windows 95, 98, NT, or 2000.

You also can map a drive at the command line using the **map** command. The syntax is as follows:

```
map driveletter:=server\volume:directory\subdirectory
```

The Novell client software also has drive-mapping functionality that allows you to map a drive as a root or as a search drive.

Shared Printers in NetWare Networks. To print to a network printer, you can use the **capture** command to redirect print jobs from the local printer port. The syntax is as follows:

```
capture L=<portnumber> Q=<queuename> P=<printername>
```

In NetWare, the *printer queue* is the stored print jobs that are waiting their turn to be printed. This is the same as the print spool in Windows networks.

UNIX and Linux Networks

The UNIX NOS has been around for a long time. It was developed in 1969, and it has evolved into numerous varieties. Because the source code is open (that is, available at no cost to anyone who wants to modify it) and because it is written in the popular C programming language, businesses, academic institutions, and even individuals can—and do—develop their own versions.

UNIX operating systems are used on high-end workstations such as Silicon Graphics and Sun machines. UNIX can run as a command-line operating system or with a graphical user interface (GUI) such as X Window.

THE OPEN SOURCE INITIATIVE

The Open Source Initiative provides a trademark for software developers who want to share their code with others, who are then free to modify and redistribute the code. To use the trademark, the software must meet certain criteria: it must be freely distributed without restriction, and the source code must be available. Examples of compliant software include Linux, the BSD version of UNIX, the X Window system, and applications developed under the GNU project. The Open Source Initiative website is located at www.opensource.org.

Linux is a UNIX-based operating system designed to run on Intel and Intel-compatible PCs. Linus Torvalds developed it in the early 1990s. Like UNIX, Linux is an open-source operating system of which there are many different varieties. In addition, like UNIX, Linux can run the X Window GUI and other graphical interfaces such as Gnome and KDE.

In the following sections, we discuss UNIX terminology, some of the UNIX and Linux distributions available, and how to perform account administration and other common tasks in UNIX and Linux.

UNIX Terminology

In UNIX and Linux distributions, the administrative account, which is used for system maintenance tasks, is called *root*. *Bin* and *sys* are accounts that own and run programs.

Server services are called *daemons*. Examples of daemons include the print daemon and the FTP daemon. There are other terms that are peculiar to the UNIX environment, and we define many of them in the following sections of this chapter.

UNIX Operating Systems

There are hundreds of different versions of UNIX. Some of the most popular are the following:

- Berkeley Software Design, Inc. (BSD UNIX, which has spawned derivatives such as FreeBSD)
- Santa Cruz Operation (SCO) UNIX
- Sun Solaris
- AIX (IBM's UNIX)
- HP-UX (Hewlett Packard's UNIX)

Open source code is both the strength and the weakness of UNIX operating systems. Developers are free to improve and customize the operating system, but this results in a lack of standardization that can be frustrating to users, administrators, and application developers. However, this is not as grim as it sounds—a large body of application software can be used across multiple UNIX and Linux platforms.

Despite the popularity of Windows and NetWare in corporate LANs, much of the Internet still runs on powerful UNIX systems. Although UNIX is usually associated with expensive hardware and is considered "user unfriendly," recent developments have changed that image. In particular, the emergence in the 1990s of Linux brought UNIX computing to the PC world.

Linux Operating Systems

Linux is sometimes referred to as "UNIX Lite." It is designed to run on Intel-compatible PCs. (It also runs on RISC machines.) Linux brings the advantages of UNIX to home and small business computers.

As with UNIX, there are numerous versions of Linux. Some are free downloads from the Web, and others are commercially distributed. The following are a few of the most popular:

- RedHat Linux, distributed by RedHat Software
- OpenLinux, distributed by Caldera
- Corel Linux
- Slackware
- Debian GNU/Linux
- SuSE Linux

A recent trend has been to create versions of Linux that fit on one or two floppy disks. One such trimmed version is LOAF (Linux On A Floppy), which fits on one disk. DOS Linux is another small, Linux NOS, and it can be installed on an existing DOS system. A third, Coyote Linux, is a small, specialized distribution designed for Internet-connection sharing.

A list of current Linux distributions can be accessed on the Web at www.linux.org.

UNIX and Linux Account Administration

Network Information System (NIS), developed by Sun Microsystems, can be used to manage UNIX servers. NIS allows single-login access to network resources, which means that a user can log in once (with a single account name and password) and access resources on computers throughout the network.

Creating and Managing User Accounts. In UNIX and Linux, you use the **adduser** command to add a new user account, as shown in Figure 10-11. You

> **NOTE**
>
> It is important to note that in UNIX, unlike Windows, commands and names are *case-sensitive*; that is, to the operating system, the filename "MyDocs" is not the same as "mydocs." In fact, these two files could exist in the same directory.
>
> You might have encountered this while typing URLs into your web browser. If the web server to which your web browser is connecting is UNIX-based, you must enter the address *exactly as shown.* If a web page is named "Web-Site.html" and you enter "web-site.html," you receive a "file not found" error message.

must be logged in as root or as supervisor to create new user accounts. The syntax is as follows:

username:/# **adduser**

FIGURE 10-11
The **adduser** command is used to create new user accounts on UNIX and Linux servers.

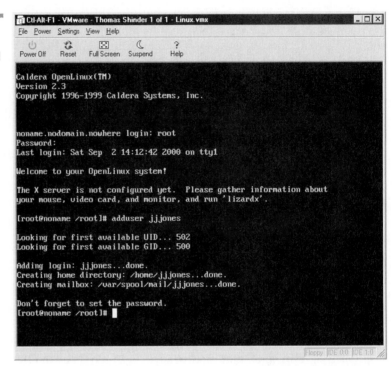

You manage user accounts by editing the /etc/passwd file. Some UNIX/Linux versions provide *scripts* that guide you through the process, and you can manually edit the file using a text editor. (vi, Pico, and Emacs are popular UNIX/Linux text editors.)

Manually editing the passwd file can be complex; it involves entering user information with this syntax:

```
deb://BimowSOF9Ev:503:100:Deb Shinder:/home/deb:/bin/bash
```

Table 10-1 shows the fields involved in the editing of the passwd file.

TABLE 10-1   **The Parts of a passwd File Entry**

Field	Explanation
deb	User name
BimowSOF9Ev	Password (displayed in the file in encrypted form so that someone opening the file cannot access users' passwords)
503	User ID
100	Group ID
Deb Shinder	Full name of user
/home/deb	User's home directory
/bin/bash	User's default shell

UNIX Groups. Like Windows and NetWare, UNIX supports groups for managing user access to resources. UNIX groups work much like local groups in Windows NT and Windows 2000.

In UNIX you add groups with the **addgroup** command, and you manage groups by modifying the /etc/groups file. If your UNIX distribution includes graphical utilities for these tasks, it is much easier and safer to use them instead of the command line.

UNIX Clients

The client/server file system used by most varieties of UNIX file servers is Network File System (NFS), which was developed by Sun Microsystems. It can be installed on Windows clients using software such as Solstice Network Client by Sun. NFS requires TCP/IP, or other NFS client software, for file transfer. Windows operating systems do not include an NFS client.

Windows clients can access UNIX servers without client software if the UNIX servers run Samba, which is a program that uses the SMB application layer protocol. Windows computers use SMB for file access across the network. Samba enables them to see the UNIX file system.

> **CAUTION**
>
> The passwd file contains system configuration information in addition to user information, so you must be careful when editing it. Fortunately, many vendors provide graphical utilities, such as User Configurator in RedHat Linux, for performing editing tasks.

Mapping Drives in UNIX Networks

Mapping a drive to a UNIX share is done by using the **mount** command. The syntax is as follows:

```
mount servername:/directory/subdirectory /localdirectory
```

The local directory designation that points to the remote share denoted by the first part of the command is called the *directory mount point*. The mount point location must already exist before you map the share to it.

Shared Printers in UNIX Networks

You can print to a printer attached to a UNIX print server by using the **lpr** command. To fulfill the print request, the print server must be running lpd software—the *line printer daemon*. The syntax for printing to a UNIX printer is as follows:

```
lpr -P printername filename
```

If you enter the command without the printer name (that is, **lpr** *filename*), the print job is sent to the default printer. Other UNIX printing commands include the following:

- **lpq**—Allows you to view the print queue, or list of jobs
- **lprm**—Removes a file from the print queue

For printing interoperability, Windows NT and Windows 2000 include TCP/IP Printing Services and Print Services for UNIX.

Other NOSs

The vast majority of PC networks run on one or more of the three NOSs discussed in this chapter. However, other NOS products are available and in use. For example, Banyan VINES, OS/2 Warp Server, the Apple NOS, and LANtastic are alternative operating systems that provide centralized administration of the network. We discuss each of these in the following sections of this chapter.

Banyan VINES

Banyan makes a product called Virtual Networking System (VINES), which is a variation of UNIX that uses its own file system—VINES—instead of NFS. Although it has waned in popularity and is now used primarily in academic environments, VINES is still significant for the fact that it introduced the first real directory service—StreetTalk. We discuss StreetTalk in Chapter 11.

OS/2 Warp Server

OS/2 is known to many as "IBM's desktop operating system that lost the race to Windows." OS/2 has all but disappeared since IBM stopped releasing new versions in 1996. Although IBM has dropped most support for the desktop operating system, it has continued to develop its OS/2 server product. Because the focus is now on e-commerce, IBM refers to the operating system as OS/2 Warp Server for E-business. OS/2 is primarily used in the banking and financial industries.

Warp Server provides file and application server functionality and features a file system called JFS (Journaled File System), which is designed for large-scale applications and increased reliability. NFS allows connectivity with AIX or other UNIX-based servers.

AppleShareIP

Apple Macintosh computers come with built-in support for peer-to-peer networking. Although Apple produced a server product called AppleShareIP, it never gained popularity outside a small niche market. AppleShareIP offers FTP, POP3/SMTP mail server, web server, and file and print server functionality.

LANtastic

Although not a server-based NOS, LANtastic is used by many small businesses to connect DOS and Windows PCs so that they can share files, modems, and Internet connections. LANtastic provides management features for peer-to-peer networking that enable you to connect up to 500 machines—far more than is feasible in the traditional workgroup environment.

Summary

In this chapter, we discussed concepts involved in network administration and the characteristics of popular NOSs. We began by examining the differences between mainframe-based centralized computing and PC-based client/server computing. We then described characteristics of the typical client/server environment and learned how client/server applications, such as SQL Server and other database "back ends," provide optimized sharing of the processing load over the network.

You discovered the importance of properly managed shared resources that ensure that authorized users can locate and access shares and that unauthorized users cannot. We discussed the specifics of sharing files, folders, printers, applications, and Internet connections.

Next we looked at each of the "Big Three" NOSs in some detail and discussed their management tools and specific terminology. In addition, we discussed how to create user accounts, map network drives, and capture printer ports in Windows NT, Windows 2000, NetWare, and UNIX/Linux.

We wrapped up with a look at some of the less widely used NOS products. These included Banyan VINES, OS/2 Warp Server, AppleShareIP, and LANtastic.

Now that you are familiar with popular server operating systems, in the next chapter, we will examine an important component of modern server products—directory services.

Further Reading

You can find support information and descriptions of Microsoft Windows NT and Windows 2000 Server products at www.microsoft.com.

NetWare information and resources can be found at Novell's website at www.novell.com.

More information about Linux distributions can be found at Linux Online! at www.linux.org.

You can download FreeBSD and find tutorials, handbooks, and FAQs at www.freebsd.org.

Review Questions

The following questions test your knowledge of the material covered in this chapter. Be sure to read each question carefully and select the *best* correct answer or answers.

1. What network applications utilize the processing power of the server to optimize tasks such as database queries?

    A. Centralized applications

    B. Front-end applications

    C. Client/server applications

    D. Shared applications

2. Which resource is made available to others for access over the network?

    A. Server

    B. Share

    C. Client

    D. Distributed resource

3. What is the name for the type of security in which every user has a user account and password, an access token, and an access control list to determine whether a user can access a specific network resource?

    A. User-level security

    B. Password-level security

    C. Share-level security

    D. Workgroup-level security

4. The master administrative account (which may be called Administrator, Admin, Supervisor, or Root depending on the operating system) has which of the following characteristics? (Select all that apply.)

    A. It is created during the installation of the operating system.

    B. It has only limited access to network resources.

    C. It should be given a strong password.

    D. It can be used to create other user accounts.

5. Which of the following could be safely used as a username in any of the three major NOSs? (Select all that apply.)

A. joesmith

B. Joe Smith

C. J+Smith

D. SMITH007

6. In a Windows server-based network, what is the name for a group of computers, users, and resources that forms a basic administrative boundary?

A. Root

B. Tree

C. Domain

D. Forest

7. What is the name of the tool with which domain user accounts are managed and password policies are set on a Windows NT 4.0 domain controller?

A. User Administrator

B. User Manager for Domains

C. User Manager

D. Account Administration Tool for Domains

8. What is the name of the directory service in which security account information is stored on a Windows 2000 network?

A. NDS

B. LDAP Directory Service

C. Active Directory

D. Directory Access Service

9. What database stores security information on a NetWare 3.*x* server?

A. The root

B. NDS

C. The organizational unit

D. The bindery

10. Which of the following is true of UNIX operating systems? (Select all that apply.)

  A. File operations are case-sensitive.

  B. The master administrative account is called the Supervisor account.

  C. Server services are called daemons.

  D. Groups in a UNIX system work much like global groups in Windows NT 4.0.

Directory Services

An important part of modern network operating systems (NOSs) is the directory service. The *directory service* enables the storing and accessing of information about network resources, network accounts, and network services.

In this chapter, you learn about directories and directory services and their expanding role in today's networks. We discuss standards and specifications governing the implementation of directory services. Specifically, we examine the Open Systems Interconnection (OSI) X.500 specifications and the Directory Access Protocol (DAP) and Lightweight Directory Access Protocol (LDAP) standards.

We then look at Directory-Enabled Networking (DEN), which is an initiative supported by Microsoft Corporation and Cisco Systems. DEN focuses on the use of directory services to improve the management of network devices, resources, and services.

You will learn about the most popular directory services that run on PC NOSs: Novell's Novell Directory Service (NDS) and Microsoft's Active Directory. We also examine directory services that run on other platforms, such as Sun Microsystems' Directory Services (SDS) and IBM's AS/400 Directory Services. In addition, we discuss interoperability of different directory services and explore the idea of a directory service for the global Internet.

What Are Directories and Directory Services?

Directory-enabled networks require two components: the directory itself and the service that manages it. Let's examine each in turn.

What Is a Directory?

A *directory* organizes information. We use directories on a daily basis. For instance, we use the telephone directory, which organizes the names of telephone service subscribers in alphabetical order, with corresponding addresses and telephone numbers.

In the computing world, a directory can be different things. You are probably familiar with the usage that relates to computer file systems, in which a directory is a collection of files grouped under an identifying name. When we talk about the directory services used by NOSs, however, we are discussing a different but related concept. In this context, a directory is a special type of database. It can contain varying types of information.

In an object-oriented operating system, the directory contains *objects* that have *attributes*. For example, a user account is an object that could be contained in a directory. Its attributes would include the username, the user's real name, the account password, and other information pertaining to the account, as shown in Figure 11-1.

FIGURE 11-1
Directories store objects, which have attributes.

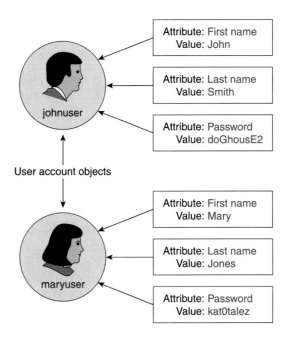

Attribute: First name
Value: John

Attribute: Last name
Value: Smith

Attribute: Password
Value: doGhousE2

johnuser

User account objects

maryuser

Attribute: First name
Value: Mary

Attribute: Last name
Value: Jones

Attribute: Password
Value: kat0talez

TIP

Directory objects can have many attributes. Some may be mandatory (for example, every user account must have a username), and others may be optional (for example, there might be a field to enter the user's job title, but this can be left blank).

To better understand the concept of directories and attributes, let's return to our example of the telephone directory. In this case, the telephone service subscriber's name is the object, and its attributes are the address and telephone number. Thus, we see that the attributes describe the object in some way.

Object classes define the attributes available for a class and its place in the directory structure or hierarchy. The definition of object classes, along with the required and allowed attributes of each, is called the *schema*. The NOS may enable authorized administrators to modify or extend the schema to add new object classes and attributes.

What Are Directory Services?

Directory services provide a way to store, update, locate, and secure information in the directory. Directory services can be *local* (that is, restricted to one machine) or *global* (that is, providing services to many machines). If the information itself is spread across multiple machines, it is referred to as *distributed*.

Using Directory Services

The benefits of using directory services on a network include the following:

- The data can be easily organized.
- The data can be easily secured.
- The data can be easily located and accessed.

To understand the advantages of using directory services, let's first look at the traditional way of accessing network resources. In the traditional way, shared files and folders are stored on the hard disks of individual workstations or file servers. To connect to the share, the user needs to know where it is located.

A directory service eliminates this requirement. Shared resources are published to the directory, and users can locate and access them without ever knowing on which machine the resources physically reside. Figure 11-2 shows the Windows 2000 network browser window. As you can see, it gives you two options:

- **Browse the Microsoft Windows Network in the traditional way**—This option enables you to browse the shares on each individual machine.
- **Browse the Directory**—This option displays all resources published to the Active Directory.

FIGURE 11-2
Windows 2000's network browser allows you to browse the network in the traditional way or to browse the Directory.

The Directory Namespace

The directory *namespace* refers to the way in which directory objects are identified. Two different types of namespaces can be used by directory services:

- Flat
- Hierarchical

Windows NT directory service (NTDS) and the NetWare 3.*x bindery* use a flat namespace. Newer, more sophisticated directory services use a hierarchical structure. This structure is often referred to as a *tree*. It is sometimes also referred to as an *inverted tree* (because the root is at the top). Most computer file systems use this type of structure.

The Directory Tree Structure. In the directory tree, objects can have parent objects and child objects. A *parent object* is directly above the object in the tree, and a *child object* is directly below it, as shown in Figure 11-3.

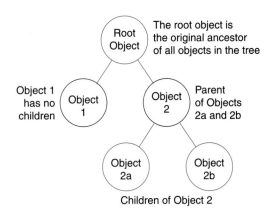

FIGURE 11-3
In a hierarchical tree, objects have parents and children.

Directory Naming Conventions. You might have noticed in Figure 11-3 that the children of Object 2 have names that include the parent's name. This is called a *contiguous namespace.* As you learned in Chapter 8, "Networking Protocols and Services," Domain Name System (DNS) names are structured in the same way. They have the same structure because DNS is a directory service that uses a hierarchical namespace. Figure 11-4 shows a DNS namespace.

In the figure, the DNS root is represented by a dot. Underneath the root are two children, the .com and .net domains. Each has child domains, which in turn can have children and grandchildren of their own. Note that each generation includes its parent's full name as part of its name.

The tree analogy can be carried further. For example, Novell's NDS terminology calls objects at the end of a branch *leaf objects.* (You will learn more about NDS later in this chapter.)

NOTE

The DNS domain structure used on the Internet is the same structure used by Windows 2000 Active Directory—minus the dot for the root domain. You will learn more about Active Directory later in this chapter.

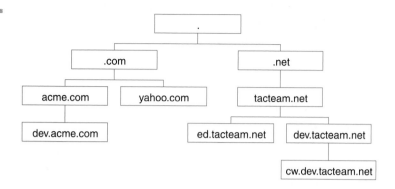

FIGURE 11-4
DNS is a directory service with a hierarchical namespace.

Directory Services Standards

For interoperability, different directory services need to have a common method of naming and referencing objects. Without standards, each application uses its own directory, which increases disk space usage, and the products of one vendor cannot use the databases compiled by the products of another vendor.

Compliance with standards enables directory services vendors to ensure that their services are compatible both over a broad range of platforms and with other directory services.

In this section, we discuss the following directory services standards:

- OSI X.500 specifications
- DAP
- LDAP

X.500

X.500 defines Electronic Directory Service (EDS) standards in ISO 9594. The directory services described in X.500 are designed to work in conjunction with X.400 messaging services.

An X.500-compliant directory has three primary components:

- **Directory System Agent (DSA)**—Manages the directory data
- **Directory User Agent (DUA)**—Gives users access to directory services
- **Directory Information Base (DIB)**—Acts as the central *data store*, or database, in which directory information is kept

The X.500 standards address how information is stored in the directory and how users and computer systems access that information. Security of data, the naming model, and the replication of directory data between servers are all defined by X.500.

X.500 specifications define the directory structure as an inverted tree, and the database is hierarchical. An X.500-compliant directory service uses DAP, which we discuss next.

DAP and LDAP

DAP enables the DUA to communicate with the DSA. DAP defines the means by which the user can search the directory and read, add, delete, and modify directory entries.

DAP is a powerful protocol, but the associated overhead is high. LDAP was developed as a subset of DAP that simplifies access to X.500-type directories. LDAP has become a popular standard, and it integrates directories from different vendors. LDAP is designed to use fewer system resources than DAP, and it is easier to implement. The current version of LDAP is LDAPv3.

LDAPv3 Specifications

RFC 2251 describes specifications for LDAPv3, including the following:

- The LDAP protocol model
- The LDAP data model
- Common elements of protocol, such as naming conventions, attribute types, and descriptions; and bind, search, add, modify, and delete operations

---

WHAT'S NEW IN LDAPv3?

LDAPv3 offers several major improvements over earlier LDAP versions. Enhanced security is a primary focus of the new version; LDAPv3 supports Secure Sockets Layer (SSL) encryption between client and server and enables X.509 certificate authentication.

LDAPv3 also enables the server to refer the LDAP client to another server if it is not able to answer the client's query itself.

Another new feature is Unicode support. This enables the encoding of more multilanguage character sets in the directory attributes; it is useful for international implementations.

LDAP Naming Conventions

LDAP-compatible directories use the standard X.500 naming convention for objects. This convention produces a *distinguished name (DN)*. With a DN, you can denote the path to an object in the directory structure. A DN looks something like this:

```
DC=net DC=tacteam OU=training CN=Users CN=John Doe
```

The name attributes in this example are described in Table 11-1.

TABLE 11-1   DN Attributes and Descriptions

DN Attribute	Description
DC	Domain component name
OU	Organizational unit (OU)
CN	Common name

Directory services such as Active Directory also can use *relative distinguished names (RDNs)*, which are shorter versions of DNs. The RDN is an attribute of the object. In the example in Table 11-1, the common name "John Doe," which is an attribute of the object, is the RDN.

Two objects in the directory might have the same RDN. For example, you can have two users with the RDN "John Doe," but only if they are in different OUs or domains. A full DN, however, cannot be shared by two objects under any circumstances.

LDAP-Compliant and LDAP-Compatible Directory Services

The first LDAP implementation occurred at the University of Michigan, and its popularity has spread all over the world. LDAP has become a standard for Internet directory services because, unlike DAP, it was designed to run over TCP.

Popular LDAP implementations include Banyan StreetTalk, Netscape Directory Server, AltaVista Directory, and Lucent Internet Directory Server. LDAP-compliant directories can be synchronized with one another, even if they are made by different vendors.

Both Novell NDS and Microsoft Active Directory support LDAP clients and use the X.500 naming conventions, although neither is fully X.500-compliant. Directory services that support LDAP clients are called *LDAP-compatible*.

LDAP Interoperability

The popularity of LDAP enables not only interoperability with all LDAP-compatible directories but also functionality as a front end to directories based on full X.500 standards.

LDAP clients are available for DOS, Windows, Macintosh, UNIX, and the X Window system. This makes LDAP and X.500 directories suitable for enterprise networks comprised of machines running on different platforms and operating systems.

Directory-Enabled Networking

DEN has become an integral part of managing resources on enterprise-level networks. Features such as quality of service (QoS) applications, groupware and collaborative computing, and process automation have increased the importance of having a centralized repository that enables users and applications to share data.

In the past, a multisite enterprise network would have numerous separate directories; different applications used their own proprietary databases, and the same information might be entered many times in different places. The more networks grew and the more networked applications were implemented, the more inefficient this method became.

Directory services that can be accessed by both applications and users save time and disk space. Another driving force behind the move toward standardized directory services is e-commerce. Directories are used in the security methods that encrypt and sign digital transactions. These security methods are called *public key infrastructure (PKI)*.

Popular Directory Services

Now that you know some of the concepts related to directories and directory services, we examine some specific implementations. The two most popular directory services for PC networking are Novell NDS and Microsoft Active Directory.

Novell NDS

Versions of NetWare up through 3.*x* use a directory database called the bindery. The biggest drawback of this directory service is its local nature. Each NetWare server on a network has to maintain an individual database, and a user has to have an account on each server to access that server's resources.

In the following sections, we examine the structure of the NDS database and discuss NDS security issues and NDS compatibility within various operating systems and hardware platforms.

The NDS Database Structure

Beginning with version 4, NetWare introduced NDS, which is a global database that is replicated between servers on the network. With it, users can log in to any server and access resources on all servers.

The NDS database is hierarchical and uses the inverted tree arrangement. It can have two basic types of objects: *container objects* and *leaf objects*. As the names imply, a container object can contain other objects within it; a leaf object is the "endpoint" of a branch—the resource itself. Shared files and printers are examples of a leaf object. OUs are examples of a container object.

NDS Security

NDS permissions to access objects are assigned to OUs, and users and groups are placed into OUs. You can change a user's permissions by moving his account from one OU to another. For example, if you move the johndoe user account from the Training OU to the Sales OU, that user no longer has the access permissions assigned to Training, but the user does acquire all permissions granted to Sales. This is different from the way in which permissions work in Microsoft Windows NT and Windows 2000 networks. (You will learn about Windows permissions later in this chapter.)

NDS Platform Compatibility

Although generally associated with the NetWare NOS, NDS can run on a variety of platforms. Novell provides NDS for the following platforms:

- NetWare 4 and 5
- Microsoft Windows NT and Windows 2000
- IBM AIX and OS/390
- Caldera OpenLinux
- SCO UNIX
- Sun Solaris

NDS eDirectory is Novell's cross-platform solution for integrated enterprise computing with directory-enabled applications.

NDS enables the use of a variety of protocols to access directory information, including the following:

- Novell Directory Access Protocol (NDAP)
- LDAP

- HTTP (when using a web server)
- Open Database Connectivity (ODBC) API
- Active Directory Services Interface (ADSI)

Microsoft Active Directory

With the release of Windows 2000 Server, Microsoft made fundamental changes in its networking components that are even more drastic than those made by Novell in the transition from NetWare 3 to 4. The Active Directory is central to these changes. Where Novell's NDS functions as a service that works with the NOS, Microsoft's Active Directory functions as an application that is deeply integrated with the operating system.

In the following sections, we examine the structure of the Active Directory database, how Active Directory is integrated with DNS and Active Directory servers, and how Active Directory information is replicated from one domain controller to another.

Active Directory Database Structure

The Active Directory information is stored in three files:

- Active Directory database
- Active Directory log files
- Shared System Volume

The database is the directory. The log files record changes made to the database. The Shared System Volume (called Sysvol) contains scripts and *group policy objects* on Windows 2000 domain controllers. *Group Policy* is the means by which Windows 2000 administrators control user desktops, automatically deploy applications, and set user rights.

Windows 2000 Domains. The logical structure of Active Directory is based on units called *domains*. Although the same terminology is used, Windows 2000 domains function differently from those in Windows NT. In both Windows NT and Windows 2000, a domain represents a security and administrative boundary, as well as a replication unit. However, Windows NT uses a flat domain structure, and Windows 2000 arranges domains in hierarchical *domain trees*.

The hierarchical tree concept works differently in Active Directory than in NDS. NDS does not divide the network into domains. Windows 2000 networks can have multiple domains, organized into domain trees. Additionally, these trees can be joined to other trees to form *forests*. Figure 11-5 shows a

Windows 2000 domain structure with two domain trees (with root domains shinder.net and tacteam.net) joined in a forest.

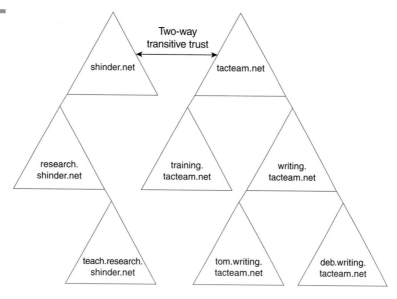

FIGURE 11-5
The Windows 2000 domain structure is a hierarchical tree.

The benefit of linking domain trees that have separate, noncontiguous name spaces is the resultant *trust relationship*. In the following sections, we discuss Windows 2000 trust relationships and how OUs function within the domain structure.

Windows 2000 Trust Relationships. All domains in the same tree and all trees in the same forest have an automatic implicit *transitive trust* in place. With such a trust, users belonging to one domain can access resources in another domain, as long as their user accounts have the appropriate permissions for those resources. Transitive trusts are a big improvement over Windows NT networks, in which an administrator was required to set up individual one-way trusts between every pair of domains in the network to achieve the equivalent effect.

Windows 2000 OUs. Active Directory, like NDS, uses OUs to organize resources within domains. Administrative authority can be delegated to individual OUs; in contrast, NT networking enables administrative privileges to be assigned only at the domain level.

Active Directory and DNS

Active Directory uses DNS naming conventions and is dependent on DNS to operate. There must be a DNS server on every Windows 2000 network. In addition, DNS zone information updates can be integrated with Active Directory replication, which is more efficient than traditional DNS update methods.

Windows 2000 supports Dynamic DNS (DDNS), which enables the automatic updating of the DNS database.

Active Directory Servers

To use Active Directory, at least one server must be configured as a *domain controller (DC)*, and it is recommended that there be at least two DCs in each domain, for fault tolerance. You promote a Windows 2000 server to DC status by running the **dcpromo.exe** command. Configuring the first domain controller on the network creates the directory for that domain.

Unlike with Windows NT, there is not one "primary" domain controller. All DCs contain a read/write copy of the Active Directory partition. This information is kept up to date and synchronized through the process of replication. We describe this process in the next section of this chapter.

OPERATIONS MASTERS

Although the primary/backup domain controller distinction in NT has been removed in Windows 2000, to avoid confusion, there are still some functions that must be the responsibility of a single domain controller. These functions are called *single-master operations.*

For example, there must be one DC that has final authority on password information in case of a conflict. This could happen when a password change has been made on one DC but has not yet been replicated to all other DCs. If there are Windows NT DCs on a Windows 2000 network, there must be a single DC from which they can obtain replication information. The DC that serves this function in a Windows 2000 network is called the PDC emulator.

The PDC emulator is one of five *operations masters* in a Windows 2000 network. Each operations master is a special DC role that is performed by only one DC in a domain (or forest). The domain-wide roles are PDC emulator, Relative ID (RID) master, and infrastructure master. The forest-wide roles are schema master and domain naming master.

Active Directory Replication

Replication is the process of copying data from one computer to one or more other computers and synchronizing that data so that it is identical on all systems.

Active Directory uses *multimaster replication* to copy directory information between the domain controllers in a domain. Changes can be made on any domain controller, and those changes are then replicated to the others, except during the performance of a single-master operation.

Windows 2000 administrators can establish replication policies that determine when and how often directory replication takes place. This enables optimum use of network bandwidth. Controlling the replication schedule is especially important when domain controllers are located on opposite sides of a slow link, such as a 56K WAN link.

Active Directory Security

Each object in Active Directory has an access control list (ACL) that contains all access permissions associated with the object. Permissions can be either explicitly allowed or denied, on a granular basis.

There are two different types of permissions:

- **Assigned permissions**—Permissions explicitly granted by a user with the authority to do so
- **Inherited permissions**—Permissions that apply to child objects because they were inherited from a parent object

Permissions can be assigned to an individual user or a group of users. Windows 2000 enables administrators to control the inheritance process, thus preventing inheritance, if desired. Note the checkbox at the bottom of the object security properties sheet in Figure 11-6.

Active Directory Compatibility

Because it is dependent on the operating system and inextricably integrated with it, Active Directory runs only on Windows 2000 servers. However, LDAP clients can access Active Directory directory services, and information can be exchanged with other LDAP directory services, because Active Directory is LDAP-compatible. Microsoft also provides tools for migrating information from other directories, such as NDS, into Active Directory.

Other Directory Services

NDS and Active Directory are well known in the PC world. There are other directories in use on various platforms, however, which are also deserving of mention. In the following sections, we take a brief look at the following:

■ IBM AS/400 Directory Services
■ Sun Directory Services
■ Banyan VINES StreetTalk

FIGURE 11-6
Administrators
control Active
Directory object
permissions.

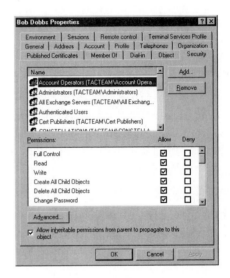

IBM OS/400 Directory Services

As part of the SecureWay Directory (also called OS/400 Directory Services), IBM provides an LDAP directory service for its AS/400 mainframe computers. This enables the use of LDAP-enabled applications, such as e-mail programs that use LDAP services to find addresses.

The OS/400 LDAP client for Windows enables interoperability with Microsoft operating systems, and the SecureWay Directory runs on OS/300, OS/400, AIX, Solaris, and Windows NT.

Sun Directory Services

Sun offers SDS for Solaris as part of the Solaris Easy Access Server. SDS is a global directory that supports global messaging and remote authentication and provides a distributed corporate directory that organizes network resources.

It supports multiple protocols and name aliases, and the directory is scalable to millions of entries. SDS is LDAPv3-compatible and is designed for access through web browsers and Windows PCs. Management is done through a Java interface.

Banyan StreetTalk

Banyan VINES StreetTalk was one of the earliest sophisticated directory services. Later implementations added LDAP support to enable integration with directory-enabled applications. Banyan ported StreetTalk to NetWare, UNIX, and Windows NT. The porting enabled these networks to share a common directory with VINES networks.

On May 1, 2000, Banyan dropped its product support programs. The company now focuses on providing e-commerce consulting and solutions.

Directory Services on the Internet

E-commerce sites are dependent on directories to catalog their goods and to track their sales. There are numerous directory services operating at individual Internet sites. For instance, www.switchboard.com provides a directory of individuals, businesses, shopping resources, maps, and other information. Users can even add their own listings to the directory.

At this time, however, there is no global directory service that spans the Internet. The Internet Engineering Task Force (IETF) has undertaken the task of defining such a global service, based on LDAP standards.

Summary

This chapter provided an overview of the role played by directory services in network computing. You learned that a directory is a database that organizes information in a logical structure. You also learned that directory services provide a way to store, locate, and secure information in a directory.

We discussed the directory namespace, which defines the way in which directory objects are identified. You learned that a directory namespace could be either flat (like the Windows NT directory service and NetWare bindery) or hierarchical (like Active Directory and NDS).

We explored the popular inverted tree structure used by hierarchical directories. In these directories, objects can have parent objects and child objects relative. The designation of "child" or "object" is relative to the position in the tree of the original object. When an object's child objects include the parent object's name as part of their own names, the namespace is contiguous.

Next, we examined the popular directory services standards: OSI X.500, DAP, and LDAP. You learned about some popular directory services—specifically, Novell's NDS and Microsoft's Active Directory.

We discussed other directory services, such as IBM's OS/400 Directory Services, SDS, and the now-obsolete Banyan StreetTalk. We also discussed the interoperability of directory services based on LDAP protocols and addressed the need for a global directory service that spans the Internet.

Now you should have a better understanding of how NOSs can use directory services to make network resources more easily available to network clients. In the next chapter, we discuss the client side of client/server networking, and you will learn some basic configuration and navigation skills for use with popular client operating systems.

Further Reading

For more information about the OSI X.500 standards, see the X.500 tutorial at www.opendirectory.com/Whitepapers/x500tut.html.

For more information on LDAP, see the LDAP World website at www.innosoft.com/ldapworld.

For more information about Novell's NDSv8, see www.nwconnection.com/may.99/nds859/index.html.

For more information about Microsoft's Active Directory, see the Active Directory guide at www.worldowindows.com/w2000/active_directory.htm.

For more information about a global directory service on the Internet, see www.isoc.org/HMP/PAPER/173/html/paper.html.

Review Questions

The following questions test your knowledge of the material covered in this chapter. Be sure to read each question carefully and select the *best* correct answer or answers.

1. A directory is a special type of what?

   A. File

   B. Folder

   C. Database

   D. Storage medium

2. What kind of database is created when a directory service spreads its information across multiple machines?

   A. An organized database

   B. A distributed database

   C. A secure database

   D. A published database

3. Which of the following uses a flat namespace? (Select all that apply.)

   A. NDS

   B. NTDS

   C. Novell bindery

   D. Active Directory

4. What kind of namespace is created when a child object includes its parent object's name as part of its own name?

   A. Flat

   B. Generational

   C. Transitive

   D. Contiguous

5. The Directory System Agent (DSA), Directory User Agent (DUA), and Directory Information Base (DIB) are primary components of which of the following?

   A. Windows 2000 Active Directory

   B. DAP

   C. OSI X.500 specifications

   D. LDAP client software

6. What is the name for the X.500/LDAP naming convention that denotes a path, such as DC=net DC=tacteam OU=training CN=Users CN=John Doe, to an object in the directory?

   A. An attribute

   B. A relative DN

   C. A DN

   D. A common name

7. What is the name for an object in the NDS tree that represents a resource, or an endpoint on a branch, rather than an object that contains other objects?

   A. A leaf object

   B. A root object

   C. A stem object

   D. A parent object

8. Which Active Directory file contains scripts and group policy objects?

   A. Active Directory log file

   B. Script file

   C. Group policy administrative file

   D. Shared System Volume file

9. Which of the following is true of Windows 2000 domains that reside in the same domain tree?

   A. They cannot share a trust relationship.

   B. They share a two-way transitive trust relationship.

   C. They share a one-way nontransitive trust relationship.

   D. They can share a trust relationship only if the relationship is explicitly created by an administrator.

10. Where are all the access permissions associated with an Active Directory object contained?

   A. Child object

   B. Replication policy

   C. ACL

   D. OU

Desktop Operating Systems

In a server-based network, *client* machines connect to and access resources on the server. These client machines run various operating systems (usually referred to as *desktop operating systems* or *client operating systems*) that distinguish them from the server operating systems.

This chapter discusses the most popular desktop operating systems:

- MS-DOS
- Windows 3.*x*
- Windows 95 and Windows 98
- Windows NT Workstation
- Windows 2000 Professional
- Linux and UNIX
- Macintosh
- IBM OS/2

It is important to understand that it is not necessary for the client computers to run a desktop operating system made by the same vendor who made the NOS that is on the server to which the client computers connect. For example, Windows 98 clients can connect to a UNIX or Linux server. Some NOS vendors, such as NetWare, don't even make a desktop operating system.

Operating System Basics

An operating system is the basic program that is initially loaded onto a computer. The loading process is called *booting*. The operating system manages all other programs (*applications*) that run on the computer, including the following:

- Productivity programs, such as word processors or spreadsheets
- Network applications, such as e-mail or web browsers
- Multimedia programs that play movie and music files or audio CDS
- Utilities that help you manage the operating system, other files, and other applications
- Reference programs, such as dictionaries and encyclopedias
- Games

The operating system performs *services* for the applications that request the services through an application programming interface (API). In a multitasking environment, the operating system allocates processor and memory resources to simultaneously running applications; the operating system acts as a liaison between the applications and the hardware devices.

Applications are often add-on programs that are purchased separately and installed on top of the operating system. These applications include word processing programs, spreadsheet and database applications, and illustration and graphics manipulation software. Operating systems also include many built-in applications, such as system tools (for example, backup utilities and disk management tools), configuration applets, and basic productivity programs such as text editors, calculators, and simple image editing programs.

Operating System Interfaces

A user interacts with an operating system and programs by using the *user interface*. User interfaces can be divided into two categories: text-based and graphical. The graphical user interface is often shortened to GUI (pronounced "gooey"). In the following sections, we will discuss the characteristics of each.

Text-Based Interfaces

The first PC operating systems used text-based (also called *character-based*) interfaces. Users typed commands at a prompt (called the *command prompt*). MS-DOS and UNIX/Linux are examples of operating systems that use text-based interfaces. Figure 12-1 shows an example of a text-based user interface.

FIGURE 12-1
You can log in to Linux using a text-based interface.

NOTE

Windows 3.*x*, although referred to as an operating system, is actually a shell that runs on top of MS-DOS.

Most text-based operating systems can run graphical *shells*, which provide GUIs. Several graphical shells, such as X Window and KDE, are available for Linux. DOSSHELL is an early graphical shell that was used with MS-DOS.

Shells differ from true GUI-interface operating systems because shells are separate programs running on top of the operating system. The operating system can function without the shell, but the shell cannot function without the operating system.

Character-based operating systems are faster and require less system resources than do GUIs.

GUIs

Operating systems such as Windows 9*x* and above, the Macintosh OS, and OS/2 are based on GUIs. A GUI displays pictures as well as text. In a GUI, you perform most commands and functions by manipulating *icons*, which are pictorial representations of programs, files, and other components. Figure 12-2 shows a GUI.

FIGURE 12-2
You log in to Windows 2000 by using a GUI.

GUIs are generally more user friendly than text-based interfaces, especially for visually oriented individuals. With a GUI, users can, for example, *drag and drop* graphical elements to move a file from one location to another.

There are disadvantages to GUIs, however. For instance, GUIs slow down the response of the system and require more system resources to display the sophisticated graphics. In some cases, interacting with the graphical elements can be awkward and less convenient than typing in commands. In addition, it is very difficult to navigate most GUIs if the computer doesn't have a pointing device (a mouse or trackball) attached.

Because of the disadvantages, GUI-based operating systems usually provide command-line programs as an alternative to using the GUI. These programs can be used to perform common administrative tasks. For example, in Windows NT, you can run the built-in backup program either by selecting its graphical icon from a menu or by typing the **ntbackup.exe** command at the command prompt.

Using Commands

You use *commands* to tell an operating system what task to perform. In a text-based interface, you type these commands as strings of characters, and in a GUI interface, you click an icon or a menu item. In either event, your input is interpreted according to the *programming language* (for example, C or Java) in which the operating system is written, and then converted to *machine language*, which are the 1s and 0s that the computer processor understands.

COMMANDS AND CASE SENSITIVITY

The file systems used by some operating systems (such as UNIX) are *case sensitive*. Even in those operating systems (such as Windows) that use file systems that are not case sensitive, some commands and command arguments are case sensitive. For example, when entering the **nbtstat** command in Windows, the switch **-r** (lowercase) lists the names resolved by broadcast and WINS, and the switch **-R** (uppercase) purges and reloads the remote cache name table.

The Importance of Syntax

For a command to be processed properly, it must be in the proper *syntax*, which is the structure of the command. The structure includes word order, spacing, and in some cases, capitalization and punctuation.

Syntax is an element of spoken and written language—part of what we call *grammar*. For example, in English, the typical sentence structure places the subject of the sentence (usually a noun or pronoun) first and then a verb (action word) and object (if there is one) follow. Adjectives and adverbs are usually placed just before the nouns or verbs that they modify. Consider the following sentence: "Mary [subject/noun] bought [verb] a new [adjective modifying *computer*] computer [object/noun]."

However, if someone whose native language is not English wanted to communicate this idea, he might look up all the words in a translation dictionary and use the syntax of his own language to create the sentence. In such a scenario, the sentence might become "Mary a new computer bought." Most of us still would understand what is being said, even though the syntax isn't correct.

Life isn't so easy with a computer, however. If the command for copying a file from a floppy disk to the hard drive is

```
copy filename a: c:
```

and we mistakenly type

filename **copy a: c:**

the computer does not understand what is being said and won't perform the task.

Our two different outcomes occur because people can think, but computers can only calculate. Therefore, command syntax must be exactly right, down to the spacing between words. For example, typing the command **netview** at the Windows 2000 command prompt gets you nothing, but typing the command **net view** (with a space between the words) displays a list of servers on the network.

Using Arguments

Operating system commands often allow definition of additional parameters by the addition of *arguments* or *switches*. For example, the **net view** command, typed alone, displays a list of Microsoft computers on the network that are running the server service, as shown in Example 12-1.

EXAMPLE 12-1 The net view Command with no Switches Displays Microsoft Servers

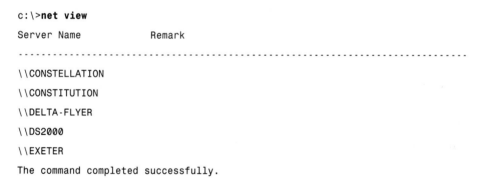

```
c:\>net view

Server Name            Remark

-------------------------------------------------------------------

\\CONSTELLATION

\\CONSTITUTION

\\DELTA-FLYER

\\DS2000

\\EXETER

The command completed successfully.
```

Adding a switch so that the command becomes **net view /network:nw** displays the NetWare servers on the network, as shown in Example 12-2.

EXAMPLE 12-2 Adding the Appropriate Switch to the net view Command Results in a Display of NetWare Servers Only

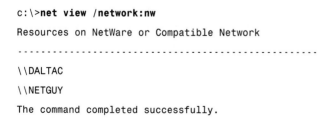

```
c:\>net view /network:nw

Resources on NetWare or Compatible Network

-----------------------------------------------

\\DALTAC

\\NETGUY

The command completed successfully.
```

An easy way to display the acceptable syntax and parameters for a command is to type [**command**] **?**, as shown in Example 12-3. To display a list of the commands themselves, type **help**. UNIX systems often provide an online manual that you can access by typing the command **man**.

EXAMPLE 12-3 Typing the Command Followed by a Question Mark Displays the Acceptable Syntax and Parameters of the Command

```
c:\>net view ?
The syntax of this command is:
NET VIEW [\\computername [/CACHE] : /DOMAIN[:domainname]]
NET VIEW /NETWORK:NW [\\computername]
```

Commands in Different Languages

In some cases, a command is the same from one operating system to the next. For example, the **arp** command displays the cached information of Address Resolution Protocol (ARP) on computers running TCP/IP, regardless of whether the operating system is Windows NT, Windows 2000, Windows 95, Windows 98, UNIX, or Linux.

On the other hand, some commands differ from one operating system to the next. To view the TCP/IP configuration information, you use an operating system-specific command, as listed in Table 12-1.

TABLE 12-1 Commands for Viewing TCP/IP Configuration Information

Operating System	Command
Windows NT and Windows 2000	ipconfig
Windows 95 and Windows 98	winipcfg
Linux and UNIX	ifconfig
NetWare	config

Common DOS Commands

All Windows operating systems include a command line that enables you to enter common MS-DOS based commands. To access the command prompt on Windows 9*x* machines, for example, you enter **command** in the Run dialog box. (You access this dialog box by choosing Start, Run from the desktop.)

On Windows NT/2000 machines, you enter **cmd**. This invokes a "DOS box" that has a prompt at which commands can be entered. (The "DOS box" is sometimes called a "c: prompt," although the directory in which the DOS prompt initiates depends on the configuration of your computer.)

Simple DOS commands include those shown in Table 12-2.

TABLE 12-2   Commonly Used DOS Commands

Command	Result
dir	Lists the files in the current directory
cd *directory name*	Changes to a different directory
time	Displays or sets the system time
date	Displays or sets the date
copy	Copies files to another location
diskcopy	Copies the contents of one floppy disk to another
attrib	Displays or changes file attributes
find *text string*	Searches for a text string in a file
help	Displays a list of other available commands and their functions

Help Commands and Help Files

GUI-based operating systems usually include Help files. These might be provided in .pdf (portable document) format for easy printing, or they might be written in HTML with clickable links to cross-referenced material. A search engine is often included. For example, the Windows 2000 operating systems include an extensive hyperlinked Help system, as shown in Figure 12-3, that can be searched by keyword, indexed list, or detailed table of contents. With it, you can easily print individual topics.

Files and File Systems

Computer information is stored in units called *files*. A file consists of a quantity of data that can be manipulated (for example, opened, viewed, copied, deleted, and moved) as one entity. Each file has a unique name within the location where it resides.

There are many different types of files. Each file type is associated with a type of application. For example, accounting information is stored in a spreadsheet file. Letters and other correspondence are stored in a word processing file. Artwork is often stored in a bitmap (BMP), Joint Photographic Experts Group (JPEG), or other type of graphics file.

Different types of files are created, opened, and modified using different types of applications. For instance, spreadsheets are manipulated using applications such as Excel or Lotus 1-2-3. Letters are manipulated using applications such as WordPad, Notepad, Word, or WordPerfect. Some artwork can be manipulated with the Paint application that comes with Microsoft operating systems. A file type is said to be *associated* with the program or programs that can be used to manipulate it.

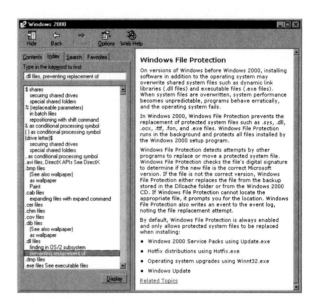

FIGURE 12-3
Modern operating systems include detailed Help files.

File Extensions and File Types

Some operating systems use *file extensions*, which are suffixes usually two or three characters in length that identify the file type and the application with which it is associated. For example, the .exe extension on the end of a filename is often used to indicate an executable (program) file, .gif identifies a graphics (picture) file, and .htm (or .html) is a file written in HyperText Markup Language (HTML). Some common file extensions are listed in Table 12-3.

TABLE 12-3   Common File Extensions

File Extension	File Type	Description	Associated Programs
.avi	Audio and video	Movie files	Media players
.bmp	Bitmap	Graphics files	Image viewers
.doc	Document	Word processing document	Word processing programs

TABLE 12-3   Common File Extensions (Continued)

File Extension	File Type	Description	Associated Programs
.jpg or .jpeg	JPEG picture	Compressed (small file size) graphics files	Image viewers and web browsers
.gif	Graphics Interchange Format (GIF) picture	Graphics files; can be combined for animations	Image viewers and web browsers
.hlp	Help	Help data files	Text editors
.htm or .html	HTML	Documents containing hypertext links	Web browsers
.ini	Initialization	Configuration files	Used by operating systems to set configurations; might be viewable in a text editor
.mid or .midi	Musical Instrument Digital Interface (MIDI) sound	Sound file; synthesized music	Media players
.pdf	Portable document format	Printable text and graphics documents	Adobe Acrobat
.ra	RealAudio	High-quality audio files	RealPlayer
.rtf	Rich text format	Formatted text files	Word processors or text editors
.tar	Tape archive	UNIX archive files	UNIX commands
.tif or .tiff	Tagged image format	High-quality graphics file	Image viewers
.wav	Waveform sound file	Sound (voice or music)	Media players

File Systems

The files stored on a computer's hard disk must be organized so that they can be located when needed by the operating system or an application program. The method used to place and retrieve files is called the *file system*.

Different operating systems use different file systems, and some operating systems can use more than one file system. For example, although Windows 3.*x* can use only the FAT16 file system, Windows 2000 can use FAT16, FAT32, or NTFS. We discuss these and other file systems later in this chapter.

The file system determines file naming conventions and the format for specifying a *path*, or route, to the file's location.

File Naming Conventions. The conventions or rules for naming files vary depending on the file system and include issues such as the following:

- Maximum number of characters allowed in a filename
- Maximum length of file extensions or suffixes
- Whether spaces are allowed between words in a filename
- Whether filenames are case sensitive
- Which characters are "legal" for use in filenames
- Format for specifying the path

Pathnames. A *pathname* can function in one of two ways:

- **Fully qualified (or absolute) pathname**—Identifies the complete path from the root partition to the file itself. An example is c:\mydirectory\subdirectory1\myfile.ext.
- **Relative pathname**—Identifies the path in relation to the directory or folder in which the operating system is currently working. For example, if the current working directory is mydirectory, the relative path is subdirectory1\myfile.ext.

NOTE

Note that in Microsoft operating systems, the drive letter is part of the path; in UNIX, it is not.

Microsoft operating systems (MS-DOS and Windows) and OS/2 use the format shown in the previous bulleted list. Backslashes separate levels of the directory structure, or *directory tree*. UNIX operating systems, on the other hand, use forward slashes, as in /mydirectory/subdirectory/myfile.

Most popular operating systems use a *tree structure* for the file system. In a tree structure, the root is at the top and containers called *directories* or *folders* are created below the root. This sometimes is referred to as an *inverted tree*.

Operating systems that use the tree structure include MS-DOS, Windows (all versions), Macintosh, OS/2, UNIX, and Linux.

Container units are called directories in DOS, Windows 3.*x*, UNIX, and Linux. They are called folders in Windows 9*x*, Windows NT 4.0, Windows 2000, and Macintosh OS. The term "folders" enables users to better understand the file system structure by relating it to an office environment in which paper files are stored in manila folders. Files are placed in containers for organizational purposes.

Directories (also called folders) can contain subdirectories (or subfolders), which can contain their own subdirectories (subfolders), and so on. Directories and folders, like files, must have unique names within their containers; that is, if you have directories named Dir1 and Dir2, each can have a subdirectory with the same name (Sub1). However, you can't have two subdirectories in Dir1 that are named Sub1 because the full pathnames would be the same. In the first case, the full pathnames will be different (c:\Dir1\Sub1 and c:\Dir2\Sub1).

Popular File Systems. In the following sections, we take a look at some popular file systems used by modern operating systems, including:

- File Allocation Table (FAT)
- NT File System (NTFS)
- High Performance File System (HPFS)
- Macintosh Hierarchical File System (HFS)
- Network File System (NFS)

FAT

There are several variants of the FAT file system, including FAT12, FAT16, FAT32, and VFAT. These file systems are so named because they use a file allocation table that is maintained on the hard disk and that provides a mapping of where files are stored. These files are stored in *clusters*, a unit of logical storage on the disk. A cluster can contain data from only one file; however, one file may be spread over multiple clusters.

You rarely see FAT12 today because it is used only on extremely small disk partitions. (We discuss disk partitioning later in this chapter.) FAT16 is a later version of the file system that was created for use on larger partitions (up to 4 GB).

Although larger disks can be formatted in FAT16, to do so is an inefficient use of disk space because in FAT, larger partitions result in larger cluster sizes. For example, with a 512 MB partition, the size of the clusters (that is, the basic storage units) is 8 KB. This means that even if a file is only 1 KB in size, it uses 8 KB of space because more than one file cannot be stored in a cluster; the extra 7 KB is wasted. To overcome this problem, FAT32 was developed. This 32-bit file system uses smaller cluster sizes on large disks. It supports partitions up to 2 *terabytes* (TB) in size.

An advantage of the FAT16 file system is the wide variety of operating systems that support it. MS-DOS, OS/2, all varieties of Windows, and other operating systems can read and write FAT16 files. Windows 95b (which you'll learn about later in the chapter), Windows 98, Windows ME, and Windows 2000 support FAT32. MS-DOS/Windows 3.*x* and Windows NT cannot use FAT32. This limits its usability in dual-boot, or multiboot, machines.

DUAL-BOOT COMPUTERS

A dual-boot, or multiboot, computer is one on which more than one operating system is installed. A boot manager program is usually used to provide a menu that allows you to select which operating system you want to load when you boot the machine. Some operating systems' installation programs include a boot manager. For example, Windows NT and Windows 2000 include the NT boot manager (with operating system options defined in a file called boot.ini), and Linux includes the LILO boot manager. Third-party boot management utilities, such as System Commander, enable you to load up to 100 operating systems on one machine.

The original FAT file systems were developed for MS-DOS, which limits filenames to eight characters with a three-character extension. *Virtual FAT (VFAT)* is a variant of FAT that was developed for Windows 95 for supporting long filenames. VFAT is implemented as a *file system driver* that extends the FAT file system's capability to use filenames that are up to 256 characters. This makes it much easier to create meaningful filenames that are recognizable later. VFAT also supports disk caching, which increases performance and reduces the time required to read from or write to the hard disk.

NTFS

Microsoft developed NTFS for Windows NT, and only Windows NT and Windows 2000 can use it. NTFS was designed to address some problems, such as lack of support for file-level security, inherent in the FAT file systems.

NTFS includes the following features, which overcome various limitations of FAT:

- **File-level security through NTFS permissions**—NTFS uses an access control list (ACL) that enables you to set specific permissions on files, regardless of whether a user is accessing the file from across the network or from the local machine. FAT files can be secured through *share permissions*, which protect the file from unauthorized network access but do not protect it from local access. (NTFS files can be protected simultaneously by both share permissions *and* NTFS file-level permissions.)

- **File-level compression**—To compress data in FAT, the entire partition must be compressed using a method that essentially turns the partition into one big file. If this file is corrupted, all data on that logical drive might be lost. NTFS files can be compressed on a file-by-file basis. If one file on the partition is corrupted, the others are not affected.

- **Sector sparing (also called *hot fixing*)**—With this feature, the file system identifies bad disk sectors, moves the data to a good sector, and marks the bad sector as unusable. This is done "on the fly," and the process is invisible to the user.

- **Unicode support**—NTFS supports the use of filenames that use Unicode characters, which enable you to display international languages.

- **Support for extremely large partitions (up to 16 *exabytes*)**—An exabyte is approximately one billion bytes of data.

- **Long File Name (LFN) support**—NTFS supports long filenames and maintains corresponding "eight dot three" names for each file. (In "eight dot three" names, there are up to eight characters plus a three-character extension, which collectively give you a name such as "file.doc.") This is done for backward compatibility with MS-DOS and Windows 3.*x*.

NTFS keeps track of file clusters with a *b-tree (binary tree) directory scheme*. B-tree indexing enables the viewing of data in sorted order. This contrasts with the *linked-list* file structure of FAT. The b-tree structure enables faster access to files in a large directory.

Where FAT stores information about a file's clusters only in the file allocation table, NTFS stores this information with each individual cluster. NTFS is less vulnerable than FAT to *file fragmentation*, which can slow performance on operations that access data on the hard disk.

> **NOTE**
>
> *Backward compatibility* is the capability of a file system, operating system, or application to work with files created by earlier versions of the software. It is important for software vendors to make their products backward compatible so that users who upgrade to the new version of a product do not lose the data they created in the earlier version.

FILE FRAGMENTATION

On an empty, or clean, disk, data is stored in clusters sequentially. If a file is too large to store all the data in one cluster, the carryover is stored in the next available cluster. When all the data for each file is stored in contiguous clusters, the disk is said to be *unfragmented*.

Fragmentation, however, occurs if data is moved or removed because such actions leave empty clusters. When new data is stored, it is stored in the first available clusters, so if the new file is larger than the one that was removed, the first part of the data is stored in the clusters left empty. Then the rest is stored in the next available clusters, which might be separated by intervening clusters on the disk.

When the operating system or an application needs to access the file, it takes longer than if the data were stored in sequential clusters on the disk. Thus, fragmentation slows performance. Utilities called *defragmenters* (such as Diskeeper, made by Executive Software) can rearrange data to reduce file fragmentation and speed performance. Windows 9x and Windows 2000 include built-in defragmentation tools.

Windows 2000 includes a new version of NTFS, called NTFS 5. Windows NT can read NTFS 5 files *if* Service Pack 4 or above has been installed. However, Windows NT cannot use the advanced features of NTFS 5, such as file encryption, that are supported by Windows 2000. NTFS 5 provides many additional features and improvements to NTFS 4, including the following:

- The capability to encrypt files on the hard disk by using the Encrypting File System (EFS).
- Support for sparse files, which enables programs to create very large files while consuming disk space only as needed.
- Support for disk quotas, which enables administrators to limit the amount of disk space used on a per-user basis.
- Distributed link-tracking, which enables programs to keep up with links when the source files are moved.
- Volume mount points, which enable you to mount a disk volume in an NTFS folder. This overcomes the limitation that stipulated that you could create only as many volumes as there were letters in the alphabet.
- Remote storage support, which makes files stored on removable media (such as tape) more accessible.

UNIX File System

The UNIX file system is organized as a hierarchy of directories and subdirectories in which files can be stored.

In UNIX, the root directory is represented by a slash (/). Thus, a directory path looks like "/dir2/subdir1"; a subdirectory called subdir1 resides in a directory called dir2, which resides in the root directory.

UNIX *system directories* are located immediately below the root directory. They contain the files used by the operating system. The standard system directories include the following:

- **/bin**—Contains *executable binary* files, which are the commands and utilities for everyday operation
- **/dev**—Contains special files that represent physical *devices* such as printers
- **/etc**—Contains commands and files used for system administration
- **/lib**—Contains *libraries* used by programs
- **/tmp**—Contains *temporary* files, which are removed when the system reboots
- **/usr**—Contains users' *home directories*, along with other files such as the online manual

The *kernel* is the operating system core, which is loaded when you boot the operating system. The UNIX root directory contains the kernel file and the *bootstrap loader*, which is a small program that begins the loading of the operating system.

The UNIX file system does not allow intervening spaces in a filename. Although you can name a file "Joe Brown Memos" in Windows 2000, in UNIX you would have to name it JoeBrownMemos, Joe_Brown_Memos, or Joe-Brown-Memos.

UNIX does allow placement of periods (or *dots)* within filenames. For example, you can name a file Joe.Brown.Memos. You can do this with the 32-bit Windows operating systems as well, but in DOS/Windows 3.x, only one dot is allowed. Whatever comes after the dot (limited to three characters) is treated as a file extension.

Filenames in UNIX may have up to 255 characters. Some characters (including # / ? " ' [ ]) are not allowed because they have special significance to the operating system.

To the user, one of the most noticeable differences between UNIX and the Microsoft file systems is *case sensitivity*. In DOS or Windows, the filename "mydocuments" is the same as "MyDocuments" or "MYDOCUMENTS." To the UNIX file system, these are three distinct names, and all three can coexist in the same directory.

While surfing the Web, you might have noticed that if you enter a URL without the exact capitalization, your web browser sometimes goes to the website anyway; other times, however, it does not. This discrepancy occurs because some web servers are running Windows NT, which does not use a case-sensitive file system, while others run UNIX, which does.

> **NOTE**
>
> Although the underscore character (_) is not prohibited in filenames, it is a good idea to avoid using it because an underscore in the name of a computer or other resource that is available on the Internet might cause problems with some Domain Name System (DNS) servers, which cannot resolve such names to IP addresses.

Other features of the UNIX file system include the following:

■ **I-node mapping**—UNIX uses an internal number called an *i-node* to identify each file or directory. The operating system maps this number to the location of the data on the physical disk. A table is maintained to match the full path name to the corresponding i-node.

■ **Hard links**—A hard link enables you to associate more than one filename with the same file. By using the **ln** command to link them, you can have two different files—one named Myfile and another named Yourfile, for example—reference the same i-node. When you do this, changes made to Myfile immediately show up in Yourfile.

■ **Flat files**—The UNIX file system does not have elaborate rules defining headers for different file types. Instead, the files are made up of data streams with no imposed structure. It is up to the application to define the structure for formatting the files.

HPFS

IBM developed HPFS for the OS/2 operating system. Although version 1.0 of OS/2 shipped with only FAT support, HPFS was included in version 1.2. Some characteristics of HPFS include the following:

■ Long filename support (up to 254 characters)

■ Faster performance than FAT

■ High reliability and recoverability

■ Less file fragmentation than FAT

HPFS supports extended character sets, and although it preserves case, it is *not* case sensitive. Thus, if you forget how you used capitalization in a filename such as "mydocuments," for example, entering myDocuments or MYDOCU-MENTS still allows you to access the file.

HPFS uses a directory structure that divides the disk into *bands*, each of which is 16 MB across. Directory structure and allocation information is located in the middle of each band. As a result, the file content can be no more than 8 MB from the control information on the disk surface. This is the basis of HPFS's high performance.

HPFS supports partitions up to 64 GB and allocates disk space using sectors instead of clusters; this creates less wasted disk space and less need for defragmentation. HPFS uses *sector signatures* to identify each disk sector; because of this, data can be recovered even from badly corrupted disks.

> **NOTE**
>
> *Reliability*, when used to describe a file system, refers to a low incidence of errors and file corruption. *Recoverability* is the capability of the file system to maintain data integrity by creating, for example, a redundant copy of data that can be used if the original data becomes corrupted.

Macintosh HFS

The Mac operating system uses HFS; in HFS, disks are partitioned into *volumes* that can contain any of the following components:

- Files
- Directories
- Directory threads
- File threads

The file system uses b-tree indexing algorithms to organize and locate the contents of the directories. In addition, HFS supports *file forking*, in which files are made up of the following parts, or *forks*:

- **Resource fork**—This file includes menu items, dialog boxes, and so on.
- **Data fork**—This file contains the data stream.

HFS uses *catalogs*, and each file or directory has *catalog records* with identification numbers that function somewhat like UNIX i-nodes. Directory threads and file threads are catalog records that include the name of the directory or file along with the identification of its parent directory. The threads provide redundancy and recoverability from disk crashes.

Utilities such as the Global File System plug-in from Charismac and MacOpener from DataViz, enable Macintosh files to be accessed from Linux, OS/2, Windows, and DOS operating systems.

NFS

NFS was developed by Sun Microsystems and has become a standard for file servers; it uses the remote-procedure call (RPC) protocols to communicate. For NFS to work, an NFS client must be installed on the requesting computer, and both client and server must run TCP/IP. WebNFS is an extension of NFS for use over the Internet; it replaces protocols such as HTTP and FTP.

Choosing the Correct PC File System

Your file system choice depends on the operating systems installed on the computer, your security needs, and your access needs. File systems are generally developed in connection with a specific operating system, but some operating systems support more than one file system. You might even be able to use two or more file systems at the same time—as long as they are on separate *disk partitions*.

> **NOTE**
>
> A *directory thread* contains the name of the directory and identification of the parent of the directory. A file thread contains the name of the file and the directory in which the file resides.

Disks and Disk Partitions. The basic storage media for PCs is the *hard disk*. The size of hard disks varies; early disks held only 5 MB of data. Modern, affordable hard disks can hold 50 GB or more.

A hard disk is made up of a stack of disks that work like phonograph records. However, where the groove on a phonograph record is one continuous spiral from the outer edge to the center, data is recorded on a disk in concentric circles called *tracks*.

The disk drive has two *heads* that read and write data. The heads are in fixed positions, and the disks rotate to enable access to different parts of the disk. The rotation speed is measured in rotations per minute, for example, 4500 rpm. The disk access time, called *seek time*, is measured in milliseconds, for example, 9 ms.

Accessing data on a disk is much slower than accessing data in RAM because disk access requires mechanical movements of physical objects (the read/write heads). Mechanical movement takes time. Accessing RAM takes only as long as necessary for electricity to flow along a circuit. This is less than the speed of light, but faster than the mechanical movement of the disk components.

Data stored on a disk is located according to its *sector*, track, and *cylinder*. As previously defined, a track is a concentric circle on a disk. A cylinder is all the tracks in the same position on each of the stacked disks. A sector is a division of a track. The file system must map the precise physical location on the disk so that data can be located again when needed.

NOTE

Note that the partitions do *not* have to be the same size. You could divide a 15 GB hard disk into partitions of 2 GB, 5 GB, 7 GB, and 1 GB.

Many of today's disks are very large and hold many gigabytes of data. To better organize the files on the disk, you can divide a disk into *partitions*, which appear to the operating system as individual *drives*. Each partition is then assigned a drive letter as if it were a separate physical disk. For instance, you might divide a disk into partitions so that you can store the operating system files on one partition, application software on another, and user data on a third. For example, if your hard disk is 15 GB, you could create three partitions of 5 GB each.

Disks are *partitioned* using utility software. Partitioning programs, such as the FDISK commands in DOS, Windows 9*x*, and Linux or the GUI Disk Management tools in Windows NT and Windows 2000, might be built into the operating system. Third-party utilities such as Partition Magic are also available.

In DOS, for example, a disk can have up to four *primary* partitions. In place of one of the primary partitions, you can create an *extended* partition and create multiple *logical drives* inside that partition. One primary partition must be marked as *active*. This is the partition from which the computer boots.

If you have many paper files (for example, several years' worth of financial records) that you want to store in a cabinet, you could put them all in one big drawer. Alternately, you could sort them and put those pertaining to 1996 in one drawer, those pertaining to 1997 in another, and so on. In a similar fashion, partitioning your disk helps you to sort and organize your electronic data.

There are two additional reasons to divide a disk into partitions:

- Different partitions can be formatted in different file systems. This means that you can have drive C formatted in FAT16, drive D in FAT32, and drive E in NTFS.
- Different operating systems can be installed on separate partitions in a multiboot configuration. Although it is possible to install multiple operating systems on the same partition (if they can use the same file system), it is not recommended because they might overwrite one another's files.

Windows 2000 introduced a new concept to Microsoft operating systems—*dynamic disks*. When you convert a disk to dynamic status, you create volumes on the disk instead of partitions. These volumes can be resized dynamically, without erasing the data. You can combine chunks of space from multiple physical disks into one volume to provide a larger storage area or to provide *fault tolerance*. We talk more about disk fault tolerance in Chapter 14, "Protecting the Network."

A volume functions as a single entity even though it is made up of two or more disks, and one drive letter is used to identify the entire aggregated space.

Common Desktop Operating Systems

In this section, we take a look at the following common desktop operating systems that function as clients in a client/server network environment:

- MS-DOS and Windows 3.*x*
- Windows 9*x*
- Windows NT Workstation
- Windows 2000 Professional
- Linux/UNIX
- Macintosh
- OS/2

The remaining sections of this chapter include step-by-step procedures and screenshots illustrating how to configure networking components on some desktop operating systems. Note that this is not meant to serve as a "how-to" guide (see the section "Further Reading" at the end of the chapter for references to detailed instructional guides). Rather, these sections are intended to provide you with a sense of how networking setup is done in each operating system and to familiarize you with the interface used for configuration.

MS-DOS and Windows 3.x

Although professionals in the information technology industry might consider them obsolete, many computers on production networks in the business world run Microsoft's "old" operating system, MS-DOS. (A *production network* is one on which business operations depend, as opposed to one used for lab or testing purposes.

There are several good reasons for using MS-DOS:

- **MS-DOS is a simple, low-overhead operating system**—Memory and processor requirements are very low. DOS runs readily on outdated hardware.
- **MS-DOS is inexpensive**—Not only is the operating system itself inexpensive, the cost of compatible hardware, as mentioned previously, also is low.
- **MS-DOS is stable and reliable**—Because it is not a multitasking operating system (that is, it runs only one program at a time), there is no need to worry about the conflicts and crashes caused by shared memory addresses.
- **MS-DOS is easy to learn and use**—Although it is not as intuitive as a GUI-based operating system, once you master the command syntax, DOS is relatively simple to use.
- **Many programs are available for MS-DOS**—Because it was a standard for many years, a large number of programs were written to run on DOS. Some companies continue to run the operating system because proprietary programs, custom-written for their business to run on MS-DOS, do not work properly on the newer operating systems.

Of course, there are many disadvantages to continuing to use this old operating system. MS-DOS is a 16-bit operating system and cannot run the sophisticated graphical programs written for 32-bit Windows operating systems. Lack of multitasking capability is, at best, a huge inconvenience in today's corporate world. The FAT file system, which is the only file system DOS uses, offers little in the way of security in modern privacy-conscious environments. In addition, in a network environment, MS-DOS clients might be unable to connect to shared resources that use long filenames. Last, many users are intimidated by the command-line interface.

Running Windows 3.x on top of MS-DOS can lessen some of these drawbacks. The Windows 3.x shell provides a GUI and supports *cooperative multitasking*, which enables users to run more than one program simultaneously.

COOPERATIVE AND PREEMPTIVE MULTITASKING

Cooperative multitasking is an environment in which programs share memory addresses and exchange information. In a cooperatively multitasked environment, applications share the use of the processor by a method known as *time slicing*. The application programs are written to give up the processor after a set amount of time so that it can be used by other programs that are running simultaneously. If the program is poorly written, it might monopolize the processor, and if one program crashes, it might bring the rest down with it.

A more efficient form of multitasking is called *preemptive multitasking*, and it is used by Windows 9*x*, Windows NT, and Windows 2000. The operating system in this case controls the allocation of processor time, and 32-bit programs run in their own separate address spaces. With preemptive multitasking, an unruly program cannot take over the system, and if one program crashes, it does not affect the others.

MS-DOS and Windows 3.1 require that you install additional *network client* software to connect to a network. Windows for Workgroups 3.11 is the first Microsoft operating system to have networking components built in. Although designed with peer-to-peer (workgroup) networking in mind, Windows 3.*x* and MS-DOS can be used, when properly configured, to connect to a Windows NT or Windows 2000 domain. Note that these machines do not have computer accounts in the domain; you can use them to log in to the domain (with the proper user account credentials) and access resources, but they cannot join the domain.

Windows 9*x*

Microsoft Windows 95 was designed for easy networkability, and the tradition was carried on and enhanced in Windows 98. These operating systems are referred to collectively as Windows 9*x* and include the following products:

- **Windows 95a**—The original release of Microsoft's first 32-bit consumer operating system.

- **Windows 95b**—Also called OSR2, which included enhancements such as FAT32 support and was made available only to original equipment manufacturers (OEM) for installation on the computers they sold.

- **Windows 98**—An upgrade to Windows 95 that added the Active Desktop technology, the Advanced Configuration and Power Interface (ACPI), support for the universal serial bus (USB) and TV-tuner cards, and setup and maintenance enhancements.

- **Windows 98 Second Edition (SE)**—Provided the Internet Explorer 5.0 web browser, stronger encryption for dialup networking, and added support for Internet Connection Sharing (ICS).

- **Windows Millennium Edition (Windows ME)**—This is the next consumer operating system in Microsoft's lineup, generally recognized as part of the 9*x* family. At the time of this writing, it had just been released to manufacturing. Features in Windows ME include the following:

  — Enhanced multimedia support, making it easy to work with movies and digital photos

  — Built-in disaster recovery features that enable you to restore the system to a predetermined state

  — Simplification of the configuration required to set up simple peer-to-peer networks

  — Faster startup and shutdown (when using new hardware that supports the FastBoot technology)

The Windows 9*x* operating systems include a client for Microsoft networks and a client for NetWare. NetBEUI, TCP/IP, and NWLink network and transport protocols also are included with the operating systems. Dialup networking for connecting to the Internet or to a remote LAN is also built in.

Because of its connectivity features, Windows 9*x* is one of the most popular client operating systems in the business world. For several years, it has been the desktop operating system of choice for both small and large companies, for peer-to-peer networks, and for use as a client to Microsoft NT, NetWare, and UNIX servers.

Windows 9*x* supports 32-bit applications, but it also includes 16-bit code for backward compatibility with DOS and Windows 3.*x* programs. It uses VFAT for long filename support, and Windows 95b, 98, and ME can use FAT32 for more efficient disk use.

Some advantages of Windows 9x as a desktop operating system and network client include the following:

- It is less expensive than Windows NT and Windows 2000.
- It runs a wide variety of DOS, 16-bit, and 32-bit Windows applications.
- Its interface is familiar to most PC computer users.
- Client software is available for Windows 9*x* to connect to most NOS types, such as Windows, NetWare, UNIX, and Linux.

In the following sections, you will learn the basics of connecting a Windows 9*x* client to a Microsoft network, a NetWare network, or a remote access server.

NOTE

Novell does not make a desktop operating system. Most client machines on NetWare networks use the Windows desktop operating systems, which have Novell's client software or the NetWare client components built in. Novell also provides a DOS client. Macintosh Connectivity Solutions for NetWare is available through Prosoft Engineering.

Connecting a Windows 9*x* Client to a Microsoft Network

Windows 9*x* has networking components built into the operating system. You can configure the computer as part of a peer-to-peer network (workgroup), or you can use it to log in to a Windows NT or Windows 2000 domain for which you have a valid domain user account.

Network settings are configured in the Network properties dialog box, shown in Figure 12-4, which is accessible by choosing Start, Settings, Control Panel, Network or by right-clicking the Network Neighborhood icon on the desktop and selecting Properties from the context menu.

FIGURE 12-4
Network settings are configured through the Network properties dialog box in Windows 9*x*.

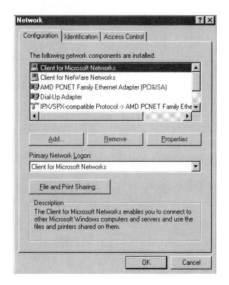

To set up a Windows 95 or Windows 98 computer as a peer in a Microsoft workgroup, perform the following steps:

1. Ensure that a network interface card (NIC) is installed and connected through cable or other media to the network.

2. Install the software drivers for the NIC according to manufacturer's instructions (be sure the drivers are written for the version of Windows that you have installed).

3. On the Configuration tab of the Network properties dialog box, ensure that Client for Microsoft Networks is installed. If it is not, you can install it by clicking the Add button and selecting it from a list. You might be prompted to insert the Windows 9*x* CD.

4. If you will use the computer to log in to a Windows NT or Windows 2000 domain, configure the domain logon by selecting Client for Microsoft Networks and clicking the Properties button. The dialog box shown in Figure 12-5 is then displayed. Check the checkbox and enter the name of the domain. You can also choose Quick logon, which does not restore mapped network drives until you use them, or Logon and restore network connections.

FIGURE 12-5
You must config-
ure the Client
properties if you
will use the com-
puter to log in to
a Windows
domain.

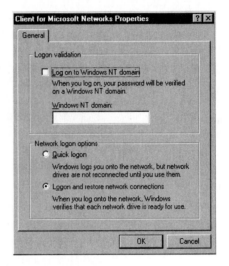

5. On the Identification tab, as shown in Figure 12-6, ensure that the computer has a unique name on the network. This name can be up to 15 alphanumeric characters. If this computer will be a member of a workgroup, enter the workgroup name here. A space also is provided for an optional computer description.

6. You must have at least one network or transport protocol installed and bound to the NIC. This protocol must be installed also on other computers on the network with which you wish to communicate. Protocols are added, removed, and configured through the Configuration tab. You might have to scroll down to see all the components installed.

7. You must enable file and printer sharing if you want to share this computer's resources across the network. This is done by clicking the File and Print Sharing button on the Configuration tab and then checking the appropriate checkboxes, as shown in Figure 12-7.

FIGURE 12-6
You configure the computer name and the workgroup name on the Identification tab.

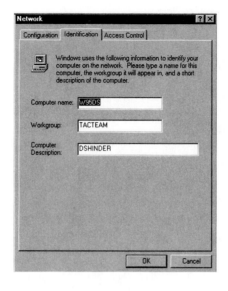

FIGURE 12-7
You must enable file and print sharing to make the computer's resources accessible across the network.

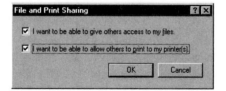

After configuring network properties, you must reboot the computer for the changes to take effect. When you boot back into Windows, you will see a network login box asking for your username and password if the configuration changes were successful. See Figure 12-8.

You can now double-click Network Neighborhood and see a list of computers on the network that are in your workgroup or domain. (Computers that have file and print sharing enabled show up on this list, and Windows NT and Windows 2000 machines that have the server service started also show up.) This list is called the *browse list*. If the computer is logged in to a domain, you might need to click the domain name to see the list of computers, as shown in Figure 12-9.

NOTE

If you will be using TCP/IP for network communications, you must configure its properties with an appropriate IP address and subnet mask (and default gateway if applicable) or configure the computer to be a Dynamic Host Configuration Protocol (DHCP) client. A DHCP client requests an IP address from a DHCP server when it initially connects to the network.

FIGURE 12-8
The network login box appears when you reboot the computer after configuring networking properties.

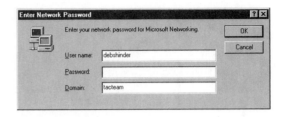

FIGURE 12-9
When networking components have been properly configured, you see a list of computers in Network Neighborhood.

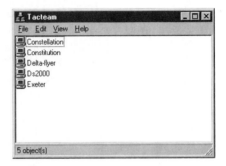

Accessing the resources of other computers on the network is as easy as double-clicking the computer name *if* your user account has the proper access permissions. We discuss access permissions in more depth in Chapter 14.

Connecting a Windows 9x Client to a NetWare Network

A Windows 9*x* computer can function as a client to a NetWare server in one of two ways:

- By using the Microsoft Client for NetWare Networks that is included on the Windows 9*x* CD (but not installed by default)
- By using the Novell client for Windows 95/98

One machine cannot have both NetWare client software packages installed.

The IPX/SPX protocol stack is required for connecting to all NetWare servers prior to version 5.0. NWLink, Microsoft's implementation of IPX/SPX, is installed automatically when you install the Microsoft Client for NetWare Networks. The Microsoft client is installed as a networking component on the Configuration tab of the Network properties dialog box.

Selecting the Client for NetWare Networks and clicking the Properties button enables you to set a preferred NetWare server, as shown in Figure 12-10. If you leave this field blank, the computer attempts to log in to the nearest NetWare server.

FIGURE 12-10
You can select a preferred Net-Ware server for your Windows 9*x* machine to log in to.

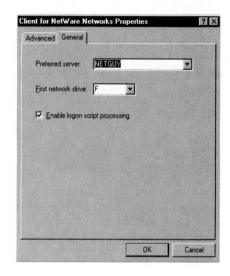

You must reboot after installing and configuring the NetWare client.

After installing and configuring the NetWare client/NWLink, you will see the NetWare tree in Network Neighborhood. This is shown as Daltac in Figure 12-11.

FIGURE 12-11
The NetWare tree appears in Net-work Neighbor-hood after you install the Net-Ware client soft-ware.

In Windows 9*x*, you can easily access NetWare resources by navigating through the tree and double-clicking the selected resource if you have the required permissions on the NetWare server. To the user, NetWare resources appear like those on a Microsoft server.

Connecting a Windows 9*x* Client to a Remote Server

It is easy to connect a Windows 9*x* computer to a remote server over telephone lines. Microsoft includes the Dialup Networking component for this purpose. To create a dialup connection, you must first install and configure a modem. Dialup connections are configured through the Dialup Networking applet, which is accessed through the My Computer icon on the desktop.

You can use dialup networking to connect to an Internet service provider (ISP) or a remote access services (RAS) server. Windows 9*x* itself can be a dialup server; this feature is installed and configured through the Add/Remove Programs applet in Control Panel.

The remote access service is discussed in more detail in Chapter 15, "Remote Access."

Windows NT Workstation

Windows NT Workstation was Microsoft's first desktop operating system aimed at the corporate market. The latest version is NT 4.0, which has a user interface similar to the one in Windows 95. Some companies still use NT 3.*x*, however, which has the Windows 3.*x* interface. Windows NT was designed to provide a more stable environment for mission-critical business use than is provided by Microsoft's consumer operating systems.

Some advantages of Windows NT Workstation as a desktop operating system and network client include the following:

- It is a true 32-bit operating system, and it supports preemptive multitasking and greater system stability.
- It includes file-level security and data compression on a file-by-file basis.
- It is backward compatible with many 16-bit programs, without sacrificing reliability. NT runs DOS and older Windows programs in virtual machines (VMs). Using this method, if one application crashes, it does not affect other applications or require a reboot of the operating system.

Network integration is a primary focus in Microsoft's design of Windows NT, and NT includes support for common NICs as well as software needed to connect to Microsoft and NetWare networks. The capability to function as a remote access client or server is also built in.

NOTE

The Microsoft Plus! Pack (a group of add-on operating system components) is required for you to use dialup networking with Windows 95. Windows 98, on the other hand, includes the dialup networking components.

NOTE

When the first version of Windows NT was released, Microsoft said the acronym stood for "New Technology." More recently, the company has stated that "NT" stands alone and is not an acronym.

Connecting a Windows NT Workstation to a Microsoft Network

Windows NT Workstation can function as a peer in a Microsoft workgroup or as a client in an NT Server-based domain. Connecting an NT Workstation machine to a Windows network involves the following steps:

1. Ensure that a NIC is properly installed and connected through cable or other media to the network.

2. Install the software drivers for the NIC according to manufacturer's instructions. Make sure that these drivers are written for Windows NT.

3. Configure network properties through the Network applet. You can access this tabbed properties configuration box by choosing Start, Settings, Control Panel, Network or by right-clicking the Network Neighborhood icon on the desktop and selecting Properties from the context menu.

4. On the Identification tab, which is shown in Figure 12-12, give the computer a unique name on the network. This name can have up to 15 alphanumeric characters.

5. Enter the name of the domain (or workgroup) to which the computer will belong, as shown in Figure 12-12.

FIGURE 12-12
A unique computer name and the name of the domain are entered in the Identification tab of the Network properties dialog box.

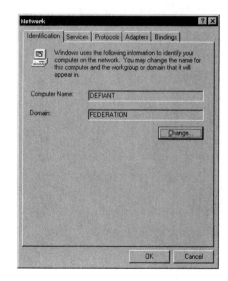

Connecting a Windows NT Workstation to a NetWare Network

As with Windows 9*x*, it is easy to connect an NT Workstation 4.0 computer to a NetWare network. Microsoft provides Client Services for NetWare (CSNW) on the NT Workstation CD; alternatively, you can download the Novell client for NT from www.novell.com. NWLink is automatically installed when you install CSNW. Figure 12-13 shows the CSNW configuration screen.

FIGURE 12-13
The CSNW service can be used to connect a Windows NT 4.0 machine to a NetWare server.

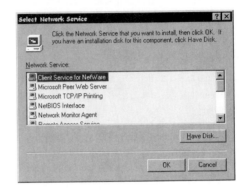

After CSNW has been installed on the workstation, an applet appears in the NT Control Panel. You configure CSNW through the Control Panel applet.

After CSNW has been installed and configured, the NetWare network appears in Network Neighborhood, as shown in Figure 12-14, and you can browse the network and connect to any resources on NetWare servers for which you have permissions and do so in the same way that you access resources on Microsoft servers.

FIGURE 12-14
After CSNW is installed, you can access the NetWare network from Network Neighborhood.

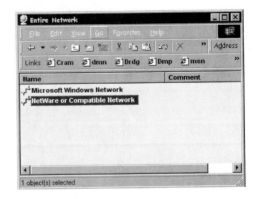

Connecting a Windows NT Workstation to a Remote Server

Configuring NT Workstation to connect to a remote server is slightly more complex than performing the same task in Windows 9x. RAS first must be installed as a service in the Network properties configuration box, which is shown in Figure 12-15.

FIGURE 12-15
RAS is installed as a service in the Network properties dialog box.

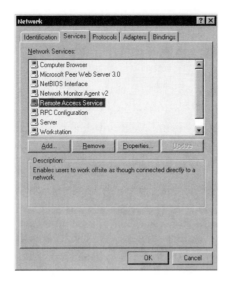

Windows 2000 Professional

Windows 2000 is Microsoft's latest operating system for the corporate desktop. Like the Windows 2000 server products, it is based on the NT kernel, but it includes many enhanced features. Unlike NT Workstation, Windows 2000 Professional supports Plug and Play technology, can be installed on hard disks formatted with FAT32, and includes file encryption for securing data on the hard disk. Unlike Windows 9x, Windows 2000 Professional provides a high level of security and stability for mission-critical tasks.

Other advantages of Windows 2000 Professional as a desktop operating system and network client include the following:

- It offers better support for mobile users through Advanced Power Management (APM) and ACPI. Windows NT does not support ACPI.
- It provides for more secure virtual private networking with the Layer 2 Tunneling Protocol (L2TP) and IP Security (IPSec). Earlier versions of

Windows supported only the Point-to-Point Tunneling Protocol (PPTP) for VPNs.

- The offline folders feature enables you to copy and synchronize documents from the network to your local system so that they can be accessed when your computer is not connected to the network.

- The Internet Printing Protocol (IPP) enables you to print to a URL and manage printers through a web browser interface.

- Built-in disk defragmenter and other tools and utilities help you maintain and manage the operating system. These have to be purchased separately from third parties for Windows NT.

- It supports Kerberos security, and you can use the features of a Windows 2000 domain as an Active Directory client.

In the following sections, you will learn how to connect a Windows 2000 Professional computer to a Microsoft network, a NetWare network, or a remote access server.

Connecting Windows 2000 Professional to a Microsoft Network

Because Windows 2000 Professional was designed for business users, networking support is an integral part of the operating system. The network adapter is detected through Plug and Play when the computer is started. A local-area connection is created automatically for each detected network card.

Hardware profiles can be created for laptops or other computers that will operate with a network connection at certain times and that will be disconnected from the network at other times. This eliminates the problem of error messages when the computer is unable to find the network.

Configuring a LAN connection involves the same basic tasks that were discussed in the "Connecting a Windows NT Workstation to a Microsoft Network" section earlier in this chapter. TCP/IP is installed as the default network/transport protocol, and IP addressing information can be set manually or the computer can be configured to be a DHCP client.

Unlike NT, Windows 2000 supports Automatic Private IP Addressing (APIPA). APIPA enables a DHCP client that can't locate a DHCP server to assign itself an IP address. The computer will then be able to communicate with any other computers on the same segment that have also assigned themselves APIPA addresses. With NT clients, if the DHCP server was down when the client came online, TCP/IP was disabled on the client.

Network configuration properties are accessed through the Network and Dialup Connections applet in Control Panel or by choosing Start, Settings, Network and Dialup Connections. Figure 12-16 shows the Local Area Connection

Properties dialog box where you add, remove, and configure the network clients, services, and protocols.

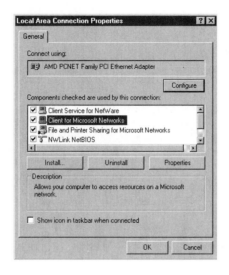

FIGURE 12-16
Windows 2000 network components are configured through the Network Services properties dialog box.

The Connection status dialog box, shown in Figure 12-17 for the configured local area connection, provides useful information that includes the following:

- Whether the network connection is active (status) and how long the computer has been connected to the network (duration)
- The connection speed in megabits per second (usually either 10 or 100 for an Ethernet connection)
- The number of packets sent and received

You can disable the connection in this dialog box, or you can click the Properties button to change the configuration.

Windows 2000 supports a wide variety of LAN and WAN connections. In addition to Ethernet, the supported connections include Token Ring, cable modem, DSL, FDDI, IP over ATM, Infrared wireless (IrDA), and ATM LAN emulation (LANE).

Connecting Windows 2000 Professional to a NetWare Network

Microsoft has extended NetWare client support to Windows 2000 Professional. CSNW works in Windows 2000 as it does in Windows NT.

In Windows 2000, CSNW is installed as a network client service in the Network properties box, as was shown in Figure 12-15.

NOTE

Note that CSNW is used to connect a Windows 2000 computer to NetWare 4.*x* and below. If the NetWare server is version 5.*x* running native IP, you cannot connect to it with CSNW. Instead, you must use a NetWare client (redirector) that is compatible with the NetWare Core Protocol (NCP) and that supports IP. An appropriate client can be downloaded from www.novell.com. Alternatively, you can run the IP/IPX gateway in NetWare 5.*x*.

FIGURE 12-17
The Connection Status dialog box provides information about the specified network connection.

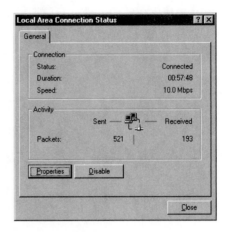

Connecting Windows 2000 Professional to a Remote Network

Windows 2000 includes a New Connection wizard that walks you through the process of setting up a connection to a remote access server. Using the wizard, you can quickly set up a dialup connection to a remote private network or to the Internet, create a VPN to "tunnel" through the Internet to a private network, or set up Windows 2000 Professional to function as a dialup server and accept incoming connections, as shown in Figure 12-18.

FIGURE 12-18
The Network Connection Wizard assists you in configuring dial-up and VPN connections and setting up remote access servers.

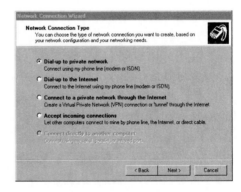

Windows 2000 can be configured to connect directly to another computer through a serial, parallel, or infrared port. This feature can be used to connect palm-size computers to a Windows 2000 computer, which enables you to upload and download files between the two.

Linux/UNIX

UNIX is a powerful operating system that is usually run on network servers rather than on desktop computers. However, UNIX computers can access the files of Microsoft and NetWare networks by using readily available software add-ons.

Linux has made significant inroads into the business world as an NOS. It is less often seen as a corporate desktop operating system. Although GUI interfaces are available to make Linux more user-friendly, as shown in Figure 12-19, a higher level of user sophistication is required than with most other desktop operating systems. However, many companies (such as RedHat, SuSE, Corel, Caldera, and TurboLinux) are striving to make Linux a viable operating system for the desktop.

FIGURE 12-19
Modern distributions of Linux provide graphical interfaces for a more user-friendly environment.

Recent distributions of Linux have networking components built in for connecting to a LAN or establishing a dialup connection to the Internet or other remote network. In fact, TCP/IP is integrated into the Linux kernel instead of being implemented as a separate subsystem.

When you implement Linux on the desktop, you must consider the application support that is available. The number of business productivity applications is limited when compared to Windows. However, some vendors provide Windows emulation software (such as WABI and WINE) that enable you to run many Windows applications on Linux. Additionally, companies such as Corel are making Linux versions of their office suites and other popular software packages.

NOTE

Although UNIX is more often implemented as a server operating system, UNIX machines can function also as network clients. In many cases, configuration and commands for UNIX are the same as they are in Linux systems. However, because both UNIX and Linux come in many different versions, the instructions in the following sections might not apply to every distribution of UNIX or Linux. Generally, you can use the **man** command to access the manual for your specific version.

Some advantages of Linux as a desktop operating system and network client include the following:

- It is a true 32-bit operating system.
- It supports preemptive multitasking and virtual memory.
- The code is open source and thus available for anyone to enhance and improve.
- It can share files with UNIX, NetWare, Windows, and Macintosh systems.

In the following sections, we discuss how to connect a Linux/UNIX client to a Microsoft network, a NetWare network, or to the Internet through a remote access dialup server.

Connecting a Linux/UNIX Client to a Microsoft Network

Linux workstations can access files on a Microsoft server by using SMB file system (SMBFS), which is based on Samba code. (We discuss Samba in more detail in Chapter 13, "Hybrid Networks.") UNIX systems can use the SMB client software that is part of the Samba suite to connect to remote SMB shares (such as those on a Microsoft server), to transfer files, and to print to remote printers.

Microsoft provides an add-on software package called Microsoft Services for UNIX, which consists of several components used to integrate UNIX and Windows networks. It uses NFS, which enables the sharing of resources between network operating systems using RPC.

The Microsoft component called Services for UNIX includes an NFS client, an NFS server, and an NFS gateway. These components provide the following functionalities:

- File and printer sharing between UNIX and Windows machines
- Remote command line access between Windows and UNIX machines
- Password synchronization between Windows and UNIX machines

NOTE

SMB is the Server Message Block protocol, which is the file-sharing protocol used by Microsoft servers.

Client for NFS is installed on Windows 2000 Professional machines to enable access to files on UNIX computers. Server for NFS is installed on computers running Windows 2000 Professional or Server to enable UNIX computers to access files on Windows machines. The NFS gateway is installed on Windows 2000 servers to enable them to act as a gateway between the CIFS protocol used by Windows 2000 and the NFS protocol used by the UNIX network, as shown in Figure 12-20. Services for UNIX works with several versions of UNIX and RedHat Linux.

FIGURE 12-20
Microsoft's Services for UNIX enables interoperability between Windows and UNIX networks.

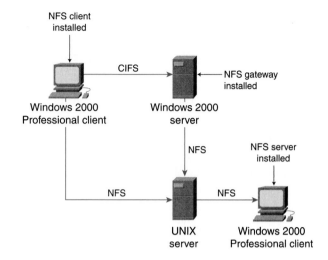

Connecting a Linux/UNIX Client to a NetWare Server

Linux or UNIX can be configured as an NCP client to access files and printers on a NetWare network. A Linux file system kernel module is available to mount NetWare volumes into the Linux file system by using NCP file system (NCPFS) software. With it installed, the Linux workstation emulates a NetWare client and can access files on a NetWare file server or print to a NetWare print queue. The NCPFS files are available for download at ftp.gwdg.de or sunsite.unc.edu. Earlier versions worked only with NetWare 3.*x* or NetWare 4.*x* in bindery emulation mode; later versions support NDS.

You can allow Linux machines to access NetWare resources by installing Novell's NFS server software on the NetWare server.

Connecting a Linux Client to a Linux/UNIX Server

Most popular distributions of Linux come with the network tools needed to configure network devices. The tools also can be downloaded from ftp.uk.linux.org. Network applications such as Telnet and FTP for Linux can be obtained from the same site.

The **ifconfig** command can be used to configure the network interface, as shown in Example 12-4. This command configures an Ethernet adapter identified as eth0 to use the IP address 192.168.1.16 with a subnet mask of

255.255.255.0 (the default Class C mask). The "up" at the end activates the interface.

EXAMPLE 12-4 You Can Use the ifconfig Command to Configure the Network Interface

```
# ifconfig eth0 192.168.1.16 netmask 255.255.255.0 up
```

NFS is the file-sharing protocol generally used in a UNIX server environment. NFS can be compiled in the Linux kernel. It is included in popular Linux distributions such as RedHat. To use a Linux machine as an NFS client, you must mount the NFS file system by using the **mount** command. This enables you to access the remote files as if they were local; the access, however, is usually slower.

Connecting a Linux/UNIX Client to the Internet

To connect the Linux or UNIX machine to the Internet through a dialup ISP account, the networking modules must be installed and a serial port must be set up for use by the modem.

You can use a program called minicom to connect directly to a shell account, if your ISP provides one. A shell account is a command-line interface (CLI) to a UNIX server that can be accessed through Telnet. The Linux computer must be configured with the following information:

- The ISP's DNS address, which is set in the /etc/revolv.conf file
- The fixed IP address (if one is assigned by the ISP), which is set up in etc/hosts
- The external mail domain, which is set up in /etc/mailname
- The user account name and password assigned by the ISP, which is set in etc/ppp/pap-secrets (if Password Authentication Protocol [PAP] is used) or /etc/ppp/chap-secrets (if Challenge Handshake Authentication Protocol [CHAP] is used)

A connection script that specifies the connection procedure is set in /etc/ppp/ chatscript, which includes the modem initialization string, the phone number of the ISP's dialup server, and other information depending on the ISP server's login procedures.

Point-to-Point Protocol (PPP) is generally used to establish the link over the phone line. In some cases, Serial Line Internet Protocol (SLIP) or UNIX-to-UNIX Copy Protocol (UUCP) can be used instead.

After the connection is established, web browsing can be done through the Lynx text-based browser. If X Window or another graphical shell is installed, the browsing can be through Netscape or other graphical browsers. Sendmail is a program used for sending e-mail, and Post Office Protocol (POP) version 3 can be used to receive e-mail.

Other UNIX/Linux e-mail programs include Pine, Elm, Fetchmail, and Smail. Procmail sorts incoming mail and handles autoreplies and similar tasks.

Macintosh

Apple Macintosh computers were designed for easy networking in a peer-to-peer (workgroup) situation. In fact, network interfaces often are included as part of the hardware and networking components built into the Macintosh operating system. Ethernet and Token Ring network adapters also are available for the Macintosh.

The Macintosh, or Mac, is popular in many educational institutions and corporate graphics departments. Macs can be connected to one another in workgroups and can access Appleshare file servers. They also can be connected to PC LANs that include Microsoft, NetWare, or UNIX servers.

In the following sections, you will learn how to connect Macintosh computers together in a workgroup; to a Windows, NetWare, or Linux/UNIX server; or to the Internet through a remote access dialup server.

Connecting Macintosh Computers in a Workgroup

Macintosh machines can be joined quickly and easily in workgroups by using the AppleTalk networking components and protocols. Earlier implementations used LocalTalk, a slower serial network connection. LocalTalk is still supported, but newer AppleTalk versions are faster and enable interoperability with other operating systems. LocalTalk uses a connector box that plugs into the serial port and phone cable.

AppleTalk utilizes the concept of *zones*, which in this context refers to logically grouped resources. Zones function like workgroups within a PC network. When you are connected to the AppleTalk network, you can access the list of zones by opening the Chooser window from the Apple menu. AppleTalk must be set to "active" in the Chooser to see the zones list. You might need to select the network type (such as LocalTalk or EtherTalk) in the Network Control Panel, which is located in the Control Panel folder inside the System folder.

Connecting Macintosh Computers to Microsoft, NetWare, and UNIX Networks

Several years ago, it was difficult or impossible to integrate Apple computers into PC networks. Today a variety of software packages enable Macintosh users to participate in Microsoft, NetWare, and UNIX networks.

Microsoft provides Services for Macintosh with its NT and Windows 2000 server products. It includes the following components:

- File server for Macintosh
- Print server for Macintosh
- AppleTalk protocol

With these services installed on the Windows server, Macintosh clients can access files and printers on the Microsoft network. The Windows server can also function as an AppleTalk router with no additional software required on the Macintosh computers.

For NetWare servers, an add-on module is available that makes the NetWare servers appear to Macintosh clients as if they were Appleshare servers. The add-on module is called NetWare for Macintosh NLM (NetWare Loadable Module). The Macintosh sends AppleTalk data packets, which are received and processed by the module. Macs also can communicate over IPX in a NetWare 4.0 network.

Software such as Syntax enables Macintosh clients (as well as DOS, Windows, and OS/2 clients) to access files, printers, and applications on a UNIX server.

Gateways or routers can be used to connect an existing AppleTalk network to a corporate LAN. Devices designed specifically for this purpose are available from companies such as Shiva.

Connecting Macintosh Computers to the Internet

Connecting a Macintosh computer to the Internet, as with any other operating system, requires that the Mac run TCP/IP. Apple offers an implementation called AppleIP, and commercial products such as MacTCP are available. Installing these protocols enables the Mac to communicate on a TCP/IP-based LAN or WAN.

As in other operating systems, TCP/IP must be configured with an IP address, a subnet mask, and a default gateway (if applicable). A DNS server address is needed to resolve host names to IP addresses. The appearance of the configuration dialog boxes differ depending on the software implementation used.

If the Macintosh is using a modem and dialup account for the Internet connection, PPP must be configured. Macintosh PPP software can be downloaded from the Web; ConfigPPP is one such program. In these programs, modem port, port speed, timeouts, and connection options are entered along with the phone number of the remote server.

iMac machines provide an Internet Setup Assistant, as shown in Figure 12-21, that walks you through the configuration process in much the same way as wizards do in Windows.

NOTE

IBM still markets
and supports OS/2
Warp Server. The
current version of
the Warp Server
product is designed
as an e-commerce
server, and it is mar-
keted to large com-
panies doing
business over the
Internet.

OS/2

Although IBM dropped support and development of its OS/2 desktop operating system in the mid-1990s, there are still many staunch users. OS/2 still can be found on some business LANs, especially in industries such as banking.

OS/2 began as a joint project of IBM and Microsoft. When the two companies parted ways, Microsoft developed Windows NT (based in part on the OS/2 technology), and IBM marketed OS/2, later changing the name to OS/2 Warp.

OS/2 can be connected to NetWare servers by using the Novell NetWare Client Kit for OS/2. IBM TCP/IP software can be used for communicating on a TCP/IP-based network, and add-on kits were produced to add NFS, NetBIOS, and IPX/SPX support.

OS/2 Warp version 4 included support for dialup networking and Internet connectivity.

Summary

In this chapter, we discussed the most commonly used desktop operating systems and how they can participate as clients on various types of networks.

We started with an overview of operating system basics, including the two types of user interface: text-based and GUI. We discussed command syntax, and you learned how switches or arguments can be added to commands to define their parameters.

We covered the roles of files and file systems, file naming conventions, and how file type extensions are used by the operating system and by applications. Popular file systems such as FAT/FAT32, NTFS, the UNIX file system, HPFS, Macintosh HFS, and NFS were discussed. Disks and disk partitioning also were addressed.

Each desktop operating system was then discussed individually. You learned about MS-DOS and the Windows client operating systems, Linux/UNIX as a desktop operating system, Apple Macintosh, and IBM's OS/2.

The preceding five chapters of this book have provided basic knowledge about networking protocols, popular NOS (server) products, the directory services used by them, and the desktop operating systems that can connect to them as clients. In the next chapter, we put all these topics together as we discuss hybrid networks, in which multiple protocols, platforms, and operating systems can coexist.

Further Reading

An overview of FAT, VFAT, FAT32, and NTFS is on Microsoft's website at www.microsoft.com/technet/winnt/filesyst.asp.

A discussion of the features of NTFS can be found at the NTFS documentation website at www.via.ecp.fr/~regis/ntfs/new.

A good tutorial on the UNIX file system is located at www.anet-stl.com/tech/unix/Pages/concepts_fsystem.html.

Partition Magic disk partitioning software can be obtained at www.powerquest.com.

The best starting point for information about Microsoft's operating systems and networking components is the TechNet web site at www.microsoft.com/technet/default.asp.

Links, how-to's, and guides to Linux and Linux networking can be found at www.linuxhq.com.

A good source for cross-platform solutions that address connecting Macintosh computers to PC networks is www.macwindows.com/Network.html.

For more information about OS/2 Warp, see the index of OS/2 Internet sites at www.nfwa.com/os2/news/e-zines.html.

Review Questions

The following questions test your knowledge of the material covered in this chapter. Be sure to read each question carefully and select the *best* correct answer or answers.

1. Which of the following are advantages of text-based operating systems? (Select all that apply.)

   A. They are generally faster than GUIs.

   B. They use fewer resources than GUIs.

   C. They are easier to use than GUIs.

   D. They generally support multitasking, which graphical operating systems do not.

2. Which of the following commands is used to display TCP/IP configuration information on a Windows 95 machine?

   A. ifconfig

   B. ipconfig

   C. winipcfg

   D. config

3. What are the two- or three-character suffixes preceded by a dot at the end of a filename called?

   A. File forks

   B. File tables

   C. File types

   D. File extensions

4. Which of the following is an advantage of using the FAT16 file system for a Microsoft operating system?

   A. It is compatible with more operating systems than any other common file system.

   B. It provides better security than other popular file systems.

   C. It is more reliable (less prone to data loss) than any other popular file system.

   D. It offers faster performance than any other file system.

5. What is the maximum partition size supported by NTFS?

    A. 2 GB

    B. 4 GB

    C. 4 TB

    D. 16 EB

6. Which of the following represents a directory path in the UNIX file system?

    A. c:/dir01/subdir02/myfile.ext

    B. \dir01\subdir02\myfile.ext

    C. /dir01/subdir02/myfile.ext

    D. /dir01/subdir02\myfile.ext

7. Which of the following file systems uses i-node mapping?

    A. FAT32

    B. UNIX file system

    C. Macintosh HFS

    D. NTFS

8. Which of the following should you install to allow a user on a Windows NT workstation computer to log in directly to a NetWare server?

    A. File and Print Services for NetWare

    B. Gateway Services for NetWare

    C. Client Services for NetWare

    D. IPX/SPX

9. Which of the following can be used to allow a Linux workstation to access files on a Microsoft server?

    A. SMBFS

    B. NCP

    C. TCP/IP

    D. PPP

10. Which of the following operating systems uses the HPFS file system?

   A. MS-DS

   B. Windows 2000

\ **C.** OS/2

   D. Windows NT 4.0

Hybrid Networks

In Part II of this book, "Networking Hardware and Software," we discussed the different networking protocols that can be used by computers to communicate with one another. You have learned about the popular network operating systems (NOSs) that run on network servers and the desktop operating systems used by network clients. You also have learned about the directory services used to organize and locate resources on today's networks and the global internetwork that connects so many LANs and WANS—the Internet.

A *hybrid network* is one in which multiple operating systems, hardware platforms, protocols, and services coexist. The Internet is the largest hybrid network of all, and in today's corporate world, it is common for even a small local-area network (LAN) to operate as a hybrid network.

This chapter provides some guidelines for working with networks that consist of different software or hardware products. Specifically, we look at three types of hybrid networks:

- Networks running multiple protocols
- Networks running multiple operating systems (NOS and client)
- Networks running multiple hardware platforms

Of course, your hybrid network might fit two or more of these categories.

Before we examine each category in detail, we discuss the general characteristics of hybrid networks and the reasons for implementing a hybrid network.

Characteristics of the Hybrid Network

Although there are advantages to implementing a "pure" network—that is, a network based on one platform, operating system, and protocol stack—there are numerous reasons for a network to combine the products of different vendors:

- The inability of a single vendor to provide all desired features
- Personal preferences of users
- Budgetary factors
- Haphazard growth

In the following sections, we look at each reason for the hybrid network.

Inability of a Single Vendor to Provide All Desired Features

One of the most common reasons for combining different platforms or operating systems in a network is the inability to obtain all desired features from the products of a single vendor.

For example, you might have a network that runs primarily on UNIX servers, but you need a particular application or feature that is available only on a Microsoft Windows NT or Windows 2000 server. If you have client machines running Windows 9x and need them to communicate with one another using NetBIOS names, you could set up a Windows NT or Windows 2000 server as a WINS server to provide NetBIOS name to IP address resolution.

In another scenario, you might have a Windows NT network with Windows 9x clients. Your graphics department, however, might need to use an application that runs only on the Macintosh platform. In that case, you could use Macintosh systems in that single department and implement Services for Macintosh on the NT Server so that the Macintosh clients can access files on the network.

Personal Preferences of Users

In some companies, individual employees are allowed to select the computer systems they will use. This is especially true of users at the executive level. If you have a Windows 2000 network with Windows 2000 Professional client machines, but the company vice president prefers Linux, you might need to integrate the Linux machine into your Microsoft network.

Budgetary Factors

Sometimes the budget won't allow for the implementation of a pure network. For example, if the company wants to migrate the network to Windows 2000 from Novell NetWare, there might not be enough money allocated for licensing all the servers at once. You might have to operate the network as a hybrid, with both Windows and NetWare servers, as an interim measure.

A similar situation exists if your organization decides to adopt Windows 2000 Professional as its client operating system but is unable to replace or upgrade the hardware at all workstations. For those machines that don't meet the Windows 2000 system requirements, you might be forced to continue using an older version of Windows or a desktop operating system such as Linux that requires fewer hardware resources.

Haphazard Growth

In many cases, there was no real plan to implement a hybrid network. Systems were purchased and operating systems were implemented gradually, depending on the preferences of whoever made the purchase or what solution seemed the best deal at the time.

Perhaps NetWare servers were used because the network administrator had Novell certification and training. Then, later, NT servers were added to the mix because the Microsoft products had become popular. Finally, the company decided to host a web site and hired a webmaster who liked the Apache software that runs on UNIX machines, so a web server running Linux was set up. To complicate matters further, your company's management might have decided that the PC network needed to communicate with the IBM mainframe network used in the accounting department. Now you, the network administrator, must bring these diverse systems together into a true hybrid network.

Multiple-Protocol Networks

Many types of computer protocols are used in networking, and they operate at different layers of the networking model.

In a sense, *all* networks run multiple protocols. When we discuss multiple protocols in the context of hybrid networks, however, we primarily are looking at two situations:

- Networks that use more than one network/transport protocol
- Networks that use more than one file-sharing protocol (sometimes referred to as the *core protocol*)

Network/Transport Protocols

To communicate with one another on a network, computers must share a common network/transport protocol stack such as TCP/IP, IPX/SPX, or NetBEUI. In many situations, a network requires more than one network/transport protocol stack. Reasons for running multiple protocols on a network include the following:

- Multiple NOSs
- Internet connectivity
- Security

Let's look at why multiple protocols are needed in these situations.

Multiple NOSs

The most common scenario in which multiple NOSs create a need for multiple protocols is the hybrid Microsoft/NetWare network.

NOTE

When you connect a small network to the Internet using Network Address Translation (NAT), each computer that accesses the Internet still requires TCP/IP, even though only the NAT host is actually directly connected to the Internet because NAT requires that IP addresses—generally from the private range—be assigned to the internal computers for identification purposes.

NOTE

Although IPX/SPX is generally associated with NetWare networks, it also can be used for LAN communications in an environment using only Microsoft operating systems. This might be a viable option if you do not need Internet connectivity but require a routable protocol stack that is easier to configure and faster than TCP/IP.

Although NetWare 5.*x* is capable of running on pure IP, there are still many NetWare 3.*x* and 4.*x* servers in use on corporate networks. These servers require the IPX/SPX protocol stack for network communication.

Typically, clients communicate with Microsoft servers on a medium or large network by using TCP/IP. If those same clients need to access files on a NetWare 3.*x* or 4.*x* server, they not only need to have either the Novell or Microsoft NetWare client software installed but also need to run an IPX/SPX protocol stack such as NWLink.

Internet Connectivity

If you have a small Microsoft network that consists of only one subnet (non-routed), you might choose to use the NetBEUI protocol for LAN communications because NetBEUI is faster, easier to configure, and easier to troubleshoot than is NWLink or TCP/IP.

However, if you want to connect some or all computers on a LAN to the Internet, they must run the protocol stack used to communicate on the global network—TCP/IP. The computers can use NetBEUI to communicate between one another (for performance purposes) while using TCP/IP for Internet communications.

The scenario also might include clients that need to access NetWare servers, communicate with other Microsoft systems, and connect to the Internet through a NAT host. In such a case, you might have all three protocol stacks—IPX/SPX, NetBEUI, and TCP/IP—installed on the same machine and bound to the same network adapter.

Security Aspects of Using Multiple Protocols

Some network administrators implement a different network/transport protocol stack than TCP/IP on the internal network (or some part of it) to provide an extra layer of security when the network is connected to the Internet.

For example, if you have a group of computers on the network that contain sensitive data, you might choose to have them communicate through IPX/SPX instead of through TCP/IP because computers with sensitive data should not require Internet access. Other computers on the internal network can communicate with them using IPX/SPX and communicate with the outside world through TCP/IP. However, a computer from outside the LAN that is not running IPX/SPX (this is the profile of the typical Internet-configured computer) would not be able to access those computers that use only IPX/SPX because there would be no common protocol. Figure 13-1 illustrates this situation.

FIGURE 13-1
Multiple protocols can be used to protect part of the network from outside intrusion.

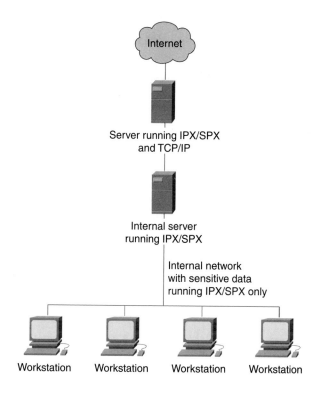

Server running IPX/SPX
and TCP/IP

Internal server
running IPX/SPX

Internal network
with sensitive data
running IPX/SPX only

Workstation   Workstation   Workstation   Workstation

The Importance of Protocol Binding Order

When multiple network/transport protocol stacks are bound to the same network card, the binding order of the protocols is important. The *binding order* of the protocols on the client machine determines which protocol is used to communicate with a server when the two machines have more than one protocol in common.

For example, if the client machine has TCP/IP, NetBEUI, and IPX/SPX bound to its network adapter in the order listed and the server has NetBEUI, IPX/SPX, and TCP/IP bound to its adapter in the order listed, the client machine attempts to communicate by first using TCP/IP (which is at the top of its binding order). If it finds TCP/IP on the server, that protocol is used for the session, even though it is at the bottom of the server's binding order. As you can see, to optimize network performance, you should ensure that the most-used protocols are at the top of the binding order on the client machines.

Figure 13-2 shows how Windows 2000 enables you to configure or change the binding order of multiple protocols in use on a particular network adapter. When you select an installed protocol, you can move it up or down in the

NOTE

Both Microsoft's Network Driver Interface Specification (NDIS) and Novell's Open Datalink Interface (ODI) specifications for network device interfaces enable multiple protocols to be bound to a single network adapter, and, conversely, for multiple network adapters to be bound to a single protocol.

binding order by using the up and down arrows on the right side of the configuration dialog box.

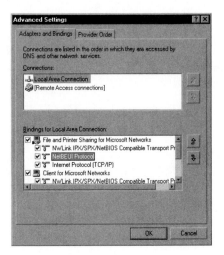

FIGURE 13-2
The protocol binding order can be changed to optimize performance when multiple protocols are in use.

Other operating systems have similar mechanisms for configuring binding order.

File-Sharing Protocols

The second type of protocol that is important in communicating on hybrid networks is the *file-sharing protocol*, which is sometimes referred to as the core protocol. Microsoft networks use Server Message Block (SMB) for file sharing; NetWare networks use NetWare Core Protocol (NCP), and UNIX systems use Network File System (NFS).

Accessing files on a server requires that a computer run the appropriate client software. For example, when you install Client Services for NetWare (or the Novell client) on a Microsoft Windows machine, this provides the NCP client software. Samba includes an SMB client for UNIX machines so that the machines can access resources on a Microsoft server using the SMB file-sharing protocol.

Multiple-Operating-System Networks

A network on which multiple operating systems are deployed might or might not also run multiple network/transport protocols. Because TCP/IP is almost universally supported (even NetWare, in version 5.0 and above, can run exclusively on TCP/IP), you might have a network with many operating systems communicating over the same protocol stack.

Hybrid networks with multiple operating systems can be divided into three types:

- Networks on which multiple NOSs are deployed
- Networks that use one server operating system but multiple client operating systems
- Networks that include multiple server and client operating systems

Multiple Server Operating Systems

A network might have servers running several different operating systems. For example, the network might have both Windows 2000 and Windows NT domain controllers, NetWare file and print servers, and UNIX or Linux web and FTP servers. Figure 13-3 shows such a common hybrid configuration.

Your job as network administrator is to create an environment in which users can access the files and other resources they need, regardless of operating system.

FIGURE 13-3
A hybrid network might have servers running different NOSs.

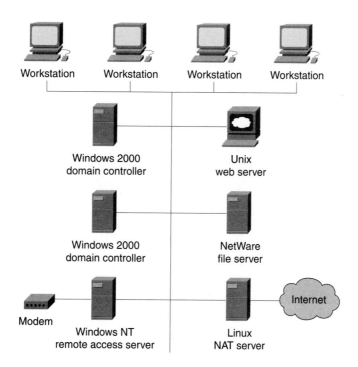

Fortunately, software packages exist to enable you to provide clients with access to different servers. Some of these software packages are included with the client operating system, and others are third-party products. The following are some of the most commonly used integration products:

- **Client Services for NetWare (CSNW)**—This is included with Windows NT Workstation and Windows 2000 Professional and allows the Windows NT or Windows 2000 client to access NetWare servers.

- **Microsoft Client for NetWare Networks**—Included with the Windows 9*x* operating systems, it serves the same function as CSNW does for Windows 95 and Windows 98 machines.

- **Gateway Service for NetWare (GSNW)**—This is included with the Windows NT Server and Windows 2000 Server operating systems. It enables clients logged in to a Windows server to access resources on a NetWare server by going through the gateway on the Windows NT or Windows 2000 server.

- **Novell Client for Windows 9*x*/NT/2000**—This is available as a free download from Novell and enables Windows computers to access files on a NetWare server.

- **Samba**—This is available as a third-party freeware product and allows SMB clients, such as Windows operating systems, to access files on a UNIX server running the Samba software.

- **SMB File System (SMBFS)**—Distributed with Samba, it allows Linux computers to map a network drive to an SMB share.

- **Microsoft Services for Macintosh**—Included with Windows NT/2000 Server, it allows Macintosh clients to access resources on Microsoft networks.

- **Linux Services for Macintosh**—Implemented through third-party products such as Columbia AppleTalk Package (CAP) and Netatalk, it allows Macintosh computers to access resources on Linux computers by adding the AppleTalk Datagram Delivery Protocol (DDP) to the Linux kernel.

Multiple Client Operating Systems

Configuring network clients that run different operating systems is not quite as complex as working with different server operating systems. How to configure popular desktop (client) machines to connect to various network operating systems is discussed in detail in Chapter 12, "Desktop Operating Systems."

Multiple Server and Multiple Client Operating Systems

In many cases, you encounter a hybrid network that includes multiple server operating systems *and* multiple client operating systems. This increases the complexity of your administration job because you need to know how to support different operating systems. In this type of complex environment, it is especially important that you obtain up-to-date information about service packs, hot fixes, and security patches for *all* operating systems that are connected to the network. Otherwise, you could inadvertently expose your entire network to security breaches or network downtime.

Multiple-Platform Networks

The term *platform* is sometimes used to refer to operating systems (as in the Windows platform or the UNIX platform). In this book, we use the term to refer to different computing architectures or hardware platforms. However, it is important to note that different platforms usually (although not always) run different operating systems.

For example, the *PC platform* uses a hardware architecture that is different from the *Macintosh platform* or the *IBM mainframe platform.* A new and increasingly popular computing platform is used by personal digital assistants (PDAs) and handheld computing devices; this platform uses a different hardware configuration.

In the following sections, we discuss how to achieve network communications between the following platforms:

- PC and Macintosh
- PC and mainframe
- PC and PDA (or handheld computer)

PC-to-Macintosh Communications

Communications between IBM-compatible PCs (so named because IBM made the first widely distributed personal computers built on this hardware platform) and Macintosh computers is a relatively simple form of cross-platform networking because the two platforms are similar in scale and use. Thus, it is usually treated as a cross-operating system issue. That is why we already addressed the situation in the "Multiple-Operating-Systems Networks" section earlier in this chapter.

PC-to-Mainframe Communications

Mainframe and "mini mainframe" systems, such as the popular IBM AS/400, are very different in concept and implementation from the personal computing model for which PCs and Macintoshes were designed. In many business situations, however, mainframes are used for crunching large amounts of data, and they often coexist with PC networks.

For example, in a municipal government operation, a mainframe might be used for processing utility bills and property tax roles. The employees in those departments probably interact with the mainframe through data entry terminals. City staff in other departments might use PCs for word processing, e-mail, spreadsheet, and database applications, and so on. However, some of those employees might occasionally need access to the data on the mainframe. One way to give them access is to place a mainframe terminal—in addition to a PC—on each desk. This solution has some disadvantages, however:

- There is extra expense for redundant hardware. (The PC already provides a monitor and keyboard—why spend money for another monitor and keyboard?)
- If office and desk space is in short supply, these components can interfere with the employee's ability to work efficiently.
- It is difficult to integrate the information from the terminal to documents composed on the PC.

A better solution is to allow the PC itself to act as a terminal to the mainframe while retaining its functionality as a desktop computer. Because mainframes and PCs use different protocols for network communications, you need *protocol gateway* software to translate between the two.

A commonly used software package for connecting PC networks to IBM mainframes is Systems Network Architecture (SNA), which we discuss later in this chapter in the "Gateways: The Hybrid Connectivity Solution" section.

PDA-to-PC and Handheld-to-PC Communications

In our increasingly mobile society, handheld devices are becoming common. PDAs are simple handheld computers that are limited to address book and contact lists, calendaring and scheduling, and the retrieval of e-mail. More sophisticated PDAs include, or allow you to add, more features through additional programs that might be loaded on a program module, usually in the form of a memory card. As more functionality is added, the lines become blurred between PDAs and full-fledged handheld computers. Examples of the latter include the Palm devices and the Windows-based Pocket PC.

Handheld devices need to communicate with desktop computers so that a user can enter new data on one and have that data synchronized to the other. For example, if you carry a handheld device and meet a new business contact, you should be able to enter the person's address, phone number, and other information into the contacts list on your handheld device and then have that information automatically transferred to the contacts list on your desktop machine.

Most handheld devices include a means of connecting to the desktop machine through serial or USB port. Synchronization software (such as Microsoft's ActiveSynch used for communication between Windows desktop and Windows CE devices) allows the systems to detect changes and to update information. Files can be transferred between the devices, and software for the handheld can be downloaded from the Internet onto the desktop computer and then installed on the handheld device over the serial or other connection.

Gateway: The Hybrid Connectivity Solution

The term *gateway* (or *gateway service*) has several meanings in the computer networking world, depending on the context. Generically speaking, a gateway is a network point that acts as an entrance to another network. Although a router might fit this definition in the sense that it functions as a way out of a subnet or as a connection point to a different subnet or network, we use the broader definition in this chapter.

Gateway software (such as Gateway Service for NetWare) enables two different types of networks to talk to one another. In other words, it serves as a link between computers using different protocols, operating systems, or platforms.

In the following sections, we discuss various types of gateway software, including the following:

- Windows-to-NetWare redirectors
- Cross-platform solutions for Macintosh-to-PC operating system connectivity
- SNA for PC-to-mainframe communication

Windows-to-NetWare Redirectors

File and Print Service for NetWare (FPNW) enables NetWare clients to access resources on Windows servers. These software packages are called *redirectors* because they intercept a request for a resource, translate it to the appropriate file-sharing protocol, and redirect it over the network to the server on which the resource resides. Because this software translates between unlike protocols, it falls into the category of gateway software.

The NetWare redirectors included with Windows operating systems include NWLink, which is an NDIS compliant, 32-bit implementation of the Novell IPX/SPX protocol stack. NWLink enables communications utilizing one of two application programming interfaces (APIs): Winsock (Windows Sockets) and NetBIOS.

NOTE

Connecting to a client/server application (such as a SQL database) does not require file and print sharing client software. For example, a NetWare client can access a client/server application on an NT Server without having FPNW installed, and a Windows client can access a client/server application on a NetWare server without CSNW, GSNW, or any other Novell client software. What *is* required, however, is a common protocol, such as IPX/SPX for NetWare machines prior to 5.*x*.

GSNW provides access to NetWare resources from Windows clients without installing any extra software on the client machines. GSNW does this by functioning as a gateway (protocol translator) between SMB, which is used on the Windows network, and NCP, which is used on the NetWare network.

When the client or gateway service is installed, the user at the Windows computer can run supported NetWare command-line utilities.

Cross-Platform Solutions

Cross-platform gateways are those that enable you to connect different platforms—for example, Macintosh machines to Windows networks. Integration of Macintosh and Windows computers requires a common protocol (typically AppleTalk) and file and print sharing services. Additional client software on the Macintosh systems is not required for communication, but client software is available for authentication of the Macintosh clients to enhance security.

Macintosh clients also can be provided with remote (dial-in) access to a Windows Server by using AppleTalk over Point-to-Point Protocol (PPP).

SNA

IBM developed SNA in the 1970s to connect incompatible systems with a layered communications architecture. Their incentive was to allow different IBM systems (such as IBM PCs and mainframes) to share data with one another.

The components of SNA include the following:

- **Node**—This is a collection of computers on the SNA network.
- **Network addressable unit (NAU)**—This represents the origination or destination point of the data that is being transmitted. An NAU can be a logical unit, a physical unit, or a system services control point (SSCP).
- **Logical unit (LU)**—This is the port that is used by network users to access the SNA network.
- **Physical unit (PU)**—A PU manages the resources of a node.
- **System services control point (SSCP)**—This is a point on the network that is used to manage services for users.

Figure 13-4 illustrates how SNA serves as a gateway from the PC network to the mainframe.

Originally, SNA networks were based on a central mainframe computer that managed dedicated minicomputers running the management software NCP. The minicomputers then managed a group of terminals, workstations, and telephone lines.

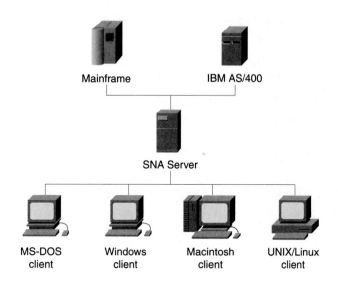

FIGURE 13-4
A Microsoft SNA server acts as a gateway between the PC network and the mainframe systems.

SNA Communications

The current implementation of SNA is called Advanced Peer-to-Peer Networking (APPN). APPN supports two node types:

- **Network nodes**—These include routers and network management systems and client and server programs.
- **End nodes**—These contain only client and server programs.

The SNA architecture requires that a session be established between a client and a server before any data can be transferred. This is in contrast to IP, which does not require fixed sessions.

SNA is a more complex protocol set than is TCP/IP. SNA is part of the AS/400 systems, but it is also implemented as Communications Manager for OS/2 (by IBM) and SNA Server for Windows NT (by Microsoft).

Microsoft SNA Server

Microsoft's SNA Server was designed to provide a gateway to link client/server networks to AS/400 and mainframe systems using IBM SNA architecture. SNA Server runs on machines running Windows NT and Windows 2000 Server; the server can be configured as a remote access server to provide dial-in or virtual private networking (VPN) access to the SNA host. Microsoft's latest version of SNA Server has been renamed Host Integration Server.

NOTE

Linux-SNA was in development stages at the time of this writing. Current information regarding beta testing and release is at www.linux-sna.org.

Samba

We have discussed Samba in this chapter and in other chapters of the book. Samba is the software package that enables Windows and UNIX machines to communicate with each other. Now is the time to go into more detail about how it works.

Samba was created by reverse-engineering Microsoft's SMB protocol, which is the so-called core protocol (or file-sharing protocol) used by Windows operating systems to share resources on the network. The goal was to make a UNIX computer look like a Windows server to Microsoft client systems. The latest versions of Samba do accomplish this goal and more.

Samba enables Microsoft and UNIX operating systems to communicate using the Common Internet File System (CIFS), which is based on the SMB file-sharing protocol. CIFS provides four services:

- Authentication and authorization
- Name resolution
- File and print sharing services
- Network browse services

Shared resources can be password protected, and NetBIOS name resolution can be performed either by broadcast messages or by using a NetBIOS name server such as WINS, if you have one on the network. The browse service provides a list of shared network resources in the Network Neighborhood on Windows 9*x* and Windows NT machines, as shown in Figure 13-5.

FIGURE 13-5
Network Neighborhood (or My Network Places in Windows 2000) displays a list of shared network resources.

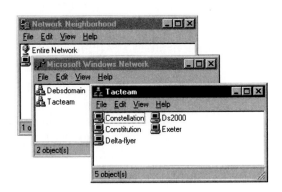

In Windows 2000, the Network Neighborhood has been renamed to My Network Places.

How Samba Works

Samba is made up of several programs. Two components provide the basic services listed in the previous bulleted list:

- The SMB daemon (SMBd)
- The NMB daemon (NMBd)

If you are familiar with UNIX, you'll recognize the "d" at the end of the program name as representing a *daemon*, or service. SMBd provides the file and print sharing services of SAMBA, authentication, and authorization. NMBd provides name resolution and browsing services.

Summary

In this chapter, we discussed different types of hybrid, or integrated, networks that combine elements from different vendors. These include networks that run multiple protocols, networks that run multiple operating systems, and networks that run on multiple hardware platforms.

You learned about some of the challenges facing a network administrator who must integrate unlike technologies and create an environment in which PCs can access data on mainframes or Apple Macintosh computers can communicate with UNIX servers.

We examined some of the reasons for operating a hybrid network environment and the solutions—such as redirectors and gateway software—that make integration easier.

We discussed the client and gateway services for NetWare that are included with Windows operating systems. We also discussed Microsoft Services for Macintosh and products that enable Macintosh clients to access Linux resources.

You learned about SNA and how SNA server software can enable PCs to communicate with IBM mainframes. Finally, we discussed how SAMBA, the SMB server and client software for UNIX, works to provide connectivity between Microsoft-based and UNIX-based networks.

Regardless of the protocols, operating systems, and hardware platforms implemented on your network, there are common administration issues that must be addressed. In Part III of this book, "Network Specialty Areas," we look at some of those specialty areas, beginning with the increasingly important topics of network security and disaster protection.

NOTE

Linux computers can use SMB File System (SMBFS) to access remote SMB shares, such as those on Windows machines. SMBFS enables the Linux user to map the share as a network drive. SMBFS is not really part of SAMBA, but it is distributed with SAMBA. It works only with Linux operating systems. SAMBA itself has been ported to work with NetWare, Virtual Memory System (VMS), and other operating systems.

Further Reading

A useful guide to integrating NetWare and Windows NT is located at www.microsoft.com/TechNet/network/int-netw.asp.

For information about Intergraph's NFS client software for Windows, see www.intergraph.com/nfs/da-br.asp.

A good synopsis of how SNA works is located at www.protocols.com/pbook/sna.htm.

Review Questions

The following questions test your knowledge of the material covered in this chapter. Be sure to read each question carefully and select the *best* correct answer or answers.

1. What is another name for the protocol used for file and resource sharing on a network?

   A. The network/transport protocol

   B. The link protocol

   C. The core protocol

   D. The Layer 2 protocol

2. Which of the following is true of IPX/SPX?

   A. IPX/SPX can be used only on NetWare networks.

   B. IPX/SPX is routable.

   C. IPX/SPX is not supported by NetWare 5.*x*.

   D. IPX/SPX is slower and more difficult to configure than is TCP/IP.

3. Which of the following enables multiple protocols to be bound to a single network adapter or for a single protocol to be bound to multiple adapters? (Select all that apply.)

   A. NDIS

   B. Winsock

   C. TDI

   D. ODI

4. Which of the following is used for file sharing by Microsoft networks?

   A. NCP

   B. SMB

   C. NFS

   D. DLC

5. Which of the following is true of the Gateway Service for NetWare (GSNW)? (Select all that apply.)

   A. GSNW is installed on a NetWare server to enable Windows clients to access its resources.

   B. GSNW is included with the Microsoft Windows NT and Windows 2000 Server operating systems.

   C. GSNW enables clients of a Windows server to connect to a NetWare server without installing anything additional on the clients or configuring anything on the NetWare server.

   D. GSNW is installed on a Windows server to enable its clients to access resources on a NetWare server.

6. Which of the following is a third-party freeware product that enables Windows and UNIX systems to exchange data across a network?

   A. CDFS

   B. Samba

   C. Client Services for UNIX

   D. SNA

7. What kind of software translates between different protocols and enables computers on different types of networks to communicate?

   A. Bridging software

   B. Server software

   C. Gateway software

   D. Routing software

8. What is the name for a software component that intercepts requests for resources and sends them out over the network instead of to the local bus?

   A. Platform

   B. Client

   C. Director

   D. Redirector

9. Which of the following are services provided by CIFS, the Common Internet File System? (Select all that apply.)

  A. Name resolution

  B. Dialup access

  C. File and print sharing services

  D. File level security

10. Which of the following components of SAMBA is responsible for providing authentication and authorization services?

  A. SMBd

  B. MBXd

  C. NMBd

  D. smbfs

Part III

Network Specialty Areas

Protecting the Network

In Part I, "Introduction to Networking Concepts," you learned the technical concepts involved in sharing data across a computer network. In Part II, "Networking Hardware and Software," we discussed the details of how the hardware components, the server and client operating systems, and the network protocols work together to make that data sharing possible.

We haven't yet examined, however, an important aspect of sharing computers' resources across a network: maintaining the integrity of the shared data. There are two broad issues involved in protecting our data from loss or misuse:

- Network security
- Disaster protection and recovery

The more that businesses become dependent on their computer networks and the information that they contain, the more vulnerable the businesses become when something goes wrong. Murphy's infamous law assures us that sooner or later, something *will* go wrong. The "something" can involve deliberate or accidental breaches of network security, up to and including corporate espionage. On the other hand, it can take the form of a hard disk crash, flood, or fire that destroys the server.

In this chapter, we examine data protection issues and discuss ways to reduce the risk of data loss without giving up the many benefits of having computers networked and connected to the outside world. You will learn that in some cases, networking even works in your favor by making data protection and recovery easier than it would be on a standalone system.

Network Security

Secure networking is a hot topic in the information technology world. Well-publicized intrusions into governmental and big business networks, widespread attacks of computer viruses, and high-profile criminal cases involving computer hackers are constantly in the news. From the administrators of multinational enterprise networks to home computer users with dialup Internet accounts, almost everyone who is "connected" is also concerned, to some degree, about the possibility of unauthorized access.

Security means different things to different people. Although the word (according to the *American Heritage Dictionary*) is synonymous with "guarantee" and "warranty," in the context of networking, security is never absolute. The only completely secure system is the one to which *no one* has access. This is obviously unworkable. *Computer security* is defined by the *Microsoft Press Computer and Internet Dictionary* as "the steps taken to protect a computer and the information it contains." No guarantees are implied in this definition.

Because the entire purpose of computer networks is to share resources, the trade-off between security and accessibility is always a delicate balancing act. The more secure your network, the less accessible it is, and the more accessible it is, the less secure it is.

Security issues can make the network administrator's relationship with network users an adversarial one. Users generally prefer more accessibility, and administrators like to err on the side of more security.

In the following sections, we discuss how you can assess the security needs of a particular network, how to assess existing and potential threats to security, and how to implement the appropriate security measures. We also take a look at how security components work and at some advanced identification and authentication technologies.

Assessing Security Needs

When it comes to a computer network, how much security is enough? The answer depends on the organization. The first step in developing a viable plan for protecting your network's data is assessing its security needs. Factors to be considered include the following:

- The type of business in which the company engages
- The type of data stored on the network
- The management philosophy of the organization

Let's take a look at these individually and discuss why each is important.

Type of Business

Some businesses, such as law or medicine, by their very nature generate confidential data. The privacy of a patient's medical records and attorney-client communications are protected by law. If sensitive documents are stored on your network, it is imperative that a high level of security be maintained. To do otherwise puts the organization at risk of civil liability and even criminal charges.

Other organization types that often produce sensitive data include the following:

- Law enforcement agencies, courts, and other governmental bodies
- Educational institutions that store student records on a network
- Hospitals, mental health facilities, and substance abuse facilities

- Companies that contract with the Department of Defense (DoD) or that perform other national security-related work

- Any organization that gathers data under a guarantee of confidentiality

- Any organization that produces a product or provides a service in a highly competitive industry or field of research

- Any organization whose network is connected to the Internet

Type of Data

Regardless of the type of business, certain types of data are considered to be private and should be protected. These types include the following:

- Payroll records and employees' personal information

- Accounting and tax information

- Trade secrets such as original code, plans and diagrams, recipes, and business strategies

If these types of information are stored on your network, you should implement a security plan to protect them.

Management Philosophy

If the data on the network is not subject to privacy laws, the security level might be dependent on the business owners' or managers' personal philosophies about how open (or closed) they want the network to be.

In some organizations, everyone is considered to be part of one big, happy family. Accessibility and ease of use enjoy a higher priority than privacy and security. Other organizations operate on a "need to know" principle; management prefers that information be accessible only to those whose jobs require it. Neither policy is right or wrong; the network administrators simply need to know and must be willing to implement network security in keeping with the organization's management style.

Assessing Security Threats

After you have decided that your business type, data type, and management philosophy require the implementation of security measures, you should assess the likely sources of threat to your data's integrity.

It is easy for organizations to underestimate, overestimate, or completely overlook the risks that make their networks vulnerable. However, there are many different types of threats to network security, and they all can be classified in one of two broad categories:

- External threats

- Internal threats

The following sections describe these types of threats.

> **NOTE**
>
> Distributed Denial of Service (DDoS) attacks work by compromising intermediary computers and surreptitiously installing software on them that will be used as part of the attack platform. Thus, your company's computers can unknowingly participate in the attack and can incur liability as a result. For this reason, it is important for all networks that are connected to the Internet to implement security policies, regardless of the sensitivity of their own data.

External Threats

Once upon a time, external threats were not a serious concern for most company LANs. The network was generally self-contained, and for an intruder to penetrate from the outside, he or she would have to dial in to a modem somewhere on the network or tap into the cabling. Now that most LANs are connected to the Internet, all that has changed. When your network can access the outside world, those outsiders also can access your network.

The motives of external intruders vary. Common motives include revenge (such as dissatisfied customers, disgruntled former employees, and angry competitors), recreation (those who hack into networks "just for fun" or to prove their technical skills), and remuneration. In this last case, the intruder is being paid to invade the network or does so for personal gain; for example, the hacker might attempt to transfer funds to his own bank account or erase records of his debts.

External security breaches can take many forms, including the following:

- Unauthorized use of passwords and keys
- Denial of Service (DoS) attacks
- IP spoofing
- Computer viruses and worms
- Trojan horse programs

We discuss each infiltration method separately in the following sections.

Unauthorized Use of Passwords and Keys. A *password* is a sequence of alphabetic, numeric, or symbol characters used to verify that a user is really the person authorized to use a particular account to access a system or network. A *key* is a number or cipher used by the system to verify the integrity of a communication.

Passwords and keys are security measures designed to keep unauthorized persons out, but they are effective only if they are kept secret. If someone knows your user account name and password and has a physical connection to the computer or network, that person can access anything to which you have access permissions. Obtaining a password is often the first step in hacking into a system.

The term *hacker* has different connotations, depending on who is using it. In the early days of computing, it meant a good programmer, but our modern news media has popularized a more negative meaning. Today it usually implies someone who breaks into computer systems, often with the intent to steal or destroy data.

Hackers are often represented as evil geniuses who use sophisticated, esoteric techniques to gain access to computers and networks. The truth is a little less exciting—in a high percentages of incidents, the intrusion is not based on high-level programming skills at all. Hackers often access the network in the same way as authorized users do—by entering a valid user account name and password. In this instance, they are often referred to as *crackers* because they "crack" or obtain the password and enter the network much as a safecracker opens a vault.

Hackers obtain the required passwords in many ways. Frequently, no technical expertise is used—the hacker simply uses observation skills or powers of persuasion to obtain the credentials from the user to whom the credentials belong.

Many users create passwords that are easy to guess (such as their birth dates or their spouses' first names). Others create—or are assigned by administrators—passwords that are less intuitive. Because this makes the passwords more difficult to remember, users write them down, often leaving them in an easily accessed desk drawer or even on a sticky note attached to the computer monitor.

Hackers can also obtain passwords by simply asking for them by posing as network technicians, company administrators, or others to whom the naive user feels safe in confiding his or her password. This is sometimes referred to as a *social engineering attack*.

The *brute-force attack* is another way to obtain passwords. This means trying every possible password until you find one that works. Hackers write scripts and programs, called password crackers, that run through lists of common words and alphanumeric combinations automatically so that the intruder doesn't have to sit there and manually enter password after password.

If these methods fail, technically savvy hackers can obtain passwords by intercepting the data packets that contain them by using a network "packet sniffer." This technique is why it is important that passwords be encrypted, rather than sent across the network as clear text. We talk about sniffer software in detail in Chapter 18, "Monitoring, Management, and Troubleshooting Tools."

Password security is an important part of establishing good overall security policies for your network. We discuss it in more detail later in this chapter in the "Password Security" section.

> **NOTE**
>
> Gaining unauthorized access by using someone else's credentials is a form of *impersonation.* This type of security breach includes IP spoofing and other methods of representing yourself as someone (or something, such as a system device) that you are not.

DoS Attacks. DoS attacks can be launched in several ways. Regardless of the method, they are designed to interrupt normal operations of the machine that is the focus of the attack. These types of attacks are also sometimes called *nuke attacks*. In February 2000, several major websites (including Amazon.com and Yahoo!) were temporarily shut down in this way.

Some DoS attacks exploit bugs in particular computer operating systems or applications, while others are aimed at the network itself. There are often patches (software provided by operating system or application program vendors to repair a problem with the program) available from the software vendor to plug the "holes" that enable attacks.

DoS attacks don't cause the computer to crash but are designed to interrupt or prevent connection to the network. They work by deluging the network with useless packets or by emulating a network problem that causes the computer to disconnect.

Some common forms of DoS attacks include the following:

- Ping/Internet Control Message Protocol (ICMP) flood
- Smurf attack
- Ping of Death
- SYN attacks

The following sections take a brief look at each.

Ping/ICMP Flood

An ICMP flood is exactly what it sounds like—a "flood" of ICMP packets that overwhelms the system. ICMP is a message and error-checking protocol used to transmit information over the Internet. The **ping** command is commonly used to send ICMP packets for the purpose of verifying that a specific computer (which is identified by IP address or host name, the latter of which is ultimately resolved to an IP address) is on the network. Ping works by sending a message called an ICMP Echo Request and then waiting for an ICMP Echo Reply from the "pinged" computer.

When a flood of packets is sent continuously to an IP address, it can become too much for the server to handle and can cause the server to slow down and eventually disconnect because of ping timeout.

Smurf Attack

A smurf attack is an ICMP flood that affects an entire service provider or an entire network segment. The ICMP messages are sent to a broadcast address, which causes all computers on that subnet to respond. When an ISP is smurfed, all connections are slowed, and all users are eventually disconnected.

Smurf attacks are a type of DoS attack. After an attacker gains access to a network, the attacker sends a broadcast into that network using an address in the target network as the source. Then all the devices in the compromised network send ICMP replies to the target address. You could have hundreds of hosts, each sending thousands of bits of ICMP echo requests into the target network. The traffic generated by this process can easily overwhelm the low-bandwidth connections used across WAN links between some ISPs and networks. The target network is affected, and often, the compromised middle network also suffers from all this traffic.

Ping of Death

The Ping of Death is a slightly more sophisticated attack that takes advantage of the maximum transmission unit (MTU) limitations of a network. The MTU depends on the media and network architecture. If a packet is sent that exceeds the MTU, it must be broken into smaller chunks and then reassembled at the destination end.

The IP packet in which the ICMP Echo Request is encapsulated is limited to 65,535 octets (an *octet* is eight bits of data). A knowledgeable attacker can send a packet that exceeds the number of octets that are allowed in the data field of the Echo Request. When the destination computer tries to reassemble this packet, it crashes.

SYN Attacks

An attacker can use the TCP synchronization sequence to disrupt communications. A process called the TCP three-way handshake is used to establish a session through TCP. See Figure 14-1.

FIGURE 14-1
TCP uses a three-way handshake to establish a communications session.

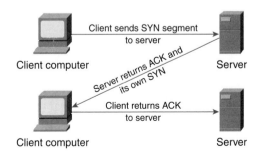

Here's how the three-way handshake works:

1. The client transmits a synchronization request (SYN) segment. This is a sequence number generated by the client.

2. The server sends an acknowledgement (ACK), which is the client's original sequence number plus 1. The server's SYN is a number generated independently by the server.

3. The client adds 1 to the server's SYN and returns it as an ACK. After both computers have acknowledged each other's communications, the connection is established.

A SYN attacker starts a large number of session requests (usually using a "spoofed" IP address, as described in the next section). The receiving computer puts these requests in a queue to wait for the completion of the process. By filling the queue and keeping it full, the attacker prevents other session requests from being established. Thus, legitimate users are unable to connect to the server.

IP Spoofing. IP spoofing involves altering the packet headers of messages being sent. This makes them appear as if they came from an IP address other than the actual originating address. Although spoofing is not in itself a form of attack, it is a method of gaining unauthorized access to a computer or network to launch an attack, to steal data, or to destroy data.

Computer Viruses and Worms. A *computer virus* is a program that can replicate and spread from one computer to another by copying its code to other files stored on the system without the user's consent or knowledge. Just as with the biological variety, some viruses are deadly and others are just annoyances. For example, the benign type might display a message on the user's screen. The more malevolent ones damage or destroy data or erase operating system files so that the computer can't be booted.

Viruses have received a great deal of media attention in the past, when programs such as Melissa, CIH (Chernobyl), Michelangelo, and the Iloveyou virus invaded thousands of computer systems all over the world.

A *worm* is a form of malicious virus that replicates itself and damages files on a computer. Worms are often disseminated as e-mail attachments, as executable files, as documents containing macros, or as HTML pages containing scripts.

Trojan Horse Programs. A *Trojan horse* is a program that presents itself as another program to obtain information. For example, there is a Trojan horse that emulates the system login screen. When a user types in his or her account name and password, the information is stored or transmitted to the originator of the Trojan horse. The username and password can then be used to gain access to the system.

Internal Threats

Many network security policies focus on the Internet and external threats almost exclusively. This is usually a mistake. Just as retail companies find that their own employees commit as much (or more) theft of merchandise as "external" shoplifters, network administrators must not discount the risk of internal security breaches. Many instances of data theft, misuse, or destruction are "inside jobs."

There are several motives for internal security breaches, including the following:

- Corporate espionage
- Internal politics
- Disgruntled employees (including ex-employees)
- Accidental breaches

Next, we look briefly at the characteristics of each and how to guard against them.

Corporate Espionage. Corporate espionage is the most sophisticated type of internal security threat. Theft of trade secrets is big business, and companies can become overnight successes or failures because of it.

Employees can be approached by competing companies and offered lucrative rewards for delivering an organization's secret information. In other instances, employees of other companies can procure a job with your company to infiltrate and gather data to take back to the competitor, and they get to draw a paycheck from both companies simultaneously.

Finally, there are freelance corporate spies who take assignments on a contract basis. In highly competitive industries, they can steal the data on their own and then auction it to the highest bidder. "Data kidnappers" can even hold your confidential data hostage, promising not to release it to another company in exchange for a "ransom" payment.

Corporate spies are often intelligent, highly skilled, technically sophisticated individuals. They are usually well financed and can evade detection until it's too late. If your business is part of a field in which corporate espionage is common (fields include the technology industry, oil and energy, research medicine, engineering, and others in which success hinges on being first to market with innovative products or services), your network can be vulnerable.

Security measures designed to thwart these professional spies must be of the highest level. You might need to call in consultants who specialize in protecting corporate networks from such infiltration.

Internal Politics. Another internal risk is the competitive employee who will do anything to get ahead and beat out his colleagues for the next promotion. This person might attempt to access and sabotage the work of those he views as personal competition. Others might attempt to harm the reputations of fellow workers by searching their e-mail or files for embarrassing messages or personal information. A particularly unscrupulous version of this ambitious person will even plant incriminating items on the victim's computer or send embarrassing e-mail that appears to originate from the victim.

Although this type of misuse of the network can pose a less serious threat to the company's important data than does espionage, it can cause a multitude of problems within the organization. Because many of these perpetrators are not highly skilled technicians, good basic network security policies (such as strong passwords and security auditing) can prevent or expose their actions.

Disgruntled Employees. A particularly destructive type of security threat is the employee or ex-employee who has a grudge against the company and wants to harm it. These people might destroy crucial data or disrupt vital network communications "just for fun" or out of a misplaced sense of "justice."

The company can be especially vulnerable to this threat when a technically knowledgeable employee is fired. It is not uncommon for an angry person to avenge his or her termination by erasing hard disks, by damaging computer hardware, or by releasing viruses onto the company network.

Your security policy should address this issue. Common sense dictates that terminated employees' user accounts be immediately deactivated and, in some instances, that their physical access to the company's computers be curtailed. The latter can be accomplished by assigning someone to escort them when they pack their personal belongings or when they otherwise reenter the company offices.

Accidental Breaches. In many cases, internal security breaches are not deliberate acts but are caused by the technical ignorance or lack of training on the part of the employees. Network administrators are well acquainted with the user who destroys necessary operating system files while trying to "fix" a minor problem or who decides to "free up some disk space" by deleting all the application program files.

Accidental breaches are why operating systems with strong security features are appropriate for the business world. By implementing file-level permissions through the System Policies feature of Windows NT or the Group Policies feature of Windows 2000, users can be prevented from deleting or moving crucial system files.

Rebellious Users. Internal security breaches can also be the result of users who disagree with security policies that they believe are too restrictive. While not "accidental," these breaches are not designed to cause harm; instead, they are intended to enable the user to do something he or she can't otherwise do. For example, if security controls don't prevent users from installing application software or hardware drivers, a rebellious user who doesn't like your Internet access policies can connect an external modem, plug in a phone line, install the drivers, and dial in to his or her own ISP. Another user can install a remote-control application such as PCAnywhere, which can open up that computer—and the internal network—to outside users who also have PCAnywhere installed on their computers.

Your response to rebellious users will depend on the company's policies and the degree of security required on the network. Implementing tighter controls might be appropriate; in other situations, it might be appropriate to evaluate whether your security policies really are unnecessarily stringent and whether you should allow users to have more legitimate access.

Implementing Security Measures

Protecting the network's data often requires that a combination of security methods be applied. In this section, we discuss how user accounts, groups, and permissions can serve as the first line of defense. Then we look at how sensitive data can be encrypted, either in files on the disk or in packets that travel across the network.

Because e-mail is one of the most widely used network applications and because it is the form of network communication most likely to contain confidential information, we focus on the technologies available to secure e-mail messages. After you learn about how security measures are implemented, we discuss how these measures actually work.

Operating System Security Levels

Some operating systems are inherently more secure than others. Older operating systems, such as MS-DOS, do not enable user accounts to access the operating system (although an account is required to access the network). Anyone can sit down at the DOS machine, boot into the operating system, and then run its programs or access its files on the hard disk.

More modern operating systems, such as Windows 95, enable you to create computer user accounts. However, the passwords might be kept in an insecure text file or accessed by booting the computer from an MS-DOS floppy. By default, if you select Cancel when prompted for a username and password, the operating system still boots to full usability.

High-security operating systems such as Windows NT, Windows 2000, and Linux *require* that you enter a valid username and password to boot into the operating system and use it. They also store passwords in an encrypted form that can't be easily accessed.

The U.S. government provides specifications for rating computer security levels. These are discussed in the "Developing Security Policies" section of this chapter.

Users, Groups, and Permissions

Modern operating systems enable multiple users to access the computer and the network by creating separate user accounts and allowing a different password to be assigned to each. The combined username and password, when entered at a login prompt, results in the following:

- The user is given access to the operating system and network.
- The user can read and write to those shares to which his or her account has been given permissions.
- The user can exercise whatever rights (such as the right to shut down the computer or to install programs) have been assigned to his or her account.
- The user's preferences, such as desktop icons and wallpaper, are loaded.

In some computing environments in which there is no sensitive data stored on computers and the attitude toward security is casual, separate user accounts might not be created. All users can use the same account to log in. This means that every user has the same access permissions. Not only does this create an open, unsecured environment, but it also means users cannot customize their desktops and other settings.

In most business organizations, it is better to create separate accounts for different users. If unauthorized access is not an issue, passwords can be left blank.

Password Security. An important part of any network security plan is ensuring that user passwords are as impenetrable as possible. If users are allowed to select their own passwords, rules should be set according to the security needs of the network.

Some examples of password policies include the following:

- Passwords should never be words or numbers easily guessed because of their association with the user (for example, the user's Social Security number or a dog's name).

- Because many brute-force attack programs use lists of common words, passwords should not be words that are listed in the dictionary. A good policy is to combine letters and numbers (for example, "heavy238").

- In most operating systems, passwords are case-sensitive, so a password that contains randomly capitalized letters is difficult to guess (for example, "mYdoGspOt").

- A password *should* be easy for its user to remember. If it's not, he or she will probably end up writing it down.

- The more characters a password has, the harder it is for someone to guess it; thus, "visualize" is a better password than "see." This factor must be balanced against the user's ability to remember a long password.

- In a high-security environment, users should be required to change their passwords periodically. The new password should not be similar to the old one. For example, the user shouldn't change a password from "panda3" to "panda6." Again, it's important to maintain balance, because users who are required to change their passwords too often will not be able to remember them, and they will write the passwords down.

- Most network operating systems enable the administrator to set criteria such as minimum password length, password history (which keeps a list of the user's previous passwords and prevents reuse), and password expiration (which forces the user to change the password at specified intervals). There are also password security programs available that enable administrators to set parameters for passwords. For example, a parameter might prevent passwords that are out of the dictionary.

NOTE

Some security-conscious operating systems (such as Windows NT and Windows 2000) will not enable you to leave passwords blank by default; an administrator has to change the password policy settings to allow this.

Access Control Policies. Modern network operating systems (NOSs) enable administrators to control access to resources on a granular basis. The mary-smith user account can be granted permission to view the contents of file1.doc but not allowed to make changes. At the same time, she might have permission to view, change, delete, or even set the access permissions on file2.doc, but no permissions to access file3.doc.

Each individual user can be given exactly the permissions needed. Using high-security file systems, permissions can be set not only on resources accessed across the network, but also on those same resources when accessed from the local machine. Local and network permissions do not have to be the same. Mary could be given full control over file4.doc when she accesses it while logged in to the machine on which it is stored, but limited to reading it if she accesses it from a remote machine across the network.

It is important to be aware of the default permissions for the NOS in use. On a Windows NT or Windows 2000 server, for example, when you share a resource, it is fully accessible to everyone on the network unless you explicitly change the permissions. On a NetWare server, the opposite is true; the share is accessible to no one until you explicitly change its permissions.

Neither method is right or wrong, but if you don't know how your NOS permissions work, you could end up allowing access to resources that you hadn't intended *or* prohibiting access to users who should have it.

In a security-sensitive organization, policies should be established to govern who should have access to which resources. Generally, access should be granted on a need-to-know basis. If the user needs access to the resource to perform his or her job duties, permissions should be granted. Otherwise, access should be denied.

Using Security Groups. Security groups are an administrative aid supported by many NOSs to make it easier to assign permissions on a large network. Groups are created, and those groups are given permission to resources. Then the appropriate user accounts are placed into the group, instantly giving the users all the permissions assigned to the group. This is easier than assigning permissions to individual users.

For example, if everyone in your sales department needs access to several folders (we'll call them salestats, salesbudget, and salesmemos), you could assign access permissions for each folder to all 20 users in the department. However, an easier method is to create a security group called sales, give it permission to all three folders, and put the 20 user accounts into it. Then if you create a new folder, salescalendars, that needs to be accessed by the entire department, all you have to do is assign permissions to the sales group. Otherwise, you would have to assign permissions for the new folder to 20 different accounts.

If you don't want a user to have access to a certain resource, don't assume that removing that permission from his user account is enough. You must also ensure that the user is not a member of any group that has permissions to access the resource. In addition, if the operating system (for example, Windows NT or Windows 2000) enables you to specifically deny access, you must explicitly do so.

File Encryption

Encryption involves converting data into a form that can't be easily understood by others. The technical aspects of encryption are discussed in more detail in the "How Security Components Work" section later in this chapter.

File encryption is a means of encrypting data stored on a computer's disk so that it is unreadable to anyone but the creator of the data. Some operating systems, such as Windows 2000, include a file-encryption function. For those that don't supply such a function (for example, Windows 9*x* and Windows NT), third-party encryption programs are available.

When documents are encrypted on the disk, only a user who has the correct key can view them. If others attempt access, either the file won't open at all or it appears as scrambled, meaningless characters. Note that sensitive data should be protected by both access permissions and encryption.

IP Security

File encryption protects data stored on a disk, but it does not offer security for data as it is sent over a network. The IP Security (IPSec) protocol was developed to remedy this shortcoming. IPSec secures data at the packet level. Because it works at the network layer of the OSI reference model, applications are not aware of it. Cisco Systems includes support for IPSec in its routers, and Windows 2000 includes IPSec in its TCP/IP stack.

IPSec uses two protocols:

- **Authentication Header (AH)**—Enables verification of the sender's identity
- **Encapsulating Security Payload (ESP)**—Ensures the confidentiality of the data itself

These two protocols can be used separately or together.

IPSec can operate in two modes: transport mode and tunnel mode. See Figure 14-2. Transport mode provides *end-to-end security;* that is, the encryption is in place from the source computer to the destination computer. Tunnel mode protects the data from the exit point of one network to the entry point of another.

FIGURE 14-2
Packet headers differ, depending on whether IPSec is used in transport mode or tunnel mode.

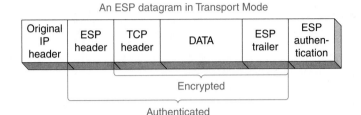

An ESP datagram in Transport Mode

| Original IP header | ESP header | TCP header | DATA | ESP trailer | ESP authentication |

Encrypted

Authenticated

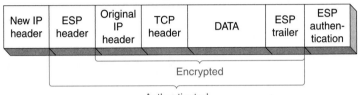

An ESP datagram in Tunnel Mode

| New IP header | ESP header | Original IP header | TCP header | DATA | ESP trailer | ESP authentication |

Encrypted

Authenticated

Secure Sockets Layer (SSL)

SSL is another means of securing communications on the network. The disadvantage of SSL is that it operates at the application layer; thus, it must be supported by the user application.

SSL was developed by Netscape to provide security for its web browser. It uses *public* and *private key encryption*. These are discussed in the "How Security Components Work" section later in this chapter.

E-mail Security

Many computer users enjoy a false sense of security about network communications in general and e-mail messages in particular. Users assume that the messages they compose and send over the local network or the Internet are read only by the recipient to whom the messages are addressed. E-mail users behave as if they have the same expectation of privacy when sending e-mail as they do when sending a letter through the postal service. A more accurate expectation would be to assume that the e-mail is like a postcard that can be read by anyone who handles it during its journey from sender to recipient.

E-mail messages are very easy to intercept (see Figure 14-3). They often travel through dozens of nodes (servers) on their way from sender to recipient. Even if a message is sent to someone within the local network, a copy of it is stored on at least three machines: the sender's computer, the recipient's computer, and the internal mail server. E-mail sent over the Internet can pass through several servers as well. Unless it is encrypted or digitally signed, the message can be easily read, copied, or altered at any point along the way.

FIGURE 14-3
E-mail messages can be intercepted at the many points through which they travel as they move across the Internet.

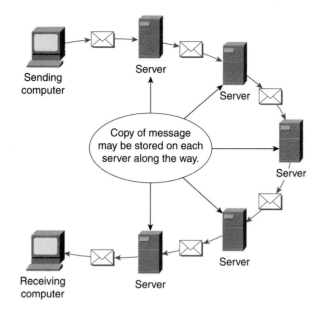

Sending computer

Server

Server

Server

Copy of message may be stored on each server along the way.

Server

Receiving computer

Server

Server

Many software products have been developed to address this problem. These products are designed to accomplish several goals:

- The message cannot be read by unauthorized parties.
- The message cannot be altered between the time it leaves the sender and the time it is opened by the recipient.
- The person identified as the sender of the message is actually who he or she purports to be.

An important factor in e-mail protection software is ease of use. If users must perform complex or time-consuming tasks to send or read secured e-mail, they are likely to abandon the security software altogether.

Popular e-mail protection programs include the following:

- Pretty Good Privacy (PGP)
- Kerberos
- Baltimore Mail Secure
- MailMarshal from Softek

Most e-mail protection software uses public key encryption (discussed in "Public/Private Key Encryption" later in this chapter)and digital signatures to provide data confidentiality and identity authentication.

How Security Components Work

Computer security technologies are based on the science of *cryptography*, which is the study of "secret writings" or *ciphers*. Encryption uses a code or key to scramble and then unscramble (or *decipher*) a message to return it to its original form. The task of analyzing and deciphering encrypted messages is called *cryptanalysis*.

Basic Cryptography Concepts

Data is encrypted using an *algorithm* or cipher. The encrypted data is referred to as *ciphertext*. To understand encryption, consider the "secret codes" used by children (and sometimes adults as well) to protect the privacy of their communications. A very simple encryption scheme assigns a number to each letter of the alphabet. If we start with A as 1, B as 2, and so forth, we can send an "encoded" message such as the following:

```
4-9-14-14-5-18 9-19 18-5-1-4-25
```

The message is easily "decoded," or *decrypted*, back to the original:

```
Dinner is ready
```

Unfortunately, this cipher is easy to crack and thus not very secure. Computer encryption is more complex. Generally a *key* is used, which is a variable of some sort that is combined with the data to be encrypted. The method of combining the key with the data is called the *algorithm*. Because computers process binary information, these calculations are applied to each bit or group of bits (see Figure 14-4).

FIGURE 14-4
Computerized encryption techniques use keys and algorithms.

The longer the encryption key, the more difficult it is to break the code. In the field of encryption, 40- and 56-bit encryption is called *standard encryption*, and 128-bit encryption is called *strong encryption*.

LAWS GOVERNING ENCRYPTION TECHNOLOGIES

Many countries have legal restrictions on the export or import of encryption technologies. The U.S. classifies encryption as "munitions" and prohibits export of strong encryption software. Cryptology up to 40 bits can be exported, and cryptology up to 56 bits can be exported under some circumstances. 128-bit encryption technologies cannot be exported. There are no restrictions on importing encryption items.

The laws in other countries range from Argentina, which has neither import nor export controls and no restrictions on the use of cryptography, to Russia, where both import and export are regulated, and the use of unauthorized encryption within the country is prohibited.

Two popular types of encryption are secret key encryption and public/private (or public) key encryption. Let's look at how each works.

Secret Key Encryption. *Secret key encryption* is often referred to as *symmetric encryption* because one key is used to both encrypt and decrypt the data. The sender and recipient agree to use a common key, or encryption algorithm, which is a *shared secret.* For example, if Ted and Carol wish to exchange private messages, they decide on the following code, or key, to represent each letter of the alphabet:

1. Convert the letter to a number using a scheme in which A = 6, B = 7, C = 8, and so forth.

2. Multiply the resulting number by 4.

This key, although by no means impossible to break, is quite a bit more secure than our first example. Now to send the message "Dinner is ready," Carol goes through the following process to arrive at the final encrypted message:

```
D = 9
9 × 4 = 36
I = 14
14 × 4 = 56
```

Eventually, she arrives at the final encrypted message:

```
36-56-76-76-40-92 56-96 92-40-24-36-120
```

Ted has the same key and knows that to decrypt the message, he need only divide each number by 4 and then apply the same A = 6, B = 7, and C = 8 table to restore the original message.

Popular secret key encryption algorithms are Data Encryption Standard (DES) and 3DES (pronounced "triple DES"). Another is RC (Rivest Cipher)-4, created by Ron Rivest. This person, along with Adi Shamir and Leonard Adleman, developed the popular RSA public key encryption scheme, which is discussed in the next section of this chapter.

There are three inherent problems with secret key encryption:

- Generating the secret keys
- Exchanging the keys between authorized parties without having them fall into the hands of unauthorized parties
- Dealing with the complexity involved in securing communications to many different parties

It is prudent to change the keys regularly to avoid compromising security. This means additional keys must be generated. There also must be a way to get the key to the party who is authorized to decipher the message. In our previous example, if Carol e-mailed the key to Ted without encryption, she would defeat the purpose of securing the communication. However, if she e-mailed it to him encrypted, he would not be able to read it, because he doesn't know the key.

Mechanisms have been developed to generate keys and exchange them securely. One example is the Diffie-Hellman algorithm, which enables two parties to create a secret known only to them, despite the fact that they are communicating on an unsecured network.

The third issue in our previous bulleted list is a bit more problematic. Carol and Ted can happily exchange (somewhat) secure messages for years using their secret key, but what happens if Carol wants to send a secure message to Bob? If she uses the same key, Ted would be able to decipher it. In addition, once Bob has the key, he can decipher Carol's messages to Ted as well.

To remedy the situation, Carol and Bob could come up with an entirely different key. For example, messages to Bob could be encrypted by converting the letter to a number using the numbering scheme A = 12, B = 13, and so on, and then adding 15 to the result. However, now Carol has to remember two keys, and if she wants to send secure messages to a large number of people, this technique quickly becomes unmanageable. A simpler solution is to use a different type of encryption: public/private key encryption.

Public/Private Key Encryption. Although often referred to as public key encryption for brevity, the more accurate term is *public/private key encryption*, because this type of encryption uses two keys, one of which is published and widely available, and the other of which is private and known only to the user. Both keys are required to complete the secure communication. This type of encryption is also referred to as *asymmetric encryption*. With this type of encryption, each user has both a public and a private key, called a *key pair*. Here's how it works:

1. Carol and Ted exchange their public keys. It doesn't matter that this is done in an insecure manner, because the messages cannot be deciphered with just the public key.

2. Carol wants to send a message to Ted, so she encrypts the message using Ted's public key. A public key is associated with only one private key. To decrypt a message that was encrypted using a public key, the associated private key is required. (The reverse also applies—to decrypt a message that was encrypted using a private key, the associated public key is required.)

3. Ted, using his private key, can decrypt the message because it was encrypted using his public key. Notice that only Ted's keys, public and private, were used in this encryption process.

If Carol had encrypted the message using her private key, anyone could decrypt the message using her public key, which is available to all.

Both keys of the same key pair must be used for this encryption to work, and there is no need for anyone to know anyone else's private key. A good way to understand this type of encryption is to think of the two pieces of information required to enter a home protected by a digital combination lock. If someone wants to enter the house, he or she must know both the street address and the number sequence to enter into the locking device. The address is public information that is published in the telephone directory. It is available to anyone, just as the user's public encryption key is available to anyone. The lock combination is analogous to the user's private key; it is known only to the owner of the house. Both keys are unique to that particular home, but one is made known to the public while the other is kept secret.

Authentication. The examples we have discussed thus far deal with protecting the *confidentiality* of the data. A separate issue is the *authentication* of the sender's identity.

Using the public/private key method, you can easily secure the data itself. However, because the public key *is* public and available to anyone, there is no way for Ted to know for sure that a message he receives, encrypted with his public key, really is from Carol. For the identity of the sender to be authenticated, Carol would have to encrypt the message with her *private* key. Ted can then decrypt it with her public key, confident that she was the actual sender because she is the only person who knows her private key.

Another way to ensure the authentication of the sender is to use *digital signatures*, which we discuss next.

Digital Signatures

Digital signatures consist of encrypted signing information appended to a document. This information verifies both the identity of the sender and the integrity of the document itself. Digital signatures don't encrypt the data. They only ensure that it has not been altered and that the sender is authentic.

Public key algorithms are used to create and verify digital signatures and *hash algorithms*. We discuss hash algorithms next.

Hash Algorithms

A *hash* is the result of a one-way mathematical calculation (the *hash algorithm*) that creates a *message digest*. The algorithm is called "one-way" because you cannot reverse-engineer the result to discover the original message.

The hash verifies the authenticity of the message in the following manner:

1. The sender hashes the message with a key that is a shared secret; that is, the key is known to both the sender and the intended recipient. The hash produces a numerical result (let's say it's 0010110010100001).

2. The message and the result, or *message digest*, are sent to the recipient.

3. To confirm that the message has not been altered, the recipient applies the same key, and he or she should get the same numerical result (0010110010100001). If the content of the message has been changed, the result of the hash does not match.

Popular hashing algorithms include the following:

- **Secure Hash Algorithm (SHA)**—Developed by the National Institute of Standards and Technology (NIST) and the National Security Agency (NSA)
- **Message Digest 5 (MD5)**—Developed by Ron Rivest at MIT

Generally, hash algorithms produce a value of at least 128 bits, making it extremely difficult or impossible to produce the same result with a different set of input data.

Digital Certificates

Digital certificates are messages that contain the digital signature of a trusted third party, or *certificate authority*. The third party warrants that a particular public key actually belongs to a specified person. Certificates are used to ensure the authenticity of messages that travel across unsecured public networks such as the Internet.

A user who has the private key that is associated with a particular public key requests a certificate from a certificate authority. The certificate authority has the responsibility for verifying that a specific public key belongs to a specific user. Certificates are valid for a specified period of time, and the certificate authority can revoke them.

Organizations can set up their own certification authorities as part of their network's *public key infrastructure (PKI)*. A PKI is a system of verifying and authenticating the identity of parties engaging in electronic communications.

Digital certificates are issued by public certificate authorities such as the following:

- Verisign
- GTE Cybertrust
- Keywitness
- TradeWave

Digital certificates can be thought of as electronic ID cards. Just as a government-issued driver's license, passport, or other identification document can be presented to establish your identity in the physical world, digital certificates perform that function in the world of network communications.

Kerberos

Kerberos is an authentication protocol that is an Internet standard for verifying the identity of a user or computer system. It was developed at MIT and named for the three-headed dog of Greek mythology that guarded the gates of Hades. Kerberos security relies on three factors: the client, the server, and a trusted authority called the *key distribution center* (KDC). The KDC maintains a database that keeps track of the participating entities.

Kerberos is based on the concept of tickets, which are encrypted messages that are used to request service from a server. Authentication is performed using symmetric encryption (also referred to as secret key encryption). See Figure 14-5.

FIGURE 14-5
The Kerberos authentication process depends on tickets to verify identity and to grant access to servers.

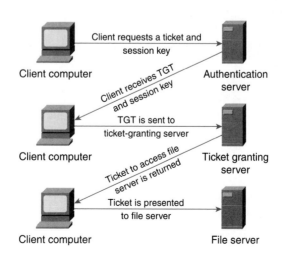

Here's how the Kerberos process works:

1. The first step involves a request from the client to an authentication server for a ticket and *session key*. This is an encryption key based on the requesting user's password, and it is combined with a random value representing the service being requested. The ticket returned to the client is called the *ticket-granting ticket* (TGT). This verifies the identity of the client.

2. The TGT is sent by the client to a ticket-granting server (which can be the same physical machine as the authentication server). Based on the TGT, the ticket-granting server returns a ticket that is presented to the file server whose resources the client wants to access.

3. The ticket is valid for a specified amount of time so that the client can make additional requests of the server without going through the process again.

Kerberos has been in use on UNIX networks for many years. Microsoft included Kerberos support in Windows 2000, and the Active Directory domain trust relationships are based on Kerberos authentication.

Advanced Identification and Authentication Technologies

Identification and authentication are important security concerns as corporate networks become larger and must support thousands of users. Establishing the identity of a user attempting to log in to the network or access a computer's resources is the foundation of a strong security plan.

Regardless of the sophistication of password encryption technologies, the problem with the username/password method is the possibility of an unauthorized party discovering and using the credentials of a legitimate user. Advanced identification and authentication technologies such as the following attempt to prevent this by basing identification on factors that can't be faked:

- Smart cards
- Biometrics, including fingerprint recognition, retinal scan and iris recognition, and voiceprint verification

Although these technologies are not yet commonly encountered in the workplace outside of government agencies, over the next decade, we can expect advanced authentication methods to become commonplace, and it will be increasingly important for network administrators to be familiar with their implementation. The following sections describe each technology.

Smart Cards

Smart cards are authentication devices that resemble credit cards and that store information such as public/private keys and passwords. The storage technology can be as simple as a magnetic strip or as complicated as an integrated circuit that is embedded in the card and that functions like a tiny computer.

Some operating systems, such as Windows 2000, have smart card support built into them. Without an operating system that has built-in support, you might need separate software before you can use smart card technologies.

A smart card is used to access the computer through a piece of hardware known as a *smart card reader*. The smart card provides extra security because a user must have possession of the physical card. Smart cards can be used in place of—or, for added security, in addition to—physically entered user credentials.

In a high-security environment, the card alone does not enable access; the user must insert the card into the reader and enter the correct login credentials before access is granted. This means a potential intruder who finds out a user's password still can't log in without the card; likewise, someone who finds or steals the card cannot gain access without knowing the correct password.

A variation on the smart card is the *I-key* from Rainbow Technologies. It is a small device that fits on a keyboard and that communicates through a USB port instead of requiring reader hardware.

Biometrics

It is still possible that an intruder could gain knowledge of the password and possession of the corresponding smart card. To counteract this possibility, fingerprint recognition, retinal scans, and voice verification technologies take security a step further. These technologies are known as *biometrics*, which is the field of biological statistics.

Biometrics work because the statistical probability of two people having the same fingerprints (or retinal patterns or voice patterns) is so small that these technologies are admissible in court in many countries as evidence in criminal proceedings. Biometric identification technologies can provide a positive identification of a user based on biological characteristics.

In the following sections, we examine how various biometric methods work.

Fingerprint Recognition. A fingerprint recognition system often operates in conjunction with card-based security. The users' fingerprints are taken and entered into the database, and when a user wants to access the computer, he must

> **NOTE**
>
> When smart cards are discussed in the context of network security, the term refers to an identification and authentication device that stores credentials that enable a user to access a system. The term "smart card" is also used in a more generic sense to indicate any plastic card that stores info on a chip or magnetic strip. These cards include credit and debit cards, medical information cards, and so forth.

place the finger (or more often, the thumb, although some systems use an entire handprint) onto a reader screen. The input from the reader is compared with the prints in the database, and access is granted or denied.

Various software and hardware systems are available for implementing fingerprint authentication. These systems include VeriPrint and U.are.U, both of which are offered by FingerSec Corporation.

Retinal Scan and Iris Recognition. Another means of identifying persons based on their unique biological characteristics is the *retinal scan*. In this technology, a low-intensity light source is used to scan the patterns of the retina, which is the delicate membrane that lines the inner eyeball.

Also based on the characteristics of the human eye is *iris recognition*. This technology involves computer analysis of the patterns found in the iris of the eye, which is the pigmented round membrane that gives the eye its color. These patterns are said to be even more unique than fingerprints or DNA. Even identical twins have distinct iris patterns.

Voiceprint Verification. Voiceprint verification operates on the principle that human voice patterns are unique to each individual and can be used to identify the speaker.

> **NOTE**
>
> Voice verification is sometimes confused with *voice recognition*. The former is used to verify the identity of the speaker. The latter does not identify the speaker, but recognizes the words spoken and, in the case of voice recognition computer software, translates them into written form on the screen.

Generally, the user is required to record a password or phrase, which is stored in the database. To log in, the user speaks the same word or phrase, and the patterns are compared. Such factors as pitch, tone, and cadence are considered. Voiceprint technology is not considered to be as accurate as retinal scans, iris scans, and fingerprint recognition. Voice verification is commonly used in situations in which identity needs to be authenticated over a phone line.

The Future of Biometrics. Some parts of the world, such as Australia, South Africa, South America, and Europe, have moved quickly to adopt biometric recognition and authentication technologies. The United States has been slower to implement them, perhaps because of privacy issues or because of market factors.

As technologies become more accurate and less intrusive and problems such as identity theft gain more attention, it is likely that the use of biometrics will grow and become commonplace in the networks of the future.

Developing Security Policies

New security technologies are emerging constantly. To develop a good security plan for a network, you must be aware of what is available. You also must be able to determine the level of security that is necessary or desirable for your situation.

Security policies should be the product of a team effort. Input should be solicited from technical personnel, management, and representative users. To be successful, a security policy must have the support of the company's managers and users. Budgetary and philosophical considerations must be weighed against the sensitivity of the data on the network and the ramifications if it were compromised.

Security policies should be in writing and should be reviewed and revised periodically as circumstances change. The first step in creating policies is to perform a detailed security analysis. You should determine what security measures are currently in place, whether they are accomplishing their purpose, and which of them should be removed, retained, or replaced.

In the following sections, we address the following important factors that you should consider when developing policies:

- Acceptable use policies
- Termination policies
- Government security ratings
- Security auditing and intrusion detection
- Firewalls and proxies
- Security through multiple protocols
- Physical security

Acceptable Use Policies

The network security policy should include an acceptable use policy that defines how users can legitimately access and use the resources on the network. This should include items such as the encryption of messages and files, web site access, the downloading of files from the Internet, bandwidth usage, the installation of programs and games, e-mail policies, and other end-user issues.

Termination Policies

A network security policy should address the procedures for ensuring continued integrity of the network data when an employee—especially one in a technical position—leaves the company either voluntarily or through termination of employment.

NOTE

Biometrics specialists make a distinction between recognition and authentication. Authentication is regarded as a voluntary activity in which the user provides a name or identifying number, along with a biometric input such as a fingerprint, usually for the purpose of gaining access to a system. The biometric is compared with a stored biometric know to belong to the user. The comparison is used to verify the user's identity, and if verification succeeds, access is granted. In recognition, the system gets only the biometric input (voice sample, retinal scan, or fingerprint) and then must search its database and find a match. For example, recognition is used when forensics experts attempt to identify a fingerprint left at a crime scene. To make the identification, experts might search for a match in a database such as the FBI's Automated Fingerprint Identification System (AFIS).

It is important that all company property be accounted for and that employees turn in smart cards and other access devices. Accounts of terminated employees should be immediately disabled. If the employee had access to sensitive data, he or she should not be allowed to take personal floppy disks, zip drives, or other data storage media without having that media checked to ensure that there has been no unauthorized copying of confidential company files.

Government Security Ratings

The U.S. government provides criteria for rating security implementations. These specifications are defined in *Department of Defense Trusted Computer System Evaluation Criteria*, which is referred to as TCSEC and sometimes called the "orange book." TCSEC is published by the National Computer Security Center (NCSC). It is used in conjunction with *Trusted Network Interpretation of the TCSEC*, which is referred to as TNI and sometimes called the "red book."

The TNI applies evaluation criteria for networks. Ratings start with A, which is the highest security rating, and go to D, which is the lowest rating. The C rating is divided into two subratings, C1 and C2; however, C1 is no longer used as a certification. A C2 rating, which is a higher rating than a C1, is sought by many businesses to obtain government contracts. A C2 rating requires that the operating system be able to track when and by whom data is accessed. A C2 operating system must have the capability to control users' access to objects, provide for unique identification of users, and include a means to audit security-related events.

If your organization requires that its computer systems have a C2 rating, you should ensure that they meet all the criteria in TCSEC and TNI. You even might have to have the security configuration certified and accredited by administrative authorities to qualify as C2-compliant for government contract work.

Table 14-1 lists various operating systems and the security ratings they have received.

NOTE

Other countries have similar security rating systems. These systems include the Canadian Trusted Computer Product Evaluation Criteria (CTCPEC) in Canada, the Australian Information Security Evaluation Programme (AISEP) in Australia, and the Information Technology Security Evaluation Criteria (ITSEC) in Western Europe.

TABLE 14-1   NSA Security Ratings for Various Operating Systems

Operating System	Vendor	NSA Certification
UNIX XTS-200 and 300	Wang Government Svcs	Orange Book B3
UNIX Trusted Xenix 3 and 4	Trusted Information Systems	Orange Book B2
UNIX HP-UX 8.04 and 9.0.9	Hewlett Packard	Orange Book B1

TABLE 14-1   NSA Security Ratings for Various Operating Systems (Continued)

Operating System	Vendor	NSA Certification
UNIX UNICOS 8.0.2	Cray Research	Red Book B1
UNIX RS/6000	IBM	Orange Book C2
Windows NT 3.5/SP3 and Windows NT 4.0	Microsoft	Orange Book C2
NetWare 4 and 4.11	Novell	Red Book C2

Merely installing the specified operating system does not guarantee that you meet the criteria of the security certification shown. There are other specifications, such as network connectivity and the enabled operating system features, that must be considered. In actuality, it is not the operating system itself that receives a security rating, but the entire hardware and software configuration.

Security Auditing and Intrusion Detection

One requirement for the C2 security rating is the capability to audit security events and the activities performed by individual users. *Auditing* is the process of tracking the activities of users and the system. For example, auditing includes monitoring which files are accessed, when, and by whom. Auditing can include information on who has logged in to or out of the system, who has accessed objects, and who has exercised user rights.

Operating systems such as Windows NT and Windows 2000 have auditing built into them, and auditing can be configured on a granular basis. Security events are not only tracked, but also recorded in a log file for easy review. Only administrators should have access to the security logs.

Passive Detection. Security auditing is referred to as a *passive* form of intruder detection. Although events affecting security are logged to a file, an administrator must suspect intrusion and check the file to learn of the breach. Examples of passive detection programs are Tripwire (for UNIX) and the built-in security-auditing feature of Windows NT and Windows 2000.

Active Detection. An environment in which network data is sensitive should not rely on passive intrusion detection alone. A security plan should include one or more forms of *active detection*. In active detection, software continuously scans the network for signs of intrusion, and some programs even alert the administrator and disconnect the suspicious session. SATAN (the ominous name stands for Security Administrator's Tool for Analyzing Networks) and NetRanger are examples of such software packages.

An updated version of SATAN has been released. It carries a more pleasant name—Security Administrator's Integrated Network Tool (SAINT). SAINT can detect additional vulnerabilities, and it is available in an easy-to-use version called WebSaint, which enables administrators to check for system vulnerabilities over the Internet.

Firewalls and Proxies

Strong perimeter security is another important consideration in establishing security policies. *Firewalls* and *proxies* can be used to create a barrier between the local internal network and the connection to the outside world. This area can be set up in its own subnet, and it is sometimes referred to as the *demilitarized zone* (DMZ) or *screened subnet*. See Figure 14-6.

FIGURE 14-6
Firewalls and proxies can be configured in a DMZ between the internal and external networks.

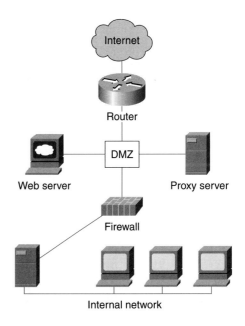

A firewall can be hardware- or software-based. It provides a means of filtering incoming and outgoing packets, and it determines (based on policies set by network administrators) whether to allow the packets through to the destination address. The firewall is typically located at the network's *gateway*, which is the point at which the network connects to another network.

Three basic types of filtering are performed by firewalls:

- Packet filtering
- Circuit filtering
- Application filtering

Packet filtering filters data packets based on the information in the IP, TCP/UDP, and ICMP headers. With packet filtering, you can enable or block specific IP addresses or port numbers. *Circuit filtering* is based on the connection at hand. If a packet isn't part of an established connection, it won't be allowed through the firewall. Finally, *application filtering* filters according to protocols used for specific IP applications. For instance, Java applets or Visual Basic scripts could be blocked.

Hardware-based firewalls are sometimes called "black boxes." They are dedicated computers that run a proprietary operating system (or, in some cases, UNIX). They function *only* as a firewall, and thus are faster and more stable than a computer that is running firewall software while providing other computer functions.

Proxy servers operate as "middlemen" in the network by performing functions similar to firewalls. Computers on the internal network communicate with the proxy, which then communicates "on their behalf" with computers on the external network (see Figure 14-7).

FIGURE 14-7
A proxy server acts as a "middleman" between the internal and external networks.

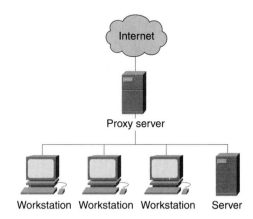

Proxy servers also provide services such as *reverse proxy* and *reverse hosting*. Reverse proxy enables a proxy server to redirect external HTTP requests to a single designated machine. This enables secure access to an internal web server without exposing the server to the external network. Reverse hosting enables the proxy server to redirect HTTP requests to more than one web server by mapping several servers to one logical address (see Figure 14-8). Proxies also provide the caching of web pages to improve web performance.

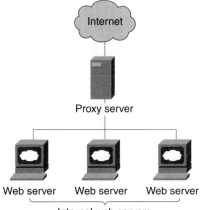

FIGURE 14-8
Reverse hosting enables a proxy server to redirect HTTP requests to multiple web servers.

NOTE

The ACLs used by the router enable or deny access based on factors such as IP addresses. This means a spoofed IP address can defeat the router's firewall protection.

Routers and Layer 3 switches can be configured with *access control lists (ACLs)* that restrict specific machines from using the router or that enable communication in one direction only. In this case, the router provides firewall protection.

Routers with configured ACLs can be thought of as a "first line of defense" for your network. They are often used to protect software firewalls from tampering.

Security Through Multiple Protocols

A network security policy should also address which protocols are allowed or required. You can provide security to the internal network by using a protocol stack other than TCP/IP, either on the LAN itself or in the DMZ subnet that separates it from the external network.

If you use IPX/SPX as the network/transport protocol on the local network instead of using TCP/IP, IP-based attacks from the Internet cannot penetrate the LAN. You simply configure a router to use TCP/IP on the side that connects to the Internet and IPX/SPX on the side that connects to the local network. If you need TCP/IP for communication between internal computers, you can use it on the LAN, but you should set up a DMZ that uses IPX/SPX between the LAN and the Internet.

Physical Security

A network security policy should control *physical access* to the network components. This is an important but often overlooked factor in developing an effective security plan. You should assess the degree of access that employees, contractors, clients, and the public have to the workstations, servers, cable, other media, routers, switches, and other physical components.

In a high-security environment, servers and connectivity devices should be kept behind locked doors. Workstations that are in nonsecured areas should have software controls that prevent access to sensitive network data. Cable should be protected by heavy conduits, not exposed on the floor or ceiling. Twisted-pair and coax are especially easy to tap into, but it is also possible to intercept data over fiber optics by using an optical splitter. Because the signal level is affected when a tap is made in this way, an observant network administrator can detect the tap with an optical time domain reflectometer (OTDR). However, experts can insert a tap that cannot be easily detected by the OTDR.

In many organizations, great pains are taken to restrict employees' and the public's access to the computer equipment—and then it is all left wide open every night when the janitorial staff comes in to clean. If security is an issue on your network, cleaning and maintenance personnel should be under the supervision of an authorized person when they are in the rooms containing network equipment.

Disaster Protection and Recovery

Intrusion is not the only threat to the network and its data. Hardware failure, natural disasters, and technical mistakes can also result in a devastating loss of important files. This is why disaster protection and recovery measures are essential for any production network.

Protecting against and recovering from catastrophic data loss involves several lines of defense:

- Power backup
- Data backup
- Disk fault tolerance
- Server fault tolerance (clustering)

We briefly review the basic principles of each and how each can be implemented on a network.

Power Backup

Numerous companies have had the experience of losing precious data when a summer thunderstorm caused the lights to flicker and the computers to reboot or when an electric company glitch created a sudden surge of high voltage. These incidents are all the more frustrating because they are preventable.

A great deal of data is lost or damaged every year because of electrical power surges and failures. In this section, we look at how you can protect the network from the dangers of power fluctuations with surge protectors, uninterruptible power supplies (UPSs), and power generators.

Surge Protectors

A power spike or surge can damage computer hardware and render data unreadable. A good surge protector and suppressor are the absolute minimum protection that you should provide for each important computer on the network, including all servers and mission-critical workstations.

UPSs

A form of power protection that is better, but more expensive, than a surge protector is a UPS. A UPS is a type of battery backup that provides a limited amount of stored electricity on which the systems can continue operating after the power fails.

A UPS is *not* designed to provide power to continue using the computer systems. Its purpose is to enable uninterrupted power for several minutes, which gives you time to close files and programs and shut the computers down "gracefully." The typical UPS provides power for 5 to 20 minutes after it kicks over to battery mode.

The UPS is plugged into the wall outlet, and the computer is plugged into the UPS. Many UPSs have multiple outlets so that several systems can be run off one UPS. The device is continually charging in normal mode. When the electricity fails, the UPS senses this and often can be configured to notify users that it is not receiving power. Notification can take the form of an audio signal (such as a beep), or software can be used to send a message to administrative accounts on the network. The same software can be configured to automatically start shutdown of the attached computer when the UPS goes to battery mode.

All crucial systems on the network should be attached to UPS devices. The cost of a good UPS system is a fraction of the cost of a new computer, and it is well

NOTE

Surge protectors are the lowest-cost power protection devices, but their effectiveness is limited to increases in power voltage. They do not protect the systems if the power voltage decreases or is turned off. Many surge protectors cannot withstand multiple power surges—after experiencing a surge and doing its job, a surge protector might need to be replaced. Unfortunately, it is not always possible to detect that this has occurred, so you might believe that you have surge protection when in fact you no longer do.

worth the expense when compared to the cost of losing your data (which can be priceless).

Generators

The next step up in power protection is the *power generator*. This device actually makes electricity by using an engine powered by gasoline, kerosene, or other fuel. A generator enables you to continue using your electrical equipment (including computers) for the duration of a power outage.

Generators are expensive, and their expense is usually not warranted except in situations in which the power is expected to be out for a long period of time or the equipment that needs the power is used for life support or other emergency purposes.

Data Backup

Despite your best efforts to prevent it, eventually it will happen: A hard disk will crash, a fire or flood will damage the server, or a malicious virus will format the drive and render your files unreadable. Simply put, data will be lost. However, if you have implemented a regular, thorough data backup program, it's not gone forever.

Devising a backup plan involves answering the following questions:

- What files should you back up?
- When should you back them up?
- How should you back them up?
- Why should you back them up?

The answer to the fourth question should be self-evident; your backup plan can mean the difference between catastrophic loss of data, time, and money and the minor inconvenience of spending a few hours restoring files to their original state. Let's look at the answers to the other three questions and see how they fit into your plan.

What to Back Up

The first step is to decide what should be backed up and to assign priorities to the files to be backed up. The ideal situation, of course, is to back up everything. However, this might not always be feasible because of time constraints and limits on the capacity of backup media.

It's not always important to back up the operating system and application files, because these can be reinstalled from the installation disks. Original data is more important to back up; original data includes word processing documents, spreadsheets, and other data created in various user applications. Creative work such as graphic art or original writing compositions should have

NOTE

Although UPS literature often uses the terminology "battery mode," in reality the computer equipment is always running off the UPS battery. It's just that the battery is always being charged as long as the power from the wall outlet is active. This is why there is no interruption to the electricity flowing to the computers when the UPS "shifts modes."

high priority, because they can be impossible to re-create exactly. Of course, mission-critical data, such as financial information on which managers depend to do their jobs, goes at the top of the "what to back up" list.

Your policies about what to back up should be in writing. Data that must be backed up should be stored in a central location, such as a specified drive on the server. If important data is scattered across the network on individual hard disks, it is too difficult to ensure that nothing is missed in the backup cycle.

When to Back Up

You should construct a schedule for periodic, *regular* backup of important data. How often to back up depends on how much data you can afford to lose: a day's worth or a week's worth.

Backups can be scheduled to take place after business hours so that you do not affect network performance. Most good backup software, as discussed in the next section, enables you to schedule automated backups so that no one has to be present to start the backup.

Most backup schedules include different types of backup. There are three basic types (although some backup utilities give you additional choices):

- **Full backup**—All data on the specified drives is backed up, regardless of whether or when it was backed up before and whether it has changed since the last backup.
- **Differential backup**—All files that have changed since the last full backup are backed up.
- **Incremental backup**—All files that have changed since the last backup of any type (not merely since the last full backup) are backed up.

The full backup requires the most time and space on the backup media, and thus, it is the most expensive. It is also the simplest method, and if you perform a full backup every night, you are ensured that all backed-up data is up to date. It is also the easiest to restore.

The differential backup saves time. It is done in conjunction with full backups. For instance, you can do a full backup once a week or once a month, and then do a differential backup every night between the full backups. To restore the data, you have to restore two tapes (the most recent full backup and the most recent differential) to ensure that all data is up to date. This method can be desirable if you have a very large amount of data to be backed up and little time in the evenings to perform the backup. The differentials take far less time. In addition, the full backups can be performed on the weekend when there is more time available.

The incremental backup is the fastest, but restoration is more complex and takes longer than with the other methods. You must restore the most recent full backup and then you restore the incremental backup for *every* day since the full backup.

How to Back Up

The "how" of backing up includes many decisions:

- What backup medium should be used?
- What backup software should be used?
- Who is responsible for performing the backup?
- Will the backup be done manually, or will it be automated?

For many years, tape was the preferred medium, and some backup software (such as the backup utility built into Windows NT) does not support any other media. Other backup programs enable you to choose from a variety of media, including removable disks such as Zip and Jaz, CD-R and CD-RW, DVD, and magneto optical (MO).

Most operating systems include a backup utility. Windows 9*x*, Windows NT, and Windows 2000 include Windows Backup; NetWare includes SBackup; and UNIX has the *tar* archiving program built in. There are many third-party backup programs available that offer a fuller feature set than those built into the operating systems. ARCserve (Cheyenne), Backup Exec (Seagate), and Norton Backup (Symantec) are popular Windows backup programs.

It is important that the responsibility for backing up critical data be specifically assigned. Ensure that the backup operator has the appropriate permissions to back up everyone's data. It is not necessary to give a person permission to read files to enable him or her to back up and even restore those files. You should also have a "backup backup operator"—someone who is trained to take over the duties if the primary backup operator is out.

Whether the backup is performed manually or automatically, it is vital that the integrity of the backup be checked periodically. Don't wait until a real disaster forces you to restore the data to find out that your tape drive hasn't been writing anything to the tapes. Do a test restore when you *don't* need it.

Finally, you should consider making multiple backups of data that is especially critical. Store at least one of these copies offsite. It does no good to have a current set of backup tapes in the desk drawer by the server if a fire, flood, or tornado destroys everything in the room. Offsite backups can be taken home with a trusted employee, stored in a bank safe deposit box, transferred daily to a branch office, or uploaded to a remote server over the phone lines or across the Internet.

> **NOTE**
>
> How does the backup software "know" which data has changed since the last backup? An *archive bit* is set on the file. This bit is a file attribute that is similar to the bit that marks a file as a hidden file or as a read-only file. This bit is removed (that is, cleared) when a file is backed up during a full backup or an incremental backup. The bit is *not* removed after a differential backup.

Disk Fault Tolerance

Another way to protect your data from hard disk failure is to implement *disk fault tolerance.* (Fault tolerance refers to the capability of a system to recover after a failure.) Fault tolerance involves combining multiple physical hard disks into a *fault-tolerant set*, which can take on one of several configurations.

Disk fault tolerance is also called *redundant array of independent* (or inexpensive) *disks (RAID).* Commonly used fault-tolerant configurations include the following:

- **Disk mirroring (RAID level 1)**—Disk mirroring requires two physical hard disks, preferably of the same size. All the data on one disk is mirrored to the second. There is an exact duplicate copy of all files and structures on the second disk. If one disk fails, the other can take over. This can be automatic, or you might have to "tell" the operating system where to find the new disk. For example, in Windows NT, this is done by editing the boot.ini file.

- **Disk duplexing (RAID level 1)**—Disk duplexing works exactly like mirroring, except that the two physical disks are attached to separate disk controllers. This adds a layer of fault tolerance, because if a controller fails, the other disk can still function, because it is on a different controller.

- **Disk striping with a parity drive (RAID level 3)**—Disk striping with a parity drive involves writing the data in stripes across multiple drives and writing parity data to another drive that is reserved for that purpose. This requires a minimum of three physical disks (two across which the data is striped and one for the parity information). If a data disk fails, the data can be regenerated using the parity information.

- **Disk striping with parity stripes (RAID level 5)**—Disk striping with parity stripes works in a manner similar to RAID 3, except that the parity (like the data) is written in stripes alternating across the disks. No one disk is designated for parity. Again, at least three disks are required, and if any one disk fails, the data can be regenerated.

Other, less commonly used fault-tolerant RAID levels include the following:

- **RAID 2**—This is similar to RAID 3 in that data is striped across multiple drives and one drive is reserved for parity information. The only difference is that the data is striped in bits; in RAID 3, it is striped in bytes.

- **RAID 4**—This also is similar to RAID 2 and 3, except that the data is striped in blocks instead of in bits or bytes.

RAID 0 is used quite often to increase the performance of reading and writing data, but it is *not* a fault-tolerant method. RAID 0 stripes data across multiple

NOTE

What is parity? The Microsoft Press Computer Dictionary defines it as "an error-checking procedure in which the number of 1s must always be the same—either even or odd—for each group of bits." In the context of disk fault tolerance, you can reconstruct the missing data on the failed drive by combining the parity information with the data on the drives that are still functioning.

disks in blocks, but it does not include parity information; thus, if one of the disks fails, there is no means of recovery.

RAID can be implemented as either a software solution or a hardware solution. Although hardware-based RAID is faster and generally more reliable, it is more expensive. Some server operating systems, such as Windows NT, and Windows 2000 Server products have built-in support for software RAID.

Clustering Technologies

The foundation of all disaster protection methods is *redundancy*. Power backup involves having redundant sources of electricity: the wall outlet and the UPS battery. Data backup involves creating redundant copies of important files on backup media. Disk fault tolerance involves writing the data to or across redundant disks. Clustering is the ultimate form of redundancy.

Clustering generally means grouping servers in *clusters*. With clusters, a group of servers is seen as one server on the network. If one of the servers goes down, another in the cluster takes over its duties. This transition is transparent to users. See Figure 14-9.

FIGURE 14-9
Server clustering is an expensive, but highly effective, way of providing fault tolerance.

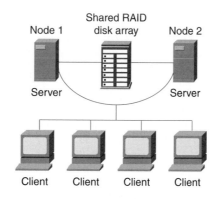

Clustering support is built into operating systems such as Windows 2000 Advanced Server, and clustering software is available to configure servers that are running other operating systems. Clustering provides fault tolerance, along with other advantages such as load balancing.

Summary

No single security measure will protect your network. Effective security is accomplished through the use of a security plan that incorporates multiple security practices, policies, and technologies.

In this chapter, we discussed various ways of protecting the network and the data that resides on and travels across it. First we examined the very broad subject of network security, and then we discussed disaster protection and recovery methods.

You learned how to assess the security needs of your network, and you learned about external security breaches such as unauthorized use of passwords and keys, DoS attacks (including Ping floods, Smurf attacks, the Ping of Death, and SYN attacks), IP spoofing, computer viruses and worms, and malicious code such as Trojan horse programs.

We then discussed internal threats, which can be attributed to corporate espionage, internal politics, disgruntled employees or ex-employees, and accidental breaches of security.

We provided an overview of cryptography concepts and how text can be "encoded" and "decoded" to thwart unauthorized interceptors. You learned to differentiate between symmetric secret key encryption and asymmetric public/private key encryption. We also discussed authentication, which is the process of determining that a message is really from the purported sender.

You learned about government security ratings and how to find information on the current ratings of popular operating systems, and we went on to discuss security auditing and intruder detection. Next we discussed firewalls and proxies and how you can create a DMZ between your internal network and the Internet (or other external network) to protect the resources on the LAN.

We also discussed methods of using different protocols on the internal and external networks to decrease the risk of intrusion from the outside. We wrapped up the first half of the chapter with a review of the importance of physical security for network components.

The second half of the chapter dealt with disaster protection and recovery, and you learned how to use multiple lines of defense against data loss, including power backup, data backup, disk fault tolerance, and clustering.

Now that you know how to protect your network to some extent from the outside world, you will learn in the next chapter how to get connected to that outside world by using phone lines.

Remote access is growing daily in popularity because more employees are telecommuting, accessing the company network after-hours, or staying connected to the corporate network when they're on the road. Chapter 15, "Remote Access," teaches you about remote access devices and how to set up remote access clients and servers. We also discuss the special security considerations that come with allowing dial-in connections to your network.

Further Reading

For more information on U.S. laws regulating the export of encryption technologies, see www.bxa.doc.gov/Encryption.

An excellent overview of IPSec is located on Cisco's website at www.cisco.com/warp/public/cc/techno/protocol/ipsecur/prodlit/ipsec_ov.htm.

A useful book that covers many aspects of creating a secure network is *Designing Network Security*, by Merike Kaeo. It is published by Cisco Press.

A good resource for information about e-mail security is at www.emailtoday.com/emailtoday/dir/email_security.htm.

Several helpful links to websites that address certificate services and other encryption technologies can be found at www.security-online.com/info/certificates.html.

A simplified explanation of Kerberos can be accessed online at www.isi.edu/gost/brian/security/kerberos.html.

For more information about developing network security policies, see www.homex.s-one.net.sg/member/itsecurity/netsec1.htm.

NCSC/NSA Security certifications are available on the Web at www.radium.ncsc.mil/tpep/epl.

Review Questions

The following questions test your knowledge of the material covered in this chapter. Be sure to read each question carefully and select the *best* correct answer or answers.

1. What is the name for the number or cipher used by the system to verify the integrity of a communication?

   A. Password

   B. Cryptography

   C. Key

   D. Authentication

2. What is the process of trying every possible combination of letters and numbers to "crack" a password?

   A. Decryption

   B. Brute-force attack

   C. Trojan horse attack

   D. Nuke attack

3. What is the name for sending a deluge of ICMP messages in an attempt to overwhelm or shut down a server or network?

   A. A SYN attack

   B. A worm

   C. A Ping of Death

   D. A Ping flood

4. Which of the following are common internal threats to network security? (Select all that apply.)

   A. Corporate espionage

   B. Accidental breaches

   C. IP spoofing

   D. Proxies

5. Which of the following is true of a good password policy in a high-security environment?

   A. It enables users to create and use the passwords that are easiest for them to remember.

   B. It requires that passwords be a minimum length, such as six characters.

   C. It prohibits using numbers or symbols in the password.

   D. It prohibits users from changing their passwords.

6. Which of the following describes the default permissions on a newly created share on a Windows 2000 server?

   A. By default, no one has permission to access the share.

   B. By default, everyone has read-only permission to the share.

   C. By default, everyone has full control permission to the share.

   D. By default, members of the administrators group have read-only access to the share.

7. Which of the following best describes file encryption?

   A. File encryption protects data stored on the hard disk.

   B. File encryption protects data sent across the network.

   C. File encryption protects data both when it is on the disk and when it is sent across the network.

   D. File encryption is available only through third-party software.

8. In the context of network security, what is ESP?

   A. Extra-Sensitive Packets

   B. Extended Security Protocol

   C. Encapsulating Security Payload

   D. External Security Properties

9. Which of the following encryption methods uses the same key to encrypt and decrypt the data?

  A. Asymmetric encryption

  B. Public key encryption

  C. Public/private key encryption

  D. Secret key encryption

10. What is the one-way mathematical calculation that creates a message digest, which is used to verify the authenticity of messages?

  A. A digital certificate

  B. A hash algorithm

  C. A ticket-granting ticket

  D. A retinal scan

Remote Access

In the traditional local-area network (LAN), computers are connected to the network through cable. On every cable type, however, there are limits on the distance that a signal can travel without significant degradation. Remote access solutions enable users to connect to the network and perform tasks as if they were directly cabled to the rest of the network—even if they're thousands of miles away. In effect, the remote computer becomes a member of the LAN, if only temporarily.

In the typical remote access connection through dialup networking, the telephone line serves the same function that an Ethernet cable serves in a direct-wired connection, and the modem or other remote access device performs the same basic function as the network card. The only practical difference between a remote connection and a cabled one is that generally the former is slower. A slow Ethernet connection has a basic transfer rate of 10 Mbps; high-speed digital subscriber line (DSL) phone lines average 1.5 Mbps.

Remote access to a network can be achieved over wireless or cable television (CATV) cable links also. In this chapter, we focus on dialup networking, the most common form of remote access.

Remote access enables you to extend a network beyond the physical boundaries of the cabled network to almost anywhere in the world. You need only a *remote access server* that is set up to accept dial-in connections and a *remote access client* that has software that enables it to dial out. Of course, both systems must have the proper hardware (typically a modem) and each must be connected to a phone line. In addition, the computers must be running a common protocol.

Most modern operating systems can act as remote clients and remote servers. They can even act as both at the same time, if there are two separate modems and if phone lines are attached.

In the following sections, we discuss the following important issues related to remote access:

- The importance of remote access as a networking option
- How remote access works
- Remote connectivity devices
- The configuration of remote access clients and servers
- Remote access security issues

Why Remote Access?

Remote access is becoming more important as network users become more mobile and as companies expand their business to multiple locations or open their resources to selected outsiders without putting those resources on the Internet.

Some popular uses of remote access include the following:

- Connecting branch offices to one another
- Providing a means for employees to connect to the network after business hours
- Allowing employees to telecommute—that is, work at home on a part-time or full-time basis
- Enabling employees who are on the road, such as traveling salespeople or executives on business trips, to connect to the corporate network
- Providing the company's clients or partners access to network resources

Let's look at how remote access services can benefit the organization in each situation.

Branch Offices

In an expanding global economy, even small businesses frequently need to open offices at multiple sites. If these locations are able to connect to the network at headquarters, up-to-date information can be easily shared and resources can be easily pooled.

When the need for access is infrequent, or when it applies only to a few computers, a dialup connection may suffice. Then, at the headquarters office, a networked computer can be set up as the dialup server. Users at the branch office can dial and connect to the network when necessary.

After-Hours Connectivity

For many corporate employees, the workday spills over into off-duty time. Executives and others often take work home. It may be useful or necessary for them to be able to connect to the network after business hours to get their work done.

With a remote access connection, an employee can dial the corporate remote access server and log in to the network with his or her regular user account. This gives the employee access to all the resources that would be available from the office desktop computer.

Using terminal services, an employee can even work on the same desktop used at the office during the day. Work that was left unfinished can be picked up in progress, without the inconvenience of transferring files from one computer to another through disks. Applications available on the terminal server also can be used from home, even though the employee does not have those applications installed on his or her own home machine. We discuss terminal services in more detail in Chapter 17, "Thin Client Networking."

Telecommuting

A large number of employees, including creative personnel, technical writers, software programmers, salespeople, and clerical staff, work from home all or part of the time. These workers *telecommute* to the office and stay in touch throughout the day through e-mail, live chat, and even audio and video conferencing.

Telecommuting is attractive to employees because it saves travel time and other costs associated with working in an office, such as business attire, lunches "out," and transportation costs. It saves the company money as well because office space for telecommuting employees is not required.

Dialup access is the most common way for telecommuting employees to connect to the company LAN, although in some cases, a dedicated connection might make more sense. If a company has many telecommuting employees, the remote access server requires multiple modems (a *modem bank*) so that numerous connections can be made simultaneously. Of course, each modem requires its own separate telephone line, as shown in Figure 15-1.

NOTE

Use of a modem bank might require the installation of a COM port adapter on the remote server. The adapter enables the operating system to recognize the multiple modem ports. Multiport cards enable as many as 128 ports with a single ISA or PCI card slot.

FIGURE 15-1
Dialup access to multiple clients can be provided through the use of a modem bank.

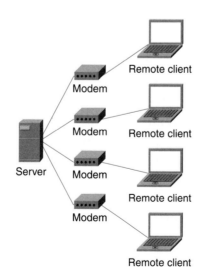

An alternate form of remote access that may be more cost-effective in this situation is *virtual private networking*, which is discussed in Chapter 16, "Virtual Private Networking."

Mobile Users

Business travel is becoming more prevalent as companies market their products on a national or international scale. Salespeople, recruiters, trainers, top-level management personnel, and others can spend a great deal of time on the road. The needs of mobile users are similar to those of after-hours users.

It can be difficult or impossible to store all the files needed on a laptop or notebook computer. It is a security threat as well because the laptop and its contents could be physically stolen. A better solution might be for the mobile user to dial in to the company LAN, where his or her user account is authenticated, and then access the data there instead of copying it to his own hard disk (see Figure 15-2).

FIGURE 15-2
A mobile user can dial in to the company LAN and access data on the desktop.

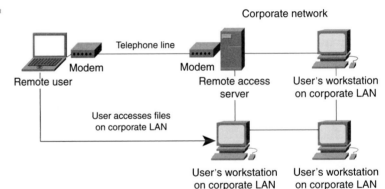
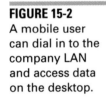

Providing Access to Clients and Partners

It has been a longstanding practice for hardware manufacturers to provide a way for their customers to dial in to a server and to download updated software drivers. Software vendors provide upgrades and patches in the same way.

The concept of allowing clients (or *partners*—that is, other companies with which your company has a mutually beneficial arrangement) to dial in to the corporate network and access selected files is growing in popularity. For security purposes, however, you must consider whether you want these "guest users" to access the network through a common account (usually termed a *guest account*) or through a unique username and password. The latter practice requires more administrative overhead, but it enables you to track who is accessing network resources and when and how they are doing so. On the other hand, allowing anonymous access is an option in a low-security environment or in one in which the remote access server is separated from the rest of the internal network by a firewall.

How Remote Access Works

There are several forms of remote access connections:

- The most common type of remote access is a dialup connection over analog or digital telephone lines.
- A *dedicated* connection is a point-to-point connection, such as a T1 line, in which a permanent circuit goes from one physical point to another. Refer to Chapter 6, "WAN Links," for more information about the available technologies.

Virtual private networking is a form of remote access that uses the Internet as the conduit for establishing a connection to a private network. Of course, both the virtual private network (VPN) client and the private network to which it connects must be connected to the Internet.

In the following sections, we take a look at the following aspects of remote access administration:

- Protocols used for remote access
- Remote access authentication methods
- How IP addresses are assigned on a remote connection that uses TCP/IP
- How bandwidth can be aggregated to provide a faster connection
- How bandwidth usage can be controlled by the administrator to prevent excessive bandwidth usage

Protocols Used for Remote Access

The remote client and the remote server must share at least one network/transport protocol (sometimes referred to as the *LAN protocol*), such as TCP/IP, IPX/SPX, AppleTalk, or NetBEUI. In addition, a link protocol (sometimes called the *WAN protocol*) is needed to establish the link across the phone line or the Internet from the client machine to the server machine.

The protocols used to establish the link include the following:

- Serial Line Internet Protocol (SLIP)
- Point-to-Point Protocol (PPP)

NOTE

A dialup connection can be made over an X.25 network. In this type of network, the client dials in to a packet assembler/disassembler (PAD). Refer to Chapter 6 for more information about the X.25 technology.

If the remote connection is through a VPN, the protocols used to establish the link include the following:

- Point-to-Point Tunneling Protocol (PPTP)
- Layer 2 Tunneling Protocol (L2TP)

The link protocols are discussed in Chapter 8, "Networking Protocols and Services."

Remote Access Authentication

The remote access server authenticates remote users according to the authentication methods specified by the administrator when the remote access connection was configured (see Figure 15-3).

FIGURE 15-3
The remote client is authenticated by the remote access server.

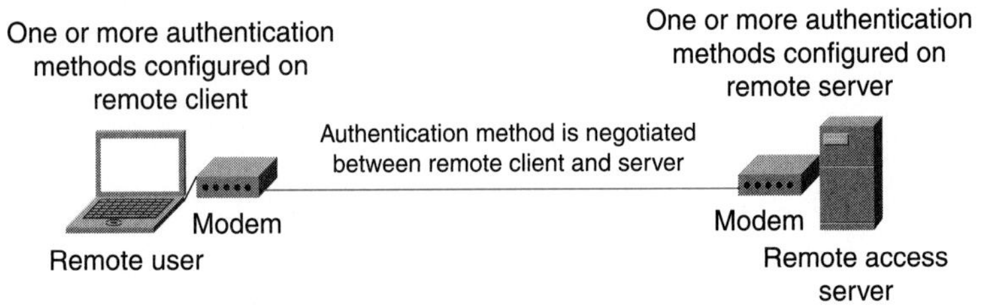

One or more authentication methods configured on remote client

One or more authentication methods configured on remote server

Authentication method is negotiated between remote client and server

Modem

Remote user

Modem

Remote access server

Examples of authentication methods include the following:

- Password Authentication Protocol (PAP), which sends passwords over the network unencrypted
- Shiva PAP (SPAP)
- Challenge Handshake Authentication Protocol (CHAP), which encrypts passwords
- Extensible Authentication Protocol (EAP), which uses MD5, smart cards, or certificates

EAP with smart cards is the most secure authentication method. See Chapter 14, "Protecting the Network," for more information about smart cards.

The Remote Authentication Dial-In User Service (RADIUS) enables authentication of remote users and provides accounting services for distributed dialup networking. See the "Remote Access Security Issues" section later in this chapter for more details about RADIUS.

It is possible to configure the server to accept unauthenticated access. In this case, the client is not required to provide a username or password. If you have clients who need to access the network from operating systems or platforms that do not support remote authentication, you will have to enable unauthenticated access or they will not be able to connect.

Assignment of IP Addresses

If TCP/IP is the protocol used on the LAN, all computers on the network must have a proper IP address to communicate. This is just as true of remote clients as it is of client computers that are cabled to the network.

Remote access servers, such as those running Windows 2000 Remote Access Server (RAS), can be configured to contact a DHCP server on the network and to obtain an IP address for the remote client. If there is no DHCP server, you can still configure the RAS server with a static address pool that consists of valid addresses for the network. Alternatively, the client can be configured with a valid static IP address for the remote network.

If the LAN protocol used by the remote client and server is NetBEUI, Apple-Talk, or IPX/SPX, an IP address is not required.

Aggregation of Bandwidth on Dialup Connections

If the operating systems on the client and the server support *bandwidth aggregation* or *multilink*, multiple physical remote links (for example, two telephone lines) can be combined to provide one connection with more bandwidth. This is most commonly used with Basic Rate ISDN (BRI), in which case, the two 64-kbps B channels (data channels) are multilinked to create one 128-kbps connection.

NOTE

Multilink is a software-based method of aggregating bandwidth. Two ISDN channels can be combined also through *bonding*, which is hardware-based.

Multilink can be used also to aggregate the bandwidth of two 56-kbps modems (each with its own phone line). Thus a dialup connection to an Internet service provider (ISP) over analog lines could attain speeds of 100 kbps or more (depending on the line condition). However, this works only if supported by the ISP.

Control of Bandwidth Usage

In conjunction with bandwidth aggregation, the Bandwidth Allocation Protocol (BAP) can be used to control the use of extra lines. This means that the additional lines are used only when needed; if the bandwidth usage drops, one or more of the aggregated lines are disconnected. If bandwidth demand increases, additional links are added automatically.

This is especially useful in situations in which service is billed on a per-unit basis because the release of the unused lines results in lower telephone charges.

Remote Access Connectivity Devices

Remote access performance is relatively slow (compared to a traditional cabled network). Although higher-bandwidth alternatives such as DSL and cable modem are becoming more widely available, typical top speeds for these high-speed technologies are 1 Mbps to 5 Mbps. The slowest Ethernet connections have transfer rates of 10 Mbps, and 100 Mbps is commonplace. The various WAN connection technologies, such as DSL and cable, are discussed in great detail in Chapter 6.

The most common means of establishing a remote connection is through a modem over an analog telephone line. In this section, we examine the characteristics of modems and other remote connectivity devices.

Modems

A modem is a hardware device whose primary function is to convert the digital signals created by the sending computer into analog signals that can travel across the telephone line. A modem on the other end of the connection then translates those analog signals back to digital signals for processing by the receiving computer, as shown in Figure 15-4. Refer to Chapter 4, "Networking Communications Methods," for a review of the difference between analog and digital signaling.

FIGURE 15-4
Modems convert digital signals to analog signals and analog signals back to digital signals.

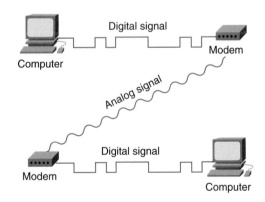

How Modems Work

The process of converting analog to digital and back again is called *modulation/demodulation* (hence the term *modem*). Recall that digital communications are based on *binary*; that is, the digital signals represent 1s and 0s. These signals must be converted to a waveform to travel across analog lines.

When a modem attempts to connect to another modem, a tone is sent by the calling modem. The tone is set to a particular modulation, which is the rapidly alternating tones of high and low pitch. The audio tones represent the 1s and 0s of the original digital signal. If the modem on the receiving end is able to use this modulation, the connection is established without further negotiation. If not, the sending modem attempts to use a lower modulation; this process continues until the sending modem discovers a modulation that the receiving computer supports. Thus, the modems are always using the highest common modulation. This process is called *fallback* because the modem falls back to a lower modulation when necessary.

Experienced modem users can identify the speed at which the connection is established by the pitch of these tones. When the modems connect, they hear the familiar "modem handshake" that is the culmination of the negotiation process.

ASYNCHRONOUS COMMUNICATION PORTS

Analog modems use a form of communication called *asynchronous communication* (refer to Chapter 4 for more information about asynchronous communication). COM ports built into the motherboards of modern computers support this type of communication. Typically, a computer has two COM port interfaces—a 9-pin connector and a 25-pin connector. Adapters are widely available to convert one to the other. An external modem connects to one of these serial ports by using a serial cable.

The chips that run the COM ports are called Universal Asynchronous Receiver/Transmitter (UART) chips. The type of UART chip determines the top speed at which devices can communicate using the port. Older UART 8259 chips have a top speed of 9600 bps. Newer UART 16450 and 16550 chips enable speeds up to 115,200 bps, and the 16650 chip supports a transmission speed of 230,400 bps.

Internal modems have their own UART chips and are not limited by the UART speed of the computers' COM ports.

Early modems used the *acoustic coupler,* which is the device into which you placed the handset of a standard telephone. These modems were not able to dial; you had to manually dial the number from the telephone pad. Connection speeds were very slow; a 2400-bps modem was considered blazingly fast. Hayes marketed the first "smart modems," which could dial the phone number for you.

Another disadvantage of older modems was the configuration for which you often had to script a *modem initialization string.* This series of characters identified and configured the method by which the two modems connected.

Today's modems are much faster and range from 14.4 kbps to 56 kbps. Acoustic couplers are still available; they provide modem access when the telephone line is hard-wired into the telephone and cannot be unplugged and then plugged into the modem.

Modem Types

Most modern modems are one of three types:

- Internal
- External
- PC Card (PCMCIA)

In all three types, you plug the phone line into a standard RJ-11 telephone jack. Each type has advantages and disadvantages, which we discuss next.

Internal Modems. Internal modems, as the name suggests, fit in a card slot inside the computer. ISA and PCI varieties are available. In addition, PCMCIA/PC card versions are available for use with laptop computers.

The internal modem takes no extra space on the desktop, but you must open the computer case to install it. In general, internal modems are slightly less expensive than the same model in an external configuration.

Configuring an internal modem might require you to set jumpers to select IRQ and I/O addresses. In this respect, configuring the modem is much like configuring a network interface card, as discussed in Chapter 7, "Physical Components of the Network." The modem must be configured to use a COM port that is not already in use. Devices that use COM ports include pointing devices, scanners, cradles for handheld computers, and other devices that use a serial connection. Software drivers for the modem also must be installed.

If the modem is a Plug and Play (PnP) model *and* both the system BIOS and the operating system support PnP, manual configuration might not be required.

External Modems. External modems typically cost a bit more than internal ones, but they offer several advantages:

- You do not need to open the case and install a card; you simply plug the modem into a serial port using a serial cable. With new USB modems, you plug it into a USB port or hub.

- The external modem uses the IRQ and I/O address assigned to the serial port to which it is attached, so there is often less configuration required, although this advantage can be negated by the use of a PnP internal modem.

- External modems usually have indicator lights, or *status lights*, that enable you to see when the modem is online, when it is sending or receiving data, and so on. Some internal modems have indicator lights as well; however, these are not usually visible to the user because they are at the back of the computer.

As with an internal modem, you must install software drivers that enable the external modem to communicate with the operating system. The drivers for popular brands, such as Motorola and U.S. Robotics, might be included on the operating system installation CD.

PC Card Modems. PC card modems, also called PCMCIA modems, are small cards that fit into special slots that are typically on laptop or notebook computers. PC card interfaces are available also for desktop machines. A PC card modem is configured in a manner similar to other modem types. The big advantage of the PC card is its small size and portability.

Customizing Modem Properties

Modem properties often can be customized. For example, if you have certain telephone company services, such as CallNotes message-taking, that interfere with a normal dial tone, you can set the modem not to wait for a dial tone before dialing.

Other customizable settings (depending on your modem model and operating system) include the following:

- The capability to adjust the volume (or have the modem dial silently)
- The capability to specify the location from which you are dialing so that the modem knows to dial an area code before long distance calls
- The capability to specify that the connection be automatically disconnected if it is not used for a certain period of time
- The capability to specify whether and how many times the modem should redial if it encounters a busy signal
- The maximum port speed for the COM port to which the modem is attached

User-friendly operating systems such as Windows 2000 make it easy to configure dialup connection properties, as shown in Figure 15-5.

FIGURE 15-5
Dialing properties can be config- ured easily in the Windows 2000 Dial-up Connec- tion Properties dialog box.

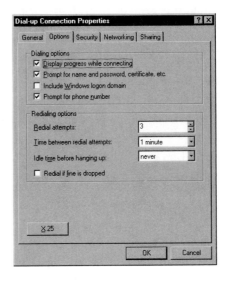

Troubleshooting Modems

Modem problems can be frustrating and range from a modem that won't dial to one that consistently connects at a very slow speed or frequently gets disconnected. The software that comes with a modem might include diagnostic utilities to help you test the functionality of your modem; in addition, operating systems such as Windows 2000 include modem diagnostic and troubleshooting tools.

We describe these modem problems in the following sections of this chapter:

- The modem won't dial.
- The modem dials, but it won't establish a connection.
- The modem connects, but then it disconnects.
- The modem connects at a low speed.
- In addition, we discuss COM port problems, which also affect a modem's capability to connect.

The Modem Won't Dial. If the modem won't dial, it is likely that the software is not communicating with the modem. This lack of communication can be caused by the operating system not recognizing the COM port to which the modem is attached. You should check the computer's BIOS to ensure that the COM port is enabled. There also could be a conflict between an internal modem's COM port and another serial device that is using the same IRQ as that COM port. Changing the COM port settings in the BIOS or changing the assigned IRQ corrects this problem.

Lack of communication can be caused also by modem drivers that are not installed, by the wrong drivers being installed, or by the driver files themselves becoming corrupt. Reinstalling the modem drivers might correct this situation.

If you are still having problems and the modem is set to wait for a dial tone before dialing, consider the possibility that the phone itself is dead. In addition, note that some phone company services, such as CallNotes voice mail, use a short signal to notify you that you have messages. This signal, when in effect, replaces the dial phone. If you have this service, you might need to set the modem not to wait for dial tone before dialing.

Finally, a common—and somewhat embarrassing—cause of the problem might be that the phone line is not plugged into the modem. Note that many modems have *two* RJ-11 jacks, and they look identical. One is for the incoming phone line, and the other is for output to a telephone. Be sure that the phone is plugged into the correct jack.

The Modem Won't Establish a Connection. If the modem dials, you know that the problem is not with the phone line or the cabling that attaches it to the modem. Instead, the most common cause is that the modem is dialing the wrong number. Check that the number is correct and that the area code is included, if required.

Another possibility is that the number you are calling is busy. If the modem volume is turned on, you should hear the busy tone. The modem can be set to automatically keep redialing when it gets a busy signal.

If another modem answers, but no connection can be established, you might have an incompatibility between the modem types. Another possibility is that the data transfer rate on your modem is set higher than that of the modem you are calling. In this case, setting the port speed to a lower rate can solve the problem.

The Modem Disconnects. If you are able to connect to the modem on the other side, but then get disconnected immediately, the remote access server might not be able to authenticate your account. Check that you have the dialup connection properties set to enter the correct username and password.

Another possibility is that your user account is set for callback security on the remote server. In that case, the server disconnects you after you enter your username and password, but should immediately call you back and reconnect. (For more information on callback security, see the "Remote Access Security Issues" section later in this chapter.) If this is the case, be sure that your modem is configured to accept incoming calls.

If you are able to connect and use the modem for a period of time, and then get disconnected, you could have "noisy" or "dirty" phone lines. If this is a recurring problem, you can have the telephone company "condition" the line. Line conditioning evens out uneven voltage on the line by boosting low voltages and stepping down high voltages.

If you have call waiting on your line, the modem can disconnect when the line receives an incoming telephone call. You can usually disable call waiting in the dialing properties. If someone picks up an extension phone on the same line, this also can disconnect the modem. You can buy devices that you attach to the phone line to prevent such disconnects.

If you get disconnected at regular intervals when accessing the Internet through an ISP, the provider might have restrictions on maximum connection times. Users can be "kicked off" automatically after a specified interval, such as six hours. This is a matter of policy and it should be taken up with your ISP. In many cases, it is permissible to redial and reconnect immediately.

The Modem Connects at a Low Speed. If the modem connects, but communicates only at a much lower speed than expected, noisy lines can be causing the problem. In some areas, you might not be able to get more than 30–35 kbps from a 56-kbps modem.

Another cause of slow connection speeds is a modem on the other end of the connection that does not support high speeds. Your 56-kbps modem connects at 28.8 kbps when the modem at the other end of the connection has a top speed of 28.8 kbps.

Incompatibility is another problem. The first 56-kbps modems came in two flavors: 56Kflex, which was supported by manufacturers such as Motorola, and X2 technology, which was used in modems by U.S. Robotics. Newer modems are designed to meet a common standard, but if you have an older device, you might have to upgrade the modem's BIOS to correct any incompatibility problems.

If you have never been able to attain high speeds with your modem, another possibility is that the drivers are outdated or incorrect. Check the manufacturer's website for updated drivers.

A faulty modem cable on an external modem might result in a slow transfer or an inability to communicate at all. It also is possible that the modem itself is defective and should be replaced.

COM Port Problems. In some cases, the problem is not with the modem but with the COM port to which it is connected. If you have a high-speed external modem that connects only at low speeds (such as 9600 bps), you should check the UART chip of the COM port to which the modem is attached.

In some cases, even if the COM port has a high-speed UART, the default port speed settings of the operating system can be set too low. In this case, you might need to manually change the port speed. Figure 15-6 shows port speed settings in a Windows 2000 dialog box.

FIGURE 15-6
The port speed can be changed in Windows 2000 through the modem properties dialog box.

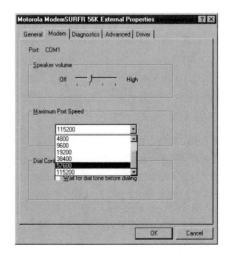

ISDN Terminal Adapters

ISDN terminal adapters are sometimes called ISDN "modems," but the application of this term is inaccurate because ISDN terminal adapters do not modulate and demodulate the signal; they do not do so because ISDN lines are digital.

ISDN adapters are made by many of the same companies that manufacture modems, and these adapters are available in internal and external models.

NOTE

The SPID is made up
of the 10-digit tele-
phone number of
the line and can
include a prefix or
suffix to identify line
features. The tele-
phone company
assigns the SPID.

Most permit the use of one or two 64-kbps B channels. Generally, the two lines have different telephone numbers, even though the wires can be enclosed in one cable.

ISDN adapters are installed in a manner that is similar to the installation of modems. Driver software must be installed and configured, and with some adapters, you must enter the *service profile IDs (SPIDs)* of both lines. Other configurations also can be required, depending on the adapter model.

ISDN routers can be used to provide Internet access to the entire LAN. This requires that each computer have a registered IP address. The ISP can assign you a block of IP addresses for this purpose. Alternately, you can use NAT software to translate private internal addresses to one registered public address, in which case, the router is not necessary. Refer to the "How Address Translation Works" section in Chapter 6 for more information about implementing NAT.

A common problem with ISDN is that sometimes only one of the two lines connects. In this case, you should ensure that you have the software correctly configured to multilink the lines.

With most ISDN adapters, you can connect analog phones to receive voice calls. The adapter can be configured so that you connect to the Internet at 128 kbps, and when a voice call comes in on one line and you answer, the Internet connection drops back to 64 kbps for the duration of the call. When you hang up, the second line automatically reconnects and returns your speed to 128 kbps.

Cable Modems

"Cable modem" is another commonly used misnomer. This device acts like a LAN interface by connecting your computer to the cable company's network through the same coax that brings CATV signals to your television set.

Cable modems, unlike analog modems and ISDN adapters, generally provide Internet access only. With analog modems and ISDN adapters, you can dial in to any service provider or remote access server on a private network. With cable, however, you are directly wired to the cable network and the only option you have for a provider is the cable company.

Cable modem service is an "always on" technology. However, if the cable company's infrastructure is one-way, you also have to establish a dialup connection to send requests upstream. See Chapter 6 for more information.

Even though the server you are contacting is at a remote location, cable modem access is more like a direct LAN connection than it is like remote access. Keep this in mind as we further discuss technology in this chapter because it is typically used for the same purpose as the remote access methods covered here.

NOTE

Some cable companies are offering or planning to offer telephone services over their CATV networks.

Cable modems, like their analog and ISDN counterparts, are available as internal and external units. The cable company usually dictates which you use, and in fact, you might be required to buy or lease the device from them and be prohibited from supplying your own.

An external cable modem is a small box to which the coax CATV cable connects. A splitter is used to divide the signal between the TV and the cable modem. In turn, the box is connected to an Ethernet card in the computer through UTP Ethernet. External USB devices are also available; these connect the modem to the computer's USB port and do not require an Ethernet card.

Internal cable modems are generally installed as PCI cards. They are less expensive, but do not work with all CATV networks, and they cannot be used with laptop computers or Macintosh machines.

The cable modem includes a tuner with a built-in duplexer so that both upstream and downstream signals can be provided. Some CATV network infrastructures support downstream signaling only. In this case, upstream transmissions must be sent through a phone line, and a phone jack will be built into the cable modem for this purpose.

The modem receives digitally modulated signals. A demodulator is built into the modem and, if it is a two-way modem, a burst modulator is used for transmitting upstream. External cable modems also include a microprocessor chip, while internal models depend on the computer's CPU to handle processing tasks, just as analog "Winmodems" do.

Unfortunately, several standards are competing for prominence in the cable access industry. Until one emerges as the clear winner, cable access will be a proprietary technology and service, speed, reliability, and configurations will vary significantly from one cable company to another.

An excellent tutorial on the technical details of cable modem technology can be found on the Web at www.cable-modems.org/tutorial/index.htm.

CSU/DSUs

The channel service unit/data service unit (CSU/DSU) is used with leased digital lines (T-carriers). It translates the digital data frames on the local network into the format used on the WAN link. The device itself resembles an external modem or ISDN terminal adapter.

There must be a CSU/DSU at both ends of the connection. The CSU protects the T-1 line from electric interference and is used to echo test signals, called *loopbacks*, from the phone company. The DSU performs control tasks that manage timing errors and the regeneration of signals. It converts incoming data signals for transmission over the line.

The CSU/DSU communicates with the computer over a data terminal equipment (DTE) interface. This is a standard RS-232C or serial interface.

Configuring Remote Access Clients and Servers

Just as you must configure your computer so that it can participate on a cabled network, you must configure the systems that communicate with one another through remote access. In the following sections, we discuss how a remote client is configured to start a connection and how a remote access server is configured to accept incoming connections.

Configuring a Remote Access Client

Before you can dial in and connect to a remote access server, such as the dialup server of an ISP or your company's RAS server, you must configure your computer to function as a remote access client. This involves several steps:

1. Install the proper hardware device (typically an analog modem).

2. Install and configure the software drivers for the device.

3. Connect the device to the telephone line.

4. Set the dialing properties for the connection. These properties include the phone number to be dialed, a username and password for accessing the remote server, the use of PPP or SLIP to make the connection, and other specifications.

You might have to install the dialup networking component if the operating system does not install it by default. You might have to install RAS as a network service on Windows NT computers. You must also install the proper protocols to communicate with the remote server.

Operating systems such as Windows 9*x* and Windows 2000 include wizards that walk you through the setup process, as shown in Figure 15-7.

Configuring a Remote Access Server

The remote server must be equipped with a modem or modems and must be configured to accept incoming calls. The exact procedure varies, depending on the operating system.

FIGURE 15-7
The Network
Connection Wiz-
ard guides you
through the pro-
cess of setting up
a new dialup con-
nection.

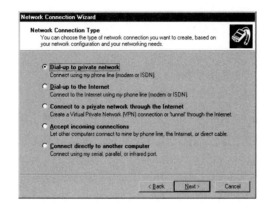

For the remote access server, you also might need to make the following decisions and make the respective changes to the settings:

- Whether to accept Multilink PPP connections.
- Whether to use the BAP to control bandwidth usage dynamically. This
  option is available only if Multilink is enabled.
- Whether to enable IP routing, or, for LAN protocols other than TCP/IP,
  whether to enable access to the server only or to the entire network.
- When using TCP/IP, whether the server will assign IP addresses from a
  static address pool or use a DHCP server.
- Which authentication method to use for remote connections.

Remote access policies can be used to control access based on group membership. For more information about remote access policies, see the next section
in this chapter, "Remote Access Security Issues."

Remote Access Security Issues

Whether you are connecting to the Internet as a dialup client or opening your
server to dial-in access, being connected to the outside world poses security risks.

In Chapter 14, we discussed general security guidelines about Internet intruders. This section addresses some of the special concerns that arise when you
enable dial-in access to a server on your network.

You can increase security in several ways while still allowing your users the
remote access they need. By using security measures in combination with file
and share permissions to control access, you can maintain a secure environment and at the same time provide users with the convenience of remote

access. The following sections discuss some of the most common security measures:

- Callback security
- RADIUS
- Remote access policies
- Account lockout
- Security hosts

Callback Security

Callback security is a feature of the remote access server that can enhance security by restricting dial-in connections to those originating from specific approved telephone numbers. With callback security enabled, the server does not believe the credentials (username and password) typed in by the user. Instead, the server attempts to verify the identity in much the same way you might if you received a telephone call from someone claiming to be a police officer. If you had suspicions that the caller was not who he claimed to be, you might hang up and call the caller back at the number listed as the local police station in the telephone book. See Figure 15-8.

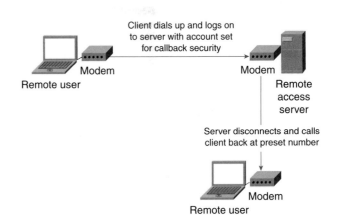

FIGURE 15-8
Callback security restricts the telephone number from which a remote user can dial in.

Here's how it works:

1. The preset telephone number, in conjunction with the user's account, is entered on the remote access server.

2. When the user dials in to the server, he is prompted for a username and password. These identify the user to the server, which then verifies whether the account is set to use callback security.

3. The server breaks the connection and then immediately dials the user back at the preset number and enables normal access to the network.

This process ensures that even if a would-be intruder learned the username and password of a legitimate user, he would not be able to access the network remotely unless he was calling from the user's home or other preset location.

RADIUS

RADIUS is a protocol that has become an industry standard for authenticating dial-in users and providing accounting services for dialup servers used by ISPs. The dialup server is configured as a RADIUS client, and the username and password information are sent by the dialup server to the RADIUS sever. The RADIUS server provides authentication.

The RADIUS server provides centralized authentication by using specified protocols, such as the following:

- PAP
- CHAP and MS-CHAP
- EAP
- Dialed Number Identification Service (DNIS)
- Automatic Number Identification (ANI) Service

We discussed the first three methods earlier in this chapter. DNIS is based on the number called by the user, and ANI (using caller ID) is based on the number from which the user called.

RADIUS also enables the logging of audit information and usage information and the management of all network access servers on the network from a centralized location. Specifications for RADIUS are provided in RFCs 2138 and 2139.

Remote Access Policies

Depending on the operating system, you might be able to control access by creating and applying *remote access policies*, which grant or deny access based on criteria such as the following:

- Time of the day (for example, restricting remote access from 8 a.m. to 5 p.m.)
- Day of the week (for example, allowing remote access on Monday through Saturday, but not on Sunday)
- Group membership (for example, denying access to all members of the Newbies group)
- Type of remote connection (for example, allowing VPN connections but denying dial-in connections, or vice versa)

Policies also can restrict the amount of time a user can be connected or the authentication methods that can be used.

Account Lockout

Account lockout can be applied to remote access connections to prevent unauthorized users from guessing a valid password by trying different passwords in succession, either manually or through brute-force software attacks.

With account lockout, after a specified number of failed attempts to log in, the account is locked out and the system does not accept more tries. You can configure this feature in the following ways:

- You can set the number of failed attempts allowed before lockout. A user might mistype a password once or even twice, but it is unlikely that the user will keep getting it wrong repeatedly, so you can set this value to 3.

- You can specify whether the account will reset after a period of time, or remain locked until an administrator unlocks it. You might want to set this value to a reasonable interval, such as 2 hours, so that if the legitimate user tries to log in after the intruder has been locked out, he or she will be able to do so.

Security Hosts

A security host is a device used to authenticate dial-in users. It is used in addition to the remote access server's own security measures. The host is a hardware device that is installed between the remote access client and the server.

There are several types of security hosts; in some instances, the host requires that the dial-in user provide a username and password that are separate and independent of the account name and password used to log in to the remote access server. For example, the Security Dynamics company offers the SecurID modem, which is a PC card modem that includes automated authentication for mobile users. The user enters a PIN number, which is sent automatically by the modem to the host for verification.

Summary

In this chapter, we discussed the growing popularity of remote access in today's business world. We reviewed situations in which remote access is appropriate, including connecting branch offices to one another, providing after-hours access to employees, telecommuting, connecting to the network while on the road, and sharing company resources with clients and partners.

You learned how remote access works, and we discussed the protocols used for remote access. You learned that the remote client and the server must share at least one common network/transport protocol and that a link protocol such as PPP or SLIP is used to make the connection over the phone line.

We discussed remote authentication methods, including PAP, SPAP, CHAP, MS-CHAP, and EAP. You also learned that a DHCP server can assign IP addresses to the dialup client and that the remote access server can be configured to contain a static address pool from which addresses are drawn.

You learned about bandwidth aggregation using Multilink PPP or bonding, both of which enable you to combine two or more lines to provide one high-speed connection. In addition, you learned about BAP, which can be used to control bandwidth usage dynamically on a multilinked connection.

We provided an overview of remote connectivity devices, including modems, ISDN terminal adapters, cable modems, and CSU/DSU devices. You learned that modems work by modulating and demodulating the signal, which is the converting of the signal from digital to analog and back. We discussed the characteristics of three modem types: internal, external, and PCMCIA. You also learned about customizing modem properties and how to troubleshoot modem problems.

Next we looked at how to configure a remote access client and how to set up a remote access server. Finally, we discussed security issues. You learned that a variety of security measures are available, including callback security, RADIUS, remote access policies, account lockout, and security hosts.

This chapter focuses on dialup access. In the next chapter, we look more closely at another type of remote access: virtual private networking.

Further Reading

A thorough discussion of modems can be found at www.teleport.com/~curt/modems.html.

You will find useful information and links at the RADIUS Resources website at www.funk.com/radius.

The homepage for the IETF working group dedicated to RADIUS is at www.ietf.org/html.charters/radius-charter.html.

RFC 2284, which addresses the EAP, is located at www.rfc-editor.org/rfc/rfc2284.txt.

3Com provides a good resource for information about BAP and Multilink PPP at infodeli.3com.com/infodeli/tools/isdn/mlppp/mlppp.htm.

For information about Shiva's remote access security management software, see www.shiva.com/images/t-products.gif.

For general information on remote access security issues, see www.list.gmu.edu/ras.htm.

Review Questions

The following questions test your knowledge of the material covered in this chapter. Be sure to read each question carefully and select the *best* correct answer or answers.

1. Which of the following may be used to provide dialup access to multiple clients simultaneously?

    A. Multilink

    B. Bandwidth Allocation Protocol

    C. Modem bank

    D. CSU/DSU

2. What is the most common type of remote access connection?

    A. Dedicated digital connection

    B. Dialup analog connection

    C. Dialup digital connection

    D. Wireless connection

3. Which of the following are called link protocols and are used to establish a connection over telephone lines? (Select all that apply.)

    A. SLIP

    B. IPX/SPX

    C. NetBEUI

    D. PPP

4. Which of the following authentication methods sends passwords over the network unencrypted?

    A. CHAP

    B. PAP

    C. EAP

    D. SPAP

5. Which of the following is used to provide a 128-kbps ISDN connection?

   A. Bandwidth Allocation Protocol

   B. Point to Point Tunneling Protocol

   C. Multilink PPP

   D. Multicasting

6. Which of the following refers to the process used by modems during the process of negotiating a connection?

   A. Fallback

   B. Bonding

   C. Remodulation

   D. Callback

7. What are the chips on which the computer's COM ports are based?

   A. USB chips

   B. UART chips

   C. UNC chips

   D. UDP chips

8. Which of the following is an advantage of internal modems over external models?

   A. Internal modems are easier to install.

   B. It is easier to monitor the status of internal modems.

   C. Internal modems are less expensive.

   D. There are no advantages to internal modems.

9. Which of the following is a common cause of a modem connecting at slow speeds? (Select all that apply.)

   A. The username and password are entered incorrectly.

   B. A call is coming in on a phone line that has the call waiting service.

   C. The phone lines are "dirty" or "noisy."

   D. The modem is incompatible with the modem at the other end of the connection.

10. Centralized authentication, accounting, and control of network access servers is provided by which of the following?

    A. NAT

    ✓ **B.** RADIUS

    C. RAID

    D. RARP

Virtual Private Networking

In Chapter 15, "Remote Access," we discussed dialup connections, but dialups are only one form of remote access. Another variety—one that is increasing in popularity as software vendors make it easier to implement and as corporations discover its benefits—is the *virtual private network (VPN)* connection.

In this chapter, we discuss this useful, cost-effective form of remote access. You will learn what virtual private networking is and how it works. We discuss the protocols used to establish a VPN and the very important topic of VPN security. Then we look at types of VPNs and performance issues and wrap up with a practical example of how to configure a VPN connection.

What Is a VPN?

If we look at the term virtual private network, we can see that it is made up of three words. Each word is a component on which the entire concept is built. The "network" is computers communicating with one another. Let's look at the other two components, "virtual" and "private," which define how virtual private networking differs from other types of networking.

Virtual Networking

We have discussed local-area networks (LANs) and wide-area networks (WANs). A common factor in both is some sort of networking *medium*—a cable or a wireless link—that directly connects the communicating computers. A virtual network does not have that direct connection. Instead, a tunnel is created through a public network—typically the Internet—and the two communicating computers are attached to the network, as shown in Figure 16-1.

Data is sent across the public network in a way that emulates a point-to-point link. This is accomplished by *encapsulating* the data. Later in this chapter, in the "The Encapsulation Process" section, we discuss how this encapsulation process works. For now, we need only know that a VPN enables you to create a logical network that is independent of location and direct physical connectivity.

Private Networking

The privacy component of virtual private networking is dependent on encryption of the data as it travels through the public network. Unencrypted data can be sent through a tunnel (established by one of the tunneling protocols discussed later in this chapter), but strictly speaking, this would create only a virtual network, not a virtual private network.

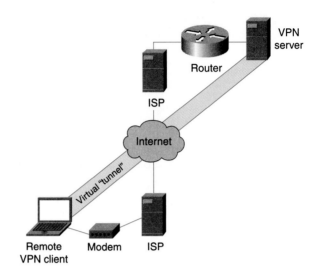

FIGURE 16-1
A VPN connection creates a tunnel through a public network such as the Internet.

Because the data is encrypted, it remains private even though it is sent through a public network. This is important, because packets traveling across the Internet are vulnerable to interception as they pass through each node (server) between the sending and destination computers. When data is encrypted, even if it is intercepted along the way, it is unreadable as long as the interceptor doesn't have the encryption key. We discuss encryption in more detail in the "VPN Security" section of this chapter.

How VPNs Work

A VPN can be configured to work over a dialup connection, or it can be configured as a router-to-router connection that uses routers with dedicated Internet connections, such as T1 lines. You can create an on-demand VPN connection between routers. In this type of connection, the answering router has a dedicated Internet connection, and the calling router uses a dialup Internet connection.

In the following sections, we examine how a VPN tunnel is established and the built-in support that is provided by modern operating systems for VPN connections.

Digging the Tunnel

The *tunnel* created in a VPN connection is really just a logical point-to-point connection that supports authentication and encryption of data from one end-point of the tunnel to the other.

Suppose your company has two buildings located across the street from one another. Employees often need to travel from one building to the other in the course of doing their jobs. To get to the other building, they could just walk outside, cross the street, and enter the other building's front door. This is comparable to routing them across a *public network*. In a public network, business data is sent across an ordinary Internet connection as, for example, an attached file. The file can be sent using Internet e-mail or a public FTP server.

Now let's suppose you want to keep the employees safe from the elements as they move from one building to the other, or you don't want them to be seen by members of the public during their journeys. One way to accomplish this is to dig a *private tunnel* underground from one building to the other. Now you have a situation that is analogous to a virtual private network.

Because you don't want members of the public wandering into the tunnel and traveling between buildings, you might build doors at each end of the tunnel that can be unlocked only by key cards issued to authorized employees. These key cards are like the authentication process that identifies a user who wants to send data over a VPN connection and then grants or denies him access.

Unfortunately, if someone did sneak into the tunnel, he could still accost the employees as they walk back and forth. We could solve this problem (albeit somewhat expensively) by building one-person vehicles to carry employees through the tunnel that lock from the inside. This is analogous to encrypting data to protect it from interception en route, as shown in Figure 16-2.

FIGURE 16-2
A tunnel offers a private way to get people and data from one point to another.

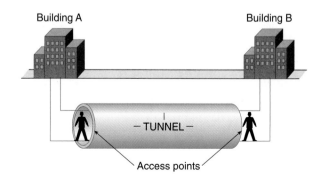

In the following sections, we discuss the encapsulation process and the characteristics of two types of tunneling: Layer 2 and Layer 3.

The Encapsulation Process

Tunneling hides the original packet inside a new packet. For routing through the tunnel, the address of the *tunnel endpoint* is provided in the outside (new) packet's header, which is called the *encapsulation header*. The final destination address is inside, in the original packet's header. When the packet reaches the tunnel's endpoint destination, the encapsulation header is stripped off. The original packet can now be delivered to the final destination. Tunneling is simply a term used to describe this encapsulation, which is the routing and decapsulation process.

Tunnels can be established at different layers of the standard networking model. In the following sections, we look at how tunneling can work at Layer 2 (the data link layer of the OSI reference model) and Layer 3 (the network layer of the OSI reference model).

Layer 2 Tunneling. VPNs most often use tunneling protocols that operate at the data link layer. These protocols provide a virtual link from one point to another. The Point-to-Point Tunneling Protocol (PPTP) works at this level.

Another data link layer tunneling protocol is Layer 2 Forwarding (L2F), which can provide tunneling over ATM and Frame Relay because it is not dependent on the Internet Protocol (IP). Unlike PPTP, an L2F tunnel can support more than one connection. Cisco Systems developed the L2F technology, and L2F is supported by the Internetwork Operating System (IOS) used by Cisco routers. In addition, Nortel and Shiva products support L2F.

The newest tunneling protocol that operates at this level is the Layer 2 Tunneling Protocol (L2TP), which combines elements of PPTP and L2F. These protocols are discussed in more detail later in this chapter, in the section titled "VPN Protocols."

Layer 3 Tunneling. Tunnels can be created at the network layer and thus provide for IP-based virtual connections. These connections work by sending IP packets encapsulated inside Internet Engineering Task Force (IETF)-specified protocol wrappers. The wrappers use IP Security (IPSec), the Internet Key Exchange (IKE), and authentication and encryption methods such as Message Digest 5 (MD5), Data Encryption Standard (DES), and Secure Hash Algorithm (SHA).

IPSec can be used in conjunction with L2TP; L2TP establishes the tunnel, and IPSec encrypts the data. In this case, IPSec is operating in *transport mode.* IPSec can also be used in *tunneling mode,* in which it provides the tunnel.

IPSec Layer 3 tunneling can be used in situations in which L2TP is not appropriate. For more information, see the following sidebar. For more information on IPSec encryption, see the "VPN Security" section later in this chapter.

IPSEC TUNNELING

It is important to understand the distinction between VPNs that use L2TP for tunneling and IPSec for encryption, and VPNs that use IPSec in tunneling mode.

One important difference is that IPSec can encapsulate only IP packets. L2TP can provide encapsulation of Internetwork Packet Exchange (IPX) and other protocol packets across the IP network.

Some gateways don't support L2TP or PPTP VPNs, and in that case, IPSec can be used to provide the tunnel. IPSec tunnels typically operate from gateway to gateway.

Operating System Support for VPNs

Modern operating systems include built-in support for virtual private networking. This enables you to create a connection to a VPN server as easily as you establish a dialup connection.

Microsoft's Windows 95, Windows 98, Windows NT, and Windows 2000 operating systems can function as VPN clients using the built-in components. Windows 9*x* and Windows NT support PPTP, and Windows 2000 supports the use of either PPTP or L2TP.

Windows 2000 uses a wizard to walk you through the steps of setting up a VPN connection, as shown in Figure 16-3.

Linux supports the use of IPSec and PPTP. In addition, you can create a "pseudo tunnel" by running Point-to-Point Protocol (PPP) through the Secure Shell (SSH), which uses the RSA public key technology to authenticate and secure the connection.

When used in conjunction with third-party software or hardware solutions, virtual private networking can be used with practically any operating system, and VPNs can function across platforms, just as remote access does.

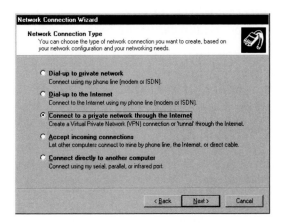

FIGURE 16-3
The Windows 2000 Network Connection Wizard makes it easy to set up a VPN connection.

Why Use Virtual Private Networking?

We have defined virtual private networking as a way for two computers (or two networks) in distant locations to communicate with each other by going across a public network. However, we haven't discussed why you might want to do this in the first place. After all, you could just set up a remote access server and have users dial in to the network. This would bypass the public network and the privacy concerns that go along with it.

In some cases, a dialup server would indeed accomplish the same objective as a VPN. Under many circumstances, however, virtual networking has distinct advantages over dialup remote access service (RAS).

In the following sections, we discuss the advantages and disadvantages of VPNs and dialup networking and then examine some common VPN scenarios.

VPN Versus Dialup Networking: Advantages and Disadvantages

Consider the remote access situations we discussed in Chapter 15. Many employees telecommute, take work home and require access to the corporate network after business hours, or need to be connected while on the road. These employees could dial in to a remote access server, but what happens if they live outside the dialing area or are traveling to another city or state? Long distance charges can make remote network access prohibitively expensive.

A VPN solution can save substantial costs in this scenario. If the corporate network is connected to the Internet, and the employee has access to a local Internet service provider (ISP), the connection can be made without incurring long distance charges. Many ISPs operate in multiple cities and can provide traveling users with local access numbers. The user need only dial the local number for the ISP and then tunnel through the Internet to the company LAN, which typically has a dedicated Internet connection, as shown in Figure 16-4.

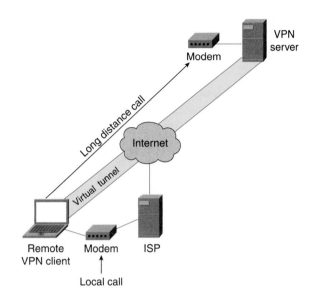

FIGURE 16-4
Using a VPN enables a user to dial in to a local ISP instead of making a long distance call to the corporate LAN.

VPNs can save money by reducing the number of telephone lines required. If many users need to access the network simultaneously through dialup connections, the company needs separate telephone lines and modems for each connection. If those same users access the network through a VPN, however, only the company's single connection to the Internet is required. Reducing the number of telephone lines can result in major cost savings every month.

Some ISPs offer VPN connections. The ISP provides and manages the link; this reduces the cost of administration at the company's end because the work is outsourced to the ISP. These ISP-based VPNs might even transport the data using the ISP's backbone network (instead of the Internet) as the "public network."

These are the advantages of virtual private networking over dialup access:

- VPNs save the cost of long distance charges when remote users are out of the dialing area.
- VPNs require fewer telephone lines to provide remote access to multiple users simultaneously.
- VPNs require less hardware equipment such as modem banks.
- VPNs that are ISP-based reduce administrative and training costs.

Of course, VPN solutions have drawbacks as well. First, both ends of the connection must have an Internet connection to establish the VPN. This can be a problem if one or both ends have an unreliable Internet connection. For example, a user who wants to access the corporate network from home might find that his ISP's server is down for maintenance. This would prevent him from using a VPN to connect to the company LAN; on the other hand, with a direct dialup connection to the LAN, the reliability of the ISP would not be an issue.

The second disadvantage of VPNs involves performance issues. This can vary from negligible to significant, depending on the type of VPN implementation and the type of Internet connections involved. Adding the VPN layer is likely to affect performance to some degree; whether the trade-off is worth the advantages of virtual networking is up to each organization to decide. Table 16-1 gives a quick summary of the advantages and disadvantages of VPN solutions.

TABLE 16-1   Advantages and Disadvantages of VPN Solutions Compared to Dialup Solutions

Advantages of VPNs	Disadvantages of VPNs
Long distance charges are avoided.	Both ends of the connection must have a reliable Internet connection.
Fewer telephone lines are required.	Performance is often slower than with dialup connections.
Fewer modems are required.	
There is a reduction in administrative and training costs if the VPN is ISP-based.	

VPN Scenarios

Virtual private networking can be used in several ways, depending on the company's needs. Most commonly, VPNs are implemented for one of the following purposes:

- To provide remote access to mobile or home-based employees
- To provide an *extranet* that is accessible to employees, clients, and partners
- To connect two offices in distant locations without incurring the cost of a dedicated direct link

In the following sections, we take a look at each situation, how the virtual network is implemented, and how privacy is best ensured.

Remote Access VPNs

Using the VPN to provide remote access to individual users is the simplest deployment scenario—in concept. Implementation can be complicated by factors such as the operating systems in use and the protocols installed at the client end.

The VPN client must be able to use the protocols supported by the VPN server (tunneling, network, and transport) and the encryption protocols used by the server. For example, non-Microsoft clients can establish a VPN to a Windows 2000 remote access server using PPTP, but if the connection is to be secure, the client must be able to use the Microsoft Point-to-Point Encryption protocol (MPPE).

Once the VPN components are installed and configured, the connection is established, as shown in Figure 16-5.

FIGURE 16-5
The mobile or home user dials in to an ISP to establish an Internet connection, through which he tunnels to the private network.

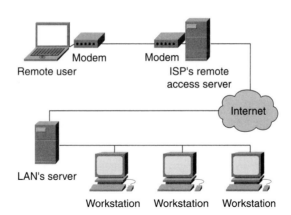

1. The mobile or home user dials in to a local ISP and logs in with a user account to establish the Internet connection. (If the client uses a dedicated or "always on" Internet connection, such as a DSL or cable modem, this step is not necessary.)

2. After the Internet connection is established, the client calls the remote access server configured to accept VPN connections (using the remote server's IP address); this action establishes the tunnel.

3. The user is authenticated on the private network, and access is granted.

A variation on this scenario works in the opposite direction in that a user with a dedicated connection can configure a home computer as a VPN server and then connect to it from the office to access files stored at home.

Virtual Private Extranets

This scenario involves making a part of the company's LAN, called the extranet, available to remote users through a VPN connection. This extranet might store, for example, technical support material for customers or shared business documents for partner companies.

An important issue is protecting the rest of the internal network from outside access. Creating a separate subnet for the extranet and placing the rest of the LAN behind a firewall can provide this security, as shown in Figure 16-6.

FIGURE 16-6
The internal network can be protected from outside access by the implementation of a firewall.

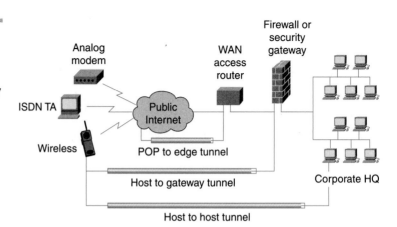

Typically, extranet users access data through a web browser, so a web server is set up in the VPN-connected subnet. File servers can be located there as well.

Existing and emerging standards make it easy for companies to share data and applications, such as groupware used for collaborative projects, on the extranet. These emerging standards include the following:

- **Hypertext Markup Language (HTML)**—This enables the sharing of documents through any web browser. Users don't have to have a particular word processing or other program to open the files.
- **Extensible Markup Language (XML) and Commerce XML (cXML)**—Like HTML, these languages offer cross-platform compatibility.
- **Open Buying on the Internet (OBI)**—This creates standards for e-commerce transactions.

VPN Connections Between Branch Offices

Creating VPN connections between branch offices uses virtual private networking to connect two offices in a router-to-router VPN configuration. This configuration is also called *gateway to gateway.* The VPN server can act as a router with IP forwarding enabled, as shown in Figure 16-7.

FIGURE 16-7
A router-to-router
VPN connects
two branch
offices.

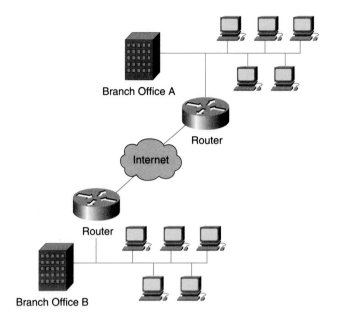

FIGURE 16-7
A router-to-router VPN connects two branch offices.

The LAN at each branch office has a routed connection to the Internet. This connection can be dial-on-demand or persistent. For a dial-on-demand connection, the router initiating the connection uses a dialup Internet connection. The router being called should have a dedicated (persistent) Internet connection, and it must be configured to accept dial-on-demand connections. Two dial-on-demand connections are configured on the calling router—one to dial the ISP and the other to connect to the VPN. If both routers have dedicated connections to the Internet, the VPN connection can be established and continuously left open, if desired.

The router-to-router VPN can be configured so that one router acts as the client and initiates the connection while the other functions as the VPN server. This is a one-way connection and is a good choice for permanent connections. Another option is a two-way connection, in which either router can initiate the connection. In this case, both routers must have a persistent Internet connection and must be set up as LAN and WAN routers.

TIP

In the router-to-router scenario, the routing tables on both routers must to be configured with the necessary routes to forward packets across the connection. The routes can be added manually, or a dynamic routing protocol can be used if the dial-on-demand interface has a permanent connection.

Software such as vpnd (VPNdaemon) can be used to connect two LANs using Linux or FreeBSD. The Blowfish encryption algorithm is used to secure the data that passes through the connection.

VPN Protocols

In this section, we look at the three protocols types used in virtual private networking:

- **A tunneling protocol**—Sometimes referred to as a VPN protocol, it is used to establish the tunnel.
- **An encryption protocol**—Sometimes referred to as a security protocol, it is used to secure the data.
- **A network/transport protocol**—Sometimes referred to as a LAN protocol, it is used to communicate on the private network.

Tunneling Protocols

The tunneling protocol encapsulates the data so that the original protocol headers are wrapped inside the encapsulation headers. In the following sections, we examine the following tunneling protocols:

- Point-to-Point Tunneling Protocol (PPTP)
- Layer 2 Forwarding (L2F)
- Layer 2 Tunneling Protocol (L2TP)
- IPSec
- Secure Shell (SSH) and Secure Shell 2 (SSH2)
- Crypto IP Encapsulation protocol (CIPE)

PPTP

Microsoft's PPTP is an established standard that is actually an extension of the PPP link protocol that is used to establish a WAN link over a remote access connection. Here's how it works:

1. PPTP encapsulates a PPP frame, which can be an IP, IPX, or NetBEUI packet inside a Generic Routing Encapsulation (GRE) header. An IP header also is added to provide source and destination IP addresses. The source address is the VPN client's and the destination address is the VPN server's.

2. The data in the original datagram is normally encrypted so that unauthorized persons cannot read it. Microsoft VPNs use the MPPE protocol

(described later in this section) in conjunction with PPTP to provide secure communications.

PPTP-linux is client software that runs on Linux or UNIX machines. It enables them to connect to PPTP servers. PPTP server software (called PoPToP) for Linux, Sun Solaris, FreeBSD, and other implementations of UNIX is available. It supports Windows clients as well as PPTP-linux clients, and it is freeware.

Macintosh clients can connect to Windows PPTP servers by using third-party software such as Network Telesystems TunnelBuilder.

L2F

Cisco developed the L2F technology in 1996 and included it in its IOS software. An alternative to PPTP, it is capable of using ATM and Frame Relay protocols for tunneling. Although PPTP requires IP to work, L2F does not. In addition, L2F provides authentication of the endpoints of the tunnel.

L2TP

Microsoft and Cisco combined the features of PPTP and L2F and created L2TP. L2TP can encapsulate data to be sent over IP, as can PPTP. L2TP can also encapsulate data to be sent over ATM, Frame Relay, and X.25. Thus, it can be used to tunnel through the Internet, or it can be used over specific WAN media without the need for IP.

Some advantages of L2TP over PPTP include the following:

- L2TP supports multiple tunnels between endpoints. This allows for the creation of separate tunnels that provide, for example, different Qualities of Service (QoS).
- L2TP supports compression of headers, which saves on overhead.
- L2TP, unlike PPTP, is capable of tunnel authentication.
- L2TP works over non-IP internetworks using ATM or Frame Relay virtual circuits.

IPSec

IPSec can be used to encrypt data that flows through a tunnel established by another protocol, such as L2TP. (We discuss that aspect in the "Encryption Protocols" section.) It can be used also to establish a tunnel when it is operating in tunneling mode. In tunneling mode, IPSec can be used to encapsulate IP packets, and an IPSec tunnel can be configured to protect data either between two IP addresses or between two IP subnets.

As you learned in Chapter 14, "Protecting the Network," IPSec can use one or both of two protocols: Authentication Header (AH) and Encapsulating Security Payload (ESP).

In the following sections, we discuss each protocol and explore how IPSec can interoperate with various operating systems.

AH Tunnel Mode. AH tunnel mode, used alone, does not provide encryption of the data that travels through the tunnel. It does, however, ensure the integrity of the data by verifying that it has not been tampered with. It also authenticates the sender. With AH, no change in the source or destination address can be made from the time the packet leaves the originating tunnel endpoint.

ESP Tunnel Mode. With ESP tunnel mode, the original source and final destination addresses are contained in the original (encapsulated) IP header. The outer header usually contains the gateway addresses. The ESP tunnel encrypts the data using algorithms such as DES or 3DES.

When ESP is used, the outer IP header is not protected, and its integrity is not guaranteed. To accomplish both encryption and authentication and integrity of the entire packet, you can use AH and ESP together.

IPSec Interoperability. Microsoft's Windows 2000 operating systems include built-in support for IPSec. IPSec is an IETF standard, and it also works with Linux, UNIX, Macintosh, and other operating systems that support the IP protocol family. IPSec authentication can be done using a variety of methods, including preshared secret keys, Kerberos, and certificate services.

FreeS/WAN for Linux is an implementation of IPSec that is open source, and it is available for download over the Internet.

SSH/SSH2

SSH was originally intended to provide a secure alternative to UNIX **r** commands such as **rsh**, **rlogin**, and **rcp**. SSH utilizes strong encryption and authentication. SSH2 has evolved into a secure tunneling protocol that can be used to create a VPN running on Linux or UNIX operating systems. The type of VPN established by SSH2 is called a *circuit-level VPN*. SSH client software is also available for Windows.

SSH can be installed on a private network's firewall, and a tunnel can be established from an SSH client with dialup Internet access to the firewall. The firewall can be configured to forward the traffic to a server on the internal network. This is a simple, easy solution for VPN connections if high performance is not an issue. SSH requires a login account, so it is best suited for

NOTE

Circuit-level gateways work at the session layer of the OSI reference model. When data is passed to a remote computer through a circuit-level gateway, it appears to have originated from the gateway itself. This enables you to conceal information about protected networks.

situations such as allowing a few trusted employees to connect to a small office network from home.

CIPE

CIPE is a Linux kernel driver that can be used to provide a secure tunnel between two IP subnets. The data is encrypted at the network layer of the OSI reference model. This is called low-level encryption. It has an advantage over high-level encryption because no changes must be made to the application software when two networks are connected by a VPN. In addition, CIPE is simpler and more efficient than IPSec.

Encryption Protocols

After the tunnel has been established, data must be encrypted before the connection can be considered secure. Protocols used to encrypt data include the following:

- MPPE
- IPSec encryption
- VPNd encryption
- SSH encryption

MPPE

MPPE is used with PPTP-based VPN connections (or PPP dialup connections), and it can use a 40-bit, 56-bit, or 128-bit key encryption algorithm. The 128-bit (strong encryption) key can be used within the United States and Canada only.

IPSec Encryption

IPSec uses DES or 3DES to encrypt the data in an L2TP tunnel. The use of a combination of cryptography-based algorithms and keys makes the information very secure. The Diffie-Hellman algorithm enables the secure exchange of a shared key without the sending of the key itself across the network connection.

VPNd Encryption: Blowfish

VPNd for Linux uses the Blowfish encryption algorithm. This is a 64-bit algorithm that can use variable-length keys, from 32 bits to 448 bits. It is fast and free; in fact, the source code is available. There are several variations, including GOLDFISH, DOSFISH, and TWOFISH.

SSH Encryption

UNIX SSH uses public key cryptography to encrypt data. Refer to Chapter 14 for more information about how public key encryption works.

LAN Protocols

For the VPN client and server to communicate, they must have a network/transport protocol stack in common. This can be TCP/IP, but it does not have to be. Even with a PPTP connection that requires IP in place on the public network through which the tunnel is constructed, the private network can use IPX/SPX or even NetBEUI for communications.

VPN Security

VPN security has three components:

- Authentication
- Authorization
- Encryption

This multicomponent implementation ensures the "private" aspect of virtual private networking. We briefly look at each in the following sections.

Authentication

Authentication of the VPN client involves verifying the identity of the machine and the user who is initiating the VPN connection. Authentication can occur at the machine level. For instance, when a Windows 2000-based VPN uses IPSec for an L2TP VPN, machine certificates are exchanged as part of establishing the IPSec security association.

The user can be authenticated using one of several authentication methods, including Extensible Authentication Protocol (EAP), Challenge Handshake Authentication Protocol (CHAP), Microsoft CHAP (MS-CHAP), Password Authentication Protocol (PAP), or Shiva PAP (SPAP), as discussed in Chapter 15.

Authorization

Authorization refers to restrictions placed on which users are granted VPN access according to set policies. Policies can be set to allow some users VPN access and to deny others the same access.

Encryption

A variety of different encryption technologies can be used to protect data in VPNs. Many VPN implementations enable you to choose the encryption method to be used. Encryption provides security for data that travels over a VPN. Without this security, the data would be vulnerable to interception as it moves over the public network.

VPN Performance Issues

Performance issues related to VPNs can be categorized in two ways: general performance issues and issues specific to particular VPN implementations.

The most serious performance concern is because of the nature of the Internet itself. System-wide or regional availability outages have been known to occur. Heavy traffic (such as during a major Internet event or a big news story) can cause slowdowns throughout the system. In addition, individual ISPs can experience server shutdowns that affect hundreds or even thousands of users.

VPN technology can also result in varying amounts of overhead that decrease performance. Circuit-level VPNs cannot match the speed of network-level virtual networks. When you use the public network to establish the connection, you will sacrifice the element of control that you have with a direct dial-in connection.

Types of VPNs

A VPN can be implemented through software or hardware. In the following sections, we briefly discuss each implementation, how they differ, and how they can be combined for added security.

Software-Based VPNs

Software-based VPNs include the use of tunneling protocols we have discussed. This category can be broken down further into third-party products and VPN software that is supported by an operating system. The obvious advantage of the latter is cost. There is nothing extra to buy, and the VPN solutions included in modern operating systems such as Windows 2000 are sufficient for many organizations' needs.

Third-party VPN software products tend to include additional features and expand the usability of the VPN, and they often provide more security options and, in some cases, easier implementation. Some software-based VPNs enable you to tunnel data based on the protocol or IP address. This type of filtering is usually not available with hardware-based products.

Third-party products include Safeguard VPN, Checkpoint SVN (Secure Virtual Networking), and NetMAX VPN Suite for Linux.

Hardware-Based VPNs

VPN hardware is made by companies such as Shiva, 3Com, and VPNet Technologies. VPN support is built into Cisco routers as well as other companies' routers. NTS TunnelBuilder provides secure VPN communications for Windows, NetWare, and Macintosh. Firewall vendors such as Raptor Systems offer VPNs that are based on firewalls and that are combined with security tools.

Hardware VPNs can generally be categorized into the following groups:

- **Router-based**—Router-based VPN solutions are routers with encryption capabilities. They offer the best network performance and are generally easy to set up and use.
- **Firewall-based**—Firewall-based solutions provide extra security measures, such as strong authentication and detailed logging. A firewall-based VPN also can perform address translation. Performance might be an issue, although in some implementations, hardware-based encryption processors solve this problem.

Configuring a VPN Connection

Configuration of a VPN connection depends on the type of VPN and whether the implementation is hardware- or software-based.

In this section, we present the steps for setting up a VPN connection in Windows 2000:

Step 1 Access Network and Dialup Connections from the Start menu, as shown in Figure 16-8.

FIGURE 16-8
Creating a VPN connection in Windows 2000 begins with the network and Dialup Connections option.

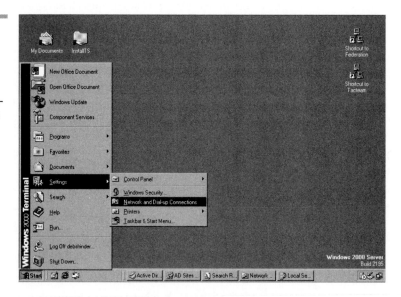

Step 2 Double-click the Make New Connection icon in the Network and Dial-up Connections window, as shown in Figure 16-9.

FIGURE 16-9
Click the Make
New Connection
icon to create a
VPN connection.

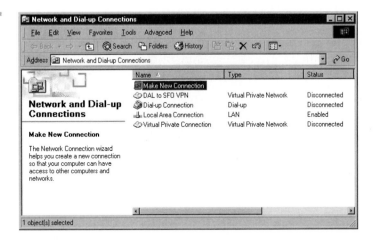

Step 3 Your action invokes the Network Connection Wizard. Select the third option, Connect to a private network through the Internet, as shown in Figure 16-3.

Step 4 Next you are asked to address the following:

- **Whether to dial in to a server to establish an initial connection to the Internet**—If you select to do so, you are asked to configure or select a dialup connection. If you have a dedicated Internet connection, you should select "do not dial."

- **The host name or IP address of the VPN server**—Enter the information for the computer or router to which you want to establish the VPN connection. Remember that host names must be resolved to IP addresses, so it is usually best to enter the IP address if you know it. This reduces the complexity of the connection.

- **Whether the connection should be available to all users who share the computer, or only to the user who is creating it**—The default is to enable all users to use the connection.

- **Whether to enable Internet Connection Sharing (ICS) to share the VPN connection over the network**—This enables other computers on the LAN to share the connection through Network Address Translation (NAT). Note that IPSec does not work with NAT.

Step 5 When you have worked your way through the wizard pages by answering these questions, you are asked to name the connection, as shown in Figure 16-10.

FIGURE 16-10
Once you have completed the wizard, you are asked to name the VPN connection.

After the VPN connection has been configured on the client computer, connecting to the VPN is easy. Simply double-click the connection's icon in Network and Dialup Connections, and you are prompted to enter your username and password for the remote VPN server. Windows 2000 makes the connection.

Using the default configuration (with VPN type set to Automatic), the software detects whether the VPN server uses PPTP or L2TP and then uses the appropriate protocol for establishing the tunnel.

You can configure or change the properties of the connection (such as which authentication protocols should be used) at any time.

Summary

In this chapter, we discussed the concept of virtual private networking in its various forms. You learned that a VPN enables you to connect to and communicate securely with a remote private network by "tunneling" through the Internet or another public network. We discussed ways in which VPNs can be implemented either over dialup connections or as router-to-router VPNs.

You learned that tunneling can occur at different layers of the OSI reference model. We discussed Layer 2 tunneling, as performed by PPTP and L2TP, and

Layer 3 tunneling, which is used by IPSec. You also learned that most modern operating systems can be used for making VPN connections, either through built-in support or through third-party software.

We discussed the cost benefits of virtual private networking, the protocols used in creating VPNs, and common LAN protocols used for communications between the VPN client and server.

We discussed VPN security and the three components involved in it: authentication, authorization, and encryption. Then we addressed VPN performance issues and looked at two types of VPN: software-based and hardware-based. We wrapped up the chapter by demonstrating the steps involved in creating a VPN connection for a Windows 2000 VPN client.

VPNs can be used also in conjunction with another technology that is rapidly growing in popularity—thin client networking. We discuss the thin client concept in Chapter 17, "Thin Client Networking." In Chapter 17, you will learn how solutions such as Microsoft terminal services, Citrix Metaframe, the NetPC, and others are saving organizations money and breathing new life into old hardware.

Further Reading

Information about the VPN mailing list and how to subscribe, as well as answers to frequently asked questions about VPNs, is at http://kubarb.phsx.ukans.edu/~tbird/vpn/FAQ.html.

A Linux mini-HOWTO document that goes into detail on setting up an SSH/PPP-based VPN can be accessed at http://sunsite.unc.edu/LDP/HOWTO/mini/VPN.html.

To learn more about NTS TunnelBuilder and TunnelMaster, see www.nts.com/products/index.html.

A concise report on virtual private networking can be found at www.core-com.com/html/vpn.html.

Review Questions

The following questions test your knowledge of the material covered in this chapter. Be sure to read each question carefully and select the *best* correct answer or answers.

1. What is the process of wrapping one protocol header inside another?

   A. Encryption

   B. Encapsulation

   C. Authentication

   D. Authorization

2. What is the name for a logical point-to-point connection that supports authentication and encryption of data from one endpoint to the other over a public network?

   A. A tunnel

   B. A protocol

   C. A gateway

   D. A remote access connection

3. Which of the following is true of PPTP? (Select all that apply.)

   A. PPTP works in conjunction with IPSec to provide a secure VPN.

   B. PPTP is based on the PPP link protocol.

   C. PPTP is a Layer 3 tunneling protocol.

   D. PPTP works in conjunction with MPPE to provide a secure VPN.

4. Which of the following can operate in either transport mode or tunnel mode?

   A. PPTP

   B. L2F

   C. IPSec

   D. SSH

5. Which of the following is an advantage of VPNs over dialup remote access? (Select all that apply.)

   A. Performance of a VPN is faster than that of a dialup connection.

   B. A VPN is more reliable than a direct dialup connection.

   C. A VPN can save you money in long distance charges when connecting from a location outside the local calling area.

   D. With a VPN, the server is not required to have a telephone line and modem for each simultaneous remote user.

6. What is the name for a part of the company's LAN that is made available to select parties such as employees, customers, or partners?

   A. The internet

   B. The intranet

   C. The extranet

   D. The subnet

7. A router-to-router VPN is often used for which of the following purposes?

   A. To provide customers access to the company LAN

   B. To provide employees access to the company network from home

   C. To provide executives access to the company network while on the road

   D. To provide a connection between two offices in distant locations

8. Which of the following is true of both PPTP and L2TP?

   A. Both can be used to create a VPN tunnel.

   B. Both can use ATM or Frame Relay for tunneling.

   C. Both work at the data link layer of the OSI reference model.

   D. Both support multiple tunnels between endpoints.

9. Which of the following is a Linux kernel driver that is used to provide a secure tunnel between two IP subnets?

   A. TunnelBuilder

   B. CIPE

   C. CIR

   D. VPN daemon

10. Which of the following is true of hardware-based VPN solutions? (Select all that apply.)

   A. Hardware-based VPNs can be divided into two categories: router-based and firewall-based.

   B. Hardware-based VPNs are generally easier to set up and use than software-based VPNs.

   C. Hardware-based VPNs are generally less expensive than software-based VPNs.

   D. Hardware-based VPNs can perform address translation.

Thin Client Networking

If virtual private networking is at the top of the list of popular technologies, thin client networking can't be far behind. Thin is "in," at least when it comes to saving a company thousands of dollars in hardware costs by using products such as Microsoft Terminal Services, Citrix MetaFrame, and Java-based computing.

Thin client solutions provide a way to use otherwise outdated or low-powered computer equipment to run popular applications that normally require many times the memory and processing capability. This utilization is done by installing software on the thin client that enables the client to connect to a server (typically called a *terminal server*) and run programs on a virtual desktop. The user works at his or her thin desktop machine, but the processing is actually taking place on the server; the screen redraws are then transmitted over the network.

In this chapter, we examine the benefits and drawbacks of using thin client solutions to reduce total cost of ownership (TCO) in corporate and small business environments. First we examine the overall concept of thin client networking, and then we look at ways in which it can be implemented.

Specifically, we discuss the client hardware options: Windows-based terminals (WBTs), Net PCs, network computers, ordinary desktop PCs, and handheld or palm computers. Then we examine hardware and software considerations involved in making the decision to deploy thin clients.

We then discuss common protocols used for communication between the thin client and the server and take a look at the these commonly used thin client solutions:

- Microsoft terminal services (including both Windows NT Terminal Server Edition and Windows 2000 Terminal Services)
- Citrix Winframe and MetaFrame
- X Window terminals
- Web-based computing and the Java desktop

Finally, we discuss application service providers (ASPs) and the "Internet is the operating system" philosophy behind such initiatives as Microsoft's new Microsoft .NET strategy.

Let's begin by defining terms and looking at some history.

The Evolution of Thin Client Networking

Traditional desktop operating systems have become more powerful, more complex, and more resource hungry over the past two decades. Table 17-1 compares the typical system configurations for Microsoft's popular operating systems. The left column of the table shows the passage of time as DOS morphed into Windows and Windows evolved into Windows 9x, Windows ME, Windows NT, and Windows 2000.

TABLE 17-1   Comparison of System Configurations in Microsoft Operating Systems*

Year Released	Operating System	Typical Memory Configuration	Typical Processor Speed
1981	MS-DOS	64 KB	4.77 MHz
1985	Windows	1–2 MB	12 MHz
1990	Windows 3.0	2–4 MB	16–25 MHz
1994	Windows NT	16 MB	33–66 MHz
1995	Windows 95	16 MB	66–90 MHz
1996	Windows NT 4.0	32 MB	100–133 MHz
1998	Windows 98	32 MB	200–233 MHz
2000	Windows ME	32–64 MB	333–450 MHz
2000	Windows 2000	64–128 MB	333–450 MHz

*   These configurations do not represent the minimum system requirements. The operating systems in question might be able to run on a lower-powered computer. These numbers indicate the "typical" system configuration for acceptable performance. Also, note that these figures are for the desktop versions (for example, Windows NT Workstation, Windows 2000 Professional), *not* the server products.

This rapid increase in typical system requirements (sometimes referred to colloquially as *bloatware*) has an unfortunate side effect: Millions of machines, still in fully functional condition, become obsolete as new "fat" operating systems are released. This means that these machines must be upgraded or replaced with machines that are more powerful; either option can add up to a large expense for a company that has hundreds or thousands of computers. Old systems are often shuffled off to sit in a storage facility, donated to nonprofit organizations that are happy to "make do" with lesser machines and older software, or salvaged for parts.

Of course, companies could simply continue to use their old systems and software or choose one of the compact operating systems such as the "tiny Linux" distributions that fit on a floppy disk and run on 4 MB of RAM. However, these solutions are unsatisfactory for most businesses because they need standardized applications such as Microsoft Word and interoperability with the software of customers and partners.

Thin client computing offers a way to utilize these "outdated" machines and still allow their users to enjoy the benefits of modern operating systems and applications. The thin client concept is simple: Use low-powered computers or terminals on the desktop, and let a high-powered server do most of the work.

This concept is not unlike the mainframe world, in which a large, powerful, centralized processor provides applications and data to multiple users. Has computing come full circle? How does the PC implementation of thin client technology differ from the mainframe model? We examine those questions in the following sections.

Thin Client Technology

How does thin client technology work? In a typical thin client implementation, software running on the server transmits the user interface over the network to the client. The desktop machine, which is running client software, transmits user input (that is, keystrokes or mouse clicks) back to the server. Processing is done on the server.

Users log in to the server with individual preconfigured accounts; thus, each user has a unique desktop customized to fit his or her needs. Multiple users can be logged in simultaneously, but users are not aware of others' sessions. Multiuser applications are installed so that each user can have his or her preferred settings. Users can access their own local drives, save to a floppy disk, print to an LPT port, and so on, as illustrated in Figure 17-1.

FIGURE 17-1
Thin client users can have their own unique desktops and settings.

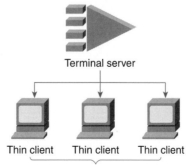

Terminal server

Thin client   Thin client   Thin client

Each user is provided with a
unique desktop and preferred settings
by the terminal server

Advantages of Thin Client Technology

An obvious advantage of the thin client model is cost savings. Because the client software generally runs on a variety of different platforms, this solution offers high flexibility. For example, users can work on a Windows 2000 desktop, which runs applications such as Office 2000, from an X386 PC or a Macintosh computer. See Figure 17-2.

FIGURE 17-2
Users can run Windows 2000 in a terminal by using older or low-powered equipment.

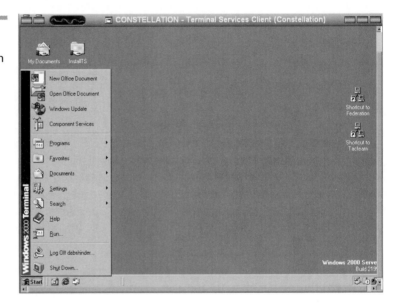

This option often is less expensive than upgrading all desktop computers to hardware that runs Windows 2000. The application server must be a relatively powerful PC. For instance, Microsoft recommends for its Windows 2000 Terminal Server a minimum configuration of a Pentium processor or equivalent and at least 128 MB of RAM, with an additional 12–21 MB for each user. However, high-end server hardware sufficient to support many clients still costs thousands of dollars less than a mainframe.

Another advantage is the user's ability to use full-fledged PCs to access the application server while still retaining the PC's local processing power for cases in which it is advantageous to run a particular application locally. The terminals typically used to access mainframes have no processing power of their own. Although gateway products such as Systems Network Architecture (SNA) can be used to provide PC access to mainframe applications, these products are costly.

For the network administrator, the deployment of thin clients offers many benefits, including the following:

- The upgrading of applications is simplified because you are upgrading the multiuser application on the server rather than upgrading hundreds or thousands of individual desktop machines.

- In some cases, there might be savings on software licensing fees. Check licensing agreements carefully; you might still be required to purchase a license for each user of the application, even though the application is being run from the terminal.

- Virus protection occurs at the server. User desktops can be locked down to prevent users from accessing the floppy drive; WBTs, which don't have floppy drives, also can be used. In addition, policies can be set to restrict users from installing software.

- When terminals are used, data is saved on the server. Data can be more easily secured and backed up when it is on the server. If PCs are used, you have the option of allowing users to store data locally.

- You can control terminal sessions. Control can even be extended to taking control of the user's cursor or shutting down the session.

- User policies can be set. These policies control the users' desktops and actions, which can be different from the policies applied to the use of the local machine.

Thin Client Protocols

Thin client solutions depend on three components: the hardware (both server and client), the software (again, both server and client), and the protocols that enable the server and client to communicate with one another.

In this section, we examine the protocols used by Windows Terminal Services and Citrix MetaFrame, two of the most popular thin client products. The protocols used by these products are the *Remote Desktop Protocol (RDP)* and the *Independent Computing Architecture (ICA)* protocol.

We also look at the X and XDM protocols, which are used by X Window terminals in the UNIX/Linux environment. Then we look at the Remote Frame Buffer (RFB) protocol and examine Bootstrap Protocol (BOOTP), Dynamic Host Configuration Protocol (DHCP), and Trivial File Transfer Protocol (TFTP). All are used to boot network PCs and other diskless workstations.

NOTE

Microsoft developed RDP for use with terminal services without Citrix add-ons. ICA comes with Citrix MetaFrame.

RDP

RDP is included in Microsoft's Windows NT Terminal Server Edition and the Windows 2000 Terminal Services, which is included with all Windows 2000 Server products. RDP works with WBTs running the Windows CE operating system and with PCs running Windows for Workgroups 3.11, Windows 95, Windows 98, Windows NT, and Windows 2000.

RDP supports the TCP/IP network transport protocol, and it works over LAN or WAN connections and dialup remote access connections. RDP also enables printing to a local LPT port, and it supports clipboard redirection, which is the ability to cut and paste between terminal and local system applications.

ICA

Citrix supplies ICA with both Winframe and MetaFrame, and ICA adds fuller functionality to Windows Terminal Services. For example, where RDP works only with Windows clients, Citrix supports DOS, Macintosh, and several versions of UNIX and Linux. It also supports the use of Internet Explorer and Netscape browsers as terminal clients. This extends terminal services to virtually all personal computing environments.

ICA works with a variety of client devices. In addition to PCs, it supports network computers, WBTs, Wyse Technology network terminals, palm and handheld computers, TV set-top devices, and network appliances.

Another advantage of the Citrix software is that it supports IPX, SPX, and NetBEUI, in addition to TCP/IP. ICA runs over LAN, WAN, dialup, and direct serial connections. Unlike RDP, ICA supports 16-bit sound so that users can play .wav, .mid, and .avi files in the terminal. The Citrix protocol enables COM port redirection and seamless drive remapping.

X and X Display Manager Communication Protocol (XDMCP)

The X protocol can enable communication between an X server and an X terminal. It is somewhat limited as a thin client protocol because it does not have the sophisticated security and compression features available with other protocols. X is not considered appropriate for WAN connections because of its lack of optimization features, although a variation called Low-Bandwidth X (LBX) attempts to address this.

The XDM Communication Protocol (XDMCP) is used by the XDM to manage the assignment of the server's resources to X terminal users.

RFB

The RFB protocol provides a terminal user with remote access to a graphical user interface (GUI). It is a cross-platform protocol that works with X, Windows, and Macintosh.

RFB qualifies as a thin client protocol because its demands on the client are minimal. The RFB server handles all processing, and the state of the session is preserved if a client disconnects. When the client reconnects to the server, the interface is in the same state as it was when the disconnection occurred. For example, whatever applications were running are still running, and any documents that were open are still open and on the screen. This is true regardless of whether the user accesses the server from the same client machine or a different one.

BOOTP, DHCP, and TFTP

BOOTP, DHCP, and TFTP are not thin client protocols, but they are used in conjunction with thin client computing to enable an extremely thin client, such as a diskless workstation, to connect to the network and to load an operating system. This process is shown in Figure 17-3.

FIGURE 17-3
The BOOTP or DHCP protocol, along with TFTP, can be used to connect a diskless workstation to the network and to load the operating system.

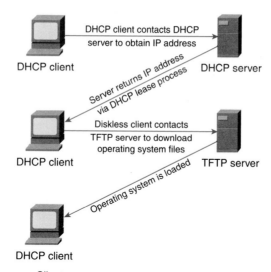

DHCP client — DHCP client contacts DHCP server to obtain IP address → DHCP server

Server returns IP address via DHCP lease process

DHCP client — Diskless client contacts TFTP server to download operating system files → TFTP server

Operating system is loaded

DHCP client

Client can now communicate on the network

BOOTP was originally developed as a way for a diskless machine to contact the network so that it could be assigned an IP address. It could then communicate with a server using TFTP to load the operating system files into memory. A BOOTP server assigns IP addresses to computers configured as BOOTP clients.

DHCP is a newer and more sophisticated form of BOOTP. A DHCP server can be used to lease addresses to DHCP client machines. The process by which

DHCP does this is discussed in Chapter 8, "Networking Protocols and Services."

After the thin client has an IP address, it can communicate on the network by using TCP/IP. This allows it to contact a TFTP server on which the boot image is stored. The TFTP server uses the User Datagram Protocol (UDP), which is faster than TCP. Diskless PCs can boot a variety of operating systems from the boot server, including Windows or Linux. Because there is no hard disk, the usual operating system loader files are located in ROM. Bootstrap code is pre-loaded in the ROM of NICs that meet the Preboot Execution Environment (PXE) standard.

PXE

Intel and other manufacturers use PXE to provide bootstrap code for thin clients and other machines that need to load an operating system from the network. The PXE code is written to a ROM chip, which can be included on the network interface adapter or as part of the thin client device.

The PXE card sends a message to the server to announce that it is PXE-capable, and the PXE-aware server then returns information allowing the client to contact a boot server where an operating system image is stored.

Thin Client Hardware

Thin client implementations can utilize many different types of hardware devices. One of the primary benefits of thin client computing is its easy portability to different platforms.

Popular choices for client hardware include the following:

- WBTs
- Network computers
- Net PCs
- Desktop computers (both PC and Macintosh, running a variety of operating systems)
- Handheld and palm computers

Next, we briefly discuss each option and how it fits into the corporate network infrastructure.

WBTs

WBTs are designed to provide a Windows desktop and Windows applications to users through a thin client computing model. Most models of WBTs have either the Microsoft terminal server software and RDP or the Citrix ICA client preloaded, and they are built to use the Windows CE or embedded NT operating system.

The WBTs are less expensive than full-fledged PCs, yet users can use them to run most applications that run on Windows PCs. The terminal of a WBT does not have a hard disk, which reduces the ability of users to introduce viruses or make unauthorized copies of company data. Another advantage of the diskless machines is that theft is unlikely. Because the device is useless without the network, it is not very attractive to thieves.

A popular vendor of WBTs is Wyse Technology, which, in 1995, was the first company to market WBTs.

Network Computers

The *Network Computer* was developed by Sun Microsystems in the mid-1990s. IBM and Oracle also joined in this endeavor. The Network Computer architecture was designed as a true thin client that consisted of only the minimal hardware that was needed to boot and connect to a network.

The Network Computer provides a web interface and a Java Virtual Machine (JVM), which provide flexibility. The Network Computer specifications have evolved into an open standard that includes the following basic characteristics:

- The Network Computer is not a proprietary computing platform. No specific operating system is required.
- The Network Computer includes a web browser interface for processing of Hypertext Transfer Protocol (HTTP) and Secure HTTP (HTTPS) requests.
- The Network Computer supports e-mail capability using the Simple Mail Transfer Protocol (SMTP).
- The Network Computer supports the execution of Java applets.
- The Network Computer supports the TCP/IP network/transport protocol stack.

A modern implementation of the Network Computer is IBM's Network Station. This device can function as a terminal for IBM mainframes and can use the Citrix ICA protocol to operate as a terminal for Windows applications.

Numerous diskless network PCs are capable of booting from the network to run Windows or Linux. The operating system loads from the network. For example, the Sun Ray client can access Java and Sun Solaris applications, as well as NT applications running on a Sun Ray server using MetaFrame.

Net PCs

Shortly after the introduction of the Network Computer, an alternative—*Net PCs*—was developed through the cooperative efforts of Microsoft, Dell, Compaq, and Hewlett Packard. Net PCs are basic PCs with low processor power and memory that include features such as Wakeup on LAN, which enables you to "wake" computers and manage them remotely, even if they've been turned off.

Because it is a full-fledged computer, the Net PC can run applications locally and still function as a standalone machine if the network is down. This is an advantage over terminal devices that are dependent on the network to boot.

Net PC specifications include a minimum of 16 MB of RAM, a Pentium 100-MHz processor (or equivalent), and Plug and Play (PnP) compliance that supports a PnP device ID for each hardware device. The case must be lockable to prevent users from tampering with components, and there should be a minimum of user interaction involved in installing and configuring devices. There is typically no floppy drive, no CD-ROM drive, and no expansion slots. However, unlike Windows-based terminals, Net PCs do have local hard disks.

Desktop Computers

An ordinary desktop computer, including high-end models, can run the Microsoft Terminal Services client or Citrix ICA client software and function as a "fat thin client." Why should an administrator bother setting this up? Well, deploying applications through a terminal server has many advantages. It enables you to control settings and preferences and to upgrade the applications easily at the server. The terminal client runs like any other application on the PC desktop, and local programs can be run at the same time.

The client software can be used on DOS, Windows, Macintosh, UNIX/Linux machines. This solution is particularly useful if you have users who are running non-Windows operating systems but who occasionally need to run Windows applications.

The disadvantage of using desktop computers as terminal clients is decreased security. Because the computers have floppy and CD-ROM drives, it is easier for users to breach security by installing unauthorized programs or by copying data across the network to a removable diskette. However, some of this risk can be reduced or eliminated by using policies to lock down the desktop and restrict users' actions.

The Thinnest Clients: Handheld PCs

By running a terminal services client for Windows CE on a handheld PC, you can create a mobile WBT. With wireless networking technologies, these portable devices can be used to access applications and data "on the go."

Portable terminals have been deployed in hospitals to provide instant access to patient records during rounds. We discuss wireless handheld networking devices in more detail in Chapter 19, "Tomorrow's Technologies," in the "Universal Connectivity" section.

Thin Client Software

In this section, we look in detail at the software used to deploy a thin client solution. Specifically, we cover Microsoft's Terminal Services as included in Windows 2000 Server products, the Citrix MetaFrame add-on for Windows NT 4.0 and Windows 2000, Winframe for Windows 3.51, and the X Window software for UNIX/Linux. We also discuss web-based computing and the JVM.

Microsoft Terminal Services

Microsoft released a Terminal Server Edition of Windows NT 4.0 based on the integration of Citrix technology. In Windows 2000, terminal services is included with all server products (Windows 2000 Server, Advanced Server, and Datacenter Server) and no longer requires the purchase of a "special edition" of the operating system.

As described in the following sections, Windows 2000 Terminal Services can be deployed in one of two modes:

- Application server mode
- Remote administration mode

Microsoft Terminal Services Application Server Mode

When configured to be an application server, the Windows 2000 terminal server functions in the traditional thin client model. The Windows 2000 desktop and the Windows applications are delivered to client machines running the terminal services client software.

You can create user groups that are specific to terminal services and user profiles that apply only to terminal sessions. Timeouts can be set to disconnect user sessions after a set period. Users must have valid accounts on the server or the network domain to log in as a terminal client. This restriction provides security.

The Terminal Services Manager, which is on a Windows 2000 server when it is running terminal services, enables you to view and control terminal sessions. See Figure 17-4.

FIGURE 17-4
Windows 2000 terminal sessions are managed through the Terminal Services Manager on the server.

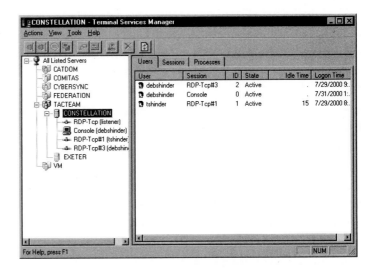

The remote control feature enables monitoring of user sessions. You can observe the selected user's activities or take control of the session and input keyboard and pointing device actions. This can be useful when troubleshooting users' problems from a remote location or for demonstrating proper procedures to users.

Microsoft Terminal Services Remote Administration Mode

You can use terminal services to connect to the server from any desktop and then manage the server from that desktop. This is a viable alternative to third-party software such as PCAnywhere.

When the terminal server is in remote administration mode, some limitations apply:

- Only members of the administrators group can log in to the terminal.
- Only two concurrent connections are allowed.

You still can run programs, manipulate the desktop, and otherwise do anything that could be done in application server mode, aside from these two restrictions.

Citrix Winframe/MetaFrame

Citrix Winframe was developed to run on top of Windows NT 3.51 Server to provide terminal services functionality. The newer version of the Citrix product, MetaFrame, adds enhanced features to Windows NT 4.0 Terminal Server Edition and Windows 2000. Citrix also provides MetaFrame for UNIX.

Because Citrix uses the ICA protocol, the MetaFrame product adds the functionalities associated with ICA. We discussed these functionalities earlier in the chapter. In a heterogeneous network environment, MetaFrame can connect to the terminal server with non-Windows clients.

MetaFrame 1.8 for Windows 2000 includes Citrix's application portal technology, which is called NFuse. It enables you to integrate interactive applications into standard web browsers such as Netscape or Microsoft Internet Explorer. We discuss this concept later in the "Web-Based Computing" section of this chapter.

NFuse also enables you to join several servers in a group to create a *server farm*. Within the farm, you can easily perform load balancing, license pooling, and application publishing. MetaFrame also features the Program Neighborhood, which is similar in appearance to the Windows Network Neighborhood and which gives you better control over application access. See Figure 17-5.

FIGURE 17-5
Citrix MetaFrame uses Program Neighborhood for managing applications and connections.

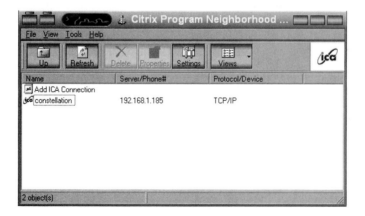

The X Window System

X Window (often incorrectly called X Window*s*) was developed at MIT to provide a graphical windowing system for UNIX operating systems (including Linux).

X creates a user environment similar to Windows, OS/2, Macintosh OS, and other graphical operating systems. It enables multiple applications to be displayed in individual windows simultaneously. X differs from many GUI operating systems, however, in that it is a network protocol; the others use programming procedure calls.

The X server accepts input from across the network and sends the graphical display back to the client. The X client software can be running either on the same computer as the server software or on a different computer. In the latter case, the client computer becomes an X terminal.

X server software and client software are available for non-UNIX machines, through vendors such as Hummingbird. Products include Exceed, a Windows-based X client, and Exceed Web, which provides web-based thin client X connectivity. We discuss web-based computing in the next section of this chapter.

Web-Based Computing

Web-based computing solutions use HTTP and the HTML scripting language to deliver applications through a web browser over the Internet or over a local-area network (LAN). Web-based applications can be accessed from any operating system on which a standard browser program runs.

A disadvantage of traditional web-based computing is the expense of developing or purchasing web applications. However, products such as Citrix offer the capability to publish Windows applications on a web server and make them available to users through the browser interface.

With Citrix application publishing, the selected applications are embedded on the web server, and access can be restricted based on user or group account. Because the web browser is a relatively small program, and because all processing is done on the web server (which might in turn access database and application servers), the client can be a "thin" machine.

The JVM

Java is a development platform that uses an object-oriented programming language. Small Java applications, or *applets*, can be written in such a way that they run from a server and that most of the processing takes place on that server.

Java-based computing runs small JavaScript applets that are launched from a server and that can be run on a low-powered client computer or terminal device. A run-time environment creates a JVM in which the applets are run. The JVM can be run on different operating system platforms. Java supports multithreading and just-in-time (JIT) compilation of the programs, which enables fast performance.

In Java computing, the code for the application is downloaded to the client on demand, where it is stored in cache or in dynamic random access memory

(DRAM). The applications can be run in a Java-capable browser, such as the current versions of Netscape and Internet Explorer. Specialized Java client devices can run a simple Java operating system and JVM, which is stored in ROM or loaded over the network.

The primary disadvantage of Java as a thin client solution is the effect on network bandwidth when the applications are downloaded to the clients. Another problem is the lack of standardization; different vendors' implementations of Java are not identical.

ASPs

The ASP model, in which applications are hosted by an outside company, is a concept that is closely related to thin client computing. The service provider manages the applications and makes them available to clients over a high-speed network connection. The ASP also handles licensing of the software and upgrade and maintenance issues.

ASPs can be beneficial to small and medium-sized businesses that might not have the resources for an in-house IT department. The option is especially appropriate for web-based services such as e-commerce. Instead of buying the software, the company rents it from the ASP. Many ASPs are using web-based computing as the platform for delivering their applications.

Another advantage of application outsourcing is the sophisticated security measures that can be implemented by the data centers and the fault tolerance afforded by their redundant hardware.

Microsoft .NET

Microsoft, as part of its business plan for the new millennium, has heavily invested in a new Internet-based software and services platform called Microsoft .NET.

With Microsoft .NET, data and applications are stored on servers accessible over the Internet. These servers can be accessed from any location and any device. Such distribution of web services enables integration of information and collaboration from anywhere in the world. This is Microsoft's vision for the future of personal computer networking.

The basis for the Microsoft .NET model is the Extensible Markup Language (XML) programming language. This language is nonproprietary, it works across platforms, and it enables the separation of data from the presentation of that same data. The goal is to distribute the data to a wide variety of devices, such as wireless handheld devices that integrate telephone, pager, and

PC functionalities. Applications software would be subscribed to as a service and delivered over the Internet. Microsoft has already announced plans for the next-generation desktop platform, Windows.NET (code-named "Whistler" while in development), which is designed specifically for this Internet-centric environment.

The success of the Microsoft .NET strategy is yet to be determined, but it is likely that in the future, networking will play an increasingly large role in business and home computing and in our everyday lives.

Summary

In this chapter, we discussed the concept of thin client networking from several perspectives. You learned that a thin client can be a low-powered computer, or terminal, that has input devices, a screen, and a connection to a server that does all processing tasks.

We discussed the advantages of thin client networking, and you learned about the protocols used for communication between a thin client and the application server. Next we discussed thin client hardware, including WBTs, Net PCs, and the network computer, and the use of ordinary desktop systems as thin clients. We also examined the use of the ultimate thin client: the handheld and palm PCs that connect to the network over wireless media and that run a slimmed-down operating system such as Windows CE.

Then we discussed thin client software, including Microsoft's Windows NT 4.0 Terminal Server Edition and Windows 2000 with terminal services built into the server products. We discussed the Citrix Winframe and MetaFrame add-ons for Windows, the X Window System, web-based computing, and the JVM as a thin client solution.

Last, we took a look at the emerging technologies behind the ASP movement and discussed the newest development—the Microsoft .NET Internet strategy—from the world's largest software company.

We discussed many exciting new technologies in the last few chapters, but we must remember that their underlying foundation is high-quality network performance. In the next chapter, we turn our attention to how we can use monitoring, management, and troubleshooting tools to keep our networks operating at peak efficiencies to take advantage of these increasingly sophisticated solutions.

Further Reading

Links to information about numerous thin client solutions can be found at the Manchester Thin Client Computing website at www.mcc.ac.uk/thin/links.htm.

A good resource for up-to-date information about thin client solutions is available at the Thin Planet website at www.thinplanet.com.

More information about Windows 2000 Terminal Services can be found at www.microsoft.com/windows2000/guide/server/features/terminalsvcs.asp.

See the Citrix website for more information about MetaFrame for Windows NT, Windows 2000, and UNIX at www.citrix.com.

For information about the X Window system, see www.x.org.

A useful paper on Java-based computing is available at www.empowermentzone.com/javacomp.txt.

For additional information about Microsoft's twenty-first century Internet strategy, see www.microsoft.net/net.

An excellent overview of terminal services is *Windows NT Terminal Server and Citrix MetaFrame* by Ted Harwood, published by New Riders.

Review Questions

The following questions test your knowledge on the material covered in this chapter. Be sure to read each question carefully and select the *best* correct answer or answers.

1. Which of the following is an advantage of PC-based thin client solutions over mainframe computing? (Select all that apply.)

   A. A PC-based server costs less than a mainframe.

   B. PCs cost less than mainframe terminals.

   C. PCs can run applications locally in addition to running them from the server.

   D. PC-based thin client solutions have no advantages over mainframe computing.

2. Which of the following is true of thin client computing?

   A. All users must have the same security settings and access permissions.

   B. Using terminals makes it more difficult to back up data.

   C. You can control or shut down users' terminal sessions.

   D. Applications must be upgraded on each individual client machine.

3. Which of the following thin client protocols is used to enable Macintosh or UNIX clients to access a Windows terminal server?

   A. RDP

   B. ICA

   C. X

   D. DHCP

4. Which of the following is true of RDP? (Select all that apply.)

   A. RDP supports printing to a local LPT port.

   B. RDP supports IPX/SPX, NetBEUI, and TCP/IP network/transport protocols.

   C. RDP enables COM port redirection.

   D. RDP enables clipboard redirection.

5. What protocol is used to manage the assignment of an X server's resources to X terminal users?

   A. X

   B. LBX

   C. XDMCP

   D. RFB

6. What is the purpose of the PXE standard?

   A. PXE (Private X Exchange) is used for communication between an X server and a Windows-based client.

   B. PXE (Preboot Execution Environment) is a means of providing boot-strap code to diskless workstations.

   C. PXE (Protocol for Extended Encapsulation) is used to create a VPN connection between a thin client and a server.

   D. PXE (Private X Window Emulator) is used to provide an X interface for Macintosh systems.

7. Which of the following is true of the Network Computer? (Select all that apply.)

   A. The Network Computer is proprietary and uses only the Sun Solaris operating system.

   B. The Network Computer supports execution of Java applets.

   C. The Network Computer supports the TCP/IP protocol stack.

   D. The Network Computer includes a web browser interface for processing of HTTP and HTTPS requests.

8. Which of the following are modes in which Microsoft's Windows 2000 Terminal Services can be run? (Select all that apply.)

   A. Remote administration mode

   B. Application server mode

   C. Local access mode

   D. Virtual machine mode

9. Which of the following is true of Citrix MetaFrame? (Select all that apply.)

    A. Citrix MetaFrame is an add-on product for Windows 3.51.

    B. Citrix MetaFrame can be used to port applications to a web server for access by a web browser.

    C. Citrix MetaFrame enables you to join multiple servers in a server farm.

    D. Citrix MetaFrame uses the Application Neighborhood for managing applications and creating new ICA connections.

10. Which of the following is true of Java-based computing?

    A. Java applets run on the server and do not have to be downloaded to the client.

    B. Java is a standardized programming language, and all vendors' implementations are identical.

    C. The Java Virtual Machine (JVM) can be run only on UNIX-based operating systems.

    D. Java supports multithreading and Just in Time (JIT) compilation, which makes it a fast performer.

Monitoring, Management, and Troubleshooting Tools

At this point in your studies, it should be obvious that computer networking—although simple in concept—can be complex in execution. Many things can go wrong, and as a network administrator, you must be prepared to detect, diagnose, and treat connectivity problems.

Following the adage the "an ounce of prevention is worth a pound of cure," you should monitor the network on a regular basis to identify and rectify potential problems. In a corporate environment, getting the computers to talk to one another is not enough. Time is an important factor in today's business world, and optimizing the network for the highest possible performance is essential. A variety of tools are available to help monitor, manage, and troubleshoot a LAN or WAN environment. These range from simple TCP/IP utilities to sophisticated third-party software packages and hardware devices.

The most important element, however, is the human element. Network administrators sometimes view the network users as adversaries—creatures who do nothing but complain or conspire to sabotage perfectly running systems. We must always remember, however, that without network users, the network would cease to have a reason to exist. In addition, the role of the network administrator would be unnecessary.

In this chapter, we discuss the basics of analyzing and optimizing performance, managing network services, and troubleshooting common problems. Then we discuss the information gathering and troubleshooting utilities included in the TCP/IP protocol suite. Finally, we look at software and hardware devices that you can use to monitor and manage your network.

We wrap up the chapter, and this section of the book, with a list of problem-solving guidelines that will help you organize the troubleshooting process.

Analyzing and Optimizing Network Performance

Administration of a computer network is often a busy, high-pressure job. This is true whether you are part of a large information technology support department for an enterprise-level network or the sole administrator of a small company's LAN.

Because there might not be a lot of downtime for network personnel, many administrators find themselves operating in *reactive* mode; that is, they are so busy addressing problems as they occur that they can't take the time to implement measures that would prevent those problems from occurring in the first place.

Although we understand why you (as an administrator) might fall into reactive mode, it still is inefficient and burdensome in the long term. Because of the disadvantages of reactive mode, you should make the time to devise a *proactive* plan for managing the network. This plan enables you to detect small problems before they mushroom into large ones. By anticipating potential trouble spots and taking measures to correct them, you will save yourself a great deal of time and aggravation. In many cases, you also will save the company a great deal of money.

Key concepts in analyzing and optimizing network performance include the following:

- Bottlenecks
- Baselines
- Best practices

In the following sections, we take a closer look at each concept and discuss another important factor in evaluating and optimizing your network: Internet connection speed. We also define some of the terms that you need to understand as we discuss performance-monitoring issues.

Bottlenecks

A *bottleneck* is exactly what the name implies—the point in the system that limits the data *throughput*, which is the amount of data that can flow through the network. A bottleneck in a network limits data just as the neck of a bottle limits the amount of liquid that can flow in or out of that bottle.

A bottleneck can be caused by a problem with a component or that component's inherent limitations. For example, if your network has 10/100-Mbps hubs and switches and all your computers have 10/100-Mbps network cards, but the cabling infrastructure is Category 3 twisted-pair that does not support a high data transfer rate, the cable is the bottleneck that slows down the network.

It is doubtful that you can fine-tune all your network components so precisely that they all operate at exactly the same speed. Nonetheless, optimizing performance involves finding the bottlenecks and upgrading, reconfiguring, or replacing the components to bring their performance up to or above the level of the rest of the network's components—thus creating a new bottleneck somewhere else. You can never eliminate bottlenecks completely; the location of the bottleneck merely changes.

Baselines

The first step in determining how efficiently a network is performing involves comparing various measurements (such as the number of bytes transferred per second or the number of packets dropped) to the same measurements taken at an earlier time. Has performance improved or degraded? What is the effect on performance of implementing a new service or feature? The only way to know the answers is to have a valid measurement against which to compare the current readings. This point of comparison is called a *baseline*, which is the level of performance that is acceptable when the system is handling a typical workload.

You should make a baseline reading at a time when the network is running normally. Don't take the measurement at the busiest time of the day, and don't wait until everyone goes home in the evening and take the reading when the network is not in use. To establish the baseline, you want to measure the network performance during typical usage. A good way to do this is to take several separate readings at spaced intervals and then average them.

In addition to helping you identify bottlenecks in the process of developing, a baseline helps you do the following:

- Identify heavy users
- Map daily, weekly, or monthly network utilization patterns
- Spot traffic patterns related to specific protocols
- Justify the cost of upgrading network components

Next we examine how each can be used to optimize network performance.

Identifying High Usage

It is not unusual to find that a handful of network users are "hogging" a large percentage of the bandwidth. Identifying these heavy users gives you the opportunity to do the following:

- Advise them of ways to conserve bandwidth
- Restrict their usage through software controls
- Plan around their heavy usage and find ways to prevent the usage from affecting the efficiency of the network

Of course, the option you choose depends on who the heavy users are, their roles in the organization, and the purpose of their heavy use.

> **NOTE**
>
> Some software applications (for example, backup programs and server-based anti-virus scans) also use a great deal of bandwidth. These should be scheduled to run during low-usage periods.

Mapping Utilization Patterns

Monitoring also enables you to map utilization patterns. You can determine not only where heavy usage occurs, but also when it occurs. This makes it easier to allocate bandwidth for expected high-usage days or peak hours. It also makes it easier to schedule network maintenance and server downtime at a time when it will have less effect on the network's users.

Pinpointing Protocol-Specific Traffic Patterns

Network monitoring devices and software enable you to pinpoint traffic patterns based on protocol and to determine what ports are being used. Thus, you can identify whether bandwidth is being used for web surfing or for playing with network gaming software.

Best Practices

Best practices are the recommended ways for performing administrative and other networking tasks in the most efficient and cost-effective way. For example, vendors of network monitoring products recommend that you save captured packets to a file when you monitor a network to establish a baseline. This enables you to analyze them later or send them to professional network analysts. It also gives you permanent documentation of your findings.

Network monitors are often referred to as *protocol analyzers*. Most analyzers are software-based, and they enable you to capture individual packets (also called frames) as they travel over the network. We discuss how the analyzers work in more detail in the "Network Monitoring and Management Tools" section later in this chapter. You should capture only as many statistics as you actually need to evaluate network performance and run network-monitoring software during low-usage periods because the monitoring software itself has an effect on system performance.

Determining Internet Connection Speed

If your network is connected to the Internet, you might want to determine your connection speed. The fact that you use a 56-kbps modem to connect does not mean that you actually establish a 56-kbps connection; it is likely, depending on line conditions, that your connection speed will be 50-kbps or below. In fact, telephone company services such as AT&T's TrueVoice prevent a 56-kbps modem from connecting at its optimum speed.

Your data throughput can vary because of factors such as the use of hardware or software compression. This compression makes it possible to get 112-kbps throughput with a 56-kbps modem over an analog phone line.

The speed of a connection is limited by its lowest-speed component (that is, the bottleneck). This means that even if your equipment is capable of a 50-kbps

NOTE

In the U.S., the Federal Communications Commission (FCC) limits the amount of electrical power that can be transmitted through phone lines. This limits a 56-kbps modem's speed to about 53 kbps, even if all other conditions are optimal.

connection, if you are dialing in to a modem that supports only 33.6 kbps, you will connect at the slower speed.

If your Internet connection seems to be slow, there can be many reasons, including the following:

- A poor connection to your ISP's remote access server, which is caused by modem problems on either end, noisy lines, and so on
- A slow web server, FTP server, or a server on the Internet to which your requests are being sent
- Congested conditions on the primary backbone lines, which can occur during events of national or international importance
- Shared bandwidth on the LAN or within the ISP's network

Occasional temporary slowdowns are to be expected, and there is little you can do about them. If overall connection speed is unacceptable on a continual basis, however, you might need to upgrade from analog lines to digital lines or switch to broadband or other high-speed access.

The dialup networking component of your operating system might indicate a connection speed, usually in bits per second (bps). For example, the 50-kbps connection we discussed earlier is shown as 50,000 bps. This might not give you a true indication of your throughput, because it measures only the initial connection rate between your modem and the remote modem. Throughput can fluctuate during a connection session.

You can download a file over the Internet and observe the download speed shown by your browser or FTP software. This is often shown as kilo*bytes* per second. There are eight bits per byte, so a 50-kbps connection will probably display a download speed of around 6.25 Kbps.

Several websites purport to test your download speed. The results of different sites can vary; you must also take into account the fact that these sites use Hypertext Transfer Protocol (HTTP), the overhead of which will affect the download speed. However, they are useful for rough comparisons. Sites that measure connection speed include the following:

- **MSN Speedtest**—Available at http://computingcentral.msn.com/topics/bandwidth/speedtest50.asp
- **Telus.net High-Speed Internet**—Available at http://speedtest.mybc.com
- **Toast.net Internet Service**—Available at www.toast.net

> **NOTE**
>
> The connection speed can be displayed as either the *port speed* (which is the modem-to-computer speed that includes compression) or the *actual connection speed* (the modem-to-modem rate). Windows can display speed in either of these formats, depending on the modem driver you have installed.

Network Monitoring and Management Tools

Many software packages are available to assist you in monitoring and managing your network. Some are included with a network operating system, some are downloadable from the Web as freeware or shareware, and some are both costly and sophisticated.

In the following sections, we take a look at some popular monitoring and management programs. We also discuss network management service providers that you can contract to manage your network.

Networking Monitoring Software

Network monitoring software ranges from simple to complex and from free to expensive. Modern operating systems such as Windows NT and Windows 2000 have built-in monitoring tools. These are not as sophisticated or full-featured as third-party products, but they can be useful in establishing performance baselines or troubleshooting network problems.

Even Windows 95 has simple monitoring tools, including Net Watcher, which is shown in Figure 18-1.

FIGURE 18-1
Windows 95 offers Net Watcher as an optional system tool.

Sophisticated network monitoring tools are called protocol analyzers. Protocol analyzers capture the packets (that is, frames) that are transmitted between two or more computer or network devices. The analyzer then decodes (interprets) the packets so that you can view the data in English (or another language) as opposed to binary language. A sophisticated protocol analyzer also provides statistics and trend information on the captured traffic.

The term *sniffer* is often used to refer to any program that enables you to "eavesdrop" on network traffic. Network Associates makes the product trademarked as Sniffer (and its enhanced version, Sniffer Pro). Both products are network analyzers.

Sniffing programs have a bad reputation in some circles because they can be used by hackers and crackers to extract usernames and passwords that are sent across a network in plain text. These credentials are then used to gain unauthorized access to systems. However, sniffers have many legitimate uses for network administrators, including the following:

- Connectivity problems analysis
- Performance analysis
- Intrusion detection

In this section, we look more closely at the Microsoft Performance Monitor and the Microsoft System Monitor. We also look at the Network Monitor. Then we discuss some add-on products, such as Sniffer Pro and Novell's LANalyzer.

The Microsoft Performance Monitor and the Microsoft System Monitor

Windows NT 4.0's Performance Monitor (called System Monitor in Windows 2000) measures the performance of a large number of system components, including counters for network components.

The monitor enables you to display values in graph format, save data to a log, and compile a report. The measurement can be viewed in real time, updated automatically, or updated on demand.

Figure 18-2 shows the Windows 2000 System Monitor being used to measure the packets sent and received (per second) as a file is being copied over the network.

The Performance Monitor and System Monitor enable you to configure alerts, which monitor specified counters and notify you when the value goes above or below a predefined limit.

To identify network bottlenecks, you should monitor network interface counters such as the following:

- Total bytes per second
- Bytes sent per second
- Bytes received per second

FIGURE 18-2
Windows 2000's
System Monitor
can be used to
measure net-
work perfor-
mance.

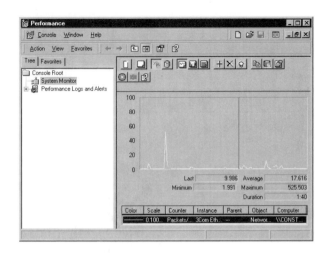

You can also monitor these protocol layer object counters:

- Segments received per second
- Segments sent per second
- Frames received per second
- Frames sent per second

Monitoring these counters helps you plan bandwidth capacity. For example, if total bytes transferred per second is close to or equals the maximum capacity of your network media, you should consider either upgrading your equipment (such as from 10-Mbps Ethernet to 100-Mbps Ethernet) or reducing the amount of network usage.

Microsoft Network Monitor

The System Monitor measures performance-related network values, but to actually capture packets as they travel across the network and then analyze them, you must use a different tool. Windows NT 4.0 and Windows 2000 include a "light" version of the Microsoft Network Monitor, which is part of Microsoft's System Management Server (SMS). We discuss SMS in the "Network Management Software" section of this chapter.

The Network Monitor that comes with Windows NT and Windows 2000 is a functional and useful tool for performing routine protocol analysis. Figure 18-3 shows Network Monitor monitoring network utilization, frames per second, and additional network statistics.

FIGURE 18-3
Microsoft includes a "light" version of Network Monitor with the Windows NT and Windows 2000 operating systems.

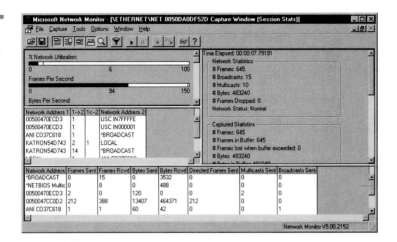

You can use Network Monitor to display the individual frames of captured data, as shown in Figure 18-4. Notice that there are packets for several different protocols captured, including TCP, UDP, and SMB.

FIGURE 18-4
Data captured by Network Monitor can be analyzed on a frame-by-frame basis.

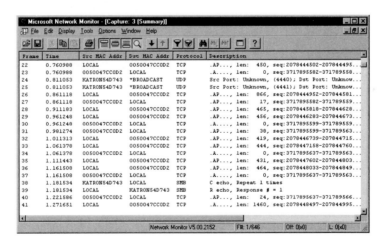

Sniffer Technologies

The popular Sniffer network analyzer has evolved into a complex suite of network tools that include the following:

- Sniffer Pro LAN and Sniffer Pro WAN
- Sniffer Pro High-Speed

■ Gigabit Sniffer Pro

■ The Sniffer Distributed Analysis Suite

The Sniffer products enable sophisticated filtering based on pattern matches, IP/IPX, or DLC addresses. Sniffer Pro includes a traffic generator to assist in testing new devices or applications; you can use it to simulate network traffic and measure response times and hop counts.

Sniffer uses a dashboard-style interface, as shown in Figure 18-5.

FIGURE 18-5
Sniffer Pro displays the capture information in a dashboard-style interface.

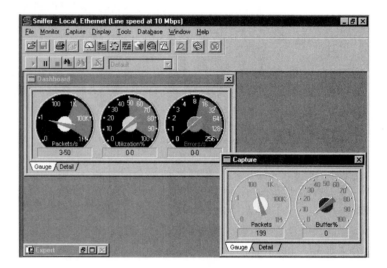

Sniffer includes built-in TCP/IP utilities such as **ping, tracert,** DNS lookup, and more. The Sniffer display is highly configurable; packet information and protocol distribution (displayed in chart form) are shown in Figure 18-6.

Sniffer includes the Expert Analyzer to assist you in diagnosing network problems, and you can run multiple instances of the program or its individual tools.

Novell LANalyzer

Novell's LANalyzer network analysis tool runs on Windows, and it includes basic network monitoring and troubleshooting capabilities for Ethernet and Token Ring networks. In addition to capturing packets, the product makes specific recommendations for troubleshooting and optimizing the performance of the network.

FIGURE 18-6
The Sniffer Pro display can be configured in several ways.

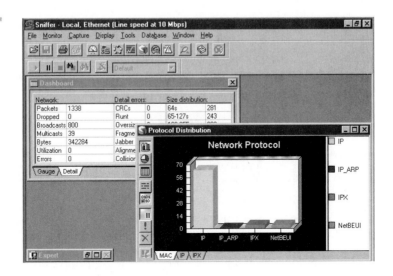

LANalyzer supports Novell Directory Services (NDS) and works with Net-Ware, AppleTalk, NFS, SNA, and TCP/IP. The LANalyzer graphical interface uses a dashboard style similar to that of Sniffer Pro, and it identifies network components by name and by MAC address.

Network Management Software

What's the difference between network monitoring software and network management software? The latter is generally more comprehensive, and although it does include monitoring components, it also enables you to do much more.

Managing network services is a large part of any network administrator's job. This is especially true in the enterprise-level environment. You should be familiar with the tools that can make this task easier, including the management features that are built into modern network operating systems and the software products offered by operating system vendors and third parties.

Managing the network includes tasks such as the following:

- Documenting the devices on the network and the status of each
- Creating an inventory of network software that allows you to deploy software and updates over the network
- Metering software to provide data on what applications are being used and how, when, and by whom they are being used
- Managing software licensing

- Remotely controlling client machines and servers over the network and managing remote desktops
- Notifying administrators of events such as failure of network components or a predefined disk capacity that is reached or exceeded

There are several network management programs (or, more accurately, suites of programs) on the market. In this section, we look at a few of the most popular, including the following:

- Microsoft SMS
- Novell ManageWise
- IBM Tivoli Enterprise
- Hewlett Packard OpenView

These products are designed with the large, multisite enterprise network in mind.

We also look at network management software that is appropriate for the small to medium-sized LAN. This software includes LANExplorer and Lanware's Network Monitoring Suite.

Microsoft SMS

Microsoft SMS is a high-end network management package that provides hardware and software inventory (see Figure 18-7), remote diagnostic capabilities, and remote desktop control and software deployment.

FIGURE 18-7
Microsoft SMS enables you to collect data for compilation of a hardware inventory by installing the client agent on target computers.

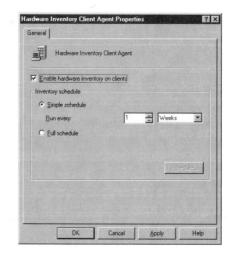

SMS also includes a more robust version of Microsoft's Network Monitor than the one built into the Windows NT and Windows 2000 operating systems. For example, the SMS Network Monitor adds the capability to find routers on the network and to resolve addresses from names.

One of the most useful features of SMS is its software distribution feature. With it, a *distribution package* is created. The package contains the information used by SMS to coordinate the distribution of the software (see Figure 18-8).

FIGURE 18-8
SMS uses software distribution packages to deploy software throughout the enterprise.

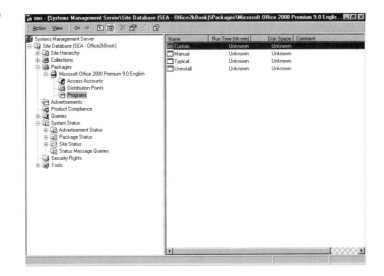

SMS uses Microsoft's SQL server for storing data, which means you can easily export the data to Microsoft Access. SMS includes support for Macintosh clients, and it can be easily integrated into a Novell NDS environment.

Novell ManageWise

Novell's ManageWise consists of an integrated group of network management services that can be used to manage NetWare servers or, with the addition of an add-on agent, Windows NT servers. Components include network traffic analysis, control of workstations and servers, and administration of network applications. Figure 18-9 shows the ManageWise console.

Like SMS, ManageWise can create an inventory of network devices; in addition, it includes an alarm/notification feature. ManageWise includes NetWare LANalyzer agent, the management agent, Intel's LANDesk Manager, and LANDesk virus protection. ManageWise includes the Desktop Manager, as shown in Figure 18-10.

FIGURE 18-9
Novell's Manage-
Wise includes
network-map-
ping capabilities.

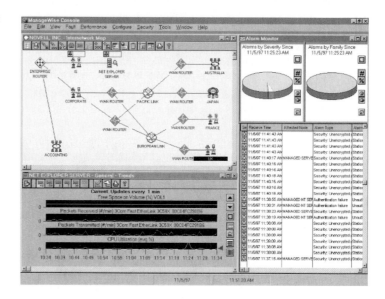

FIGURE 18-10
The Manage-
Wise Desktop
Manager pro-
vides a graphical
interface for man-
agement tasks.

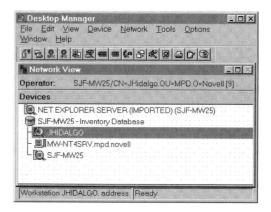

The Desktop Manager enables you to view the hardware and software inventories of the workstation, transfer files to and from it, remotely control its desktop, chat with the user, and reboot the computer.

IBM Tivoli Enterprise

Tivoli Enterprise is a popular network management package that includes tools designed to provide asset management, availability management, change management, operations management, security management, service management, and storage management. Tivoli Enterprise makes it easy to implement these components in phases.

Tivoli Enterprise is capable of providing a complete view of the network topology. Reporting tools enable you to customize the view in which the data is presented, and you can create "smart sets" that group data logically and that help you analyze the health of the network (see Figure 18-11).

FIGURE 18-11
Tivoli Enterprise enables customized presentation of collected data.

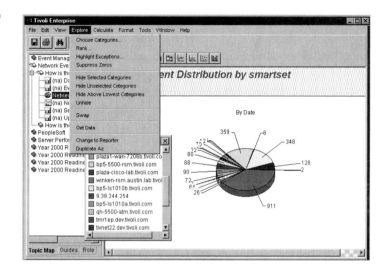

Tivoli also offers solutions for small businesses (with Tivoli IT Director) and for medium-sized organizations (with Tivoli management suites).

Hewlett Packard OpenView

Hewlett Packard's OpenView management tools include OpenView Enterprise for large-scale enterprise solutions and OpenView Express for medium-sized companies. OpenView Enterprise is designed for networks that have thousands of servers and more than 5000 workstations and that run Windows NT, Windows 2000, or UNIX network operating systems. OpenView Express provides web server management, management of Exchange mail servers, and Windows NT and Windows 2000 mixed-mode networks.

The OpenView ManageX component is a server and performance management tool that can be used in NT and NetWare environments.

Management Software for Small and Medium-Sized Networks

In addition to the network management products offered by major software companies such as Microsoft, Novell, IBM, and Hewlett Packard, numerous smaller companies make third-party products aimed at the small- to medium-sized network market. These include Lanware's Network Monitoring Suite (NMS), which uses Simple Network Management Protocol (SNMP) and that provides features such as the capability to restart services, schedule events, and reboot servers. NuLink's ViewLAN is another relatively simple SNMP management and monitoring tool.

In the following sections, we discuss the protocols—SNMP and Common Management Information Protocol (CMIP)—on which many of these simple software solutions are based.

SNMP

SNMP is a utility that is included in most implementations of TCP/IP. It has several advantages as a network management solution:

- It is simple.
- It is inexpensive.
- It is relatively easy to implement.
- Its overhead on the network is low.
- It is supported by most network hardware devices.

SNMP uses a hierarchical database called a management information base (MIB) to organize the information it gathers about the network. Software called the SNMP manager is installed on a host computer that is used to collect the data. SNMP agent software is installed on the computers on the network from which the data is collected. There are freeware versions of both SNMP managers and agents for various operating systems.

CMIP

CMIP was designed to improve on SNMP and expand its functionality. It works in much the same way as SNMP, but it has better security features, and it enables notification when specified events occur.

The overhead for CMIP is considerably greater than that which is required for SNMP; thus, it is less widely implemented. CMIP is based on the OSI protocol suite; SNMP is considered part of the TCP/IP suite.

Management Service Providers

In Chapter 17, "Thin Client Networking," we discussed the concept of application service providers (ASPs), which are companies that deliver software applications over the network. A new development in network management is a variation on that theme: the management service provider (MSP).

A company subscribes to an MSP service, which provides performance monitoring and network management. This saves the organization the cost of buying, installing, and learning to use monitoring and management software.

An example of a company that provides outsourcing of network management tasks is Luminate.Net, which provides a web-based interface for interaction with customers over the Internet.

Hardware Monitoring and Troubleshooting Devices

Most hardware devices that are used for network monitoring and management are merely dedicated computers (often portable) that run proprietary protocol analysis or network management software. Some devices that can be useful in troubleshooting network problems include the following:

- **Tone generator/locator (also called** *fox and hound*)—The "fox" portion can be attached to one end of the cable, and a tone is generated. A locator (the "hound") at the other end receives the tone, which indicates that you have the correct cable.

- **Crossover cable**—This is an Ethernet unshielded twisted-pair (UTP) cable in which the wire pairs are crossed. Instead of pin 1 connecting to pin 1 on the other end, pin 2 connecting to pin 2, and so on (as in normal UTP), pins 1 and 2 connect to pins 3 and 6 on the opposite end, and pins 3 and 6 connect to pins 1 and 2. The crossover cable is used to connect two computers without going through a hub or to connect two hubs when there is no uplink port.

- **Time domain reflectometer (TDR)**—A sonar-type pulse is transmitted through the cable. The pulse is measured to locate shorts or breaks in the cable.

- **Hardware loopback**—This device is connected to the serial port to send data, which is then "looped back" to be received by the same computer. This enables you to determine whether the serial port is functioning correctly and lets you do so without attaching a modem or other device.

- **Digital volt-ohm meter**—The volt-ohm meter (or voltmeter) is used to measure electronic pulses through cable and to determine if there are shorts or breaks in the cable.

- **Cable tester**—A cable tester is used to detect breaks and shorts, and an *advanced cable tester* can display additional information about the cable's condition and properties.

- **Oscilloscope**—An oscilloscopes is used in electronics calibration and to measure how much signal voltage passes through a cable over a set period of time. The display is output to a small monitor as a waveform. This can indicate shorts and breaks in the cable and crimped wires and attenuation.

- **LAN meter**—A LAN meter can check for broadcasts, collisions, usage levels, and errors on Ethernet and Token Ring LANs, and it can measure throughput across WANs. It also can identify devices connected to the network.

Troubleshooting Network Problems

Despite your best preventive efforts, it is inevitable that as an administrator, you will encounter problems with the network. These range from gradual slowdowns that annoy users to a complete loss of connectivity across the entire network that brings the work of thousands of employees to a halt.

All products that we have discussed can be used in troubleshooting network problems. Because most modern networks run on TCP/IP, you have at your disposal several useful troubleshooting utilities. They can be used without the need for purchasing, installing, and learning a complex and expensive network management product.

In this section, we discuss some troubleshooting basics, how to use log files in troubleshooting, and the tools and utilities included in most implementations of TCP/IP. We then discuss how they can be used in troubleshooting network connectivity problems. Finally, we provide a list of more detailed network troubleshooting guidelines to assist you in tracking down and solving network connectivity and performance problems.

Troubleshooting Basics

The most basic networking problem is the inability of one computer to communicate with another. There can be many causes of loss of connectivity, and they can be both hardware- and software-related.

The first rule of troubleshooting is to check for physical connectivity. Don't overlook the simple explanation. More than one networking professional has spent hours reconfiguring protocols, reinstalling software, and perhaps even reinstalling the operating system, only to discover that the reason the computer couldn't communicate over the network was that someone had unplugged the cable from the NIC. Therefore, before embarking on a complex troubleshooting mission, ensure that the cables are properly plugged in at *both* ends, that the network adapter is functioning (check the link light on the NIC), that the hub's status lights are on, and that the communication problem isn't a simple hardware malfunction.

Another common cause of network problems is euphemistically referred to as "operator error." Perhaps the reason the workstation can't see the rest of the network is that the user logged in to the local machine and did not log in to the network. Be sure that users are using the correct username and password and that their accounts are not restricted in a way that prevents them from being able to connect to the network. For example, login times might be limited to business hours on weekdays, or the user might be restricted to logging in only from a specified workstation.

Hardware problems are relatively simple to deal with once they are discovered. You must turn on or plug in the device and then repair or replace it if it is malfunctioning.

Software problems can be much more difficult to track down. Software misconfiguration is a common culprit. Software settings might have been changed by the installation routine of a recently installed program, or the user might have been experimenting with the settings. Missing or corrupt files can cause problems of many kinds, including network connectivity problems. Users accidentally (or otherwise) delete files, and power surges or shutting down the computer abruptly can damage file data. Also, don't overlook the possibility of a virus.

Whatever the suspected origin of the problem, following a set of steps for each troubleshooting scenario ensures that you cover all bases. The Network+ certification program recommends the following sequence of troubleshooting steps:

1. Identify the problem, gathering as much information as possible.

2. Attempt to re-create the problem. Determine whether the problem can be re-created on a different computer or whether it is specific to the machine in question.

3. Try to isolate the cause of the problem. Formulate possible explanations for the problem, and eliminate them one by one.

4. Come up with a response to correct the problem, based on your experience and research.

5. Implement your correction plan.

6. Test to verify that the plan worked.

7. Document the problem and solution for future reference. Documentation should include a log of any configuration changes.

8. Provide feedback to the user.

> **NOTE**
>
> One of the most common reasons that a user's password "doesn't work" is because of the case-sensitive nature of passwords on most operating systems. Accidentally pressing the Caps Lock key before entering the password will cause the password to be rejected. Even operating systems that do not have case-sensitive file systems, such as Windows, usually impose case sensitivity on user passwords.

NOTE

When you provide feedback to the user, be sure to make clear what you want done if the problem occurs again. If it is a very simple matter and you think the user can correct it, give detailed step-by-step instructions, and perhaps even do so in writing. Otherwise, make it clear that you're providing information only and that company policy requires that the user notify you if problems occur again.

While the first six steps might seem like common sense, many network professionals skip Steps 7 and 8. Once the problem is "fixed," they believe that the job is over. However, the last two steps are critical in a networking environment.

After spending two days troubleshooting a problem and finally solving it, you can think you'll never forget the excruciating details. But a network administrator's life is a busy one, and it's likely that when the same problem occurs again, perhaps a year later, all you'll be able to remember is that it happened before and you were *somehow* able to resolve it. Documenting the steps you took not only can save you time, but also a great deal of frustration.

Providing feedback to users is also important. Don't miss the opportunity to educate them; this is a key element in preventing problems in the first place. You may believe that the user doesn't care *what* was wrong, only that it's been fixed. However, most people appreciate information—especially if that information can help change their habits or understand what signs of trouble to look for and report before the problem becomes worse. When you supply feedback, be careful to use the level of language that is appropriate for the user's technical knowledge.

Using Operating System Log Files

Most operating systems provide a means of logging to a file device failures, failed communications attempts, and other error conditions. The information is a useful starting point for troubleshooting problems. For example, Windows NT and Windows 2000 provide the Event Viewer, which enables you to view a list of system events, as shown in Figure 18-12.

FIGURE 18-12
The Event Viewer in Windows NT Server displays error conditions.

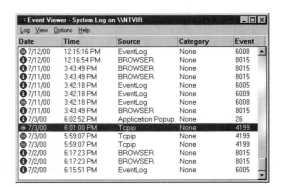

By selecting a specific event, such as the TCP/IP error shown in Figure 18-12, you will receive more details about the event, as shown in Figure 18-13. The information in this server tells us that an IP address conflict occurred, which could explain why this computer is not able to communicate on the network.

FIGURE 18-13
When you select a specific event, more detailed information about that event is displayed.

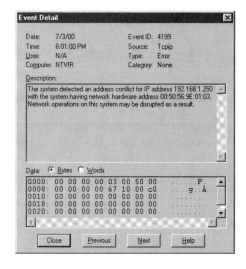

Other operating systems have logging mechanisms as well. NetWare's SYS$LOG.ERR file is a log of server errors. The CONSOLE.LOG file contains errors and informational messages that have been displayed at the server console. NetWare also keeps a log called ABEND.LOG; it records Abnormal End errors, which cause the server to cease operation or to shut down a NetWare Loadable Module (NLM).

Using TCP/IP Utilities

Although they can differ somewhat in name and functionality, most TCP/IP implementations include a suite of utilities that can be used to gather configuration information, test connectivity, and troubleshoot network problems.

In the following sections, we look at several categories of TCP/IP utilities: those that test connectivity, those used for configuration, and those that provide information that can be useful in troubleshooting network problems.

Connectivity Testing Utilities

The first step in troubleshooting a lost connection is to determine whether it is really lost. Less-experienced network users are quick to assume that they aren't connected to the server if they can't see the server's name in the Windows Network Neighborhood. Often this is merely a browsing issue; the server is not registering itself with the master browser, which is the computer that keeps track of network resources for display in the browse list. However, if you attempt to access the server by entering its universal naming convention (UNC) path, you will find that the connection is fine.

TCP/IP tools that let you test connectivity to another machine and determine the path that a packet takes to reach the destination include the following:

- **ping** and **pathping**
- Tracing utilities

We examine these tools in the following sections.

ping and pathping. **ping** stands for packet internetwork groper. This command is a simple utility that sends a message called an Echo Request, using Internet Control Message Protocol (ICMP), to a designated destination computer. The destination computer responds by sending an ICMP Echo Reply.

The first step in checking for a suspected connectivity problem is to ping the host. If it's your Internet connection that you want to check, you should ping a reliable host on the Internet, such as www.yahoo.com. If you receive a reply, you know that the physical connection between the two computers is intact and working. Example 18-1 shows an example of a **ping** request and response.

EXAMPLE 18-1 The ping Command Is Used to Test Connectivity Between Two Computers

```
G:\>ping www.yahoo.com


Pinging www.yahoo.akadns.net [216.32.74.52] with 32 bytes of data:


Reply from 216.32.74.52: bytes=32 time=110ms TTL=241

Reply from 216.32.74.52: bytes=32 time=141ms TTL=241

Reply from 216.32.74.52: bytes=32 time=100ms TTL=241

Reply from 216.32.74.52: bytes=32 time=100ms TTL=241


Ping statistics for 216.32.74.52:

    Packets: Sent = 4, Received = 4, Lost = 0 (0% loss),

Approximate round trip times in milli-seconds:

    Minimum = 100ms, Maximum =  141ms, Average =  112ms
```

The **ping** command can be issued using either the IP address or the name of the destination computer. To test connectivity, use the IP address. If you are able to ping by IP address, but you receive no response when pinging the same computer by name, this indicates a problem with your name resolution server or configuration. Such a problem might occur when your computer does not use DHCP and it does not have a DNS server address entered into its TCP/IP properties. On the other hand, when your computer is a DHCP client, the DHCP server can assign the DNS server address.

ping can also be used to test whether the computer's TCP/IP stack is properly installed and functioning. To perform the test, **ping** the 127.0.0.1 loopback address. (We discussed this address in Chapter 8, "Networking Protocols and Services.") If you get a response, you know the stack is working.

A command-line version of **ping** is included with the TCP/IP stacks of all Windows operating systems and with UNIX and Linux distributions. On a NetWare server, two versions are included: **ping** and **tping** (which stands for *trivial ping*). They are loaded as NLMs at the server console.

pathping is included with Windows 2000, but not with Windows 9*x* or NT. It combines the features of **ping** with those of **tracert** and provides additional information that is not displayed by either utility. With **pathping**, you can detect which routers are causing problems on the network and measure how many packets are lost at a particular router.

NOTE

The term *ping time* refers to the amount of time that elapses between the sending of the Echo Request and receipt of the Echo Reply. A low ping time indicates a fast connection.

Tracing Utilities. Tracing utilities are used to discover the route taken by a packet to reach its destination. Table 18-1 shows the tracing commands used in different operating systems.

TABLE 18-1   Tracing Utilities in Various Operating Systems*

Operating System	Tracing Command
Windows (9*x*, NT, and 2000)	Enter **tracert** at the command prompt
Linux/UNIX	Enter **traceroute** at the command line
NetWare	Enter **load iptrace** at the server console

* Remember that to access the command prompt in Windows 9*x*, you must enter **command** at the Run line. In Windows NT and Windows 2000, you enter **cmd.**

The tracing utility shows all the routers through which the packet passes as it travels through the network from sending computer to destination computer (see Example 18-2). The route tracing utility can be useful for determining at what point connectivity is lost or slowed.

EXAMPLE 18-2 The tracert Command Shows the Route Taken by a Packet Sent by One Host to Another

```
G:\>tracert www.yahoo.com


Tracing route to www.yahoo.akadns.net [216.32.74.52]
over a maximum of 30 hops:


  1    <10 ms    <10 ms    <10 ms   STARBLAZER [192.168.1.16]
  2    131 ms     60 ms     60 ms   dal-isdn0.august.net [216.87.128.117]
  3     60 ms    110 ms     61 ms   dal-gw-eth0.august.net [216.87.128.126]
  4     60 ms     60 ms     60 ms   dal-gw2-fe2-0.august.net [216.87.128.86]
  5    100 ms     70 ms     90 ms   500.Serial2-7.GW6.DFW9.ALTER.NET [157.130.216.157]

  6    110 ms     70 ms    111 ms   158.at-5-0-0.XR1.DFW9.ALTER.NET [152.63.100.186]

  7     60 ms    100 ms     61 ms   285.at-1-0-0.XR1.DFW7.ALTER.NET [152.63.96.205]

  8     60 ms     80 ms     91 ms   191.ATM6-0.GW6.DFW7.ALTER.NET [146.188.242.81]
  9     90 ms     60 ms     70 ms   exodus-oc3-dfw.customer.alter.net
                                    [157.130.141.74]
 10     60 ms    130 ms     60 ms   bbr01-g4-0.dlls01.exodus.net [216.34.160.205]
 11     90 ms    120 ms    110 ms   bbr02-p5-0.atln01.exodus.net [209.185.9.38]
 12     90 ms     90 ms    130 ms   bbr01-g6-0.atln01.exodus.net [216.35.162.19]
 13    110 ms    120 ms    120 ms   bbr02-p5-0.stng01.exodus.net [209.185.9.42]
 14    110 ms    110 ms    120 ms   dcr04-g9-0.stng01.exodus.net [216.33.96.146]
 15    130 ms    431 ms    170 ms   csr22-ve243.stng01.exodus.net [216.33.98.26]
 16    150 ms    210 ms    240 ms   216.35.210.126
 17    120 ms    151 ms    120 ms   www3.dcx.yahoo.com [216.32.74.52]
```

Configuration Utilities

Connectivity problems often turn out to be configuration problems. Perhaps the IP address assigned to the computer is not in the correct subnet range, or perhaps the subnet mask, default gateway, DNS address, or other pieces of configuration information were entered incorrectly. If any of these entries is wrong, or is accidentally deleted, the computer cannot properly communicate on a TCP/IP network.

Each operating system includes a utility to display the IP configuration being used by the system or network adapter. Table 18-2 lists the commands used by various operating systems.

TABLE 18-2 IP Configuration Commands in Various Operating Systems

Operating System	Configuration Display Command
NetWare	config
Windows NT and Windows 2000	ipconfig
Linux and UNIX	ifconfig
Windows 95 and Windows 98	winipcfg

Although the format and exact information may differ slightly, each utility displays basic configuration information such as the IP address in use, the net mask (the subnet mask) and gateway, and information such as DNS servers, MAC (physical) address, and more.

NetWare config. You enter the NetWare **config** command at the server console. See Example 18-3 for an illustration of the NetWare **config** command.

EXAMPLE 18-3 The config Command at the NetWare Server Console Displays IP Configuration Information

```
File server name: NETGUY
IPX internal network number: 394CEC29
    Node address: 000000000001
    Frame type: VIRTUAL_LAN
    LAN protocol: IPX network 394CEC29
Server Up Time: 1 Minute 22 Seconds


AMD PCNTNW
    Version 3.20   June 27, 1996
    Hardware setting: Slot 2, I/) ports 1000b to 101Fh. Interrupt 9h
    Node address: 005056AC01BA
    Frame type: ETHERNET_802.2
    Board name: PCNTNW_1_E82
```

continues

**EXAMPLE 18-3 The config Command at the NetWare Server Console Displays IP
Configuration Information (Continued)**

```
    LAN protocol: IPX network 66745DBA


AMD PCNTNW
    Version 3.20   June 27, 1996
    Hardware setting: Slot 2, I/) ports 1000b to 101Fh. Interrupt 9h
    Node address: 005056AC01BA
    Frame type: ETHERNET_802.3
    Board name: PCNTNW_1_E82
    LAN protocol: IPX network 66745DBA


<Press ESC to terminate or any other key to continue>
```

Windows NT and Windows 2000 ipconfig. The **ipconfig** command is used in
Windows NT and Windows 2000 to display the IP address, subnet mask, and
default gateway for which a network adapter is configured. To see more
detailed information, you use the **/all** switch. Example 18-4 shows the results
of using the **ipconfig /all** command on a Windows NT server.

**EXAMPLE 18-4 The ipconfig Command with the /all Switch Is Used to Display Detailed
Configuration Information in Windows NT and Windows 2000**

```
C:\>ipconfig /all


Windows 2000 IP Configuration


        Host Name . . . . . . . . . . . . : DS2000
        Primary DNS Suffix  . . . . . . . : tacteam.net
        Node Type . . . . . . . . . . . . : Hybrid
        IP Routing Enabled. . . . . . . . : Yes
        WINS Proxy Enabled. . . . . . . . : No
        DNS Suffix Search List. . . . . . : tacteam.net


Ethernet adapter Local Area Connection:


        Connection-specific DNS Suffix  . :
        Description . . . . . . . . . . . : 3Com EtherLink XL 10/100 PCI TX NIC
                                            (3C905B-TX)
```

EXAMPLE 18-4 **The ipconfig Command with the /all Switch Is Used to Display Detailed Configuration Information in Windows NT and Windows 2000 (Continued)**

```
Physical Address. . . . . . . . . : 00-50-04-7C-C0-D2

DHCP Enabled. . . . . . . . . . . : No

IP Address. . . . . . . . . . . . : 192.168.1.201

Subnet Mask . . . . . . . . . . . : 255.255.255.0

Default Gateway . . . . . . . . . : 192.168.1.16

DNS Servers . . . . . . . . . . . : 192.150.87.2

                                    216.87.128.131

Primary WINS Server . . . . . . . : 192.168.1.185
```

If the computer is configured as a DHCP client, two additional switches can be used with **ipconfig**. The first is **/renew**. It causes the lease for the IP address to be renewed. The second is the **/release** switch, which causes the IP address to be released so that the DHCP server can reassign it.

Linux/UNIX ifconfig. You use the **ifconfig** command on a UNIX or Linux computer to view configuration information. The configuration can be changed with this utility by using command arguments.

Example 18-5 shows the results of using the **ifconfig** command on a Linux machine.

EXAMPLE 18-5 **Linux and UNIX Use the ifconfig Command to Display Configuration Information**

```
[root@noname /root]# ifconfig

eth0     Link encap: Ethernet   HWaddr 00:50:56:8Z:01:C9

         inet addr:192.168.1.128 Bcast:192.168.1.255  Mask:255.255.255.128

         UP BROADCAST RUNNING MULTICAST  MTU:1500   Metric:1

         RX packets:154 errors:0 dropped: 0 overruns:0 frame:0

         TX packets:0 errors:0 dropped:0 overruns:0 frame:0

         collisions:0 txqueuelen:100

         Interrupt:9 Base address:0x1000


lo       Link encap:Local Loopback

         inet addr:127.0.0.1  Mask:255.0.0.0

         UP LOOPBACK RUNNING   MTU:3924   Metric:1

         RX packets:24 errors:0 dropped:0 overruns:0 frame:0
```

continues

TIP

Unlike the Windows and NetWare commands, the **ifconfig** command in UNIX and Linux is case-sensitive. If you enter **IFCONFIG** in all caps, the command is not recognized.

EXAMPLE 18-5 Linux and UNIX Use the ifconfig Command to Display Configuration Information (Continued)

```
TX packets:24 errors:0 dropped:0 overruns:0 carrier:0
collisions:0 txqueuelen:0
```

Windows 9x winipcfg. The Windows 95 and Windows 98 operating systems implement the configuration utility with a graphical interface. Entering **winipcfg** at the command line displays the screen shown in Figure 18-14. **winipcfg** can be used with the **/all** switch to provide more detailed information.

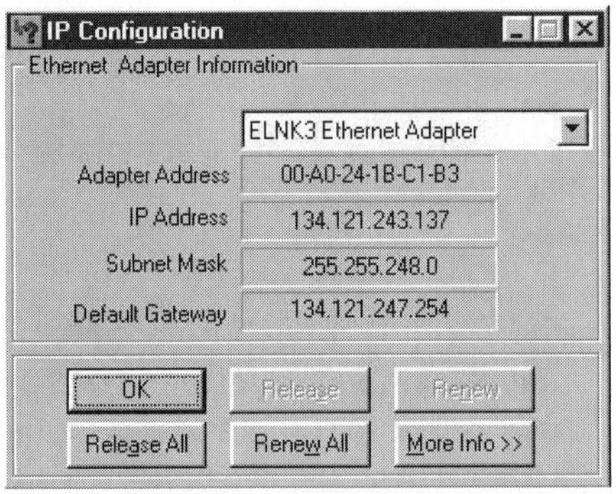

FIGURE 18-14
The Windows 9x operating systems use winipcfg, a GUI-based utility.

Other TCP/IP Utilities

Testing connectivity and checking configuration information are the most common uses of the TCP/IP utilities when troubleshooting network problems. However, several additional tools can be used to gather specific information:

- **Netstat and Nbtstat**—They display TCP/IP and NetBIOS statistical information.
- **ARP (or "arp" in Linux and UNIX)**—This is used to display and manipulate the Address Resolution Protocol (ARP) cache.
- **ROUTE (or "route" in Linux and UNIX)**—This is used to view and change the routing table entries.

Problem-Solving Guidelines

Troubleshooting a network requires problem-solving skills. Your chances of success are greatest if you use a structured method to detect, analyze, and address each problem as you encounter it. Troubleshooting should be done in a step-by-step manner.

Good problem solving skills are not specific to computer networking. Consider the way in which a doctor approaches a perplexing medical problem or the way in which an investigator solves a crime. Regardless of the field, the steps are the same:

1. **Gather information**—A physician takes a medical history and asks the patient to describe symptoms. A police detective questions victims and witnesses. Both rely on their own observations and might have to turn to books or other experts to research specific facts involved in the case. As a network troubleshooter, you should learn to listen to your users describe their experiences and to formulate good questions to help you get all the information you need to diagnose the problem.

2. **Analyze the information**—This is where your experience and knowledge come into play. Eliminate the most obvious possible causes first. If a patient complains of headache, the doctor doesn't begin by performing brain surgery, but first considers the simpler factors from which the symptoms can originate. As mentioned earlier, you should verify whether the cable is plugged in before reformatting the hard disk and reinstalling the operating system. As you eliminate possibilities, you narrow your search.

3. **Formulate and implement a "treatment" plan**—Based on your analysis, come up with a plan to rectify the problem. Your plan should include a contingency plan, in case the first attempt doesn't work. Proceed with the plan in an organized fashion. *Try only one solution at a time.*

4. **Test to verify the results of the treatment**—Even if you are absolutely certain that you know what the problem, the solution, and the required corrections are, it is essential that you confirm the success of your actions. You also should verify that your "cure" didn't have side effects that caused additional or different problems.

5. **Document everything**—Take the time to record the details of the problem and the steps you took to correct it. It is a good idea to keep a hard copy of this record. Remember that even if you have a flawless, photographic memory, you might one day move on to another job. Your successor will be grateful that he or she doesn't have to repeat your trial and error.

When you are troubleshooting network problems or striving to optimize network performance, remember to set realistic goals and priorities. Perform a cost-benefit analysis if you are unsure which problems should take precedence. Keep in mind that the "costs" are not always monetary; although your priorities can be dependent on budgetary factors, they also can be influenced by efficiency issues, time pressures and deadlines, and even internal politics.

Troubleshooting is one of the most difficult jobs of the network administrator. It is also the area in which a good administrator proves his or her worth and earns both the salary and the title.

Summary

In this chapter, we discussed the importance of preventive maintenance and how to monitor, manage, and troubleshoot our busy network environments. You learned how to identify network bottlenecks and establish baselines against which network performance can be measured.

We discussed how to measure your Internet connection speed and how to use network monitoring software such as Microsoft's Network Monitor, Novell's LANalyzer, and third-party solutions such as Sniffer Pro to gather information about network performance.

Next we looked at network management software and how it can be used to document the network's hardware, software, and topology. We also looked at how to deploy software, manage licensing, remotely control user desktops, and notify administrators of significant network events. Specifically, we discussed popular management packages such as Microsoft's SMS, Novell's ManageWise, IBM's Tivoli, and Hewlett Packard's OpenView. We also looked at both the SNMP utility included with the TCP/IP protocol suite and CMIP, TCP/IP's OSI cousin.

You learned about hardware devices that can be used to monitor and trouble-shoot connectivity problems. These devices include tone generators and locators, crossover cables, TDRs, hardware loopbacks, cable testers, and oscilloscopes. We then turned to software aids and discussed the use of log files and the TCP/IP utilities to isolate our network problems. These utilities included ping, pathping, the tracing utilities, the configuration utilities, and others. Finally, we walked through some basic problem-solving guidelines to help you organize your optimization and troubleshooting efforts.

Over the course of this book, you learned how to build a network from the ground up, starting with the physical layer. You learned about the hardware and the software that go together to make up a modern computer network. In the next and final chapter, we explore the ways in which the network administrator's job evolves and grows as the world becomes even more interconnected by the technologies of tomorrow.

Further Reading

A good discussion of sniffing and sniffer software is available at http://secinf.net/info/misc/sniffingfaq.html.

For more information about Tivoli network management solutions, see www.tivoli.com.

You can download a demonstration of HP's OpenView software at www.openview.hp.com.

A tutorial about the ping utility is online at www.hgmp.mrc.ac.uk/Embnetut/ Universl/ping.html.

Review Questions

The following questions test your knowledge of the material covered in this chapter. Be sure to read each question carefully and select the *best* correct answer or answers.

1. What is the name for the amount of data that can actually be transmitted over a network?

   A. Bandwidth

   B. Throughput

   C. Committed information rate

   D. Baseline

2. Which of the following are software-based tools that enable you to capture individual frames or packets as they travel over the network?

   A. Protocol analyzers

   B. Performance monitors

   C. Time domain reflectometers

   D. Packet filters

3. Which of the following is a protocol analyzer? (Select all that apply.)

   A. Microsoft's Network Monitor

   B. Simple Network Management Protocol

   C. Sniffer Pro

   D. Novell's TCPCON

4. Which of the following contains a full-featured, robust version of Microsoft's Network Monitor?

   A. OpenView

   B. Tivoli

   C. SMTP

   D. SMS

5. Which of the following monitoring programs uses a dashboard-style interface? (Select all that apply.)

   A. Network Monitor

   B. LANanalyzer

   C. Sniffer Pro

   D. Performance Monitor

6. Which of the following is true of SMS? (Select all that apply.)

   A. SMS can be used to deploy software.

   B. SMS is included with Windows NT and Windows 2000, but not with Windows 9*x*.

   C. SMS is used to provide connectivity between a Windows network and an IBM mainframe network.

   D. SMS includes a robust version of Microsoft's Network Monitor.

7. Which of the following uses a MIB to organize information that it gathers about the network?

   A. Network Monitor

   B. SNMP

   C. Protocol Analyzer

   D. ASP

8. Which of the following is also known as a "fox and hound"?

   A. Time domain reflectometer

   B. Oscilloscope

   C. Tone generator and locator

   D. Digital volt-ohm meter

9. What is the first thing you should check when you encounter a network connectivity problem?

   A. The protocol configuration

   B. The operating system files for corruption

   C. The server to ensure the user's account is valid

   D. Physical connectivity

10. If you are using a UNIX system, which of the following is used to determine the path that a packet takes from the sending computer to the destination computer?

   A. TRACERT

   B. TRACEROUTE

   C. tracert

   ∕ **D.** traceroute

The Future of Networking

Chapter 19 Tomorrow's
Technologies

Tomorrow's Technologies

This book has taken you from the early stages of computer networking, when just getting two systems to transfer a bit of data was a challenge, to the twenty-first century, where a second-grader can easily send instantaneous communications halfway around the world.

The rate at which computer and networking technologies have developed in recent years is astounding, and the progress shows no signs of slowing. This chapter discusses what lies in that future and the many ways in which we can expect the growing presence of networking to affect our lives. As with any technological development, it is likely that some of the changes will be positive and others will be negative, but it is almost certain that many of them will be profound.

We look at new and exciting technologies that are already emerging, as well as some that are still on the drawing board and that might never become reality. The past has taught us that yesterday's science fiction often becomes today's scientific fact. Computer networking holds the potential for limitless possibilities, and the evolution—or, some would say, the revolution—has already begun.

Ubiquitous Computing

"Ubiquitous computing"—which means, literally, that computers are everywhere—is the concept that serves as a foundation for the ambitious dreams of networking futurists. As difficult as it might have been to imagine just a decade ago, ubiquitous computing is quickly becoming a reality in many parts of the world.

In the United States, it is difficult for anyone to avoid contact and interaction with computers—although many of these systems are not the monitor-and-keyboard variety that we might first associate with the word computer. For example, embedded chips permeate our society; if you punch an elevator button, use the telephone, or drive a late-model car, and you are using computer technology.

Each day, more and more of these "invisible computers" are networked. Consider the automatic teller machine at the shopping mall. It is communicating over a vast network with your bank to complete a transaction without human intervention. Modern motor vehicles include global positioning system (GPS) technology to guide you to your destination. Hundreds of thousands of people each day connect to the huge wireless telephone networks. Grocery store clerks, for example, operate networked cash registers equipped with sophisticated bar code scanners. Children surf the Internet at school and then come home to watch their favorite television program broadcast over the local cable television (CATV) network. The goal of ubiquitous networking is closer to reality than many might think.

In the following sections of this chapter, we discuss these aspects of networking technology:

- Bringing networking home
- Overcoming the limits of the Internet Protocol (IP)
- New directions in networking technologies

Bringing Networking Home

One of the hottest new marketing ideas in the computer industry is home networking. Products designed to connect two or more computers quickly and simply in the home are being advertised as the next must-have technology.

Many of these home networking solutions use traditional Ethernet cabling. In fact, some home builders now include Ethernet cabling as part of the infrastructure, just as they include plumbing, electricity, and phone wiring.

Other home networking technologies are based on more innovative ideas, such as using the existing telephone wire or electrical wiring in the house to transmit the signal. Wireless networking is another option that is being marketed to home network users; this alternative is especially attractive to people who don't want to bother with running new cables through the walls.

By far the most common form of home networking is still the dialup remote access connection to an Internet service provider (ISP). Many users don't even realize that when they dial in to an ISP, their computers become remote nodes on the provider's local network. Internet connectivity is important to many people who otherwise aren't interested in networking their computers. It is this global connectivity to the Internet that is the basis of emerging technologies.

Before ubiquitous Internet connectivity is possible, however, some very real technical limitations must be overcome. The most pressing is the shortage of available IP addresses. The Internet is a TCP/IP network, and every computer that communicates through TCP/IP must have a unique IP address.

As discussed in previous chapters, the current version of IP, IPv4, uses 32-bit addresses. That means that there are "only" 4,294,967,296 possible addresses. It might seem as if over four billion addresses would be enough; in fact, those who designed the protocol in the early days of the ARPAnet didn't anticipate that the demand for addresses would grow to such an extent.

The world population is now over six billion, however, and it is growing rapidly. If the futurists' dream of universal connectivity is to happen, and if every person on earth is to have a connection to the global network (not to mention having one for each "smart" toaster, refrigerator, and so on), the limitations of IPv4 must be overcome.

Overcoming the Limits of IP

Plans for implementing the next generation of IP—IPv6 (also called IPng, for "IP next generation")—have been in the works for many years. The Internet Engineering Task Force (IETF) has been working on specifications for the new IP since 1994.

As discussed in Chapter 8, "Networking Protocols and Services," the use of classless interdomain routing (CIDR) and IP-sharing solutions such as Network Address Translation (NAT) has slowed the depletion of available addresses. However, these are only temporary solutions. Despite the difficulties that are sure to result from making a change of such magnitude, the Internet will eventually make the transition to the new version of IP.

To make the conversion as painless as possible, the focus in developing IPv6 has been on compatibility with the current system. The goal is to enable IPv4 and IPv6 systems to communicate with one another during the interim period before the new IP is fully deployed. This is critical to the success of the IPv6 effort. The failure of the OSI suite to replace TCP/IP was primarily caused by the lack of a coherent transition plan.

How Is IPv6 Better Than IPv4?

The most significant difference between the old and new versions of IP is the address space. In contrast to the 32-bit addresses used by IPv4, the next generation of IP will use a 128-bit address space. This would allow 3.4^{38} IP addresses. It is difficult to grasp the size of this number. When written out, it looks like this:

340,282,366,920,938,463,463,374,607,431,768,211,456

In other words, there would be 3,911,873,538,269,506,102 addresses for every square meter of the earth's surface. This address space should provide accessibility for the foreseeable future, even if every person on earth owns dozens of devices that require individual IP addresses.

How Secure Is IPv6?

The new IP supports new security mechanisms such as the IPng Authentication Header (AH) and the IPng Encapsulating Security Header. You might recognize AH from our discussion of IPSec in Chapter 14, "Protecting the Network." IPv6 also reduces broadcast messages on the network, which improves both performance and security.

Implementing IPv6

It is not possible to shut down the Internet for a few days or weeks to make the changeover to IPv6. Thus, several methods have been proposed, and are likely to be used in combination, to make the transition from IPv4 to IPv6. They involve making the change gradually, and they include the following:

- **Dual stacking**—This method enables both versions of IP to run on the same devices and within the same network. IPv6 software runs alongside IPv4 in a manner that is similar to the way in which different protocols (for example, IPX and TCP/IP) run on the same device.

- **Translation**—With this method, IPv6 would communicate with IPv4 devices by a conversion process that translates the new IP's communications to the old format. This is comparable to the way in which NAT translates private IP addresses to public addresses.

- **Tunneling**—Using this method, IPv6 packets can be tunneled inside IPv4. This would enable the new version to run on a network running IPv4 devices until the devices are updated. In effect, this creates a virtual IPv6 network over the IPv4 Internet.

The 6bone is a test IPv6 network that began as a virtual network that tunneled through the Internet. It was implemented as part of the IETF's IPng project. The 6bone is a worldwide network with nodes in most industrialized countries. Experimentation with IPv6 addressing and routing is conducted over this network.

The IPv6 Forum is an organization devoted to issues involving the new version of IP. Its web site, www.ipv6forum.com, contains a wealth of information about the next generation of IP.

New Directions in Networking Technologies

The new version of IP, as exciting as it is, still is based on traditional networking technologies. As we look further into the future, we must consider the possibility that the networks of tomorrow will be based on entirely new computing and networking technologies. Although many of networking ideas sound like science fiction now, there is serious study going on in the areas of neural networking, which is based on the way the human brain communicates with its "nodes" throughout the body, and quantum networking, which is based on the theories of quantum physics, which deals with matter at the atomic and subatomic levels. The following sections describe some of these possibilities.

Neural Networking

Neural network has become a buzzword in the computing industry; the original concept of creating an artificial neural network is based on modeling computer and network architectures after the human brain. This involves connecting multiple, relatively simple processors in a configuration that emulates the neurons in the brain.

The neural network model is built on the concept of parallel processing. Its use of vast numbers of small processors, instead of one or two very powerful processing units, is very different from traditional computing architecture.

Neural networking would provide the foundation for the development of true *artificial intelligence,* which we might consider the ultimate in computer technology. (We discuss the idea of artificial intelligence more in the last section of this chapter.) See Figure 19-1.

FIGURE 19-1
Neural networking uses multiple small processors that work together like the neurons in the human brain.

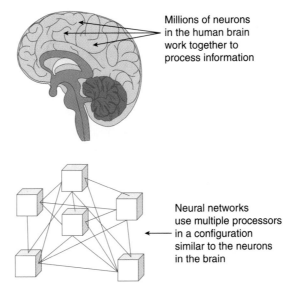

Millions of neurons in the human brain work together to process information

Neural networks use multiple processors in a configuration similar to the neurons in the brain

Quantum Networking

Quantum theory is based on the idea that the laws of physics applicable to the *macro* world that we can see do not necessarily apply to the *micro* world of the incredibly small bits of matter that make up atoms.

A basic premise of quantum mechanics is that subatomic particles such as electrons and protons can exist in multiple states simultaneously. This concept could drastically change the way in which computers process information. Traditional computers are based on binary code, and they depend on the fact that a bit can be seen in one of two states: on (represented by 1) or off (represented by 0).

In the world of quantum physics, a quantum bit (called a *qubit*) can be both on *and* off at the same time. In addition, multiple qubits can be strung together to enable you to manipulate multiple values simultaneously. Laser and magnetic resonance imaging technologies were developed based on studies of quantum physics.

Quantum theory encompasses the idea of branching universes (called *multiverses*) and paradoxical ideas such as the principle of *Schrödinger's Cat,* in which physicist Erwin Schrödinger postulated that a cat inside a box was both dead and alive at the same time. Other scientists who contributed to quantum research include Max Planck (said to be the originator of quantum theory), Werner Heisenberg, and Neils Bohr (who is recognized as having solidified the acceptance of quantum theory in scientific circles, although Albert Einstein disagreed with his views).

A detailed discussion of quantum theory is far beyond the scope of this book, but it makes for fascinating speculation about the future of computing and computer networking. See the "Further Reading" section at the end of this chapter for more information.

Universal Connectivity

If ubiquitous computing is to become reality, we must achieve a state of almost *universal connectivity*, which is the state in which every person in the world who desires to be connected to the global network has access to an Internet connection. Although it might seem impossible to achieve, we have made enormous headway toward that goal in the past decade alone.

According to a survey conducted by e-land, the number of users of the global Internet has been doubling every year since 1995 (see www.e-land.com). If this trend continues, universal—or almost universal—connectivity could become a reality in the not-too-distant future. Within the next two decades, it is likely that an Internet connection will be as commonplace in most households as telephone service is today.

Hardware, software, and Internet service have become less expensive over time. In the early 1980s, a personal computer (far less powerful than today's under-$500 machines) cost over $10,000, and a dialup connection to an online service such as CompuServe (at a blazing 900–1200 bps) was over $20 an hour. Today a high-end multimedia PC with all the bells and whistles costs under $3000, and basic Internet-ready systems sell for only a few hundred. ISPs offer unlimited-access dialup accounts for $10 a month or less, high-speed DSL or cable modem accounts that rival a T-1 line cost less than $50 a month, and numerous advertiser-supported free Internet services are available in many areas.

The Internet of tomorrow is likely to be a much more integrated part of our lives than today's Internet. No longer will we have to sit down at a keyboard and monitor and power up a CPU to venture into cyberspace. In fact, those on the cutting edge of technology don't have to do that even today.

The wireless Internet, accessed through cell phones and small handheld computers, is in its infancy but growing rapidly. Some pagers are actually tiny computers that can receive e-mail. We can expect tomorrow's Internet to be made up of a variety of connected devices, many of which bear little resemblance to a traditional computer.

In the following sections, we discuss "smart" appliances and how networking is bringing changes to family life and the entertainment industry. We also address privacy issues that have emerged in our globally connected society.

"Smart" Everything

The term *Internet appliance* describes a compact, dedicated system that runs only specific software, such as a web browser and e-mail client, and that provides an easy means of accessing the Internet to surf or send messages. Little configuration is required (or possible), and user friendliness, rather than computing power, is the top priority.

The term might take on new meaning, however, in the context of tomorrow's technological advances. Software companies such as Microsoft and Sun Microsystems are collaborating with home appliance vendors such as Maytag and Whirlpool to create smart refrigerators and microwave ovens. In their vision of the future, these common kitchen appliances will be outfitted with microprocessors and networked to one another—and to the Internet.

What possible reason would your coffeepot have to go online? Well, consider this scenario: You're on the way home from the office on a cold winter day and craving a cup of steaming coffee. Wouldn't it be nice if a fresh pot were brewed and waiting for you when you arrived? In our futuristic vision, all you have to do is use your Internet-connected wireless phone to contact your Internet-connected coffeepot and tell it to start a pot of your favorite French Roast.

Smart coffeemakers are only the beginning. The idea of smart appliances is part of a more ambitious goal: the "smart house." Emware, a company in Utah, makes networking software for devices with embedded chips. The software makes it possible to connect these devices to the Internet, and it enables them to exchange information. This can be done even with devices such as thermostats, sprinkler systems, and vending machines that use 8- or 16-bit processors. Emware has joined with other major companies, including Hitachi, Phillips, SAP, Sybase, and others, in a consortium devoted to "embedding the Internet."

The possibilities are limited only by our imaginations. Smart refrigerators have already been built that can detect when you're low on specific food items and then contact the supermarket to place an order.

Networking the Family

The prevalence of networking technology is changing family life in subtle and not-so-subtle ways. Much of the media attention has focused on the negative impact, such as marriages that have broken up because of one spouse's "Internet addiction" or online infidelity. However, the Internet has also been pivotal in bringing and keeping families close together.

E-mail, live chat, videoconferencing, and Internet phone technologies have made it possible for family members and friends to keep in touch regardless of geographic separation. The family LAN enables the sharing of files, printers, and an Internet connection. A common interest in networking has become a point of conversation and has even provided the impetus for more than one family business.

Ten years ago, no one would have thought it possible for any person—save the very rich—to monitor a babysitter or day care center in real time from the workplace. Today, it is economically feasible and has been implemented in several areas. In the future, we can expect networking to permeate family life to an even greater degree and in ways we can't currently imagine.

That's Entertainment

One area in which the Internet is already making a big impact is the entertainment industry. Legal controversies have already come up over the sharing of MP3 music files. Other legal issues concern online gambling casinos. These and similar cases are complicated by the jurisdictional ambiguity in which the web sites exist. Often they are operated in countries in which their activities are legal and are accessible from other countries in which those actions are against the law. The resolution of these conflicting laws is one of the biggest challenges facing an increasingly globally interconnected world.

Downloadable e-books are becoming commonplace, and with high-speed broadband connections, even entire movies can be transferred across a network. Major videotape rental firms are already testing pilot programs to make feature films available for download, which would eliminate the need to leave the house to rent a movie.

The Web itself has become a major source of entertainment, with sites such as ITEN (Internet Talk and Entertainment Network) and dozens of traditional entertainment publications such as *Variety* and *Hollywood Reporter* now available online. In fact, the Internet is also a driving force in the rising popularity of the concept known as "infotainment." The term refers to the presentation of information and news in an entertaining format.

Privacy Issues: Big Brother Is Watching

Universal connectivity brings with it a great many questions about the right to privacy, especially about governmental agencies' monitoring and use of information transmitted across the Internet and other networks. The FBI's Carnivore e-mail surveillance system and the British intelligence agency MI5's monitoring of Internet traffic have raised concerns among privacy advocates.

Exploitation of information gathered over the Internet by corporations for commercial purposes is another much-debated issue. The technology exists to collect information and track visitors to websites without their knowledge or consent. It is possible to obtain access to users' hard disks and the data stored there and to take control of their systems by surreptitiously installing malicious programs that might be disseminated by e-mail or by scripts running on web pages.

Many employers monitor their employees' Internet activities, and courts have ruled in many cases that they have the right to do so when company property and time are involved.

Numerous organizations have been formed that are devoted to preserving online privacy, and legislatures have formulated laws such as the Children's

Online Privacy Protection Act. This piece of legislation went into effect in April 2000. It is aimed at regulating the collection of consumer information. Some states have passed laws to protect Internet users from "cyberstalkers" who use electronic communications to harass or threaten others.

It is likely that the twenty-first century will see many new laws passed to govern the interception, collection, and use of transmitted data, by both private- and public-sector entities.

Networking at Work

In addition to raising issues concerning employer surveillance of employees' online communications, networking technologies have changed the face of the modern workplace in many ways. This is especially true in specific occupations, as we will discuss in the following sections, and the impact of networking will be felt in more fields as time goes on.

E-commerce is having an impact on retailing, and web-based advertising is affecting businesses of all types. Consumers can now shop at their leisure and make both large and small purchases from their computer screens without ever leaving home. Telecommuting and computer-dependent home businesses are becoming commonplace. From the one-person office to the government-sponsored space exploration program, networks are changing the way we work.

In the following sections, we look at how modern technology has affected governmental bodies, the legal and medical professions, and the publishing industry.

The Impact of Networking Technologies on Government

Local, state, and federal governments are increasingly using the Internet to disseminate information to their citizens and to utilize their internal networks to increase the productivity of their employees. The following sections discuss these impacts.

Providing Better Service to Citizens

Many cities now put forms such as zoning change applications and building permit paperwork on the Web in downloadable, printable format. This saves citizens a trip to city hall, and it saves the time of employees who otherwise would have to hand out the paper forms. Other services provided over the Web by local governments include the following:

- Directories of phone numbers for various municipal departments
- E-mail addresses for citizen complaints or questions

- Postings of job openings for public positions
- Maps and directions to city facilities
- Calendars of city events
- Property tax information
- Searchable databases of city ordinances, minutes of council and committee meetings, and other public documents

State governments post similar information. In addition, they post travel and tourism information, online versions of the state statutes, contact information for elected and appointed officials, resources for obtaining copies of birth certificates, drivers licensing information, and data generated by other state programs and services.

Individual agencies of the federal government provide websites, FTP sites, and Telnet access to citizens. For example, the Internal Revenue Service provides tax forms in downloadable format. A good starting point for federal government information in the United States is www.fedword.gov.

Easing the Burden on Government Workers

Technology has affected the operation of government offices and processes. Data-intensive tasks such as the collection and compilation of census information and the maintenance of tax rolls are simplified by the network of computers used to correlate the data. Members of legislative bodies, from the local level to the national level, can use the private and public networks to gather information quickly and easily to assist the policymaking process.

Computer Warfare and Terrorism

As countries around the globe become more technology-dependent, how will that affect the darker side of nationalism—the waging of war? Some predict that in the future, wars will be fought in cyberspace instead of on the battleground. Networked robots, instead of citizens, could be sent to invade foreign shores.

To the optimist, new technologies offer the possibility of warfare without bloodshed. The fighting could take place entirely between virtual soldiers on the network. This practice already is commonplace in the context of computer games. Human nature being what it is, the ambitious dream of completely bloodless warfare might never be realized. However, it is entirely feasible that technological developments could greatly reduce the number of lives lost on the battlefield. For instance, the Space and Naval Warfare Center at San Diego has developed unmanned ground, air, and undersea vehicles, as well as autonomous land robots and virtual reality-controlled "manipulators" that could be used for long distance hand-to-hand combat and other tasks.

To the more pessimistic, technological progress creates an opportunity for cyber-terrorists to wreak havoc in the all-too-real world. They point out that universal access and increased technological sophistication could result in a doomsday scenario. Hackers could penetrate the computerized controls of nuclear missiles and hold entire nations hostage. Hostile powers could gain access to sensitive military secrets. Oppressive governments could monitor and control every aspect of their citizens' lives.

Networking technology could also be part of "smart bombs" and missiles that acquire and use information in flight and then correct their courses to hit their targets. Warfare experts and futurists predict that human soldiers in the not-too-distant future will carry GPS devices and other network-connected gear.

Computer networking technologies—especially wireless communications—have provided a means of gathering information and getting that information to those in command. Such information gathering has always been a basic requirement for successfully waging war. In the future, instead of wars being won based on the size of an army, they might be won or lost based on which side most strategically uses technology.

Government Support for Technology Research

The U.S. government has been instrumental in the development and support of the Internet infrastructure since the Department of Defense (DoD) sponsored the construction of the ARPAnet. In recent years, the creation of an information superhighway that provides broadband access throughout the nation has been high on the list of the federal government's priorities.

On February 15, 2000, the U.S. House of Representatives passed The Networking and Information Technology Research and Development Act, which authorizes $126 million for federal high-performance computing research in fiscal year 2000. In addition, the Clinton administration requested $2.3 billion in the fiscal year 2001 budget for information technology research and development.

If the past is an indicator, we can expect the governments of the world to be involved in the development of new technologies and to implement those technologies as they emerge.

The Impact of Networking Technologies on Law

The easy availability of information through computer networks has profoundly affected the daily life of the practicing attorney. Legal research, once a tedious task, has become faster, more complete, and more accurate. Computers can search through thousands of pages of case and statutory law in a fraction of the time required for a human to read the text.

As described in the following sections, new technologies are changing not only how law is practiced, but also how it is made and enforced.

Information-Based Legislation

Information is the basis of legislative and regulatory decisions, and universal connectivity brings more information, more quickly, to the decision makers. Members of the U.S. Congress, state legislatures, city councils, and other law-making bodies can use the Internet and private networks to do the following:

- Research issues involved in particular bills before voting on them
- Communicate quickly and efficiently with one another
- Receive real-time input from constituents

In some states, legislators have access to computer and network technology from the floor of the statehouse. Representatives can check web polls or e-mail while participating in the legislative session.

In the future, it is conceivable that not only voter registration, but also voting itself, could take place online. Numerous security and authentication issues would have to be worked out first, but in a completely connected society, there would be many advantages to the electronic ballot box.

Enforcement Evolution

The process of making law is not the only legal area that is adapting to new technologies. The law enforcement world also has been tremendously affected, especially by the advent of wireless networking.

Many modern police departments have mobile display terminals (MDTs) and full-featured laptop computers mounted in squad cars. These are used to communicate over wireless media with other MDTs and with the network at the police station. Officers can use the terminals to connect to state and national databases to verify license plate registrations, driving records, and criminal histories. In the past, the officer had to radio a dispatcher at the police station, who in turn used the computers there to gather this information and then verbally return it to the officer.

Police vehicles now can be equipped with GPSs to provide precise location information and to improve response time to emergency calls. Another interesting use of technology that combines law enforcement and commercial interests is the LoJack system, in which a hidden transmitter is implanted in cars to enable police to track and recover stolen vehicles. We can expect to see more use of similar technologies in law enforcement efforts in the future.

The Impact of Networking Technologies on Medicine

The medical field has been one of the first to adopt networked handheld computers on a wide scale. Doctors and nurses can make entries in patients' charts, and these entries are synchronized immediately to other systems on the network, thus increasing efficiency and accuracy of medical records. Clinical references such as the Merck manual and the *Physician's Desk Reference* also can be made available on the system.

Long-Distance Doctoring

Surgeons are already performing "long-distance surgery" across a network by remotely controlling robotic devices. Telemedicine—the concept of having doctors perform preliminary examinations of patients through videoconferencing—is an exciting, if controversial, new possibility.

Physicians on the Internet

Publications such as *MD netguide* are dedicated to providing information about online resources for physicians, and there are numerous private data services in to which doctors can dial and access medical information or obtain a cyber-consultation with another physician.

Many doctors are creating their own websites, which provide their patients access to them through e-mail or live chat. The sites also are used to provide information to patients about common medical conditions, what to expect in case of hospitalization, standard medical procedures, warnings about drug interactions, and other healthcare tips. The goal is to foster better doctor-patient relationships and to open up the communications that lead to better diagnoses and treatment.

Patients on the Internet

Numerous online support groups are available for persons who need help in coping with chronic illness, both physiological and psychological. Patients and their family members can communicate with others suffering from the same conditions and exchange their experiences and information about their treatment programs, doctors, and hospitals.

Popular 12-step organizations such as Alcoholics Anonymous sponsor websites and run mailing lists and newsgroups for members. In addition, a plethora of health-related commercial and nonprofit websites exist. These sites offer those who are ill many options and a wealth of information that they never had access to in the past.

Fully Informed Consent

Not only can patients now research their medical conditions using a large store of information made available by medical schools and medical libraries, but they also can obtain information about their physicians. Numerous "watchdog" websites function as a clearinghouse for information about doctors, hospitals, and problems encountered by patients.

In the future, databases such as the National Physicians Database, which contains information about medical board actions against doctors in each state, might be opened to the public over the Internet. In addition, future computer networking technologies promise more ways in which healthcare providers can interact with patients.

The Impact of Networking Technologies on Publishing

The latest buzzword in the publishing industry is "e-book," and the growing availability of electronic books, magazines, and online newspapers is slowly but surely changing the publishing industry.

Products such as the Glassbook Reader for PCs and the Microsoft Reader (with versions for both PCs and handheld computers) make it easy to read a novel or consult a reference book in electronic format. The advantages of the technology are obvious:

- Hundreds or thousands of books can be stored in a small amount of space. The same number of print books would require entire rooms.
- Many electronic books can easily be carried from place to place.
- The creation of electronic books doesn't involve cutting down trees, and thus, they are more environmentally friendly.
- Electronic publications can be sold at a lower price because the costs of printing and distribution are avoided.
- Errors in electronic versions of a book can be corrected easily and almost instantaneously.
- Authors can more easily self-publish electronic books.
- Worldwide distribution of electronic books through the Web or FTP is fast and easy.

Of course, there are drawbacks to electronic publishing. For instance, copyright violations are easier to accomplish, and some people are physically uncomfortable with reading from the screen.

There are other, more practical disadvantages. For example, some of the handheld devices are difficult to read in bright sunlight, and if the battery dies, the book becomes unavailable. Nonetheless, some futurists predict that within the next century, paper books will become obsolete, and most or all data will be in electronic format.

> **NOTE**
>
> Many of the issues surrounding the publishing industry apply to the music industry as well. To gain wide acceptance, publishers and readers must negotiate the terms of any new access model. Consumers who are free to dispose of a book or CD as they see fit after they purchase it have difficulty understanding why they can't legally give away or sell an electronic piece of writing or music for which they have already paid.

New Ways of Learning

Technology is not only changing the way we read; it also is providing new ways to obtain an informal or formal education. Networking and the Internet are making it easier and more convenient to take a class or even get a degree, without ever leaving home.

Online universities, both accredited and unaccredited, are plentiful. Many traditional schools, from the Ivy League to the local community college, offer *distance learning* opportunities. For example, the Harvard University Extension School offers computer science courses over the Internet.

Virtual classes can be conducted through web sites, in which professors post reading assignments and host online chat sessions. Students submit work through e-mail, and audio and videoconferencing technologies enable live class participation.

The "classroom without walls" is likely to become a common learning environment in the future. This educational model offers students the convenience of studying on their own schedule instead of being required to travel to classes, and it is more cost-effective for educators who no longer must maintain brick-and-mortar facilities.

According to studies (Moore & Thompson, 1990, Penn State American Center for the Study of Distance Education; and Verduin & Clark, 1991, *Distance Education: The Foundations of Effective Practice,* Jossey-Bass), distance learning can be just as effective as traditional methods of instruction when the technologies are appropriate to the instructional tasks and when there is student-to-student interaction and teacher-to-student feedback.

Artificial Intelligence

Artificial intelligence (AI) is defined as "the simulation of human intelligence processes by machines, especially computer systems. These processes include learning, reasoning, and self-correction" (from the Whatis.com IT encyclopedia).

A computer program that can emulate the judgment and behavior of a human who has expertise in a specific topic or field is referred to as an *expert system*. The system relies on an extensive database, and it includes a set of programmed rules that define how to apply the knowledge base to predefined situations. Expert system examples include the Deep Blue chess-playing program developed by IBM to compete against world chess champion Gary Kasparov.

In fiction, expert system examples include the holographic doctor aboard the starship *Voyager* on the *Star Trek: Voyager* television series.

Computers That Think

True AI is capable of not only sorting data and providing preprogrammed responses, but also of learning from its previous experiences. In other words, the machine would be able to think and be capable of recognizing relationships, making generalizations, and comprehending nuances—skills that no computer has yet been able to master.

The effort to create an intelligent computer has intensified over the past decade. Most major universities, including prestigious schools such as MIT, have programs devoted to this goal. Military agencies (for example, the U.S. Navy's Center for Applied Research in Artificial Intelligence) are deeply involved in AI projects. Billions of dollars in research funding have been spent. Yet, as amazing as the capabilities of modern computers might be, thus far, they still fall far short of the human brain.

Computers do one thing very well and very quickly: processing numbers. However, computers as we know them today are slaves to their programmers; they cannot make decisions or take actions for which they were not programmed. A computer that thinks will be an entirely new and different kind of device.

If and when such machines become reality, it is inevitable that they will be networked to share their information. Some researchers believe that eventually, not only will such machines be joined to one another, but also that they will be joined with human beings to produce a part-organic, part-technological being.

Cybernetic Life-Forms: The Ultimate Network

Cybernetic life-forms—humans, or *cyborgs*, with electronic and mechanical implants—networked to share a "collective consciousness" is a common theme in modern science fiction. In addition, the field of cybernetics is an area of serious research in universities around the world. In fact, some researchers believe that linking body and computer might be the means by which people finally achieve immortality.

Summary

In this chapter, we discussed the future of networking and how the technologies of tomorrow will change the world in which we live today.

We started with a discussion of how the goal of ubiquitous computing is quickly becoming a reality and how the concept of computers everywhere will change the way the Internet and other networks operate. You learned about the ways in which the limitations of the Internet Protocol can be overcome, including temporary solutions such as NAT and CIDR that already are implemented widely.

We then discussed the ultimate solution to the IP address shortage: a new version of IP called IPv6. You learned about the characteristics of the new protocol and the methods for making the transition from the current version, IPv4, smoother.

We then touched on some new directions in networking technology and future possibilities such as neural networking and networks based on quantum computing.

Next we addressed the concept of universal Internet connectivity and how it will impact our lives both at home and at work. You learned about the "smart appliance" and "smart home" projects that already are underway, and we discussed social and legal issues that are sure to come up as the world becomes even more "connected."

Specifically, we outlined some of the ways in which networking technologies of today have impacted the fields of government, law, medicine, and publishing. We also looked at how future technologies might change these professions even more. In addition, we addressed the new ways of learning made possible by Internet access and how traditional educational models are adapting to the new technologies.

Finally, we wrapped up the chapter and this book with a look into the future and considered the implications of current "impossible dreams" such as true artificial intelligence and cybernetic life-forms coming true.

This book has taken you from the bare basics of computer networking into areas that are, at present, only theoretical. We close with a tenet we have been able to depend on since the inception of personal computing and PC networking: The technologies of today, as complex and sophisticated as they might seem, will pale in comparison to the technologies of tomorrow.

Further Reading

An excellent paper on IPv6 is located at http://playground.sun.com/pub/ipng/html/INET-IPng-Paper.html#CH1.

A comprehensive discussion of the IPv6 6bone network is at www.6bone.net.

A good short, simple explanation of quantum physics is online at www.jracademy.com/~jtucek/science/what.html.

For more information about Internet privacy issues, see the Electronic Privacy Information Center website at www.epic.org.

The government technology website is located at www.govtech.net.

A detailed synopsis of the Chinese views of twenty-first century warfare is available at the Institute for National Strategic Studies' website at www.ndu.edu/inss/books/chinview/chinapt4.html.

For information about handheld computers for medical professionals, see www.handheldmed.com.

A good resource for information and links related to distance learning is at the Distance Learning Resource Network (DLRN) at www.dlrn.org.

The *Journal of Artificial Intelligence Research* is online at www.cs.washington.edu/research/jair/home.html.

The homepage of the American Society for Cybernetics is at http://gwis.circ.gwu.edu/~asc/asc-cyber.html.

Parting Questions

As you complete this phase of your studies and move toward a career in computer networking technology, here are some thought-provoking questions to consider:

- How will you be using computers at your job three years from now? How will this differ from the ways in which you are using computers now?
- How will your personal relationships be affected by computers? Will they be affected at all?
- What changes, if any, will you experience in your life—emotionally, physically, financially, or otherwise—due to developments in computer technology?
- How much of your time will you devote to learning how to use computer technology over the next decade?
- How much of what you currently know about computers will still be useful three years from now? Ten years from now?
- How can you make money on the Internet, with your own private business, one year from now? What Internet business could you set up that would,

within one year, provide you with at least a modest but worthwhile part-time income?

- What job, working for a company in the technology industry, could you realistically hold one year from now that will provide you with a good living?
- Will you ever vote for a cyborg for president?
- Will you become the next Bill Gates or Steve Jobs and achieve fame and fortune as an outrageously successful information technology entrepreneur?

Chapter Review Answer Key

This appendix contains answers to the chapter review questions at the end of each chapter.

Chapter 1

1. **B.** The optical telegraph network was developed by the French in the early 1800s and was capable of transmissions of 20 characters per second. During this period, Samuel Morse demonstrated the electrical telegraph in the United States. The telephone network did not begin to be built until the late 1800s, and Ethernet networks were first implemented by the Palo Alto Research Center (PARC) in the 1960s. The ARPAnet also came into being in the 1960s.

2. **D.** Telephone communications travel over switched circuits. This means that a circuit is established for the duration of the session, but if you disconnect and reconnect, an entirely different circuit can be used. Packet switching is a newer technology, used in computer networking. Layer 2 and Layer 3 switching refer to technologies used in LANs to improve performance by creating dedicated pathways from one computer to another.

3. **A.** The packet-switching technology developed by researchers at MIT, the RAND Institute, and the NPL was designed to handle bursty transmission in which data is sent in intermittent chunks. Circuit switching is more appropriate for voice transmission, which is more continuous. Analog refers to the signaling method used, and switchboards are used to manually connect circuits.

4. **A and C.** Mainframe hardware is generally more expensive than PCs. Mainframes are traditionally less fault tolerant because the mainframe processing unit represents a single point of failure. Terminals have no processing power of their own and are useless if the mainframe is down. Mainframes are capable of processing huge amounts of data and are appropriate in data-intensive situations. PCs are less secure than mainframes because they contain local hard disks and floppy drives that enable users to load programs (possibly introducing viruses) or to copy sensitive information and carry it away.

5. A, B, C, and **D.** Networked computers can share both hardware and software components. Users can send data to printers across the network, share modem connections (with the appropriate software), access data stored anywhere on the network (if their user accounts have the appropriate access permissions), and run applications that are installed on application servers.

6. B and **C.** Fax machines can be classified as both input and output devices, depending upon whether the fax data is incoming or outgoing. Digital cameras are input devices that are used to capture digital images and then transfer those images to the computer. Plotters and printers are output devices; they receive data from the computer and create a paper representation of that data.

7. D. The Domain Name System (DNS) was developed in the 1980s, as the number of host computers on the ARPAnet increased to a level that made it necessary to find an efficient way of resolving computers' host names to IP addresses. The DoD is the Department of Defense, which was instrumental in creating the ARPAnet. DHCP is the Dynamic Host Configuration Protocol, a method of automatically assigning IP addresses to computers. DSL is the Digital Subscriber Line, a high-speed broadband service offered by telephone companies in many areas for data and voice transfer.

8. B. Telephony applications combine telecommunications and computer technologies, such as those implemented in accordance with Microsoft's TAPI (Telephony Applications Programmers Interface). The ITC is the Internet and Telecoms Convergence Consortium, which sets standards related to telephony communications.

9. C. In client/server networking, the computer that requests data from another computer is called a client. The computer that shares its data with the client is called a server. A workstation can also be a client computer, but some workstations are standalone systems that do not access network resources. A terminal is not a computer, but merely a set of input and output devices connected to a computer (often a central mainframe).

10. A. Rules by which computers communicate with one another are called protocols. These rules determine the format of the sent data and the sequence of processing. A media type refers to the physical means by which data signals are sent by cable, airwaves, lightwaves, and so on. A byte is a unit of measure that describes the size of a data file or sent unit of data, and consists of eight bits (a smaller unit of measure). Topology is the layout of the network.

Chapter 2

1. **B.** The categories used to classify networks according to physical scope are WAN, LAN, and MAN. 10Base2 is a classification used when categorizing according to architecture. IPX/SPX is used when categorizing by protocol. A ring network is a type defined when categorizing by topology.

2. **C and D.** LANs are the smallest of the network types categorized by physical scope and are generally confined to a limited geographic area, with the computers in close proximity to one another. Large networks comprised of many small networks are MANs or, more typically, WANs. A WAN, not a LAN, would typically have nodes in different cities, states, or countries.

3. **A.** An internet (short for internetwork) is a group of networks that are networked together. The best example is the global Internet. Intranets and extranets use Internet technologies, such as Web browsers and FTP, but they are private networks limited to specific users. A workgroup is a group of computers whose users often access the same resources.

4. **B, C, and D.** Client/server networks provide centralized data storage on network servers, making it easier to back up data. A dedicated network administrator is generally required because client/server networks run complicated NOS software on the servers. The centralized client/server administrative model provides better security. However, client/server networks are more expensive to implement because of specialized server software and the need to employ one or more network administrators.

5. **C.** Microsoft client/server networks are divided into groups of computers and resources called *domains*, and the server on which users log to access the domain is the domain controller. A daemon is a UNIX term for a program that runs continuously and handles requests for services. The security accounts manager (SAM) is the database that holds security information for users and groups on a Windows NT computer. A cluster server runs software that enables multiple servers to be joined in a group that works together like one computer for fault tolerance and load balancing purposes.

6. **C and D.** In a workgroup, each computer maintains an individual local security database. A user must have an account on every machine he or she wishes to access. Passwords are assigned to each shared resource; this is called share-level security. Unlike a client/server environment, security is not centralized and cannot be controlled by a network administrator, but is managed locally by the user of each machine that has shared

resources. Because of this, security is not as strong as in a client/server network, and it is easier to defeat.

7. **A** and **D.** Unlike Windows NT, which was based on a security account manager (SAM) database located on the primary domain controller, Windows 2000 domains are based on the Active Directory. There can be multiple domain controllers in a Windows 2000 network, and each can both read and write to the directory database. Windows NT enabled only the PDC to write to the security database. The Bindery is the security database used by older NetWare servers (version 3.*x*). *Windows NT domains are sometimes referred to as downlevel domains.*

8. **A** and **B.** TCP/IP is an appropriate protocol choice for medium- to large-size networks. Small networks may benefit from running on a less-complex, faster protocol such as NetBEUI or IPX/SPX. The global Internet is a TCP/IP network. There are many tools and utilities available for monitoring, troubleshooting, and administering TCP/IP networks. Despite the availability of these tools, it is more difficult to administer a network running TCP/IP than one running on NetBEUI because of the complexity of the addressing scheme, the routing issues, and the larger typical size of the network.

9. **C.** A linear bus topology is laid out in a line, with cable proceeding from one computer to the next. The cable requires a device called a terminator at each end, to prevent signals from bouncing back when they reach the end and interfering with network communications. A star network is one in which all computers join to a central hub. A hybrid mesh network has redundant links between some, but not all, computers. A Token Ring network is an architecture rather than a topology, which typically is implemented as a physical star with all computers joined to a central unit called a multistation access unit, inside which the signal travels in a logical ring.

10. **B.** Specifications for 10BaseT networks include a star topology and UTP cable, typically Cat 5. A 10Base2 network uses thin coaxial cable in a linear bus configuration. 100BaseFL networks run on fiber-optic cable. A Token Ring network typically uses IBM shielded twisted-pair cabling.

Chapter 3

1. **B.** The hexadecimal numbering system uses digits 0-9 and alphabetic characters A-F to represent numerical values. It often is used in the computer industry because it is easier to convert between hex and binary (the

numbering system that is the basis of digital processing) than between decimal and binary. Decimal is the base 10 numbering system that we use for everyday transactions. Machine code refers to the streams of bits (binary digits) that are processed by the computer.

2. A. A binary digit is called a bit. A byte is generally equal to 8 bits (in the microcomputer world). A qubit is a quantum bit, which—rather than being in a discrete state of off or on—remains in an indeterminate state until it is observed. Gig is an abbreviated term for gigabyte, which represents 1024 megabytes, or 1,073,741,824 bytes.

3. C. In the binary number 10010001, the bits for the values 1, 16, and 128 are turned on (represented by ones). Adding these values gives you a result of 145. The values that are turned off (represented by 0s) have a value of 0 and thus do not affect the result. Converting binary to decimal involves adding the values of all bits that are represented by 1s. The decimal number 256 would be represented in binary as 100000000, 128 in binary is 10000000, and 64 in binary is 1000000.

4. B. A unit of data that is a manageable chunk to be sent over the network is called a packet, or, alternately, a frame or segment. Hexadecimal is a numbering system often used in computing. Headers are units of information that are affixed to the front of a data packet by network protocols and that contain addressing, sequencing, or other relevant information. Although bits are indeed sent across the network, data files are not broken into individual bits, but into groups of bits (packets).

5. D. The error-checking component in the trailer of a data packet is called a cyclical redundancy check (CRC). It is a means of performing binary calculations on the packet at the source computer and again at the destination computer, and comparing the results to ensure that the data has not changed. There is no verification bit in the trailer. A frame is a unit of data, such as a packet, to be sent over the network. UDP is the User Datagram Protocol, a connectionless transport layer protocol that is part of the TCP/IP suite.

6. B. A model is "a schematic description of a system, theory, or phenomenon that accounts for its known or inferred properties and can be used for further study of its characteristics." Networking models are used to graphically represent the networking communication process. Protocols are sets of rules that enable computers to communicate. A process is a series of actions, changes, or functions bringing about a result. Layers are different levels at which protocols within a suite operate, and the popular OSI and DoD networking models are referred to as layered models.

7. B. The data link layer (Layer 2) is divided into the Media Access Control (MAC) sublayer and the Logical Link Control (LLC) sublayer. The physical, network, and transport layers are not divided into sublayers.

8. A. The physical layer does not add header information because it deals with the networking hardware and signaling. The data link, session, and application layers (and the presentation and network layers) all add header information, which is processed by the corresponding layer on the receiving computer.

9. C. NetBIOS and Winsock are the two popular session layer protocols. NetBIOS enables two computers to establish a connection and provides error detection and recovery. TCP (Transmission Control Protocol), like UDP, is a transport layer protocol. IPX, like IP, is a network layer protocol. Telnet is an application layer protocol.

10. D. An active hub is a repeater that has ports to which multiple stations can be attached. It regenerates the signal before sending it out to the other computers on the network. A bridge is a Layer 2 device that is used to segment the network and reduce traffic. A router is a Layer 3 device that forwards packets from one subnet to another. A switch is a device (Layer 2, 3, or 4, depending on the implementation) that sends the signal out only on the port attached to the computer to which the packet is addressed.

Chapter 4

1. B. The process of turning the binary data produced by a computer into pulses of energy (electricity or light) is called modulation or encoding. Encrypted data is that which is scrambled to protect it from unauthorized access. Secured data is protected by encryption, access permissions, or other methods. Pulsation is merely the act of rhythmically expanding and contracting or throbbing.

2. D. Digital signaling is called discrete-state signaling because the signals change from one state to another almost instantaneously, with no gradual variations. An electronic wave that is constantly changing is an analog signal, and analog signals are measured in cycles according to three characteristics: amplitude, frequency, and phase.

3. C and D. Analog signals are generally easier to multiplex (combined to increase bandwidth) than digital signals, and analog signaling is less vulnerable to attenuation (weakening of a signal over distance). However, analog signals tend to be more vulnerable to interference such as EMI, and digital devices are less expensive to make because digital signaling is inherently simpler.

4. **A.** Baseband technologies such as Ethernet use the entire capacity of the cable to send the data in a single channel. Broadband technologies, such as DSL, split the signal into multiple channels. Multiplexed transmissions combine signals to increase bandwidth, and multilink technology can be used to provide a greater aggregate bandwidth over analog phone lines or ISDN.

5. **A and D.** Baseband signaling is bidirectional; the signal can flow both ways, so you can send and receive over the same channel. Baseband is usually associated with digital signaling technologies, although it can also be used with analog transmissions. CATV is broadband technology; the signal is split into dozens of different channels. Broadband is unidirectional, although the bandwidth can be divided into two channels with one used for sending and one for receiving.

6. **C.** Dense Wavelength Division Multiplexing (DWDM) is used with fiber optic cable and it carries each signal on a separate wavelength of light. Frequency Division Multiplexing (FDM) combines multiple channels on a single line for transmission, with each line assigned a different frequency. TDM (Time Division Multiplexing) breaks each signal into segments of short duration and sends them over the line in alternating time slots. MPPE is the Microsoft Point to Point Encryption protocol, which has nothing to do with multiplexing.

7. **D.** Asynchronous transmissions are characterized by a start bit and stop bit to identify the beginning and end of the transmission and to synchronize the timing. Synchronous transmissions include a built-in timing mechanism and can use different types of synchronization, including guaranteed state change (the most common) and oversampling.

8. **B.** Citizens' band radio, police emergency radio, and similar two-way radio technologies are examples of half-duplex transmission because the signal can go in both directions, but not at the same time. Traditional television broadcasts are simplex, in which the signal goes only in one direction. Regular telephone communications and DSL technologies are full-duplex transmissions, in which the signal can go in both directions simultaneously.

9. **A.** UTP is the most vulnerable to EMI, although the twisting of the wire pairs inside the cable helps to reduce that vulnerability. Coaxial cable and STP both have shielding that protects against EMI, although all copper

cable is susceptible to interference to some degree. Fiber-optic cable, because it uses light pulses instead of pulses of electricity to carry a signal, is not vulnerable to EMI and is the best choice in an environment in which there is a great deal of electromagnetic energy.

10. **B.** CSMA/CD is the access method specified for Ethernet networks. CSMA/CA is used on AppleTalk networks. Token passing is the access method used on Token Ring networks, and demand priority is an access method used by the infrequently implemented 100VG-AnyLAN network.

Chapter 5

1. **B.** 802.3 specifications address the CSMA/CD access method used by Ethernet networks. Token Ring and FDDI are based on the 802.5 specifications, and ARCnet is loosely mapped to the 802.4 specifications. The 802 Committee of the Institute of Electrical and Electronics Engineers developed the IEEE 802 standards to define standards for the physical and data link layer protocols.

2. **A.** CSMA/CD is the access method used by Ethernet networks. In this method, a computer with data to transmit "listens" to the wire and sends the data if there is no traffic on the cable. If another computer does the same action simultaneously, both sense the collision, and each waits a random amount of time and then resends the data. CSMA/CA is used by AppleTalk networks; Token Passing is used by Token Ring, ARCnet, and FDDI, and demand priority is used by 100VG-AnyLAN.

3. **A.** The specifications for 10Base2 Ethernet networks, using thin coaxial cable, limit the number of nodes on a cable segment (length of cable between repeaters) to 30. A node is a computer or other network device that transmits and receives data across the network.

4. **C.** BNC bayonet-style connectors are used with thin coax cable in Ethernet 10Base2 networks. Unshielded twisted-pair (UTP) cable in a 10BaseT network uses RJ connectors, usually RJ-45. Thick coax cable in a 10Base5 network uses 15-pin AUI connectors to connect to an external transceiver, which in turn is connected to the cable through a "vampire tap." Fiber optic cable uses SMA or FSMA connectors.

5. **D.** The term standard Ethernet refers to 10Base5, or thicknet networks. Although thicknet is less popular than other Ethernet architectures today (UTP-based architectures being the most widely used), 10Base5 was the

"standard" when Ethernet was developed in the 1960s, and thus it is still referred to as such in the industry.

6. **B.** 10Base5 specifications for networks using thick coax limit the segment length to 500 meters, as compared to the 100-meter limitation for 10BaseT and the 185-meter limitation for 10Base2. This greater segment distance makes thicknet an appropriate choice for "backbone" segments. The IEEE cable length specifications are given in meters. In U.S. measurements, the 10Base5 specification is equivalent to 1640 feet.

7. **B and C.** Token Ring networks can run at 4 or 16 Mbps (depending on the network card and hub). The Token Ring hub, or concentrator, is called a multistation access unit (MAU or MSAU). Token Ring is an active topology, in that each station regenerates the signal before passing it around the ring. Like Ethernet, Token Ring is a baseband architecture; the entire bandwidth of the cable is used to transmit one signal.

8. **C.** The monitor computer sends a frame called a beacon, and each computer anticipates receipt of the beacon. If it fails to arrive when expected, the computer notifies the monitor of its own address and that of its nearest active upstream neighbor (NAUN). The Token Ring MSAU can then reconfigure the signal path to exclude the nonfunctioning station, and communications are restored to the rest of the ring. The token is a signal that circulates, for which a station must wait before it can transmit data. The data frame contains the information being transmitted.

9. **B.** LocalTalk is the original data link layer protocol, designed for quick and easy (but slow) networking of Macintosh computers through cables attached to their printer ports. LocalTalk transmits at only 230.4 Kbps, and it has been replaced by Ethernet on many Macintosh networks. EtherTalk is a protocol that enables Macintoshes running the AppleTalk upper-layer protocols to participate on Ethernet coax cable. TokenTalk enables Macintoshes to connect to Token Ring networks.

10. **A.** Standard ARCnet is relatively slow, running at only 2.5 Mbps. Of the popular networking architectures, only LocalTalk is slower. An enhanced version of ARCnet was developed to overcome this limitation; ARCnet Plus runs at 20 Mbps, twice the speed of standard Ethernet and faster than "high speed" Token Ring networks that operate at 16 Mbps.

Chapter 6

1. A, C, and **D.** The I/O address, IRQ, and virtual com port must commonly be configured on non-Plug and Play internal modems. These settings can be changed through jumpers, dip switches, or software. IP addresses can be assigned to a modem connection (the external network adapter) when the computer participates on a TCP/IP network, but this is not a hardware configuration.

2. B. They are examples of customer premises equipment. The CSU/DSU is used to provide an interface to a T-carrier line. The CSU receives and transmits signals to and from the WAN line. The DSU manages line control, timing errors, and signal regeneration.

3. A. The named technologies are all circuit-switching technologies. In a circuit-switched network, a connection is established (a circuit) over which the data is sent for the duration of the session. In a packet-switched network, individual packets might take different routes to reach the destination. Switched 56 is a type of packet switched network. All the technologies named are WAN technologies.

4. B, C, and **E.** ISDN lines must be installed by the telephone company and are generally more expensive than PSTN analog telephone lines. Special equipment that handles digital transmission must be installed at the telephone company's CO that services the location, and an ISDN terminal adapter (sometimes called an ISDN modem) must be installed at the customer's premise. ISDN can transfer both voice and data. With a BRI line consisting of two B (data) channels, voice calls can be placed or received over one channel while data is simultaneously being transferred over the other.

5. C. The star topology is the most scalable because adding additional nodes to the network does not require reconfiguring the network. The ring topology is more difficult to "grow" because adding a node means interrupting the connection between two existing nodes. The point-to-point topology, by definition, cannot be expanded.

6. B. The first packet-switching technology was X.25. Frame Relay is a newer technology that was passed on the X.25 scheme, adding improvements. ATM is a more recent packet switching technology that provides high speed. DSL is a circuit-switched technology.

7. A, C, and **D.** Frame Relay offers higher performance than X.25, up to 45 Mbps. It does not include the extensive error checking used by X.25, which is not necessary because it uses more reliable digital signaling. X.25 used analog. Both Frame Relay and X.25 use packet switching.

8. **B, C, and D.** The 53 byte fixed cell length is a distinguishing characteristic of ATM. It is a high-speed technology that is capable of transferring video, voice, and data simultaneously, using predefined circuits.

9. **D.** OC-SONET rated OC-48 has a top transmission rate of 2.488 Gbps. ADSL implementations range from 384 Kbps to about 6 Mbps. T-1 has a top transmission rate of 1.544 Mbps. ISDN BRI has a maximum rate of 128 Kbps (two 64 Kbps channels multilinked).

10. **C and D.** NAT uses a table to map multiple private internal IP addresses to one or more external public addresses, thus avoiding the necessity of registered public address for every computer on the internal network. However, NAT cannot be used with encryption technologies that do not allow changing of the IP header, and NAT is not compatible with certain applications.

Chapter 7

1. **C.** The NIC is the most basic hardware component. A network interface is required for every computer that connects to the network. Most NICs fit into a card slot using an ISA/EISA, PCI, or PCMCIA (PC card) bus. Some NICs are built into the computer's motherboard. A router is used to forward packets from one network to another. Cable is the media used for traditional networks; however, wireless networks do not require cable. A hub connects computers when a star topology is used.

2. **B.** Networks using thicknet cable in compliance with the 10Base5 specifications use an external transceiver that connects to the NIC through an AUI connector and that connects to the thick coax cable with vampire taps. 10Base2 (thinnet) and 10BaseT (UTP) networks use NICs that have the transceiver built onto the card.

3. **A.** IRQ 5 is often used for sound cards; however, this computer's sound card is set to use IRQ 10. IRQ 7 is the default IRQ for the primary parallel (printer) port (LPT1), which is in use. IRQ 12 is the default IRQ for a PS/2 mouse. The computer's primary IDE controller uses IRQ 14. There is no mention of a secondary parallel port in use on this computer; thus, IRQ 5 should be free for the NIC.

4. **D.** The term for the space between floors is the plenum, and special plenum grade cable, made of Teflon or similar fire-resistant material (instead

of Polyvinyl chloride, the material of which the covering of regular cable is made), is required by most fire or building codes when cable is installed in this area.

5. **B.** RG-58 A/U, thin coax with a stranded wire core, is specified for 10Base2 networks. RG-58 /U is similar in appearance, but has a solid copper core and does not meet 10Base2 specifications. RG-58 C/U is the military-grade equivalent to RG-58 A/U and has a thicker outer covering. It can be used for 10Base2 networks, but it is not the typical choice. RG-59 is cable TV (CATV) coax.

6. **C.** Thick coax (thicknet) is used on 10Base5 networks, which use external transceivers that are connected to the NICs through AUI connectors and to the cables through vampire taps. UTP, STP, and thin coax use NICs that have transceivers built into the adapter card.

7. **D.** Crosstalk is the leaking of signal from one wire to another when wires are in close proximity. Twisting the wires around one another diminishes or prevents this. The degree of protection from crosstalk is increased as the number of twists per foot increases. RFI is radio frequency interference, which comes from radio signals. Attenuation is signal loss over distance. Distortion is any lack of fidelity in reception or any undesired change in the waveform of a signal.

8. **A.** Ethernet Cat 5 cabling generally uses RJ-45 modular plugs and jacks, which resemble telephone plugs and jacks (RJ-11) except that they are slightly larger. BNC connectors are used with thin coax cables on 10Base2 networks. An F connector is used to join two lengths of cable TV coax.

9. **B** and **D.** Fiber-optic cable is more secure than copper cable because it is more difficult for intruders to tap into the cable and intercept signals because the signals are light instead of electrical impulses. Single-mode fiber-optic cable is faster than multimode because of the dispersion caused by light pulses arriving at the end of the cable at different times. Fiber-optic cable is more difficult to work with and install than copper, and its installation requires special training because tiny strands of glass or plastic must be perfectly aligned. Fiber-optic cable is less susceptible to attenuation than is copper cable, and thus can travel longer distances.

10. **C.** A repeater is used to connect two cable segments and repeat (regenerate) the signal as it is passed from one segment to the other. This counters the effect of attenuation and lengthens the distance of the network. Barrel connectors, patch panels, and passive hubs are simple connection devices

that do not regenerate the signal. Active hubs, however, function as multi-port repeaters.

Chapter 8

1. **C.** NetBEUI is a low-overhead, high-performance protocol that is simple to set up. Because it does not use logical addressing, it cannot be routed to other networks/subnets. It is used on small workgroups running Microsoft operating systems.

2. **A.** IPX calls the part of the address that identifies the device and incorporates the MAC address a node number. *It is denoted in hexadecimal notation and is used, in conjunction with the network number, to route an IPX packet to the proper destination.*

3. **A and D.** Both TCP and SPX operate at the transport layer of the OSI reference model and provide the establishment of a connection before sending data. UDP is a transport-layer connectionless protocol, and IP and IPX are network-layer connectionless protocols.

4. **B and C.** An IP address is a 32-bit binary number, made up of four octets containing eight bits each. Although the computer processes them in binary, IP addresses are commonly notated in dotted-decimal format.

5. **C.** Classful addressing enables 16,384 Class B networks, each of which can have 65,535 host computers. There can be 126 Class A networks with over 16 million hosts each and 2,097,152 Class C networks limited to 254 host computers.

6. **B.** In an unsubnetted Class C network, the first three octets identify the network. The network ID bits are "masked" by 1s, resulting in eight ones for each of the three octets: 11111111.11111111.11111111. In decimal, that translates to 255.255.255. The host ID bits (the last octet) are "open" as indicated by 0s: 00000000. In decimal, this translates to 0. Thus the decimal notation for the subnet mask is 255.255.255.0.

7. **B.** The high-order bits in a Class B address are 10. This means that the decimal range for the first octet is 128–191. Class A addresses use the 0–127 range, Class C addresses use the 192–223 range, and Class D addresses use the 224–239 range.

8. **C.** CIDR provides for more efficient use of IP addresses by doing away with the old address classes and enabling network sizes that fall among the Class A, B, and C designations.

9. **D.** DHCP provides for automatic assignment of IP addresses to computers configured as DHCP clients, through a four-step lease negotiation process (discover, offer, request, and acknowledgment).

10. **C.** ARP resolves IP addresses to physical hardware (MAC) addresses. The ARP command-line utility enables you to view the cache of addresses that have been resolved, delete entries, and add permanent IP-to-MAC mappings.

Chapter 9

1. **B.** The connection points that make up the backbones are called nodes. Hosts are individual computers on the Internet. Subnets are parts into which networks are divided. Servers are computers that share resources with other computers across a network.

2. **D.** The NAPs are the locations where access providers are connected together through switching facilities. ISPs are companies that connect to the Internet backbone and that provide dial-in or dedicated access through their network to customers. vBNS is part of the Internet2 Project, a joint effort of U.S. universities and the U.S. government that is aimed at developing a high-speed backbone that can be used as a test bed for deployment of new technologies. Five supercomputer centers are connected to make up the vBNS.

3. **C.** Hypertext refers to the ability to embed links into the document to other text files, graphics, sounds, and so on. Hypertext files can be, but do not have to be, located on a web server and accessed through a URL address. (HTML Help is an example of hypertext.) Hypertext files can, and often do, contain embedded graphics.

4. **C.** http://bigserver.acme.com/ has the correct syntax to access the default web page on a web server named bigserver in the second-level domain called acme that has been registered in the top-level domain .com. Although many web servers are named "www," this is *not required*. The HTTP protocol is used in this example; HTML is the markup language in which pages are encoded.

5. **B.** Portals are websites designed to serve as starting points for web users. A metasearch engine combines results of multiple search engines, and a default gateway is the IP address of a router on a TCP/IP network. Hyperlinks are pointers to other files that are encoded into HTML documents.

6. D. IMAP is a sophisticated service that allows users to view and manipulate messages without downloading them to the local machine. SMTP is the protocol used for sending mail across the Internet. SNMP is a monitoring, information gathering, and management utility included in the TCP/IP suite. POP is used to download e-mail messages from a mail server to an e-mail client program on a user's computer.

7. C. NNTP (sometimes referred to as Usenet) is used for hosting and accessing newsgroups. Software such as Listserv and Majordomo is used to manage mailing lists. Telnet is the protocol used to connect to a remote computer to view files and run applications. NetWare 5.*x* is capable of running on TCP/IP without IPX/SPX.

8. A. The IRC system allows users to connect to IRC servers and sign on to "channels," in which they can conduct text-based real-time discussions with one or more other users. Telnet is used to connect to a remote computer and view its files or run applications. IGMP is used in multicast communications. FTP is used to download files from other computers or upload files from your computer to other computers across the network.

9. B. The H.323 standard of the ITU pertains to multimedia communications over IP and IPX, including videoconferencing technologies, that do not provide QoS.

10. A and D. RIP for IP is a distance-vector, dynamic routing protocol; it is suitable for small and medium-sized networks, but it is less efficient and scalable than OSPF, which is a link-state dynamic routing protocol that divides the network into areas.

Chapter 10

1. C. Client/server applications use a front end, which is a user application on a client machine, to request data from a back end, which is a database server. Sorting and processing of the query takes place on the server and only the results are returned to the client.

2. B. A resource, such as a file, folder, or printer, that is made available to others across the network is called a shared resource, or share.

3. A. User-level security, which requires a user to remember only one login password, is more secure and easier to administer than share-level security, in which a separate password is assigned to every shared resource.

4. **A, C, and D.** The master administrative account is created during installation of the operating system, and it is used to log in to the operating system for the first time. Far from having only limited access, the master account has full access to all network resources; this is why it should be given a strong password. The administrative account is used when you wish to perform management tasks such as creating new user accounts.

5. **A and D.** Uppercase and lowercase alpha and numeric characters are generally acceptable in user account names, but spaces and symbols, such as +, should be avoided. Some operating systems restrict the number of characters that can be used, but an eight-character name is recognizable even on MS-DOS machines.

6. **C.** Windows domains are collections of users, computers, and resources over which an administrator exercises administrative authority. Domains in Windows 2000 (but not in Windows NT) can be organized into hierarchical structures called trees, and trees can be grouped into forests.

7. **B.** User Manager for Domains is the tool used to create domain user accounts on a Windows NT 4.0 domain controller. A tool called User Manager is available on Windows NT 4.0 Workstation and standalone server machines, but it is used for creating local user accounts that are valid only on that particular machine.

8. **C.** Active Directory is Microsoft's new directory service upon which Windows 2000 networks are built. AD is similar in some ways to NDS, Novell's directory services, and both are compatible with LDAP standards.

9. **D.** NetWare 3.x servers use a flat database called the bindery, which stores security information for that server on which it resides. It is not replicated to other servers on the network. NetWare 4.x and above uses NDS, a hierarchical distributed database that allows access through a single user account to all resources on the network.

10. **A and C.** UNIX operating systems are case-sensitive, unlike Windows and NetWare. Service services, such as the print server service, are called daemons. The master administrative account in UNIX is called root, and groups in a UNIX system work much like local groups in Windows NT 4.0, which are valid only on that server.

Chapter 11

1. **C.** A directory is a database that can contain various types of information. In an object-oriented system, the directory contains objects, and each object has attributes.

2. B. When the data is spread across two or more physical machines on the network, the database is distributed.

3. B and C. Windows NT's NTDS and the Novell bindery used for NetWare 3.*x* are flat databases; Novell's NDS and Microsoft's Windows 2000 Active Directory are hierarchical.

4. D. A contiguous namespace is one in which the child objects have the parent object's name as part of their own name. A Windows 2000 domain tree is an example of a contiguous namespace.

5. C. The OSI X.500 standards specify a directory built on a DSA, which manages the directory data, a DUA, which gives users access to the directory services, and a DIB, which is where directory information is stored.

6. C. The distinguished name (DN) is the means of identifying the full path to a directory object, using attributes such as DC (DomainComponent-Name), OU (OrganizationalUnit) and CN (CommonName).

7. A. NDS has two basic object types: container objects (which can contain other objects) and leaf objects, which represent the resources at the end of the branch.

8. D. The Shared System Volume (SysVol) file stores the scripts and group policy objects that are used by administrators to control the user environment and restrict user rights.

9. B. Within a Windows 2000 domain tree, all domains share two-way transitive trust relationships. This means that users belonging to one domain can access resources in another domain, provided that the user account has the proper access permissions.

10. C. The ACL is the accumulation of all access permissions that are assigned to an Active Directory object.

Chapter 12

1. A and B. Text-based operating systems such as DOS and UNIX are generally faster than graphical operating systems such as Windows because there is less system overhead and fewer system resources being used. However, graphical interfaces are easier for most users to learn and use, and graphical interfaces provide for multitasking, which is the running of more than one application at a time.

2. C. The **winipcfg** command invokes a graphic display of TCP/IP configuration information on Windows 95 and Windows 98 computers. **ifconfig** is used for the same purpose on Linux and UNIX computers; **ipconfig** is used on Windows NT and 2000 machines, and **config** is the command used on NetWare servers running TCP/IP.

3. D. The suffix, which can be used to identify the file type, is called the file extension. File forks are the two parts of a Macintosh file. File tables are databases maintained by file systems to keep track of where data that makes up each file is located physically on the disk.

4. A. Unlike FAT32 and NTFS, FAT16 can be used by all Microsoft operating systems, including DOS, Windows 3.*x*, Windows 9*x*, Windows NT, and Windows 2000. FAT16 does not offer the file-level security available in NTFS, and it is less reliable because it does not include features such as hot fixing. Although FAT16 has less overhead and thus might perform better on very small partitions, FAT32 and NTFS provide better performance under most circumstances.

5. D. NTFS supports partitions up to 16 exabytes, or approximately 16 billion bytes. 2 GB is the partition limit imposed by DOS, and FAT16 cannot use partitions over 4 GB, regardless of the operating system. 4 TB is the maximum partition size supported by FAT32.

6. C. UNIX represents the root directory as a forward slash (/) and does not use the drive letter as part of the path. Each level of the hierarchy is separated by forward slashes, instead of the backslashes (\)used in FAT and NTFS file systems.

7. B. The UNIX file system uses an internal number called an i-node to identify each file or directory and maps the number to the location of the data on the physical disk. The other file systems named do not use this system, although the Macintosh HFS's catalog records function in a manner similar to i-node mapping.

8. C. CSNW is included with Windows NT Workstation, although it is not installed by default. Once installed, it enables you to log in to and access files on a NetWare server. Gateway Services for NetWare is installed on an NT Server to enable its clients to access NetWare files in an indirect manner. File and Print Services for NetWare is a product that can be purchased from Microsoft to enable NetWare clients to access files on an NT or Windows 2000 server. Although an IPX/SPX compatible protocol must be used to communicate with the NetWare server, NWLink is installed automatically when you install CSNW; thus you do not have to install it explicitly.

9. A. The SMB (Server Message Block) file system, based on Samba code, can be installed on Linux to provide access to Microsoft resources. NCP is the NetWare Core Protocol, the file sharing protocol used by NetWare servers. Although the Linux machine can communicate on the network using TCP/IP as the network transport protocol, it cannot access the Microsoft server's files without an application layer SMB client. The Point to Point Protocol (PPP) is used for establishing a link over a dialup connection and is not a file sharing protocol.

10. C. OS/2 uses the High Performance File System (it can also use FAT16). Windows NT 3.*x* included supported for HPFS, but later versions of NT and other Microsoft operating systems do not.

Chapter 13

1. C. The file-sharing protocol is also referred to as the core protocol because sharing of resources is at the core of computer networking; we connect computers in networks so that they can share resources. The network/transport protocol is the set of protocols (called the protocol stack) used for LAN/WAN communications. The link protocol (or data link protocol) is used to establish the link between computers and this term is often used in relation to remote access WAN protocols such as Point-to-Point Protocol (PPP) and Serial Line Interface Protocol (SLIP). Layer 2 is merely the data link layer of the OSI model, so Layer 2 protocols are link protocols.

2. B. Like TCP/IP (and unlike NetBEUI), the IPX/SPX protocol is routable. Although it is often associated with NetWare networks, it also can be used on Microsoft networks, and it is sometimes implemented on internal networks for security purposes. NetWare 5.*x* is the first version that can run on pure IP and that does not require IPX/SPX; however, the latter is still supported and must be used if there are older NetWare servers on the network with which the 5.x machines must communicate. IPX/SPX is faster and easier to configure than TCP/IP, although slower and more difficult to set up than NetBEUI.

3. A and **D.** The Network Driver Interface Specification (NDIS), which was devised by Microsoft, and the Open Driver Interface (ODI), enable binding of multiple protocols to a single adapter or for a single protocol to be bound to multiple adapters. Winsock is an application programming interface (API) and the Transport Driver Interface (TDI) is a boundary layer in the Windows NT networking model.

4. B. The Server Message Block (SMB) protocol is used for file sharing on Microsoft networks. SMB client and server software also is available for other network operating systems to provide integration with Microsoft computers. NCP is the NetWare Core Protocol used on Novell networks. NFS is the Network File System used for file sharing by UNIX machines. DLC is the Data Link Control protocol that can be used for communication with network-connected laser printers and IBM mainframes.

5. B and **D.** GSNW is included with Windows NT and Windows 2000 Server products and is installed on the Windows server to enable Microsoft clients to access resources on a NetWare server through the gateway. Additional software is not required on the clients; however, the NetWare server must be configured with a group called NTGATEWAY and a user account in that group which is used by all the gateway clients. GSNW is not installed on the NetWare server.

6. B. Samba enables SMB clients (such as Windows computers) to access files on UNIX servers, and it includes an SMB client to enable UNIX machines to access SMB shares. CDFS is the file system used on CD-ROMs. There is no such thing as Client Services for UNIX. Systems Network Architecture (SNA) is a protocol set developed by IBM to enable unlike architectures, such as PCs and mainframes, to communicate.

7. C. A gateway is a software package that links two different types of networks that use entirely different protocols and then translates between the protocols to enable computers on each side to communicate with one another. A bridge provides a means of segmenting a network to reduce traffic. Server software, or NOS, is the operating system that runs on a server system and that provides login authentication to the network and centralized file storage and administration. Routing software enables packets to be forwarded from one network (subnet) to another, using a device (such as a dedicated router or a PC functioning as a router) that has a network interface on both networks.

8. D. The redirector software intercepts requests for resources and redirects the request over the network rather than to the computer's local bus. A platform is hardware architecture (such as Macintosh, IBM mainframe, or PC). A client is a program that accesses the resources on a server. There is no such thing as a director.

9. A and **C.** CIFS, based on the SMB file-sharing protocol, provides name resolution, file and print sharing services, authentication and authorization, and a network browse service. Dialup access and file level security are not services that are provided by CIFS.

10. A. The SMB daemon, SMBd, is one of the two major components of SAMBA. It provides authentication, authorization, and file and print sharing. The second major component, NMBd, provides browsing services and name resolution. There is no MBXd. SMBFS is a product that enables Linux machines to map a network drive to an SMB share. It is distributed with SAMBA but is not part of SAMBA.

Chapter 14

1. C. Keys are numbers or ciphers used to verify the integrity of electronic communications. A password is a sequence of alpha, numeric, or symbol characters used to verify that a user really is the owner of the account associated with the password. Cryptography is the study of secret writings. Authentication refers to the entire process of verifying identity.

2. B. A brute force attack simply keeps trying different password possibilities until one works. The passwords can be entered manually or, more often, by a program or script. Decryption is the act of using the encryption code to return a scrambled message back into its original form. A Trojan horse is a program that appears to be something it is not, and it usually contains malicious code. A nuke attack is another word for a DoS attack.

3. D. A Ping flood (or ICMP flood) sends a "flood" of ICMP packets that eventually overwhelms the system. When the ICMP messages are sent to a broadcast address with the intent of affecting the entire network segment, it is called a Smurf attack. A SYN attack uses the TCP three-way handshake sequence to fill the queue of the server so that it cannot accept additional, legitimate connection requests. A worm is a type of malicious code that replicates itself. The Ping of Death involves sending an ICMP packet that exceeds the Maximum Transfer Unit (MTU) limits of the system.

4. A and B. Both corporate espionage, in which an insider sells network data to an unauthorized party for monetary compensation, and accidental breaches of security, which are caused by employee incompetence or carelessness, are common internal threats. IP spoofing is more often an external threat, in which someone on the Internet emulates an internal IP address to gain access. Proxies (or proxy servers) enhance security rather than present a threat.

5. B. Longer passwords are more difficult to guess, so a good policy requires a minimum length for passwords. The passwords that are easiest for users to remember are also usually the easiest for someone else to guess. Including numbers and symbols in the password (along with a combination of upper and lowercase letters) makes it more difficult to guess and should be encouraged or required. In a high-security environment, passwords should be changed on a regular basis.

6. **C.** Windows 2000 grants everyone full control permission to a new share by default. This permission can be removed or changed. NetWare servers work in the opposite manner; by default, no one has permission to the share. You must explicitly assign permissions for NetWare shares before anyone can access them.

7. **A.** File encryption protects data when it is stored on the disk, not when it is sent across the network. You must use another method, such as IPSec, to protect data during network transit. Although third-party encryption software is available, the encryption function is built into some operating systems, such as Windows 2000.

8. **C.** ESP is the Encapsulating Security Payload protocol, which, along with AH (Authentication Header), is used by IPSec to protect data as it traverses the network. ESP ensures the confidentiality of the data itself, and AH is used only to authenticate the identity of the sender. ESP and AH can be used independently or in combination with each other.

9. **D.** Secret key encryption, also called symmetric encryption, uses a single key (called a shared secret) to encrypt and decrypt the data. Public key encryption (also called asymmetric encryption) uses two keys: a public key that is published and distributed freely and a private key known only to the owner of the key pair. Public key encryption is also called public/private key encryption.

10. **B.** A hash algorithm is a mathematical computation that cannot be reverse-engineered; it is performed on a message at the sending and receiving sides. If the results are the same, the message has not been altered. A digital certificate is issued by a trusted third party to verify the identity of the holder of a key pair. A ticket granting ticket is issued in Kerberos authentication to verify the identity of a user or system to a server.

Chapter 15

1. **C.** A modem bank enables multiple incoming phone lines to the remote access server; thus, multiple clients can be connected simultaneously.

Multilink is a means of aggregating bandwidth. BAP works with multilink to enable dynamic control over bandwidth usage. A CSU/DSU is a device used with a T-carrier line.

2. **B.** The dialup analog connection that uses a modem and ordinary telephone lines is the most common form of remote access. Dialup digital, dedicated digital, and wireless connections all can be used to access a network remotely; however, they are all more expensive and the equipment is more difficult to obtain, configure, and maintain.

3. **A and D.** The Serial Line Internet Protocol (SLIP) and the Point to Point Protocol (PPP) are protocols used to establish a link over a telephone network. IPX/SPX and NetBEUI are both network/transport protocols, which the remote client and server can use to communicate after the WAN link is established.

4. **B.** The Password Authentication Protocol (PAP) sends plain text, unencrypted passwords over the network, and thus, it is the least secure of the listed methods. The Challenge Handshake Authentication Protocol (CHAP), Extensible Authentication Protocol (EAP), and Shiva PAP (SPAP) all use encryption to protect the integrity of passwords as the passwords travel across the network.

5. **C.** Multilink PPP combines the bandwidth of the two 64-Kbps B channels provided with Basic Rate ISDN service into one 128-Kbps connection. The remote server to which you are connecting must be configured to accept multilink connections. BAP is used to dynamically allocate bandwidth usage on a multilinked connection. PPTP is used to create a tunnel through the Internet for virtual private networking. Multicasting is a means of sending the same message simultaneously to all computers that are members of a multicast group.

6. **A.** The process of decreasing modulation until the calling modem finds a modulation that is supported by the receiving modem is called fallback because the modem incrementally falls back to lower modulations. Bonding is a hardware method of aggregating bandwidth. Remodulation is not a term used in modem negotiations. Callback is a form of remote access security.

7. **B.** The Universal Asynchronous Receiver/Transmitter (UART) chip controls the COM port and determines its maximum speed. USB is the Universal Serial Bus, an interface that provides more convenience and speed than standard serial and parallel port interfaces. UNC stands for the Universal Naming Convention, which defines the syntax for specifying a path to a network resource. UDP is the User Datagram Protocol, a connection-

less transport layer protocol used for communications when the overhead of TCP is not desirable.

8. **C.** Internal modems are generally a little less expensive than their external counterparts. External modems are easier to install because you are not required to open the computer case or configure jumper settings. External modems are also easier to monitor because they often include status lights that indicate the activity in which the modem is engaged.

9. **C and D.** Dirty or noisy telephone lines can prevent your modem from connecting at the maximum speeds of which it is capable. Another possibility is that the modem is incompatible with the modem on the other end, especially if you have an older 56-kbps modem that uses the 56Kflex or X2 technology and the remote server's modem uses the other. If the username and password were entered incorrectly, you would not be able to connect at all. An incoming call on a line that has call waiting can cause the modem to disconnect, but call waiting itself would not cause a slow connection speed.

10. **B.** The Remote Authentication Dial-In User Service (RADIUS) is an industry standard protocol that provides centralization of authentication, accounting and NAS control. The dialup server is configured as a RADIUS client, and authentication is performed by a RADIUS server. Network Address Translation (NAT) is a means of sharing an Internet connection with an entire LAN by translating private internal addresses to one external public address. Redundant Array of Independent Disks (RAID) is a method for providing disk fault tolerance and high performance. The Reverse Address Resolution Protocol (RARP) is used by a computer to learn its IP address based on its physical MAC address.

Chapter 16

1. **B.** When a protocol header is wrapped or hidden inside another, this is called encapsulation, and it is the process by which the tunnel is created. Encryption is the process of scrambling data so that it is unreadable to unauthorized persons. Authentication is the process of establishing the identity of a user or machine. Authorization is allowing only users with predefined accounts access to the network resources.

2. **A.** A tunnel is a logical point-to-point connection that supports authentication and encryption of data from one endpoint to the other. A protocol is a set of rules by which computers communicate with one another. The term gateway is used to refer to the router through which packets intended for a different subnet pass. A gateway, such as Gateway Services for NetWare, is also a means of translating from one network protocol to another. Although a remote access connection is a logical point-to-point connection, it does not necessarily provide for authentication and encryption, nor does it necessarily pass through a public network. A VPN is one type of remote access connection.

3. **B and D.** PPTP is an extension of the PPP link protocol. As such, it operates at the data link layer (Layer 2) of the OSI reference model. PPTP uses the Microsoft Point-to-Point Encryption (MPPE) protocol to provide security by encrypting data; it does not use IPSec. IPSec is used in conjunction with L2TP.

4. **C.** IPSec can operate in transport mode, for example when it provides data encryption while L2TP provides encapsulation. It can also operate in tunnel mode, during which it performs encapsulation itself. PPTP and L2F are tunneling protocols that do not operate in two modes. SSH is the Secure Shell used to create VPNs in UNIX environments.

5. **C and D.** The biggest advantage of VPN connections is the cost savings, which comes from reduced long distance charges. These charges are reduced because users are dialing their local ISPs instead of making long distance calls to the remote server. Costs are reduced also because you do not need telephone lines and modems for each user. VPN performance, however, is usually somewhat slower than a direct remote connection because of the overhead of creating the tunnel. VPNs that rely on the Internet, especially using a dialup connection, are generally not as reliable as a direct dialup connection.

6. **C.** An extranet is a part of the company LAN that is made available to others. When access is provided by tunneling through the public network, you have a VPN extranet. An internet (with lowercase *i*) is any network of networks. An intranet is similar to an extranet, but generally is accessed from inside the corporate network. It is for the use of company employees rather than for outside clients and partners. A subnet is a division of the network.

7. **D.** The router-to-router configuration connects two separate LANs to one another and enables users to access resources on each side. In the other three scenarios, it is likely that the user is initiating the VPN connection from a dialup Internet connection instead of going through a router.

8. **A and C.** Both PPTP and L2TP can be used to create VPN tunnels, and both work at the data link layer (Layer 2) of the OSI reference model. However, PPTP requires IP and cannot use ATM or Frame Relay virtual

circuits for tunneling over non-IP networks. Only L2TP supports multiple tunnels between endpoints.

9. **B.** The CryptoIP Encapsulation protocol (CIPE) is implemented as a Linux kernel driver, and it can be used to provide a secure tunnel between two IP subnets. TunnelBuilder is a third-party VPN product. CIR stands for Committed Information Rate and does not directly relate to VPNs. The VPN daemon (VPNd) is a Linux/UNIX tunneling software that uses the Blowfish encryption algorithm.

10. **A, B,** and **D.** Hardware-based VPNs come in two flavors: router-based and firewall-based. Router-based VPNs are generally quite easy to set up and use—some to the point of "plug-and- play" operability. Firewall-based VPNs can perform address translation. However, many software-based VPN solutions are freeware or are included with the operating system. Hardware-based VPNs tend to be more expensive.

Chapter 17

1. **A** and **C.** Even a high-end PC-based server used as an application server costs thousands of dollars less than a mainframe computer. Using PCs as clients provides users with the ability to run some applications locally while running others from the server. PCs are more costly than mainframe terminals, but they have more functionality.

2. **C.** With most thin client implementations, such as Microsoft Terminal Services, you have control over user sessions and can take over the keyboard and mouse input or disconnect the session. Users do not have to have the same security settings and access permissions; these are configured based on user account or group membership. Using terminals actually makes it easier to back up data because it is all stored in a central location on the server. Applications are upgraded only on the server, not on individual client machines.

3. **B.** The Independent Computing Architecture (ICA) protocol, which is used by Citrix for their MetaFrame product, enables non-Windows clients to connect to a Windows terminal server. The Remote Desktop Protocol (RDP), which is used by Microsoft and included with Windows NT and Windows 2000 Terminal Services, enables only Windows clients to access the terminal server. The X protocol is typically used for UNIX clients to access UNIX X servers. The Dynamic Host Configuration Protocol (DHCP) is used to assign IP addresses to computers (including thin clients) when they connect to a TCP/IP network.

4. A and D. The Remote Desktop Protocol(RDP), which is used by Microsoft Terminal Services, supports printing to a local LTP (parallel) port by clients, and it enables clipboard redirection, which is the copying and pasting of data between the terminal window and the local desktop. Only ICA supports COM port redirection and the IPX/SPX and NetBEUI protocols.

5. C. The XDMCP (X Display Manager Communication Protocol) is used to assign X server resources to the X terminal clients. X is the protocol used for communication between client and server. LBX (Low Bandwidth X) is a variation of X designed for slow WAN links. RFB is the Remote Frame Buffer protocol, which is used to provide remote access to a GUI interface across platforms.

6. B. The Preboot Execution Environment is a standard implemented by Intel and other manufacturers that defines the means of providing bootstrap code to diskless workstations or other computers that boot an operating system from the network. The other three definitions of PXE are incorrect.

7. B, C, and D. The Network Computer, which was developed by Sun Microsystems in cooperation with Oracle and IBM, supports the TCP/IP protocol stack and the execution of Java applets. Network Computers include web browser software for processing of HTTP and HTTPS requests. The Network Computer is a nonproprietary system that does not require a specific platform or operating system.

8. A and B. Windows 2000 Terminal Services can run in either remote administration mode, which enables you to manage the server from a remote workstation, or application server mode, in which multiple users can connect to the terminal server to run applications on a Windows 2000 desktop. Terminal Services does not have a local access or virtual machine mode.

9. B and C. Citrix MetaFrame features the Nfuse technology, an application portal technology that enables integration of applications into the standard web browser interface. Another feature of MetaFrame is the ability to group servers into server farms for load balancing and license pooling. MetaFrame is an add-on product for Windows NT 4.0 and Windows 2000; the Citrix product for NT 3.51 is Winframe. MetaFrame uses the Program Neighborhood for management of applications and creation of new ICA connections.

10. D. Java's high performance is based in part on its multithreading capability and support of JIT compilation. Java applets must be downloaded to the client machine, although some or all processing can take place on the server. Java standards are not yet universal; the implementations by different vendors can differ considerably. The JVM can run on almost any platform, including Windows and Macintosh; it is not limited to UNIX-based machines.

Chapter 18

1. **B.** The amount of data that actually can be transmitted from the source computer to the destination computer over a network is its measured throughput. The bandwidth is the theoretical amount of signal available. A Committed Information Rate (CIR) is a guarantee from the service provider that your connection will have a specified minimum data transfer rate. A baseline is an established performance standard against which future measurements can be made.

2. **A.** A protocol analyzer (sometimes called a network monitor) is a tool, usually a software package, that captures individual frames or packets for analysis. Performance monitors are software tools that use counters to measure specified criteria, such as the number of bytes transferred per second. Time domain reflectometers (TDRs) are hardware devices used to detect broken or shorted cables. Packet filters are components that can be used on protocol analyzers to view packets of a specific protocol or those sent to or from a specified address.

3. **A and C.** Microsoft's Network Monitor, Novell's LANalyzer, and Network Associates' Sniffer Pro are software protocol analyzers. SNMP (the Simple Network Management Protocol) is a TCP/IP utility used to perform management tasks, but it does not provide packet and protocol analysis. Novell's TPCON is a NetWare Loadable Module (NLM) used to view TCP/IP configuration and statistics.

4. **D.** Microsoft's System Management Server (SMS) contains a more robust version of the Network Monitor than the one included with the Windows NT and Windows 2000 operating systems. OpenView is a Hewlett Packard network management product, and Tivoli is a similar product made by IBM. SMTP is the Simple Mail Transfer Protocol, used to transfer e-mail messages over the Internet.

5. **B and C.** Both Novell's LANalyzer and Network Associates' Sniffer Pro use the dashboard-style interface with gauges to indicate packets sent and received. Network Monitor displays the information in a text format, and Performance Monitor uses a graph or chart to display performance data.

6. **A** and **D.** Systems Management Server can be used to gather hardware and software inventory data, document the devices on the network, meter software, manage licenses, remotely control user desktops, notify administrators of events, and deploy software over the network. SMS includes a more robust version of the Network Monitor program that is provided with Windows NT and Windows 2000. SMS itself is an add-on program and does not come with any version of the Windows operating system. SMS cannot provide connectivity between a Windows network and an IBM mainframe network; such connectivity is the function of a Systems Network Architecture (SNA) server.

7. **B.** Simple Network Management Protocol (SNMP) uses three components to collect data about the network: a manager, an agent, and a MIB. Network Monitor and other protocol analyzers capture packets and save captured data, but they do not use SNMP. An Application Service Provider rents software applications over a network.

8. **C.** A tone generator and locator is called a "fox and hound" by electronics technicians because the "hound" (the tone locator) chases the "fox" (the tone generator). TDRs, oscilloscopes, and digital volt-ohm meters also are hardware devices used to troubleshoot cable problems, but they are nicknamed after animals.

9. **D.** The first thing to check is whether the cables are properly plugged into the NICs and hubs and whether any cables are broken or crimped. Only after you have eliminated the physical problems should you check the protocol configuration, suspect corrupt files, or check the user's account for validity.

10. **D.** The proper command for route tracing on a UNIX or Linux computer is **traceroute**. Because UNIX commands are case-sensitive, you must enter the command in lowercase letters for it to be recognized. **TRACERT** is the appropriate command for a Windows 9*x*, Windows NT, or Windows 2000 system. Because the Windows commands are not case sensitive, **tracert** will work on those machines as well.

This glossary defines many common terms and abbreviations related to computer networking that are used in this book. Terms that are commonly denoted as acronyms or abbreviations are defined under the commonly used form, with the full term spelled out in parentheses following the acronym or abbreviation.

Numerics

3DES (triple DES)   A strong form of the Data Encryption Standard algorithm and used to encrypt data. 3DES can use three separate encryption keys, and DES uses only one.

10Base2   A 10-Mbps baseband Ethernet specification using 50-ohm thin coaxial cable. 10Base2, which is part of the IEEE 802.3 specification, has a distance limit of 185 meters per segment. *See* Ethernet and IEEE 802.3.

10Base5   A 10-Mbps baseband Ethernet specification using standard (thick) 50-ohm baseband coaxial cable. 10Base5, which is part of the IEEE 802.3 baseband physical layer specification, has a distance limit of 500 meters per segment. *See* Ethernet and IEEE 802.3.

10BaseF   A 10-Mbps baseband Ethernet specification that refers to the 10BaseFB, 10BaseFL, and 10BaseFP standards for Ethernet over fiber-optic cabling. *See* 10BaseFB, 10BaseFL, and Ethernet.

10BaseFB   A 10-Mbps baseband Ethernet specification using fiber-optic cabling, with a maximum segment length of 2000 meters and maximum of 1024 stations per segment. Typically uses 62.5/125 micron duplex FDDI compliant fiber optic cable, with ST or SMA connector.

10BaseFL   A 10-Mbps baseband Ethernet specification using fiber-optic cabling. 10BaseFL is part of the IEEE 10BaseF specification and, although able to interoperate with FOIRL, is designed to replace the FOIRL specification. 10BaseFL segments can be up to 1000 meters long if used with FOIRL and up to 2000 meters if 10BaseFL is used exclusively. *See* 10BaseF and Ethernet.

10BaseT   A 10-Mbps baseband Ethernet specification using two pairs of twisted-pair cabling (Category 3, 4, or 5); one pair is for transmitting data and the other is for receiving data. 10BaseT, which is part of the IEEE 802.3 specification, has a distance limit of approximately 100 meters per segment. *See* Ethernet and IEEE 802.3.

100BaseFX   A 100-Mbps baseband Fast Ethernet specification using two strands of multimode fiber-optic cable per link. To guarantee proper signal timing, a 100BaseFX link cannot exceed 400 meters in length. Based on the IEEE 802.3 standard. *See* 100BaseX, Fast Ethernet, and IEEE 802.3.

100BaseT A 100-Mbps baseband Fast Ethernet specification using UTP wiring. Like the 10BaseT technology on which it is based, 100BaseT sends link pulses over the network segment when no traffic is present. However, these link pulses contain more information than do those used in 10BaseT. Based on the IEEE 802.3 standard. *See* 10BaseT, Fast Ethernet, and IEEE 802.3.

100BaseT4 A 100-Mbps baseband Fast Ethernet specification using four pairs of Category 3, 4, or 5 UTP wiring. To guarantee proper signal timing, a 100BaseT4 segment cannot exceed 100 meters in length. Based on the IEEE 802.3 standard. *See* Fast Ethernet and IEEE 802.3.

100BaseTX A 100-Mbps baseband Fast Ethernet specification using two pairs of either UTP or STP wiring. The first pair of wires is used to receive data; the second is used to transmit. To guarantee proper signal timing, a 100BaseTX segment cannot exceed 100 meters in length. Based on the IEEE 802.3 standard. *See* 100BaseX, Fast Ethernet, and IEEE 802.3.

100BaseX A 100-Mbps baseband Fast Ethernet specification that refers to the 100BaseFX and 100BaseTX standards for Fast Ethernet over fiber-optic cabling. Based on the IEEE 802.3 standard. *See* 100BaseFX, 100BaseTX, Fast Ethernet, and IEEE 802.3.

100VG-AnyLAN A 100-Mbps Fast Ethernet and Token Ring media technology using four pairs of Category 3, 4, or 5 UTP cabling. This high-speed transport technology, developed by Hewlett-Packard, can be made to operate on existing 10BaseT Ethernet networks. Based on the IEEE 802.12 standard. *See* IEEE 802.12.

A

access control list *See* ACL.

access layer The layer at which a LAN or a group of LANs, typically Ethernet or Token Ring, provide users with frontline access to network services.

access method 1. The way in which network devices access the network medium. 2. Software within an SNA processor that controls the flow of information through a network.

ACK *See* acknowledgment.

acknowledgment A notification sent from one network device to another to acknowledge that some event (for example, receipt of a message) has occurred. Sometimes abbreviated as ACK.

ACL (access control list) A list kept by a Cisco router to control access to or from the router for many services (for example, to prevent packets with a certain IP address from leaving a particular interface on the router).

Active Directory The directory services used by Windows 2000 networks, in which information is stored in a hierarchical database.

adapter *See* NIC.

Address Resolution Protocol *See* ARP.

address resolution Generally, a method for resolving differences between computer addressing schemes. Address resolution usually specifies a method for mapping network layer (Layer 3) addresses to data link layer (Layer 2) addresses.

address A data structure or logical convention used to identify a unique entity, such as a particular process or network device.

ADSL (asymmetric digital subscriber line) A high-speed broadband service offered by telephone companies in some areas that runs over traditional copper line and that can transmit data and voice.

Advanced Peer-to-Peer Networking *See* APPN.

Advanced Research Projects Agency Network *See* ARPAnet.

Advanced Resource Computer Network *See* ARCnet.

AI (artificial intelligence) The simulation of human intelligence processes by machines, especially computer systems. These processes include learning, reasoning, and self-correction.

American National Standards Institute *See* ANSI.

American Standard Code for Information Interchange *See* ASCII.

analog A signaling method that uses a continuously variable waveform representing an infinite number of incremental values. Standard telephone lines carry data in analog form.

ANSI (American National Standards Institute) A voluntary organization composed of corporate, government, and other members that coordinates standards-related activities, approves U.S. national standards, and develops positions for the United States in international standards organizations. ANSI helps develop international and U.S. standards relating to, among other things, communications and networking. ANSI is a member of the IEC and the International Organization for Standardization.

API (application programming interface) A process, consisting of programming routines, by which an application program interfaces with the operating system and requests services.

APIPA (Automatic Private IP Addressing) A feature included in Windows 98 and Windows 2000 by which computers configured as DHCP clients can assign themselves IP addresses if a DHCP server is unavailable.

AppleTalk A network architecture used by Apple Macintosh computers, the software for which is included with the Macintosh operating systems.

AppleTalk Transaction Protocol *See* ATP.

application layer Layer 7 of the OSI reference model. This layer provides network services to user applications. For example, a word processing application is serviced by file transfer services at this layer. *See* OSI reference model.

application programming interface *See* API.

application A program that performs a function directly for a user. FTP and Telnet clients are examples of network applications.

APPN (Advanced Peer-to-Peer Networking) An enhancement to the original IBM SNA architecture. APPN handles session establishment between peer nodes, dynamic transparent route calculation, and traffic prioritization for APPC traffic.

ARCnet (Advanced Resource Computer Network) A token-passing bus architecture designed for small LANs.

ARP (Address Resolution Protocol) A protocol that is part of the TCP/IP suite, which resolves IP addresses to physical hardware (MAC) addresses.

ARPAnet (Advanced Research Projects Agency Network) A WAN launched in the 1960s by the U.S. Department of Defense in conjunction with major universities; it evolved into the Internet.

artificial intelligence *See* AI.

ASCII (American Standard Code for Information Interchange) An eight-bit code (seven bits plus parity) for character representation.

asymmetric digital subscriber line *See* ADSL.

asymmetric encryption An encryption scheme that uses two keys, one called the public key, which is made available freely, and the other called the private key, which is known only to the user. One key is used to encrypt the message and the other is used to decrypt it.

asynchronous communication A method of sending data in which the signals are sent and received at irregular intervals, using start bits and stop bits to indicate when the bits of a character begin and end.

Asynchronous Transfer Mode *See* ATM.

ATM (Asynchronous Transfer Mode)　A packet-switching technology that uses fixed-length 53-byte cells to send data at high speeds, by using multiplexers to enable multiple computers to send data over the network at the same time.

ATP (AppleTalk Transaction Protocol)　A transport-level protocol that provides a loss-free transaction service between sockets. The service enables exchanges between two socket clients in which one client requests the other to perform a particular task and to report the results. ATP binds the request and response together to ensure the reliable exchange of request/response pairs.

attenuation　Weakening of signal strength over distance.

audit　To track and log use and attempted use of user rights, login privileges, and access to objects; this is done for security purposes.

authentication　Verification of the identity of a user, traditionally based on a predefined user account and corresponding password. Other means of authentication include use of advanced technologies such as fingerprint comparison, voice pattern analysis, and retinal scanning.

authorization　The process of confirming that a user has permission to access a resource on the network.

Automatic Private IP Addressing　*See* APIPA.

B

B (bearer) channel　In an ISDN line, a channel that carries data, that works in conjunction with a D channel, and that carries signaling information. A typical BRI line has one 16-kbps D channel and two B channels that transmit at 64 kbps each.

back up　To make a copy of data and programs, which can be restored if the original becomes lost or corrupted.

backbone　A trunk, or main cable, to which hubs, switches, or routers are connected and off of which network segments run.

backup domain controller　*See* BDC.

Bandwidth Allocation Protocol　*See* BAP.

bandwidth　The difference between the highest and lowest frequencies available for network signals. Also, the rated throughput capacity of a given network medium or protocol.

Banyan VINES　*See* VINES.

BAP (Bandwidth Allocation Protocol)   A method of controlling the use of multiple lines using multilink by dropping extra lines when the bandwidth is not required and reconnecting when bandwidth demand becomes heavier.

basic rate ISDN   *See* BRI.

baud   A unit of measurement indicating the speed of data transmission over analog lines. It is based on the speed of oscillation of a waveform on which the data is carried and is named after a French telegraph engineer named Baudot.

BDC (backup domain controller)   In a Windows NT network, a server that contains a read-only copy of the security accounts database (SAM) for the domain, which is used to authenticate user logins. The SAM information is replicated to the BDCs by a PDC (primary domain controller), on which changes to the database are made.

Berkeley Internet Name Domain   *See* BIND.

binary   A numbering system that uses two digits, 0 and 1, to represent all values.

BIND (Berkeley Internet Name Domain)   A version of DNS that runs on UNIX systems to perform host name to IP address resolution.

bind   To establish a connection between a protocol and a NIC.

bindery   The flat database used in NetWare 3.x servers that contains security account information.

bit   A unit of data that represents either a 0 or a 1 in binary notation; it is the smallest unit of data processed by a computer.

Boot Protocol   *See* BOOTP.

BOOTP (Boot Protocol)   A protocol originally devised to provide a way for diskless workstations to obtain an IP address and download the operating system on a TCP/IP network; the predecessor of DHCP.

Bootstrap Protocol   *See* BOOTP.

bootstrap   A simple, preset operation to load instructions that in turn cause other instructions to be loaded into memory or that cause entry into other configuration modes.

BRI (basic rate ISDN)   An ISDN line composed of two B channels and one D channel for circuit-switched communication of voice, video, and data. Compare with PRI.

bridge   A device that connects and passes packets between two network segments that use the same communications protocol. Bridges operate at the data link layer (Layer 2) of the OSI reference model. In general, a bridge filters, forwards, or floods an incoming frame based on the MAC address of that frame.

bridging   A technology in which a bridge connects two or more LAN segments.

broadcast   A message that is sent to all computers on a segment or subnet, rather than to a specific destination computer.

broadcast address   A special address reserved for sending a message to all stations. Generally, a broadcast address is a MAC destination address of all ones. Compare with multicast address and unicast address. *See* broadcast.

broadcast domain   The set of all devices that will receive broadcast frames originating from any device within the set. Broadcast domains are typically bounded by routers because routers do not forward broadcast frames. *See* broadcast.

broadcast storm   An undesirable network event in which many broadcasts are sent simultaneously across all network segments. A broadcast storm uses substantial network bandwidth and, typically, causes network timeouts. *See* broadcast.

bus topology   A linear LAN architecture in which transmissions from network stations propagate the length of the medium and are received by all other stations. Compare with ring topology, star topology, and tree topology.

byte   Eight bits.

C

cache   Data that is temporarily stored to speed access. For example, web browsers stored web pages that have been accessed in cache files so that if you want to return to the same page, it can be retrieved from the local disk, rather than from its Internet location.

caching   A form of replication in which information learned during a previous transaction is used to process later transactions.

callback security   A means by which a server verifies the validity of a remote caller by disconnecting and calling the user back at a predefined telephone number after the user enters a username and password.

carrier network   A service provider's network.

carrier sense multiple access collision detect   *See* CSMA/CD.

carrier   An electromagnetic wave or alternating current of a single frequency, suitable for modulation by another, data-bearing signal.

Category 1 cabling   One of five grades of UTP cabling described in the EIA/TIA 568B standard. Category 1 cabling is used for telephone communications and is not suitable for transmitting data. *See* UTP.

Category 2 cabling   One of five grades of UTP cabling described in the EIA/TIA 568B standard. Category 2 cabling is capable of transmitting data at speeds up to 4 Mbps. *See* UTP.

Category 3 cabling   One of five grades of UTP cabling described in the EIA/TIA 568B standard. Category 3 cabling is used in 10BaseT networks and can transmit data at speeds up to 10 Mbps. *See* UTP.

Category 4 cabling   One of five grades of UTP cabling described in the EIA/TIA 568B standard. Category 4 cabling is used in Token Ring networks and can transmit data at speeds up to 16 Mbps. *See* UTP.

Category 5 cabling   One of five grades of UTP cabling described in the EIA/TIA 568B standard. Category 5 cabling can transmit data at speeds up to 100 Mbps. *See* UTP.

Category 5e cabling   An enhanced implementation of Category 5 UTP cabling that can transmit data at 1.55 Mbps. *See* UTP.

CCIE   Cisco Certified Internet Expert.

CCITT (Committee for International Telegraph and Telephone)   International committee based in Geneva, Switzerland that recommends telecommunications standards.

CCNA   Cisco Certified Network Associate.

CCNP   Cisco Certified Network Professional.

central office   *See* CO.

certificate   Information that is used to authenticate and secure the exchange of data on a nonsecure network, using public key encryption.

Challenge Handshake Authentication Protocol   *See* CHAP.

channel service unit/digital service unit   *See* CSU/DSU.

CHAP (Challenge Handshake Authentication Protocol)   A security feature supported on lines using PPP encapsulation that prevents unauthorized access. CHAP does not itself prevent unauthorized access, but it identifies the remote end; the router or access server then determines whether that user is allowed access.

CIDR (classless interdomain routing)   A means of defining the network and host portions of an IP address that is more efficient and flexible than the older "classful" addressing method. CIDR uses a network prefix, whose length is specified as part of the IP address based on the number of bits used to identify the network.

CIFS (Common Internet File System)   A file system based on the SMB file-sharing protocol, which is used by Samba to enable Microsoft and UNIX computers to communicate. CIFS provides authentication and authorization, name resolution, file and print sharing services, and network browse services.

cipher   An encoding or encryption method that produces ciphertext, or a scrambled message that cannot be easily deciphered by unauthorized parties.

CIR (committed information rate)   The rate, in bits per second, at which the Frame Relay switch agrees to transfer data.

circuit switching   A switching system in which a dedicated physical circuit path must exist between the sender and the receiver for the duration of the "call." Used heavily in the telephone company network, circuit switching can be contrasted with contention and token passing as a channel-access method and with message switching and packet switching as a switching technique.

circuit   A communications path between two or more points.

circuit-switched network   A networking technology that establishes a connection by closing a switch (for example, the public telephone network). The circuit is dedicated for the duration of the session, although if you disconnect and reconnect, a different circuit might be used.

Cisco IOS software   The software platform that runs on the majority of Cisco routers and switches to deliver network services and enable networked applications.

classless interdomain routing   *See* CIDR.

client/server application   An application that is stored centrally on a server and accessed by workstations, thus making it easy to maintain and protect.

client/server computing   Distributed computing (processing) network systems in which transaction responsibilities are divided into two parts: client (front end) and server (back end). Both terms (client and server) can be applied to software programs or to actual computing devices. Also called distributed computing (processing). Compare with peer-to-peer computing.

client/server   The architecture of the relationship between a workstation and a server in a network.

client   The computer or application program that requests access to the resources or services of another computer (the server).

cluster   To group computers to provide a service, in which the computers in the group act as if they were one computer. Clustering can be implemented for the purposes of load balancing or fault tolerance.

CO (central office)   The local telephone company office to which all local loops in a given area connect and in which circuit switching of subscriber lines occurs.

coaxial cable   Cable consisting of a hollow outer cylindrical conductor that surrounds a single inner wire conductor. Two types of coaxial cable are currently used in LANs: 50-ohm cable, which is used for digital signaling, and 75-ohm cable, which is used for analog signal and high-speed digital signaling.

coding   Electrical techniques used to convey binary signals.

collision domain   In Ethernet, the network area within which frames that have collided are propagated. Repeaters and hubs propagate collisions; LAN switches, bridges, and routers do not.

collision   In Ethernet, the result of two nodes transmitting simultaneously. The frames from each device collide and are damaged when they meet on the physical medium.

committed information rate   *See* CIR.

Common Internet File System   *See* CIFS.

concentrator   *See* hub.

congestion   Traffic in excess of network capacity.

connectionless protocol   A protocol that does not require that a connection be established before data is sent (for example, UDP).

connection-oriented protocol   A protocol that requires the establishment of a connection between the sending and receiving computers before data is sent. An example of this protocol is TCP.

console   A DTE through which commands are entered into a host.

contention   An access method in which network devices compete for permission to access the physical medium.

convergence   The speed and capability of a group of internetworking devices running a specific routing protocol to agree on the topology of an internetwork after a change in that topology.

CPE (customer premises equipment)   Terminating equipment, such as terminals, telephones, and modems, supplied by the telephone company, installed at customer sites, and connected to the telephone company network.

cracker   A hacker who specializes in breaking passwords or licenses and otherwise intentionally breaches computer security. *See* hacker.

CRC (cyclical redundancy check)   A means of verifying that characters in a data packet are intact by using a mathematical calculation.

crossover cable   A length of UTP Ethernet cable in which the pin contacts are reversed, which can be used to directly connect two computers without a hub (or to connect two hubs without uplink ports). Also referred to as null modem cable.

cryptography   The process of securing data so that only authorized persons can access the data. This involves encoding and encryption.

CSMA/CD (carrier sense multiple access collision detect)   A media-access mechanism in which devices ready to transmit data first check the channel for a carrier. If no carrier is sensed for a specific period of time, a device can transmit. If two devices transmit at one time, a collision occurs and is detected by all colliding devices. This collision subsequently delays retransmissions from those devices for some random length of time. CSMA/CD access is used by Ethernet and IEEE 802.3.

CSU/DSU (channel service unit/digital service unit)   A digital interface device that connects end-user equipment to the local digital telephone loop.

customer premises equipment   *See* CPE.

cybernetics   Defined by its founder, Norbert Weiner, as "the theory of control in engineering, whether human, animal or mechanical." General usage of the term includes futuristic technologies such as sophisticated robotics and cyborgs (entities that include both biological and technological components).

cyborg   A human with electronic and mechanical implants, networked to other such lifeforms to share a collective memory and consciousness.

cyclical redundancy check   *See* CRC.

D

D (data) channel   In an ISDN line, a channel that carries signaling information and that works in conjunction with the B channels, which carry data. Also called the Delta channel. A typical BRI line has one 16-kbps D channel and two B channels that transmit at 64-kbps each.

daemon   A program on a UNIX or Linux computer that runs continuously for the purpose of responding to requests for services. Usually denoted by a "d" at the end of the program name. For example, HTTPd (the HTTP daemon) runs on web servers to respond to HTTP requests.

data circuit-terminating equipment   *See* DCE.

Data Encryption Standard   *See* DES.

data link layer   Layer 2 of the OSI networking reference model; responsible for moving data in and out across the network's physical link, and it is divided into two sublayers: the MAC sublayer and the LLC sublayer.

data store   A database where information is kept.

data terminal equipment   *See* DTE.

data warehouse   A centralized storage location for large amounts of data in an enterprise network, often located on a mainframe or on a powerful PC or group of PCs running special data warehousing software (for example, Microsoft's Windows 2000 Datacenter Server).

data   Information that has been changed into digital or binary form for processing by computers or transmitting across a network.

datagram   A unit of data along with the required information for routing the datagram from the sending to the destination computer. Datagrams are referred to as "self contained" because a connection does not have to be established before sending. IP datagrams are the primary information units in the Internet. The terms cell, frame, message, packet, and segment are also used to describe logical information groupings at various layers of the OSI reference model and in various technology circles.

DCE (data circuit-terminating equipment)   The device used to convert the user data from the DTE into a form acceptable to the WAN service's facility. Compare with DTE.

DDNS (Dynamic DNS)   A form of DNS that dynamically updates host-to-IP address mappings and that is implemented in Windows 2000.

dedicated connection   A communications link that is indefinitely reserved for transmissions, rather than switched as transmission is required. *See* leased line.

default gateway   The address of the router to which packets with a destination outside the sending computer's subnet are sent by default.

default route   A routing table entry that is used to direct frames for which a next hop is not explicitly listed in the routing table.

demarcation point   The point at which the CPE ends and the local loop portion of the service begins. Often occurs at the POP of a building.

Department of Defense   *See* DoD.

DES (Data Encryption Standard)   A popular encryption method that uses secret key cryptography. DES works by using a 56-bit key, which is applied to data in 64-bit blocks. A stronger version is called 3DES (triple DES).

desktop operating system   A computer operating system designed for workstation or standalone machines on which work is done by users. Desktop operating systems run productivity applications such as word processing, spreadsheet, and graphics manipulation programs. Contrast with NOS.

destination address   An address of a network device that is receiving data. *See* source address.

DHCP (Dynamic Host Configuration Protocol)   A protocol that provides a mechanism for allocating IP addresses dynamically so that addresses can be reused automatically when hosts no longer need them.

dialup connection   A network connection that is established through telephone lines and in which the remote node disconnects at the end of the session. *See* dedicated connection and remote access.

digital subscriber line   *See* DSL.

digital   A signal that consists of discrete values, with no transition between them (for example, on and off or 1 and 0).

directory service   A network service that provides a means for accessing a central database containing information about network resources (for example, Microsoft's Active Directory and Novell's NDS).

discrete state signaling   A signaling method in which the signal is either on or off, with no variables in between. Compare with waveform signaling.

dispersion   Scattering or separation of a complex wave into components according to wavelength or frequency.

distance-vector routing protocol   A routing protocol that iterates on the number of hops in a route to find a shortest-path spanning tree. Distance-vector routing protocols call for each router to send its entire routing table in each update, but only to its neighbors. Distance-vector routing protocols can be prone to routing loops, but they are computationally simpler than link-state routing protocols. Also called the Bellman-Ford routing algorithm. Compare with link-state routing protocol.

DNS (Domain Name System)   A system used in the Internet for translating names of network nodes into addresses.

DoD (Department of Defense)   The U.S. government organization that is responsible for national defense. The DoD has frequently funded communication protocol development.

Domain Name System *See* DNS.

domain   In Microsoft Windows networking, a group of computers that share a security accounts database, providing login authentication and centralized administration.

dotted-decimal notation   The common notation for IP addresses in the form a.b.c.d, where each number represents, in decimal, one byte of the four-byte IP address. Also called dotted notation or four-part dotted notation.

DSL (digital subscriber line)   Digital service that provides high-speed data transfer over copper telephone lines. Variations include Asymmetric DSL (ADSL), High-Speed DSL (HDSL), Symmetric DSL (SDSL) and Very High-Speed DSL (VDSL).

DTE (data terminal equipment)   The interface used by a computer to pass data to or from a modem or other serial device.

dual homing   A network topology in which a device is connected to the network by way of two independent access points (points of attachment). One access point is the primary connection, and the other is a standby connection that is activated if a primary connection fails. Also called multihoming.

dumb terminal   Input and output devices (typically a keyboard and monitor) that send input to a central computer such as a mainframe and that return output. A dumb terminal does not have any computing power of its own.

Dynamic DNS   *See* DDNS.

Dynamic Host Configuration Protocol   *See* DHCP.

dynamic routing   Routing that adjusts automatically to network topology or traffic changes. Also called adaptive routing. Compare with static routing.

E

electromagnetic interference   *See* EMI.

encapsulate   To wrap data in a particular protocol header. For example, Ethernet data is wrapped in a specific Ethernet header before network transit. Also, when bridging dissimilar networks, the entire frame from one network is simply placed in the header used by the data link layer protocol of the other network.

Encapsulating Security Header   *See* ESP.

EMI (electromagnetic interference)   Interference from outside electromagnetic impulses that can disrupt the transmission of data over copper cable.

Encapsulating Security Payload *See* ESP.

encapsulation Wrapping of data in a particular protocol header. For example, upper-layer data is wrapped in a specific Ethernet header before network transit. Also, when bridging dissimilar networks, the entire frame from one network can simply be placed in the header used by the data link layer protocol of the other network. *See* tunneling.

encoding The process by which bits are represented by voltages.

enterprise network A corporation, agency, school, or other organization's network that ties together its data, communication, computing, and file servers.

ESP (Encapsulating Security Header) A new security mechanism used by IPv6, also called IPng Encapsulating Security Header.

ESP (Encapsulating Security Payload) A protocol used by IPSec to protect data that travels across the network through the IP network layer protocol. ESP provides both authentication and encryption.

Ethernet A baseband LAN specification invented by Xerox Corporation and developed jointly by Xerox, Intel, and Digital Equipment Corporation. Ethernet networks use CSMA/CD and run over a variety of cable types at 10 Mbps. Ethernet is similar to the IEEE 802.3 series of standards. *See* Fast Ethernet.

exabyte A unit of measurement equal to 10^{18}, or 1,000,000,000,000,000,000 bytes.

F

failover In server clustering, a system in which a secondary or failover server is connected to a primary server for the purpose of taking over the server function if the primary server fails.

Fast Ethernet Any 100-Mbps Ethernet specification. Fast Ethernet offers speed that is 10 times that of the 10BaseT Ethernet specification and does so while preserving qualities such as frame format, MAC mechanisms, and MTU. Such similarities enable the use of existing 10BaseT applications and network management tools on Fast Ethernet networks. Based on an extension to the IEEE 802.3 specification. *See* Ethernet.

fault tolerance The capability of a system to recover with data intact after a failure. Fault tolerance is usually based on redundancy. For example, disk fault tolerance uses multiple disks on which the same data is mirrored or across which data is written. This enables regeneration if one disk in the set fails.

FDDI (Fiber Distributed Data Interface) A LAN standard, defined by ANSI X3T9.5, specifying a 100-Mbps token-passing network using fiber-optic cable with transmission distances of up to 2 km. FDDI uses a dual-ring architecture to provide redundancy. Compare with FDDI II.

Fiber Distributed Data Interface   *See* FDDI.

fiber-optic cable   A physical medium capable of conducting modulated light transmission. Compared with other transmission media, fiber-optic cable is more expensive, but it is not susceptible to electromagnetic interference, and it is capable of higher data rates. Sometimes called optical fiber.

File and Print Services for NetWare (FPNW)   A service that can be installed on a Windows NT or Windows 2000 server to provide access to its files for NetWare clients.

File Transfer Protocol   *See* FTP.

filter   Generally, a process or device that screens network traffic for certain characteristics, such as source address, destination address, or protocol, and that determines whether to forward or discard that traffic based on the established criteria.

firewall   A router, an access server, or several routers or access servers that are designated as a buffer between any connected public networks and a private network. A firewall router uses access control lists and other methods to ensure the security of the private network.

flat addressing   A scheme of addressing that does not use a logical hierarchy to determine location.

flooding   A traffic-passing technique used by switches and bridges in which traffic received on an interface is sent out all the interfaces of that device except the interface on which the information was originally received.

flow   A stream of data traveling between two endpoints across a network (for example, from one LAN station to another). Multiple flows can be transmitted on a single circuit.

FQDN (fully qualified domain name)   A network name consisting of both the host name (name of the individual computer) and the name of the domain in which it resides.

fragment   A piece of a larger packet that has been broken down into smaller units. In Ethernet networks, sometimes referred to as a frame less than the legal limit of 64 bytes.

fragmentation   The process of breaking a packet into smaller units when transmitting over a network medium that cannot support the original size of the packet.

frame   A logical grouping of information sent as a data link layer unit over a transmission medium. Often refers to the header and trailer that is used for synchronization and error control and that surround the user data contained in the unit. The terms datagram, message, packet, and segment also are used to describe logical information groupings at various layers of the OSI reference model and in various technology circles.

Frame Relay   An industry-standard, switched, data link layer protocol that handles multiple virtual circuits using HDLC encapsulation between connected devices. Frame Relay is more efficient than X.25, the protocol for which it is generally considered a replacement.

FTP (File Transfer Protocol)   An application protocol, part of the TCP/IP protocol stack, used for transferring files between network nodes. FTP is defined in RFC 959.

full duplex   The capability for simultaneous data transmission between a sending station and a receiving station. Compare with half duplex and simplex.

fully qualified domain name   *See* FQDN.

G

Gateway Service for NetWare   A service that can be installed on a Windows NT or Windows 2000 server, enabling the Window's server's clients to access resources on a NetWare server by translating SMB protocol requests into NetWare's file sharing protocol, NCP.

gateway   In the IP community, an older term referring to a routing device (*see* default gateway). Today, the term router is more often used to describe nodes that perform this function, and gateway refers to a special-purpose device or software that performs an application layer conversion of information from one protocol stack to another. Compare with router.

Gb (gigabit)   Approximately 1,000,000,000 bits.

GB (gigabyte)   1,073,741,824 bytes. (A byte consists of eight bits.)

Gbps (gigabits per second)   A rate of transfer speed.

GBps (gigabytes per second)   A rate of transfer speed.

Ghost   A product made by Symantec that is used to copy (called cloning) all the data and data structure from one disk to another by maintaining the formatting and partitioning information to create an exact replica.

GHz   A measurement of the frequency of electromagnetic waves or alternating current that is used to measure microwave and UHF signals and computer microprocessor speed. *See* Hertz.

gigabit   *See* Gb.

gigabits per second   *See* Gbps.

gigabyte   *See* GB.

gigabytes per second   *See* GBps.

gigahertz   *See* GHz.

global positioning system   *See* GPS.

GNOME (GNU Network Object Model Environment)   A GUI and group of applications for Linux that uses a Windows-like desktop.

GNU Network Object Model Environment   *See* GNOME.

GPS (global positioning system)   A means of determining geographic location based on a receiver that triangulates its position in relation to three of the twenty-four earth-orbiting satellites owned and operated by the DoD.

graphical user interface   *See* GUI.

group   A way of organizing user accounts for easier administration, in which users are members of groups and access permissions are assigned to the group rather than to individual users.

groupware   Application programs devised for collaboration, enabling users to work collectively on the same documents or projects. Examples include Microsoft Exchange, Lotus Notes, and Novell Groupwise.

GUI (graphical user interface)   A user environment that uses pictorial and textual representations of the input and output of applications and the hierarchical or other data structure in which information is stored. Conventions such as buttons, icons, and windows are typical, and many actions are performed using a pointing device (such as a mouse). Microsoft Windows and the Apple Macintosh are prominent examples of platforms utilizing GUIs.

H

hacker   A person who is expert at a programming language and who is capable of solving programming problems by using reverse engineering programs and by defeating computer security methods. *See* cracker.

HAL (Hardware Abstraction Layer) The part of the Windows NT or Windows 2000 architecture that interfaces with the hardware. This protects the applications from directly accessing the hardware and provides better operating system stability.

half duplex A capability for data transmission in only one direction at a time between a sending station and a receiving station. Compare with full duplex and simplex.

handheld computer A portable computer that fits conveniently in the palm of the hand or that can be carried in a pocket. Examples include the Palm Pilot and the Pocket PC.

handshake A sequence of messages exchanged between two or more network devices to ensure transmission synchronization before sending user data.

Hardware Abstraction Layer *See* HAL.

hardware address *See* MAC address.

hardware loopback A device that connects the transmission pins to the receiving pins and that is used in testing network interface cards to determine whether the NIC is capable of transmitting and receiving.

hash function A mathematical computation performed on an original input that results in a fixed-length string of bits, which cannot be reversed to produce the original input.

HDLC (High-Level Data Link Control) A bit-oriented synchronous data link layer protocol developed by ISO. HDLC specifies a data encapsulation method on synchronous serial links by using frame characters and checksums.

header Control information placed before data when encapsulating that data for network transmission.

Hertz A unit of frequency change of one cycle per second (abbreviated Hz).

hexadecimal (base 16) A number representation using the digits 0 through 9, with their usual meaning, plus the letters A through F to represent hexadecimal digits with values 10 to 15. The rightmost digit counts ones, the next counts multiples of 16, the next is $16^2 = 256$, and so on.

High-Level Data Link Control *See* HDLC.

hop The passage of a data packet between two network nodes (for example, between two routers).

hop count A routing metric used to measure the distance between a source and a destination. RIP uses hop count as its sole metric.

host   A computer system on a network. Similar to node, except that host usually implies a computer system, whereas node generally applies to any networked system, including access servers and routers. *See* node.

host address   *See* host number.

host number   The portion of an IP address assigned to the individual machine, or host.

host-to-host layer   The term used in the DoD networking model for the layer that corresponds to the transport layer in the OSI reference model.

HTML (Hypertext Markup Language)   A simple hypertext document formatting language that uses tags to indicate how a given part of a document should be interpreted by a viewing application, such as a Web browser.

HTTP (Hypertext Transfer Protocol)   The protocol used by web browsers and web servers to transfer files, such as text and graphics files.

hub   1. A device that serves as the center of a star-topology network. Also called a multiport repeater. 2. A hardware or software device that contains multiple independent but connected modules of network and internetwork equipment. Hubs can be active (where they repeat signals sent through them) or passive (where they do not repeat, but merely split, signals sent through them).

hybrid network   An internetwork made up of more than one type of network technology, including LANs and WANs.

hyperlink   An association, in a hypertext document, with a file or marked location in a hypertext document, which when activated (typically by clicking it with a pointing device) displays the associated document, file, or location.

Hypertext Markup Language   *See* HTML.

Hypertext Transfer Protocol   *See* HTTP.

I

IAB (Internet Architecture Board)   A board of internetwork researchers who discuss issues pertinent to Internet architecture. Responsible for appointing a variety of Internet-related groups such as the IANA, IESG, and IRSG. The IAB is appointed by the trustees of the ISOC. *See* IANA, IESG, IRSG, and ISOC.

IANA (Internet Assigned Numbers Authority)   An organization operated under the auspices of the ISOC as a part of the IAB. IANA delegates authority for IP address-space allocation and domain-name assignment to the InterNIC and other organizations. IANA also maintains a database of assigned protocol identifiers used in the TCP/IP stack, including autonomous system numbers.

ICANN (Internet Corporation for Assigned Names and Numbers) A private non-profit corporation that has responsibility for IP address space allocation, DNS, and root server management that was previously performed by IANA. *See* IANA.

ICMP (Internet Control Message Protocol) A network layer Internet protocol that reports errors and that provides other information relevant to IP packet processing. Documented in RFC 792.

IEEE (Institute of Electrical and Electronic Engineers) A professional organization whose activities include the development of communications and network standards. IEEE LAN standards are the predominant LAN standards today.

IEEE 802.1 IEEE LAN protocol that introduces standards for LAN and MAN management, bridges that operate at the MAC sublayer, and STA, the Spanning-Tree Algorithm that prevents a communications problem called bridge looping.

IEEE 802.10 IEEE LAN protocol that pertains to virtual private networking, which is a way of establishing a secure connection to a private network over the public Internet.

IEEE 802.11 IEEE LAN protocol that provides guidelines for implementing wireless (noncabled) LAN technologies.

IEEE 802.12 IEEE LAN protocol that pertains to the demand priority media access method developed by Hewlett Packard to combine advantages of Ethernet, Token Ring, and ATM technologies in a high-speed LAN solution.

IEEE 802.2 An IEEE LAN protocol that specifies an implementation of the LLC sublayer of the data link layer. IEEE 802.2 handles errors, framing, flow control, and the network layer (Layer 3) service interface. Used in IEEE 802.3 and IEEE 802.5 LANs. *See* IEEE 802.3 and IEEE 802.5.

IEEE 802.3 An IEEE LAN protocol that specifies an implementation of the physical layer and the MAC sublayer of the data link layer. IEEE 802.3 uses CSMA/CD access at a variety of speeds over a variety of physical media. Extensions to the IEEE 802.3 standard specify implementations for Fast Ethernet. Physical variations of the original IEEE 802.3 specification include 10Base2, 10Base5, 10BaseF, 10BaseT, and 10Broad36. Physical variations for Fast Ethernet include 100BaseTX and 100BaseFX.

IEEE 802.5 An IEEE LAN protocol that specifies an implementation of the physical layer and MAC sublayer of the data link layer. IEEE 802.5 uses token passing access at 4 Mbps or 16 Mbps over STP or UTP cabling and is functionally and operationally equivalent to IBM Token Ring. *See* Token Ring.

IEEE 802.6 IEEE LAN protocol that sets standards for networks that are larger than LANs and smaller than WANs.

IEEE 802.7   IEEE LAN protocol that addresses networking with broadband transmission technologies such as CATV and by using Frequency Division Multiplexing (FDM) to send different signals on separate frequencies using the same cable.

IEEE 802.8   IEEE LAN protocol that provides specifications for networks using fiber-optic cabling, including Fiber Distributed Data Interface (FDDI).

IEEE 802.9   A IEEE LAN protocol that is sometimes called "integrated services," this standard addresses transmission of voice and data over ISDN.

IESG (Internet Engineering Steering Group)   A subdivision of the IETF that provides leadership and ratifies the output from the IETF's working groups.

IETF (Internet Engineering Task Force)   A task force consisting of more than 80 working groups responsible for developing Internet standards. The IETF operates under the auspices of ISOC.

IGRP (Interior Gateway Routing Protocol)   A protocol developed by Cisco to address the problems associated with routing in large, heterogeneous networks.

IIS (Internet Information Server)   Microsoft's web and ftp server software that runs on Windows NT and Windows 2000. *See* web server.

information technology   *See* IT.

infrared radiation   *See* IR.

inode (or i-node)   The description of an individual file, including information required to locate the file on the disk in a UNIX system.

input/output   A device or program that transfers data to or from a computer system. Also called I/O.

Institute of Electrical and Electronic Engineers   *See* IEEE.

Integrated Services Digital Network   *See* ISDN.

integration   Combining different vendors' products into a functioning network.

interface   1. A connection between two systems or devices. 2. In routing terminology, a network connection. 3. In telephony, a shared boundary defined by common physical interconnection characteristics, signal characteristics, and meanings of interchanged signals. 4. A boundary between adjacent layers of the OSI reference model.

Interior Gateway Routing Protocol   *See* IGRP.

International Organization for Standardization   *See* ISO.

International Telecommunication Union Telecommunication Standardization Sector *See* ITU-T.

Internet Architecture Board *See* IAB.

Internet Assigned Numbers Authority *See* IANA.

Internet Control Message Protocol *See* ICMP.

Internet Corporation for Assigned Names and Numbers *See* ICANN.

Internet Engineering Task Force *See* IETF.

Internet Information Server *See* IIS.

Internet protocol Any protocol that is part of the TCP/IP protocol stack. *See* IP and TCP/IP.

Internet service provider *See* ISP.

Internet Society *See* ISOC.

internet Short for internetwork. Not to be confused with the Internet. *See* internetwork.

Internet The largest global internetwork, connecting tens of thousands of networks worldwide and having a culture that focuses on research and standardization based on real-life use. Many leading-edge network technologies come from the Internet community. The Internet evolved in part from ARPAnet. At one time, it was called the DARPA Internet, not to be confused with the general term internet.

Internetwork Operating System *See* IOS.

Internetwork Packet Exchange *See* IPX.

internetwork A collection of networks interconnected by routers and other devices that functions (generally) as a single network.

internetworking The industry devoted to connecting networks together. The term can refer to products, procedures, and technologies.

InterNIC An organization that serves the Internet community by supplying user assistance, documentation, training, registration service for Internet domain names, network addresses, and other services. Formerly called NIC.

interoperability The capability of computing equipment manufactured by different vendors to communicate with one another successfully over a network.

intranet   An internal network that is to be accessed by users who have access to an organization's internal LAN.

IOS (Internetwork Operating System)   *See* Cisco IOS software.

IP (Internet Protocol)   A network layer protocol in the TCP/IP stack offering a connectionless internetwork service. IP provides features for addressing, type-of-service specification, fragmentation and reassembly, and security. Defined in RFC 791. IPv4 (Internet Protocol version 4) is a connectionless, best-effort packet switching protocol. *See* IPv6.

IP address   A 32-bit address assigned to hosts by using TCP/IP. An IP address belongs to one of five classes (A, B, C, D, or E) and is written as four octets separated by periods (that is, dotted-decimal format). Each address consists of a network number, an optional subnetwork number, and a host number. The network and subnetwork numbers together are used for routing, and the host number is used to address an individual host within the network or subnetwork. A subnet mask is used to extract network and subnetwork information from the IP address. Also called an Internet address.

IP next generation   *See* IPv6.

IP Security   *See* IPSec.

IP spoofing   The act of a packet illegally claiming to be from an address from which it was not actually sent. Spoofing is designed to foil network security mechanisms such as filters and ACLs.

IP version 6   *See* IPv6.

ipconfig   A command-line utility used in Windows NT and Windows 2000 to determine TCP/IP configuration information for the network adapter.

IPng (IP next generation)   *See* IPv6.

IPSec (IP Security)   A standard for protecting data transmitted across a network by using authentication and encryption protocols.

IPv6 (IP version 6)   A replacement for the current version of IP (version 4). IPv6 includes support for flow ID in the packet header, which can be used to identify flows. Formerly called IPng.

IPX (Internetwork Packet Exchange)   A NetWare network layer (Layer 3) protocol used for transferring data from servers to workstations. IPX is similar to IP and XNS.

IR (infrared radiation)   A frequency range that is higher than microwaves but lower than visible light. It is used for wireless networking and communications, remote controls, motion detectors, night vision devices, medical equipment, and missile guidance systems.

IRSG (Internet Research Steering Group)   Group that oversees various research groups and holds workshops focused on research areas of importance to the evolution of the Internet.

ISDN (Integrated Services Digital Network)   A communication protocol, offered by telephone companies, that enables telephone networks to carry data, voice, and other source traffic.

ISO (International Organization for Standardization)   An international organization that is responsible for a wide range of standards, including those relevant to networking. ISO developed the OSI reference model, a popular networking reference model.

ISOC (Internet Society)   An international nonprofit organization, founded in 1992, that coordinates the evolution and use of the Internet. In addition, ISOC delegates authority to other groups, such as the IAB, that are related to the Internet. ISOC is headquartered in Reston, Virginia. *See* IAB.

ISP (Internet service provider)   A company that provides Internet access to other companies or individuals through dialup remote access or dedicated links.

IT (information technology)   A term used to denote the industry encompassing all the various technologies, including computer and telephony, used to create, store, and use information.

ITU-T (International Telecommunication Union Telecommunication Standardization Sector)   Formerly the Committee for International Telegraph and Telephone (CCITT), an international organization that develops communication standards. *See* CCITT.

J

Java   A programming language that was specifically designed for use on the Internet to create applications or "applets" (small applications that can be embedded on web pages or distributed among servers and clients on the network).

Java Virtual Machine (JVM)   Sun Microsystems's software used to create a virtual Java computer, on which Java applications can be run.

JPEG or JPG   A compressible graphic image file format, often used for images embedded in web pages because it is supported by web browsers and because it downloads relatively quickly because of the small file size.

K

Kb (kilobit)   Approximately 1000 bits.

KB (kilobyte)   Approximately 1000 bytes.

KBps (kilobytes per second)   A rate of transfer speed.

Kbps (kilobits per second)   A rate of transfer speed.

Kerberos   A security method used for authentication that relies on an encrypted "ticket," so that the user's password is not required to be sent across the network. Kerberos is an Internet standard and is the means of authentication used by Windows 2000's Active Directory.

kernel   The core of the computer's operating system that provides the basic services for other parts of the operating system. Compare with shell.

kilobit   *See* Kb.

kilobits per second   *See* Kbps.

kilobyte   *See* KB.

kilobytes per second   *See* KBps.

L

LAN (local area network)   A high-speed, low-error data network covering a relatively small geographic area (up to a few thousand meters). LANs connect workstations, peripherals, terminals, and other devices in a single building or other geographically limited area. LAN standards specify cabling and signaling at the physical and data link layers of the OSI reference model. Ethernet, FDDI, and Token Ring are widely used LAN technologies. Compare with MAN and WAN. *See* VLAN.

LAN link   Technology used to connect computers in a local network that is sometimes referred to as the LAN architecture. Examples include Ethernet, Token Ring, FDDI, AppleTalk, and ARCnet.

latency   The delay between the time a device requests access to a network and the time it is granted permission to transmit.

layering   The separation of networking functions used by the OSI reference model, which simplifies the tasks required for two computers to communicate with each other.

LDAP (Lightweight Directory Access Protocol)   A "light" version of the Directory Access Protocol (DAP), which is standard for network directory services. LDAP compatible directories use a hierarchical tree structure and common naming conventions.

leased line   A transmission line reserved by a communications carrier for the private use of a customer. A leased line is a type of dedicated line. *See* dedicated connection.

legacy   Hardware, applications, or data that were inherited from earlier technologies.

Lightweight Directory Access Protocol   *See* LDAP.

link-layer address   *See* MAC address.

link layer   *See* data link layer.

link   A network communications channel consisting of a circuit or transmission path and all related equipment between a sender and a receiver. Most often used to refer to a WAN connection. Sometimes referred to as a line or transmission link.

link-state routing protocol   A routing protocol in which each router broadcasts or multicasts information to all nodes in the internetwork about the cost of reaching each of its neighbors. Link-state protocols create a consistent view of the network and are therefore not prone to routing loops, but they achieve this at the cost of relatively greater computational difficulty and more widespread traffic (compared with distance-vector routing protocols). Compare with distance-vector routing protocol.

Linux   An operating system based on UNIX that was designed as a low-cost, open-source personal computer operating system by Linus Torvalds at the University of Helsinki, Finland.

LLC (logical link control)   The higher of the two data link layer sublayers defined by the IEEE. The LLC sublayer handles error control, flow control, framing, and MAC-sublayer addressing. The most prevalent LLC protocol is IEEE 802.2, which includes both connectionless and connection-oriented variants.

load balancing   In routing, the capability of a router to distribute traffic over all its network ports that are the same distance from the destination address. Good load-balancing algorithms use both line speed and reliability information. Load balancing increases the use of network segments, thus increasing effective network bandwidth.

load   The amount of activity on a network resource such as a router or link.

local loop   Cabling (usually copper wiring) that extends from the demarc into the WAN service provider's central office.

log   A list of access requests, errors, or other activities that can be analyzed to obtain information for security, optimization, or troubleshooting purposes.

logical addressing   The addressing scheme used by network layer protocols such as IP and IPX.

logical link control   *See* LLC.

logical topology   The pathway by which information flows, regardless of the physical layout of the network.

login   The process of identifying oneself to an operating system or application to gain access. Typically this involves entering a user account name and password.

loop   A route in which packets never reach their destination but simply cycle repeatedly through a constant series of network nodes.

loopback test   A test in which signals are sent and then directed back toward their source from some point along the communications path. Loopback tests are often used to test network interface usability.

M

MAC (Media Access Control)   The part of the data link layer that includes the 66-byte (48-bit) address of the source and destination and the method of getting permission to transmit. *See* data link layer and LLC.

MAC address   A standardized data link layer address that is required for every port or device that connects to a LAN. Other devices in the network use these addresses to locate specific ports in the network and to create and update routing tables and data structures. MAC addresses are each six bytes long, and they are controlled by the IEEE. Also known as a hardware address, a MAC-layer address, or a physical address. Compare with network address.

Mac OS   The operating system used by the Apple Macintosh.

machine language   The stream of 0s and 1s that are processed by a computer. The output of programming languages such as BASIC or C++ are compiled or assembled into binary code, which is read and interpreted by the microprocessor.

mainframe   A large centralized computer, such as those made by IBM, that is used for processing large amounts of data.

MAN (metropolitan area network)   A network that spans a metropolitan area. Generally, a MAN spans a larger geographic area than a LAN, but a smaller geographic area than a WAN. Compare with LAN and WAN.

MAPI (Messaging Application Program Interface)   A programming interface developed by Microsoft for sending e-mail; it is supported by many popular applications such as the Eudora e-mail client.

mask   *See* subnet mask.

master boot record   *See* MBR.

MAU (media attachment unit)   A device used in Ethernet and IEEE 802.3 networks that provides the interface between the AUI port of a station and the common medium of the Ethernet. The MAU, which can be built into a station or be a separate device, performs physical layer functions including the conversion of digital data from the Ethernet interface, collision detection, and the injection of bits onto the network. Sometimes referred to as a media access unit or as a transceiver; sometimes it is abbreviated as MSAU.

maximum transmission unit   *See* MTU.

Mb (megabit)   Approximately 1,000,000 bits.

MB (megabyte)   Approximately 1,000,000 bytes.

Mbone   A part of the Internet used for sending multicast messages (messages sent to multiple users at the same time), typically streaming audio or video. *See* multicast.

Mbps (megabits per second)   A rate of transfer speed.

MBps (megabytes per second)   A rate of transfer speed.

MBR (master boot record)   Data stored in the first sector of a disk that provides information on where the operating system files are located, which is required for the computer to load the files into memory (called booting the operating system).

MCP   Microsoft Certified Professional.

MCSE   Microsoft Certified Systems Engineer.

MCT   Microsoft Certified Trainer.

MD5 (Message Digest 5)   A one-way hashing algorithm that generates a 128-bit output.

Media Access Control   *See* MAC.

media attachment unit   *See* MAU.

media Plural of medium. The various physical environments through which transmission signals pass. Common network media include twisted-pair, coaxial, fiber-optic cable, and the atmosphere through which microwave, laser, and infrared transmission occurs. Sometimes called physical media.

megabit *See* Mb.

megabits per second *See* Mbps.

megabyte *See* MB.

megabytes per second *See* MBps.

megahertz One million cycles of electromagnetic current per second; used as a measure of microprocessor speed. *See* Hertz.

memory buffer The area of memory in which the switch stores the destination and transmission data.

memory The location where data is stored on a computer for fast access. Often refered to as RAM. Memory is a temporary holding place for data, and the contents of memory are lost when the computer is rebooted. Contrast this to disk storage, in which the data remains intact when the computer is turned off.

mesh A network topology in which devices are organized in a manageable, segmented manner with many, often redundant, interconnections strategically placed between network nodes. Topology can be arranged in either full mesh (all nodes connected to one another) or partial mesh (some redundant connections).

Message Digest 5 *See* MD5.

message An application layer logical grouping of information, often composed of several lower-layer logical groupings such as packets. The terms datagram, frame, packet, and segment are also used to describe logical information groupings at various layers of the OSI reference model and in various technology circles.

Messaging Application Program Interface *See* MAPI.

metadata A definition or description of data.

metropolitan area network *See* MAN.

MHz *See* megahertz.

MIB (Management Information Base) A database of network management information that is used and maintained by a network management protocol such as SNMP. The value of a MIB object can be changed or retrieved by using SNMP commands, usually through a GUI network management system. MIB objects are organized in a tree structure that includes public (standard) and private (proprietary) branches.

modem (modulator-demodulator)   A device that converts digital and analog signals. At the source, a modem converts digital signals to a form suitable for transmission over analog communication facilities. At the destination, the analog signals are returned to their digital form. Modems enable data to be transmitted over voice-grade telephone lines.

modulator-demodulator   *See* modem.

MSAU (multistation access unit)   *See* MAU.

MTU (maximum transmission unit)   Maximum packet size, in bytes, that a particular interface can handle.

multicast address   A single address that refers to multiple network devices. Synonymous with group address. Compare with broadcast address and unicast address. *See* multicast.

multicast   Single packets copied by a network and sent out to a set of network addresses. These addresses are specified in the destination address field. Compare with broadcast and unicast.

multiplexing   A scheme that enables multiple logical signals to be transmitted simultaneously across a single physical channel. Compare with demultiplexing.

multistation access unit   *See* MSAU.

multivendor network   A network using equipment from more than one vendor. Multivendor networks pose many more compatibility problems than single-vendor networks. Compare with single-vendor network.

N

NAK (negative acknowledgment)   A response sent from a receiving device to a sending device indicating that the information received contained errors. Compare with acknowledgment.

name resolution   Generally, the process of associating a name with a network address.

name server   A server connected to a network that resolves network names into network addresses.

NAT (Network Address Translation)   A mechanism for reducing the need for globally unique IP addresses. NAT enables an organization with addresses that are not globally unique to connect to the Internet by translating those addresses into globally routable address space. Also known as network address translator.

NCP (NetWare Core Protocol)   The file sharing protocol used to provide access to resources on a NetWare server.

NCP (Network Control Program)   A program that routes and controls the flow of data between a communications controller and other network resources.

NDIS (Network Driver Interface Specification)   Microsoft's driver specification for network interfaces that enables the binding of multiple protocols to a single adapter or the binding of multiple adapters to a single protocol.

NDS (Novell Directory Service)   The LDAP-compatible directory service used by NetWare 4.x and above.

negative acknowledgment   *See* NAK.

NetBEUI (NetBIOS Extended User Interface)   An enhanced version of the NetBIOS protocol used by network operating systems such as LAN Manager, LAN Server, Windows for Workgroups, and Windows NT. NetBEUI formalizes the transport frame and adds additional functions. NetBEUI implements the OSI LLC2 protocol.

NetBIOS (Network Basic Input/Output System)   An application programming interface used by applications on an IBM LAN to request services from lower-level network processes. These services might include session establishment and termination and information transfer.

NetBIOS Extended User Interface   *See* NetBEUI.

NetWare Core Protocol   *See* NCP.

NetWare Link Services Protocol   *See* NLSP.

NetWare Loadable Module   *See* NLM.

NetWare   A popular distributed NOS developed by Novell. Provides transparent remote file access and numerous other distributed network services.

Network Address Translation   *See* NAT.

network address   A network layer address referring to a logical, rather than a physical, network device. Also called a protocol address.

network administrator   A person responsible for the operation, maintenance, and management of a network.

network analyzer   A hardware or software device offering various network troubleshooting features, including protocol-specific packet decodes, specific preprogrammed troubleshooting tests, packet filtering, and packet transmission.

Network Basic Input/Output System   *See* NetBIOS.

Network Control Program   *See* NCP.

Network Driver Interface Specification   *See* NDIS.

Network File System   *See* NFS.

network interface card   *See* NIC.

network interface   The boundary between a carrier network and a privately owned installation.

network layer   Layer 3 of the OSI reference model. This layer provides connectivity and path selection between two end systems. The network layer is the layer at which routing occurs. Corresponds roughly with the path control layer of the SNA model. *See* OSI reference model.

network number   The part of an IP address that specifies the network to which the host belongs.

network operating system   *See* NOS.

network   A collection of computers, printers, routers, switches, and other devices that are able to communicate with each other over some transmission medium.

networking   The interconnection of workstations, peripherals such as printers, hard drives, scanners, CD-ROMs, and other devices.

neural network   A network based on modeling the computer and network architecture after the human brain by connecting multiple, relatively simple processors together.

NFS (Network File System)   As commonly used, a distributed file system protocol suite developed by Sun Microsystems that enables remote file access across a network. In actuality, NFS is simply one protocol in the suite. NFS protocols include RPC and XDR. These protocols are part of a larger architecture that Sun refers to as ONC.

NIC (network interface card)   A board that provides network communication capabilities to and from a computer system. Also called an adapter.

NLM (NetWare Loadable Module)   An individual program that can be loaded into memory and function as part of the NetWare NOS.

NLSP (NetWare Link Services Protocol)   A link-state routing protocol based on IS-IS. The Cisco implementation of NLSP also includes MIB variables and tools to redistribute routing and SAP information between NLSP and other IPX routing protocols.

node   An endpoint of a network connection or a junction common to two or more lines in a network. Nodes can be processors, controllers, or workstations. Nodes, which vary in routing and other functional capabilities, can be interconnected by links and serve as control points in the network. Node is sometimes used generically to refer to any entity that can access a network, and it is frequently used interchangeably with "device."

NOS (network operating system)   The operating system used to run a network such Novell NetWare and Windows NT.

Novell Directory Service   *See* NDS.

Novell IPX   *See* IPX.

NWLink   The Microsoft implementation of the IPX/SPX protocol stack, which is included with Windows operating systems and is automatically installed when a Microsoft client for NetWare is installed. This enables communication between a Microsoft client and a NetWare server.

O

Open System Interconnection   *See* OSI.

octet   Eight bits. In networking, the term octet (rather than byte) is often used rather than byte because some machine architectures employ bytes that are not eight bits long.

ODI (Open Data Link Interface)   A Novell specification providing a standardized interface for NICs that enables multiple protocols to use a single NIC.

ohm   The unit used to measure electrical resistance. A resistance of one ohm will pass one ampere of current when a voltage of one volt is applied.

Open Data Link Interface   *See* ODI.

Open Shortest Path First   *See* OSPF.

operating system   The "master" program on a computer, which is loaded by a boot loader, on top of which the application programs run. The operating system provides services to applications and acts as a liaison between the computer hardware and the applications.

OSI (Open System Interconnection)   An international standardization program created by ISO and ITU-T to develop standards for data networking that facilitate multivendor equipment interoperability.

OSI reference model   A network architectural model developed by ISO and ITU-T. The model consists of seven layers, each of which specifies particular network functions such as addressing, flow control, error control, encapsulation, and reliable message transfer. The lowest layer (the physical layer) is closest to the media technology. The lower two layers are implemented in hardware and software, and the upper five layers are implemented only in software. The highest layer (the application layer) is closest to the user. The OSI reference model is used universally as a method for teaching and understanding network functionality. Similar in some respects to SNA. *See* application layer, data link layer, network layer, physical layer, presentation layer, session layer, and transport layer.

OSPF (Open Shortest Path First)   A link-state, hierarchical routing protocol proposed as a successor to RIP in the Internet community. OSPF features include least-cost routing, multipath routing, and load balancing.

P

packet internet groper   *See* ping.

packet switching   A networking method in which nodes share bandwidth with each other by sending packets.

packet   A logical grouping of information that includes a header containing control information and (usually) user data. Packets are most often used to refer to network layer units of data. The terms datagram, frame, message, and segment are also used to describe logical information groupings at various layers of the OSI reference model and in various technology circles.

PAP (Password Authentication Protocol)   An authentication protocol that enables PPP peers to authenticate one another. The remote router attempting to connect to the local router is required to send an authentication request. Unlike CHAP, PAP passes the password and host name or username in clear-text (that is, unencrypted). PAP does not itself prevent unauthorized access, but it identifies the remote end; the router or access server then determines whether that user is allowed access. PAP is supported only on PPP lines. Compare with CHAP.

Password Authentication Protocol   *See* PAP.

patch panel   An assembly of pin locations and ports that can be mounted on a rack or wall bracket in the wiring closet. Patch panels act like switchboards that connect workstations' cables to each other and to the outside environment.

patch   A small program that is provided by an operating system or application program vendor to be installed as a "quick fix" to repair problems with the program.

PDA (personal digital assistant)   A handheld low-powered computing device used to store address and contact information, to maintain a calendar and schedule, and to perform similar tasks.

PDC (primary domain controller)   In a Microsoft Windows NT network, the NT server that maintains a master copy of the Security Accounts Management database (SAM) database and that replicates a read-only copy to each backup domain controller (BDC).

peer-to-peer computing   Peer-to-peer computing calls for each network device to run both client and server portions of an application. Also describes communication between implementations of the same OSI reference model layer in two different network devices. Compare with client/server computing.

permanent virtual circuit   *See* PVC.

personal digital assistant   *See* PDA.

PGP (Pretty Good Privacy)   A shareware version of RSA encryption.

physical layer   Layer 1 of the OSI reference model. This layer defines the electrical, mechanical, procedural, and functional specifications for activating, maintaining, and deactivating the physical link between end systems. Corresponds with the physical control layer in the SNA model. *See* OSI reference model.

ping (packet internet groper)   An ICMP echo message and its reply. Often used in IP networks to test the reachability of a network device.

point-to-multipoint connection   One of two fundamental connection types. In ATM, a point-to-multipoint connection is a unidirectional connection in which a single source end system (known as a root node) connects to multiple destination end systems (known as leaves). Compare with point-to-point connection.

point-to-point connection   One of two fundamental connection types. In ATM, a point-to-point connection can be unidirectional or bidirectional with point connection between two ATM end systems. Compare with point-to-multipoint connection.

point-to-point link   A link that provides a single, preestablished WAN communications path from the customer premises through a carrier network, such as a telephone company, to a remote network. Also called a dedicated link or a leased line.

Point-to-Point Protocol   *See* PPP.

POP (Post Office Protocol)   A protocol used for downloading e-mail from a mail server to an e-mail client application. The current version is POP3.

port 1. An interface on an internetworking device (such as a router). 2. A female plug on a patch panel that accepts the same size plug as an RJ-45 jack. Patch cords are used in these ports to cross-connect computers wired to the patch panel. It is this cross-connection that enables the LAN to function. 3. In IP terminology, an upper-layer process that receives information from lower layers. Ports are numbered, and many are associated with a specific process. For example, SMTP is associated with port 25. A port number of this type is called a well-known address. 4. To rewrite software or microcode so that it rund on a different hardware platform or in a different software environment than that for which it was originally designed.

Post Office Protocol *See* POP.

PPP (Point-to-Point Protocol) A successor to SLIP, a protocol that provides router-to-router and host-to-network connections over synchronous and asynchronous circuits.

PPTP (Point-to-Point Tunneling Protocol) A protocol based on PPP, which enables establishment of virtual private networks (VPNs), through which a user can "tunnel" through a public network such as the Internet to access a private network.

presentation layer Layer 6 of the OSI reference model. This layer provides data representation and code formatting, along with the negotiation of data transfer syntax. It ensures that the data that arrives from the network can be used by the application, and it ensures that information sent by the application can be transmitted on the network. *See* OSI reference model.

Pretty Good Privacy *See* PGP.

PRI (primary rate interface) An ISDN interface to primary rate access. Primary rate access consists of a single 64-kbps D channel plus 23 (T1) or 30 (E1) B channels for voice or data. Compare with BRI.

primary domain controller *See* PDC.

primary rate interface *See* PRI.

private key encryption A security method in which a private key, called a shared secret, is used to encrypt and decrypt messages. Also called secret key encryption or symmetric encryption.

protocol address *See* network address.

protocol analyzer *See* network analyzer.

protocol stack A set of related communications protocols that operate together and, as a group, address communication at some or all of the seven layers of the OSI reference model. Not every protocol stack covers each layer of the model, and often a single protocol in the stack addresses several layers at once. TCP/IP is a typical protocol stack.

protocol suite   A set of related communications protocols (*see* protocol stack) that includes extra utilities and other protocols not required for communication.

protocol   A formal description of a set of rules and conventions that govern how devices on a network exchange information.

proxy   An entity that, in the interest of efficiency, essentially stands in for another entity.

PSTN (public switched telephone network)   The U.S. telephone network, also colloquially referred to in the telecom industry as POTS (plain old telephone service).

public key encryption   A security method in which two separate keys are used: a public and a private key. The first is used to encrypt messages and the other is used to decrypt messages. Also called public/private key encryption or asymmetric encryption.

public switched telephone network   *See* PSTN.

PVC (permanent virtual circuit)   A virtual circuit that is permanently established. PVCs save bandwidth associated with circuit establishment and teardown in situations in which certain virtual circuits must exist all the time. Compare with SVC.

Q

QoS (Quality of Service)   A measure of performance for a transmission system that reflects its transmission quality and service availability.

Quality of Service   *See* QoS.

quantum physics   A branch of physics that involves the study of units of energy called quanta and the interactions between subatomic objects such as electrons and protons.

qubit   A quantum bit.

queue   1. Generally, an ordered list of elements waiting to be processed. 2. In routing, a backlog of packets waiting to be forwarded over a router interface.

R

radio frequency interference   *See* RFI.

RADIUS (Remote Authentication Dial-In User Service) A service that provides for secure communication between remote access clients and servers.

RAID (redundant array of independent [or inexpensive] disks) A fault tolerance method, in which multiple hard disks are used in various configurations to ensure the integrity of data in case one disk fails.

RAM (random-access memory) Volatile memory that can be read and written by a microprocessor.

random-access memory *See* RAM.

RARP (Reverse Address Resolution Protocol) A protocol in the TCP/IP stack that provides a method for finding IP addresses based on MAC addresses. Compare with ARP.

RAS (remote access service) A service that enables client computers to dial in to or establish a VPN connection to a remote server and be authenticated on the network. *See* remote access.

read-only memory *See* ROM.

reassembly The putting back together of an IP datagram at the destination after it has been fragmented either at the source or at an intermediate node.

redirector A software component that intercepts requests for services or resources and determines that the request should go out over the network rather than to the computer's local bus.

redundancy 1. In internetworking, the duplication of devices, services, or connections so that in the event of a failure, the redundant devices, services, or connections can perform the work of those that failed. 2. In telephony, the portion of the total information contained in a message that can be eliminated without loss of essential information or meaning.

redundant array of independent [or inexpensive] disks *See* RAID.

registered jack *See* RJ (registered jack) connector.

Registry In Windows operating systems, the hierarchical database in which initialization information is stored.

remote access service *See* RAS.

remote access A network connection between a client and server that is established over dialup telephone lines, a dedicated connection, or through a VPN link over the Internet.

Remote Authentication Dial-In User Service *See* RADIUS.

remote-procedure call *See* RPC.

repeater   A device that regenerates and propagates electrical signals between two network segments.

Request for Comments   *See* RFC.

Reverse Address Resolution Protocol   *See* RARP.

RFC (Request for Comments)   A document series used as the primary means for communicating information about the Internet. Some RFCs are designated by the IAB as Internet standards. Most RFCs document protocol specifications, such as Telnet and FTP, but some are humorous or historical. RFCs are available online from numerous sources.

RFI (radio frequency interference)   Interference with data transmission over copper cable that is caused by radio transmissions.

ring topology   A network topology that consists of a series of repeaters connected to one another by unidirectional transmission links to form a single closed loop. Each station on the network connects to the network at a repeater. Although they are logical rings, ring topologies are most often organized in a closed-loop star. Compare with bus topology, star topology, and tree topology.

ring   A connection of two or more stations in a logically circular topology. Information is passed sequentially between active stations. Token Ring, FDDI, and CDDI are based on this topology.

RIP (Routing Information Protocol)   A protocol supplied with UNIX BSD systems. The most common Interior Gateway Protocol (IGP) in the Internet. RIP uses hop count as a routing metric.

RJ (registered jack) connector   A modular connector used with copper wire. RJ-11 connectors are typically used with analog telephone lines, and RJ-45 connectors are used with UTP Ethernet.

ROM (read-only memory)   Nonvolatile memory that can be read, but not written, by the microprocessor.

routed protocol   A protocol that can be routed by a router. A router must be able to interpret the logical internetwork as specified by that routed protocol. Examples of routed protocols include AppleTalk, DECnet, and IP. Compare with routing protocol.

router   A network layer device that uses one or more metrics to determine the optimal path along which network traffic should be forwarded. Routers forward packets from one network to another based on network layer information. Occasionally called a gateway (although this definition of gateway is becoming increasingly outdated).

Routing Information Protocol   *See* RIP.

routing protocol   A protocol that accomplishes routing through the implementation of a specific routing protocol. Examples of routing protocols include IGRP, OSPF, and RIP. Compare with routed protocol.

routing table   A table stored in a router or some other internetworking device that keeps track of routes to particular network destinations and, in some cases, metrics associated with those routes.

routing   The process of finding a path to a destination host. Routing is very complex in large networks because of the many potential intermediate destinations a packet might traverse before reaching its destination host.

RPC (remote-procedure call)   The technological foundation of client/server computing. RPCs are procedure calls that are built or specified by clients and executed on servers, with the results returned over the network to the clients.

S

SAM (Security Accounts Database)   On Windows NT operating systems, a database that stores information about user accounts, groups, and associated permissions.

Samba   A software package that enables Windows and UNIX machines to communicate with one another, using the SMB file-sharing protocol.

SAP (Service Advertising Protocol)   An IPX protocol that provides a means of informing network clients, through routers and servers, of available network resources and services.

scalability   The capability of a network to grow, without any major changes to the overall design.

SDLC (Synchronous Data Link Control)   An SNA data link layer communications protocol. SDLC is a bit-oriented, full-duplex serial protocol that has spawned numerous similar protocols, including HDLC and LAPB.

Secure Hash Algorithm   *See* SHA1.

Security Accounts Database   *See* SAM.

segment   A section of a network that is bounded by bridges, routers, or switches. 2. In a LAN using a bus topology, a continuous electrical circuit that is often connected to other such segments with repeaters. 3. In the TCP specification, a single transport layer unit of information. The terms datagram, frame, message, and packet are also used to describe logical information groupings at various layers of the OSI reference model and in various technology circles.

segmentation The process of splitting a single collision domain into two or more collision domains to reduce collisions and network congestion.

Sequenced Packet Exchange *See* SPX.

Serial Line Internet Protocol *See* SLIP.

serial transmission A method of data transmission in which the bits of a data character are transmitted sequentially over a single channel. Compare with parallel transmission.

server A node or software program that provides services to clients. *See* client.

Service Advertising Protocol *See* SAP.

service profile identifier *See* SPID.

session layer Layer 5 of the OSI reference model. This layer establishes, maintains, and manages sessions between applications. *See* OSI reference model.

session 1. A related set of connection-oriented communications transactions between two or more network devices. 2. In SNA, a logical connection enabling two network addressable units to communicate.

SHA1 (Secure Hash Algorithm) A one-way hash algorithm designed by NIST that has a 160-bit digest.

share A resource on a computer that is made available for access from other computers on the network.

share-level security A means of controlling access to network shares by assigning individual passwords to each share.

shielded twisted-pair *See* STP.

Simple Mail Transfer Protocol *See* SMTP.

Simple Network Management Protocol *See* SNMP.

simplex The capability for transmission in only one direction between a sending station and a receiving station. Broadcast television is an example of a simplex technology. Compare with full duplex and half duplex.

single-vendor network A network using equipment from only one vendor. Single-vendor networks rarely suffer compatibility problems. *See* multivendor network.

sliding window   A window whose size is negotiated dynamically during the TCP session.

SLIP (Serial Line Internet Protocol)   A standard protocol for point-to-point serial connections using a variation of TCP/IP. The predecessor of PPP.

small office/home office   *See* SOHO.

smart card   In the context of computer security, a plastic card the size of a credit card that contains authentication credentials on an embedded chip or magnetic strip. It is used in place of or in conjunction with account name and password information to gain access to a system.

smart technology   Embedding small microprocessors into household appliances, office machines, and so forth to enable them to be programmed to perform tasks and to be networked together to communicate with one another.

SMTP (Simple Mail Transfer Protocol)   A protocol used for sending e-mail on the Internet.

SNA (Systems Network Architecture)   A large, complex, feature-rich network architecture developed in the 1970s by IBM. Similar in some respects to the OSI reference model, but with a few differences. SNA is essentially composed of seven layers. *See* data flow control layer, data link control layer, path control layer, physical control layer, presentation services layer, transaction services layer, and transmission control layer.

SNMP (Simple Network Management Protocol)   A network management protocol used almost exclusively in TCP/IP networks. SNMP provides a means to monitor and control network devices and to manage configurations, statistics collection, performance, and security.

socket number   An eight-bit number that identifies a socket. A maximum of 254 socket numbers can be assigned in an AppleTalk node.

socket   1. A software structure operating as a communications endpoint within a network device (similar to a port). 2. An addressable entity within a node connected to an AppleTalk network; sockets are owned by software processes known as socket clients. AppleTalk sockets are divided into two groups: SASs, which are reserved for clients such as AppleTalk core protocols, and DASs, which are assigned dynamically by DDP upon request from clients in the node. An AppleTalk socket is similar in concept to a TCP/IP port.

SOHO (small office/home office)   A small office or home office consisting of a few users requiring a connection that provides faster, more reliable connectivity than an analog dialup connection.

Solaris   A UNIX-based operating system developed by Sun Microsystems.

source address   An address of a network device that is sending data. *See* destination address.

spanning tree   A loop-free subset of a Layer 2 (switched) network topology.

Spanning-Tree Algorithm   An algorithm used by the Spanning-Tree Protocol to create a spanning tree. Sometimes abbreviated as STA.

Spanning-Tree Protocol   A bridge protocol that utilizes the spanning-tree algorithm, enabling a learning bridge to dynamically work around loops in a network topology by creating a spanning tree. Bridges exchange BPDU messages with other bridges to detect loops, and then remove the loops by shutting down selected bridge interfaces. Refers to both the IEEE 802.1 Spanning-Tree Protocol standard and the earlier Digital Equipment Corporation Spanning-Tree Protocol on which it is based. The IEEE version supports bridge domains and enables the bridge to construct a loop-free topology across an extended LAN. The IEEE version is generally preferred over the Digital version.

SPID (service profile identifier)   A number that some service providers use to define the services to which an ISDN device subscribes. The ISDN device uses the SPID when accessing the switch that initializes the connection to a service provider.

split horizon   An IGRP feature designed to prevent routers from picking up erroneous routes. Split horizon prevents loops between adjacent routers and keeps down the size of update messages.

spoofing   1. A scheme used by routers to cause a host to treat an interface as if it were up and supporting a session. The router spoofs replies to keepalive messages from the host to convince that host that the session still exists. Spoofing is useful in routing environments such as DDR, in which a circuit-switched link is taken down when there is no traffic to be sent across it to save toll charges. The term also is used to refer to IP spoofing. *See* IP spoofing.

SPX (Sequenced Packet Exchange)   A reliable, connection-oriented protocol that supplements the datagram service provided by network layer protocols. Novell derived this commonly used NetWare transport protocol from the SPP of the XNS protocol suite.

SQL (Structure Query Language)   A programming language used for interacting with a database, which is a standard under the American National Standards Institute and the ISO. Microsoft SQL Server is often referred to as "SQL"; it is a client/server database application that uses the Structured Query Language.

standard   A set of rules or procedures that are either widely used or officially specified.

star topology   A LAN topology in which endpoints on a network are connected to a common central switch by point-to-point links. A ring topology that is organized as a star implements a unidirectional closed-loop star, instead of point-to-point links. Compare with bus topology, ring topology, and tree topology.

static routing   Routing that is explicitly configured and entered into the routing table. Static routes take precedence over routes chosen by dynamic routing protocols. Compare with dynamic routing.

store-and-forward   A packet-switching technique in which frames are completely processed before being forwarded out the appropriate port. This processing includes calculating the CRC and checking the destination address. In addition, frames must be temporarily stored until network resources (such as an unused link) are available to forward the message.

STP (shielded twisted-pair)   A two-pair wiring medium used in a variety of network implementations. STP cabling has a layer of shielded insulation to reduce EMI. Compare with UTP. *See* twisted-pair.

Structure Query Language   *See* SQL.

subnet address   A portion of an IP address that is specified as the subnetwork by the subnet mask.

subnet mask   A mask used to extract network and subnetwork information from the IP address.

subnet   *See* subnetwork.

subnetwork   1. A network that is segmented into a series of smaller networks. 2. In IP networks, a network sharing a particular subnet address. Subnetworks are networks arbitrarily segmented by a network administrator to provide a multilevel, hierarchical routing structure while shielding the subnetwork from the addressing complexity of attached networks. Sometimes called a subnet. 3. In OSI networks, a collection of ESs and ISs under the control of a single administrative domain and using a single network access protocol.

surge   Any voltage increase above 110 percent of the normal voltage carried by a power line.

SVC (switched virtual circuit)   A virtual circuit that is dynamically established on demand and that is torn down when transmission is complete. SVCs are used in situations in which data transmission is sporadic. Compare with PVC.

switch   A network device that filters, forwards, and floods frames based on the destination address of each frame. The switch operates at the data link layer of the OSI reference model.

switched virtual circuit   *See* SVC.

switching The process of taking an incoming frame from one interface and delivering it out through another interface.

synchronous circuit A signal that is transmitted with precise clocking. Such signals have the same frequency, with individual characters encapsulated in control bits (called start bits and stop bits) that designate the beginning and end of each character.

Synchronous Data Link Control *See* SDLC.

Systems Network Architecture *See* SNA.

T

T1 A digital WAN carrier facility that transmits data formatted as DS-1 at 1.544 Mbps through the telephone-switching network, using AMI or B8ZS coding. Compare with E1.

T3 A digital WAN carrier facility that transmits data formatted as DS-3 at 44.736 Mbps through the telephone switching network. Compare with E3.

TA (terminal adapter) A device used to connect ISDN BRI connections to existing interfaces such as EIA/TIA-232. Essentially, an ISDN modem.

TCP (Transmission Control Protocol) A connection-oriented transport layer protocol that provides reliable full-duplex data transmission. TCP is part of the TCP/IP protocol stack.

TCP/IP (Transmission Control Protocol/Internet Protocol) A common name for the suite of protocols developed by the U.S. DoD in the 1970s to support the construction of worldwide internetworks. TCP and IP are the two best-known protocols in the suite.

TDM (time-division multiplexing) A circuit-switching signal used to determine the call route, which is a dedicated path between the sender and the receiver.

TDR (time domain reflectometer) A type of cable testing device that sends a sonar-like signal and measures the time required for it to return. Used to locate breaks or shorts in the cable.

telephony Technologies that combine telecommunications and computer technology.

Telnet A standard terminal emulation protocol in the TCP/IP protocol stack. Telnet is used for remote terminal connection, enabling users to log in to remote systems and use resources as if they were connected to a local system. Telnet is defined in RFC 854.

terabyte   A unit of measure equal to 10^{12}, or 1,000,000,000,000 bytes.

terminal adapter   *See* TA.

terminator   A device attached to the end of a coax cable, to prevent signal bounce.

TFTP (Trivial File Transfer Protocol)   A simplified version of FTP that enables files to be transferred from one computer to another over a network.

thin client   A term referring to a low-powered computer running software that enables it to connect to a server, access a desktop, and run applications, with all processing being done by the server instead of the client.

throughput   The rate of information arriving at, and possibly passing through, a particular point in a network system.

time domain reflectometer   *See* TDR.

time-division multiplexing   *See* TDM.

timeout   An event that occurs when one network device expects to hear from another network device within a specified period of time but does not. The resulting timeout usually results in a retransmission of information or the dissolving of the session between the two devices.

token bus   A LAN architecture using token passing access over a bus topology. This LAN architecture is the basis for the IEEE 802.4 LAN specification.

token passing   An access method by which network devices access the physical medium in an orderly fashion based on possession of a small frame called a token. Compare with circuit switching and contention.

Token Ring   A token-passing LAN developed and supported by IBM. Token Ring runs at 4 or 16 Mbps over a ring topology. Similar to IEEE 802.5.

token   A frame that contains control information. Possession of the token enables a network device to transmit data onto the network.

TokenTalk   Apple Computer's data-link product that enables an AppleTalk network to be connected by Token Ring cables.

tone generator and locator   A set of devices used to test UTP cable by sending a signal down a set of wires. Sometimes colloquially referred to as a fox and hound.

topology   A physical arrangement of network nodes and media within an enterprise networking structure.

traceroute   A program available on many systems that traces the path a packet takes to a destination. It is mostly used to debug routing problems between hosts. There is also a traceroute protocol defined in RFC 1393.

tracert   *See* traceroute.

trailer   Control information appended to data when encapsulating the data for network transmission. Compare with header.

transceiver   The part of a network interface that transmits and receives. Some NICs have the transceiver built into the card, while others use an external transceiver.

Transmission Control Protocol/Internet Protocol   *See* TCP/IP.

Transmission Control Protocol   *See* TCP.

transport layer   Layer 4 of the OSI reference model. This layer segments and reassembles data into a data stream. The transport layer has the potential to guarantee a connection and offer reliable transport. *See* OSI reference model.

trap   A message sent by an SNMP agent to an NMS, a console, or a terminal to indicate the occurrence of a significant event, such as a specifically defined condition or a threshold that was reached.

tree topology   A LAN topology similar to a bus topology, except that tree networks can contain branches with multiple nodes. Transmissions from a station propagate the length of the medium and are received by all other stations. Compare with bus topology, ring topology, and star topology.

triple DES   *See* 3DES.

Trivial File Transfer Protocol   *See* TFTP.

troubleshooting   The process of recognizing, analyzing, diagnosing, and repairing problems with a computer system or network.

TTL (Time To Live)   A field in an IP header that indicates how long a packet is considered valid.

tunneling   An architecture that is designed to provide the services necessary to implement any standard point-to-point encapsulation scheme.

U

UDP (User Datagram Protocol)   A connectionless transport layer protocol in the TCP/IP protocol stack. UDP is a simple protocol that exchanges datagrams without acknowledgments or guaranteed delivery. It requires that error processing and retransmission be handled by other protocols. UDP is defined in RFC 768.

unicast address   An address specifying a single network device. Compare with broadcast address and multicast address.

unicast   A message sent to a single network destination.

uniform resource locator   *See* URL.

uninterruptible power supply   *See* UPS.

universal serial bus   *See* USB.

UNIX   A powerful text-based operating system that originated at Bell Labs in 1969 as an interactive time-sharing system. It has evolved into an open source product, often used to run servers on large enterprise-level networks.

UPS (uninterruptable power supply)   A backup device designed to provide an uninterrupted power source in the event of a power failure. UPSs are commonly installed on file servers and wiring hubs.

URL (uniform resource locator)   A standardized addressing scheme for accessing hypertext documents and other services using a browser.

USB (universal serial bus)   An interface between peripherals and computers, that provides "plug-and-play" functionality and that supports a transfer rate of 12 Mbps.

User Datagram Protocol   *See* UDP.

user-level security   A means of securing network shares by assigning each user a user account and by assigning permissions to users for access to particular resources.

UTP (unshielded twisted-pair)   A four-pair wire medium used in a variety of networks. UTP does not require the fixed spacing between connections that is necessary with coaxial-type connections. There are five types of UTP cabling commonly used: Category 1 cabling, Category 2 cabling, Category 3 cabling, Category 4 cabling, and Category 5 cabling. Compare with STP.

V

virtual circuit   A logical circuit created to ensure reliable communication between two network devices. A virtual circuit is defined by a VPI/VCI pair, and can be either permanent (a PVC) or switched (an SVC). Virtual circuits are used in Frame Relay and X.25. In ATM, a virtual circuit is called a virtual channel. Sometimes abbreviated VC.

Virtual Integrated Network Service   *See* VINES.

virtual LAN   *See* VLAN.

virtual private network   *See* VPN.

VINES (Virtual Integrated Network Service)   A NOS developed and marketed by Banyan Systems.

virus   A program that propagates itself, and in some cases, it is intended to cause damage to other programs or files.

VLAN (virtual LAN)   A group of devices on a LAN that are configured (using management software) so that they can communicate as if they were attached to the same wire, when in fact they are located on several different LAN segments. Because VLANs are based on logical instead of physical connections, they are extremely flexible.

Voice over IP   *See* VoIP.

VoIP (Voice over IP)   A method for sending voice over a LAN, a WAN, or the Internet using TCP/IP packets. VoIP is also called Voice over Internet Protocol.

volume   A means of organizing the space on a disk.

VPN (virtual private network)   A connection between a remote client and a private network, such as a company LAN, that uses the public Internet as a conduit. A VPN is established using tunneling and encryption protocols to enable data to travel across the public network to the private network in a secure manner.

W

WAN (wide area network)   A data communications network that serves users across a broad geographic area and often uses transmission devices provided by common carriers. Frame Relay, SMDS, and X.25 are examples of WAN technologies. Compare with LAN and MAN.

WAN link   A WAN communications channel consisting of a circuit or transmission path and all related equipment between a sender and a receiver.

waveform signaling   A signaling method in which the signal follows a continuously variable wave pattern, which an infinite number of values along the wave. Compare with discrete state signaling.

web server   A server on which web pages are stored, which can be accessed through software called a web browser using the HTTP protocol.

wide area network   *See* WAN.

window size   The number of messages that can be transmitted while awaiting an acknowledgment.

window   The number of octets that the sender is willing to accept.

Windows Internet Name Server   *See* WINS.

Windows Sockets   *See* Winsock.

Windows   A family of operating systems marketed by Microsoft, that use a GUI in which multiple applications can run simultaneously, each in its own window. Includes Windows 1.*x* through 3.*x*, Windows 95, Windows 98, Windows ME, Windows NT, and Windows 2000.

WINS (Windows Internet Name Server)   Microsoft's implementation of the NetBIOS name server (NBNS) that resolves NetBIOS names to IP addresses on a Microsoft network.

Winsock (Windows Sockets)   An API used to handle input and output requests for Internet applications on a computer using a Windows operating system.

workgroup server   A server that supports a specific set of users and that offers services such as word processing and file sharing, which are services that only a few groups of people would need. Compare with enterprise server.

workgroup   A group of computers and network devices that share resources. Sometimes referred to as a peer-to-peer network.

worm   A type of virus that propagates itself over a network.

X

X Window   A GUI used on UNIX and Linux operating systems.

X.25   An ITU-T standard that defines how connections between DTEs and DCEs are maintained for remote terminal access and computer communications in public data networks. Frame Relay has to some degree superseded X.25.

X.500   A set of standards defining a distributed directory service that uses DAP.

Xerox Network Systems   *See* XNS.

XNS (Xerox Network Systems)   A protocol suite originally designed by PARC. Many PC networking companies, such as 3Com, Banyan, Novell, and UB Networks used or currently use a variation of XNS as their primary transport protocol.

Z

zone   In AppleTalk, a logical group of network devices. Similar to the function of a domain or workgroup in Microsoft networks. In a DNS database, it is a subtree of the DNS database that is administered as a single separate entity.